The Practice of System and Network Administration

Second Edition

The Practice of System and Network Administration

Second Edition

Thomas A. Limoncelli
Christina J. Hogan
Strata R. Chalup

♦ Addison-Wesley

Upper Saddle River, NJ • Boston • Indianapolis • San Francisco
New York • Toronto • Montreal • London • Munich • Paris • Madrid
Capetown • Sydney • Tokyo • Singapore • Mexico City

Many of the designations used by manufacturers and sellers to distinguish their products are claimed as trademarks. Where those designations appear in this book, and the publisher was aware of a trademark claim, the designations have been printed with initial capital letters or in all capitals.

The authors and publisher have taken care in the preparation of this book, but make no expressed or implied warranty of any kind and assume no responsibility for errors or omissions. No liability is assumed for incidental or consequential damages in connection with or arising out of the use of the information or programs contained herein.

The publisher offers excellent discounts on this book when ordered in quantity for bulk purchases or special sales, which may include electronic versions and/or custom covers and content particular to your business, training goals, marketing focus, and branding interests. For more information, please contact:

U.S. Corporate and Government Sales, (800) 382-3419, corpsales@pearsontechgroup.com

For sales outside the United States please contact:

International Sales, international@pearsoned.com

Visit us on the Web: www.awprofessional.com

Library of Congress Cataloging-in-Publication Data

Limoncelli, Tom.
  The practice of system and network administration / Thomas A. Limoncelli, Christina J. Hogan, Strata R. Chalup.—2nd ed.
      p. cm.
  Includes bibliographical references and index.
  ISBN-13: 978-0-321-49266-1 (pbk. : alk. paper)
  1. Computer networks—Management. 2. Computer systems.
  I. Hogan, Christine. II. Chalup, Strata R. III. Title.
  TK5105.5.L53 2007
  004.6068–dc22

                                                                                    2007014507

ISBN 13: 978-0-321-49266-1

ISBN 10:   0-321-49266-8

Text printed in the United States on recycled paper at RR Donnelley in Crawfordsville, Indiana.
Tenth Printing, July 2015

Contents at a Glance

Contents

Preface

Our goal for this book has been to write down everything we've learned from our mentors and to add our real-world experiences. These things are beyond what the manuals and the usual system administration books teach.

This book was born from our experiences as SAs in a variety of organizations. We have started new companies. We have helped sites to grow. We have worked at small start-ups and universities, where lack of funding was an issue. We have worked at midsize and large multinationals, where mergers and spin-offs gave rise to strange challenges. We have worked at fast-paced companies that do business on the Internet and where high-availability, high-performance, and scaling issues were the norm. We've worked at slow-paced companies at which high tech meant cordless phones. On the surface, these are very different environments with diverse challenges; underneath, they have the same building blocks, and the same fundamental principles apply.

This book gives you a framework—a way of thinking about system administration problems—rather than narrow how-to solutions to particular problems. Given a solid framework, you can solve problems every time they appear, regardless of the operating system (OS), brand of computer, or type of environment. This book is unique because it looks at system administration from this holistic point of view; whereas most other books for SAs focus on how to maintain one particular product. With experience, however, all SAs learn that the big-picture problems and solutions are largely independent of the platform. This book will change the way you approach your work as an SA.

The principles in this book apply to all environments. The approaches described may need to be scaled up or down, depending on your environment, but the basic principles still apply. Where we felt that it might not be obvious how to implement certain concepts, we have included sections that illustrate how to apply the principles at organizations of various sizes.

This book is not about how to configure or debug a particular OS and will not tell you how to recover the shared libraries or DLLs when someone accidentally moves them. Some excellent books cover those topics, and we refer you to many of them throughout. Instead, we discuss the principles, both basic and advanced, of good system administration that we have learned through our own and others' experiences. These principles apply to all OSs. Following them *well* can make your life a lot easier. If you improve the way you approach problems, the benefit will be multiplied. Get the fundamentals right, and everything else falls into place. If they aren't done well, you will waste time repeatedly fixing the same things, and your customers[1] will be unhappy because they can't work effectively with broken machines.

Who Should Read This Book

This book is written for system administrators at all levels. It gives junior SAs insight into the bigger picture of how sites work, their roles in the organizations, and how their careers can progress. Intermediate SAs will learn how to approach more complex problems and how to improve their sites and make their jobs easier and their customers happier. Whatever level you are at, this book will help you to understand what is behind your day-to-day work, to learn the things that you can do now to save time in the future, to decide policy, to be architects and designers, to plan far into the future, to negotiate with vendors, and to interface with management. These are the things that concern senior SAs. None of them are listed in an OS's manual. Even senior SAs and systems architects can learn from our experiences and those of our colleagues, just as we have learned from each other in writing this book. We also cover several management topics for SA trying to understand their managers, for SAs who aspire to move into management, and for SAs finding themselves doing more and more management without the benefit of the title.

Throughout the book, we use examples to illustrate our points. The examples are mostly from medium or large sites, where scale adds its own problems. Typically, the examples are generic rather than specific to a particular OS; where they are OS-specific, it is usually UNIX or Windows.

One of the strongest motivations we had for writing this book is the understanding that the problems SAs face are the same across all OSs. A new

---

1. Throughout the book, we refer to the end users of our systems as *customers* rather than *users*. A detailed explanation of why we do this is in Section 31.1.2.

OS that is significantly different from what we are used to can seem like a black box, a nuisance, or even a threat. However, despite the unfamiliar interface, as we get used to the new technology, we eventually realize that we face the same set of problems in deploying, scaling, and maintaining the new OS. Recognizing that fact, knowing what problems need solving, and understanding how to approach the solutions by building on experience with other OSs lets us master the new challenges more easily.

We want this book to change your life. We want you to become so successful that if you see us on the street, you'll give us a great big hug.

Basic Principles

If we've learned anything over the years, it is the importance of simplicity, clarity, generality, automation, communication, and doing the basics first. These six principles are recurring themes in this book.

1. *Simplicity* means that the smallest solution that solves the entire problem is the best solution. It keeps the systems easy to understand and reduces complex component interactions that can cause debugging nightmares.

2. *Clarity* means that the solution is straightforward. It can be easily explained to someone on the project or even outside the project. Clarity makes it easier to change the system, as well as to maintain and debug it. In the system administration world, it's better to write five lines of understandable code than one line that's incomprehensible to anyone else.

3. *Generality* means that the solutions aren't inherently limited to a particular case. Solutions can be reused. Using vendor-independent open standard protocols makes systems more flexible and makes it easier to link software packages together for better services.

4. *Automation* means using software to replace human effort. Automation is critical. Automation improves repeatability and scalability, is key to easing the system administration burden, and eliminates tedious repetitive tasks, giving SAs more time to improve services.

5. *Communication* between the right people can solve more problems than hardware or software can. You need to communicate well with other SAs and with your customers. It is your responsibility to initiate communication. Communication ensures that everyone is working

toward the same goals. Lack of communication leaves people concerned and annoyed. Communication also includes documentation. Documentation makes systems easier to support, maintain, and upgrade. Good communication and proper documentation also make it easier to hand off projects and maintenance when you leave or take on a new role.

6. *Basics first* means that you build the site on strong foundations by identifying and solving the basic problems before trying to attack more advanced ones. Doing the basics first makes adding advanced features considerably easier and makes services more robust. A good basic infrastructure can be repeatedly leveraged to improve the site with relatively little effort. Sometimes, we see SAs making a huge effort to solve a problem that wouldn't exist or would be a simple enhancement if the site had a basic infrastructure in place. This book will help you identify what the basics are and show you how the other five principles apply. Each chapter looks at the basics of a given area. Get the fundamentals right, and everything else will fall into place.

These principles are universal. They apply at all levels of the system. They apply to physical networks and to computer hardware. They apply to all operating systems running at a site, all protocols used, all software, and all services provided. They apply at universities, nonprofit institutions, government sites, businesses, and Internet service sites.

What Is an SA?

If you asked six system administrators to define their jobs, you would get seven different answers. The job is difficult to define because system administrators do so many things. An SA looks after computers, networks, and the people who use them. An SA may look after hardware, operating systems, software, configurations, applications, or security. A system administrator influences how effectively other people can or do use their computers and networks.

A system administrator sometimes needs to be a business-process consultant, corporate visionary, janitor, software engineer, electrical engineer, economist, psychiatrist, mindreader, and, occasionally, a bartender.

As a result, companies calls SAs different names. Sometimes, they are called network administrators, system architects, system engineers, system programmers, operators and so on.

This book is for "all of the above."

We have a very general definition of system administrator: one who manages computer and network systems on behalf of another, such as an employer or a client. SAs are the people who make things work and keep it all running.

Explaining What System Administration Entails

It's difficult to define system administration, but trying to explain it to a nontechnical person is even more difficult, especially if that person is your mom. Moms have the right to know how their offspring are paying their rent. A friend of Christine Hogan's always had trouble explaining to his mother what he did for a living and ended up giving a different answer every time she asked. Therefore, she kept repeating the question every couple of months, waiting for an answer that would be meaningful to her. Then he started working for WebTV. When the product became available, he bought one for his mom. From then on, he told her that he made sure that her WebTV service was working and was as fast as possible. She was very happy that she could now show her friends something and say, "That's what my son does!"

System Administration Matters

System administration matters because computers and networks matter. Computers are a lot more important than they were years ago. What happened?

The widespread use of the Internet, intranets, and the move to a web-centric world has redefined the way companies depend on computers. The Internet is a 24/7 operation, and sloppy operations can no longer be tolerated. Paper purchase orders can be processed daily, in batches, with no one the wiser. However, there is an expectation that the web-based system that does the process will be available all the time, from anywhere. Nightly maintenance windows have become an unheard-of luxury. That unreliable machine room power system that caused occasional but bearable problems now prevents sales from being recorded.

Management now has a more realistic view of computers. Before they had PCs on their desktops, most people's impressions of computers were based on how they were portrayed in film: big, all-knowing, self-sufficient, miracle machines. The more people had direct contact with computers, the more realistic people's expectations became. Now even system administration itself is portrayed in films. The 1993 classic *Jurassic Park* was the first mainstream movie to portray the key role that system administrators play in large systems.

The movie also showed how depending on one person is a disaster waiting to happen. IT is a team sport. If only Dennis Nedry had read this book.

In business, nothing is important unless the CEO feels that it is important. The CEO controls funding and sets priorities. CEOs now consider IT to be important. Email was previously for nerds; now CEOs depend on email and notice even brief outages. The massive preparations for Y2K also brought home to CEOs how dependent their organizations have become on computers, how expensive it can be to maintain them, and how quickly a purely technical issue can become a serious threat. Most people do not think that they simply "missed the bullet" during the Y2K change but that problems were avoided thanks to tireless efforts by many people. A CBS Poll shows 63 percent of Americans believe that the time and effort spent fixing potential problems was worth it. A look at the news lineups of all three major network news broadcasts from Monday, January 3, 2000, reflects the same feeling.

Previously, people did not grow up with computers and had to cautiously learn about them and their uses. Now more and more people grow up using computers, which means that they have higher expectations of them when they are in positions of power. The CEOs who were impressed by automatic payroll processing are soon to be replaced by people who grew up sending instant messages and want to know why they can't do all their business via text messaging.

Computers matter more than ever. If computers are to work and work well, system administration matters. We matter.

Organization of This Book

This book has the following major parts:

- Part I: Getting Started. This is a long book, so we start with an overview of what to expect (Chapter 1) and some tips to help you find enough time to read the rest of the book (Chapter 2).

- Part II: Foundation Elements. Chapters 3–14 focus on the foundations of IT infrastructure, the hardware and software that everything else depends on.

- Part III: Change Processes. Chapters 15–21 look at how to make changes to systems, starting with fixing the smallest bug to massive reorganizations.

- Part IV: Providing Services. Chapters 22–29 offer our advice on building seven basic services, such as email, printing, storage, and web services.
- Part V: Management Practices. Chapters 30–36 provide guidance—whether or not you have "manager" in your title.
- The two appendixes provide an overview of the positive and negative roles that SAs play and a list of acronyms used in the book.

Each chapter discusses a separate topic; some topics are technical, and some are nontechnical. If one chapter doesn't apply to you, feel free to skip it. The chapters are linked, so you may find yourself returning to a chapter that you previously thought was boring. We won't be offended.

Each chapter has two major sections. *The Basics* discusses the essentials that you simply have to get right. Skipping any of these items will simply create more work for you in the future. Consider them investments that pay off in efficiency later on. *The Icing* deals with the cool things that you can do to be spectacular. Don't spend your time with these things until you are done with the basics. We have tried to drive the points home through anecdotes and case studies from personal experience. We hope that this makes the advice here more "real" for you. Never trust salespeople who don't use their own products.

What's New in the Second Edition

We received a lot of feedback from our readers about the first edition. We spoke at conferences and computer user groups around the world. We received a lot of email. We listened. We took a lot of notes. We've smoothed the rough edges and filled some of the major holes.

The first edition garnered a lot of positive reviews and buzz. We were very honored. However, the passing of time made certain chapters look passé.

The first edition, in bookstores August 2001, was written mostly in 2000. Things were very different then. At the time, things were looking pretty grim as the dot-com boom had gone bust. Windows 2000 was still new, Solaris was king, and Linux was popular only with geeks. Spam was a nuisance, not an industry. Outsourcing had lost its luster and had gone from being the corporate savior to a late-night comedy punch line. Wikis were a research idea, not the basis for the world's largest free encyclopedia. Google was neither a household name nor a verb. Web farms were rare, and "big sites" served millions of hits per day, not per hour. In fact, we didn't have a chapter on running web servers, because we felt that all one needed to know could be inferred by reading the right combination of the chapters: Data Centers, Servers, Services, and Service Monitoring. What more could people need?

My, how things have changed!

Linux is no longer considered a risky proposition, Google is on the rise, and offshoring is the new buzzword. The rise of India and China as economic superpowers has changed the way we think about the world. AJAX and other Web 2.0 technologies have made the web applications exciting again.

Here's what's new in the book:

- *Updated chapters:* Every chapter has been updated and modernized and new anecdotes added. We clarified many, many points. We've learned a lot in the past five years, and all the chapters reflect this. References to old technologies have been replaced with more relevant ones.

- *New chapters:*
  - Chapter 9: Documentation
  - Chapter 25: Data Storage
  - Chapter 29: Web Services

- *Expanded chapters:*
  - The first edition's Appendix B, which had been missed by many readers who didn't read to the end of the book, is now Chapter 1: What to Do When . . . .
  - The first edition's Do These First section in the front matter has expanded to become Chapter 2: Climb Out of the Hole.

- *Reordered table of contents:*
  - Part I: Getting Started: introductory and overview material
  - Part II: Foundation Elements: the foundations of any IT system
  - Part III: Change Processes: how to make changes from the smallest to the biggest
  - Part IV: Providing Services: a catalog of common service offerings
  - Part V: Management Practices: organizational issues

What's Next

Each chapter is self-contained. Feel free to jump around. However, we have carefully ordered the chapters so that they make the most sense if you read the book from start to finish. Either way, we hope that you enjoy the book. We have learned a lot and had a lot of fun writing it. Let's begin.

Thomas A. Limoncelli
Google, Inc.
tom@limoncelli.org

Christina J. Hogan
BMW Sauber F1 Team
chogan@chogan.com

Strata R. Chalup
Virtual.Net, Inc.
strata@virtual.net

P.S. Books, like software, always have bugs. For a list of updates, along with news and notes, and even a mailing list you can join, please visit our web site: www.EverythingSysAdmin.com.

Acknowledgments

Acknowledgments for the First Edition

We can't possibly thank everyone who helped us in some way or another, but that isn't going to stop us from trying. Much of this book was inspired by Kernighan and Pike's *The Practice of Programming* (Kernighan and Pike 1999) and John Bentley's second edition of *Programming Pearls* (Bentley 1999).

We are grateful to Global Networking and Computing (GNAC), Synopsys, and Eircom for permitting us to use photographs of their data center facilities to illustrate real-life examples of the good practices that we talk about.

We are indebted to the following people for their helpful editing: Valerie Natale, Anne Marie Quint, Josh Simon, and Amara Willey.

The people we have met through USENIX and SAGE and the LISA conferences have been major influences in our lives and careers. We would not be qualified to write this book if we hadn't met the people we did and learned so much from them.

Dozens of people helped us as we wrote this book—some by supplying anecdotes, some by reviewing parts of or the entire book, others by mentoring us during our careers. The only fair way to thank them all is alphabetically and to apologize in advance to anyone that we left out: Rajeev Agrawala, Al Aho, Jeff Allen, Eric Anderson, Ann Benninger, Eric Berglund, Melissa Binde, Steven Branigan, Sheila Brown-Klinger, Brent Chapman, Bill Cheswick, Lee Damon, Tina Darmohray, Bach Thuoc (Daisy) Davis, R. Drew Davis, Ingo Dean, Arnold de Leon, Jim Dennis, Barbara Dijker, Viktor Dukhovni, Chelle-Marie Ehlers, Michael Erlinger, Paul Evans, Rémy Evard, Lookman Fazal, Robert Fulmer, Carson Gaspar, Paul Glick, David "Zonker" Harris, Katherine "Cappy" Harrison, Jim Hickstein, Sandra Henry-Stocker, Mark Horton, Bill "Whump" Humphries, Tim Hunter, Jeff Jensen, Jennifer Joy, Alan Judge, Christophe Kalt, Scott C. Kennedy, Brian Kernighan, Jim Lambert, Eliot Lear,

Steven Levine, Les Lloyd, Ralph Loura, Bryan MacDonald, Sherry McBride, Mark Mellis, Cliff Miller, Hal Miller, Ruth Milner, D. Toby Morrill, Joe Morris, Timothy Murphy, Ravi Narayan, Nils-Peter Nelson, Evi Nemeth, William Ninke, Cat Okita, Jim Paradis, Pat Parseghian, David Parter, Rob Pike, Hal Pomeranz, David Presotto, Doug Reimer, Tommy Reingold, Mike Richichi, Matthew F. Ringel, Dennis Ritchie, Paul D. Rohrigstamper, Ben Rosengart, David Ross, Peter Salus, Scott Schultz, Darren Shaw, Glenn Sieb, Karl Siil, Cicely Smith, Bryan Stansell, Hal Stern, Jay Stiles, Kim Supsinkas, Ken Thompson, Greg Tusar, Kim Wallace, The Rabbit Warren, Dr. Geri Weitzman, PhD, Glen Wiley, Pat Wilson, Jim Witthoff, Frank Wojcik, Jay Yu, and Elizabeth Zwicky.

Thanks also to Lumeta Corporation and Lucent Technologies/Bell Labs for their support in writing this book.

Last but not least, the people at Addison-Wesley made this a particularly great experience for us. In particular, our gratitude extends to Karen Gettman, Mary Hart, and Emily Frey.

Acknowledgments for the Second Edition

In addition to everyone who helped us with the first edition, the second edition could not have happened without the help and support of Lee Damon, Nathan Dietsch, Benjamin Feen, Stephen Harris, Christine E. Polk, Glenn E. Sieb, Juhani Tali, and many people at the League of Professional System Administrators (LOPSA). Special 73s and 88s to Mike Chalup for love, loyalty, and support, and especially for the mountains of laundry done and oceans of dishes washed so Strata could write. And many cuddles and kisses for baby Joanna Lear for her patience.

Thanks to Lumeta Corporation for giving us permission to publish a second edition.

Thanks to Wingfoot for letting us use its server for our bug-tracking database.

Thanks to Anne Marie Quint for data entry, copyediting, and a lot of great suggestions.

And last but not least, a big heaping bowl of "couldn't have done it without you" to Mark Taub, Catherine Nolan, Raina Chrobak, and Lara Wysong at Addison-Wesley.

About the Authors

Tom, Christine, and Strata know one another through attending USENIX conferences and being actively involved in the system administration community. It was at one of these conferences that Tom and Christine first spoke about collaborating on this book. Strata and Christine were coworkers at Synopsys and GNAC, and coauthored Chalup, Hogan et al. (1998).

Thomas A. Limoncelli

Tom is an internationally recognized author and speaker on system administration, time management, and grass-roots political organizing techniques. A system administrator since 1988, he has worked for small and large companies, including Google, Cibernet Corp, Dean for America, Lumeta, AT&T, Lucent/Bell Labs, and Mentor Graphics. At Google, he is involved in improving how IT infrastructure is deployed at new offices. When AT&T trivested into AT&T, Lucent, and NCR, Tom led the team that split the Bell Labs computing and network infrastructure into the three new companies.

In addition to the first and second editions of this book, his published works include *Time Management for System Administration* (2005), and papers on security, networking, project management, and personal career management. He travels to conferences and user groups frequently, often teaching tutorials, facilitating workshops, presenting papers, or giving invited talks and keynote speeches.

Outside of work, Tom is a grassroots civil-rights activist who has received awards and recognition on both state and national levels. Tom's first published paper (Limoncelli 1997) extolled the lessons SAs can learn from activists. Tom doesn't see much difference between his work and activism careers—both are about helping people.

He holds a B.A. in computer science from Drew University. He lives in Bloomfield, New Jersey.

For their community involvement, Tom and Christine shared the 2005 Outstanding Achievement Award from USENIX/SAGE.

Christina J. Hogan

Christine's system administration career started at the Department of Mathematics in Trinity College, Dublin, where she worked for almost 5 years. After that, she went in search of sunshine and moved to Sicily, working for a year in a research company, and followed that with 5 years in California.

She was the security architect at Synopsys for a couple of years before joining some friends at GNAC a few months after it was founded. While there, she worked with start-ups, e-commerce sites, biotech companies, and large multinational hardware and software companies. On the technical side, she focused on security and networking, working with customers and helping GNAC establish its data center and Internet connectivity. She also became involved with project management, customer management, and people management. After almost 3 years at GNAC, she went out on her own as an independent security consultant, working primarily at e-commerce sites.

Since then, she has become a mother and made a career change: she now works as an aerodynamicist for the BMW Sauber Formula 1 Racing Team. She has a Ph.D. in aeronautical engineering from Imperial College, London; a B.A. in mathematics and an M.Sc. in computer science from Trinity College, Dublin; and a Diploma in legal studies from the Dublin Institute of Technology.

Strata R. Chalup

Strata is the owner and senior consultant of Virtual.Net, Inc., a strategic and best-practices IT consulting firm specializing in helping small to midsize firms scale their IT practices as they grow. During the first dot-com boom, Strata architected scalable infrastructures and managed some of the teams that built them for such projects as talkway.net, the Palm VII, and mac.com. Founded as a sole proprietorship in 1993, Virtual.Net was incorporated in 2005. Clients have included such firms as Apple, Sun, Cimflex Teknowledge, Cisco, McAfee, and Micronas USA.

Strata joined the computing world on TOPS-20 on DEC mainframes in 1981, then got well and truly sidetracked onto administering UNIX by 1983, with Ultrix on the VAX 11-780, Unisys on Motorola 68K micro systems, and a dash of Minix on Intel thrown in for good measure. She has the unusual perspective of someone who has been both a user and an administrator of Internet services since 1981 and has seen much of what we consider the modern Net evolve, sometimes from a front-row seat. An early adopter and connector, she was involved with the early National Telecommunications Infrastructure Administration (NTIA) hearings and grant reviews from 1993–1995 and demonstrated the emerging possibilities of the Internet in 1994, creating NTIA's groundbreaking virtual conference. A committed futurist, Strata avidly tracks new technologies for collaboration and leverages them for IT and management.

Always a New Englander at heart, but marooned in California with a snow-hating spouse, Strata is an active gardener, reader of science fiction/fantasy, and emergency services volunteer in amateur radio (KF6NBZ). She is SCUBA-certified but mostly free dives and snorkles. Strata has spent a couple of years as a technomad crossing the country by RV, first in 1990 and again in 2002, consulting from the road. She has made a major hobby of studying energy-efficient building construction and design, including taking owner-builder classes, and really did grow up on a goat farm.

Unlike her illustrious coauthors, she is an unrepentent college dropout, having left MIT during her sophmore year. She returned to manage the Center for Cognitive Science for several years, and to consult with the EECS Computing Services group, including a year as postmaster@mit-eddie, before heading to Silicon Valley.

Part I

Getting Started

Chapter 1

What to Do When . . .

In this chapter, we pull together the various elements from the rest of the book to provide an overview of how they can be used to deal with everyday situations or to answer common questions system administrators (SAs) and managers often have.

1.1 Building a Site from Scratch

- Think about the organizational structure you need—Chapter 30.
- Check in with management on the business priorities that will drive implementation priorities.
- Plan your namespaces carefully—Chapter 8.
- Build a rock-solid data center—Chapter 6.
- Build a rock-solid network designed to grow—Chapter 7.
- Build services that will scale—Chapter 5.
- Build a software depot, or at least plan a small directory hierarchy that can grow into a software depot—Chapter 28.
- Establish your initial core application services:
  - Authentication and authorization—Section 3.1.3
  - Desktop life-cycle management—Chapter 3
  - Email—Chapter 23
  - File service, backups—Chapter 26
  - Network configuration—Section 3.1.3
  - Printing—Chapter 24
  - Remote access—Chapter 27

1.2 Growing a Small Site

- Provide a helpdesk—Chapter 13.
- Establish checklists for new hires, new desktops/laptops, and new servers—Section 3.1.1.5.
- Consider the benefits of a network operations center (NOC) dedicated to monitoring and coordinating network operations—Chapter 22.
- Think about your organization and whom you need to hire, and provide service statistics showing open and resolved problems—Chapter 30.
- Monitor services for both capacity and availability so that you can predict when to scale them—Chapter 22.
- Be ready for an influx of new computers, employees, and SAs—See Sections 1.23, 1.24, and 1.25.

1.3 Going Global

- Design your wide area network (WAN) architecture—Chapter 7.
- Follow three cardinal rules: scale, scale, and scale.
- Standardize server times on Greenwich Mean Time (GMT) to maximize log analysis capabilities.
- Make sure that your helpdesk really is 24/7. Look at ways to leverage SAs in other time zones—Chapter 13.
- Architect services to take account of long-distance links—usually lower bandwidth and less reliable—Chapter 5.
- Qualify applications for use over high-latency links—Section 5.1.2.
- Ensure that your security and permissions structures are still adequate under global operations.

1.4 Replacing Services

- Be conscious of the process—Chapter 18.
- Factor in both network dependencies and service dependencies in transition planning.
- Manage your Dynamic Host Configuration Protocol (DHCP) lease times to aid the transition—Section 3.1.4.1.

- Don't hard-code server names into configurations, instead, hard-code aliases that move with the service—Section 5.1.6.
- Manage your DNS time-to-live (TTL) values to switch to new servers—Section 19.2.1.

1.5 Moving a Data Center

- Schedule windows unless everything is fully redundant and you can move first half of a redundant pair and then the other—Chapter 20.
- Make sure that the new data center is properly designed for both current use and future expansion—Chapter 6.
- Back up every file system of any machine before it is moved.
- Perform a fire drill on your data backup system—Section 26.2.1.
- Develop test cases before you move, and test, test, test everything after the move is complete—Chapter 18.
- Label every cable before it is disconnected—Section 6.1.7.
- Establish minimal services—redundant hardware—at a new location with new equipment.
- Test the new environment—networking, power, uninterruptable power supply (UPS), heating, ventilation, air conditioning (HVAC), and so on—before the move begins—Chapter 6, especially Section 6.1.4.
- Identify a small group of customers to test business operations with the newly moved minimal services, then test sample scenarios before moving everything else.
- Run cooling for 48–72 hours, and then replace all filters before occupying the space.
- Perform a dress rehearsal—Section 18.2.5.

1.6 Moving to/Opening a New Building

- Four weeks or more in advance, get access to the new space to build the infrastructure.
- Use radios or walkie-talkies for communicating inside the building—Chapter 6 and Section 20.1.7.3.

- Use a personal digital assistant (PDA) or nonelectronic organizer—Section 32.1.2.
- Order WAN and Internet service provider (ISP) network connections 2–3 months in advance.
- Communicate to the powers that be that WAN and ISP connections will take months to order and must be done soon.
- Prewire the offices with network jacks during, not after, construction—Section 7.1.4.
- Work with a moving company that can help plan the move.
- Designate one person to keep and maintain a master list of everyone who is moving and his or her new office number, cubicle designation, or other location.
- Pick a day on which to freeze the master list. Give copies of the frozen list to the moving company, use the list for printing labels, and so on. If someone's location is to be changed after this date, don't try to chase down and update all the list copies that have been distributed. Move the person as the master list dictates, and schedule a second move for that person after the main move.
- Give each person a sheet of 12 labels preprinted with his or her name and new location for labeling boxes, bags, and personal computer (PC). (If you don't want to do this, at least give people specific instructions as to what to write on each box so it reaches the right destination.)
- Give each person a plastic bag big enough for all the PC cables. Technical people can decable and reconnect their PCs on arrival; technicians can do so for nontechnical people.
- Always order more boxes than you think you'll be moving.
- Don't use cardboard boxes; instead, use plastic crates that can be reused.

1.7 Handling a High Rate of Office Moves

- Work with facilities to allocate only one move day each week. Develop a routine around this schedule.
- Establish a procedure and a form that will get you all the information you need about each person's equipment, number of network and telephone connections, and special needs. Have SAs check out nonstandard equipment in advance and make notes.

- Connect and test network connections ahead of time.

- Have customers power down their machines before the move and put all cables, mice, keyboards, and other bits that might get lost into a marked box.

- Brainstorm all the ways that some of the work can be done by the people moving. Be careful to assess their skill level; maybe certain people shouldn't do anything themselves.

- Have a moving company move the equipment, and have a designated SA move team do the unpacking, reconnecting, and testing. Take care in selecting the moving company.

- Train the helpdesk to check with customers who report problems to see whether they have just moved and didn't have the problem before the move; then pass those requests to the move team rather than the usual escalation path.

- Formalize the process, limiting it to one day a week, doing the prep work, and having a move team makes it go more smoothly with less downtime for the customers and fewer move-related problems for the SAs to check out.

1.8 Assessing a Site (Due Diligence)

- Use the chapters and subheadings in this book to create a preliminary list of areas to investigate, taking the items in the Basics section as a rough baseline for a well-run site.

- Reassure existing SA staff and management that you are here not to pass judgment but to discover how this site works, in order to understand its similarities to and differences from sites with which you are already familiar. This is key in both consulting assignments and in potential acquisition due-diligence assessments.

- Have a private document repository, such as a wiki, for your team. The amount of information you will collect will overwhelm your ability to remember it: document, document, document.

- Create or request physical-equipment lists of workstations and servers, as well as network diagrams and service workflows. The goal is to generate multiple views of the infrastructure.

- Review domains of authentication, and pay attention to compartmentalization and security of information.

- Analyze the ticket-system statistics by opened-to-close ratios month to month. Watch for a growing gap between total opened and closed tickets, indicating an overloaded staff or an infrastructure system with chronic difficulties.

1.9 Dealing with Mergers and Acquisitions

- If mergers and acquisitions will be frequent, make arrangements to get information as early as possible, even if this means that designated people will have information that prevents them from being able to trade stock for certain windows of time.

- Some mergers require instant connectivity to the new business unit. Others are forbidden from having full connectivity for a month or so until certain papers are signed. In the first case, set expectations that this will not be possible without some prior warning (see previous item). In the latter case, you have some breathing room, but act quickly!

- If you are the chief executive officer (CEO), you should involve your chief information officer (CIO) before the merger is even announced.

- If you are an SA, try to find out who at the other company has the authority to make the big decisions.

- Establish clear, final decision processes.

- Have one designated go-to lead per company.

- Start a dialogue with the SAs at the other company. Understand their support structure, service levels, network architecture, security model, and policies. Determine what the new model is going to look like.

- Have at least one initial face-to-face meeting with the SAs at the other company. It's easier to get angry at someone you haven't met.

- Move on to technical details. Are there namespace conflicts? If so, determine how are you going to resolve them—Chapter 8.

- Adopt the best processes of the two companies; don't blindly select the processes of the bigger company.

- Be sensitive to cultural differences between the two groups. Diverse opinions can be a good thing if people can learn to respect one another—Sections 32.2.2.2 and 35.1.5.

- Make sure that both SA teams have a high-level overview diagram of both networks, as well as a detailed map of each site's local area network (LAN)—Chapter 7.

- Determine what the new network architecture should look like—Chapter 7. How will the two networks be connected? Are some remote offices likely to merge? What does the new security model or security perimeter look like?—Chapter 11.

- Ask senior management about corporate-identity issues, such as account names, email address format, and domain name. Do the corporate identities need to merge or stay separate? What implications does this have on the email infrastructure and Internet-facing services?

- Learn whether any customers or business partners of either company will be sensitive to the merger and/or want their intellectual property protected from the other company—Chapter 7.

- Compare the security policies, mentioned in Chapter 11—looking in particular for differences in privacy policy, security policy, and how they interconnect with business partners.

- Check router tables of both companies, and verify that the Internet Protocol (IP) address space in use doesn't overlap. (This is particularly a problem if you both use RFC 1918 address space [Lear et al. 1994, Rekhler et al. 1996].)

- Consider putting a firewall between the two companies until both have compatible security policies—Chapter 11.

1.10 Coping with Frequent Machine Crashes

- Establish a temporary workaround, and communicate to customers that it is temporary.

- Find the real cause—Chapter 15.

- Fix the real cause, not the symptoms—Chapter 16.

- If the root cause is hardware, buy better hardware—Chapter 4.

- If the root cause is environmental, provide a better physical environment for your hardware—Chapter 6.

- Replace the system—Chapter 18.

- Give your SAs better training on diagnostic tools—Chapter 15.

- Get production systems back into production quickly. Don't play diagnostic games on production systems. That's what labs and preannounced maintenance windows—usually weekends or late nights—are for.

1.11 Surviving a Major Outage or Work Stoppage

- Consider modeling your outage response on the Incident Command System (ICS). This ad hoc emergency response system has been refined over many years by public safety departments to create a flexible response to adverse situations. Defining escalation procedures *before an issue arises* is the best strategy.

- Notify customers that you are aware of the problem on the communication channels they would use to contact you: intranet help desk "outages" section, outgoing message for SA phone, and so on.

- Form a "tiger team" of SAs, management, and key stakeholders; have a brief 15- to 30-minute meeting to establish the specific goals of a solution, such as "get developers working again," "restore customer access to support site" and so on. Make sure that you are working toward a goal, not simply replicating functionality whose value is nonspecific.

- Establish the costs of a workaround or fallback position versus downtime owing to the problem, and let the businesspeople and stakeholders determine how much time is worth spending on attempting a fix. If information is insufficient to estimate this, do not end the meeting without setting the time for the next attempt.

- Spend no more than an hour gathering information. Then hold a team meeting to present management and key stakeholders with options. The team should do hourly updates of the passive notification message with status.

- If the team chooses fix or workaround attempts, specify an order in which fixes are to be applied, and get assistance from stakeholders on verifying that the each procedure did or did not work. Document this, even in brief, to prevent duplication of effort if you are still working on the issue hours or days from now.

- Implement fix or workaround attempts in small blocks of two or three, taking no more than an hour to implement total. Collect error message or log data that may be relevant, and report on it in the next meeting.

- Don't allow a team member, even a highly skilled one, to go off to try to pull a rabbit out of his or her hat. Since you can't predict the length of the outage, you must apply a strict process in order to keep everyone in the loop.

- Appoint a team member who will ensure that meals are brought in, notes taken, and people gently but firmly disengaged from the problem if they become too tired or upset to work.

1.12   What Tools Should Every SA Team Member Have?

- A laptop with network diagnostic tools, such as network sniffer, DHCP client in verbose mode, encrypted TELNET/SSH client, TFTP server, and so on, as well as both wired and wireless Ethernet.
- Terminal emulator software and a serial cable. The laptop can be an emergency serial console if the console server dies or the data center console breaks or a rogue server outside the data center needs console access.
- A spare PC or server for experimenting with new configurations— Section 19.2.1.
- A portable label printer—Section 6.1.12.
- A PDA or nonelectronic organizer—Section 32.1.2.
- A set of screwdrivers in all the sizes computers use.
- A cable tester.
- A pair of splicing scissors.
- Access to patch cables of various lengths. Include one or two 100-foot (30-meter) cables. These come in handy in the strangest emergencies.
- A small digital camera. (Sending a snapshot to technical support can be useful for deciphering strange console messages, identifying model numbers, and proving damage.)
- A portable (USB)/firewire hard drive.
- Radios or walkie-talkies for communicating inside the building— Chapter 6 and Section 20.1.7.3.
- A cabinet stocked with tools and spare parts—Section 6.1.12.
- High-speed connectivity to team members' home and the necessary tools for telecommuting.
- A library of the standard reference books for the technologies the team members are involved in—Sections 33.1.1, 34.1.7, and bibliography.
- Membership to professional societies such as USENIX and LOPSA— Section 32.1.4.

- A variety of headache medicines. It's really difficult to solve big problems when you have a headache.
- Printed, framed, copies of the SA Code of Ethics—Section 12.1.2.
- Shelf-stable emergency-only snacky bits.
- A copy of this book!

1.13 Ensuring the Return of Tools

- Make it easier to return tools: Affix each with a label that reads, "Return to [your name here] when done."
- When someone borrows something, open a helpdesk ticket that is closed only when the item is returned.
- Accept that tools won't be returned. Why stress out about things you can't control?
- Create a team toolbox and rotate responsibility for keeping it up to date and tracking down loaners.
- Keep a stash of PC screwdriver kits. When asked to borrow a single screw driver, smile and reply, "No, but you can have this kit as a gift." Don't accept it back.
- Don't let a software person have a screwdriver. Politely find out what the person is trying to do, and do it. This is faster than fixing the person's mistakes.
- If you are a software person, use a screwdriver only with adult supervision.
- Keep a few inexpensive eyeglass repair kits in your spares area.

1.14 Why Document Systems and Procedures?

- Good documentation describes the *why* and the *how to*.
- When you do things right and they "just work," even you will have forgotten the details when they break or need upgrading.
- You get to go on vacation—Section 32.2.2.
- You get to move on to more interesting projects rather than being stuck doing the same stuff because you are the only one who knows how it works—Section 22.2.1.

- You will get a reputation as being a real asset to the company: raises, bonuses, and promotions, or at least fame and fortune.
- You will save yourself a mad scramble to gather information when investors or auditors demand it on short notice.

1.15 Why Document Policies?

- To comply with federal health and business regulations.
- To avoid appearing arbitrary, "making it up as you go along," and senior management doing things that would get other employees into trouble.
- Because other people can't read your mind—Section A.1.17.
- To communicate expectations for your own team, not only your customers—Section 11.1.2 and Chapter 12.
- To avoid being unethical by enforcing a policy that isn't communicated to the people that it governs—Section 12.2.1.
- To avoid punishing people for not reading your mind—Section A.1.17.
- To offer the organization a chance to change their ways or push back in a constructive manner.

1.16 Identifying the Fundamental Problems in the Environment

- Look at the Basics section of each chapter.
- Survey the management chain that funds you—Chapter 30.
- Survey two or three customers who use your services—Section 26.2.2.
- Survey all customers.
- Identify what kinds of problems consume your time the most—Section 26.1.3.
- Ask the helpdesk employees what problems they see the most—Sections 15.1.6 and 25.1.4.
- Ask the people configuring the devices in the field what problems they see the most and what customers complain about the most.
- Determine whether your architecture is simple enough to draw by hand on a whiteboard; if its not, maybe it's too complicated to manage—Section 18.1.2.

1.17 Getting More Money for Projects

- Establish the need in the minds of your managers.
- Find out what management wants, and communicate how the projects you need money for will serve that goal.
- Become part of the budget process—Sections 33.1.1.12 and 34.1.6.
- Do more with less: Make sure that your staff has good time-management skills—Section 32.1.2.
- Manage your boss better—Section 32.2.3.
- Learn how your management communicates with you, and communicate in a compatible way—Chapters 33 and 34.
- Don't overwork or manage by crisis. Show management the "real cost" of policies and decisions.

1.18 Getting Projects Done

- Usually, projects don't get done because the SAs are required to put out new fires while trying to do projects. Solve this problem first.
- Get a management sponsor. Is the project something that the business needs, or is it something the SAs want to implement on their own? If the former, use the sponsor to gather resources and deflect conflicting demands. If a project isn't tied to true business needs, it is doubtful whether it should succeed.
- Make sure that the SAs have the resources to succeed. (Don't guess; ask them!)
- Hold your staff accountable for meeting milestones and deadlines.
- Communicate priorities to the SAs; move resources to high-impact projects—Section 33.1.4.2.
- Make sure that the people involved have good time-management skills—Section 32.1.2.
- Designate project time when some staff will work on nothing but projects, and the remaining staff will shield them from interruptions—Section 31.1.3.
- Reduce the number of projects.
- Don't spend time on the projects that don't matter—Figure 33.1.
- Prioritize → Focus → Win.

- Use an external consultant with direct experience in that area to achieve the highest-impact projects—Sections 21.2.2, 27.1.5, and 30.1.8.
- Hire junior or clerical staff to take on mundane tasks, such as PC desktop support, daily backups, and so on, so that SAs have more time to achieve the highest-impact projects.
- Hire short-term contract programmers to write code to spec.

1.19 Keeping Customers Happy

- Make sure that you make a good impression on new customers—Section 31.1.1.
- Make sure that you *communicate more* with existing customers—Section 31.2.4 and Chapter 31.
- Go to lunch with them and listen—Section 31.2.7.
- Create a System Status web page—Section 31.2.1.
- Create a local Enterprise Portal for your site—Section 31.2.1.
- Terminate the worst performers, especially if their mistakes create more work for others—See Chapter 36.
- See whether a specific customer or customer group generates an unusual proportion of complaints or tickets compared to the norm. If so, arrange a meeting with the customer's manager and your manager to acknowledge the situation. Follow this with a solution-oriented meeting with the customer's manager and the stakeholders that manager appoints. Work out priorities and an action plan to address the issues.

1.20 Keeping Management Happy

- Meet with the managers in person to listen to the complaints: *don't* try to do it via email.
- Find out your manager's priorities, and adopt them as your own—Section 32.2.3.
- Be sure that you know how management communicates with you, and communicate in a compatible way—Chapters 33 and 34.
- Make sure that the people in specialized roles understand their roles—Appendix A.

1.21 Keeping SAs Happy

- Make sure that their direct manager knows how to manage them well—Chapter 33.
- Make sure that executive management supports the management of SAs—Chapter 34.
- Make sure that the SAs are taking care of themselves—Chapter 32.
- Make sure that the SAs are in roles that they want and understand—Appendix A.
- If SAs are overloaded, make sure that they manage their time well—Section 32.1.2; or hire more people and divide the work—Chapter 35.
- Fire any SAs who are fomenting discontent—Chapter 36.
- Make sure that all new hires have positive dispositions—Section 13.1.2.

1.22 Keeping Systems from Being Too Slow

- Define *slow*.
- Use your monitoring systems to establish where the bottlenecks are—Chapter 22.
- Look at performance-tuning information that is specific to each architecture so that you know what to monitor and how to do it.
- Recommend a solution based on your findings.
- Know what the real problem is before you try to fix it—Chapter 15.
- Make sure that you understand the difference between latency and bandwidth—Section 5.1.2.

1.23 Coping with a Big Influx of Computers

- Make sure that you understand the *economic difference* between *desktop* and *server* hardware. Educate your boss or chief financial officer (CFO) about the difference or they will balk at high-priced servers—Section 4.1.3.
- Make sure that you understand the *physical differences* between desktop and server hardware—Section 4.1.1.
- Establish a small number of standard hardware configurations, and purchase them in bulk—Section 3.2.3.

- Make sure that you have automated host installation, configuration, and updates—Chapter 3.

- Check power, space, and heating, ventilating, and air conditioning (HVAC) capacity for your data center—Chapter 6.

- Ensure that even small computer rooms or closets have a cooling unit— Section 2.1.5.5.

- If new machines are for new employees, see Section 1.24.

1.24 Coping with a Big Influx of New Users

- Make sure that the hiring process includes ensuring that new computers and accounts are set up before the new hires arrive—Section 31.1.1.

- Have a stockpile of standard desktops preconfigured and ready to deploy.

- Have automated host installation, configuration, and updates— Chapter 3.

- Have proper new-user documentation and adequate staff to do orientation—Section 31.1.1.

- Make sure that every computer has at least one simple game and a CD/DVD player. It makes new computer users feel good about their machines.

- Ensure that the building can withstand the increase in power utilization.

- If dozens of people are starting each week, encourage the human resources department to have them all start on a particular day of the week, such as Mondays, so that all tasks related to information technology (IT) can be done in batches and therefore assembly-lined.

1.25 Coping with a Big Influx of New SAs

- Assign mentors to junior SAs—Sections 33.1.1.9 and 35.1.5.

- Have an orientation for each SA level to make sure the new hires understand the key processes and policies; make sure that it is clear whom they should go to for help.

- Have documentation, especially a wiki—Chapter 9.

- Purchase proper reference books, both technical and nontechnical— time management, communication, and people skills—Chapter 32.

- Bulk-order the items in Section 1.12.

1.26 Handling a High SA Team Attrition Rate

- When an SA leaves, completely lock them out of all systems—Chapter 36.
- Be sure that the human resources department performs exit interviews.
- Make the group aware that you are willing to listen to complaints in private.
- Have an "upward feedback session" at which your staff reviews your performance.
- Have an anonymous "upward feedback session" so that your staff can review your performance.
- Determine what you, as a manager, might be doing wrong—Chapters 33 and 34.
- Do things that increase morale: Have the team design and produce a T-shirt together—a dozen dollars spent on T-shirts can induce a morale improvement that thousands of dollars in raises can't.
- Encourage everyone in the group to read Chapter 32.
- If everyone is leaving because of one bad apple, get rid of him or her.

1.27 Handling a High User-Base Attrition Rate

- Make sure that management signals the SA team to disable accounts, remote access, and so on, in a timely manner—Chapter 36.
- Make sure that exiting employees return all company-owned equipment and software they have at home.
- Take measures against theft as people leave.
- Take measures against theft of intellectual property, possibly restricting remote access.

1.28 Being New to a Group

- Before you comment, ask questions to make sure that you understand the situation.
- Meet all your coworkers one on one.
- Meet with customers both informally and formally—Chapter 31.
- Be sure to make a good first impression, especially with customers—Section 31.1.1.

- Give credence to your coworkers when they tell you what the problems in the group are. Don't reject them out of hand.

- Don't blindly believe your coworkers when they tell you what the problems in the group are. Verify them first.

1.29 Being the New Manager of a Group

- That new system or conversion that's about to go live? Stop it until you've verified that it meets your high expectations. Don't let your predecessor's incompetence become your first big mistake.

- Meet all your employees one on one. Ask them what they do, what role they would like to be in, and where they see themselves in a year. Ask them how they feel you can work with them best. The purpose of this meeting is to listen to them, not to talk.

- Establish weekly group staff meetings.

- Meet your manager and your peers one on one to get their views.

- From day one, show the team members that you have faith in them all—Chapter 33.

- Meet with customers informally and formally—Chapter 31.

- Ask everyone to tell you what the problems facing the group are, listen carefully to everyone, and then look at the evidence and make up your own mind.

- Before you comment, ask questions to make sure that you understand the situation.

- If you've been hired to reform an underperforming group, postpone major high-risk projects, such as replacing a global email system, until you've reformed/replaced the team.

1.30 Looking for a New Job

- Determine why you are looking for a new job; understand your motivation.

- Determine what role you want to play in the new group—Appendix A.

- Determine which kind of organization you enjoy working in the most—Section 30.3.

- Meet as many of your potential future coworkers as possible to find out what the group is like—Chapter 35.

- Never accept the first offer right off the bat. The first offer is just a proposal. Negotiate! But remember that there usually isn't a third offer—Section 32.2.1.5.

- Negotiate in writing the things that are important to you: conferences, training, vacation.

- Don't work for a company that doesn't let you interview your future boss.

- If someone says, "You don't need to have a lawyer review this contract" and isn't joking, you should have a lawyer review that contract. We're not joking.

1.31 Hiring Many New SAs Quickly

- Review the advice in Chapter 35.

- Use as many recruiting methods as possible: Organize fun events at the appropriate conferences, use online boards, sponsor local user groups, hire famous people to speak at your company and invite the public, get referrals from SAs and customers—Chapter 35.

- Make sure that you have a good recruiter and human resources contact who knows what a good SA is.

- Determine how many SAs of what level and what skills you need. Use the SAGE level classifications—Section 35.1.2.

- *Move quickly* when you find a good candidate.

- After you've hired one person, refine the other job descriptions to fill in the gaps—Section 30.1.4.

1.32 Increasing Total System Reliability

- Figure out what your target is and how far you are from it.

- Set up monitoring to pinpoint uptime problems—Chapter 22.

- Deploy end-to-end monitoring for key applications—Section 24.2.4.

- Reduce dependencies. Nothing in the data center should rely on anything outside the data center—Sections 5.1.7 and 20.1.7.1.

1.33 Decreasing Costs

- Decrease costs by centralizing some services—Chapter 21.
- Review your maintenance contracts. Are you still paying for machines that are no longer critical servers? Are you paying high maintenance on old equipment that would be cheaper to replace?—Section 4.1.4.
- Reduce running costs, such as remote access, through outsourcing—Chapter 27 and Section 21.2.2.
- Determine whether you can reduce the support burden through standards and/or automation?—Chapter 3.
- Try to reduce support overhead through applications training for customers or better documentation.
- Try to distribute costs more directly to the groups that incur them, such as maintenance charges, remote access charges, special hardware, high-bandwidth use of wide-area links—Section 30.1.2.
- Determine whether people are not paying for the services you provide. If people aren't willing to pay for the service, it isn't important.
- Take control of the ordering process and inventory for incidental equipment such as replacement mice, minihubs, and similar. Do not let customers simply take what they need or direct your staff to order it.

1.34 Adding Features

- Interview customers to understand their needs and to prioritize features.
- Know the requirements—Chapter 5.
- Make sure that you maintain at least existing service and availability levels.
- If altering an existing service, have a back-out plan.
- Look into building an entirely new system and cutting over rather than altering the running one.
- If it's a really big infrastructure change, consider a maintenance window—Chapter 20.
- Decentralize so that local features can be catered to.
- Test! Test! Test!
- Document! Document! Document!

1.35 Stopping the Hurt When Doing "This"

- Don't do "that."
- Automate "that."

If It Hurts, Don't Do It

A small field office of a multinational company had a visit from a new SA supporting the international field offices. The local person who performed the SA tasks when there was no SA had told him over the telephone that the network was "painful." He assumed that she meant painfully slow until he got there and got a powerful electrical shock from the 10Base-2 network. He closed the office and sent everyone home immediately while he called an electrician to trace and fix the problem.

1.36 Building Customer Confidence

- Improve follow-through—Section 32.1.1.
- Focus on projects that matter to the customers and will have the biggest impact—Figure 33.1.
- Until you have enough time to complete the ones you need to, discard projects that you haven't been able to achieve.
- Communicate more—Chapter 31.
- Go to lunch with customers and listen—Section 31.2.7.
- Create a good first impression on the people entering your organization—Section 31.1.1.

1.37 Building the Team's Self-Confidence

- Start with a few simple, achievable projects; only then should you involve the team in more difficult projects.
- Ask team members what training they feel they need, and provide it.
- Coach the team. Get coaching on how to coach!

1.38 Improving the Team's Follow-Through

- Find out why team members are not following through.
- Make sure that your trouble-ticket system assists them in tracking customer requests and that it isn't simply for tracking short-term requests.

Be sure that the system isn't so cumbersome that people avoid using it—Section 13.1.10.

- Encourage team members to have a single place to list all their requests—Section 32.1.1.
- Discourage team members from trying to keep to-do lists in their heads—Section 32.1.1.
- Purchase PDAs for all team members who want them and promise to use them—Section 32.1.1.

1.39 Handling an Unethical or Worrisome Request

- See Section 12.2.2.
- Log all requests, events, and actions.
- Get the request in writing or email. Try a a soft approach, such as "Hey, could you email me exactly what you want, and I'll look at it after lunch?" Someone who knows that the request is unethical will resist leaving a trail.
- Check for a written policy about the situation—Chapter 12.
- If there is no written policy, absolutely get the request in writing.
- Consult with your manager *before* doing anything.
- If you have any questions about the request, escalate it to appropriate management.

1.40 My Dishwasher Leaves Spots on My Glasses

- Spots are usually the result of not using hot enough water rather than finding a special soap or even using a special cycle on the machine.
- Check for problems with the hot water going to your dishwasher.
- Have the temperature of your hot water adjusted.
- Before starting the dishwasher, run the water in the adjacent sink until it's hot.

1.41 Protecting Your Job

- Look at your most recent performance review and improve in the areas that "need improvement"—whether or not you think that you have those failings.

- Get more training in areas in which your performance review has indicated you need improvement.
- Be the best SA in the group: Have positive visibility—Chapter 31.
- Document everything—policies and technical and configuration information and procedures.
- Have good follow-through.
- Help everyone as much as possible.
- Be a good mentor.
- Use your time effectively—Section 32.1.2.
- Automate as much as you can—Chapter 3 and Sections 16.2, 26.1.9, and 31.1.4.3.
- Always keep the customers' needs in mind—Sections 31.1.3 and 32.2.3.
- Don't speak ill of coworkers. It just makes you look bad. Silence is golden. A closed mouth gathers no feet.

1.42 Getting More Training

- Go to training conferences like LISA.
- Attend vendor training to gain specific knowledge and to get the inside story on products.
- Find a mentor.
- Attend local SA group meetings
- Present at local SA group meetings. You learn a lot by teaching.
- Find the online forums or communities for items you need training on, read the archives, and participate in the forums.

1.43 Setting Your Priorities

- Depending on what stage you are in, certain infrastructure issues should be happening.
  - Basic services, such as email, printing, remote access, and security, need to be there from the outset.
  - Automation of common tasks, such as machine installations, configuration, maintenance, and account creation and deletion, should happen early; so should basic policies.
  - Documentation should be written as things are implemented, or it will never happen.

- Build a software depot and deployment system.
- Monitor before you think about improvements and scaling, which are issues for a more mature site.
- Think about setting up a helpdesk—Section 13.1.1.

- Get more in touch with your customers to find out what their priorities are.

- Improve your trouble-ticket system—Chapter 13.

- Review the top 10 percent of the ticket generators—Section 13.2.1.

- Adopt better revision control of configuration files—Chapter 17, particularly Section 17.1.5.1.

1.44 Getting All the Work Done

- Climb out of the hole—Chapter 2.

- Improve your time management; take a time-management class—Sections 32.1.2 and 32.1.2.11.

- Use a console server so that you aren't spending so much time running back and forth to the machine room—Sections 6.1.10 and 4.1.8 and 20.1.7.2.

- Batch up similar requests; do as a group all tasks that require being in a certain part of the building.

- Start each day with project work, not by reading email.

- Make informal arrangements with your coworkers to trade being available versus finding an empty conference room and getting uninterrupted work done for a couple of hours.

1.45 Avoiding Stress

- Take those vacations! (Three-day weekends are not a vacation.)

- Take a vacation long enough to learn what hasn't been documented well. Better to find those issues when you are returning in a few days than when you're (heaven forbid) hit by a bus.

- Take walks; get out of the area for a while.

- Don't eat lunch at your desk.

- Don't forget to have a life outside of work.

- Get weekly or monthly massages.

- Sign up for a class on either yoga or meditation.

1.46 What Should SAs Expect from Their Managers?

- Clearly communicated priorities—Section 33.1.1.1
- Enough budget to meet goals—Section 33.1.1.12
- Feedback that is timely and specific—Section 33.1.3.2
- Permission to speak freely in private in exchange for using decorum in public—Section 31.1.2

1.47 What Should SA Managers Expect from Their SAs?

- To do their jobs—Section 33.1.1.5
- To treat customers well—Chapter 31
- To get things done on time, under budget
- To learn from mistakes
- To ask for help—Section 32.2.2.7
- To give pessimistic time estimates for requested projects—Section 33.1.2
- To set honest status of milestones as projects progress—Section 33.1.1.8
- To participate in budget planning—Section 33.1.1.12
- To have high ethical standards—Section 12.1.2
- To set at least one long vacation per year—Section 32.2.2.8
- To keep on top of technology changes—Section 32.1.4

1.48 What Should SA Managers Provide to Their Boss?

- Access to monitoring and reports so that the boss can update himself or herself on status at will
- Budget information in a timely manner—Section 33.1.1.12
- Pessimistic time estimates for requested projects—Section 33.1.2
- Honest status of milestones as projects progress—Section 33.1.1.8
- A reasonable amount of stability

Chapter 2

Climb Out of the Hole

System administration can feel pretty isolating. Many IT organizations are stuck in a hole, trying to climb out. We hope that this book can be your guide to making things better.

The Hole

A guy falls into a hole so deep that he could never possibly get out. He hears someone walking by and gets the person's attention. The passerby listens to the man's plight, thinks for a moment, and then jumps into the hole.

"Why did you do that? Now we're both stuck down here!"

"Ah" says the passerby, "but now at least you aren't alone."

In IT prioritizing problems is important. If your systems are crashing every day, it is silly to spend time considering what color your data center walls should be. However, when you have a highly efficient system that is running well and growing, you might be asked to make your data center a showcase to show off to customers; suddenly, whether a new coat of paint is needed becomes a very real issue.

The sites we usually visit are far from looking at paint color samples. In fact, time and time again, we visit sites that are having so many problems that much of the advice in our book seems as lofty and idealistic as finding the perfect computer room color. The analogy we use is that those sites are spending so much time mopping the floor, they've forgotten that a leaking pipe needs to be fixed.

2.1 Tips for Improving System Administration

Here are a few things you can do to break this endless cycle of floor mopping.

- Use a trouble-ticket system
- Manage quick requests right
- Adopt three time saving policies
- Start every new host in a known state
- Our other tips

If you aren't doing these things, you're in for a heap of trouble elsewhere. These are the things that will help you climb out of your hole.

2.1.1 Use a Trouble-Ticket System

SAs receive too many requests to remember them all. You need software to track the flood of requests you receive. Whether you call this software *request management* or *trouble-ticket tracking*, you need it. If you are the only SA, you need at least a PDA to track your to-do list. Without such a system, you are undoubtedly forgetting people's requests or not doing a task because you thought that your coworker was working on it. Customers get really upset when they feel that their requests are being ignored.

Fixing the Lack of Follow-Through

Tom started working at a site that didn't have a request-tracking system. On his first day, his coworkers complained that the customers didn't like them. The next day, Tom had lunch with some of those customers. They were very appreciative of the work that the SAs did, *when* they completed their requests! However, the customers felt that most of their requests were flat-out ignored.

Tom spent the next couple days installing a request-tracking system. Ironically, doing so required putting off requests he got from customers, but it wasn't like they weren't already used to service delays. A month later, he visited the same customers, who now were much happier; they felt that they were being heard. Requests were being assigned an ID number, and customers could see when the request was completed. If something wasn't completed, they had an audit trail to show to management to prove their point; the result was less finger pointing. It wasn't a cure-all, but the tracking system got rid of an entire class of complaints and put the focus on the tasks at hand, rather than not managing the complaints. It unstuck the processes from the no-win situations they were in.

> The SAs were happier too. It had been frustrating to have to deal with claims that a request was dropped when there was no proof that a request had ever been received. Now the complaints were about things that SAs could control: Are tasks getting done? Are reported problems being fixed? There was accountability for their actions. The SAs also discovered that they now had the ability to report to management how many requests were being handled each week and to change the debate from "who messed up," which is rarely productive, to "how many SAs are needed to fulfill all the requests," which turned out to be the core problem.

Section 13.1.10 provides a more complete discussion of request-tracking software. We recommend the open source package Request Tracker from Best Practical (http://bestpractical.com/rt/); it is free and easy to set up.

Chapter 13 contains a complete discussion of managing a helpdesk. Maybe you will want to give that chapter to your boss to read. Chapter 14 discusses how to process a single request. The chapter also offers advice for collecting requests, qualifying them, and getting the requested work done.

2.1.2 Manage Quick Requests Right

Did you ever notice how difficult it is to get anything done when people keep interrupting you? Too many distractions make it impossible to finish any long-term projects. To fix this, organize your SA team so that one person is your *shield*, handling the day-to-day interruptions and thereby letting everyone else work on their projects uninterrupted.

If the interruption is a simple request, the shield should process it. If the request is more complicated, the shield should delegate it—or *assign* it, in your helpdesk software—or, if possible, start working on it between all the interruptions. Ideally, the shield should be self-sufficient for 80 percent of all requests, leaving about 20 percent to be escalated to others on the team.

If there are only two SAs, take turns. One person can handle interruptions in the morning, and the other can take the afternoon shift. If you have a large SA team that handles dozens or hundreds of requests each day, you can reorganize your team so that some people handle interruptions and others deal with long-term projects.

Many sites still believe that every SA should be equally trained in everything. That mentality made sense when you were a small group, but specialization becomes important as you grow.

Customers generally do have a perception of how long something should take to be completed. If you match that expectation, they will be much happier. We expand on this technique in Section 31.1.3. For example, people expect password resets to happen right away because not being able to log in delays a lot of other work. On the other hand, people expect that deploying a new desktop PC will take a day or two because it needs to be received, unboxed, loaded, and installed. If you are able to handle password resets quickly, people will be happy. If the installation of a desktop PC takes a little extra time, nobody will notice.

The order doesn't matter to you. If you reset a password and then deploy the desktop PC, you will have spent as much time as if you did the tasks in the opposite order. However, the order does matter to others. Someone who had to wait all day to have a password reset because you didn't do it until after the desktop PC was deployed would be very frustrated. You just delayed all of that person's other work one day.

In the course of a week, you'll still do the same amount of work, but by being smart about the order in which you do the tasks, you will please your customers with your response time. It's as simple as aligning your priorities with customer expectations.

You can use this technique to manage your time even if you are a solo SA. Train your customers to know that you prefer interruptions in the morning and that afternoons are reserved for long-term projects. Of course, it is important to assure customers that emergencies will always be dealt with right away. You can say it like this: "First, an emergency will be my top priority. However, for nonemergencies, I will try to be interrupt driven in the morning and to work on projects in the afternoon. Always feel free to stop by in the morning with a request. In the afternoon, if your request isn't an emergency, please send me an email, and I'll get to it in a timely manner. If you interrupt me in the afternoon for a nonemergency, I will record your request for later action."

Chapter 30 discusses how to structure your organization in general. Chapter 32 has a lot of advice on time-management skills for SAs.

It can be difficult to get your manager to buy into such a system. However, you can do this kind of arrangement unofficially by simply mentally following the plan and not being too overt that this is what you are doing.

2.1.3 Adopt Three Time-Saving Policies

Your management can put three policies in writing to help with the floor mopping.

1. How do people get help?
2. What is the scope of responsibility of the SA team?
3. What's our definition of *emergency*?

Time and time again, we see time wasted because of disconnects in these three issues. Putting these policies in writing forces management to think them through and lets them be communicated throughout the organization. Management needs to take responsibility for owning these policies, communicating them, and dealing with any customer backlash that might spring forth. People don't like to be told to change their ways, but without change, improvements won't happen.

First is a policy on how people get help. Since you've just installed the request-tracking software, this policy not only informs people that it exists but also tells them how to use it. The important part of this policy is to point out that people are to change their habits and no longer hang out at your desk, keeping you from other work. (Or if that is still permitted, they should be at the desk of the current shield on duty.) More tips about writing this policy are in Section 13.1.6.

The second policy defines the scope of the SA team's responsibility. This document communicates to both the SAs and the customer base. New SAs have difficulty saying no and end up overloaded and doing other people's jobs for them. Hand holding becomes "let me do that for you," and helpful advice soon becomes a situation in which an SA is spending time supporting software and hardware that is not of direct benefit to the company. Older SAs develop the habit of curmudgeonly saying no too often, much to the detriment of any management attempts to make the group seem helpful. More on writing this policy is in Section 13.1.5.

The third policy defines an emergency. If an SA finds himself unable to say no to customers because they claim that every request is an emergency, using this policy can go a long way to enabling the SAs to fix the leaking pipes rather than spend all day mopping the floor. This policy is easier to write in some organizations than in others. At a newspaper, an emergency is anything that will directly prevent the next edition from getting printed and delivered on time. That should be obvious. In a sales organization, an emergency might be something that directly prevents a demo from happening or the end-of-quarter sales commitments from being achieved. That may be more difficult to state concretely. At a research university, an emergency might be anything that will directly prevent a grant request from being submitted on time. More on this kind of policy is in Section 13.1.9.

> **Google's Definition of Emergency**
>
> Google has a sophisticated definition of *emergency*. A *code red* has a specific definition related to service quality, revenue, and other corporate priorities. A *code yellow* is anything that, if unfixed, will directly lead to a red alert. Once management has declared the emergency situation, the people assigned to the issue receive specific resources and higher-priority treatment from anyone they deal with. The helpdesk has specific service-level agreements (SLAs) for requests from people working on code reds and yellows.

These three policies can give an overwhelmed SA team the breathing room they need to turn things around.

2.1.4 Start Every New Host in a Known State

Finally, we're surprised by how many sites do not have a consistent method for loading the operating system (OS) of the hosts they deploy. Every modern operating system has a way to automate its installation. Usually, the system is booted off a server, which downloads a small program that prepares the disk, loads the operating system, loads applications, and then installs any locally specified installation scripts. Because the last step is something we control, we can add applications, configure options, and so on. Finally, the system reboots and is ready to be used.[1]

Automation such as this has two benefits: time savings and repeatability. The time saving comes from the fact that a manual process is now automated. One can start the process and do other work while the automated installation completes. Repeatability means that you are able to accurately and consistently create correctly installed machines every time. Having them be correct means less testing before deployment. (You do test a workstation before you give it to someone, right?) Repeatability saves time at the helpdesk; customers can be supported better when helpdesk staff can expect a level of consistency in the systems they support. Repeatability also means that customers are treated equally; people won't be surprised to discover that their workstation is missing software or features that their coworkers have received.

There are unexpected benefits, too. Since the process is now so much easier, SAs are more likely to refresh older machines that have suffered entropy and would benefit from being reloaded. Making sure that applications are

---

1. A cheap substitute is to have a checklist with detailed instructions, including exactly what options and preferences are to be set on various applications and so on. Alternatively, use a disk-cloning system.

configured properly from the start means fewer helpdesk calls asking for help getting software to work the first time. Security is improved because patches are consistently installed and security features consistently enabled. Non-SAs are less likely to load the OS by themselves, which results in fewer ad hoc configurations.

Once the OS installation is automated, automating patches and upgrades is the next big step. Automating patches and upgrades means less running from machine to machine to keep things consistent. Security is improved because it is easier and faster to install security patches. Consistency is improved as it becomes less likely that a machine will accidentally be skipped.

The case study in Section 11.1.3.2 (page 288) highlights many of these issues as they are applied to security at a major e-commerce site that experiences a break-in. New machines were being installed and broken into at a faster rate than the consultants could patch and fix them. The consultants realized that the fundamental problem was that the site didn't have an automated and consistent way to load machines. Rather than repair the security problems, the consultants set up an automatic OS installation and patching system, which soon solved the security problems.

Why didn't the original SAs know enough to build this infrastructure in the first place? The manual explains how to automate an OS installation, but knowing how important it is comes from experience. The e-commerce SAs hadn't any mentors to learn from. Sure, there were other excuses—not enough time, too difficult, not worth it, we'll do it next time—but the company would not have had the expense, bad press, and drop in stock price if the SAs had taken the time to do things right from the beginning.

In addition to effective security, inconsistent OS configuration makes customer support difficult because every machine is full of inconsistencies that become trips and traps that sabotage an SA's ability to be helpful. It is confusing for customers when they see things set up differently on different computers. The inconsistency breaks software configured to expect files in particular locations.

If your site doesn't have an automated way to load new machines, set up such a system right now. Chapter 3 provides more coverage of this topic.

2.1.5   Other Tips

2.1.5.1   Make Email Work Well

The people who approve your budget are high enough in the management chain to use only email and calendaring if it exists. Make sure that these applications work well. When these applications become stable and reliable, management will have new confidence in your team. Requests for resources will become easier. Having a stable email system can give you excellent cover as you fight other battles. Make sure that management's administrative support people also see improvements. Often, these people are the ones running the company.

2.1.5.2 Document as You Go

Documentation does not need to be a heavy burden; set up a wiki, or simply create a directory of text files on a file server. Create checklists of common tasks such as how to set up a new employee or how to configure a customer's email client. Once documented, these tasks are easier to delegate to a junior person or a new hire.

Lists of critical servers for each application or service also are useful. Labeling physical devices is important because it helps prevent mistakes and makes it easier for new people to help out. Adopt a policy that you will pause to label an unlabeled device before working on it, even if you are in a hurry. Label the front and back of machines. Stick a label with the same text on both the power adapter and its device. (See Chapter 9.)

2.1.5.3 Fix the Biggest Time Drain

Pick the single biggest time drain, and dedicate one person to it until it is fixed. This might mean that the rest of your group has to work a little harder in the meantime, but it will be worth it to have that problem fixed. This person should provide periodic updates and ask for help as needed when blocked by technical or political dependencies.

Success in Fixing the Biggest Time Drain

When Tom worked for Cibernet, he found that the company's London SA team was prevented from any progress on critical, high-priority projects because it was drowning in requests for help with people's individual desktop PCs. He couldn't hire a senior SA to work on the high-priority projects, because the training time would exceed the project's deadline. Instead, he realized that entry-level Windows desktop support technicians were plentiful and inexpensive and wouldn't require much training beyond normal assimilation. Management wouldn't let him hire such a person but finally agreed to bring someone in on a temporary 6-month contract. (Logically, within 6 months, the desktop environment would be cleaned up enough that the person would no longer be needed.) With that person handling the generic desktop problems—virus cleanup, new PC deployment, password resets, and so on—the remaining SAs were freed to complete the high-priority projects that were key to the company.

By the end of the 6-month contract, management could see the improvement in the SAs' performance. Common outages were eliminated both because the senior SAs finally had time to "climb out of the hole" and because the temporary Windows desktop technician had cleaned up so many of the smaller problems. As a result, the contract was extended and eventually made permanent when management saw the benefit of specialization.

2.1.5.4 Select Some Quick Fixes

The remainder of this book tends to encourage long-term, permanent solutions. However, when stuck in a hole, one is completely justified in strategically selecting short-term solutions for some problems so that the few important, high-impact projects will get completed. Maintain a list of long-term solutions that get postponed. Once stability is achieved, use that list to plan the next round of projects. By then, you may have new staff with even better ideas for how to proceed. (For more on this, see Section 33.1.1.4.)

2.1.5.5 Provide Sufficient Power and Cooling

Make sure that each computer room has sufficient power and cooling. Every device should receive its power from an uninterruptible power supply (UPS). However, when you are trying to climb out of a hole, it is good enough to make sure that the most important servers and network devices are on a UPS. Individual UPS—one in the base of each rack—can be a great short-term solution. UPSs should have enough battery capacity for servers to survive a 1-hour outage and gracefully shut themselves down before the batteries have run down. Outages longer than an hour tend to be very rare. Most outages are measured in seconds. Small UPSs are a good solution until a larger-capacity UPS that can serve the entire data center is installed. When you buy a small UPS, be sure to ask the vendor what kind of socket is required for a particular model. You'd be surprised at how many require something special.

Cooling is even more important than power. Every watt of power a computer consumes generates a certain amount of heat. Thanks to the laws of thermodynamics, you will expend more than 1 watt of energy to provide the cooling for the heat generated by 1 watt of computing power. That is, it is very typical for more than 50 percent of your energy to be spent on cooling.

Organizations trying to climb out of a hole often don't have big data centers but do have small computer closets, often with no cooling. These organizations scrape by simply on the building's cooling. This is fine for one server, maybe two. When more servers are installed, the room is warm, but the building cooling seems sufficient. Nobody notices that the building's cooling isn't on during the weekend and that by Sunday, the room is very hot. A long weekend comes along, and your holiday is ruined when all your servers have overheated on Monday. In the United States, the start of summer unofficially begins with the three-day Memorial Day weekend at the end of May. Because it is a long weekend and often the first hot weekend of the year means, that is often when people realize that their cooling isn't sufficient. If you have a failure on this weekend, your entire summer is going to be bad. Be smart; check all cooling systems in April.

For about $400 or less, you can install a portable cooler that will cool a small computer closet and exhaust the heat into the space above the ceiling or out a window. This fine temporary solution is inexpensive enough that it does not require management approval. For larger spaces, renting a 5- or 10-ton cooler is a fast solution.

2.1.5.6 Implement Simple Monitoring

Although we'd prefer to have a pervasive monitoring system with many bells and whistles, a lot can be gained by having one that pings key servers and alerts people of a problem via email. Some customers have the impression that servers tend to crash on Monday morning. The reality is that without monitoring, crashed machines accumulate all weekend and are discovered on Monday morning. With some simple monitoring, a weekend crash can be fixed before people arrive Monday. (If nobody hears a tree fall in the forest, it doesn't matter whether it made a noise.) Not that a monitoring system should be used to hide outages that happen over the weekend; always send out email announcing that the problem was fixed. It's good PR.

2.2 Conclusion

The remainder of this book focuses on more lofty and idealistic goals for an SA organization. This chapter looked at some high-impact changes that a site can make if it is drowning in problems.

First, we dealt with managing requests from customers. Customers are the people we serve: often referred to as users. Using a trouble-ticket system to manage requests means that the SAs spend less time tracking the requests and gives customers a better sense of the status of their requests. A trouble-ticket system improves SAs ability to have good follow-through on users' requests.

To manage requests properly, develop a system so that requests that block other tasks get done sooner rather than later. The mutual interrupt shield lets SAs address urgent requests while still having time for project work. It is an organizational structure that lets SAs address requests based on customer expectations.

Often, many of the problems we face arise from disagreements, or differences in expectations, about how and when to get help. To fix these mismatches, it is important to lessen confusion by having three particular policies in writing how to get computer support, scope of the SAs' responsibility, and what constitutes an IT emergency.

It is important to start each host in a known state. Doing so makes machine deployment easier, eases customer support, and gives more consistent service to customers.

Some smaller tips too are important. Make email work well: Much of your reputation is tied to this critical service. Document as you go: The more you document, the less relearning is required. Fix the biggest time drain: You will then have more time for other issues. When understaffed, focusing on short-term fixes is OK. Sufficient power and cooling help prevent major outages.

Now that we've solved all the burning issues, we can focus on larger concepts: the foundation elements.

Exercises

1. What request-tracking system do you use? What do you like or dislike about it?

2. How do you ensure that SAs follow through on requests?

3. How are requests prioritized? On a given day, how are outstanding requests prioritized? On a quarterly or yearly basis, how are projects prioritized?

4. Section 2.1.3 describes three policies that save time. Are these written policies in your organization? If they aren't written, how would you describe the ad hoc policy that is used?

5. If any of the three policies in Section 2.1.3 aren't written, discuss them with your manager to get an understanding of what they would be if they were written.

6. If any of the three policies in Section 2.1.3 are written, ask a coworker to try to find them without any hints. Was the coworker successful? How can you make the policies easier to find?

7. List all the operating systems used in your environment in order of popularity. What automation is used to load each? Of those that aren't automated, which would benefit the most from it?

8. Of the most popular operating systems in your environment, how are patches and upgrades automated? What's the primary benefit that your site would see from automation? What product or system would you use to automate this?

9. How reliable is your CEO's email?

10. What's the biggest time drain in your environment? Name two ways to eliminate this.

11. Perform a simple audit of all computer/network rooms. Identify which do not have sufficient cooling or power protection.

12. Make a chart listing each computer/network room, how it is cooled, the type of power protection, if any, and power usage. Grade each room. Make sure that the cooling problems are fixed before the first day of summer.

13. If you have no monitoring, install an open source package, such as Nagios, to simply alert you if your three most important servers are down.

Part II

Foundation Elements

Chapter 3

Workstations

If you manage your desktop and laptop workstations correctly, new employees will have everything they need on their first day, including basic infrastructure, such as email. Existing employees will find that updates happen seamlessly. New applications will be deployed unobtrusively. Repairs will happen in a timely manner. Everything will "just work."

Managing operating systems on workstations boils down to three basic tasks: loading the system software and applications initially, updating the system software and applications, and configuring network parameters. We call these tasks the Big Three.

If you don't get all three things right, if they don't happen uniformly across all systems, or if you skip them altogether, everything else you do will be more difficult. If you don't load the operating system *consistently* on hosts, you'll find yourself with a support nightmare. If you can't update and patch systems *easily*, you will not be motivated to deploy them. If your network configurations are not administered from a centralized system, such as a DHCP server, making the smallest network change will be painful. Automating these tasks makes a world of difference.

We define a **workstation** as computer hardware dedicated to a single customer's work. Usually, this means a customer's desktop or laptop PC. In the modern environment, we also have remotely accessed PCs, virtual machines, and dockable laptops, among others.

Workstations are usually deployed in large quantities and have long life cycles (birth, use, death). As a result, if you need to make a change on all of them, doing it right is complicated and critical. If something goes wrong, you'll probably find yourself working late nights, blearily struggling to fix a big mess, only to face grumpy users in the morning.

Consider the life cycle of a computer and its operating system. Rémy Evard produced an excellent treatment of this in his paper "An Analysis

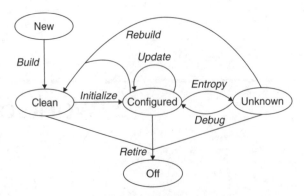

Figure 3.1 Evard's life cycle of a machine and its OS

of Unix System Configuration" (Evard 1997). Although his focus was Unix hosts, it can be extrapolated to others. The model he created is shown in Figure 3.1.

The diagram depicts five states: new, clean, configured, unknown, and off.

- **New** refers to a completely new machine.
- **Clean** refers to a machine on which the OS has been installed but no localizations performed.
- **Configured** means a correctly configured and operational environment.
- **Unknown** is a computer that has been misconfigured or has become out of date.
- **Off** refers to a machine that has been retired and powered off.

There are many ways to get from one lifestyle state to another. At most sites, the machine *build* and *initialize* processes are usually one step; they result in the OS being loaded and brought into a usable state. *Entropy* is deterioration that we don't want that leaves the computer in an unknown state, which is fixed by a *debug* process. Updates happen over time, often in the form of patches and security updates. Sometimes, it makes sense to wipe and reload a machine because it is time for a major OS upgrade, the system needs to be recreated for a new purpose, or severe entropy has plainly made it the only resort. The *rebuild* process happens, and the machine is wiped and reloaded to bring it back to the configured state.

These various processes repeat as the months and years roll on. Finally, the machine becomes obsolete and is retired. It dies a tragic death or, as the model describes, is put into the off state.

What can we learn from this diagram? First, it is important to acknowledge that the various states and transitions exist. We plan for installation time, accept that things will break and require repair, and so on. We don't act as if each repair is a surprise; instead, we set up a repair process or an entire repair department, if the volume warrants it. All these things require planning, staffing, and other resources.

Second, we notice that although there are many states, the computer is usable only in the configured state. We want to maximize the amount of time spent in that state. Most of the other processes deal with bringing the computer to the configured state or returning it to that state. Therefore, these set-up and recovery processes should be fast, efficient, and, we hope, automated.

To extend the time spent in the configured state, we must ensure that the OS degrades as slowly as possible. Design decisions of the OS vendor have the biggest impact here. Some OSs require new applications to be installed by loading files into various system directories, making it difficult to discern which files are part of which package. Other OSs permit add-ons to be located nearly anywhere. Microsoft's Windows series is known for problems in this area. On the other hand, because UNIX provides strict permissions on directories, user-installed applications can't degrade the integrity of the OS.

An architectural decision made by the SA can strengthen or weaken the integrity of the OS. Is there a well-defined place for third-party applications to be installed outside the system areas (see Chapter 28)? Has the user been given `root`, or Administrator, access and thus increased the entropy? Has the SA developed a way for users to do certain administrative tasks without having the supreme power of `root`?[1] SAs must find a balance between giving users full access and restricting them. This balance affects the rate at which the OS will decay.

Manual installation is error prone. When mistakes are made during installation, the host will begin life with a head start into the decay cycle. If installation is completely automated, new workstations will be deployed correctly.

Reinstallation—the rebuild process—is similar to installation, except that one may potentially have to carry forward old data and applications (see Chapter 18). The decisions the SA makes in the early stages affect how easy or difficult this process will become. Reinstallation is easier if no data is stored on the machine. For workstations, this means storing as much data as possible

---

1. "To err is human; to really screw up requires the `root` password."—Anonymous

on a file server so that reinstallation cannot accidentally wipe out data. For servers, this means putting data on a remote file system (see Chapter 25).

Finally, this model acknowledges that machines are eventually retired. We shouldn't be surprised: Machines don't last forever. Various tasks are associated with retiring a machine. As in the case of reinstallation, some data and applications must be carried forward to the replacement machine or stored on tape for future reference; otherwise, they will be lost in the sands of time.

Management is often blind to computer life-cycle management. Managers need to learn about financial planning: Asset depreciation should be aligned with the expected life cycle of the asset. Suppose most hard goods are depreciated at your company on a 5-year schedule. Computers are expected to be retired after 3 years. Therefore, you will not be able to dispose of retired computers for 2 years, which can be a big problem. The modern way is to depreciate computer assets on a 3-year schedule. When management understands the computer life cycle or a simplified model that is less technical, it becomes easier for SAs to get funding for a dedicated deployment group, a repair department, and so on.

In this chapter, we use the term **platform** to mean a specific vendor/OS combination. Some examples are an AMD Athlon PC running Windows Vista, a PPC-based Mac running OS X 10.4, an Intel Xeon desktop running Ubuntu 6.10 Linux, a Sun Sparc Ultra 40 running Solaris 10, and a Sun Enterprise 10000 running Solaris 9. Some sites might consider the same OS running on different hardware to be different platforms; for example, Windows XP running on a desktop PC and a laptop PC might be two different platforms. Usually, different versions of the same OS are considered to be distinct platforms if their support requirements are significantly different.[2]

3.1 The Basics

Three critical issues are involved in maintaining workstation operating systems:

1. Loading the system software and applications initially
2. Updating the system software and applications
3. Configuring network parameters

---

2. Thus, an Intel Xeon running SUSE 10 and configured as a web server would be considered a different platform from one configured as a CAD workstation.

If your site is to be run in a cost-effective manner, these three tasks should be automated for any platform that is widely used at your site. Doing these things well makes many other tasks easier.

If your site has only a few hosts that are using a particular platform, it is difficult to justify creating extensive automation. Later, as the site grows, you may wish you had the extensive automation you should have invested in earlier. It is important to recognize—whether by intuition, using business plan growth objectives, or monitoring customer demand—when you are getting near that point.

First-Class Citizens

When Tom was at Bell Labs, his group was asked to support just about every kind of computer and OS one could imagine. Because it would be impossible to meet such a demand, it was established that some platforms would receive better support than others, based on the needs of the business. "First-class citizens" were the platforms that would receive full support. SAs would receive training in hardware and software for these systems, documentation would be provided for users of such systems, and all three major tasks—loading, updating, and network configuration—would be automated, permitting these hosts to be maintained in a cost-effective manner. Equally important, investing in automation for these hosts would reduce SAs' tedium, which would help retain employees (see Section 35.1.11).

All other platforms received less support, usually in the form of providing an IP address, security guidelines, and best-effort support. Customers were supposed to be on their own. An SA couldn't spend more than an hour on any particular issue involving these systems. SAs found that it was best to gently remind the customer of this time limit before beginning work rather than to surprise the customer when the time limit was up.

A platform could be promoted to "first-class citizen" status for many reasons. Customer requests would demonstrate that certain projects would bring a large influx of a particular platform. SAs would sometimes take the initiative if they saw the trend before the customers did. For example, SAs tried not to support more than two versions of Windows at a time and promoted the newest release as part of their process to eliminate the oldest release.

Sometimes it was cheaper to promote a platform rather than to deal with the headaches caused by customers' own botched installations. One platform installed by naive engineers that would enable everything and could take down the network accidentally created a machine that acted like an 802.3 Spanning Tree Protocol bridge. ("It sounded like a good idea at the time!") After numerous disruptions resulting from this feature's being enabled, the platform was promoted to take the installation process away from customers and prevent such outages. Also, it is sometimes cheaper to promote OSs that have insecure default configurations than to deal with the security problems they create. Universities and organizations that live without firewalls often find themselves in this situation.

Creating such automation often requires a large investment of resources and therefore needs management action. Over the years, the Bell Labs management was educated about the importance of making such investments when new platforms were promoted to first-class status. Management learned that making such investments paid off by providing superior service.

It isn't always easy to automate some of these processes. In some cases, Bell Labs had to invent them from scratch (Fulmer and Levine 1998) or build large layers of software on top of the vendor-provided solution to make it manageable (Heiss 1999). Sometimes, one must sacrifice other projects or response time to other requests to dedicate time to building such systems. It is worth it in the long run.

When vendors try to sell us new products, we always ask them whether and how these processes can be automated. We reject vendors that have no appreciation for deployment issues. Increasingly, vendors understand that the inability to rapidly deploy their products affects the customers' ability to rapidly purchase their products.

3.1.1 Loading the OS

Every vendor has a different name for its systems for automated OS loading: Solaris has JumpStart; RedHat Linux has KickStart; SGI IRIX has RoboInst; HP-UX has Ignite-UX; and Microsoft Windows has Remote Installation Service. Automation solves a huge number of problems, and not all of them are technical. First, automation saves money. Obviously, the time saved by replacing a manual process with an automated one is a big gain. Automation also obviates two hidden costs. The first one relates to *mistakes:* Manual processes are subject to human error. A workstation has thousands of potential settings, sometimes in a single application. A small misconfiguration can cause a big failure. Sometimes, fixing this problem is easy: If someone accesses a problem application right after the workstation is delivered and reports it immediately, the SA will easily conclude that the machine has a configuration problem. However, these problems often lurk unnoticed for months or years before the customer accesses the particular application. At that point, why would the SA think to ask whether the customer is using this application for the first time. In this situation, the SA often spends a lot of time searching for a problem that wouldn't have existed if the installation had been automated. Why do you think "reloading the app" solves so many customer-support problems?

The second hidden cost relates to *nonuniformity:* If you load the operating system manually, you'll never get the same configuration on all your machines, ever. When we loaded applications manually on PCs, we discovered that no amount of SA training would result in all our applications being configured exactly the same way on every machine. Sometimes, the technician forgot one or two settings; at other times, that another way was better. The result was that customers often discovered that their new workstations weren't properly configured, or a customer moving from one workstation to the next didn't have the exact same configuration, and applications failed. Automation solves this problem.

Case Study: Automating Windows NT Installation Reduces Frustration

Before Windows NT installation was automated at Bell Labs, Tom found that PC system administrators spent about 25 percent of their time fixing problems that were a result of human error at time of installation. Customers usually weren't productive on new machines until they had spent several days, often as much as a week, going back and forth with the helpdesk to resolve issues. This was frustrating to the SAs, but imagine the customer's frustration! This made a bad first impression: Every new employee's first encounter with an SA happened because his or her machine didn't work properly from the start. Can't they can't get anything right?

Obviously, the SAs needed to find a way to reduce their installation problems, and automation was the answer. The installation process was automated using a home-grown system named AutoLoad (Fulmer and Levine 1998), which loaded the OS, as well as all applications and drivers.

Once the installations were automated, the SAs were a lot happier. The boring process of performing the installation was now quick and easy. The new process avoided all the mistakes that can happen during manual installation. Less of the SAs' time was spent debugging their own mistakes. Most important, the customers were a lot happier too.

3.1.1.1 Be Sure Your Automated System Is Truly Automated

Setting up an automated installation system takes a lot of effort. However, in the end, the effort will pay off by saving you more time than you spent initially. Remember this fact when you're frustrated in the thick of setup. Also remember that if you're going to set up an automated system, do it properly; otherwise, it can cause you twice the trouble later.

The most important aspect of automation is that it must be *completely* automated. This statement sounds obvious, but implementing it can be another story. We feel that it is worth the extra effort to not have to return to the machine time and time again to answer another prompt or start the next phase. This means that prompts won't be answered incorrectly and that steps won't be forgotten or skipped. It also improves time management for the SA, who can stay focused on the next task rather than have to remember to return to a machine to start the next step.

Machine Says, "I'm done!"

One SA modified his Solaris JumpStart system to send email to the helpdesk when the installation is complete. The email is sent from the newly installed machine, thereby testing that the machine is operational. The email that is generated notes the hostname, type of hardware, and other information that the helpdesk needs in order to add the machine to its inventory. On a busy day, it can be difficult to remember to return to a host to make sure that the installation completed successfully. With this system, SA did not have to waste time checking on the machine. Instead, the SA could make a note in their to-do list to check on the machine if email hadn't been received by a certain time.

The best installation systems do all their human interaction at the beginning and then work to completion unattended. Some systems require zero input because the automation "knows" what to do, based on the host's Ethernet media access control (MAC) address. The technician should be able to walk away from the machine, confident that the procedure will complete on its own. A procedure that requires someone to return halfway through the installation to answer a question or two isn't truly automated, and loses efficiency. For example, if the SA forgets about the installation and goes to lunch or a meeting, the machine will hang there, doing nothing, until the SA returns. If the SA is out of the office and is the only one who can take care of the stuff halfway through, everyone who needs that machine will have to wait. Or worse, someone else will attempt to complete the installation, creating a host that may require debugging later.

Solaris's JumpStart is an excellent example of a truly automated installer. A program on the JumpStart server asks which template to use for a new client. A senior SA can set up this template in advance. When the time comes to install the OS, the technician—who can even be a clerk sent to start the process—need only type `boot net - install`. The clerk waits to make sure that the process has begun and then walks away. The machine is loaded, configured, and ready to run in 30 to 90 minutes, depending on the network speed.

Remove All Manual Steps from Your Automated Installation Process

Tom was mentoring a new SA who was setting up JumpStart. The SA gave him a demo, which showed the OS load happening just as expected. After it was done, the SA showed how executing a simple script finished the configuration. Tom congratulated him on the achievement but politely asked the SA to integrate that last step into the JumpStart process. Only after four rounds of this procedure was the new JumpStart system completely automated.

An important lesson here is that the SA hadn't made a mistake, but had not actually fully automated the process. It's easy to forget that executing that simple script at the end of the installation is a manual step detracting from your automated process. It's also important to remember that when you're automating something, especially for the first time, you often need to fiddle with things to get it right.

When you think that you've finished automating something, have someone unfamiliar with your work attempt to use it. Start the person off with one sentence of instruction but otherwise refuse to help. If the person gets stuck, you've found an area for improvement. Repeat this process until your cat could use the system.

3.1.1.2 Partially Automated Installation

Partial automation is better than no automation at all. Until an installation system is perfected, one must create stop-gap measures. The last 1 percent can take longer to automate than the initial 99 percent.

A lack of automation can be justified if there are only a few of a particular platform, if the cost of complete automation is larger than the time savings, or if the vendor has done the world a disservice by making it impossible (or unsupported) to automate the procedure.

The most basic stop-gap measure is to have a well-documented process, so that it can be repeated the same way every time.[3] The documentation can be in the form of notes taken when building the first system, so that the various prompts can be answered the same way.

One can automate parts of the installation. Certain parts of the installation lend themselves to automation particularly well. For example, the initialize process in Figure 3.1 configures the OS for the local environment after initially loading the vendor's default. Usually, this involves installing particular files, setting permissions, and rebooting. A script that copies a

---

3.   This is not to imply that automation removes the need for documentation.

fixed set of files to their proper place can be a lifesaver. One can even build a `tar` or `zip` file of the files that changed during customization and extract them onto machines after using the vendor's install procedure.

Other stop-gap measures can be a little more creative.

Case Study: Handling Partially Completed Installations

Early versions of Microsoft Windows NT 4.0 AutoLoad (Fulmer and Levine 1998) were unable to install third-party drivers automatically. In particular, the sound card driver had to be installed manually. If the installation was being done in the person's office, the machine would be left with a note saying that when the owner received a log-on prompt, the system would be usable but that audio wouldn't work. The then note indicated when the SA would return to fix that one problem. Although a completely automated installation procedure would be preferred, this was a workable stop-gap solution.

❖ **Stop-Gap Measures**   Q: How do you prevent a stop-gap measure from becoming a permanent solution?

A: You create a ticket to record that a permanent solution is needed.

3.1.1.3 Cloning and Other Methods

Some sites use cloned hard disks to create new machines. **Cloning hard disks** means setting up a host with the exact software configuration that is desired for all hosts that are going to be deployed. The hard disk of this host is then cloned, or copied, to all new computers as they are installed. The original machine is usually known as a **golden host**. Rather than copying the hard disk over and over, the contents of the hard disk are usually copied onto a CD-ROM, tape, or network file server, which is used for the installation. A small industry is devoted to helping companies with this process and can help with specialized cloning hardware and software.

We prefer automating the loading process instead of copying the disk contents for several reasons. First, the hardware of the new machine is significantly different from that of the old machine, you have to make a separate master image. You don't need much imagination to envision ending up with many master images. Then, to complicate matters, if you want to make even a single change to something, you have to apply it to each master image. Finally, having a spare machine of each hardware type that requires a new image adds considerable expense and effort.

Some OS vendors won't support cloned disks, because their installation process makes decisions at load time based on, factors such as what hardware is detected. Windows NT generates a unique security ID (SID) for each machine during the install process. Initial cloning software for Windows NT wasn't able to duplicate this functionality, causing many problems. This issue was eventually solved.

You can strike a balance here by leveraging both automation and cloning. Some sites clone disks to establish a minimal OS install and then use an automated software-distribution system to layer all applications and patches on top. Other sites use a generic OS installation script and then "clone" applications or system modifications on to the machine.

Finally, some OS vendors don't provide ways to automate installation. However, home-grown options are available. SunOS 4.x didn't include anything like Solaris's JumpStart, so many sites loaded the OS from a CD-ROM and then ran a script that completed the process. The CD-ROM gave the machine a known state, and the script did the rest.

PARIS: Automated SunOS 4.x Installation

Given enough time and money, anything is possible. You can even build your own install system. Everyone knows that SunOS 4.x installations can't be automated. Everyone except Viktor Dukhovni, who created Programmable Automatic Remote Installation Service (PARIS) in 1992 while working for Lehman Brothers. PARIS automated the process of loading SunOS 4.x on many hosts in parallel over the network long before Sun OS 5.x introduced JumpStart.

At the time, the state of the art required walking a CD-ROM drive to each host in order to load the OS. PARIS allowed an SA in New York to remotely initiate an OS upgrade of all the machines at a branch office. The SA would then go home or out to dinner and some time later find that all the machines had installed successfully. The ability to schedule unattended installs of groups of machines is a PARIS feature still not found in most vendor-supplied installation systems.

Until Sun created JumpStart, many sites created their own home-grown solutions.

3.1.1.4 Should You Trust the Vendor's Installation?

Computers usually come with the OS preloaded. Knowing this, you might think that you don't need to bother with reloading an OS that someone has already loaded for you. We disagree. In fact, we think that reloading the OS makes your life easier in the long run.

Reloading the OS from scratch is better for several reasons. First, you probably would have to deal with loading other applications and localizations on top of a vendor-loaded OS before the machine would work at your site. Automating the entire loading process from scratch is often easier than layering applications and configurations on top of the vendor's OS install. Second, vendors will change their preloaded OS configurations for their own purposes, with no notice to anyone; loading from scratch gives you a *known state* on every machine. Using the preinstalled OS leads to deviation from your standard configuration. Eventually, such deviation can lead to problems.

Another reason to avoid using a preloaded OS is that eventually, hosts have to have an OS reload. For example, the hard disk might crash and be replaced by a blank one, or you might have a policy of reloading a workstation's OS whenever it moves from one to another. When some of your machines are running preloaded OSs and others are running locally installed OSs, you have two platforms to support. They will have differences. You *don't* want to discover, smack in the middle of an emergency, that you can't load and install a host without the vendor's help.

The Tale of an OS That Had to Be Vendor Loaded

Once upon a time, Tom was experimenting with a UNIX system from a Japanese company that was just getting into the workstation business. The vendor shipped the unit preloaded with a customized version of UNIX. Unfortunately, the machine got irrecoverably mangled while the SAs were porting applications to it. Tom contacted the vendor, whose response was to send a new hard disk preloaded with the OS—all the way from Japan! Even though the old hard disk was fine and could be reformatted and reused, the vendor hadn't established a method for users to reload the OS, even from backup tapes.

Luckily for Tom, this workstation wasn't used for critical services. Imagine if it had been, though, and Tom suddenly found his network unusable, or, worse yet, payroll couldn't be processed until the machine was working! Those grumpy customers would not have been amused if they'd had to live without their paychecks until a hard drive arrived from Japan.

If this machine had been a critical one, keeping a preloaded replacement hard disk on hand would have been prudent. A set of written directions on how to physically install it and bring the system back to a usable state would also have been a good idea.

The moral of this story is that if you *must* use a vendor-loaded OS, it's better to find out right after it arrives, rather than during a disaster, whether you can restore it from scratch.

The previous anecdote describes an OS from long ago. However, history repeats itself. PC vendors preload the OS and often include special applications, add-ons, and drivers. Always verify that add-ons are included in the OS reload disks provided with the system. Sometimes, the applications won't be missed, because they are free tools that aren't worth what is paid for them. However, they may be critical device drivers. This is particularly important for laptops, which often require drivers that do not come with the basic version of the OS. Tom ran into this problem while writing this book. After reloading Windows NT on his laptop, he had to add drivers to enable his PCMCIA slots. The drivers couldn't be brought to the laptop via modem or Ethernet, because those were PCMCIA devices. Instead they had to be downloaded to floppies, using a different computer. Without a second computer, there would have been a difficult catch-22 situation.

This issue has become less severe over time as custom, laptop-specific hardware has transitioned to common, standardized components. Microsoft has also responded to pressure to make its operating systems less dependent on the hardware it was installed on. Although the situation has improved over time from the low-level driver perspective, vendors have tried to differentiate themselves by including application software unique to particular models. But doing that defeats attempts to make one image that can work on all platforms.

Some vendors will preload a specific disk image that you provide. This service not only saves you from having to load the systems yourself but also lets you know exactly what is being loaded. However, you still have the burden of updating the master image as hardware and models change.

3.1.1.5 Installation Checklists

Whether your OS installation is completely manual or fully automated, you can improve consistency by using a written checklist to make sure that technicians don't skip any steps. The usefulness of such a checklist is obvious if installation is completely manual. Even a solo system administrator who feels that "all OS loads are consistent because I do them myself" will find benefits to using a written checklist. If anything, your checklists can be the basis of training a new system administrator or freeing up your time by training a trustworthy clerk to follow your checklists. (See Section 9.1.4 for more on checklists.)

Even if OS installation is completely automated, a good checklist is still useful. Certain things can't be automated, because they are physical acts, such as starting the installation, making sure that the mouse works, cleaning the screen before it is delivered, or giving the user a choice of mousepads. Other related tasks may be on your checklist: updating inventory lists, reordering network cables if you are below a certain limit, and a week later checking whether the customer has any problems or questions.

3.1.2 Updating the System Software and Applications

Wouldn't it be nice if an SA's job was finished once the OS and applications were loaded? Sadly, as time goes by, people identify new bugs and new security holes, all of which need to be fixed. Also, people find cool new applications that need to be deployed. All these tasks are **software updates**. Someone has to take care of them, and that someone is you. Don't worry, though; you don't have to spend all your time doing updates. As with installation, updates can be automated, saving time and effort.

Every vendor has a different name for its system for automating software updates: Solaris, AutoPatch; Microsoft Windows, SMS; and various people have written layers on top of Red Hat Linux's RPMs, SGI IRIX's RoboInst, and HP-UX's Software Distributor (SD-UX). Other systems are multiplatform solutions (Ressman and Valdés 2000).

Software-update systems should be general enough to be able to deploy new applications, to update applications, and to patch the OS. If a system can only distribute patches, new applications can be packaged as if they were patches. These systems can also be used for small changes that must be made to many hosts. A small configuration change, such as a new `/etc/ntp.conf`, can be packaged into a patch and deployed automatically. Most systems have the ability to include **postinstall scripts**—programs that are run to complete any changes required to install the package. One can even create a package that contains *only* a postinstall script as a way of deploying a complicated change.

Case Study: Installing New Printing System

An SA was hired by a site that needed a new print system. The new system was specified, designed, and tested very quickly. However, the consultant spent weeks on the menial task of installing the new client software on each workstation, because the site had no automated method for rolling out software updates. Later, the consultant was hired to install a similar system at another site. This site had an excellent—and documented!—software-update system. *En masse* changes could be made easily. The client software was packaged and distributed quickly. At the first site, the cost of building a new print system was mostly deploying to desktops. At the second site, the main cost was the same as the main focus: the new print service. The first site thought they were saving money by not implementing a method to automate software rollouts. Instead, they spent large amounts of money every time new software needed to be deployed. This site didn't have the foresight to realize that in the future, it would have other software to roll out. The second site saved money by investing some money up front.

3.1.2.1 Updates Are Different from Installations

Automating software updates is similar to automating the initial installation but is also different in many important ways.

- *The host is in usable state.* Updates are done to machines that are in good running condition, whereas the initial-load process has extra work to do, such as partitioning disks and deducing network parameters. In fact, initial loading must work on a host that is in a disabled state, such as with a completely blank hard drive.

- *The host is in an office.* Update systems must be able to perform the job on the native network of the host. They cannot flood the network or disturb the other hosts on the network. An initial load process may be done in a laboratory where special equipment may be available. For example, large sites commonly have a special **install room**, with a high-capacity network, where machines are prepared before delivery to the new owner's office.

- *No physical access is required.* Updates shouldn't require a physical visit, which are disruptive to customers; also, coordinating them is expensive. Missed appointments, customers on vacation, and machines in locked offices all lead to the nightmare of rescheduling appointments. Physical visits can't be automated.

- *The host is already in use.* Updates involve a machine that has been in use for a while; therefore, the customer assumes that it will be usable when the update is done. You can't mess up the machine! By contrast, when an initial OS load fails, you can wipe the disk and start from scratch.

- *The host may not be in a "known state."* As a result, the automation must be more careful, because the OS may have decayed since its initial installation. During the initial load, the state of the machine is more controlled.

- *The host may have "live" users.* Some updates can't be installed while a machine is in use. Microsoft's System Management Service solves this problem by installing packages after a user has entered his or her user name and password to log in but before he or she gets access to the machine. The AutoPatch system used at Bell Labs sends email to a customer two days before and lets the customer postpone the update a few days by creating a file with a particular name in /tmp.

- *The host may be gone.* In this age of laptops, it is increasingly likely that a host may not always be on the network when the update system is running. Update systems can no longer assume that hosts are alive but must either chase after them until they reappear or be initiated by the host itself on a schedule, as well as any time it discovers that it has rejoined its home network.

- *The host may be dual-boot.* In this age of dual-boot hosts, update systems that reach out to desktops must be careful to verify that they have reached the expected OS. A dual-boot PC with Windows on one partition and Linux on another may run for months in Linux, missing out on updates for the Windows partition. Update systems for both the Linux and Windows systems must be smart enough to handle this situation.

3.1.2.2 One, Some, Many

The ramifications of a failed patch process are different from those of a failed OS load. A user probably won't even know whether an OS failed to load, because the host usually hasn't been delivered yet. However, a host that is being patched is usually at the person's desk; a patch that fails and leaves the machine in an unusable condition is much more visible and frustrating.

You can reduce the risk of a failed patch by using the **one, some, many** technique.

- *One.* First, patch one machine. This machine may belong to you, so there is incentive to get it right. If the patch fails, improve the process until it works for a single machine without fail.

- *Some.* Next, try the patch on a few other machines. If possible, you should test your automated patch process on all the other SAs' workstations before you inflict it on users. SAs are a little more understanding. Then test it on a few friendly customers outside the SA group.

- *Many.* As you test your system and gain confidence that it won't melt someone's hard drive, slowly, slowly, move to larger and larger groups of risk-averse customers.

An automated update system has potential to cause massive damage. You *must* have a well-documented process around it to make sure that risk is managed. The process needs to be well defined and repeatable, and you *must* attempt to improve it after each use. You can avoid disasters if you follow this system. Every time you distribute something, you're taking a risk. Don't take unnecessary risks.

An automated patch system is like a clinical trial of an experimental new anti-influenza drug. You wouldn't give an untested drug to thousands of people before you'd tested it on small groups of informed volunteers; likewise, you shouldn't implement an automated patch system until you're sure that it won't do serious damage. Think about how grumpy they'd get if your patch killed their machines and they hadn't even noticed the problem the patch was meant to fix!

Here are a few tips for your first steps in the update process.

- Create a well-defined update that will be distributed to all hosts. Nominate it for distribution. The nomination begins a buy-in phase to get it approved by all stakeholders. This practice prevents overly enthusiastic SAs from distributing trivial, non-business-critical software packages.

- Establish a communication plan so that those affected don't feel surprised by updates. Execute the plan the same way *every time,* because customers find comfort in consistency.

- When you're ready to implement your *Some* phase, define (and use!) a success metric, such as *If there are no failures, each succeeding group is about 50 percent larger than the previous group. If there is a single failure, the group size returns to a single host and starts growing again.*

- Finally, establish a way for customers to stop the deployment process if things go disastrously wrong. The process document should indicate who has the authority to request a halt, how to request it, who has the authority to approve the request, and what happens next.

3.1.3 Network Configuration

The third component you need for a large workstation environment is an automated way to update **network parameters,** those tiny bits of information that are often related to booting a computer and getting it onto the network. The information in them is highly customized for a particular subnet or even for a particular host. This characteristic is in contrast to a system such as application deployment, in which the same application is deployed to all hosts in the same configuration. As a result, your automated system for updating network parameters is usually separate from the other systems.

The most common system for automating this process is DHCP. Some vendors have DHCP servers that can be set up in seconds; other servers take considerably longer. Creating a global DNS/DHCP architecture with dozens or hundreds of sites requires a lot of planning and special knowledge. Some DHCP vendors have professional service organizations that will help you through the process, which can be particularly valuable for a global enterprise.

A small company may not see the value in letting you spend a day or more learning something that will, apparently, save you from what seems like only a minute or two of work whenever you set up a machine. Entering an IP address manually is no big deal, and, for that matter, neither is manually entering a netmask and a couple of other parameters. Right?

Wrong. Sure, you'll save a day or two by not setting up a DHCP server. But there's a problem: Remember those hidden costs we mentioned at the beginning of this chapter? If you don't use DHCP, they'll rear their ugly heads sooner or later. Eventually, you'll have to renumber the IP subnet or change the subnet netmask, Domain Name Service (DNS) server IP address, or modify some network parameter. If you don't have DHCP, you'll spend weeks or months making a single change, because you'll have to orchestrate teams of people to touch every host in the network. The small investment of using DHCP makes all future changes down the line nearly free.

Anything worth doing is worth doing well. DHCP has its own best and worst practices. The following section discusses what we've learned.

3.1.3.1 Use Templates Rather Than Per-Host Configuration

DHCP systems should provide a templating system. Some DHCP systems store the particular parameters given to each individual host. Other DHCP systems store templates that describe what parameters are given to various classes of hosts. The benefit of templates is that if you have to make the same change to many hosts, you simply change the template, which is much better than scrolling through a long list of hosts, trying to find which ones require the change. Another benefit is that it is much more difficult to introduce a syntax error into a configuration file if a program is generating the file. Assuming that templates are syntactically correct, the configuration will be too.

Such a system does not need to be complicated. Many SAs write small programs to create their own template systems. A list of hosts is stored in a database—or even a simple text file—and the program uses this data to program the DHCP server's configuration. Rather than putting the individual host information in a new file or creating a complicated database, the information can be embedded into your current inventory database or file. For example, UNIX sites can simply embed it into the /etc/ethers file that is already being maintained. This file is then used by a program that automatically generates the DHCP configuration. Sample lines from such a file are as follows:

```
8:0:20:1d:36:3a      adagio       #DHCP=sun
0:a0:c9:e1:af:2f     talpc        #DHCP=nt
0:60:b0:97:3d:77     sec4         #DHCP=hp4
0:a0:cc:55:5d:a2     bloop        #DHCP=any
0:0:a7:14:99:24      ostenato     #DHCP=ncd-barney
0:10:4b:52:de:c9     tallt        #DHCP=nt
0:10:4b:52:de:c9     tallt-home   #DHCP=nt
0:10:4b:52:de:c9     tallt-lab4   #DHCP=nt
0:10:4b:52:de:c9     tallt-lab5   #DHCP=nt
```

The token #DHCP= would be treated as a comment by any legacy program that looks at this file. However, the program that generates the DHCP server's configuration uses those codes to determine what to generate for that host. Hosts adagio, talpc, and sec4 receive the proper configuration for a Sun workstation, a Windows NT host, and an HP LaserJet 4 printer respectively. Host ostenato is an NCD X-Terminal that boots off a Trivial File Transfer Protocol (TFTP) server called barney. The NCD template takes a parameter, thus making it general enough for all the hosts that need to read a configuration file from a TFTP server. The last four lines indicate that Tom's laptop should get a different IP address, based on the four subnets to which it may be connected: his office, at home, or the fourth- or fifth-floor labs. Note that even though we are using static assignments, it is still possible for a host to hop networks.[4]

By embedding this information into an /etc/ethers file, we reduced the potential for typos. If the information were in a separate file, the data could become inconsistent.

Other parameters can be included this way. One site put this information in the comments of its UNIX /etc/hosts file, along with other tokens

---

4. SAs should note that this method relies on an IP address specified elsewhere or assigned by DHCP via a pool of addressees.

that indicated JumpStart and other parameters. The script extracts this information for use in JumpStart configuration files, DHCP configuration files, and other systems. By editing a single file, an SA was able to perform huge amounts of work! The open source project HostDB[5] expands on this idea, you edit one file to generate DHCP and DNS configuration files, as well as to distribute them to appropriate servers.

3.1.3.2 Know When to Use Dynamic Leases

Normally, DHCP assigns a particular IP address to a particular host. The **dynamic leases** DHCP feature lets one specify a range of IP addresses to be handed out to hosts. These hosts may get a different IP address every time they connect to the network. The benefit is that it is less work for the system administrators and more convenient for the customers.

Because this feature is used so commonly, many people think that DHCP *has* to assign addresses in this way. In fact, it doesn't. It is often better to lock a particular host to a particular IP address; this is particularly true for servers whose IP address is in other configuration files, such as DNS servers and firewalls. This technique is termed **static assignment** by the RFCs or **permanent lease** by Microsoft DHCP servers.

The right time to use a dynamic pool is when you have many hosts chasing a small number of IP addresses. For example, you may have a remote access server (RAS) with 200 modems for thousands of hosts that might dial into it. In that situation, it would be reasonable to have a dynamic pool of 220 addresses.[6] Another example might be a network with a high turnover of temporary hosts, such as a laboratory testbed, a computer installation room, or a network for visitor laptops. In these cases, there may be enough physical room or ports for only a certain number of computers. The IP address pool can be sized slightly larger than this maximum.

Typical office LANs are better suited to dynamically assigned leases. However, there are benefits to allocating static leases for particular machines. For example, by ensuring that certain machines always receive the same IP address, you prevent those machines from not being able to get IP addresses when the pool is exhausted. Imagine a pool being exhausted by a large influx of guests visiting an office and then your boss being unable to access anything because the PC can't get an IP address.

---

5. http://everythingsysadmin.com/hostdb/
6. Although in this scenario you need a pool of only 200 IP addresses, a slightly larger pool has benefits. For example, if a host disconnects without releasing the lease, the IP address will be tied up until its lease period has ended. Allocating 10 percent additional IP addresses to alleviate this situation is reasonable.

Another reason for statically assigning IP addresses is that it improves the usability of logs. If people's workstations always are assigned the same IP address, logs will consistently show them at a particular IP address. Finally, some software packages deal poorly with a host changing its IP address. Although this situation is increasingly rare, static assignments avoid such problems.

The exclusive use of statically assigned IP addresses is not a valid security measure. Some sites disable any dynamic assignment, feeling that this will prevent uninvited guests from using their network. The truth is that someone can still manually configure network settings. Software that permits one to snoop network packets quickly reveals enough information to permit someone to guess which IP addresses are unused, what the netmask is, what DNS settings should be, the default gateway, and so on.

IEEE 802.1x is a better way to do this. This standard for **network access control** determines whether a new host should be permitted on a network. Used primarily on WiFi networks, network access control is being used more and more on wired networks. An Ethernet switch that supports 802.1x keeps a newly connected host disconnected from the network while performing some kind of authentication. Depending on whether the authentication succeeds or fails, traffic is permitted, or the host is denied access to the network.

3.1.3.3 Using DHCP on Public Networks

Before 802.1x was invented, many people crafted similar solutions. You may have been in a hotel or a public space where the network was configured such that it was easy to get on the network but you had access only to an authorization web page. Once the authorization went through—either by providing some acceptable identification or by paying with a credit card—you gained access. In these situations, SAs would like the plug-in-and-go ease of an address pool while being able to authenticate that users have permission to use corporate, university, or hotel resources. For more on early tools and techniques, see Beck (1999) and Valian and Watson (1999) Their systems permit unregistered hosts to be registered to a person who then assumes responsibility for any harm these unknown hosts create.

3.1.4 Avoid Using Dynamic DNS with DHCP

We're unimpressed by DHCP systems that update dynamic DNS servers. This flashy feature adds unnecessary complexity and security risk.

In systems with dynamic DNS, a client host tells the DHCP server what its hostname should be, and the DHCP server sends updates to the DNS server. (The client host can also send updates directly to the DNS server.) No matter what network the machine is plugged in to, the DNS information for that host is consistent with the name of the host.

Hosts with static leases will always have the same name in DNS because they always receive the same IP address. When using dynamic leases, the host's IP address is from a pool of addresses, each of which usually has a formulaic name, in DNS, such as `dhcp-pool-10`, `dhcp-pool-11`, `dhcp-pool-12`. No matter which host receives the tenth address in the pool, its name in DNS will be `dhcp-pool-10`. This will most certainly be inconsistent with the hostname stored in its local configuration.

This inconsistency is unimportant unless the machine is a server. That is, if a host isn't running any services, nobody needs to refer to it by name, and it doesn't matter what name is listed for it in DNS. If the host is running services, the machine should receive a permanent DHCP lease and always have the same fixed name. Services that are designed to talk directly to clients don't use DNS to find the hosts. One such example is peer-to-peer services, which permit hosts to share files or communicate via voice or video. When joining the peer-to-peer service, each host registers its IP address with a central registry that uses a fixed name and/or IP address. H.323 communication tools, such as Microsoft Netmeeting, use this technique.

Letting a host determine its own hostname is a security risk. Hostnames should be controlled by a centralized authority, not the user of the host. What if someone configures a host to have the same name as a critical server? Which should the DNS/DHCP system believe is the real server? Most dynamic DNS/DHCP systems let you lock down names of critical servers, which means that the list of critical servers is a new namespace that must be maintained and audited (see Chapter 8, name spaces.) If you accidentally omit a new server, you have a disaster waiting to occur.

Avoid situations in which customers are put in a position that allows their simple mistakes to disrupt others. LAN architects learned this a long time ago with respect to letting customers configure their own IP addresses. We should not repeat this mistake by letting customers set their own hostnames. Before DHCP, customers would often take down a LAN by accidentally setting their host's IP address to that of the router. Customers were handed a list of IP addresses to use to configure their PCs. "Was the first one for 'default gateway,' or was it the second one? Aw, heck, I've got a 50/50 chance of getting it right." If the customer guessed wrong, communication with the router essentially stopped.

The use of DHCP greatly reduces the chance of this happening. Permitting customers to pick their own hostnames sounds like a variation on this theme that is destined to have similar results. We fear a rash of new problems related to customers setting their host's name to the name that was given to them to use as their email server or their domain name or another common string.

Another issue relates to how these DNS updates are authenticated. The secure protocols for doing these updates ensure that the host that inserted records into DNS is the same host that requests that they are deleted or replaced. The protocols do little to prevent the initial insertion of data and have little control over the format or lexicon of permitted names. We foresee situations in which people configure their PCs with misleading names in an attempt to confuse or defraud others—a scam that commonly happens on the Internet[7]—coming soon to an intranet near you.

So many risks to gain one flashy feature! Advocates of such systems argue that all these risks can be managed or mitigated, often through additional features and controls that can be configured. We reply that adding layers of complicated databases to manage risk sounds like a lot of work that can be avoided by simply not using the feature.

Some would argue that this feature increases accountability, because logs will always reflect the same hostname. We, on the other hand, argue that there are other ways to gain better accountability. If you need to be able to trace illegal behavior of a host to a particular person, it is best to use a registration and tracking system (Section 3.1.3.3).

Dynamic DNS with DHCP creates a system that is more complicated, more difficult to manage, more prone to failure, and less secure in exchange for a small amount of aesthetic pleasantness. It's not worth it.

Despite these drawbacks, OS vendors have started building systems that do not work as well unless dynamic DNS updates are enabled. Companies are put in the difficult position of having to choose between adopting new technology or reducing their security standards. Luckily, the security industry has a useful concept: containment. **Containment** means limiting a security risk so that it can affect only a well-defined area. We recommend that dynamic DNS should be contained to particular network subdomains that

---

7.   For many years, www.whitehouse.com was a porn site. This was quite a surprise to people who were looking for www.whitehouse.gov.

will be treated with less trust. For example, all hosts that use dynamic DNS might have such names as myhost.dhcp.corp.example.com. Hostnames in the dhcp.corp.example.com zone might have collisions and other problems, but those problems are isolated in that one zone. This technique can be extended to the entire range of dynamic DNS updates that are required by domain controllers in Microsoft ActiveDirectory. One creates many contained areas for DNS zones with funny-looking names, such as _tcp.corp.example.com and _udp.corp.example.com (Liu 2001).

3.1.4.1 Managing DHCP Lease Times

Lease times can be managed to aid in propagating updates. DHCP client hosts are given a set of parameters to use for a certain amount of time, after which they must renew their leases. Changes to the parameters are seen at renewal time.

Suppose that the lease time for a particular subnet is 2 weeks. Suppose that you are going to change the netmask for that subnet. Normally, one can expect a 2-week wait before all the hosts have this new netmask.

On the other hand, if you know that the change is coming, you can set the lease time to be short during the time leading up to the change. Once you change the netmask in the DHCP server's configuration, the update will propagate quickly. When you have verified that the change has created no ill effects, you can increase the lease time to the original value (2 weeks). With this technique, you can roll out a change much more quickly.

DHCP for Moving Clients Away from Resources

At Bell Labs, Tom needed to change the IP address of the primary DNS server. Such a change would take only a moment but would take weeks to propagate to all clients via DHCP. Clients wouldn't function properly until they had received their update. It could have been a major outage.

He temporarily configured the DHCP server to direct all clients to use a completely different DNS server. It wasn't the optimal DNS server for those clients to use, but it was one that worked. Once the original DNS server had stopped receiving requests, he could renumber it and test it without worry. Later, he changed the DHCP server to direct clients to the new IP address of the primary DNS server.

Although hosts were using a slower DNS server for a while, they never felt the pain of a complete outage.

The optimal length for a default lease is a philosophical battle that is beyond the scope of this book. For discussions on the topic, we recommend

The DHCP Handbook (Lemon and Droms 1999) and *DHCP: A Guide to Dynamic TCP/IP Network Configuration* (Kercheval 1999).

Case Study: Using the Bell Labs Laptop Net

The Computer Science Research group at Bell Labs has a subnet with a 5-minute lease in its famous UNIX Room. Laptops can plug in to the subnet in this room for short periods. The lease is only 5 minutes because the SAs observed that users require about 5 minutes to walk their laptops back to their offices from the UNIX Room. By that time, the lease has expired. This technique is less important now that DHCP client implementations are better at dealing with rapid change.

3.2 The Icing

Up to this point, this chapter has dealt with technical details that are basic to getting workstation deployment right. These issues are so fundamental that doing them well will affect nearly every other possible task. This section helps you fine-tune things a bit.

Once you have the basics in place, keep an eye open for new technologies that help to automate other aspects of workstation support (Miller and Donnini 2000a). Workstations are usually the most numerous machines in the company. Every small gain in reducing workstation support overhead has a massive impact.

3.2.1 High Confidence in Completion

There are automated processes, and then there is process automation. When we have exceptionally high confidence in a process, our minds are liberated from worry of failure, and we start to see new ways to use the process.

Christophe Kalt had extremely high confidence that a Solaris JumpStart at Bell Labs would run to completion without fail or without the system unexpectedly stopping to ask for user input. He would use the UNIX at to schedule hosts to be JumpStarted[8] at times when neither he nor the customer would be awake, thereby changing the way he could offer service to customers. This change was possible only because he had high confidence that the installation would complete without error.

---

8. The Solaris command reboot -- 'flnet - installfl' eliminates the need for a human to type on the console to start the process. The command can be done remotely, if necessary.

3.2.2 Involve Customers in the Standardization Process

If a standard configuration is going to be inflicted on customers, you should involve them in specifications and design.[9] In a perfect world, customers would be included in the design process from the very beginning. Designated delegates or interested managers would choose applications to include in the configuration. Every application would have a service-level agreement detailing the level of support expected from the SAs. New releases of OSs and applications would be tracked and approved, with controlled introductions similar to those described for automated patching.

However, real-world platforms tend to be controlled either by management, with excruciating exactness, or by the SA team, which is responsible for providing a basic platform that users can customize. In the former case, one might imagine a telesales office where the operators see a particular set of applications. Here, the SAs work with management to determine exactly what will be loaded, when to schedule upgrades, and so on.

The latter environment is more common. At one site, the standard platform for a PC is its OS, the most commonly required applications, the applications required by the parent company, and utilities that customers commonly request and that can be licensed economically in bulk. The environment is very open, and there are no formal committee meetings. SAs do, however, have close relationships with many customers and therefore are in touch with the customers' needs.

For certain applications, there are more formal processes. For example, a particular group of developers requires a particular tool set. Every software release developed has a tool set that is defined, tested, approved, and deployed. SAs should be part of the process in order to match resources with the deployment schedule.

3.2.3 A Variety of Standard Configurations

Having multiple standard configurations can be a thing of beauty or a nightmare, and the SA is the person who determines which category applies.[10] The more standard configurations a site has, the more difficult it is to maintain them all. One way to make a large variety of configurations scale well is to

---

9. While SAs think of standards as beneficial, many customers consider standards to be an annoyance to be tolerated or worked around.

10. One Internet wog has commented that "the best thing about standards is that there are so many to choose from."

be sure that every configuration uses the same server and mechanisms rather than have one server for each standard. However, if you invest time into making a single generalized system that can produce multiple configurations and can scale, you will have created something that will be a joy forever.

The general concept of managed, standardized configurations is often referred to as **Software Configuration Management** (SCM). This process applies to servers as well as to desktops.

We discuss servers in the next chapter; here, it should be noted that special configurations can be developed for server installations. Although they run particularly unique applications, servers always have some kind of base installation that can be specified as one of these custom configurations. When redundant web servers are being rolled out to add capacity, having the complete installation automated can be a big win. For example, many Internet sites have redundant web servers for providing static pages, Common Gateway Interface (CGI) (dynamic) pages, or other services. If these various configurations are produced through an automated mechanism, rolling out additional capacity in any area is a simple matter.

Standard configurations can also take some of the pain out of OS upgrades. If you're able to completely wipe your disk and reinstall, OS upgrades become trivial. This requires more diligence in such areas as segregating user data and handling host-specific system data.

3.3 Conclusion

This chapter reviewed the processes involved in maintaining the OSs of desktop computers. Desktops, unlike servers, are usually deployed in large quantities, each with nearly the same configuration. All computers have a life cycle that begins with the OS being loaded and ends when the machine is powered off for the last time. During that interval, the software on the system degrades as a result of entropy, is upgraded, and is reloaded from scratch as the cycle begins again. Ideally, all hosts of a particular platform begin with the same configuration and should be upgraded in parallel. Some phases of the life cycle are more useful to customers than others. We seek to increase the time spent in the more usable phases and shorten the time spent in the less usable phases.

Three processes create the basis for everything else in this chapter. (1) The initial loading of the OS should be automated. (2) Software updates should be automated. (3) Network configuration should be centrally administered via a system such as DHCP. These three objectives are critical to economical management. Doing these basics right makes everything that follows run smoothly.

Exercises

1. What constitutes a *platform*, as used in Section 3.1? List all the platforms used in your environment. Group them based on which can be considered the same for the purpose of support. Explain how you made your decision.

2. An anecdote in Section 3.1.2 describes a site that repeatedly spent money deploying software manually rather than investing once in deployment automation. It might be difficult to understand why a site would be so foolish. Examine your own site or a site you recently visited, and list at least three instances in which similar investments had not been made. For each, list why the investment hadn't been made. What do your answers tell you?

3. In your environment, identify a type of host or OS that is not, as the example in Section 3.1 describes, a first-class citizen. How would you make this a first-class citizen if it was determined that demand would soon increase? How would platforms in your environment be promoted to first-class citizen?

4. In one of the examples, Tom mentored a new SA who was installing Solaris JumpStart. The script that needed to be run at the end simply copied certain files into place. How could the script—whether run automatically or manually—be eliminated?

5. DHCP presupposes IP-style networking. This book is very IP-centric. What would you do in an all-Novell shop using IPX/SPX? OSI-net (X.25 PAD)? DECnet environment?

Chapter 4

Servers

This chapter is about servers. Unlike a workstation, which is dedicated to a single customer, multiple customers depend on a server. Therefore, reliability and uptime are a high priority. When we invest effort in making a server reliable, we look for features that will make repair time shorter, provide a better working environment, and use special care in the configuration process.

A server may have hundreds, thousands, or millions of clients relying on it. Every effort to increase performance or reliability is amortized over many clients. Servers are expected to last longer than workstations, which also justifies the additional cost. Purchasing a server with spare capacity becomes an investment in extending its life span.

4.1 The Basics

Hardware sold for use as a server is qualitatively different from hardware sold for use as an individual workstation. Server hardware has different features and is engineered to a different economic model. Special procedures are used to install and support servers. They typically have maintenance contracts, disk-backup systems, OS, better remote access, and servers reside in the controlled environment of a data center, where access to server hardware can be limited. Understanding these differences will help you make better purchasing decisions.

4.1.1 Buy Server Hardware for Servers

Systems sold as servers are different from systems sold to be clients or desktop workstations. It is often tempting to "save money" by purchasing desktop hardware and loading it with server software. Doing so may work in the short term but is not the best choice for the long term or in a large installation you would be building a house of cards. Server hardware usually costs more but has additional features that justify the cost. Some of the features are

- *Extensibility.* Servers usually have either more physical space inside for hard drives and more slots for cards and CPUs, or are engineered with high-through put connectors that enable use of specialized peripherals. Vendors usually provide advanced hardware/software configurations enabling clustering, load-balancing, automated fail-over, and similar capabilities.

- *More CPU performance.* Servers often have multiple CPUs and advanced hardware features such as pre-fetch, multi-stage processor checking, and the ability to dynamically allocate resources among CPUs. CPUs may be available in various speeds, each linearly priced with respect to speed. The fastest revision of a CPU tends to be disproportionately expensive: a surcharge for being on the cutting edge. Such an extra cost can be more easily justified on a server that is supporting multiple customers. Because a server is expected to last longer, it is often reasonable to get a faster CPU that will not become obsolete as quickly. Note that CPU speed on a server does not always determine performance, because many applications are I/O-bound, not CPU-bound.

- *High-performance I/O.* Servers usually do more I/O than clients. The quantity of I/O is often proportional to the number of clients, which justifies a faster I/O subsystem. That might mean SCSI or FC-AL disk drives instead of IDE, higher-speed internal buses, or network interfaces that are orders of magnitude faster than the clients.

- *Upgrade options.* Servers are often upgraded, rather than simply replaced; they are designed for growth. Servers generally have the ability to add CPUs or replace individual CPUs with faster ones, without requiring additional hardware changes. Typically, server CPUs reside on separate cards within the chassis, or are placed in removable sockets on the system board for case of replacement.

- *Rack mountable.* Servers should be rack-mountable. In Chapter 6, we discuss the importance of rack-mounting servers rather than stacking them. Although nonrackable servers can be put on shelves in racks, doing so wastes space and is inconvenient. Whereas desktop hardware may have a pretty, molded plastic case in the shape of a gumdrop, a server should be rectangular and designed for efficient space utilization in a rack. Any covers that need to be removed to do repairs should be removable while the host is still rack-mounted. More importantly, the server should be engineered for cooling and ventilation in a rack-mounted setting. A system that only has side cooling vents will not maintain its temperature as well in a rack as one that vents front to back. Having the word *server* included in a product name is not sufficient; care must be taken to make sure that it fits in the space allocated. Connectors should support a rack-mount environment, such as use of standard cat-5 patch cables for serial console rather then db-9 connectors with screws.

- *No side-access needs.* A rack-mounted host is easier to repair or perform maintenance on if tasks can be done while it remains in the rack. Such tasks must be performed without access to the sides of the machine. All cables should be on the back, and all drive bays should be on the front. We have seen CD-ROM bays that opened on the side, indicating that the host wasn't designed with racks in mind. Some systems, often network equipment, require access on only one side. This means that the device can be placed "butt-in" in a cramped closet and still be serviceable. Some hosts require that the external plastic case (or portions of it) be removed to successfully mount the device in a standard rack. Be sure to verify that this does not interfere with cooling or functionality. Power switches should be accessible but not easy to accidentally bump.

- *High-availability options.* Many servers include various high-availability options, such as dual power supplies, RAID, multiple network connections, and hot-swap components.

- *Maintenance contracts.* Vendors offer server hardware service contracts that generally include guaranteed turnaround times on replacement parts.

- *Management options.* Ideally, servers should have some capability for remote management, such as serial port access, that can be used to diagnose and fix problems to restore a machine that is down to active service. Some servers also come with internal temperature sensors and other hardware monitoring that can generate notifications when problems are detected.

Vendors are continually improving server designs to meet business needs. In particular, market pressures have pushed vendors to improve servers so that is it possible to fit more units in **colocation centers**, rented data centers that charge by the square foot. Remote-management capabilities for servers in a colo can mean the difference between minutes and hours of downtime.

4.1.2 Choose Vendors Known for Reliable Products

It is important to pick vendors that are known for reliability. Some vendors cut corners by using consumer-grade parts; other vendors use parts that meet MIL-SPEC[1] requirements. Some vendors have years of experience designing servers. Vendors with more experience include the features listed earlier, as well as other little extras that one can learn only from years of market experience. Vendors with little or no server experience do not offer maintenance service except for exchanging hosts that arrive dead.

It can be useful to talk with other SAs to find out which vendors they use and which ones they avoid. The System Administrators' Guild (SAGE) (www.sage.org) and the League of Professional System Administrators (LOPSA) (www. lopsa.org) are good resources for the SA community.

Environments can be homogeneous—all the same vendor or product line—or heterogeneous—many different vendors and/or product lines. Homogeneous environments are easier to maintain, because training is reduced, maintenance and repairs are easier—one set of spares—and there is less finger pointing when problems arise. However, heterogeneous environments have the benefit that you are not locked in to one vendor, and the competition among the vendors will result in better service to you. This is discussed further in Chapter 5.

4.1.3 Understand the Cost of Server Hardware

To understand the additional cost of servers, you must understand how machines are priced. You also need to understand how server features add to the cost of the machine.

Most vendors have three[2] product lines: home, business, and server. The home line is usually the cheapest initial purchase price, because consumers tend to make purchasing decisions based on the advertised price. Add-ons and future expandability are available at a higher cost. Components are specified in general terms, such as video resolution, rather than particular

---

1. **MIL-SPECs**—U.S. military specifications for electronic parts and equipment—specify a level of quality to produce more repeatable results. The MIL-SPEC standard usually, but not always, specifies higher quality than the civilian average. This exacting specification generally results in significantly higher costs.

2. Sometimes more; sometimes less. Vendors often have specialty product lines for vertical markets, such as high-end graphics, numerically intensive computing, and so on. Specialized consumer markets, such as real-time multiplayer gaming or home multimedia, increasingly blur the line between consumer-grade and server-grade hardware.

video card vendor and model, because maintaining the lowest possible purchase price requires vendors to change parts suppliers on a daily or weekly
basis. These machines tend to have more game features, such as joysticks,
high-performance graphics, and fancy audio.

The business desktop line tends to focus on total cost of ownership. The
initial purchase price is higher than for a home machine, but the business
line should take longer to become obsolete. It is expensive for companies
to maintain large pools of spare components, not to mention the cost of
training repair technicians on each model. Therefore, the business line tends
to adopt new components, such as video cards and hard drive controllers,
infrequently. Some vendors offer programs guaranteeing that video cards will
not change for at least 6 months and only with 3 months notice or that spares
will be available for 1 year after such notification. Such specific metrics can
make it easier to test applications under new hardware configurations and
to maintain a spare-parts inventory. Much business-class equipment is leased
rather than purchased, so these assurances are of great value to a site.

The server line tends to focus on having the lowest cost per performance
metric. For example, a file server may be designed with a focus on lowering the cost of the SPEC SFS97[3] performance divided by the purchase price
of the machine. Similar benchmarks exist for web traffic, online transaction
processing (OLTP), aggregate multi-CPU performance, and so on. Many of
the server features described previously add to the purchase price of a machine, but also increase the potential uptime of the machine, giving it a more
favorable price/performance ratio.

Servers cost more for other reasons, too. A chassis that is easier to service may be more expensive to manufacture. Restricting the drive bays and
other access panels to certain sides means not positioning them solely to minimize material costs. However, the small increase in initial purchase price
saves money in the long term in mean time to repair (MTTR) and ease of
service.

Therefore, because it is not an apples-to-apples comparison, it is inac-
curate to state that a server costs more than a desktop computer. Understanding these different pricing models helps one frame the discussion when
asked to justify the superficially higher cost of server hardware. It is common to hear someone complain of a $50,000 price tag for a server when a
high-performance PC can be purchased for $5,000. If the server is capable of

---

3.   Formerly LADDIS.

serving millions of transactions per day or will serve the CPU needs of dozens of users, the cost is justified. Also, server downtime is more expensive than desktop downtime. Redundant and hot-swap hardware on a server can easily pay for itself by minimizing outages.

A more valid argument against such a purchasing decision might be that the performance being purchased is more than the service requires. Performance is often proportional to cost, and purchasing unneeded performance is wasteful. However, purchasing an overpowered server may delay a painful upgrade to add capacity later. That has value, too. Capacity-planning predictions and utilization trends become useful, as discussed in Chapter 22.

4.1.4 Consider Maintenance Contracts and Spare Parts

When purchasing a server, consider how repairs will be handled. All machines eventually break.[4] Vendors tend to have a variety of maintenance contract options. For example, one form of maintenance contract provides on-site service with a 4-hour response time, a 12-hour response time, or next-day options. Other options include having the customer purchase a kit of spare parts and receive replacements when a spare part gets used.

Following are some reasonable scenarios for picking appropriate maintenance contracts:

- *Non-critical server.* Some hosts are not critical, such as a CPU server that is one of many. In that situation, a maintenance contract with next-day or 2-day response time is reasonable. Or, no contract may be needed if the default repair options are sufficient.

- *Large groups of similar servers.* Sometimes, a site has many of the same type of machine, possibly offering different kinds of services. In this case, it may be reasonable to purchase a spares kit so that repairs can be done by local staff. The cost of the spares kit is divided over the many hosts. These hosts may now require a lower-cost maintenance contract that simply replaces parts from the spares kit.

- *Controlled introduction.* Technology improves over time, and sites described in the previous paragraph eventually need to upgrade to newer

---

4. Desktop workstations break, too, but we decided to cover maintenance contracts in this chapter rather than in Chapter 3. In our experience, desktop repairs tend to be less time-critical than server repairs. Desktops are more generic and therefore more interchangeable. These factors make it reasonable not to have a maintenance contract but instead to have a locally maintained set of spares and the technical know-how to do repairs internally or via contract with a local repair depot.

models, which may be out of scope for the spares kit. In this case, you might standardize for a set amount of time on a particular model or set of models that share a spares kit. At the end of the period, you might approve a new model and purchase the appropriate spares kit. At any given time, you would have, for example, only two spares kits. To introduce a third model, you would first decommission all the hosts that rely on the spares kit that is being retired. This controls costs.

- *Critical host.* Sometimes, it is too expensive to have a fully stocked spares kit. It may be reasonable to stock spares for parts that commonly fail and otherwise pay for a maintenance contract with same-day response. Hard drives and power supplies commonly fail and are often interchangeable among a number of products.

- *Large variety of models from same vendor.* A very large site may adopt a maintenance contract that includes having an on-site technician. This option is usually justified only at a site that has an extremely large number of servers, or sites where that vendor's servers play a keen role related to revenue. However, medium-size sites can sometimes negotiate to have the regional spares kit stored on their site, with the benefit that the technician is more likely to hang out near your building. Sometimes, it is possible to negotiate direct access to the spares kit on an emergency basis. (Usually, this is done without the knowledge of the technician's management.) An SA can ensure that the technician will spend all his or her spare time at your site by providing a minor amount of office space and use of a telephone as a base of operations. In exchange, a discount on maintenance contract fees can sometimes be negotiated. At one site that had this arrangement, a technician with nothing else to do would unbox and rack-mount new equipment for the SAs.

- *Highly critical host.* Some vendors offer a maintenance contract that provides an on-site technician and a duplicate machine ready to be swapped into place. This is often as expensive as paying for a redundant server but may make sense for some companies that are not highly technical.

There is a trade-off between stocking spares and having a service contract. Stocking your own spares may be too expensive for a small site. A maintenance contract includes diagnostic services, even if over the phone. Sometimes, on the other hand, the easiest way to diagnose something is to swap in spare parts until the problem goes away. It is difficult to keep staff trained on the full range of diagnostic and repair methodologies for all the models used, especially for nontechnological companies, which may find such an endeavor to be distracting. Such outsourcing is discussed in Section 21.2.2 and Section 30.1.8.

Sometimes, an SA discovers that a critical host is not on the service contract. This discovery tends to happen at a critical time, such as when it needs to be repaired. The solution usually involves talking to a salesperson who will have the machine repaired on good faith that it will be added to the contract immediately or retroactively. It is good practice to write purchase orders for service contracts for 10 percent more than the quoted price of the contract, so that the vendor can grow the monthly charges as new machines are added to the contract.

It is also good practice to review the service contract, at least annually if not quarterly, to ensure that new servers are added and retired servers are deleted. Strata once saved a client several times the cost of her consulting services by reviewing a vendor service contract that was several years out of date.

There are three easy ways to prevent hosts from being left out of the contract. The first is to have a good inventory system and use it to cross-reference the service contract. Good inventory systems are difficult to find, however, and even the best can miss some hosts.

The second is to have the person responsible for processing purchases also add new machines to the contract. This person should know whom to contact to determine the appropriate service level. If there is no single point of purchasing, it may be possible to find some other choke point in the process at which the new host can be added to the contract.

Third, you should fix a common problem caused by warranties. Most computers have free service for the first 12 months because of their warranty and do not need to be listed on the service contract during those months. However, it is difficult to remember to add the host to the contract so many months later, and the service level is different during the warranty period. To remedy these issues, the SA should see whether the vendor can list the machine on the contract immediately but show a zero dollar charge for the first 12 monthly statements. Most vendors will do this because it locks in revenue for that host. Lately, most vendors require a service contract to be purchased at the time of buying the hardware.

Service contracts are reactive, rather than proactive, solutions. (Proactive solutions are discussed in the next chapter.) Service contracts promise spare parts and repairs in a timely manner. Usually, various grades of contracts are available. The lower grades ship replacement parts to the site; more expensive ones deliver the part and do the installation.

Cross-shipped parts are an important part of speedy repairs, and ideally should be supported under any maintenance contract. When a server has hardware problems and replacement parts are needed, some vendors require the old, broken part to be returned to them. This makes sense if the replacement is being done at no charge as part of a warranty or service contract. The returned part has value; it can be repaired and returned to service with the next customer that requires that part. Also, without such a return, a customer could simply be requesting part after part, possibly selling them for profit.

Vendors usually require notification and authorization for returning broken parts; this authorization is called **returned merchandise authorization (RMA)**. The vendor generally gives the customer an RMA number for tagging and tracking the returned parts.

Some vendors will not ship the replacement part until they receive the broken part. This practice can increase the time to repair by a factor of 2 or more. Better vendors will ship the replacement immediately and expect you to return the broken part within a certain amount of time. This is called **cross-shipping**; the parts, in theory, cross each other as they are delivered.

Vendors usually require a purchase order number or request a credit card number to secure payment in case the returned part is never received. This is a reasonable way to protect themselves. Sometimes, having a service contract alleviates the need for this.

Be wary of vendors claiming to sell servers that don't offer cross-shipping under any circumstances. Such vendors aren't taking the term *server* very seriously. You'd be surprised which major vendors have this policy.

For even faster repair times, purchasing a **spare-parts kit** removes the dependency on the vendor when rushing to repair a server. A kit should include one part for each component in the system. This kit usually costs less than buying a duplicate system, since, for example, if the original system has four CPUs, the kit needs to contain only one. The kit is also less expensive, since it doesn't require software licenses. Even if you have a kit, you should have a service contract that will replace any part from the kit used to service a broken machine. Get one spares kit for each model in use that requires faster repair time.

Managing many spare-parts kits can be extremely expensive, especially when one requires the additional cost of a service contract. The vendor may have additional options, such as a service contract that guarantees delivery of replacement parts within a few hours, that can reduce your total cost.

4.1.5 Maintaining Data Integrity

Servers have critical data and unique configurations that must be protected.

Workstation clients are usually mass-produced with the same configuration on each one, and usually store their data on servers, which eliminates the need for backups. If a workstation's disk fails, the configuration should be identical to its multiple cousins, unmodified from its initial state, and therefore can be recreated from an automated install procedure. That is the theory. However, people will always store some data on their local machines, software will be installed locally, and OSs will store some configuration data locally. It is impossible to prevent this on Windows platforms. Roaming profiles store the users' settings to the server every time they log out but do not protect the locally installed software and registry settings of the machine.

UNIX systems are guilty to a lesser degree, because a well-configured system, with no `root` access for the user, can prevent all but a few specific files from being updated on the local disk. For example, crontabs (scheduled tasks) and other files stored in `/var` will still be locally modified. A simple system that backs up those few files each night is usually sufficient.

Backups are fully discussed in Chapter 26.

4.1.6 Put Servers in the Data Center

Servers should be installed in an environment with proper power, fire protection, networking, cooling, and physical security (see Chapter 5). It is a good idea to allocate the physical space of a server when it is being purchased. Marking the space by taping a paper sign in the appropriate rack can safeguard against having space double-booked. Marking the power and cooling space requires tracking via a list or spreadsheet.

After assembling the hardware, it is best to mount it in the rack immediately before installing the OS and other software. We have observed the following phenomenon: A new server is assembled in someone's office and the OS and applications loaded onto it. As the applications are brought up, some trial users are made aware of the service. Soon the server is in heavy use before it is intended to be, and it is still in someone's office without the proper protections of a machine room, such as UPS and air conditioning. Now the people using the server will be disturbed by an outage when it is moved into the machine room. The way to prevent this situation is to mount the server in its final location as soon as it is assembled.[5]

Field offices aren't always large enough to have data centers, and some entire companies aren't large enough to have data centers. However, everyone should have a designated room or closet with the bare minimums: physical security, UPS—many small ones if not one large one—and proper cooling. A telecom closet with good cooling and a door that can be locked is better than having your company's payroll installed on a server sitting under someone's desk. Inexpensive cooling solutions, some of which remove the need for drainage by reevaporating any water they collect and exhausting it out the exhaust air vent, are becoming available.

4.1.7 Client Server OS Configuration

Servers don't have to run the same OS as their clients. Servers can be completely different, completely the same, or the same basic OS but with a different configuration to account for the difference in intended usage. Each is appropriate at different times.

A web server, for example, does not need to run the same OS as its clients. The clients and the server need only agree on a protocol. Single-function network appliances often have a mini-OS that contains just enough software to do the one function required, such as being a file server, a web server, or a mail server.

Sometimes, a server is required to have all the same software as the clients. Consider the case of a UNIX environment with many UNIX desktops and a series of general-purpose UNIX CPU servers. The clients should have similar cookie-cutter OS loads, as discussed in Chapter 3. The CPU servers should have the same OS load, though it may be tuned differently for a larger number of processes, pseudoterminals, buffers, and other parameters.

It is interesting to note that what is appropriate for a server OS is a matter of perspective. When loading Solaris 2.x, you can indicate that this host is a server, which means that all the software packages are loaded, because diskless clients or those with small hard disks may use NFS to mount certain packages from the server. On the other hand, the server configuration when loading Red Hat Linux is a minimal set of packages, on the assumption that you simply want the base installation, on top of which you will load the

---

5. It is also common to lose track of the server rack-mounting hardware in this situation, requiring even more delays, or to realize that power or network cable won't reach the location.

specific software packages that will be used to create the service. With hard disks growing, the latter is more common.

4.1.8 Provide Remote Console Access

Servers need to be maintained remotely. In the old days, every server in the machine room had its own console: a keyboard, video monitor or hardcopy console, and, possibly, a mouse. As SAs packed more into their machine rooms, eliminating these consoles saved considerable space.

A **KVM switch** is a device that lets many machines share a single keyboard, video screen, and mouse (KVM). For example, you might be able to fit three servers and three consoles into a single rack. However, with a KVM switch, you need only a single keyboard, monitor, and mouse for the rack. Now more servers can fit there. You can save even more room by having one KVM switch per row of racks or one for the entire data center. However, bigger KVM switches are often prohibitively costly. You can save even more space by using IP-KVMs, KVMs that have no keyboard, monitor, or mouse. You simply connect to the KVM console server over the network from a software client on another machine. You can even do it from your laptop while connected by VPNed into your network from a coffee shop!

The predecessor to KVM switches were for serial port–based devices. Originally, servers had no video card but instead had a serial port to which one attached an terminal.[6] These terminals took up a lot of space in the computer room, which often had a long table with a dozen or more terminals, one for each server. It was considered quite a technological advancement when someone thought to buy a small server with a dozen or so serial ports and to connect each port to the console of a server. Now one could log in to the console server and then connect to a particular serial port. No more walking to the computer room to do something on the console.

Serial console concentrators now come in two forms: home brew or appliance. With the home-brew solution, you take a machine with a lot of serial ports and add software—free software, such as ConServer,[7] or commercial equivalents—and build it yourself. Appliance solutions are prebuilt

---

6. Younger readers may think of a *VT-100 terminal* only as a software package that interprets ASCII codes to display text, or a feature of a *TELNET* or *SSH* package. Those software packages are emulating actual devices that used to cost hundreds of dollars each and be part of every big server. In fact, before PCs, a server might have had dozens of these terminals, which comprised the only ways to access the machine.

7. www.conserver.com

vendor systems that tend to be faster to set up and have all their software in firmware or solid-state flash storage so that there is no hard drive to break.

Serial consoles and KVM switches have the benefit of permitting you to operate a system's console when the network is down or when the system is in a bad state. For example, certain things can be done only while a machine is booting, such as pressing a key sequence to activate a basic BIOS configuration menu. (Obviously, IP-KVMs require the network to be reliable between you and the IP-KVM console, but the remaining network can be down.)

Some vendors have hardware cards to allow remote control of the machine. This feature is often the differentiator between their server-class machines and others. Third-party products can add this functionality too.

Remote console systems also let you simulate the funny key sequences that have special significance when typed at the console: for example, CTRL-ALT-DEL on PC hardware and L1-A on Sun hardware.

Since a serial console is receiving a single stream of ASCII data, it is easy to record and store. Thus, one can view everything that has happened on a serial console, going back months. This can be useful for finding error messages that were emitted to a console.

Networking devices, such as routers and switches, have only serial consoles. Therefore, it can be useful to have a serial console in addition to a KVM system.

It can be interesting to watch what is output to a serial port. Even when nobody is logged in to a Cisco router, error messages and warnings are sent out the console serial port. Sometimes, the results will surprise you.

Monitor All Serial Ports

Once, Tom noticed that an unlabeled and supposedly unused port on a device looked like a serial port. The device was from a new company, and Tom was one of its first beta customers. He connected the mystery serial port to his console and occasionally saw status messages being output. Months went by before the device started having a problem. He noticed that when the problem happened, a strange message appeared on the console. This was the company's secret debugging system! When he reported the problem to the vendor, he included a cut-and-paste of the message he was receiving on the serial port. The company responded, "Hey! You aren't supposed to connect to that port!" Later, the company admitted that the message had indeed helped them to debug the problem.

When purchasing server hardware, one of your major considerations should be what kind of remote access to the console is available and determining which tasks require such access. In an emergency, it isn't reasonable or timely to expect SAs to travel to the physical device to perform their work. In nonemergency situations, an SA should be able to fix at least minor problems from home or on the road and, optimally, be fully productive remotely when telecommuting.

Remote access has obvious limits, however, because certain tasks, such as toggling a power switch, inserting media, or replacing faulty hardware, require a person at the machine. An on-site operator or friendly volunteer can be the eyes and hands for the remote engineer. Some systems permit one to remotely switch on/off individual power ports so that hard reboots can be done remotely. However, replacing hardware should be left to trained professionals.

Remote access to consoles provides cost savings and improves safety factors for SAs. Machine rooms are optimized for machines, not humans. These rooms are cold, cramped, and more expensive per square foot than office space. It is wasteful to fill expensive rack space with monitors and keyboards rather than additional hosts. It can be inconvenient, if not dangerous, to have a machine room full of chairs.

SAs should never be expected to spend their typical day working inside the machine room. Filling a machine room with SAs is bad for both. Rarely does working directly in the machine room meet ergonomic requirements for keyboard and mouse positioning or environmental requirements, such as noise level. Working in a cold machine room is not healthy for people. SAs need to work in an environment that maximizes their productivity, which can best be achieved in their offices. Unlike a machine room, an office can be easily stocked with important SA tools, such as reference materials, ergonomic keyboards, telephones, refrigerators, and stereo equipment.

Having a lot of people in the machine room is not healthy for equipment, either. Having people in a machine room increases the load put on the heating, ventilation, and air conditioning (HVAC) systems. Each person generates about 600 BTU of heat. The additional power required to cool 600 BTU can be expensive.

Security implications must be considered when you have a remote console. Often, host security strategies depend on the consoles being behind a locked door. Remote access breaks this strategy. Therefore, console systems should have properly considered authentication and privacy systems. For example, you might permit access to the console system only via an encrypted channel, such as SSH, and insist on authentication by a one-time password system, such as a handheld authenticator.

When purchasing a server, you should expect remote console access. If the vendor is not responsive to this need, you should look elsewhere for equipment. Remote console access is discussed further in Section 6.1.10.

4.1.9 Mirror Boot Disks

The **boot disk,** or disk with the operating system, is often the most difficult one to replace if it gets damaged, so we need special precautions to make recovery faster. The boot disk of any server should be mirrored. That is, two disks are installed, and any update to one is also done to the other. If one disk fails, the system automatically switches to the working disk. Most operating systems can do this for you in software, and many hard disk controllers do this for you in hardware. This technique, called RAID 1, is discussed further in Chapter 25.

The cost of disks has dropped considerably over the years, making this once luxurious option more commonplace. Optimally, all disks should be mirrored or protected by a RAID scheme. However, if you can't afford that, at least mirror the boot disk.

Mirroring has performance trade-offs. Read operations become faster because half can be performed on each disk. Two independent spindles are working for you, gaining considerable throughput on a busy server. Writes are somewhat slower because twice as many disk writes are required, though they are usually done in parallel. This is less of a concern on systems, such as UNIX, that have write-behind caches. Since an operating system disk is usually mostly read, not written to, there is usually a net gain.

Without mirroring, a failed disk equals an outage. With mirroring, a failed disk is a survivable event that you control. If a failed disk can be replaced while the system is running, the failure of one component does not result in an outage. If the system requires that failed disks be replaced when the system is powered off, the outage can be scheduled based on business needs. That makes outages something we control instead of something that controls us.

Always remember that a RAID mirror protects against hardware failure. It does not protect against software or human errors. Erroneous changes made on the primary disk are immediately duplicated onto the second one, making it impossible to recover from the mistake by simply using the second disk.

More disaster recovery topics are discussed in Chapter 10.

Even Mirrored Disks Need Backups

A large e-commerce site used RAID 1 to duplicate the system disk in its primary database server. Database corruption problems started to appear during peak usage times. The database vendor and the OS vendor were pointing fingers at each other. The SAs ultimately needed to get a memory dump from the system as the corruption was happening, to track down who was truly to blame. Unknown to the SAs, the OS was using a signed integer rather than an unsigned one for a memory pointer. When the memory dump started, it reached the point at which the memory pointer became negative and started overwriting other partitions on the system disk. The RAID system faithfully copied the corruption onto the mirror, making it useless. This software error caused a very long, expensive, and well-publicized outage that cost the company millions in lost transactions and dramatically lowered the price of its stock. The lesson learned here is that mirroring is quite useful, but never underestimate the utility of a good backup for getting back to a known good state.

4.2 The Icing

With the basics in place, we now look at what can be done to go one step further in reliability and serviceability. We also summarize an opposing view.

4.2.1 Enhancing Reliability and Service Ability

4.2.1.1 Server Appliances

An **appliance** is a device designed specifically for a particular task. Toasters make toast. Blenders blend. One could do these things using general-purpose devices, but there are benefits to using a device designed to do one task very well.

The computer world also has appliances: file server appliances, web server appliances; email appliances; DNS appliances; and so on. The first appliance was the dedicated network router. Some scoffed, "Who would spend all that money on a device that just sits there and pushes packets when we can easily add extra interfaces to our VAX and do the same thing?" It turned out that quite a lot of people would. It became obvious that a box dedicated to a single task, and doing it well, was in many cases more valuable than a general-purpose computer that could do many tasks. And, heck, it also meant that you could reboot the VAX without taking down the network.

A server appliance brings years of experience together in one box. Architecting a server is difficult. The physical hardware for a server has all the requirements listed earlier in this chapter, as well as the system engineering and performance tuning that only a highly experienced expert can do. The software required to provide a service often involves assembling various packages, gluing them together, and providing a single, unified administration system for it all. It's a lot of work! Appliances do all this for you right out of the box.

Although a senior SA can engineer a system dedicated to file service or email out of a general-purpose server, purchasing an appliance can free the SA to focus on other tasks. Every appliance purchased results in one less system to engineer from scratch, plus access to vendor support in the unit of an outage. Appliances also let organizations without that particular expertise gain access to well-designed systems.

The other benefit of appliances is that they often have features that can't be found elsewhere. Competition drives the vendors to add new features, increase performance, and improve reliability. For example, NetApp Filers have tunable file system snapshots, thus eliminating many requests for file restores.

4.2.1.2 Redundant Power Supplies

After hard drives, the next most failure-prone component of a system is the power supply. So, ideally, servers should have redundant power supplies.

Having a redundant power supply does not simply mean that two such devices are in the chassis. It means that the system can be operational if one power supply is not functioning: $n + 1$ redundancy. Sometimes, a fully loaded system requires two power supplies to receive enough power. In this case, *redundant* means having three power supplies. This is an important question to ask vendors when purchasing servers and network equipment. Network equipment is particularly prone to this problem. Sometimes, when a large network device is fully loaded with power-hungry fiber interfaces, dual power supplies are a minimum, not a redundancy. Vendors often do not admit this up front.

Each power supply should have a separate power cord. Operationally speaking, the most common power problem is a power cord being accidentally pulled out of its socket. Formal studies of power reliability often overlook such problems because they are studying utility power. A single power cord for everything won't help you in this situation! Any vendor that provides a single power cord for multiple power supplies is demonstrating ignorance of this basic operational issue.

Another reason for separate power cords is that they permit the following trick: Sometimes a device must be moved to a different power strip, UPS, or circuit. In this situation, separate power cords allow the device to move to the new power source one cord at a time, eliminating downtime.

For very-high-availability systems, each power supply should draw power from a different source, such as separate UPSs. If one UPS fails, the system keeps going. Some data centers lay out their power with this in mind. More commonly, each power supply is plugged into a different power distribution unit (PDU). If someone mistakenly overloads a PDU with two many devices, the system will stay up.

Benefit of Separate Power Cords

Tom once had a scheduled power outage for a UPS that powered an entire machine room. However, one router absolutely could not lose power; it was critical for projects that would otherwise be unaffected by the outage. That router had redundant power supplies with separate power cords. Either power supply could power the entire system. Tom moved one power cord to a non-UPS outlet that had been installed for lights and other devices that did not require UPS support. During the outage, the router lost only UPS power but continued running on normal power. The router was able to function during the entire outage without downtime.

4.2.1.3 Full versus $n + 1$ Redundancy

As mentioned earlier, $n + 1$ **redundancy** refers to systems that are engineered such that one of any particular component can fail, yet the system is still functional. Some examples are RAID configurations, which can provide full service even when a single disk has failed, or an Ethernet switch with additional switch fabric components so that traffic can still be routed if one portion of the switch fabric fails.

By contrast, in **full redundancy**, two complete sets of hardware are linked by a fail-over configuration. The first system is performing a service and the second system sits idle, waiting to take over in case the first one fails. This *failover* might happen manually—someone notices that the first system failed and activates the second system—or automatically—the second system monitors the first system and activates itself (if it has determined that the first one is unavailable).

Other fully redundant systems are **load sharing**. Both systems are fully operational and both share in the service workload. Each server has enough capacity to handle the entire service workload of the other. When one system fails, the other system takes on its failed counterpart's workload. The systems may be configured to monitor each other's reliability, or some external resource may control the flow and allocation of service requests.

When n is 2 or more, $n + 1$ is cheaper than full redundancy. Customers often prefer it for the economical advantage.

Usually, only server-specific subsystems are $n + 1$ redundant, rather than the entire set of components. Always pay particular attention when a vendor tries to sell you on $n + 1$ redundancy but only parts of the system are redundant: A car with extra tires isn't useful if its engine is dead.

4.2.1.4 Hot-Swap Components

Redundant components should be hot-swappable. **Hot-swap** refers to the ability to remove and replace a component while the system is running. Normally, parts should be removed and replaced only when the system is powered off. Being able to hot-swap components is like being able to change a tire while the car is driving down a highway. It's great not to have to stop to fix common problems.

The first benefit of hot-swap components is that new components can be installed while the system is running. You don't have to schedule a downtime to install the part. However, installing a new part is a planned event and can usually be scheduled for the next maintenance period. The real benefit of hot-swap parts comes during a failure.

In $n + 1$ redundancy, the system can tolerate a single component failure, at which time it becomes critical to replace that part as soon as possible or risk a *double component failure*. The longer you wait, the larger the risk. Without hot-swap parts, an SA will have to wait until a reboot can be scheduled to get back into the safety of $n + 1$ computing. With hot-swap parts, an SA can replace the part without scheduling downtime. RAID systems have the concept of a *hot spare* disk that sits in the system, unused, ready to replace a failed disk. Assuming that the system can isolate the failed disk so that it doesn't prevent the entire system from working, the system can automatically activate the hot spare disk, making it part of whichever RAID set needs it. This makes the system $n + 2$.

The more quickly the system is brought back into the fully redundant state, the better. RAID systems often run slower until a failed component has been replaced and the RAID set has been rebuilt. More important, while the system is not fully redundant, you are at risk of a second disk failing; at that point, you lose all your data. Some RAID systems can be configured to shut themselves down if they run for more than a certain number of hours in nonredundant mode.

Hot-swappable components increase the cost of a system. When is this additional cost justified? When eliminated downtimes are worth the extra expense. If a system has scheduled downtime once a week and letting the system run at the risk of a double failure is acceptable for a week, hot-swap components may not be worth the extra expense. If the system has a maintenance period scheduled once a year, the expense is more likely to be justified.

When a vendor makes a claim of hot-swappability, always ask two questions: Which parts aren't hot-swappable? How and for how long is service interrupted when the parts are being hot-swapped? Some network devices have hot-swappable interface cards, but the CPU is not hot-swappable. Some network devices claim hot-swap capability but do a full system reset after any device is added. This reset can take seconds or minutes. Some disk subsystems must pause the I/O system for as much as 20 seconds when a drive is replaced. Others run with seriously degraded performance for many hours while the data is rebuilt onto the replacement disk. Be sure that you understand the ramifications of component failure. Don't assume that hot-swap parts make outages disappear. They simply reduce the outage.

Vendors should, but often don't, label components as to whether they are hot-swappable. If the vendor doesn't provide labels, you should.

Hot-Plug versus Hot-Swap

Be mindful of components that are labeled **hot-plug**. This means that it is electrically safe for the part to be replaced while the system is running, but the part may not be recognized until the next reboot. Or worse, the part can be plugged in while the system is running, but the system will immediately reboot to recognize the part. This is very different from hot-swappable.

Tom once created a major, but short-lived, outage when he plugged a new 24-port FastEthernet card into a network chassis. He had been told that the cards were hot-pluggable and had assumed that the vendor meant the same thing as hot-swap. Once the board was plugged in, the entire system reset. This was the core switch for his server room and most of the networks in his division. Ouch!

> You can imagine the heated exchange when Tom called the vendor to complain. The vendor countered that if the installer had to power off the unit, plug the card in, and then turn power back on, the outage would be significantly longer. Hot-plug was an improvement.
>
> From then on until the device was decommissioned, there was a big sign above it saying, "Warning: Plugging in new cards reboots system. Vendor thinks this is a good thing."

4.2.1.5 Separate Networks for Administrative Functions

Additional network interfaces in servers permit you to build separate administrative networks. For example, it is common to have a separate network for backups and monitoring. Backups use significant amounts of bandwidth when they run, and separating that traffic from the main network means that backups won't adversely affect customers' use of the network. This separate network can be engineered using simpler equipment and thus be more reliable or, more important, be unaffected by outages in the main network. It also provides a way for SAs to get to the machine during such an outage. This form of redundancy solves a very specific problem.

4.2.2 An Alternative: Many Inexpensive Servers

Although this chapter recommends paying more for server-grade hardware because the extra performance and reliability are worthwhile, a growing counterargument says that it is better to use many replicated cheap servers that will fail more often. If you are doing a good job of managing failures, this strategy is more cost-effective.

Running large web farms will entail many redundant servers, all built to be exactly the same, the automated install. If each web server can handle 500 queries per second (QPS), you might need ten servers to handle the 5,000 QPS that you expect to receive from users all over the Internet. A load-balancing mechanism can distribute the load among the servers. Best of all, load balancers have ways to automatically detect machines that are down. If one server goes down, the load balancer divides the queries between the remaining good servers, and users still receive service. The servers are all one-tenth more loaded, but that's better than an outage.

What if you used lower-quality parts that would result in ten failures? If that saved 10 percent on the purchase price, you could buy an eleventh machine to make up for the increased failures and lower performance of the slower machines. However, you spent the same amount of money, got the same number of QPS, and had the same uptime. No difference, right?

In the early 1990s, servers often cost $50,000. Desktop PCs cost around $2,000 because they were made from commodity parts that were being mass-produced at orders of magnitude larger than server parts. If you built a server based on those commodity parts, it would not be able to provide the required QPS, and the failure rate would be much higher.

By the late 1990s, however, the economics had changed. Thanks to the continued mass-production of PC-grade parts, both prices and performance had improved dramatically. Companies such as Yahoo! and Google figured out how to manage large numbers of machines effectively, streamlining hardware installation, software updates, hardware repair management, and so on. It turns out that if you do these things on a large scale, the cost goes down significantly.

Traditional thinking says that you should never try to run a commercial service on a commodity-based server that can process only 20 QPS. However, when you can manage many of them, things start to change. Continuing the example, you would have to purchase 250 such servers to equal the performance of the 10 traditional servers mentioned previously. You would pay the same amount of money for the hardware.

As the QPS improved, this kind of solution became less expensive than buying large servers. If they provided 100 QPS of performance, you could buy the same capacity, 50 servers, at one-fifth the price or spend the same money and get five times the processing capacity.

By eliminating the components that were unused in such an arrangement, such as video cards, USB connectors, and so on, the cost could be further contained. Soon, one could purchase five to ten commodity-based servers for every large server traditionally purchased and have more processing capability. Streamlining the physical hardware requirements resulted in more efficient packaging, with powerful servers slimmed down to a mere rack-unit in height.[8]

This kind of massive-scale cluster computing is what makes huge web services possible. Eventually, one can imagine more and more services turning to this kind of architecture.

---

8. The distance between the predrilled holes in a standard rack frame is referred to as a rack-unit, abbreviated as U. This, a system that occupies the space above or below the bolts that hold it in would be a 2U system.

Case Study: Disposable Servers

Many e-commerce sites build mammoth clusters of low-cost 1U PC servers. Racks are packed with as many servers as possible, with dozens or hundreds configured to provide each service required. One site found that when a unit died, it was more economical to power it off and leave it in the rack rather than repair the unit. Removing dead units might accidentally cause an outage if other cables were loosened in the process. The site would not need to reap the dead machines for quite a while. We presume that when it starts to run out of space, the site will adopt a monthly day of reaping, with certain people carefully watching the service-monitoring systems while others reap the dead machines.

Another way to pack a large number of machines into a small space is to use **blade server** technology. A single chassis contains many slots, each of which can hold a card, or blade, that contains a CPU and memory. The chassis supplies power and network and management access. Sometimes, each blade has a hard disk; others require each blade to access a centralized storage-area network. Because all the devices are similar, it is possible to create an automated system such that if one dies, a spare is configured as its replacement.

An increasingly important new technology is the use of virtual servers. Server hardware is now so powerful that justifying the cost of single-purpose machines is more difficult. The concept of a server as a set of components (hardware and software) provide security and simplicity. By running many virtual servers on a large, powerful server, the best of both worlds is achieved. Virtual servers are discussed further in Section 21.1.2.

Blade Server Management

A division of a large multinational company was planning on replacing its aging multi-CPU server with a farm of blade servers. The application would be recoded so that instead of using multiple processes on a single machine, it would use processes spread over the blade farm. Each blade would be one node of a vast compute farm that jobs could be submitted to and results consolidated on a controlling server. This had wonderful scalability, since a new blade could be added to the farm within minutes via automated build processes, if the application required it, or could be repurposed to other uses just as quickly. No direct user logins were needed, and no SA work would be needed beyond replacing faulty hardware and managing what blades were assigned to what applications. To this end, the SAs engineered a tightly locked-down minimal-access solution that could be deployed in minutes. Hundreds of blades were purchased and installed, ready to be purposed as the customer required.

The problem came when application developers found themselves unable to manage their application. They couldn't debug issues without direct access. They demanded shell access. They required additional packages. They stored unique state on each machine, so automated builds were no longer viable. All of a sudden, the SAs found themselves managing 500 individual servers rather than a blade farm. Other divisions had also signed up for the service and made the same demands.

Two things could have prevented this problem. First, more attention to detail at the requirements-gathering stage might have foreseen the need for developer access, which could then have been included in the design. Second, management should have been more disciplined. Once the developers started requesting access, management should have set down limits that would have prevented the system from devolving into hundreds of custom machines. The original goal of a utility providing access to many similar CPUs should have been applied to the entire life cycle of the system, not just used to design it.

4.3 Conclusion

We make different decisions when purchasing servers because multiple customers depend on them, whereas a workstation client is dedicated to a single customer. Different economics drive the server hardware market versus the desktop market, and understanding those economics helps one make better purchasing decisions. Servers, like all hardware, sometimes fail, and one must therefore have some kind of maintenance contract or repair plan, as well as data backup/restore capability. Servers should be in proper machine rooms to provide a reliable environment for operation (we discuss data center requirements in Chapter 5, Services). Space in the machine room should be allocated at purchase time, not when a server arrives. Allocate power, bandwidth, and cooling at purchase time as well.

Server appliances are hardware/software systems that contain all the software that is required for a particular task preconfigured on hardware that is tuned to the particular application. Server appliances provide high-quality solutions engineered with years of experience in a canned package and are likely to be much more reliable and easier to maintain than homegrown solutions. However, they are not easily customized to unusual site requirements.

Servers need the ability to be remotely administered. Hardware/software systems allow one to simulate console access remotely. This frees up machine room space and enables SAs to work from their offices and homes. SAs can respond to maintenance needs without the overhead of traveling to the server location.

To increase reliability, servers often have redundant systems, preferably in $n + 1$ configurations. Having a mirrored system disk, redundant power supplies, and other redundant features enhances uptime. Being able to swap dead components while the system is running provides better MTTR and less service interruption. Although this redundancy may have been a luxury in the past, it is often a requirement in today's environment.

This chapter illustrates our theme of completing the basics first so that later, everything else falls into place. Proper handling of the issues discussed in this chapter goes a long way toward making the system reliable, maintainable, and repairable. These issues must be considered at the beginning, not as an afterthought.

Exercises

1. What servers are used in your environment? How many different vendors are used? Do you consider this to be a lot of vendors? What would be the benefits and problems with increasing the number of vendors? Decreasing?

2. Describe your site's strategy in purchasing maintenance and repair contracts. How could it be improved to be cheaper? How could it be improved to provide better service?

3. What are the major and minor differences between the hosts you install for servers versus clients' workstations?

4. Why would one want hot-swap parts on a system without $n + 1$ redundancy?

5. Why would one want $n + 1$ redundancy if the system does not have hot-swap parts?

6. Which critical hosts in your environment do not have $n + 1$ redundancy or cannot hot-swap parts? Estimate the cost to upgrade the most critical hosts to $n + 1$.

7. An SA who needed to add a disk to a server that was low on disk space chose to wait until the next maintenance period to install the disk rather than do it while the system was running. Why might this be?

8. What services in your environment would be good candidates for replacing with an appliance (whether or not such an appliance is available)? Why are they good candidates?

9. What server appliances are in your environment? What engineering would you have to do if you had instead purchased a general-purpose machine to do the same function?

Chapter 5

Services

A **server** is hardware. A **service** is the function that the server provides. A service may be built on several servers that work in conjunction with one another. This chapter explains how to build a service that meets customer requirements, is reliable, and is maintainable.

Providing a service involves not only putting together the hardware and software but also making the service reliable, scaling the service's growth, and monitoring, maintaining, and supporting it. A service is not truly a service until it meets these basic requirements.

One of the fundamental duties of an SA is to provide customers with the services they need. This work is ongoing. Customers' needs will evolve as their jobs and technologies evolve. As a result, an SA spends a considerable amount of time designing and building new services. How well the SA builds those services determines how much time and effort will have to be spent supporting them in the future and how happy the customers will be.

A typical environment has many services. Fundamental services include DNS, email, authentication services, network connectivity, and printing.[1] These services are the most critical, and they are the most visible if they fail. Other typical services are the various remote access methods, network license service, software depots, backup services, Internet access, DHCP, and file service. Those are just some of the generic services that system administration teams usually provide. On top of those are the business-specific services that serve the company or organization: accounting, manufacturing, and other business processes.

---

1. DNS, networking, and authentication are services on which many other services rely. Email and printing may seem less obviously critical, but if you ever do have a failure of either, you will discover that they are the lifeblood of everyone's workflow. Communications and hardcopy are at the core of every company.

Services are what distinguish a structured computing environment that is managed by SAs from an environment in which there are one or more stand-alone computers. Homes and very small offices typically have a few stand-alone machines providing services. Larger installations are typically linked through shared services that ease communication and optimize resources. When it connects to the Internet through an Internet service provider, a home computer uses services provided by the ISP and the other people that the person connects to across the Internet. An office environment provides those same services and more.

5.1 The Basics

Building a solid, reliable service is a key role of an SA, who needs to consider many basics when performing that task. The most important thing to consider at all stages of design and deployment is the customers' requirements. Talk to the customers and find out what their needs and expectations are for the service.[2] Then build a list of other requirements, such as administrative requirements, that are visible only to the SA team. Focus on the *what* rather than the *how*. It's easy to get bogged down in implementation details and lose sight of the purpose and goals.

We have found great success through the use of open protocols and open architectures. You may not always be able to achieve this, but it should be considered in the design.

Services should be built on server-class machines that are kept in a suitable environment and should reach reasonable levels of reliability and performance. The service and the machines that it relies on should be monitored, and failures should generate alarms or trouble tickets, as appropriate.

Most services rely on other services. Understanding in detail how a service works will give you insight into the services on which it relies. For example, almost every service relies on DNS. If machine names or domain names are configured into the service, it relies on DNS; if its log files contain the names of hosts that used the service or were accessed by the service, it uses DNS; if the people accessing it are trying to contact other machines through the service, it uses DNS. Likewise, almost every service relies on the network, which is also a service. DNS relies on the network; therefore, anything that relies on DNS also relies on the network. Some services rely on email, which relies on DNS and the network; others rely on being able to access shared files on other

---

2. Some services, such as name service and authentication service, do not have customer requirements other than that they should always work and they should be fast and unintrusive.

computers. Many services also rely on the authentication and authorization service to be able to distinguish one person from another, particularly where different levels of access are given based on identity. The failure of some services, such as DNS, causes cascading failures of all the other services that rely on them. When building a service, it is important to know the other services on which it relies.

Machines and software that are part of a service should rely only on hosts and software that are built to the same standards or higher. A service can be only as reliable as the weakest link in the chain of services on which it relies. A service should not gratuitously rely on hosts that are not part of the service.

Access to server machines should be restricted to SAs for reasons of reliability and security. The more people who are using a machine and the more things that are running on it, the greater the chance that bad interactions will happen. Machines that customers use also need to have more things installed on them so that the customers can access the data they need and use other network services.

Similarly, a system is only as secure as its weakest link. The security of client systems is no stronger than the weakest link in the security of the infrastructure. Someone who can subvert the authentication server can gain access to clients that rely on it; someone who can subvert the DNS servers could redirect traffic from the client and potentially gain passwords. If the security system relies on that subverted DNS, the security system is vulnerable. Restricting login and other kinds of access to machines in the security infrastructure reduces these kinds of risk.

A server should be as simple as possible. Simplicity makes machines more reliable and easier to debug when they do have problems. Servers should have the minimum that is required for the service they run, only SAs should have access to them; and the SAs should log in to them only to do maintenance. Servers are also more sensitive from a security point of view than desktops are. An intruder who can gain administrative access to a server can typically do more damage than with administrative access to a desktop machine. The fewer people who have access and the less that runs on the machine, the lower the chance that an intruder can gain access, and the greater the chance that an intruder will be spotted.

An SA has several decisions to make when building a service: from what vendor to buy the equipment, whether to use one or many servers for a complex service, and what level of redundancy to build into the service. A service should be as simple as possible, with as few dependencies as possible, to increase reliability and make it easier to support and maintain. Another method of easing support and maintenance for a service is to use standard hardware, standard software, and standard configurations and to have documentation in a standard location. Centralizing services so that there are one or two large primary print servers, for example, rather than hundreds of small ones scattered throughout the company, also makes the service more supportable. Finally, a key part of implementing any new service is to make it independent of the particular machine that it is on, by using service-oriented names in client configurations, rather than, for example, the actual hostname. If your OS does not support this feature, tell your OS vendor that it is important to you, and consider using another OS in the meantime. (Further discussion is in Chapter 8.) Once the service has been built and tested, it needs to be rolled out slowly to the customer base, with further testing and debugging along the way.

Case Study: Tying Services to a Machine

In a small company, all services run on one or two central machines. As the company grows, those machines will become overloaded, and some services will need to be moved to other machines, so that there are more servers, each of which runs fewer services. For example, assume that a central machine is the mail delivery server, the mail relay, the print server, and the calendar server. If all these services are tied to the machine's real name, every client machine in the company will have that name configured into the email client, the printer configuration, and the calendar client. When that server gets overloaded, and both email functions are moved to another machine with a different name, every other machine in the company will need to have its email configuration changed, which requires a lot of work and causes disruption. If the server gets overloaded again and printing is moved to another machine, all the other machines in the company will have to be changed again. On the other hand, if each service were tied to an appropriate global alias, such as `smtp` for the mail relay, `mail` for the mail delivery host, `calendar` for the calendar server, and `print` for the print server, only the global alias would have to be changed, with no disruption to the customers and little time and effort beyond building the service.

5.1.1 Customer Requirements

When building a new service, you should always start with the customer requirements. The service is being built for the customers. If the service does not meet their needs, building the service was a wasted effort.

A few services do not have customer requirements. DNS is one of those. Others, such as email and the network, are more visible to customers. Customers may want certain features from their email clients, and different customers put different loads on the network, depending on the work they do and how the systems they use are set up. Other services are very customer oriented, such as an electronic purchase order system. SAs need to understand how the service affects customers and how customer requirements affect the service design.

Gathering customer requirements should include finding out how customers intend to use the new service, the features they need and would like, how critical the service will be to them, and what levels of availability and support they will need for the service. Involve the customers in usability trials on demo versions of the service, if possible. If you choose a system that they will find cumbersome to use, the project will fail. Try to gauge how large the customer base for this service will be and what sort of performance they will need and expect from it, so that you can create it at the correct size. For example, when building an email system, try to estimate how many emails, both inbound and outbound, will be flowing through the system on peak days, how much disk space each user would be permitted to store, and so on.

This is a good time to define a service-level agreement for the new service. An SLA enumerates the services that will be provided and the level of support they receive. It typically categorizes problems by severity and commits to response times for each category, perhaps based on the time of day and day of week if the site does not provide 24/7 support. The SLA usually defines an escalation process that increases the severity of a problem if it has not been resolved after a specified time and calls for managers to get involved if problems are getting out of hand. In a relationship in which the customer is paying for a certain service, the SLA usually specifies penalties if the service provider fails to meet a given standard of service. The SLA is always discussed in detail and agreed on by both parties to the agreement.

The SLA process is a forum for the SAs to understand the customers' expectations and to set them appropriately, so that the customers understand what is and isn't possible and why. It is also a tool to plan what resources will be required for the project. The SLA should document the customers' needs and set realistic goals for the SA team in terms of features, availability, performance, and support. The SLA should document future needs and capacity so that all parties will understand the growth plans. The SLA is a document that the SA team can refer to during the design process to make sure that they meet team customers' and their own expectations and to help keep them on track.

SLA discussions are a consultative process. The ultimate goal is to find the middle ground between what the customer ideally wants, what is technically possible, what is financially affordable, and what the SA team can provide.

A feature that will take years to develop is not reasonable for a system that must be deployed in 6 months. A feature that will cost a million dollars is not reasonable for a project with a multi-thousand-dollar budget. A small company with only one or two SAs will not get 24/7 support, no matter how much the company wants. Never be upset when a customer asks for something technically unreasonable; if the customer knew the technology as well as you do, the customer would be an SA. Instead, remember that it is a consultative process, and your role is to educate the customer and work together to find a middle ground.

Kick-off Meetings

Although it is tempting to do everything by email, we find that having at least one in-person meeting at the beginning makes things run a lot better. We call this the kick-off meeting. Having such a meeting early in the process sets the groundwork for a successful project.

Although painfully low-tech, in-person meetings work better. People skim email or ignore it completely. Phone calls don't convey people's visual cues. A lot of people on a conference call press Mute and don't participate.

A kick-off meeting should have all the key people affected or involved—the **stakeholders**—present. Get agreement on the goal of the new service, a time line for completion, and budget, and introduce similar big-picture issues. You won't be able to resolve all these issues, but you can get them into the open. Assign unresolved issues to participants.

Once everyone is on the same page, remaining communication status meetings can be by phone and updates via email.

5.1.2 Operational Requirements

The SA team may have other new-service requirements that are not immediately visible to the customers. SAs need to consider the administrative interface of the new service: whether it interoperates with existing services and can be integrated with central services, such as authentication or directory services.

SAs also need to consider how the service scales. Demand for the service may grow beyond what was initially anticipated and will almost certainly grow along with the company. SAs need to think of ways that the service can be scaled up without interrupting the existing service.

A related consideration is the upgrade path for this service. As new versions become available, what is the upgrade process? Does it involve an interruption of service? Does it involve touching every desktop? Is it possible to roll out the upgrade slowly, to test it on a few willing people before inflicting it on the whole company? Try to design the service so that upgrades are easy, can be performed without service interruption, don't involve touching the desktops, and can be rolled out slowly.

From the level of reliability that the customers expect and what the SAs predict as future reliability requirements for the system, the SAs should be able to build a list of desired features, such as clustering, slave or redundant servers, or running on high-availability hardware and OSs. SAs also need to consider network performance issues related to the network between where the service is hosted and where the users are located. If some customers will be in remote locations across low-bandwidth, high-latency links, how will this service perform? Are there ways to make it perform equally well, or close to that, in all locations, or does the SLA need to set different expectations for remote customers? Vendors rarely test their products over high-latency links—links with a large round-trip time (RTT)—and typically everyone from the programmers to the salespeople are equally ignorant about the issues involved. In-house testing is often the only way to be sure.

❖ **Bandwidth versus Latency**   The term **bandwidth** refers to how much data can be transmitted in a second; **latency** is the delay before the data is received by the other end. A high-latency link, no matter what the bandwidth, will have a long round-trip time: the time for a packet to go and the reply to return. Some applications, such as noninteractive (streaming) video, are unaffected by high latency. Others are affected greatly.

Suppose that a particular task requires five database queries. The client sends a request and waits for the reply. This is done four more times. On an Ethernet, where latency is low, these five queries will happen about as quickly as the database server can process them and return the result. The complete task might take a second. However, what if the same server is in India and the client is running on a machine in New York? Suppose that it takes half a second between for the last bit of the request to reach India. Light can travel only so fast, and routers and other devices add delays. Now the task is going to take 5 seconds (one-half second for each request and each reply) plus the amount of time the server takes to process the queries. Let's suppose that this is now 6 seconds. That's a lot slower than the original Ethernet time. This kind of task done thousands or millions of times each day takes a significant amount of time.

Suppose that the link to India is a T1 (1.5Mbps). Would upgrading the link to a T3 (45Mbps) solve the problem? If the latency of the T3 is the same as the T1, the upgrade will not improve the situation.

Instead, the solution is to launch all five queries at the same time and wait for the replies to come back as each of them completes. Better yet is when five queries can be replaced by a single high-level operation that the server can perform locally. For example, often SQL developers use a series of queries to gather data and sum them. Instead, send a longer SQL query to the server that gathers the data, sums them, and returns just the result.

Mathematically speaking, the problem is as follows. The total time to completion (T) is the sum of the time each request takes to complete. The time it takes to complete each request is made up of three components: sending the request (S), computing the result (C), and receiving the reply (R). This is depicted mathematically as

$$T = (S_1 + C_1 + R_1) + (S_2 + C_2 + R_2) + (S_3 + C_3 + R_3)$$
$$+ \cdots + (S_n + C_n + R_n)$$

In a low-latency environment, $S_n + R_n$ is nearly zero, thus leading programmers to forget it exists, or worse, thinking that the formula is

$$T = C_1 + C_2 + C_3 + C_n$$

when it most certainly is not.

Programs written under the assumption that latency is zero or near-zero will benchmark very well on a local Ethernet, but terribly once put into production on a global high-latency wide area network (WAN). This can make the product too slow to be usable. Most network providers do not sell latency, just bandwidth. Therefore their salesperson's only solution is to sell the customer more bandwidth, and as we have just shown, more bandwidth won't fix a latency problem. We have seen many sites unsuccessfully try to fix this kind of problem by purchasing more bandwidth.

The real solution is to improve the software. Improving the software usually is a matter of rethinking algorithms. In high-latency networks, one must change the algorithms so that requests and replies do not need to be in lock-step. One solution (batched requests) sends all requests at once, preferably combined into a small number of packets, and waits for the replies to arrive. Another solution (windowed replies) involves sending many requests in a way that is disconnected from waiting for replies. A program may be able to track a "window" of n outstanding replies at any given moment.

Applications like streaming video and audio are not as concerned with latency because the video or audio packets are only being sent in one direction. The delay is unnoticed once the broadcast begins. However, for interactive media, such as voice communication between two people, the latency is noticed as a pause between when one person stops speaking and the other person starts.

Even if an algorithm sends only one request and waits for one reply, how they are sent can make all the difference.

Case Study: Minimizing the Number of Packets in High-Latency Networks

A global pharmaceutical company based in New Jersey had a terrible performance problem with a database application. Analysis found that a single 4,000-byte Structured Query Language (SQL) request sent over a transatlantic link was being sent in fifty 80-byte packets. Each packet was sent only when the previous one was acknowledged. It took 5 minutes just to log in. When the system administrators reconfigured the database connector to send fewer larger packets, the performance problem went away. The developers had been demanding additional transatlantic bandwidth, which would have taken months to order, been very expensive, and disappointing when it didn't solve the problem.

Every SA and developer should be aware of how latency affects the services being created. SAs should also look at how they can monitor the service in terms of availability and performance. Being able to integrate a new service into existing monitoring systems is a key requirement for meeting the SLA. SAs and developers should also look at whether the system can generate trouble tickets in the existing trouble-ticket system for problems that it detects, if that is appropriate.

The SA team also needs to consider the budget that has been allocated to this project. If the SAs do not believe that they can meet the service levels that the customers want on the current budget, that constraint should be presented as part of the SLA discussions. Once the SLA has been ratified by both groups, the SAs should take care to work within the budget allocation constraints.

5.1.3 Open Architecture

Wherever possible, a new service should be built around an architecture that uses **open** protocols and file formats. In particular, we're referring to protocols and file formats that are documented in a public forum so that many vendors can write to those standards and make interoperable products. Any service with an open architecture can be more easily integrated with other services that follow the same standards.

By contrast a **closed** service uses proprietary protocols and file formats that will interoperate with fewer products because the protocols and file formats are subject to change without notice and may require licensing from the creator of the protocol. Vendors use proprietary protocols when they are covering new territory or are attempting to maintain market share by preventing the creation of a level playing field.

Sometimes, vendors that use proprietary protocols do make explicit licensing agreements with other vendors; typically, however, a lag exists between the release of a new version from one vendor and the release of the compatible new version from the second vendor. Also, relations between the two vendors may break down, and they may stop providing the interface between the two products. That situation is a nightmare for people who are using both products and rely on the interface between them.

❖ **The Protocol versus the Product**   SAs need to understand the difference between the protocol and the product. One might standardize on Simple Mail Transfer Protocol (SMTP) (Crocker 1982) for email transmission, for example. SMTP is not a product but rather a document, written in English, that explains how bits are to be transmitted over the wire. This is different from a product that uses SMTP to transmit email from one server to another. Part of the confusion comes from the fact that companies often have internal standards that list specific products that will be deployed and supported. That's a different use of the word *standard*.

The source of this confusion is understandable. Before the late 1990s, when the Internet became a household word, many people had experience only with protocols that were tied to a particular product and didn't need to communicate with other companies, because companies were not interconnected as freely as they are now. This situation gave rise to the notion that a protocol is something that a particular software package implements and does not stand on its own as an independent concept. Although the Internet has made more people aware of the difference between protocols and products, many vendors still take advantage of customers who lack awareness of open protocols. Such vendors fear the potential for competition and would rather eliminate competition by locking people in to systems that make migration to other vendors difficult. These vendors make a concerted effort to blur the difference between the protocol and the product.

Also, beware of vendors that *embrace and extend* a standard in an attempt to prevent interoperability with competitors. Such vendors do this so they can claim to support a standard without giving their customers the benefits of interoperability. That's not very *customer oriented*. A famous case of this occurred when Microsoft adopted the Kerberos authentication system, which was a very good decision, but extended it in a way that prevented it from interoperating with non-Microsoft Kerberos systems. All the servers had to be Microsoft based. The addition that Microsoft made was gratuitous, but it successfully forced sites to uproot their security infrastructures and replace them with Microsoft products if they were to use Kerberos clients of either flavor. Without this "enhancement," customers could choose their server vendor, and those vendors would be forced to compete for their business.

The business case for using open protocols is simple: It lets you build better services because you can select the best server and client, rather than being forced to pick, for example, the best client and then getting stuck with a less than optimal server. Customers want an application that has the features and ease of use that they need. SAs want an application whose server is easy to manage. These requirements are often conflicting. Traditionally, either the customers or the SAs have more power and make the decision in private, surprising the other with the decision. If the SAs make the decision, the customers consider them fascists. If the customers make the decision, it may well be a package that is difficult to administer, which will make it difficult to give excellent service to the customers.

A better way is to select protocols based on open standards, permitting each side to select its own software. This approach decouples the client-application-selection process from the server-platform selection process. Customers are free to choose the software that best fits their own needs, biases, and even platform. SAs can independently choose a server solution based on their needs for reliability, scalability, and manageability. The SAs can now choose between competing server products rather than being locked in to the potentially difficult-to-manage server software and platform required for a particular client application. In many cases, the SAs can even choose the server hardware and software independently, if the software vendor supports multiple hardware platforms.

We call this the ability to decouple the client and server selections. Open protocols provide a level playing field that inspires competition between vendors. The competition benefits you.

For comparison, the next anecdote illustrates what can happen when the customers select a proprietary email system that does not use open protocols but fits their client-side needs.

Hazards of Proprietary Email Software

A New Jersey pharmaceutical company selected a particular proprietary email package for its PC user base after a long evaluation. The selection was based on user interface and features, with no concern for ease of server management, reliability, or scalability. The system turned out to be very unreliable when scaled to a large user base. The system stored all messages from all users in a single large file that everyone had to have write access to, which was a security nightmare. Frequent data-corruption problems resulted in having to send the email database to the vendor across the Internet for demangling. This meant that potentially sensitive information was being exposed to people outside the company and that the people within the company could have no expectation of privacy for email. It also caused long outages of the email system, because it was unusable while the database was being repaired.

Because the package was not based on open protocols, the system support staff could not seek out a competing vendor that would offer a better, more secure, and more reliable server. Because of the lack of competition, the vendor considered server management low priority and ignored the requests for server-related fixes and improvements. If the company had selected an open protocol and then let customers and SAs independently select their solutions, it would have realized the best of both worlds.

Open protocols and file formats typically are either static or change only in upwardly compatible ways and are widely supported, giving you the maximum product choice and maximum chance of reliable, interoperable products. The other benefit to using open systems is that you won't require gateways to the rest of the world. Gateways are the "glue" that connects different systems. Although a gateway can save your day, systems based on a common, open protocol avoid gateways altogether. Gateways are additional services that require capacity planning, engineering, monitoring, and, well, everything else in this chapter. Reducing the number of services is a good thing.

Protocol Gateways and Reliability Reduction

In college, Tom's email system was a proprietary system that was not based around Internet standard protocols, such as SMTP. Instead, the system was sold with a software package to gateway email to and from the Internet. The gateway used its proprietary protocol to communicate with the mail server and SMTP to communicate with the rest of the world. This gateway was slow, unreliable, and expensive. It seemed that the vendor had engineered the gateway with the assumption that only a tiny fraction of the email traffic would go through the gateway. The gateway was yet another thing to manage, debug, do capacity planning for, and so on. The vendor had little incentive to improve the gateway, because it let customers communicate with systems that were considered to be the competition. The mail system had many outages, nearly all of which were gateway outages. None of these problems would have arisen if the system had used open protocols rather than requiring a gateway.

History repeated itself nearly a decade later when Microsoft's Exchange mail server was introduced. It used a nonstandard protocol and offered gateways for communicating with other sites on the Internet. These gateways added to the list of services that SAs needed to engineer, configure, plan capacity for, scale, and so on. Many of the highly publicized Exchange bugs were related to the gateway.

These examples may seem outdated, since nobody would now sell an email system that is ignorant of the Internet. However, it is important to remember these lessons the next time a salesperson tries to sell you a calendar management system, directory service, or other product that ignores Internet and other industry standards but promises excellent gateways at an extra (or even zero) cost. Using standard protocols means using open standards, such as Internet Engineering Task Force (IETF) and Institute of Electrical and Electronic Engineers (IEEE), not vendor-proprietary standards. Vendor-proprietary protocols lead to big future headaches. A vendor that offers gateways is probably not using open standards. If you are unsure, directly ask what open standards the gateways interoperate with.

5.1.4 Simplicity

When architecting a new service, your foremost consideration should be simplicity. The simplest solution that satisfies all the requirements will be the most reliable, easiest to maintain, easiest to expand, and easiest to integrate with other systems. Undue complexity leads to confusion, mistakes, and potential difficulty of use and may well make everything slower. It will be more expensive in set-up cost and maintenance costs.

As a system grows, it will become more complex. That is a fact of life. Therefore, starting out as simple as possible delays the day when a system becomes *too* complex. Consider two salespeople proposing to provide systems. One system has 20 basic features, and the other has an additional 200 features. One can expect that the more feature-rich software will have more bugs, and the vendor will have a more difficult time maintaining the code for the system.

Sometimes, one or two requirements from the customers or SAs may add considerably to the complexity of the system. During the architecture phase, if you come across such requirements, it is worth going back to the source and reevaluating the importance of the requirement. Explain to the customers or SAs that these requirements can be met but at a cost to reliability, support levels, and ongoing maintenance. Then ask them to reevaluate those requirements in that light and decide whether they should be met or dropped.

Let's return to our example of the proposals from two salespeople. Sometimes, the offer with the 20 basic features does not include certain required features, and you might be tempted to reject the bid. On the other hand, customers who understand the value of simplicity may be willing to forego those features and gain the higher reliability.

5.1.5 Vendor Relations

When choosing the hardware and software for a service, you should be able to talk to sales engineers from your vendors to get advice on the best configuration for your application. Hardware vendors sometimes have product configurations that are tuned for particular applications, such as databases or web servers. If the service you are building is a common one, your vendor may have a suitable canned configuration.

If more than one server vendor is in your environment and more than one of your server vendors has an appropriate product, you should use this situation to your advantage. You should be able to get those vendors bidding against each other for the business. Because you probably have a fixed budget, you may be able to get more for the same price, which you can use to improve performance, reliability, or scalability. Or, you may get a better price and be able to invest the surplus in improving the service in some other way. Even if you know which vendor you will choose, don't reveal your choice until you are convinced that you have the best deal possible.

When choosing a vendor, particularly for a software product, it is important to understand the direction in which the vendor is taking the product. If you have a large installation, it should be possible to get involved in beta trials and to influence the product direction by telling the product manager what features will be important to you in the future. For key, central services, such as authentication or directory services, it is essential to stay in touch with the product direction, or you may suddenly discover that the vendor no longer supports your platform. The impact of having to change a central piece of infrastructure can be huge. If possible, try to stick to vendors that develop the product primarily on the platform that you use, rather than port it to that platform. The product will typically have fewer bugs, receive new features first, and be better supported on its primary development platform. Vendors are much less likely to discontinue support for that platform.

5.1.6 Machine Independence

Clients should always access a service that uses a generic name based on the function of the service. For example, clients should point their shared calendar clients to the server called `calendar`, their email clients to a Post Office Protocol (POP) (Myers and Rose 1996) server called `pop`, an Internet Message Access Protocol (IMAP) (Crispin 1996) server named `imap`, and an SMTP server named `mail`. Even if some of these services initially reside on the same machine, they should be accessed through function-based names to enable you to scale by splitting the service across multiple machines without reconfiguring each client.

The machine should never have a function-based primary name. For example, the calendar server could have a primary name of `dopey`, and also be referred to as `calendar` but should never have a primary name of `calendar`, because ultimately, the function may need to move to another machine. Moving the name with the function is more difficult because other things that are tied to the primary name (`calendar`) on the original machine are not meant to move to the new machine. Naming and namespace management issues are discussed in more detail in Chapter 8.

For services that are tied to an IP address rather than to a name, it is also generally possible to give the machine that the service runs on multiple virtual IP addresses in addition to its primary real IP address and to use a virtual address for each service. Then the virtual address and the service can be moved to another machine relatively easily.

When building a service on a machine, think about how you will move it to another machine in the future. Someone will have to move it at some point. Make that person's life as simple as possible by designing it well from the beginning.

5.1.7 Environment

A reliable service needs a reliable environment. A service is something that your customers rely on, either directly or indirectly through other machines and services that rely on it. Customers have an expectation that the service will be available when they want to use it. A fundamental piece of building a service is providing a reasonably high level of availability, which means placing all the equipment associated with that service into a data center environment built for reliability.

A data center provides protected power, plenty of cooling, controlled humidity—vital in dry or damp climates—fire suppression, and a secure location where the machine should be free from accidental damage or disconnection. Data centers are described in more detail in Chapter 6.

There are also technical reasons for having a data center. One reason to locate servers in the data center is that a server often needs much higher-speed network connections than its clients because it needs to be able to communicate at reasonable speeds with many clients simultaneously. A server also is often connected to multiple networks, including some administrative ones, to reduce traffic across the network backbone. High-speed network cabling and hardware typically are expensive to deploy when they first come out and so will be installed in the limited area of the data center first, where it is relatively cheap to deploy to many hosts, and is the most critical. All the servers that make up your service should be in the data center, to take advantage of the higher-speed networking there.

None of the components of the service should rely on anything that runs on a machine not located in the data center. The service is only as reliable as the weakest link in the chain of components that need to be working for the service to be available. A component on a machine that is not in a protected environment, is more likely to fail and bring your service down with it. If you discover that you are relying on something that is running on a machine that is not in the data center, find a way to change the situation: Move the machine into the data center, replicate that service onto a data center machine, or remove the dependence on the less reliable server.

NFS Dependencies Outside the Data Center

NFS, the network file system protocol commonly used on UNIX systems, has a feature whereby the server goes down, the clients will pause until it comes back up. This feature is useful in situations in which one would rather wait than have client software get confused because a server went away, or lose data because the server isn't responding.

When Tom was at Bell Labs, a customer configured his desktop machine to be an NFS server and started providing some useful data there. Soon, many machines had mounted the disk volume from his machine, including some very important servers in the data center.

Then the customer powered off his desktop machine and left on vacation. All the machines that had accessed the data froze, waiting for the desktop machine to become live again.

For precisely this reason servers usually don't mount NFS file systems from other servers. In hindsight, the servers should have been configured to mount NFS volumes only from machines directly managed by the SA team. The SAs had to decide whether to get corporate security to open his office door to boot up his machine or to reboot all the clients, which included some very important machines that shouldn't have been rebooted without a good reason.

Fundamental services, such as DNS servers, should particularly avoid dependencies on other systems.

Catch-22 Dependencies

A start-up web company found itself short of disk space and, to save money, exported some free disk space from a UNIX desktop via NFS. This disk ended up being mounted on all the servers, since it provided a common component. After a blockwide power failure that outlasted the UPS, the company's network would not come up. The workstation couldn't finish booting without the DNS server running, and the DNS server required the NFS partition to be available in order to complete its own boot process. Shortly afterward, the company hired an SA.

5.1.8 Restricted Access

Have you ever had a customer wander into your computer room, sit down at the keyboard and monitor of a critical server, and log in just to check email? When done, did the customer power off the machine, thinking that it was just another desktop? Now nobody can access the primary billing database.

Restrict direct login access on the servers that are part of the service. Permit only SAs responsible for the service to log in to the machine, whether it is at the console or via some remote access method. This restriction is important because interactive users on a machine can overload it. The user may crash the machine, reboot it, or shut it down. Worst of all, whoever is logged in via the console may thereby gain privileged access. For example, at least one Windows-based email system permits a person logged in to the console to read all email on the system.

The more people who log in directly to a machine, the more likely it is to crash. Even OSs known for being unreliable can stay up for months at a time offering a network service if there are no interactive users.

A customer who becomes accustomed to logging in to a particular server for a light task, such as checking email, may eventually start running other programs that hog the CPU, memory, and I/O system. Without realizing it, that person may be adversely affecting the service. For example, suppose that a server is providing file service through NFS and that customers start experiencing NFS performance problems. The correct thing to do is to open a ticket with the SA group and get them to fix the performance problems. However, the quick and easy thing for the customer to do is simply log in to the server and run the jobs on the server; the application will now access the data as a local disk, avoiding any network delays. The customer who is able to log in will probably do so, without considering the impact on the system. As more customers start running their jobs on the NFS server, the performance of the NFS service will deteriorate, becoming more unstable and less reliable, resulting in more people running their jobs directly on the server. Clearly, this situation does not benefit anyone. It is far better to know about the situation and start fixing the root problem as soon as the first customer notices it.

We recommend restricting server access to the SA team from the outset.

5.1.9 Reliability

Along with environmental and access concerns are several things to consider when architecting a service for reliability. In Chapter 4, we explained how to build an individual server to make it more reliable. Having reliable servers as components in your service is another part of making the service reliable as a whole.

If you have redundant hardware available, use it as effectively as you can. For example, if a system has two power supplies, plug them into different power strips and different power sources. If you have redundant machines, get the power and also the network connectivity from different places—for example, different switches—if possible. Ultimately, if this service is meant to be available to people at several sites, think about placing redundant systems at another site that will act as a fallback if the main site has a catastrophic failure.

All the components of each service, other than the redundant pieces, should be tightly coupled, sharing the same power source and network infrastructure, so that the service as a whole depends on as few components as possible. Spreading nonredundant parts across multiple pieces of infrastructure simply means that the service has more single points of failure, each of which can bring the whole service down. For example, suppose that a remote access service is deployed and that part of that service is a new, more secure authentication and authorization system. The system is designed with three components: the box that handles the remote connections, the server that makes sure that people are who they say they are (authentication), and the server that determines what areas people are allowed to access (authorization). If the three components are on different power sources, a failure of any one power source will cause the whole service to fail. Each one is a single point of failure. If they are on the same power source, the service will be unaffected by failures of the other power sources. Likewise, if they are on the same network switch, only a failure of that switch will take the service down. On the other hand, if they are spread across three networks, with many different switches and routers involved in communications between the components, many more components could fail and bring the service down.

The single most effective way to make a service as reliable as possible is to make it as simple as possible. Find the simplest solution that meets all the requirements. When considering the reliability of a service you are building, break it down into its constituent parts and look at what each of them relies on and the degree of reliability, until you reach servers and services that do not rely on anything else. For example, many services rely on name service, such as DNS. How reliable is your name service? Do your name servers rely on other servers and services? Other common central services are authentication services and directory services.

The network is almost certainly one of the components of your system. When you are building a service at a central location that will be accessed from remote locations, it is particularly important to take network topology into account. If connectivity to the main site is down, can the service still be made available to the remote site? Does it make sense to have that service still available to the remote site? What are the implications? Are there resynchronization issues? For example, name service should remain available on both sides when a link is severed, because many things that people at the remote site do rely only on machines at that site. But people won't be able to do those things if they can't resolve names. Even if their name server database isn't getting updates, the stale database can still be useful. If you have a centralized remote access authentication service with remote access systems at other offices, those remote access systems probably still should be able to authenticate people who connect to them, even if the link to the central server is down. In both of these cases, the software should be able to provide secondary servers at remote offices and cope with resynchronizing databases when connectivity is restored. However, if you are building a large database or file service, ensuring that the service is still available in remote offices when their connectivity has been lost is probably not realistic.

Soft outages still provide some functionality. For example, a DNS server can be down and customers can still function, though sometimes a little more slowly or unable to do certain functions.

Hard outages, on the other hand, disrupt all other services, making it impossible for people to get any work done. It's better to group customers and servers/services such that hard outages disrupt only particular customer groups, not all customers. The funny thing about computers is that if one critical function, such as NFS, isn't working, often no work can be done. Thus, being 90 percent functional can be the same as being 0 percent functional. Isolate the 10 percent outage to well-partitioned subsets.

For example, a down NFS server hangs all clients that are actively connected. Suppose that there are three customer groups and three NFS file servers. If the customers' data is spread over the file servers randomly, an outage on one file server will affect all customers. On the other hand, if each customer group is isolated to a particular file server, only one-third of the customers, at most, will be unable to work during an outage.

Grouped Power Cords

This same technique relates to how hardware is connected. A new SA was very proud of how neatly he wired a new set of servers. Each server had three components: a CPU, an external disk chassis, and a monitor. One power strip was for all the CPUs, one for all the disk chassis, and one for all the monitors. Every wire was neatly run and secured with wire ties—a very pretty sight. His mentor complimented him on a job well done but, realizing that the servers weren't in use yet, took the opportunity to shut off the power strip with all the disks. All the servers crashed. The SA learned his lesson: It would be better to have each power strip supply power to all the components of a particular machine. Any single power strip failure would result in an outage of one-third of the devices. In both cases, one-third of the components were down, but in the latter case, only one-third of the service became unusable.

❖ **Windows Login Scripts** Another example of reliability grouping relates to how one architects MS Windows login scripts. Everything the script needs should come from the same server as the script. That way, the script can be fairly sure that the server is alive. If users receive their login scripts from different servers, the various things that each login script needs to access should be replicated to all the servers rather than having multiple dependencies.

5.1.10 Single or Multiple Servers

Independent services, or daemons, should always be on separate machines, cost and staffing levels permitting. However, if the service that you are building is composed of more than one new application or daemon and the communication between those components is over a network connection, you need to consider whether to put all the components on one machine or to split them across many machines.

This choice may be determined by security, performance, or scaling concerns. For example, if you are setting up a web site with a database, you will want to put the database on a separate machine, so that you can tune it for database access, protect it from general Internet access, and scale up the front end of your service by adding more web servers in parallel without having to touch the database machine.

In other cases, one of the components will initially be used only for this one application but may later be used by other applications. For example, you could introduce a calendar service that uses a Lightweight Directory Access Protocol (LDAP) (Yeong, Howes and Kille 1995) directory server and is the first LDAP-enabled service. Should the calendar server and the directory server reside on the same machine or different ones? If a service, such as LDAP, may be used by other applications in the future, it should be placed on a dedicated machine, rather than a shared one, so that the calendar service can be upgraded and patched independently of the (ultimately more critical) LDAP service.

Sometimes, two applications or daemons may be completely tied together and will never be used separately. In this situation, all other things being equal, it makes sense to put them both on the same machine, so that the service is dependent on only one machine rather than two.

5.1.11 Centralization and Standards

An element of building a service is centralizing the tools, applications, and services that your customers need. Centralization means that the tools, applications, and services are managed primarily by one central group of SAs on a single central set of servers rather than by multiple corporate groups that duplicate one another's work and buy their own servers. Support for these services is provided by a central helpdesk. Centralizing services and building them in standard ways make them easier to support and lowers training costs.

To provide good support for any service that a customer relies on, the SA team as a whole needs to understand it well. This means that each service should be properly integrated into the helpdesk process and should use your standard vendor's hardware, where possible. The service should be designed and documented in some consistent way, so that the SA answering the support call knows where to find everything and thus can respond more quickly. Having many instances of the same service can be more difficult to support. One must provide a way for the helpdesk workers to determine, for example, which print server a particular customer calling with a problem is connected to.

Centralization does not preclude centralizing on regional or organizational boundaries, particularly if each region or organization has its own support staff. Some services, such as email, authentication, and networks, are part of the infrastructure and need to be centralized. For large sites, these services can be built with a central core that feeds information to and from distributed regional and organizational systems. Other services, such as file services and CPU farms, are more naturally centralized around departmental boundaries.

5.1.12 Performance

Nobody likes a slow service, even if it has every imaginable feature. From a customer's perspective, two things are important in any service: Does it work,[3] and is it fast? When designing a service, you need to pay attention to its performance characteristics, even though many other difficult technical challenges need to be overcome. If you solve all those difficult problems but the service is slow, the people using it will not consider it a success.

Performance expectations increase as networks, graphics, and processors get faster. Performance that is acceptable now may not be so 6 months or a

---

3. *Work* covers such areas as reliability, functionality, and user interface.

year from now. Bear that in mind when designing the system. You do not want to have to upgrade it for years, if possible. You have other work to do. You want the machine to outlast the depreciation being paid on it.

To build a service that performs well, you need to understand how it works and perhaps look at ways of splitting it effectively across multiple machines. From the outset, you also need to consider how to scale the performance of the system as usage and expectations rise above what the initial system can do.

With **load testing**, you generate an artificial load on a service and see how it reacts. For example, generate 100 hits per second on a web server, and measure the latency, or the average time to complete a single request. Then generate 200 hits per second, and see how the behavior is affected. Increase the member of hits until you see how much load the service can take before response time becomes unacceptable.

If your testing shows that the system runs fine with a few simultaneous users, how many resources—RAM, I/O, and so on—will be consumed when the service goes into production and is being used by hundreds or thousands of users simultaneously? Your vendor should be able to help with these estimates, but conduct your own tests, if possible. Don't expect perfect accuracy from a vendor's predictions of how your organization will use its product.

Bad Capacity Planning/Bad First Impression

Always purchase servers with enough extra capacity to handle peak utilization, as well as a growing number of customers. A new electronic voucher system deployed at one site was immediately overwhelmed by the number of users accessing it simultaneously. Customers trying to use the system found it impossibly slow and unreliable and therefore switched back to the old paper method. This situation gave a bad first impression of the service. A memo was sent out stating that a root-cause analysis was performed and that the system needed more RAM, which would arrive shortly. Even when the new RAM arrived, the customers did not adopt the new system, because everyone "knew" that it was too slow and unreliable. They preferred to stick with what they knew worked.

This new system had been projected to save millions of dollars per year, yet management had skimped on purchasing enough RAM for the system. The finance group had hoped that the new system would be wildly popular and the basis for numerous future applications, yet the performance was specified for an initial small capacity rather than leaving some room for growth. This new service had been given a lot of internal publicity, so the finance group shouldn't have been surprised that so many people would be trying the service on the very first day, rather than having a slowly increasing number of customers. Finally, the finance group had decided to flash-cut the new service rather than gradually introduce it to more divisions of the company over time. (This is something we discuss more, and advocate against, in Section 19.1.6.) The finance group learned a lot about introducing new electronic services from this experience. Most important, the group learned that with customers, "once burned, twice shy" holds true. It is very difficult to get customers to accept a service that has failed once already.

When choosing the machines that run the service, consider how the service works. Does it have processes that do a lot of disk accesses? If so, choose servers with fast disk I/O and fast disks to run those processes. Optimize that further by determining whether the disk access is more reads than writes or vice versa. If the service keeps large tables of data in memory, look at servers with a lot of fast memory and large memory caches. If it is a network-based service that sends large amounts of data to clients or between servers in the service, get a lot of high-speed network interfaces, and look at ways of balancing the traffic across those interfaces. Ways to do that include having a separate network for server-to-server communications, having dedicated network interfaces on key client networks, and using technology that enables the client to transparently communicate with the closest available interface. Also look at clustering options and devices that allow loosely tied clusters or machines running the same service to appear as a single entity.

Performance of the service for remote sites may also be an issue because of low-bandwidth and high-latency connections (see Section 5.1.2 for advice about latency). You may need to become very creative in providing reasonable remote performance if the service has a lot of network traffic, particularly if it has not been designed for placing a server or two at each remote site. In some cases, quality of service (QoS) or intelligent queuing mechanisms can be sufficient to make the performance acceptable. In others, you may need to look at ways of reducing the network traffic.

Performance at Remote Sites

A large company was outsourcing some of its customer-support functions, hardware support in particular. The company needed to provide people at several locations around the world, with interactive access to the customer-support systems and the service that was used for ordering replacement parts for customers. These both had graphical interfaces that ran on the client PCs and talked to the servers. Previously, the clients and servers were all on the same campus network, but now long-distance links were being introduced.

One of the applications transferred huge bitmaps to the client display rather than more concise pieces of data that the client software would then display; for example, it would send a bitmap of what a window should look like rather than instructions to put a button here, a text string there, and so on. This feature of the server software made the usual client/server configuration completely unusable over slow links. The people architecting the service discovered that they could run the client application on a machine on the same network as the server and remotely display the results across the wide-area link to the end user's desktop, resulting in much better interactive performance for the end user. So they bought some new server-class machines to act as the client machines at the central site. The real clients connected to these new machines, which displayed the results back to the real clients over the WAN, yielding acceptable performance.

The performance issue over wide-area links and the solution that yielded acceptable performances were found through systematic testing of a prototype early in the project. If this problem had been discovered at the last minute, it would have delayed the project considerably, because it would have required a complete redesign of the whole system, including the security systems. If it had been discovered when it was rolled out to an end user of the service, the project would have visibly failed.

5.1.13 Monitoring

A service is not complete and cannot properly be called a service unless it is being monitored for availability, problems, and performance, and capacity-planning mechanisms are in place. (Monitoring is the topic of Chapter 22.)

The helpdesk, or front-line support group, must be automatically alerted to problems with the service in order to start fixing them before too many people are affected by the problems. A customer who always has to notice a major problem with a service and call up to report it before anyone starts looking into the problem is getting a very low standard of service. Customers do not like to feel that they are the only ones paying attention to problems in the system. On the other hand, problems you can detect and fix before they are noticed are like trees that fall in the woods with nobody around to hear them. For example, if an outage happens over the weekend and you are alerted in time to fix it before Monday morning, your customers don't even need to know that anything went wrong. (In this case, one should announce by email that the problem has been resolved, so that you receive credit. See Section 31.2).

Likewise, the SA group should monitor the service on an ongoing basis from a capacity-planning standpoint. Depending on the service, capacity planning can include network bandwidth, server performance, transaction rates, licenses, and physical-device availability. As part of any service, SAs can reasonably be expected to anticipate and plan for growth. To do so effectively, usage monitoring needs to be built in as a part of the service.

5.1.14 Service Rollout

The way that a new service is rolled out to the customers is every bit as important as the way that it is designed. The rollout and the customers' first experiences with the service will color the way that they view the service in the future. So make sure that their first impressions are positive.

One of the key pieces of making a good impression is having all the documentation available, the helpdesk familiar with and trained on the new service, and all the support procedures in place. Nothing is worse than having a problem with a new application and finding out that no one seems to know anything about it when you look for help.

The rollout also includes building and testing a mechanism to install whatever new software and configuration settings are needed on each desktop. Methods for rolling out new software to the desktops (see Section 3.1.2), include using a slow-rollout technique that we named "one, some, many," which uses well-chosen test groups that gradually increase in number. Ideally, no new desktop software or configuration should be required for the service, because that is less disruptive for your customers and reduces maintenance, but installing new client software on the desktops is frequently necessary.

5.2 The Icing

Besides building a service that is reliable, monitored, easy to maintain and support, and meets all your and the customers' basic requirements for a service, some extra things should be considered. If possible, you should use dedicated machines for each service. Doing so makes them easier to maintain and support. In large companies, using dedicated machines is one of the basics. In smaller companies, the cost may be prohibitive.

The other ideal that you should aim for in building services is to have them fully redundant. Some services are so critical that they need full redundancy, no matter what the size of the company. You should aim to make the others fully redundant as the company grows.

5.2.1 Dedicated Machines

Ideally, services should be built on dedicated machines. Large sites should be able to justify this structure, based on demands on the services, but small sites will have a much more difficult time justifying it. Having dedicated machines for each service makes them more reliable, makes debugging easier when there are reliability problems, reduces the scope of outages, and ensures that upgrades and capacity planning are much easier.

Sites that grow generally end up with one central administrative machine that is the core of all the critical services. It provides name, authentication, print, email, and other services. Eventually, this machine will have to be split up and the services spread across many servers because of the increased load. Often, by the time that the SAs get funding for more administrative machines, this machine has so many services and dependencies that it is very difficult to split it apart.

IP address dependencies are the most difficult to deal with when splitting services from one machine to many. Some services have IP addresses hard-coded into all the clients; network products, such as firewalls and routers, often have many IP addresses hard-coded into their configurations.

Splitting the Central Machine

As a small company, Synopsys started with the typical configuration of one central administrative machine. It was the Network Information Service (NIS) master, DNS master, time server, print server, console server, email server, SOCKS relay, token-card authentication server, boot server, NetApp admin host, file server, Columbia Appletalk Protocol (CAP) server, and more. It was also the only head—keyboard and monitor—in the machine room, so it was the machine that SAs used when they had to work in there. As the group grew and new SAs were working at its console, using the console server software to access other hosts' consoles, a new SA would occasionally accidentally type a `halt` key sequence on the central server rather than use the appropriate sequence to send a `halt` message through the console server software. Because everything relied on this machine, this accident effectively brought down the whole company at once.

The time had come to split the functionality of the machine across multiple servers, not only because of those occasional slips but also because the machine was becoming increasingly unreliable and overloaded. At this point, the central machine had so many services running on it that just figuring out what they all were was a large task in itself.

The primary services of NIS and DNS were moved to three machines with lots of network interfaces, so that each network had two of these machines connected to it. Other services were moved onto still more machines, with each new machine being the primary machine for one service and a secondary one for another. Some services moved relatively easily because they were associated with a service-based name. Others were more difficult because they were tied to IP addresses. In some cases, machines in other parts of the company had been built to rely on the real hostname rather than the service-based name.

Years later, the original central machine was still in existence, though not nearly so critical or overloaded, as the SAs continued to find dependencies that remote offices had built into their local infrastructure servers and desktops in nonstandard ways.

Splitting a center-of-the-universe host into many different hosts is very difficult and becomes more so the longer it exists and the more services that are built onto it. Using service-based names helps, but they need to be standardized and used universally and consistently throughout the company.

5.2.2 Full Redundancy

Having a duplicate server or set of servers ready to take over from the primary set in the case of failure is called **full redundancy**. Having a secondary take over service from a failed primary can happen different ways: It may require human intervention, it may be automatic after the primary fails, or the primary and secondary may share workload until one fails, at which time the remaining server is responsible for the entire workload.

The type of redundancy that you choose depends on the service. Some services, such as web servers and compute farms, lend themselves well to running on large farms of cloned machines. Other services, such as huge databases, do not and require a more tightly coupled failover system. The software you are using to provide a service may dictate that your redundancy be in the form of a live passive slave server that responds to requests only when the master server fails. In all cases, the redundancy mechanism must ensure that data synchronization occurs and that data integrity is maintained.

In the case of large farms of cloned servers and other scenarios in which redundant servers run continuously alongside the primary servers, the redundant machines can be used to share the load and increase performance when everything is operating normally. If you use this approach, be careful not to allow the load to reach the point at which performance would be unacceptable if one of the servers were to fail. Add more servers in parallel with the existing ones before you reach that point.

Some services are so integral to the minute-to-minute functioning of a site that they are made fully redundant very early on in the life of the site. Others remain largely ignored until the site becomes very large or has some huge, visible failure of the service.

Name and authentication services are typically the first ones to have full redundancy, in part because the software is designed for secondary servers and in part because they are so critical. Other critical services, such as email, printing, and networks, tend to be considered much later because they are more complicated or more expensive to make completely redundant.

As with everything that you do, consider which services will benefit your customers most to have completely redundant, and start there.

Case Study: Designing Email Service for Reliability

Bob Flandrena engineered an interesting redundant way for email to flow into and out of Bell Labs. Mail coming in from the Internet was spooled to a group of machines inside the firewall, which then forwarded the messages to the appropriate internal mail server. An external machine queued mail if the firewall was down. This external machine had a large spool area and could hold a couple of days' worth of mail. Logging, spam control, and various security-related issues were therefore focused on the small set of internal hosts guaranteed to see all incoming email.

Internal mail servers routed email between each other. However, their configurations were simplified by the fact that more difficult routing decisions could be deferred to two routing hosts, both inside the firewall. These routing hosts had more complicated configurations and could determine whether email should be routed to the Internet.

Outbound mail, destined for the Internet, was sent by the routing hosts to two redundant hosts, outside the firewall, dedicated to repeatedly retrying message delivery to external Internet domains. The Internet was unreliable, and retrying email is a huge burden. Spool space was sufficient on the routing hosts in case these two external relays were inaccessible and on the external machines in case they had to retry some messages for a long time.

The firewall rules permitted only outbound email (SMTP) traffic from the routing hosts to the external relays. The inbound rules permitted only the appropriate paths for incoming email. All these hosts used the same hardware and software, with slightly different configurations. A spare set of hardware was kept on hand so that broken hosts could be replaced quickly.

The system was slower when a single host was down, but as long as the firewall was operating, email went through. If the firewall was down, it took a simultaneous failure of a complete set of redundant systems before incoming or outgoing mail was not spooled.

The system scaled very well. Each potential bottleneck was independently monitored. If it became overloaded, the simple addition of more hosts and appropriate DNS MX records added capacity. It was a simple, clear design that was reliable and easy to support.

The only remaining points of failure were the mail delivery hosts within the company. Failure of any one of those affected only part of the company, however. This was the trickiest part to address.

Another benefit of such redundancy is that it makes upgrades easier: A **rolling upgrade** can be performed. One at a time, each host is disconnected, upgraded, tested, and brought back into service. The outage of the single host does not stop the entire service, though it may affect performance.

5.2.3 Dataflow Analysis for Scaling

If you understand the individual components of a typical transaction in a service, you can scale the service with much greater precision and efficiency. Strata's experiences building scalable Internet services for ISPs and ASPs led her to create a dataflow model for individual transactions and combine them into spreadsheets to get an overall dataflow picture, which sounds more complicated than it really is.

A dataflow model is simply a list of transactions and their dependencies, with as much information as can be acquired about resource usages for each transaction. That information might include the amount of memory used on the server hosting that transaction, the size and number of packets used in a transaction, the number of open sockets used to service a transaction, and so on.

In modeling an individual service transaction with dataflow, all the pieces of the transaction necessary to make it happen are included, even such pieces as Internet name lookups via DNS, in order to get a true picture of the transaction. Even things technically outside your control, such as the behavior of the root-level name servers in DNS, can affect what you're trying to model. If a transaction bottleneck occurred in the name-lookup phase, for instance, you could internally run a caching name server, thus saving some time doing external lookups. Sites that keep and analyze web service logs or other external access logs routinely do this, as it speeds up logging. For even faster logging, sites may simply record the external host by IP address and do the name lookups in a postprocessing phase for analysis.

A nice thing about a service is that it is generally transaction based. Even file sharing consists of multiple transactions as blocks are read and written across the network. The key part of dataflow modeling to remember is that service transactions almost always depend on infrastructure transactions. It's fairly common to investigate a scaling problem with a service and discover that the service itself has a bottleneck somewhere in the infrastructure.

Once the dataflow model is accurately depicting the service, you can address performance and scaling problems by seeing what part of the dataflow model is the weakest point, monitoring each piece, under real or simulated conditions, and see how they act or how they fail. For example, if your database can handle up to 100 queries per second and if you know that every access to your web site's home page requires three database queries, you can predict that the web site will work only if there are no more than 33 hits per second. However, you also now know that if you can improve the performance of the database to be 200 QPS—possibly by replicating it on a second server and dividing the queries between the two—the web site can handle twice as many hits per second, assuming that no other bottleneck is involved.

Resources on the server can also be an issue. Suppose that a server provides email access via IMAP. You might know, from direct observation or from vendor documentation, that each client connected to the server requires about 300K of RAM. Looking at the logs, you can get an idea of the usage patterns of the server: how many users are on simultaneously during which parts of the day versus the total number of server users.

Knowing how many people are using the service is only part of the process. In order to analyze resources, you also should consider whether the IMAP server process loads an index file of some type, or even the whole mailbox, into memory. If so, you need to know the average size of the data that will be loaded, which can be calculated as a strict average of all the customers' index files; as a mean or median, based on where in the size curve most index files occur, or even by adding up only the index files used during peak usage times and doing those calculations on them. Pick what seems like the most realistic case for your application. The monitoring system can be used to validate your predictions. This might show unexpected things, such as whether the average mailbox size grows faster than expected. This might affect index size and thus performance.

Finally, step back and do this kind of analysis for all the steps in the dataflow. If a customer desktop makes an internal name-lookup query to find the mail server rather than caching info on where to find it, that should be included in your dataflow analysis as load on the name server. Maybe the customer is using a webmail application, in which case the customer will be using resources on a web server, whose software in turn makes an IMAP connection to the mail server. In this case, there are probably at least two name lookups per transaction, since the customer desktop will look up the webmail server, and the webmail server will look up the IMAP server. If the webmail server does local authentication and passes credentials to the IMAP server, there would be an additional name lookup, to the directory server, then a directory transaction.

Dataflow modeling works at all levels of scale. You can successfully design a server upgrade for a 30-person department or a multimedia services cluster for 3 million simultaneous users. It might take some traffic analysis on a sample setup, as well as vendor information, system traces, and so on, to get exact figures of the type you'd want for the huge-scale planning.

An Example of Dataflow Analysis

Strata once managed a large number of desktops accessing a set of file servers on the network. A complaint about files being slow to open was investigated, but the network was not clogged, nor were there unusual numbers of retransmits or lags in the file server statistics on the hosts serving files. Further investigation revealed that all the desktops were using the same directory server to get the server-to-file mapping when opening a file and that the directory server itself was overloaded. No one had realized that although the directory server could easily handle the number of users whose desktops mapped to it, each user was generating dozens, if not hundreds, of file-open requests to compile large jobs. When the requests per user figures were calculated and the number of simultaneous users estimated, it was then easy to see that an additional directory server was required for good performance.

5.3 Conclusion

Designing and building a service is a key part of every SA's job. How well the SA performs this part of the job determines how easy each service is to support and maintain, how reliable it is, how well it performs, how well it meets customer requirements, and ultimately how happy the customers will be with the performance of the SA team.

You build services to provide better service to your customers, either directly by providing a service they need or indirectly by making the SA team more effective. Always keep the customers' requirements in mind. They are ultimately the reason you are building the service.

An SA can do a lot of things to build a better service, such as building it on dedicated servers, simplifying management, monitoring the servers and the service, following company standards, and centralizing the service onto a few machines. Some ways to build a better service involve looking beyond the initial requirements into the future of upgrade and maintenance projects. Making the service as independent as possible of the machines it runs on is one key way of keeping it easier to maintain and upgrade.

Services should be as reliable as the customer requirements specify. Over time, in larger companies, you should be able to make more services fully redundant so that any one component can fail and be replaced without bringing the service down. Prioritize the order in which you make services fully redundant, based on the return on investment for your customers. You will have a better idea of which systems are the most critical only after gaining experience with them.

Rolling out the service smoothly with minimal disruption to the customers is the final, but possibly most visible, part of building a new service. Customers are likely to form their opinion of the new service on the basis of the rollout process, so it is important to do that well.

Exercises

1. List all the services that you can think of in your environment. What hardware and software make up each one? List their dependencies.

2. Select a service that you are designing or can predict needing to design in the future. What will you need to do to make it meet the recommendations in this chapter? How will you roll out the service to customers?

3. What services rely on machines that do not live in the machine room? How can you remove those dependencies?

4. What services do you monitor? How would you expand your monitoring to be more service based rather than simply machine based? Does your monitoring system open trouble tickets or page people as appropriate? If not, how difficult would it be to add that functionality?

5. Do you have a machine that has multiple services running on it? If so, how would you go about splitting it up so that each service runs on dedicated machines? What would the impact on your customers be during that process? Would this help or hurt service?

6. How do you do capacity planning? Is it satisfactory, or can you think of ways to improve it?

7. What services do you have that have full redundancy? How is that redundancy provided? Are there other services that you should add redundancy to?

8. Reread the discussion of bandwidth versus latency (Section 5.1.2). What would the mathematical formula look like for the two proposed solutions: batched requests and windowed requests?

Chapter 6

Data Centers

This chapter focuses on building a data center. A **data center** is the place where you keep machines that are shared resources. A data center is more than simply the room that your servers live in, however. A data center also typically has systems for cooling, humidity control, power, and fire suppression. These systems are all part of your data center. The theory is that you put all your most important eggs in one basket and then make sure that it is a really good basket.

These places go by different terms, and each implies something slightly different. Data centers are often stand-alone buildings built specifically for computing and network operations. *Machine room* or *computer room* evokes a smaller image, possibly a designated room in an otherwise generic office. The very smallest such places are often referred to humorously as *computer closets*.

Building a data center is expensive, and doing it right is even more expensive. You should expect your company's management to balk at the cost and to ask for justification. Be prepared to justify spending the extra money up front by showing how it will save time and money in the years to come. Some anecdotes in this chapter should help.

Small sites will find it difficult to justify many of the recommendations in this chapter. However, if your small site is intending to grow into a larger one, use this chapter as a road map to the data center that your company will need when it is larger. Plan for improving the data center as the company grows and can afford to spend more to get higher reliability. Do what you can now for relatively little cost, such as getting decent racks and cable management, and look for opportunities to improve.

Many organizations choose to rent space in a **colocation facility**, a data center run by a management company that rents space out to companies that need it. This option can be much more economical, and it leverages the facility's expertise in such esoteric topics as power and cooling. In that case, this chapter will help prepare you to speak knowledgeably about data center issues and to ask the right questions.

Because the equipment in the data center is generally part of a shared infrastructure, it is difficult to upgrade or fundamentally alter a data center in any way without scheduling at least one maintenance window (see Chapter 20 for tips on doing that), so it is best to get it right the first time, when you initially build the data center. Obviously, as technologies change, the data center requirements will change, but you should aim to predict your needs 8 to 10 years into the future. If 10 years sounds like a long time, consider that most data centers last 30 years. Ten years is in fact pessimistic and suggests a forklift upgrade twice in the life of the building.

In the early days of computing, computers were huge and could be operated only by a few trained people. Their size alone required that the computers be accommodated in a dedicated data center environment. Large mainframes had special cooling and power requirements and therefore had to live in a special data center environment. Minicomputers generated less heat and had lower power requirements and also were housed in special computer rooms. Supercomputers generally needed water cooling, had special power requirements, and typically had to be housed in a data center with a specially strengthened and reinforced raised floor. Early desktop computers, such as Apple IIs and PCs running DOS, were not used as servers but rather resided on people's desks without special power or cooling. These computers were the radical, antimainframe tool, and their users prided themselves on being far from the data center. UNIX workstations were used as desktops and servers from the beginning. Here, the line between what should be in a data center versus what can be on or under a desk elsewhere in the building becomes less obvious and must be determined by function and customer access requirements rather than by type of machine. We have come full circle: The PC world is now being required to build reliable 24/7 systems and is learning to put its PCs in the data centers that they had previously rebelled against.

6.1 The Basics

At first glance, it may seem fairly easy to build a data center. You simply need a big room with tables, racks, or wire shelves in there and voilà! In fact, the basics of building a good, reliable data center that enables SAs to work efficiently is a lot more complicated than that. To start with, you need to select good racks, you need good network wiring, you need to condition the power that you send to your equipment, you need lots of cooling, and you need to consider fire suppression. You also should plan for the room to survive natural disasters reasonably well. Organizing the room well means thinking ahead about wiring, console service, labeling, tools, supplies, and workbenches and designating parking places for mobile resources. You also need to consider security mechanisms for the data center and how you will move equipment in and out of the room.

6.1.1 Location

First, you need to decide where the data center will be. If it is to be a hub for worldwide offices or for a geographic area, this will first involve picking a town and a building within that town. Once the building has been chosen, a suitable place within the building must be selected. For all these stages, you should take into consideration as part of the decision process the natural disasters that the area is subject to.

Selecting a town and a building is typically out of the hands of the SA staff. However, if the data center is to serve a worldwide or significant geographic area and will be located in an area that is prone to earthquakes, flooding, hurricanes, lightning storms, tornados, ice storms, or other natural disasters that may cause damage to the data center or loss of power or communications, you must prepare for these eventualities. You also must be prepared for someone with a backhoe to accidentally dig up and break your power and communication lines, no matter how immune your site is from natural disasters (Anonymous 1997). (Preparing for power loss is discussed further in Section 6.1.4.) For communications loss, you can deploy technologies for communication backups should your primary links fail. Such precautions can be as simple as diversely routed lines—redundant connections run through different conduits, all the way to the provider—or as complicated as satellite backup connections. You can also raise the issue of having another site to take over the data center services completely if the primary site fails. This approach is expensive and can be justified only if loss of this data center for a time will have a considerable adverse impact on the company (see Chapter 10).

Location and Political Boundary

Sometimes, a site a few miles from another is significantly better because it is in another state or county. For example, one company leasing new data center space in the late 1990s needed many data centers for redundancy. One of the company's decisions was not to lease any space in counties that were participating in California's proposed power-deregulation plan. This often meant disqualifying one space that was just miles from another, similar space. Someone not following the regulatory politics wouldn't see the difference.

When the deregulation plan led to the famous California power problems of 2000/2001, what had previously looked like paranoia turned out to prevent significant power-related outages.

When it comes to selecting the location for the data center within the building, the SA team should have influence. Based on the requirements you build from the rest of this chapter, you should be able to discuss your space needs. You should also be able to provide the facilities department with requirements that will help it select an appropriate location. At a basic level, you should make sure that the floor will be strong enough for the weight of the equipment. There are, however, other factors to consider.

If the area is prone to flooding, you will want to avoid having the data center in a basement or even at ground level, if possible. You should also consider how this affects the location of the support infrastructure for the data center, such as the UPS systems, automatic transfer switches (ATSs), generators, and cooling systems. If these support systems have to be shut down, the data center will, too. Remember, the data center is more than simply the room in which your servers live.

Case Study: Bunkers as the Ultimate Secure Data Center

When you need a secure building, you can't go wrong following the U.S. military as an example. A federal agency provides insurance for members and families of the U.S. military. Most of the people who work there are ex-military, and their data center is in the strongest kind of building they could think of: a military bunker. People who have visited the site say that they have to stifle a chuckle or two, but they appreciate the effort. These buildings will survive all kinds of weather, natural disasters, and, most likely, terrorist attacks and mortar fire. Multiple vendors now provide colocation space in bunker-style facilities.

HavenCo

Being *too* secure can have its own problems. For example, HavenCo took a WWII-era sea fortress, which looks like an oil rig, and converted it into a data center. The company suffered years of logistical problems, such as the need to transport all its equipment and supplies via fishing trawler, and staffing issues, since few people want to live in a concrete tower 7 miles offshore. The company also had poor sales because most customers are satisfied with traditional data center service. Ultimately, the facility suffered massive damage in late June 2006 when stored fuel for the generator caught fire. As if this writing, the company's web site says HavenCo is rebuilding and looking for new investors.

Having a data center in an earthquake zone affects several things. You must choose racks that can withstand a reasonable amount of shaking, and you must ensure that equipment is secured in the rack and will not fall out during an earthquake. You should install appropriate earthquake bracing that provides support but is not too rigid. If you have a raised floor, you should make sure that it is sufficiently strong and compliant to building codes. Consider how power and network cables are run through the data center. Are they able to cope with some stretching and compressing forces, or will they come apart?

There are various levels of earthquake readiness for a data center. A good data center consultant should be able to discuss possibilities and costs with you, so that you can decide what is appropriate for your company. We've also found that a good rack salesperson will walk you through much of the design decisions and legal safety requirements and often know good cooling engineers and good power and cable companies. A good rack salesperson can hook you up with all the experts you need to design your data center.

Areas exposed to a lot of lightning require special lightning protection. Architects can offer advice about that.

Lightning Protection

A hill in New Jersey has a large amount of iron ore in it. On top of the hill is a very large building that has an all-copper roof. Because the hill and the roof attract many lightning strikes, the building has an extremely large amount of lightning protection. However, when unexplainable outages happen in that building, the SAs have a fun time blaming the iron ore and the copper roof even when it isn't raining. Hey, you never know!

Redundant Locations

Extremely large web-based service organizations deploy multiple, redundant data centers. One such company has many data centers around the world. Each of the company's products, or properties, is split between different data centers, each handling a share of the workload. One property might be popular enough that being in four data centers provides the capacity to provide the service at peak times. A more popular property might exist in eight data centers to provide enough capacity. The policy at this company is that all production services must exist in enough data centers that any two may be offline at a given time and still have enough capacity to provide service. Such $n + 2$ redundancy permits one data center to be down for maintenance while another goes down unexpectedly, yet the service will still survive.

6.1.2 Access

Local laws will determine to some degree the access to your data center and, for example, may require at least two exits or a wheelchair ramp if you have a raised floor. Aside from those considerations, you also must examine how you will move racks and equipment into the room. Some pieces of equipment are wider than standard door widths, so you may want extrawide doors. If you have double doors, make sure that they don't have a post in the middle. You also may want to look at the spacing between racks for getting the equipment into place. If you have a raised floor, you will need a ramp for wheeling in equipment. You may need to strengthen certain areas of the floor and the path to them for supporting extraheavy equipment. You also need to consider access from the delivery dock all the way to the data center. Remember that equipment is usually delivered in a box that is larger than the equipment itself. We've seen equipment unboxed at the delivery dock so that it could be wheeled into the elevator and to its final destination.

Delivery Dock

One Silicon Valley start-up company had no delivery dock. One day, a large shipment of servers arrived and was delivered onto the street outside the building because there was no immediate way to get them inside the building from the truck. Some of the servers were on pallets that could be broken down, and individual pieces were carried up the entrance stairs into the building. Other pieces were small enough that they could be wheeled up the narrow wheelchair ramp into the building. But some pieces were too large for either of these approaches and were wheeled down the steep ramp into the parking garage, where they could be squeezed into the small elevator and brought up to the entrance level where the computer room was. Fortunately, because it was summer in California, it didn't start to rain during this rather lengthy process.

6.1.3 Security

Insofar as possible, your data center should have good physical security that does not impede the SAs' work. Access should be granted only to people whose duties require physical access: hardware technicians, tape-backup operators, network administrators, physical plant and safety personnel, as well as a limited number of managers. The fire safety wardens or, in some places, the emergency search teams, assigned to that area should be drawn from people who have access already.

Restricting data center access increases the reliability and availability of the equipment in there and increases the chance that wiring and rack-mounting standards will be followed. Servers, by definition, have high-availability requirements and therefore should be subject to all the change-management processes and procedures that the SA group abides by to meet or exceed their service-level commitments. Non-SA people do not have those commitments and will not have been trained on the SA group's key processes. Because these people spend less time maintaining infrastructure equipment, they are more likely to make mistakes that could cause a costly outage. If some of your customers need physical access to machines in the data center, they cannot be considered highly reliable or infrastructure machines and so should be moved to a lab environment, where your customers can have access to them; alternatively, use remote access technology, such as KVM switches.

Locking a data center with keys is not ideal, because keys are cumbersome to use, too easy to copy, and too difficult to trace. Instead, consider proximity badge systems, which are more convenient and automatically record accesses. Data centers with very high security requirements, such as banks or medical centers, sometimes use both keys and proximity badges, require two people to badge in together so that nobody is in the room unsupervised, or use motion detectors to make sure that the room is empty when the badge records say it should be.

When designing a data center, consider the height of proximity badge readers. If a card reader is at an appropriate height, the badge can be kept on a chain or in a back pocket and brought close to the card reader without requiring the use of your hands. SAs with style do this with Elvis-like precision. Others look plain silly.

Biometric locks introduce many new concerns. Is it ethical to install a security system that can be bypassed by cutting off an authorized person's finger? If the data is sufficiently valuable, the biometric lock system may put the lives of authorized personnel in danger. Most biometric security systems also check for life by looking for a pulse or body heat from the finger. Other systems also require a PIN or do voice recognition, in addition to the biometric scan. If you do install such a security system, we recommend that you select one that checks whether the person is still alive. Even so, ethical issues relate to the fact that employees cannot change their fingerprints, voices, or DNA when they leave a company: The biometric is an **irrevocable key.** Last but not least, people with special physical needs often cannot use these systems.

The effectiveness of biometric systems has been called into question recently. Tsutomu Matsumoto, a Japanese cryptographer, showed that leading fingerprint-scanning systems can be reliably fooled with a little ingenuity and $10 worth of household supplies: He used gelatin, the stuff that Gummi Bears are made out of, to make a fake finger (SPIE 2002).

Also important to the security of a room is visitor policy. Should visitors be left alone? What if a vendor has been hired to do an installation or repair in a room for many hours? Will an SA have to babysit the vendor for the duration?

I Don't Pay You to Watch People Point

The walls of a data center were to be painted. The painting company was selected because it claimed to have experience working in data centers.

The SAs proposed that they take shifts watching the crew to make sure that nothing was broken or damaged. The manager replied, "I don't pay you to stand around watching other people paint all day!" and said that the painters were to be left alone to do their job.

You can imagine the result.

Repairing the damage was more costly than a week's salary.

6.1.4 Power and Cooling

Power and cooling in your data center are directly related. Power makes equipment run; cooling removes the heat generated by the equipment so that it stays within operating temperature. Equipment malfunctions and can even catch on fire when it gets too hot.

In general, for every watt of power consumed by your equipment, you will need to spend at least 1 watt on cooling. The heat generated by equipment consuming 10 kilowatts will require a cooling system that uses 10 kilowatts—in fact, more like 11 or 12 kilowatts, owing to inefficiencies in the system. It's the law of thermodynamics. This means that half of your electricity bill will be spent on cooling and half on powering your equipment. It also means that using lower-powered equipment saves twice as much energy, since you don't have to cool it as much.

You can direct the airflow in a data center in two general ways. One way is to use a raised floor as the conduit for the cold air. The airflow system pushes the cold air, creating enough pressure to force the air up holes in the raised floor. These holes are strategically placed to blow up into the equipment, carrying the heat up and away. This works because heat rises. Many people think that raised floors are to make it easier to run cables. Cables block airflow and shouldn't be run under a raised floor used for cooling. If your raised floor is part of your cooling architecture, overhead racks should be used to run cables and power. You will continually need to remind people that cables and other airflow-blocking devices should not be placed under the floor.

The alternative is to have the cold air output from the ceiling and blow down onto the machines. Since hot air rises, it is less work to force cold air to flow down. With a system like this, cables can be distributed via overhead trays as before, or a raised floor can be used exclusively for cables.

When deciding how much power and cooling a data center needs, you should aim to reach capacity on your power systems at the same time as you reach capacity on your cooling systems, which should be at the same time as you run out of space.

Cooling Rules

In 2001, a common rule of thumb was that a typical office computer room not packed very densely required 5 tons (60,050 BTU) of cooling for every 5,000 square feet of data center.

Bear in mind that equipment tends to get smaller over time, so in a few years, the same amount of space will be capable of consuming more power and needing more cooling. With the popularity of high-density blade farms, all the old rules are going away.

Humidity control is another component of air conditioning. The humidity in the data center needs to be regulated because high humidity leads to condensation and equipment failure, and low humidity causes static discharge that can damage equipment. A humidity level between 45 and 55 percent is ideal. Power systems and HVAC[1] systems are large, complicated

---

1. One rarely needs to heat the data center. The computers at Amundsen-Scott South Pole Station are reported to not need heating. However, the computers at the top of the ski slopes in Nagano at the 1998 Winter Olympics did have electric blankets because everything was turned off at night (Guth and Radosevich 1998).

to replace, and will almost certainly require outages, so you want to plan for these systems to last at least 8 to 10 years.

Data center power must be conditioned, or **cleaned,** to protect equipment from the spikes, brownouts, and power cuts that are a fact of life with utility power. Clean alternating-current power also means a steady sine wave and a constant number of volts. Achieving all this requires at least one UPS that provides sufficient power at a constant voltage to the whole data center. A UPS normally supplies power from battery banks, which it is continually recharging from its in-bound power feed, when that feed is clean enough to use. Power from the UPS is then brought to distribution panels in the data center and any other locations that get protected power. A UPS with modular battery banks is pictured in Figure 6.1.

UPS systems should be able to notify staff in case of failure or other problems. Smaller UPS systems have the ability to notify servers to power themselves off when the batteries are getting low.

The most important thing you can know when purchasing a UPS is this: Studies show that power outages tend to be extremely short—seconds—or extremely long—half a day or longer. The majority of power outages last less than 10 seconds. Statistically speaking, if an outage lasts longer than 10 minutes, it will likely last the rest of the day, and you should consider sending staff home.

Figure 6.1 A modular UPS at GNAC, Inc.

Therefore, purchasing a UPS that can last significantly longer than an hour is, statistically speaking, a waste of money. If the outage lasts more than an hour, it is likely going to last a day or so, and a UPS with that much capacity is very expensive. If your SLAs require services to withstand a power outage longer than an hour, your data center should have a generator.

Therefore, you can design your UPS system to last either an hour or much longer. If you purchase a UPS with enough capacity to last an hour, that will cover the frequent, short outages and give you enough time to power down all the systems in the occasional multihour outage. This solution is less expensive, since the cooling system does not need to be on the UPS, because a data center can typically last an hour without cooling. From our earlier cooling and power discussion, it is clear that putting the cooling system on the UPS would double the capacity required, which would approximately double the cost of the UPS.

Data centers that provide 24/7 service require a more sophisticated UPS system. A smaller UPS that lasts for a shorter amount of time is combined with a generator and an ATS that switches between the two. This type of UPS system will survive multihour outages. The UPS will handle the frequent, short outages and give you enough time to power up the generator. Emergency refueling service can be prearranged to allow the building to run on generator power indefinitely. Figures 6.2 and 6.3 show a fuel tank and a generator, respectively.

Figure 6.2 A 1,000-gallon tank to power the generators at GNAC, Inc.

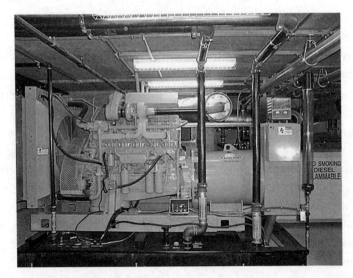

Figure 6.3 The redundant generators at GNAC, Inc., each have a 200-gallon tank that is filled from the main 1,000-gallon tank.

An ATS is a device that controls whether the UPS gets its power from the power utility or from a generator. The ATS monitors utility power and, if it is within tolerances, connects it to the UPS. If the ATS is out of tolerance, it disconnects the UPS from utility power, turns on the generator, and when the generator is producing clean power, connects it to the UPS. When utility power returns to within tolerance, the ATS switches the power feed to the UPS back to utility power and turns the generator off. An ATS usually has a manual switch as well, so you can force it to feed utility power—or generator power—to the UPS, if necessary. The control panel of an ATS is pictured in Figure 6.4.

Always install a switch that allows you to bypass the UPS if it fails. All power for the data center runs through the UPS. Therefore, you will need to bypass it if it fails or if you need to do maintenance on it. This switch must be external to the UPS and a reasonable distance away from it. A UPS is full of batteries, and if it catches fire, you do not want to go into the UPS room to bypass it. The UPS will probably come with a bypass switch that is integral to the unit. That switch is insufficient, particularly in the case of a fire.

When purchasing the UPS, you should also consider its maintenance and environmental requirements. The UPS may need periodic maintenance, will certainly need to have its batteries replaced about once every 3 years, and may

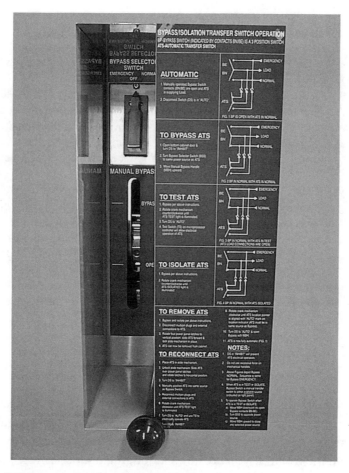

Figure 6.4 ATS bypass switch at GNAC, Inc.

require cooling and humidity control, which may dictate its location within the building. Also consider whether the UPS can be forced to trickle-charge its batteries rather than to charge them as quickly as it can. A UPS fast-charging batteries, puts a huge load on the rest of the power system, which may bring the power down. With trickle-charging, a much lower additional load is placed on the rest of the power system.

Generators have to be carefully maintained, tested monthly, and periodically refueled. Otherwise, they will not work on the few occasions when they are needed, and you will have wasted your money.

If a data center has a generator, the HVAC system also must be on protected power. Otherwise, the systems will overheat.

Case Study: A Failing HVAC System

A small start-up biotechnology company of about 50 people was building its first data center, having just moved into a large building where it was planning to stay in for at least 10 years. The company did not have a senior SA on staff. The facilities manager didn't realize how much heat a data center can generate and decided to save some money on the HVAC system by getting a less powerful one than recommended by the data center contractors. Instead, the company went with the unit recommended by the HVAC salesperson, who apparently was not familiar with data center planning.

A few years later, the data center was full of equipment, and the HVAC system was failing every few months. Each time this happened, the SAs shut down the less essential machines, got huge buckets of ice (which the labs had lots of) and fans, and tried to keep the most critical parts of the data center running for the rest of the day. The SAs then shut everything off overnight. Over the following 2 or 3 weeks, a multitude of hardware failures, mostly disks, occurred. Then things would even out for a while until the next HVAC failure. The HVAC engineers told the SAs the problem was that the unit was unable to keep up with the amount of heat the room was generating.

The problem persisted until additional cooling capacity was installed.

Heat sensors distributed around the data center and connected to the monitoring system are useful for detecting hot spots. A quick, cheap alternative is to move digital thermometers that record the high and low temperatures around the room. If you are good at judging temperatures, you can also check for hot spots with your hand. Hot spots with no airflow are particularly problematic because they will get hotter faster. When there are known hot spots, the problem can be addressed by moving equipment or altering the HVAC system. If hot spots go unnoticed, they can be the source of equipment failure. Some hardware vendors provide a way to monitor the temperature at one or more points inside their equipment. If this feature is provided, it should be used because doing so can provide better coverage than deploying heat sensors.

HVAC systems often fail silently and sometimes return to service without anyone noticing. Because HVAC failures cause hardware to fail more quickly, it is important to notice when the HVAC system fails. If an HVAC system itself does not provide a monitoring mechanism that can automatically alert the helpdesk systems, the network-monitoring systems should be configured to monitor heat sensors.

Monitor Room Temperature to Detect Foot Traffic

You should monitor room temperature not only for emergency situations, such as HVAC failures and fires, but also to prevent the development of bad habits. For example, a manager was concerned that his SAs were leaving a machine room door open occasionally. He noticed that sometimes when he entered the room, it was nearly normal room temperature and the HVAC system was running on high, trying to compete with the open door.

At a staff meeting, he was assured by everyone that nobody was leaving the door open. He configured Cricket, an SNMP monitoring tool, to collect temperature data from the routers in this and other machine rooms. At the next staff meeting, he presented graphs of the data showing that the temperature rose 10° during the day but was fine during weekends and holidays. More revealing was that the other machine rooms did not have such variations in temperature. At the next staff meeting, he presented graphs showing that the problem had disappeared and thanked everyone for being more mindful of the door.

In addition to having the HVAC systems on generator power, it can be useful to put other building circuits onto power circuits that have generator backup. These circuits should be tolerant of small outages and spikes. Lights are good candidates, particularly in the operations and helpdesk areas. For groups such as the helpdesk, operations (for example, shipping and receiving), or a customer-service center that needs to stay up during power outages, it can be useful to have the light and power circuits on generator backup with small deskside UPS systems. All areas should at least have emergency lighting that comes on automatically when the power fails, even if it is not part of the building code in that region. If you have the luxury of being able to switch off utility power to the building, it can be useful to try it and see what else you would like to have on emergency power. In the absence of a full trial, mime all the things that you would do in a power outage, and note what you rely on that would not be available.

The Importance of Lighting

One site did not have emergency power brought to the lights in the generator room. This omission was discovered when a power outage occurred, and the site needed to refuel the diesel generator in the dark.

Maximum load is more than simply what the equipment in the data center can draw. All the components of the electrical system, as well as the wiring and trip switches between them, must have the capacity to deal with your data center at maximum load and the HVAC system running at maximum capability, with the added load of the UPS charging its batteries.

❖ **Extra Capacity** A small company moved into new premises and had the foresight to allocate a large area for data center space, knowing that its data center needs would grow a lot during the coming years. At the time, the company did not have enough money to build in all the power and air conditioning capability that it would eventually need and therefore put in a temporary system that would be replaced in a year or two with the full-capacity system.

Adding the extra electrical capacity involved getting new service from the local power company to a new dedicated transformer, which meant cutting power to the building. It also involved new generators, a new ATS unit, new UPS systems, and new power-distribution panels in the data center.

The local power utility company would switch the service to the new transformer only in the middle of the day on a midweek day. The power company claimed that it would take half an hour, but the SAs at the company assumed that it would take at least 2 hours. The SAs already had a UPS, an ATS, and a generator for the data center, so planned to run on generator power during the outage. However, because the generator had sometimes proved unreliable in running under load for more than a few minutes, the SAs wisely decided to rent a second generator for the day in case their primary one stopped working.

When the second generator arrived, the SAs ran the cables from it to the ATS ahead of time, so that they would be on hand if they needed to be connected. They also had their electrical contractors on site that day to deal with that eventuality.

When the day arrived, they manually switched over to generator power a couple of minutes before the utility company cut power to the building. The generator ran fine for about ten minutes and then failed. The electrical contractors sprang into action, pulled out the failed generator's cables from the ATS, quickly connected the second generator's cables, powered up the new generator, waited for its power to stabilize, and finally switched on the electrical feed from the generator to the ATS. All the while, a person was standing by the UPS in the data center on a cell phone to another person on a cell phone, who was with the electrical contractors. The person in the data center was giving the UPS' count-down time (for power remaining) to the people downstairs, who in turn were letting him know their progress.

As in all the best action films, the drama ran to the last possible moment. The power feed from the generator to the ATS was turned on with two seconds of remaining time showing on the UPS display. The feeling of having just averted a disaster was short-lived, however. The UPS did not like the power that it was getting from the new generator, so it ran down its batteries completely and then went into bypass mode, feeding the generator power directly through to the data center.

In the rush, the three-phase power cables from the generator were connected to the ATS the wrong way around because the ATS had been mounted upside-down on the wall. So, despite having prepared very well for the event, they still had to take a small power hit later in the day when they switched back to utility power because the UPS had no battery power available during the transition.

That was not the end of the problems, however. It also turned out that the temporary electrical system had a thermal circuit breaker that was undersized and could not deal with the load of charging the UPS batteries on top of the load of the data center. After the data center was switched back to utility power and everything remained stable, the SAs started charging the UPS batteries. A few minutes later, the thermal breaker overheated and tripped. The UPS ran its batteries down again, and a few seconds before the circuit breaker had cooled down enough to be reset, the data center lost power for a second time.

The rest of the electrical cut-over involved switching to a new UPS, ATS, generators, and power distribution panels. For those remaining components, everything was comprehensively tested with load banks for a couple of weeks before the switch was made. Lots of bugs were worked out, and the switch went flawlessly.

Even if you are installing a system that you know will be temporary, you must still examine every component with the same attention to detail as if it were your permanent system. No component should be undersized. No component should be installed in a nonstandard way. Otherwise, no matter how much you try to prepare for every eventuality, the unexpected quirks of the system will bite you when you least expect it.

❖ **Smaller Cooling Solutions**   Small companies often have a computer closet with a single server and a couple small pieces of network equipment. Often, the building cooling is enough for so little equipment. However, since cooling is not provided during weekends, the first 3-day weekend of summer becomes a meltdown. Alternatively, the company grows to four or five servers, and the room overheats all the time.

In these situations, **spot coolers** can provide up to 10,000 BTU of cooling with only a standard 110 V socket and conduit to a nearby external window. Newer models reevaporate any water condensation into the exhaust air, eliminating the need to empty a condensation bucket every day. In some buildings, the exhaust hose can be directed into the ceiling space, to be exhausted by the building ventilation system.

Small units cost as little as $300. For a tiny computer closet or telecom room, this is inexpensive enough that a second unit can be purchased as a backup. Often, this can all be done at a price low enough to not require management purchase approval.

For larger rooms with five to ten racks of equipment, mobile cooling units can be rented at reasonable rates. Sometimes, a year of rental costs less than the installation and construction costs associated with permanent units.

These portable units can be rolled into a computer room and set up in an afternoon. For a small start-up, it can be reasonable to rent a 5-ton (65,050 BTU) unit for a year or two, replacing it with a larger ones as needs grow, until the company is large enough to afford a permanent solution.

The price of a cooling system can be shocking if you have previously purchased only consumer, or household, cooling units. An industrial or office unit is a very different device. A household unit is expected to run for a few hours per day during the summer months. An industrial unit runs 24/7 all year long. Because they have to run continuously, they are engineered differently, with their more reliable motors and parts driving up the price.

Once you have the appropriate amount of conditioned power in the data center, you need to distribute it to the racks. An overhead power bus is a good way to do that, giving you the option of bringing different voltages into each rack, in case you have equipment that requires nonstandard power, as some high-end equipment does. Overhead power also mitigates the risks associated with anything that may cause water to be on the floor or under a raised floor, such as a leak from an air conditioning unit or overhead pipes. Power outlets can be located away from anything that might drip on them and protected with something to deflect dripping water. Sites with raised floors must install water sensors under the floor. A builder should be able to help you locate the low spots where water will accumulate first. Sensors also should be placed under the air conditioning units.

Overhead power also provides some flexibility in how much power can be brought into a rack, as some racks may need more than others, and you should avoid running power cords between racks. Equipment that takes power from another rack may be inadvertently deprived of power if someone working in the next rack is unaware of the interrack dependency. Good practice dictates keeping everything within the rack as much as possible.

A power-distribution unit (PDU) may look like a power strip but has internal wiring that connects different sockets onto different circuits. A PDU reduces the chance of overload, whereas a simple power strip won't.

Figures 6.5 and 6.6 show two examples of overhead power infrastructure and PDUs, respectively. Figure 6.5 also shows what a neat network cable infrastructure can look like.

Some PDUs include **remote power management**, which simply means that there is a way to remotely control each individual power port. The ability to turn a particular port on or off can save a trip to the data center when a machine needs more than a basic reboot. These PDUs are very expensive, and it is difficult to justify using them for all equipment. Use of this kind of PDU is often reserved for networking equipment that connects a remote data center to the rest of the world plus the equipment required to do remote management of other equipment.

> ❖ **PDUs with Remote Power Management**   PDUs with remote power management are also common at locations with no people—**lights-out** operation—or offices that lack on-site technical personnel, such as small sales offices. Some PDUs can be controled from a Touch-Tone telephone. The ability to power cycle a host remotely can make a big difference in the time it takes to get an unreachable server back online.

The power should be properly distributed using PDUs within the rack. If there are different power sources within the data center, such as protected and unprotected power or power from two separate UPS and generator systems,

Figure 6.5 Host racks at GNAC, Inc., with a patch panel at the top and consoles wired into the patch panels. (A different color is used to differentiate console cables from network cables.)

they should be clearly identified, using different color sockets or PDUs. Many kinds of PDUs are available, including vertical and horizontal rack-mount options. If they work with your racks and equipment depths, the vertical ones can be nice, as discussed in Section 6.1.7.

In all cases, look at where the power switch on the PDU is located and how easy it is to accidentally turn off. Some PDUs have switches that are protected inside a small box that must be lifted to trip the switch. You do not want someone to accidentally cut power to the whole rack.

Figure 6.6 The GNAC, Inc., data center with prewired overhead network and power

---

Upside-Down PDUs

The technical lead at Synopsys always mounted the horizontally rack-mounted PDUs upside-down in the racks. The reason was that each PDU had a large trip switch on it that cut the power to that PDU when pushed down. He had realized that it was easy to accidentally lean on the PDU and knock the switch into the off position. However, having the unit the other way up made it much less likely that someone would accidentally knock the switch upward.

One PDU did not get mounted upside-down by a new SA, who had not been told about this practice and had not read the documentation. A few months later, as fate would have it, another SA accidentally bumped this PDU and tripped the switch, shutting down several important servers. After that, everyone made it a point to indicate this feature to all new SAs.

6.1.5 Fire Suppression

It's a good idea to have a fire-suppression system in your data center, even if local laws do not require it. Power supplies, UPS batteries, and disks can all burn out or catch on fire. Electrical wiring can develop a fault that sparks and ignites nearby materials.

Typically, local laws not only require a fire-suppression system but also are very explicit about what systems you can and can't use. This list changes continually as dangers of new systems, particularly to those in the room when they are activated, are discovered. If you do have a choice, consider the dangers to the people working in the room, environmental hazards of the system, the damage that it might do to the equipment that is not on fire, and how well that system deals with electrical fires.

Another thing to consider is whether to link activation of the fire-suppression system with a switch for turning off power in the computer room. If you are going to dump water on all the equipment, for example, you need to cut the power to the equipment first. Such a harsh method of turning off the equipment may cause some hardware fatalities but not as many as dumping water on live equipment.

Find out whether your choice of fire-suppression system will allow other equipment to continue operating. If not, can the fire suppression be localized to a small set of racks? Some systems have a preactivation facility that enables on-site staff to check on a small amount of localized smoke before the fire-suppression system activates. This feature permits staff to turn off the equipment that is smoking before a fire starts and the fire-suppression system activates fully.

In addition to the technology of your fire-suppression system, you need to put in place some important procedural components. If your fire-suppression system is linked to your operations center, you need to train the operations staff on what to do if there is an alert. If the people who are on-site 24 hours a day are not computer professionals, you need to train them on the process they should follow in response to a fire alert. If the fire-suppression system activates, you are probably going to be without fire suppression until the system is recharged; if the fire reignites after the fire-suppression system has activated, you may lose the whole building. You need a procedure to both minimize the chance of the fire reactivating and for monitoring it and dealing with it effectively if it does.

6.1.6 Racks

Equipment in a data center is generally mounted in racks. At first glance, one would think that racks aren't important. They're simply sheet metal and bolts. In fact, however, they're so important as to dictate nearly every other aspect of data centers. Racks are to data centers what your spine is to your body. Your spine determines your body's shape, which affects all other aspects. Each kind of rack has a specific purpose. Some types are better for servers; other, for network equipment.

Racks organize your equipment. Being well organized means that you can fit more computers into the same-size room. The higher density is because racks stack equipment vertically. Data centers would have to be considerably larger if machines were sitting on the floor or on tables. When machines are literally stacked on top of each other, working on a lower machine is difficult without jostling the top machines.

Racks are part of your cooling system. The airflow of the room is greatly determined by the arrangement of racks. Inside the rack itself, good airflow means that computers get cooled properly. Racks with bad internal airflow make it more difficult to cool your equipment.

Racks are part of your wiring infrastructure. Your ability to have a sane, managed cable plant is largely determined by whether your racks encourage good cable-management practices. Messy wiring is both ugly and inefficient. Without racks, cables from different machines will become tangled and often end up on the floor, being walked on, because there are no facilities for cable management. This results in cable damage and accidental disconnection of cables. It will be difficult, if not impossible, to trace cables without the risk of pulling another cable and disconnecting or damaging it.

Racks are part of your power infrastructure. PDUs generally sit inside racks. Without racks, power provisioning will be haphazard and may increase the risk of fire caused by chaining power strips. The resulting mess will be unreliable and a nightmare to support. Racks facilitate keeping power cables away from network cables, which reduces network problems.

Rack selection and layout will influence the amount and type of space you need.

A Great Rack Salesperson

When Tom built Lumeta's computer room, the rack salesperson he contacted practically designed the entire space, including cooling, power, and cable plant. The salesperson explained that if anything was wrong with the cooling, the cooling engineer would blame the racks. Same for power distribution and cable management. He figured that if people were going to blame him for cooling, power, and cables, he had to take responsibility for making sure that it was done right, too. Even though it was above and beyond what a rack salesperson usually did, and he received no compensation for it, he helped evaluate the other designs and plans for the room. Tom was very happy with the extra service and the racks!

Rack selection is not as simple as it may appear on the surface. Many factors need to be considered. The most major are the number of posts—two or four—and the height, width, and depth of the rack. You also will want to look at air circulation in the rack, strength of the rack, whether it has threaded mounting holes, and the options for the vertical rails and shelves. You need to consider whether you want fronts, backs, or sides for the racks, and what the options for cable management are.

6.1.6.1 Rack Overview

Racks are often called *19-inch racks* because of their origins in the telecommunications world, where they were 19 inches across. The vertical pieces onto which equipment is mounted are called *rails*. Usually, either two or four rails are placed 17.75 inches (0.45 meters) apart. Along with their own thickness, this traditionally totals 19 inches.[2] Modern racks have additional cable management on the sides, increasing their width.

The holes in the rails are arranged in repeating sets of three: After the first hole, the second one is 0.5 inches (12.7 mm) above it, the next is 0.625 inches (15.875 mm) above that, the next is 0.625 inch (15.875 mm) higher. The pattern repeats like that.

The vertical space of three holes is called a *rack unit*, or *U* (for unit). 1U is 1.75 inches. The height of equipment is described in terms of rack units, or Us. A disk chassis might be 4U; a large server, 8U, 16U, or even bigger. Small PC-style servers are often 2U, if they have many disks, or 1U if they don't. A device that is 1U is often called a *pizza box*, due to it's shape. A typical full-height rack is 42U.

This is confusing to new SAs, but if you mount a piece of equipment starting at the first hole in the set of three, equipment above and below will mount perfectly. Visually speaking, what looks like the first hole is usually the third hole of the previous set of three. If you start on the wrong hole, you'll find that the next piece of equipment will not line up correctly unless you leave a gap that brings it up to the first hole in the next set of three.

Better racks include marks that indicate which is the first of each group of three holes. Better racks also number each hole; if you need to find the mate of a hole on the left, you simply find the hole with the same number on the right. Without numbers, this seemingly simple task can make the smartest SA feel like an idiot when a piece of equipment is lifted into a rack only to find

---

2. See http://en.wikipedia.org/wiki/19-inch_rack.

that what visually looked correct is off by one. Amazingly enough, numbering holes is a recent innovation. (If this paragraph seems odd to you, consult an older SA.)

Older racks have threaded, round holes for bolting equipment into. These holes sometimes get dirty or damaged, and that part of the rack becomes unusable. Some rack manufacturers have a different hole size, which makes it frustrating to find the right size bolt. Racks with unthreaded holes solve this problem by simply requiring a nut and bolt. If the threads get worn, the nut and bolt are replaced.

Modern racks are boltless; they have square holes. Equipment has phalanges that protrude into the square hole diagonally. The equipment rests in the rack, held down by gravity. Larger equipment is stabilized by additional screws that secure the device from moving. Older equipment can mount in these racks with the help of a **cage nut**, a square bit of metal with a threaded hole in it. A cage nut is inserted into the square mounting hole, and the equipment is bolted into the nut's hole. When the bolt is screwed tightly into the cage nut, the nut is locked into place and is secure. If the threads of the cage nut get dirty or abused, you can replace the nut. Since you purchase the cage nuts and bolts at the same time, you know they will be of matching size. Now you simply have to be careful not to hurt your fingers when inserting the cage nuts. (A **cage nut insertion tool** and a **cage nut removal tool** can be the best $40 you've ever spent.) Boltless equipment can be mounted in older, threaded-hole racks, with adapter kits. These kits are often expensive.

6.1.6.2 Posts
The rails on each side of a rack are also known as *posts*. Racks have either two or four posts.

Two-post racks are often used for networking and telecommunication equipment, which is often designed to be center-mountable, as well as front- and/or rear-mountable. However, it is often easier and safer to mount some of the heavier networking and telecommunications equipment in a four-post rack, which provide more protection for the equipment from accidental knocks that may loosen or damage cables. Four-post racks typically provide better horizontal cable-management options.

Most server equipment is only front-mountable, although some servers have options for center or rear mounting. Front-mounted equipment in two-post racks sticks out at the back, and different-depth equipment sticks out different distances. This can be hazardous for people walking behind the racks and for the equipment. Full-depth shelves for two-post racks are center-mounted, often as two half-depth shelves, one at the front of the rack and one at the back. Having front-mounted equipment with either shelves or center-mounted equipment in the same rack or row of racks means that the effective depth of the rack, with equipment, is more than the depth of a four-post rack, in which everything lines up at the front.

Two-post racks are cheaper than four-post racks, so many sites use them. However, four-post racks are nicer to work with.

If your site decides to get two-post racks, make sure that you leave lots of space between the rows. The aisles must be wide enough to accommodate the depth of one and a half pieces of equipment plus the width of the aisle where people will walk. A minimum aisle width usually is specified in fire safety regulations. The machines can't protrude into that space. The reason for a depth of one and a half machines plus the regulation aisle width is that sufficient aisle space must be left when a deep machine is front-mounted in one rack and a center-mounted piece of equipment or a shelf in the rack is immediately behind it.

Racks may have additional feet that stick out into the aisle. This prevents them from toppling forward when servers on rails slide out.

Case Study: Insufficient Aisle Space

One company rented a cage and some racks in a data center selected on the basis of the cost of the rack space. The two-post racks didn't have much aisle space between them. Once the equipment was installed in both rows of racks, it was impossible to access the equipment in the back rack. In fact, the cables for the back row of machines were so close to the edge of the cage that they could be reached from outside the cage, which defeated the point of having a secured cage. The SAs who had to work on machines in the cage hated it but were stuck with it. The contract specified the number of racks and the size of the cage. The SAs should have measured carefully before they signed the contract.

6.1.6.3 Height
The height of the rack may have an impact on reliability if it is very tall and an SA has to stretch across other equipment to access a machine. Taller racks also may not fit beneath anything that might be attached to the ceiling,

such as power buses, cooling systems, or fire-suppression apparatus, and may not give adequate clearance for overhead air circulation or fire-suppression systems to work correctly. It may not be safe to pull roll-out shelves from the high part of the rack. On the other hand, tall racks use data center floor space more efficiently.

6.1.6.4 Width

Most equipment fits into 19-inch racks, but telecommunications equipment is usually in racks that are Network Equipment Building System (NEBS) compliant. These racks are 21 inches between poles. However, NEBS-compliant equipment tends to come in its own rack, so one need allocate space only for the rack and not worry about purchasing the rack itself. Based on the type of equipment you will have, you need to allocate an appropriate mix of spaces on your floor plans, which may include only one width, if that is appropriate.

When we have the choice, we prefer wider racks. The additional width makes cable management easier.

6.1.6.5 Depth

For four-post racks, several rack depths are available because of the various machine depths. You want to have racks that are deep enough for your equipment to fit completely inside, so that the cables are more protected from accidental knocks and so that horizontal cable management can be used within the rack where necessary. Having machines protrude into the aisles is a safety hazard and may be contravene local safety laws if it causes the aisle to be less than the regulation width. It also looks neater and more professional to have the equipment fully contained within the rack. However, if the racks are too deep, you may consume floor space too rapidly and not be able to accommodate enough equipment in the room. Having excess unused space may tempt people to mount extra equipment into the back of the rack, if they can squeeze it in. This makes it difficult to access the cables or rear panels of other machines or to perform maintenance on other machines in the rack and may cause equipment in the rack to overheat as a result of insufficient air circulation.

In an effort to pack more and more functionality into 1U servers, vendors are making them deeper and deeper. Some servers won't fit into older, shallow racks at all.

A Bad Use of Wasted Space

A company had a shortage of space in its data center while an additional data center was under construction. But in the meantime, SAs still had to install machines. The SAs realized that many of the older, free-standing machines had unused space inside where extra boards or disks could have been installed. The SAs started installing smaller machines inside the still running older machines, diligently labeling the main machine with its own name and listing the machines that were inside. It was an unusual practice and made machines more difficult to find if SAs didn't remember to look at the larger machines as additional racks. However, the only real problem was that they were consuming more power per square foot than the UPS could manage, because they had outgrown that data center. Ideally, the new data center should have been commissioned before they reached this point.

6.1.6.6 Air Circulation

Heat is drown away from equipment through air circulation. Some racks have fans built into them to increase air flow. If you are considering such racks, consider how air will reach them. They may require raised perforated floors with air pushed into the rack from below. If it is a simpler rack that does not have its own air-circulation system, you probably don't want to get doors for the front, back, or side panels, because they will restrict airflow to equipment in the rack. Having doors and side panels can make the data center look neater but also can hide many cabling sins, and it makes neat interrack wiring more difficult unless it is all prewired (see Section 6.1.7). Neat wiring is possible, as shown in Figures 6.5 and 6.7, but requires discipline.

❖ **Racks with Doors** Tom prefers racks with doors: "If the door doesn't close, you're not done." This keeps SAs from leaving dangling wires after they make changes. As it is difficult to properly cool racks with doors, he does this only for racks that don't require cooling, such as racks that contain only network patch panels.

Christine prefers no doors; she can see at a glance what has not been done correctly and get it fixed before things get out of hand.

6.1.6.7 Cable Management

Always consider cable management while purchasing a rack. Generally, you will want to buy cable-management tools at the same time. To decide what you need in this department, you should consider how you are wiring your data center, as discussed in Section 6.1.7. Consider both horizontal and

Figure 6.7 Network racks in GNAC, Inc., have patch panels in one rack and the network gear in the adjacent rack.

vertical cable-management options. Keeping cables neatly organized within and between racks is vital for being able to work efficiently without disturbing other equipment. Cleaning up a rat's nest of cables is painful and cannot be done without taking equipment down. If you don't provide reasonable cable management, people will wire equipment in all sorts of interesting ways, and you will later discover that you can't take a piece of equipment out of the rack to replace broken hardware without bringing down three other critical pieces of equipment that have nothing to do with the machine you are trying to work on.

Horizontal cable management usually screws into the mounting rails and can be open or closed. Open cable management has a series of large split hoops that all the cables go behind. Cables are slotted through the gaps in the hoops as they are run from one place to the other. The hoops keep the cables within a confined channel or area. Closed cable management consists of a channel with a cover. The cover is removed, cables are placed in the channel, and then the cover is replaced. Open cable management can look messier if not maintained well, but closed cable management often is used to hide huge loops of cables that are too long. When closed cable management fills up, it becomes difficult or impossible to replace the covers, so they are left off, and it becomes even messier than open cable management. Closed cable management is also more tedious to work with and becomes a nuisance for very little gain.

Some racks are designed to have vertical cable management as a recessed channel between the racks. Others can have it within the rack, going down the sides just inside the back posts. Others can have cable management attached only externally to the back posts. Cable management that is between the racks makes cables take up more valuable floor space. Cable management that attaches to the back of the racks protrudes into the aisles, which makes the cables more vulnerable and may be a safety concern. Cable management that goes within the rack requires racks that are deep enough to contain the cable management, in addition to the deepest piece of equipment. Wherever it is placed, the cable management can be either open or closed.

Cable management also comes in a variety of widths. A data center typically requires different widths for different rack functions. Racks that have lots of patch panels and network or console equipment will have lots of cables in them and require much wider and deeper cable management than racks that contain a few hosts with a few network and console connections. Racks with lots of wires also require lots of horizontal cable management well distributed between the pieces of equipment and the various patch panels. Having too little cable-management space is frustrating and encourages adhoc solutions that are difficult to manage. That makes it difficult to access the cables, and SAs may damage cables by trying to force them into the cable management. It is better to overestimate rather than to underestimate your space requirements.

6.1.6.8 Strength

The racks must be strong enough to carry the weight of the equipment that will be mounted in them. As stated before, earthquake zones may have special strength requirements.

6.1.6.9 Environment

If your racks are going to be deployed in remote locations, consider the atmosphere of the location. For example, in China, the pervasive use of coal results in air pollution that is high in sulfur. The sulfur leads to high water vapor content in the air, which leads to racks rusting. Special coatings are available that prevent rusting.

6.1.6.10 Shelves

Smaller equipment not designed to mount in a rack can sit on a shelf. Shelves that mount into racks are available.

Be careful how shelves and various pieces of rack-mount equipment will fit into the rack and how, or whether, you can combine different rack-mount units in the same rack or whether you can still mount shelves in the rack when a rack-mount unit requires the vertical rails to be moved forward or backward. Often, large rack-mount units need the vertical rails to be a particular distance apart so they can be attached at all four corners. In some cases, the positioning of these rails may prevent you from mounting other pieces of equipment that require a different spacing of the rails. Worse yet, the shelves may require these vertical rails to have an exact positioning that is not compatible with your rack-mount equipment. Make sure that the racks you choose allow mounting the shelves with the vertical rails in various positions. You also may want to get extra vertical rails so that you can mount a couple of units with different depths in the same rack.

6.1.6.11 Extra Floor Space

Consider how many large freestanding pieces of equipment you might have, with a footprint the size of a rack or larger, that cannot be rack-mounted. Leaving space for these items will affect the number of racks that you order and how you wire the data center.

6.1.7 Wiring

It is difficult to keep data center wiring tidy. However, when you are designing the data center, you have several ways to make it easier for all the SAs to keep the wiring neat.

Hiding the mess does not mean that it is not there or that it will not affect SAs trying to work in the data center. A raised floor can hide sloppy cabling, with cables following all sorts of random paths to go between two points. When you go to pull cables out from under the floor, you will find them tangled up in many others, and extracting them probably will be difficult. This may cause some people to simply leave them there "until later, when I have time."

Cables Under a Raised Floor

At one company, the oldest data center had a raised floor. Wiring was done under the floor as needed and old cables were never removed. They simply accumulated layer after layer. Not long after a new SA started, he set about pulling out all the unused cables from under the floor in his spare time, because some places had so many cables that it was difficult for them all to fit. He pulled out 2 miles of cable over the course of 3 months.

The biggest gain that you can make is by prewiring the racks as much as possible. Choose a section of your data center that will house only network equipment—for example, the back row. Then put a clearly labeled patch panel at the top of each rack, with more jacks than you think you will need, and clearly label the rack.

Racks should be labeled based on their row and position within the row. Put these labels high on the walls so that they can be seen from anywhere and the racks will be easy to locate. Figures 6.8 and 6.9 show this form of rack-location labeling and how it is used on patch panels.

Wire the rack's patch panel to a patch panel in your network row that has corresponding labels and is clearly labeled with the rack number. If you

Figure 6.8 Numbering high on the walls of the data center in Synopsys is used for rack naming and makes it easy to locate a given rack.

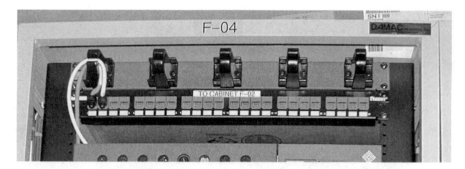

Figure 6.9 Racks at Synopsys are clearly labeled at the top and have a patch panel that indicates the rack to which it is wired.

are using serial console servers, put one of them at the top of every rack too, if they are small. If they are large, put a patch panel for the serial consoles in every rack that is connected to a console server box mounted a couple of racks away, or, increase the number of jacks you have wired to the back of the room, and put the console servers with the network equipment. An example of this is pictured in Figure 6.10.

Some sites choose to color code their network cables. At the very least, cables of different qualities (Category 5, Category 6) and cables with different wiring (straight through, crossover) should be different colors. Some sites choose to have different subnets use different colors. We recommend reserving red for networks that are "live" on the Internet with no firewall protection.

❖ **Patch Cable Tips**   The short network cables that one uses to connect from a network outlet to a machine or between two patch panels, or from a patch panel to a machine are called **patch cables**, or simply **patches**. These cables are typically 1, 2, or 3 meters long.

If you color code by network type or copper category, you should use the same color-coding system for patches. Some people prefer to make their own patches, which can be done by buying the right parts and a tool called a **crimper**. They are very inexpensive to make, an excellent justification. However, time and time again we find erratic network behavior and outages being traced to handmade cables. As networks get faster, tolerances get smaller. Making a Cat-5 cable that passes certification is very difficult. A Cat-6 cable can fail certification

Figure 6.10 Synopsys stores serial console concentrators in the network racks and uses special cables to wire them directly into the patch panel.

for minor reasons; for example, each pair of wire needs to be twisted at a specific number of twists per meter, and each twist reduces crosstalk by a certain amount. To attach the modular RJ-45 connectors on each end one must untwist each pair, but if you untwist more than a few inches the crosstalk will be high enough that the cable will fail certification. It really is that demanding. How much time do you want to spend making and re-making cables until they pass certification?

When purchased in bulk, the price of a patch is quite reasonable. We don't recommend making them by hand.

As an aside, people often wonder why each individual patch cable they purchase has two tie-wraps. Why is this? It isn't just so that they don't get tangled during transport. It isn't to annoy you when you are trying to quickly unpack a large number of cables. It is so that you can make your installation neat and clean. When you go to use the patch, undo the tie-wraps and install the cable. Now recycle the tie-wraps and use them to latch the patch to the rack or other cable-management rail. Your cables will always be tidy.

All network and console wiring for servers in a rack should stay within that rack, other than what has been prewired. Make sure that there is adequate cable-management space within the rack for the intrarack cabling. Get cables in a variety of lengths so that you will always be able to find a cable that is almost the right length. It always should be possible to find a cable that will run through the cable management with sufficient slack for sliding the machine forward a little and for seismic events. The cable should not have so much slack that it leaves a long trailing loop. If your hosts are on shelves that pull out, make sure that there is enough slack in the cables so the machines can keep functioning even when the shelves are completely extended. Cables should never run diagonally across the rack, where they will get in the way of someone working in the rack later. Make it easy for people to do the right thing by having a full selection of cable lengths in stock. Otherwise, you will have to deal with either a rat's nest of cables on the floor or a web of crisscrossing cables at the back of the rack.

The cabling in the network row will require a lot of cable management and discipline, but at least it is confined to one area. You also may be able to optimize this area if networks are common to most or all machines, such as a dedicated network for backups, an administrative network, or serial console connections. If you know that a certain percentage of connections from a rack will be going to particular destinations, you can have all those connections prewired, live, and ready to go, which will reduce entropy in your cabling. Alternatively, if you can configure your network equipment to map a particular port to a particular network, you may be able to prewire everything. A set of network patch panels is pictured in Figure 6.11.

A word of caution, however, about doing too much prewiring within your network racks. You need to be able to deal gracefully with hardware failures, so you may need to be able to rapidly move a lot of connections to a different piece of hardware while you get replacement parts. You also need to

Figure 6.11 Network racks at GNAC, Inc. (Patch panels are connected to overhead cabling to prewired patch panels at the top of each host rack.)

be able to deal with the exceptions that will inevitably crop up. Don't paint yourself into a corner by making your wiring too inflexible.

Case Study: The Payoff for Good Wiring

Prewiring a dozen network connections to every rack may sound expensive, but the payback is immeasurable. Once Tom oversaw two machine rooms in two different buildings. Only one of the rooms was prewired. In the data center that was not prewired, installing any new machine was an all-day event. Running the networking and console cables took hours, often an entire day. Over the years, the continual wear and tear on the floor tiles caused them to become wobbly and dangerous. The difficulty and danger of working in the room made SAs procrastinate. It was difficult to find a 2- to 3-hour block of free time to do an installation, especially since often it required two people. New hosts might be delayed by a week as a result. The successful installation of a host was a cause for celebration.

Conversely, the other data center was prewired with a dozen Cat5 cables to each rack drawn back to an orderly patch panel near all the network equipment. Installing a new host in this room was a breeze, usually taking less than 15 minutes. The installations were done without procrastination or fanfare. The cost of the prewiring is more than compensated for by the productivity it affords.

❖ **Cable Bundling**   In a computer room that isn't prewired, you will find yourself running a cable each time you set up a new machine. Consider making a bundle of 6 or 12 cables and running the entire bundle. It takes only a little longer than running 1 cable, and the next time a new machine is being installed, there's a good chance that there will be an unused cable available for use . We find it useful to run a bundle from the network rack/row to a rack with a lot of empty space.

To make a bundle, follow these steps.

1. Get 12 cables of the same type and length. Remove any packaging, but leave them tie-wrapped.

2. Label both ends of each cable. For example, label each end of the first cable A-1. Then label the ends of the second cable A-2. Continue until each end of every cable is labeled. (To make things easier, the next bundle can be B-1 through B-12). It is important to label them before this next step; trying to accurately label cables after they are run can take hours.

3. Find a long room or hallway without a lot of traffic.

4. Remove the tie-wrap from a cable, saving the tie. Run the cable down the hallway.

5. Repeat the process with the other cables.

6. Use the tie-wraps you've collected to bundle the cables. You should have enough wraps for one every couple of feet. Leave a meter or two free on each end.

7. That's it!

The major trade-offs for prewiring are rack-space consumption and up-front cost. But the increases in reliability, productivity, and manageability from not having to deal with rat's nests and cables crossing all over the place at the backs of the racks are huge.

Some places may not be able to prewire their racks. For example, a colocation center that will have customer equipment in the racks cannot know when building the data center what kind of equipment will be in the racks and how many connections will be leaving a set of racks to be connected to other sets of racks or to the colocation center's own network equipment.

Another trick for optimizing your cabling is to have vertical power distribution units, with lots of outlets, mounted at the sides of the racks. Buy a lot of really short power cords in a couple of lengths—for example, 1 foot and 2 feet—and plug each piece of equipment into the power socket next to it. As depicted in Figure 6.12, this avoids having long power cords trailing all over the rack next to the data cables and possibly causing interference problems in addition to the mess.

Separation of Power and Data Cables

At a site where Christine performed consultant work, an SA received a report of a network problem. The customer who reported the problem found that data transfer between two hosts was very slow. The SA verified the problem and did further tests. She found that the network interface of one of the machines was recording a lot of errors. She went down to the data center to check the cabling. It all seemed solid, and replacing the cables made no difference. While she was doing that, however, she noticed that the power cord of the machine that she had installed in a rush earlier in the day was crossing over the network cable that went into the interface that was having problems. All the other power cords were carefully kept away from network cables and neatly run through the cable management. She remembered Christine telling her about keeping network and data cables apart because of electromagnetic interference, so she took the extra minute or so to run the power cord through the cable-management system with the rest of the power cords. When she tested again, the network problem had vanished.

6.1.8 Labeling

Good labeling is essential to a smooth-running data center. All equipment should be labeled on both the front and the back with its full name as it appears in the corporate namespace (see Chapter 8) and in the console server system (see Section 6.1.10).

If a machine has multiple connections of the same kind and it is not obvious from looking at the machine which one is used for what function, such

Figure 6.12 Vertical PDUs at GNAC, Inc., with short power cables are convenient and help to keep the wiring neat.

as multiple network interfaces that belong on different networks, both the interfaces and the cables should be labeled. Color coding the network cables can also help, perhaps using a different color for each security domain.[3] For example, a firewall may have three network interfaces: one for the internal, protected network; one for the external, unprotected network; and one for a service network that is accessed from untrusted networks through the firewall. The interfaces should at least have *int*, *ext*, and *serv* next to them, and cables should have labels with corresponding tags attached. When you are debugging a problem, you will then be able to easily say, "The external network card has no link light." When you have to pull it out of the rack to

---

work on a hardware fault, you will be able to put it back in and reconnect all the cables without having to think about it or trace cables.

For high-port-density network equipment, labeling every port will be impractical. However, maintaining a label on the equipment that associates ports with networks or virtual LANs (VLANs) should be possible. For example, such a label might read "192.168.1/24: cards 1-3; 192.168.15/24: cards 4,5,8; 192.168.27/24: cards 6,7."

For network equipment that connects to WANs, both the name of the other end of the connection and the link vendor's identity number for the link should be on the label. This labeling should be on the piece of equipment that has the error lights for that link. For example, (CSU/DSU) for a T1 would have a label that reads "T1 to San Diego office" or "512K link to WAN Frame Relay cloud," as appropriate, and the T1 provider's circuit ID and telephone number. Listing the phone number saves having to find it when there is an outage.

Network equipment typically also has facilities for labeling ports in software. The software-labeling facility should be used to its full potential, providing at least as much information as is available from the physical labels. As network equipment becomes smaller and more integrated, and as detailed physical labeling becomes more difficult, the software labels will become the most convenient way to store information that you need for debugging.

Using both physical labeling and software labeling leads to having multiple sources of the "truth." It is important to make sure that they are synchronized so they give the same information. Make someone responsible for ensuring that physical and software labels match, finding out the correct information, and fixing the labels when they do not match. Nothing is worse than having multiple sources of information all disagreeing when you are trying to debug a problem. It takes diligence, time, and effort to keep labeling up to date, but it saves lots of time during an outage, when it is important to be able to respond quickly. It can also prevent accidental outages from happening when someone traces a cable to the wrong spot.

Labeling both ends of every cable becomes tedious, especially when cables get reused and old labels must be removed and new ones attached. Cables are also notoriously difficult to label because not many labels stick well to their PVC shells over the long term. A useful alternative is to get prelabeled cables that have their type and their length encoded into the label, along with a unique sequence number, and have the same label at each end. Your cable vendor should be able to do this for you, including tracking the sequence numbers. You then have an easier way of finding the other end of the cable—if you know approximately where it is already—rather than tracing it. Even if you have to trace it, you can confirm that you have the right cable before disconnecting it, by checking the numbers. Another alternative is to find cable ties with a flat tab at the end that normal labels will stick to. The cable ties can be permanently attached to either end of the cable, and labels on the tabs can be changed relatively easily.

If you are labeling the cables by hand, label them before you run the cables. This bears repeating: Label, then run. Otherwise, you will spend half a day playing guessing games until all the runs are labeled. We know this from experience.

Policy for Enforcing Labeling Standards

Eircom has a very strict labeling policy. Servers must be labeled front and back, and every power cord must be labeled at the far end with the name of the machine it is attached to. Network cables are color coded rather than labeled. The policy is briefly and clearly described in a sign on the data center wall (see Figure 6.13). Periodic sweeps to check labels are made; any server or power cord that is not labeled will be removed. This policy makes it very clear that any resulting problems are the fault of the person who installed the machine without labeling it or the power cord, rather than the fault of the person who disconnected the machine. Because these sweeps happen frequently, however, machines that do not comply with labeling standards are typically disconnected only before they have gone into production.

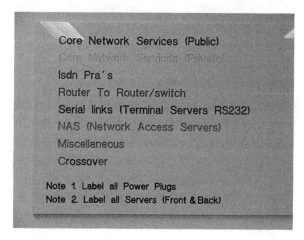

Figure 6.13 The Eircom data center sign showing the cabling and labeling policy.

6.1.9 Communication

SAs working in the data center often need to communicate with customers, other SAs outside the data center, and vendors. The SAs may need someone else to test whether a problem has been fixed, someone to monitor service availability, or someone to find information, equipment, or another person. Sometimes, vendors prefer to talk someone through a diagnostic procedure.

We recommend that some communication method be provided. Some SAs carry radios or mobile phones to facilitate communication, because many SAs are rarely at their desks. Mobile phones with push-to-talk features are becoming more and more popular. However, radios and mobile phones often do not work well in data centers because of high levels of electromagnetic interference or, at some sites, because of RF shielding. Simple telephone extensions sometimes work better. In these situations, we recommend putting a telephone at each end of a row of racks, with a cord to the receiver long enough to enable SAs to work on any part of the row and still be able to talk on the phone, if necessary (see Figure 6.14).

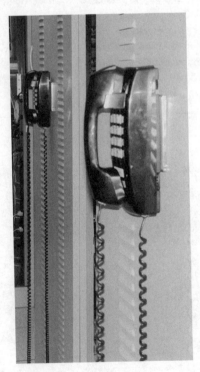

Figure 6.14 SAs at Synopsys all have radios but find that phone extensions at the end of each row work better in the data center. (Note the extremely long cord.)

❖ **Warning: Mobile Phones with Cameras**   Rented colocation facilities often forbid cameras and therefore forbid mobile phones that include cameras.

6.1.10 Console Access

Certain tasks can be done only from the console of a computer. Console servers and KVM switches make it possible to remotely access a computer's console. For an in-depth discussion, refer to Section 4.1.8.

Console servers allow you to maintain console access to all the equipment in the data center, without the overhead of attaching a keyboard, video monitor, and mouse to every system. Having lots of monitors, or heads, in the data center is an inefficient way to use the valuable resource of data center floor space and the special power, air conditioning, and fire-suppression systems that are a part of it. Keyboards and monitors in data centers also typically provide a very unergonomic environment to work in if you spend a lot of time on the console of a server attached to a head in a data center.

Console servers come in two primary flavors. In one, switch boxes allow you to attach the keyboard, video monitor, and mouse ports of many machines through the switch box to a single keyboard, video, and mouse (KVM). Try to have as few such heads in the data center as you can, and try to make the environment they are in an ergonomic one.

The other flavor is a console server for machines that support serial consoles. The serial port of each of these machines is connected to a serial device, such as a terminal server. These terminal servers are on the network. Typically, some software on a central server controls them all (Fine and Romig 1990) and makes the consoles of the machines available by name, with authentication and some level of access control. The advantage of this system is that an SA who is properly authenticated can access the console of a system from anywhere: desk, home, and on the road and connected by remote access. Installing a console server improves productivity and convenience, cleans up the data center, and yields more space (Harris and Stansell 2000).

It can also be useful to have a few carts with dumb terminals or laptops that can be used as portable serial consoles. These carts can be conveniently wheeled up to any machine and used as a serial console if the main console server fails or an additional monitor and keyboard are needed. One such cart is shown in Figure 6.15.

Figure 6.15 Synopsys has several serial console carts that can be wheeled up to a machine if the main console server fails or if the one machine with a head in the machine room is in use.

6.1.11 Workbench

Another key feature for a data center is easy access to a workbench with plenty of power sockets and an antistatic surface where SAs can work on machines: adding memory, disks, or CPUs to new equipment before it goes into service or perhaps taking care of something that has a hardware fault. Ideally, the workbench should be near the data center but not part of it, so that it is not used as temporary rack space and so that it does not make the data center messy. These work spaces generate a lot of dust, especially if new hardware is unboxed there. Keeping this dust outside the data center is important.

Lacking space to perform this sort of work, SAs will end up doing repairs on the data center floor and new installs at their desk, leading to unprofessional, messy offices or cubicles with boxes and pieces of equipment lying around. A professionally run SA group should look professional. This means having a properly equipped and sufficiently large work area that is designated for hardware work.

> ❖ **People Should Not Work in the Data Center**   Time and time again, we meet SAs whose offices are desks inside the data center, right next to all the machines. We strongly recommend against this.
>
> It is unhealthy for people to work long hours in the data center. The data center has the perfect temperature and humidity for computers, not people. It is unhealthy to work in such a cold room and dangerous to work around so much noise.
>
> It is also bad for the systems. People generate heat. Each person in the data center requires an additional 600 BTU of cooling. That is 600 BTU of additional stress on the cooling system and the power to run it.
>
> It is bad financially. The cost per square meter of space is considerably more expensive in a data center.
>
> SAs need to work surrounded by reference manuals, ergonomic desks, and so on: an environment that maximizes their productivity. Remote access systems, once rare, are now inexpensive and easy to procure.
>
> People should enter the room only for work that can't be done any other way.

6.1.12   Tools and Supplies

Your data center should be kept fully stocked with all the various cables, tools, and spares you need. This is easier to say than to do. With a large group of SAs, it takes continuous tracking of the spares and supplies and support from the SAs themselves to make sure that you don't run out, or at least run out only occasionally and not for too long. An SA who notices that the data center is running low on something or is about to use a significant quantity of anything should inform the person responsible for tracking the spares and supplies.

Ideally, tools should be kept in a cart with drawers, so that it can be wheeled to wherever it is needed. In a large machine room, you should have multiple carts. The cart should have screwdrivers of various sizes, a couple of electric screwdrivers, Torx drivers, hex wrenches, chip pullers, needle-nose pliers, wire cutters, knives, static straps, a label maker or two, and anything else that you find yourself needing, even occasionally, to work on equipment in the data center.

Spares and supplies must be well organized so that they can be quickly picked up when needed and so that it is easy to do an inventory. Some people hang cables from wall hooks with labels above them; others use labeled bins of varying sizes that can be attached to the walls in rows. A couple of these arrangements are shown in Figures 6.16 and 6.17. The bins provide a more compact arrangement but need to be planned for in advance of laying out the racks in the data center, because they will protrude significantly into the aisle. Small items, such as rack screws and terminators, should be in bins or small drawers. Many sites prefer to keep spares in a different room with easy access from the data center. A workroom near the data center is ideal. Keeping spares in another room may also protect them from the event that killed

Figure 6.16 Various sizes of labeled blue bins are used to store a variety of data center supplies at GNAC, Inc.

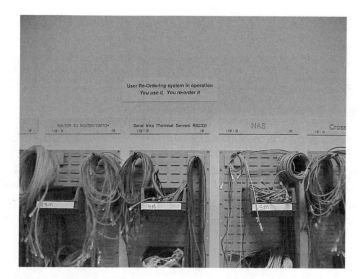

Figure 6.17 Eircom uses a mixture of blue bins and hanging cables.

the original. Large spares, such as spare machines, should always be kept in another room so that they don't use valuable data center floor space. Valuable spares, such as memory and CPUs, are usually kept in a locked cabinet.

If possible, you should keep spares for the components that you use or that fail most often. Your spares inventory might include standard disk drives of various sizes, power supplies, memory, CPUs, fans, or even entire machines if you have arrays of small, dedicated machines for particular functions.

It is useful to have many kinds of carts and trucks: two-wheel hand-trucks for moving crates, four-wheel flat carts for moving mixed equipment, carts with two or more shelves for tools, and so on. Mini-forklifts with a hand-cranked winch are excellent for putting heavy equipment into racks, enabling you to lift and position the piece of equipment at the preferred height in the rack. After the wheels are locked, the lift is stable, and the equipment can be mounted in the rack safely and easily.

6.1.13 Parking Spaces

A simple, cheap, effective way to improve the life of people who work in the data center is to have designated parking spaces for mobile items. Tools that are stored in a cart should have their designated place on the cart labeled. Carts should have labeled floor space where they are to be kept when unused. When someone is done using the floor tile puller, there should be a labeled spot to return the device. The chargers for battery-operated tools should have a secure area. In all cases, the mobile items should be labeled with their return location.

Case Study: Parking Space for Tile Pullers

Two tile pullers were in the original Synopsys data center that had a raised floor. However, because there was no designated place to leave the tile pullers, the SAs simply put them somewhere out of the way so that no one tripped over them. Whenever SAs wanted a tile puller, they had to walk up and down the rows until they found one. One day, a couple of SAs got together and decided to designate a parking space for them. They picked a particular tile where no one would be in danger of tripping over them, labeled the tile to say, "The tile pullers live here. Return them after use," and labeled each tile puller with, "Return to tile at E5," using the existing row and column labeling on the walls of the data center. The new practice was not particularly communicated to the group, but as soon as they saw the labels, the SAs immediately started following the practice: It made sense, and they wouldn't have to search the data center for tile pullers any more.

6.2 The Icing

You can improve your data center above and beyond the facilities that we described earlier. Equipping a data center properly is expensive, and the improvements that we outline here can add substantially to your costs. But if you are able to, or your business needs require it, you can improve your data center by having much wider aisles than necessary and by having greater redundancy in your power and HVAC systems.

6.2.1 Greater Redundancy

If your business needs require very high availability, you will need to plan for redundancy in your power and HVAC systems, among other things. For this sort of design, you need to understand circuit diagrams and building blueprints and consult with the people who are designing the system to make sure that you catch every little detail, because it is the little detail you miss that is going to get you.

For the HVAC system, you may want to have two independent parallel systems that run all the time. If one fails, the other will take over. Either one on its own should have the capacity to cool the room. Your local HVAC engineer should be able to advise you of any other available alternatives.

For the power system, you need to consider many things. At a relatively simple level, consider what happens if a UPS, a generator, or the ATS fails. You can have additional UPSs and generators, but what if two fail? What if one of the UPSs catches fire? If all of them are in the same room, they will all need to be shut down. Likewise, the generators should be distributed. Think about bypass switches for removing from the circuit, pieces of equipment that have failed, in addition to the bypass switch that, ideally, you already have for the UPS. Those switches should not be right next to the piece of equipment that you want to bypass, so that you can still get to them if the equipment is on fire. Do all the electrical cables follow the same path or meet at some point? Could that be a problem?

Within the data center, you may want to make power available from several sources. You may want both alternating current (AC) and direct current (DC) and power, but you may also want two different sources of AC power for equipment that can have two power supplies or to power each half of a redundant pair of machines. Equipment with multiple power supplies should take power from different power sources (see Figure 6.18).

❖ **High-Reliability Data Centers**   The telecommunications industry has an excellent understanding about how to build a data center for reliability, because the phone system is used for emergency services and must be reliable. The standards were also set forth when telecommunication monopolies had the money to go the extra distance to ensure that things were done right. Network Equipment Building System (NEBS) is the U.S. standard for equipment that may be put in a phone company's central office. In Europe, the equipment must follow the European Telecommunication Standards Institute (ETSI) standard. NEBS and ETSI set physical requirements and testing standards for equipment, as well as minimums for the physical room itself. These document in detail topics such as space planning, floor and heat loading, temperature and humidity, earthquake and vibration, fire resistance, transportation and installation, airborne contamination, acoustic noise, electrical safety, electromagnetic interference, electrostatic discharge (ESD) immunity, lightning protection, DC potential difference, and bonding and grounding. We only mention this to show how anal retentive the telecom industry is. On the other hand, when was the last time you picked up your telephone and didn't receive a dial tone in less than a second? The

Figure 6.18 GNAC, Inc., brings three legs of UPS power into a single power strip. Redundant power supplies in a single piece of equipment are plugged into different legs to avoid simultaneous loss of power to both power supplies if one leg fails.

NEBS and ETSI standards are good starting places when creating your own set of requirements for a very-high-availability data center.

For a high-availability data center, you also need good process. The SAS-70 standard applies to service organizations and is particularly relevant to companies providing services over the Internet. SAS-70 stands for Statement of Auditing Standards No. 70, which is entitled "Reports on the Processing of Transactions by Service Organizations." It is an auditing standard established by the American Institute of Certified Public Accountants (AICPA).

6.2.2 More Space

If space is not at a premium, it is nice to have more aisle space than you need in your computer room to meet safety laws and to enable you to move equipment around. One data center that Christine visited had enough aisle space to pull a large piece of equipment out of a rack onto the floor and wheel another one behind it without knocking into anything. Cray's data center in Eagan, Minnesota, had aisles that were three times the depth of the deepest machine. If you are able to allocate this much space, based on your long-term plans—so that you will not have to move the racks later—treat yourself. It is a useful luxury, and it makes the data center a much more pleasant environment.

6.3 Ideal Data Centers

Different people like different features in a data center. To provide some food for thought, Tom and Christine have described the features each would like in a machine room.

6.3.1 Tom's Dream Data Center

When you enter my dream data center, the first thing you notice is the voice-activated door. To make sure that someone didn't record your voice and play it back, you are prompted for a dictionary word, which you must then repeat back. The sliding door opens. It is wide enough to fit a very large server, such as an SGI Challenge XL, even though those servers aren't sold any more. Even though the room has a raised floor, it is the same height as the hallway, which means that no ramp is required.

The room is on the fourth floor of a six-story building. The UPS units and HVAC systems are in the sixth-floor attic, with plenty of room to grow and plenty of conduit space if additional power or ventilation needs to be brought to the room. Flooding is unlikely.

The racks are all the same color and from the same vendor, which makes them look very nice. In fact, they were bought at the same time, so the paint fades evenly. A pull-out drawer at the halfway point of every third rack has a pad of paper and a couple of pens. (I never can have too many pens.) Most of the servers mount directly in the rack, but a few have five shelves: two below the drawer, one just above the drawer, and two farther up the rack. The shelves are at the same height on all racks so that it looks neat and are strong enough to hold equipment and still roll out. Machines can be rolled out to do maintenance on them, and the cables have enough slack to permit this. When equipment is to be mounted, the shelves are removed or installed on racks that are missing shelves. Only now do you notice that some of the racks—the ones at the far end of the room—are missing shelves in anticipation of equipment that will be mounted and not require shelves.

The racks are 19-inch, four-post racks. The network patch-panel racks, which do not require cooling, have doors on the front and open in the back. The racks are locked together so that each row is self-stable.

Each rack is as wide as a floor-tile: 2 feet, or one rack per floor tile. Each rack is 3 feet deep, or 1.5 floor tiles deep. A row of racks takes up 1.5 tiles, and the walkway between them takes an equal amount of space. Thus, every three tiles is a complete rack and walkway combination that includes one tile that is completely uncovered and can therefore be removed when access is required. If we are really lucky, some or all rows have an extra tile between them. Having the extra 2 feet makes it much easier to rack-mount bulky equipment (see Figure 6.19).

The racks are in rows that are no more than 12 racks long. Between every row is a walkway large enough to bring the largest piece of equipment through. Some rows are missing or simply missing a rack or two nearest the walkway. This space is reserved for machines that come with their own rack or are floor-standing servers.

If the room is large, it has multiple walkways. If the room is small, its one walkway is in the middle of the room, where the door is. Another door, used less frequently, is in the back for fire safety reasons. The main door gives an excellent view of the machine room when tours come through. The machine room has a large shatterproof plastic window. Inside the room, by the window, is a desk with three monitors that display the status of the LAN, WAN, and services.

The back of each rack has 24 network jacks cable certified for Cat-6 cable. The first 12 jacks go to a patch panel near the network equipment. The next 12 go to a different patch panel near the console consolidator. Although the consoles do not require Cat-6 copper, using the same copper consistently means that one can overflow network connections into the console space. If perhaps fiber may someday be needed, every rack—or simply every other rack—has six pairs of fiber that run back to a fiber patch panel. The popularity of storage-area networks (SANs) is making fiber popular again.

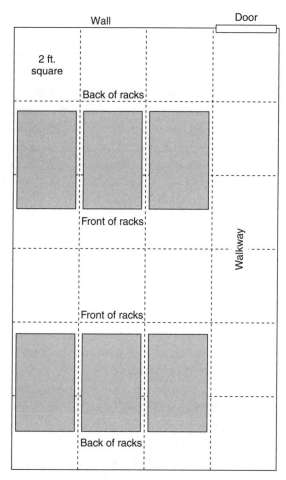

Figure 6.19 Simple floor plan that provides open space

The last row of racks is dedicated for network equipment. The patch panels have so much wire coming into them that they can never be moved, so this row is in the far back corner. Also, in this part of the room is a table with three monitors and keyboards. Two are for the KVM switch; the third connects to the serial console concentrator directly. One rack is dedicated to connections that go out of the room. Near it is a row of fiber-to-copper adapters. Vendors now make a single unit that supplies power to many such adapters that slide into it, thus eliminating the rat's nest of power cables and power bricks.

The network equipment rack also has a couple of non-UPS outlets. They are colored differently and are well labeled. Sometimes, the UPS will be down, but the network must be up, and the redundant power supplies can be plugged into these non-UPS outlets.

Air conditioning is fed under the floor. Every other floor tile in the walkways has pin holes to let air out. The tiles under each rack have large holes to let air in, so air can flow up the back of each piece of equipment. The system forces the air with enough pressure to properly cool every rack. The cold air flows up the front of the rack, and each machine's fans pull the air toward the back of the rack. Rows of racks alternate which is front and which is back. That is, if you walk down an aisle, you'll see either all fronts or all backs. The aisle with all fronts is a "cold row" and receives the cold air from holes in the floor. The aisle with all backs is a "hot row" and receives the hot air coming from the backs of the machines, which is then exhausted up and out the room through vents in the ceiling.

Along the left and right sides of the back of each rack is a PDU with widely spaced outlets. Each pair of racks is on a different circuit that comes from the UPS. Each circuit is marked with a circuit number so that redundant services can be placed on different circuits.

Every cable is labeled on each end with a unique number, and every host is labeled with name, IP address, and MAC address. The two label printers in the room are labeled with the room number of the data center and a warning that stealing the device will lead to certain death.

Also under the floor are cable trays, with separate ones for power and for networking. Because power and networking are prewired, there should be little need to ever open the floor.

Outside the machine room through the other door is a work area. It is separated from the main room to keep out the dust. This room has wide wire shelves that hold new machines being installed. There are workbenches with power sockets and an antistatic surface where repairs can be done without doing more damage to the equipment. Also in this room is a set of drawers filled with tools, spare parts, and bins of cables of various lengths and types. There are 20 extra pairs of wire cutters, 40 extra Phillips screwdrivers, and 30 extra flathead screwdrivers. (At the rate they are stolen, that supply should last a year.)

This ends our tour of Tom's dream data center. As you leave, the tour guide hands you a complimentary Linux box.

❖ **The Floor Puller Game**   Here's a great game to play in a wide open space in a room with a raised floor, such as the open area behind the desk at a helpdesk. This game should be played when your boss isn't around. You will need two people and one floor puller.

Each person sits or stands at a different end of the room. One player throws the floor puller at a tile. If it sticks, the player removes the tile and accumulates it in a pile in his or her end of the room. The two players alternate, taking turns until all the floor tiles are missing. You must walk on the grid and not touch the floor below the tiles. If you fall into the floor, you must return a floor tile to one place. When all the tiles are removed, whoever has the larger pile of floor tiles wins.

If you play this enough, the edges of the tiles will be damaged in a year, and you will need to purchase a new floor. We don't recommend that you play this game, but if you are in the business of installing and repairing raised floors, teaching it to your customers might increase your sales. (You didn't hear that from us!)

6.3.2 Christine's Dream Data Center

Christine's dream data center has double doors that are opened with a hands-free security system, such as proximity badges or voice activation, so that it is easy for people carrying equipment to get access. The double doors are wide enough to get even the largest piece of equipment through and is on the same level as, and is convenient to, the receiving area, with wide corridors between the two.

The data center has backup power from a generator with enough capacity to hold the machines and lighting in the data center, the HVAC system, the UPS charging, the phone switches, the SA work area, and the customer service center. The security-access system is also on the protected power system. The generator has large tanks that can be refueled while it is running. The generator is tested once a week.

An ATS is tunable for what is considered to be acceptable power.[4] A UPS protects the data center and has enough power to run for 30 minutes, which

---

4. Christine once saw an ATS that found utility power acceptable when the UPS didn't, so the UPS ran off batteries, and the generator didn't get switched on—what a nightmare.

should be enough to manually switch to a backup generator, provided that the backup generator is there already.

The data center does not have a raised floor. The air is pumped in from overhead units. The room has a high ceiling with no tiles. The room is painted matte black from a foot above the racks, with drop-down lights that are at the level where the black paint starts. This makes the overhead HVAC inconspicuous.

An overhead power bus supports two power sources—different UPS, ATS, generator, and power distribution panels and power bus for each, with different physical locations for each set of equipment, but that couldn't be justified for the average site data center.

The data center is prewired with one 36-port, 2U patch panel at the top of each rack, brought back to racks in the network row. In the network row, patch-panel racks are interspersed between racks that hold the network equipment. There is lots of wire management.

The data center has 7-foot-tall, four-post racks (black), with 19-inch-wide rack-mount spaces that are 36 inches deep with no backs, fronts, or sides. They have threaded mounting holes, and the sides of the shelves mount onto vertical rails, which can be moved just about anywhere. The shelves are not as deep as the racks—just 30 inches—to leave room for cables that are plugged into the machines and PDUs and vertical wire management within the racks. Extra vertical rails can be moved for rack mounting different-depth equipment. The racks have vertical PDUs with lots of outlets down one side. If different power sources are in the machine room, the racks have power available from both. Lots of 1- and 2-foot power cables are available, so no power cords dangle. Vertical wire management goes down the other side and horizontally on an as-needed basis. Several short stepladders are available so that vertically challenged SAs can reach the top.

The data center has network patch cables from 3 feet to 10 feet at every 1-foot interval, plus a few that are 15, 20, 25, 30, 35, 40, 45, and 50 feet long. All network cables are prelabeled with unique serial numbers that also encode length and type. There are blue bins for storing all the various kinds of cables and connectors in the data center where it is convenient.

The machines are labeled front and back with the DNS name. Network interfaces are labeled with the network name or number.

A couple of carts with drawers have all the tools you could possibly need. There are battery-powered screwdrivers, as well as manual ones. Each cart has a label maker. A work area off the machine room has a nice wide bench, lots of power, and static protection. Sets of tools are kept to hand in there also.

6.4 Conclusion

A data center takes a lot of planning to get right, but whatever you build, you will be stuck with it for a long time, so it is worth doing right. A badly designed, underpowered, or undercooled data center can be a source of reliability problems; a well-designed data center should see you safely through many problems.

Power, air conditioning, and fire-suppression systems are relatively immutable key components of the data center. They can also have the greatest effects if they go wrong. Messy wiring is something that everyone has experienced and would rather not have to deal with. With good advance planning, you can reduce your nightmares in that area.

Access to the room for getting equipment in and moving it around is another key area that you need to plan in advance. And along with access comes security. The data center is a business-critical room that holds a lot of valuable equipment. The security-access policies must reflect that, but the mechanism selected should be convenient for people with armloads of equipment to use.

Building a good, reliable data center is costly but has significant payback. However, you can do simple, inexpensive things to make the data center a nicer and more efficient environment to work in. Everyone appreciates having a convenient place to work on broken equipment with all the tools, spares, and supplies that you need on hand, and, relatively speaking, the cost for that is very low. Labeling all equipment well and having designated parking spaces for mobile resources will provide you with inexpensive time-saving benefits. Seek ideas from the SAs; all of them will have features that they particularly like or dislike. Incorporate the good ones, and learn from the negative experiences of others.

For companies with lots of space, it is nice to make the data center more spacious than it needs to be. And for those with lots of money and very high reliability requirements, you can do much with the key systems of power and air conditioning to add greater redundancy that will make the room even more reliable.

To get the most out of a data center, you need to design it well from the start. If you know that you are going to be building a new one, it is worth spending a lot of time up front to get it right.

Exercises

1. What natural disasters might occur in your area? What precautions have you taken for natural disasters, and what improvements could you make?

2. What problems have you found with your racks? What would you like to change?

3. Could you make use of prewiring in your current data center, if you had it? If not, what would you have to do to make it useful? How much do you think prewiring would help in cleaning up the wiring in your data center?

4. What is the power capacity of your data center? How close are you to reaching it?

5. If you have separate power circuits from different UPSs in your data center, how well are they balanced? What could you do to balance them better?

6. How much space is occupied with monitors in your data center? How many could you pull out with the use of serial console servers? How many could you pull out by deploying KVM switch boxes?

7. Where do you work on broken machines? Is there an area that could be turned into a workbench area?

8. What tools would you want in a cart in the data center?

9. What supplies do you think you would want in the data center, and how many of each? What should the high and low supply levels be for each item?

10. What spares would you want, and how many of each?

11. What equipment do you have that is always "walking off"? Can you think of good parking spaces for it?

Chapter 7

Networks

A site's network is the foundation of its infrastructure. A poorly built network affects everyone's perception of all other components of the system. A network cannot be considered in isolation. Decisions made as part of the network design and implementation process influence how infrastructure services are implemented. Therefore, the people who are responsible for designing those services should be consulted as part of the network design process.

We cannot explain every detail of network design and implementation in this short chapter. Entire shelves of books are devoted to the topic. However, we can relate the points we have found to be the most important. An excellent starting point is Perlman (1999). For Transmission Control Protocol/Internet Protocol (TCP/IP), we recommend Stevens (1994) and Comer (2000). To understand how routers and switches work, see Berkowitz (1999). Berkowitz (1998) also has written a book on network addressing architectures. For more information on specific technologies, see Black (1999). For WANs, see Marcus (1999) and Feit (1999). For routing protocols, see Black (2000). Other books concentrate on a single protocol or technology, such as Open Shortest Path First (OSPF) [Moy 2000, Thomas 1998a]; Enhanced Interior Gateway Routing Protocol (EIGRP) [Pepelnjak 2000]; Border Gateway Protocol (BGP) [Stewart 1999, Halabi and McPherson 2000]; Multi Protocol Label Switching (MPLS), VPNs, and QoS [Black 2001, Guichard and Pepelnjak 2000, Lee 1999, Vegesna 2001, Keagy 2000, and Maggiora et al. 2000]; multicast [Williamson 2000]; Asynchronous Transfer Mode (ATM) [Pildush 2000]; and Ethernet [Spurgeon 2000].

Networking is an area of rapid technological development, and therefore the approaches and implementation possibilities change significantly over the years. In this chapter, we identify areas that change over time, as well as some of the constants in the networking realm.

187

This chapter is primarily about an e-commerce organization's internal LANs and WANs, but we also look at a campus environment.

7.1 The Basics

When building a network, your basic goal is to provide a reliable, well-documented, easy-to-maintain network that has plenty of capacity and room for growth. Sounds simple, doesn't it?

Many pieces at different layers combine to help you reach—or fail to reach—that goal. This section discusses those building blocks, covering physical-network issues, logical-network topologies, documentation, host routing, routing protocols, monitoring, and administrative domains. This section also discusses how components of the network design interact with one another and with the design of the services that run on top of the network.

WAN and LAN designs differ significantly. Over time, cyclic trends make them more similar, less similar, then more similar again. For example, at one time, it was popular for LAN topologies to be dual-connected rings of Fiber-Distributed Data Interface (FDDI) connections to provide fault tolerance. This lost popularity as Fast (100MB) Ethernet arose, which was a bus architecture. Meanwhile, WANs were adopting ring architectures, such as synchronous optical network (SONET) and multiwavelength optical network (MONET). In early 2007, draft proposals for 10GB Ethernet LAN technology return to ring architectures. We have come full circle.

7.1.1 The OSI Model

The Open Systems Interconnection (OSI) reference model for networks has gained widespread acceptance and is used throughout this chapter. The model looks at the network as logical layers and is briefly described in Table 7.1.

Network devices decide the path that data travels along the physical network, which consists of cables, wireless links, and network devices (*layer 1*). A network device that makes those decisions based on hardware or MAC address of the source or destination host is referred to as a *layer 2 device*. A device that makes decisions based on the IP (or AppleTalk or DECnet) address of the source or destination host is known as a *layer 3 device*. One that uses transport information, such as TCP port numbers, is a *layer 4 device*.

Engineers more familiar with TCP/IP networking often simplify this as follows: layer 1, the physical cable; layer 2, devices that deal with a particular

Table 7.1 The OSI Model

Layer	Name	Description
1	Physical	The physical connection between devices: copper, fiber, radio, laser
2	Data link	Interface (or MAC) addressing, flow control, low-level error notification
3	Network	Logical addressing (e.g., IP addresses) and routing (e.g., RIP, OSPF, IGRP)
4	Transport	Data transport, error checking and recovery, virtual circuits (e.g., TCP sessions)
5	Session	Communication-session management (e.g., AppleTalk name binding, or PPTP)
6	Presentation	Data formats (e.g., ASCII, Unicode, HTML, MP3, MPEG), character encoding, compression, encryption
7	Application	Application protocols, e.g., SMTP (email), HTTP (web), and FTP (file transfer)

LAN; layer 3, the routers and gateways that route packets between LANs; layer 4, the protocol being used.

Layer 5 is a layer that doesn't map well into the world of TCP/IP. Layer 6 is the data format: ASCII, HTML, MP3, or MPEG. Encryption and compression are usually handled here also.

Layer 7 is the application protocol itself: HyperText Transfer Protocol (HTTP) for web serving, SMTP for email transmission, IMAP4 for email access, File Transfer Protocol (FTP) for file transfer, and so on.

The OSI model is a useful guideline for understanding the way networks are intended to work, but many layering violations occur in the real world. For example, a VPN connection made through an HTTPS proxy is sending layers 3 and 4 traffic over a layer 7 application protocol.

❖ **Layers 8, 9, and 10** A common joke is that the OSI model has three additional layers:

- Layer 8: User
- Layer 9: Financial
- Layer 10: Political

Many corporate network architectures focus on solving problems at layer 10 but are limited by layer 9 in what they can achieve.

7.1.2 Clean Architecture

A network architecture should be as clean and simple to understand as it can
be. It should be possible to briefly describe the approach used in designing the
network and draw a few simple pictures to illustrate that design. A clean architecture makes debugging network problems much easier. You can quickly
tell what path traffic should take from point A to point B. You can tell which
links affect which networks. Having a clear understanding of the traffic flow
on your network puts you in control of it. Not understanding the network
puts you at the mercy of its vagaries.

A clean architecture encompasses both physical- and logical-network
topologies and the network protocols that are used on both hosts and network
equipment. A clean architecture also has a clearly defined growth strategy for
both adding LAN segments and connecting new remote offices. A clean network architecture is a core component behind everything discussed later in
this chapter.

Case Study: Complexity and Vendor Support

A network architecture that can't be explained easily makes it difficult to get support
from vendors when you have a problem. A network administrator discovered that
the hard way. When an outage in an overly complicated network occurred, anyone
he talked to, either locally or at a vendor, spent a lot of time trying to understand
the configuration, let alone come up with suggestions to fix the problem. Calling
vendor support lines wasn't very useful, because the front-line support people could
not understand the network being debugged; sometimes, the vendor simply had
difficulty believing that anyone would use such a complicated design! After being
escalated to higher levels of customer support, he was told that the products weren't
supported in such odd configurations and was urged to simplify the design rather
than push so many different vendors' products to their limits.

Case Study: Complexity and Support by Network Administrators

When debugging a complicated network, the network administrator at one site found
herself spending more time figuring out what network paths existed than debugging
the problem. Once the network architecture was simplified, problems were debugged
in less time.

We recommend limiting the number of network protocols on a given WAN. Most networks have done this in recent years, migrating all data networks to TCP/IP rather than trying to mix it with Novell IPX, AppleTalk, and other protocols. If needed, those protocols can be tunneled over TCP/IP, using various encapsulation protocols. This approach is also less expensive than having a different WAN for each protocol.

7.1.3 Network Topologies

Network topologies change as technologies and cost structures change, as well as when companies grow, set up large remote offices, or buy other companies. We introduce some of the common topologies here.

One topology often seen in wide-area, campus-area, and local-area networks is a *star*, whereby one site, building, or piece of network hardware is at the center of the star, and all other sites, buildings, or networks are connected to the center. For example, a single building or a campus might have one layer 2 or layer 3 device to which all hosts or all networks are connected. That device is the center of a star. A LAN with a star topology is illustrated in Figure 7.1. For a WAN, if all wide-area connectivity is brought into one building, that building is the center of the star, as illustrated in Figure 7.2. A star topology has an obvious single-point-of-failure problem: A failure at the center of the star disrupts all connectivity between the points of the star. In other words, if all hosts in a building are connected to a single switch,

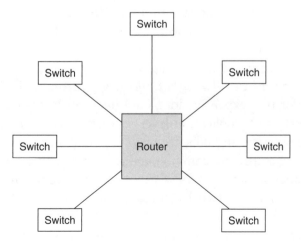

Figure 7.1 A local-area or campus-area network with a star topology

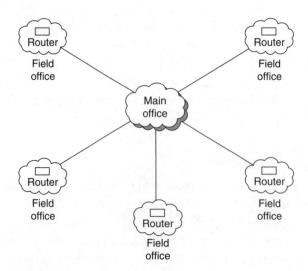

Figure 7.2 A wide-area network with a star topology

all connectivity is lost. If all wide-area sites are connected through one building that loses power, they cannot communicate with one another or with the site they connect through, but communication within each individual wide-area site still works. However, a star topology is easy to understand, simple, and often cost-effective to implement. It may be the appropriate architecture to use, particularly for relatively small organizations. One simple improvement on this design is to have each link be redundant between the two end points and have a spare for the center point.

A common variant of the star topology consists of multiple stars, the centers of which are interconnected with redundant high-speed links (Figure 7.3). This approach limits the effects of a failure of a single star-center point. Companies with geographically disparate offices often use this approach to concentrate all long-distance traffic from a single geographic area onto one or two expensive long-haul lines. Such a company also typically provides lots of application-layer services at each star-center site to reduce long-haul traffic and dependence on the long-distance links.

Ring topologies also are common and are most often used for particular low-level topologies, such as SONET rings. Ring topologies are also found in LANs and campus-area networks and are sometimes useful for WANs. In a ring topology, each network entity—piece of network hardware, building, or site—is connected to two others so that the network connectivity forms a ring,

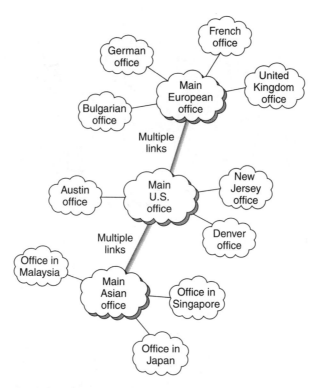

Figure 7.3 A multiple-star topology for a WAN, based on geographic hubs

as shown in Figure 7.4. Any one link or network entity can fail without affecting connectivity between functioning members of the ring. Adding members to the ring, particularly in a WAN, can involve reconfiguring connectivity at multiple sites, however.

Another architecture that sites concerned about redundancy and availability use looks like a multistar topology, but each leaf node[1] has a backup connection to a second star center, as shown in Figure 7.5. If any star-center node fails, its leaf nodes revert to using their backup connections until the primary service has been restored. This hybrid model permits an organization to manage cost/reliability trade-offs for each site.

---

1.   A leaf node is a network entity that handles only traffic originating at or destined for local machines and does not act as a conduit for other traffic. In a simple star topology, every node except the center node is a leaf node.

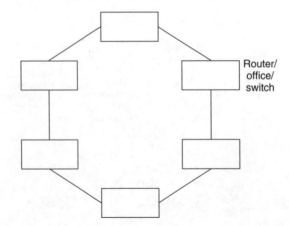

Figure 7.4 A ring topology, with each network device connected to two others

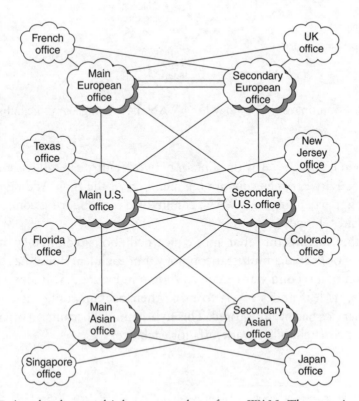

Figure 7.5 A redundant multiple-star topology for a WAN. The core is a ring, for reliability. Small sites connect in star topology for cost and simplicity.

Many other network topologies are possible, including the *chaos* topology, which largely describes the topology of the Internet. A chaotic topology ensues when each node can pick any one or more willing upstream nodes to use as a path to the rest of the networks. However, you cannot expect anyone to accurately describe or draw a connectivity map for a chaotic network without the aid of complicated mapping software. Attempts to produce maps of the Internet have generated interesting and useful pictures (Cheswick's 1998).

An architecture that cannot be drawn or described without aids is not clean. The Internet survives, however, because it is highly adaptive and fault tolerant: The rest does not stop working because of an outage elsewhere. In fact, outages occur all over the Internet all the time, but because they are small and affect only specific, usually downstream, sites, they go unnoticed by the greater network. That is not true in a corporate or university network, where each part is often heavily dependent on other parts. The chaos approach is not a reliable model to use in a network where availability of every component matters.

What is normally drawn as the network map is the **logical network topology**. It generally shows only network devices, such as routers, that operate at layer 3 and above, and represents each subnetwork that is handled by one or more layer 2 devices, such as switches, as a single entity. The logical-network topology that makes the most sense for any given site varies with technologies and cost structures. Differing logical-network maps of a single network may sometimes be drawn depending on what specific features need to be highlighted for the audience.

A simple rule of thumb about limiting network complexity is that a site's network architects and senior network administrators should all be able to sketch, without aids, the key features and basic structure of the network topology. If other sources of information are needed, the architecture is not clean and easy to understand.

The logical-network topology cannot be designed in isolation. It influences, and is influenced by, other aspects of the computing infrastructure. In particular, the logical-network design, its physical implementation, and the routing topologies that will be used across that network are all interdependent. In addition, the architecture of network services, such as email, Internet access, printing, and directory services, must influence and be influenced by the network architecture.

Case Study: Inconsistent Network Architecture

A large multinational computer manufacturing company needed to redesign its WAN to bring it up to date with current technologies. Both the implementation of the physical intersite connectivity and the routing architecture for the site were to be re-designed. The new routing protocol was chosen relatively quickly by evaluating the constraints and requirements. The physical architecture—in particular, the bandwidth between certain key sites—was later chosen independently of the routing protocol choice. The metrics used by the routing protocol for path determination were not taken into consideration.[2] As a result, some high-bandwidth links were underused, and some low-bandwidth connections suffered delays and packet loss as a result of overuse. Incorrectly sizing the connections is an expensive mistake to make.

  The network must be considered as a unit. Choices made in one area affect other areas.

Case Study: Network Services Design

A large multinational software company had a core-services team, a field office team, and a network team that worked closely together. The network team determined that it would connect small field offices to the corporate backbone through small, inex-pensive, wide-area links. Redundancy through Integrated Services Digital Network (ISDN) backup connections would be provided at a later date, so network hardware that would be able to accommodate a backup ISDN link was used from the outset. Based on this decision and discussions with the network team, the core-services and field office teams decided to make the field offices as independent as possible so that they would be able to conduct the majority of their business while connectivity to the corporate backbone was unavailable.

  Each field office, however small, had a server that handled local email, authentica-tion, name service, file service, and printing, as well as a remote access box configured to fall back to a local authentication server if it could not contact the primary corpo-rate authentication server. This architecture worked well because the field office sites were almost fully functional even when they were cut off from the rest of the com-pany. For the few tasks requiring connection on to another site, ordinary corporate remote access was available, if necessary.

  If all the field offices had had high-speed redundant connectivity to the corporate backbone, they could have chosen an alternative service architecture that relied on that network connectivity more heavily, though this would have been much more expensive.

The star, multistar, and ring topologies described previously can appear at the physical level, the logical level, or both. Other topologies that are common

---

2. The protocol chosen did not take bandwidth into consideration, only hop-counts.

at the logical-network level include a flat network topology, a functional group–based topology, and a location-based topology.

A flat topology is one big network of all layer 2 devices; in TCP/IP terms, just one big switched area, one big broadcast domain. No routers. A *broadcast domain* means that when one machine sends a broadcast to that network, all machines on that network receive the broadcast. A flat topology has only one network address block with all the machines in it. All services, such as file, print, email, authentication, and name services, are provided by servers on that network.

In a location-based topology, layer 2 networks are assigned based on physical location. For example, a company might build a layer 2 network on each floor of a building and use layer 3 devices to connect the floors. Each floor of the building would have a layer 2 switch, and each switch would have a high-speed connection to a layer 3 device (router). All the machines on the same floor of a building would be in the same network address block. Machines on different floors would be in different network address blocks and communicate through at least one layer 3 device.

In a functional group–based topology, each member of a functional group is connected to the same (flat) network, regardless of location, within reason. For example, a building may have four LANs: sales, engineering, management, and marketing. Network ports at each group member's desk would be patched from wiring closet to wiring closet, potentially across interbuilding links, until reaching a place where there was a layer 2 switch for that network. The group network typically also includes file, name, and authentication services to that group on that same network, which means that the network would also extend into the data center. One or more layer 3 devices connect the group network to the main company network, which also provides services to the group network, such as email, intranet, and Internet access. Some of the services provided on the group network, such as authentication and name services, will exchange information with master servers on the main company network.

7.1.4 Intermediate Distribution Frame

An **intermediate distribution frame** (IDF) is a fancy name for a wiring closet. This distribution system is the set of network closets and wiring that brings network connectivity out to the desktops. The need for IDFs and how to design them and lay them out have not changed rapidly over time. The technologies and wiring specifics are what change with time.

New innovations in network hardware require higher-quality copper or fiber wiring to operate at increased speeds. If you use the newest, highest-specification wiring available when you build your cable plant, it is reasonable to expect it to last for 5 years before networking technology outpaces it. However, if you try to save money by using older, cheaper, lower-specification wiring, you will need to go through the expense and disruption of an upgrade sooner than if you had selected better cabling. Sites that tried to save money by installing Category 3 copper when Category 5 was available paid heavily to convert their cable plants when Fast Ethernet became commonplace.

> ❖ **Cable Categories**   Category 3 cable is rated for 10M Ethernet up to 100 meters. Category 5 is rated for 100M (Fast Ethernet) up to 100 meters. Category 6 is rated for 1,000M (Gigabit Ethernet) up to 90 meters. Catogory 7 is required for the new 10 Gigabit Ethernet standard. All these are backward compatible. They are commonly abbreviated to Cat3, Cat5, and so on.

More modern IDFs make it easy to connect the cable coming from a network jack to the proper network. One simply connects a short patch cable from an RJ-45 socket that represents that jack to the RJ-45 socket of the Ethernet switch on that network.

Older IDFs make such connections by using a **punch block.** Rather than modular RJ-45 connectors, the wires of each cable are individually punched, or connected, to terminals. The other side of the terminal is connected to a wire that connects to the destination network. Each network jack may require four or eight punches. We recommend using patch panels, not punch blocks, for networking.

Making a connection between two IDFs can be done in two ways. One way is to run bundles of cables between IDFs within a building. However, if there are large numbers of IDFs, the number of links can make this very expensive and complicated to maintain. The other way is to have a central location and run bundles from IDFs only to this central location. Then, to connect any two IDFs, one simply creates a cross-connect in the central location. This central location is referred to as a **main distribution frame** (MDF) and is discussed later.

You generally get a chance to lay out and allocate space for your IDFs only before moving into a building. It is difficult and expensive to change at a later date if you decide that you did the wrong thing. Having to run from one floor to another to debug a network problem at someone's desk is frustrating and time consuming. You should have at least one IDF per floor, more if the floors are large. You should align those IDFs vertically within the building— located in the same place on each floor so that they stack throughout the building. Vertical alignment means that cabling between the IDFs and the MDF is simpler and cheaper to install, and it is easier to add cabling between the IDFs at a later date, if necessary. It also means that support staff need to learn only one floor layout, which eases the support burden. Likewise, if a campus consists of several similar buildings, the IDFs should be located at the same place in each of them. Figure 7.6 illustrates the connections between the IDFs and an MDF.

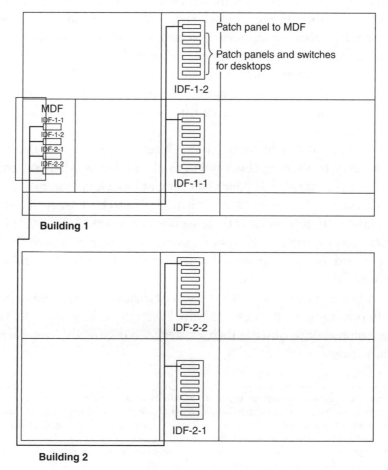

Figure 7.6 A patch panel in each IDF connects back to a patch panel in the MDF.

The IDFs should be numbered with the building, floor, and closet numbers. The closet numbers should be consistent across all the floors and all the buildings. Network jacks that are served by the IDFs should be labeled with the IDF number and a location number.[3] If multiple network jacks are at a single location, a common convention is to use letters after the location number. The location numbers and letters must correspond to the location number and letters on the corresponding jacks in the IDF. When that numbering is inconsistent or nonexistent, debugging desktop network problems becomes very difficult. Color coding multiple jacks in a single location works well for people who are not color blind but can cause problems for those who are. If you want to color code the jacks, you should also use letters to avoid those problems. Each wiring closet should have, solidly mounted on the wall, a permanent, laminated floorplan for the area that it serves, showing the locations and location numbers of the network jacks. You will be surprised how often it gets used. It is also a good idea to install a small whiteboard in dynamic locations to track changes. For example, in an IDF that serves training rooms that are used for both in-house and customer training, a whiteboard could be used to track rooms for classes, dates, attendees, and network connections. The board should also have an area for free-form text for tracking current issues.

IDFs always should be locked and subject to restricted access. It is easy to wreak havoc in a wiring closet if you think you know what you are doing but have not been trained. If your environment has a high volume of changes made by a team with large turnover, it is advisable to have frequent, but brief, wiring-closet training classes. If these sessions are regularly scheduled for the same time and location each month, people who have access to the closets but rarely work in them can attend whenever they feel the need and keep up to date with what is happening.[4]

Security is another reason for IDFs to be locked. IDFs are good places to hide network snooping devices, typically having little human traffic and lots of other equipment to obscure their existence. IDFs are also easy targets for malicious changes.

---

3. A location is a network drop point, where one or more cables are terminated. Typically, an individual office or cubicle will have a single location number corresponding to a single point in the room that has one or more network jacks. But a larger room, such as a conference room, may have multiple network drops and therefore multiple location numbers.

4. We suggest monthly meetings in fast-growing environments so that new people get training shortly after joining. More static environments may want to have such training less frequently.

The IDF closets themselves should be larger than you expect to need for your networking equipment but not so large that people will be tempted to store servers or noncomputer equipment there. The IDF closet should contain only the network equipment for the area that it serves. If stored in unexpected places, such as wiring closets, servers are more likely to suffer problems as a result of accidental knocks or cable disconnections and will be more difficult to locate when they do have problems.

Sometimes, more people have access to the wiring closets than the server room. Perhaps some trusted, trained people from your customer base may have access to the closet to bring ports live in a lab that has a high equipment turnover, for example. Very large labs may be configured similarly to an IDF and even be labeled as one in network diagrams. That should bring sufficient networking to the lab. In some situations, smaller labs can be configured as substations of the IDF by connecting the IDF to a network switch in the lab via a high-speed connection.

Wiring closets should be on protected power. Network equipment, like all computer equipment, should be protected from power spikes and surges. If your data center is on UPS, so too should the network equipment in the wiring closets, which are an extension to your data center. You don't want the embarrassing situation in which there is a power outage and your data center and people's computers are up, but the intervening network devices are down. Considering that laptops have batteries, and desktop computers are often connected to small, single-person UPSs, having the network be up during power outages is becoming more and more important. (For more on UPS and power issues, see Section 6.1.4.)

IDF closets should have special cooling beyond what the building air conditioning can supply. Network equipment is compact, so you will have lots of heat-generating devices packed into a small area. Network devices are typically robust, but they do have operating limits. A small IDF closet can get very hot without extra cooling.

You should also provide remote console access to all the devices located in the IDFs that support that functionality. The console ports on all devices should be appropriately protected using strong authentication, if available, or passwords at a minimum.

It is less expensive to install jacks at construction time than to add them one at a time afterward as needed. Therefore, it is reasonable to install at every desk one or two more jacks than you think any of your customers will ever need. The expensive part of wiring an office is not the cables but the construction cost of ripping up walls. If the jacks can be installed at construction time, considerable cost savings can be achieved.

Dead Presidents

When rewiring a building, the construction costs tend to dominate all others. The phrase used in the industry is that the cost of the installation dominates; thus, it doesn't matter whether you are "filling the walls with Category 5 copper or dead presidents," slang for dollar bills.

Rather than trying to determine, for example, that engineering offices will have more jacks than marketing offices, install the same number of jacks at every desk, and have the same number in the ceiling. Initial location assignments are never permanent. Over time, engineers will end up in what used to be the marketing area, and you will need to bring the cable plant in that area up to the standard of the rest of the engineering locations.

Similar economics are true when running fiber to the desktop. Fiber to the desktop is very rare, often seen only in research facilities. As with copper, the expensive part is the construction work required to open the walls. However, another expensive part is **fiber termination**, which involves polishing the end points and attaching the proper connector; this work is very difficult and expensive. If one must run fiber, do it before the walls are built or when the walls are open for another project. Run fiber to each desktop, but terminate only the runs that are going to be in use immediately. Later, if more desktops require fiber connections, terminate at that time. The termination cost is less than the cost and disruption of new fiber runs to the IDFs.

Cabling should be tested after it is installed. Vendors have sophisticated test equipment and should be able to provide a book of test printouts, one page per network jack. The graph will have a line or mark that indicates loss; above that point indicates that the jack is not certified. We recommend including in the installation contract that such a book will be delivered as a condition of payment. It is the only way to know that such testing was performed. We have seen companies install cabling without doing any testing.

To evaluate a vendor, ask for a customer reference and a past deployment that you can visit, examine the work, and talk with the customer. Look at the work that was performed, look for neatness in the IDFs. Ask to see the vendor's test book. Building wiring is expensive and is not a place for cost savings. Fixing a problem later is much more expensive than fixing it while the installers are still on site. Saving a few dollars at installation time is not worth the pain of debugging seemly random network problems. It is not uncommon to find faults, particularly with the second or third jacks at a desk, years after the wiring contractor has left, and realize that the network jack could never have worked or passed a test.

Case Study: The Value of Cable Test Printouts

A company in Oregon maintained a catalog of the cable tests performed on every jack in its campus. When inconsistent or difficult-to-reproduce problems were reported with a particular jack, the company found that a quick review of the jack's test results usually revealed that it had passed the quality tests only marginally. The debugging process would be short-circuited by trying a different jack and labeling the old jack as "do not use." The connections for the bad jack would be scheduled for retermination. The added cost of paying to receive the full book of test results easily paid for itself in a short period of time.

The short cable from the jack to the device is called a **patch cable**. As discussed in Section 6.1.7, we recommend buying premade patch cables rather than making them by hand. A bad cable can create reliability problems that seem random and difficult to track down. Replacing a handmade patch cable with one professionally made and tested can magically improve otherwise unsolved reliability issues.

Something else to consider about installing network jacks is their orientation. Jacks are installed in some kind of termination box or faceplate, which determines which way the jacks face. If the faceplate is flush, a cable that plugs into it will stick out from the wall, requiring space to make sure that the cable is not bent or crimped. Make sure that space is available. Termination boxes tend to be mounted on the wall and therefore stick out. If the jacks are on the side of the box, they can face up, down, left, or right. Jacks that face upward become buckets that catch dust and construction particles. That's bad. If jacks face down, it can be difficult for people to see how to insert cables into them, and loose connections will fall out. That's not good either. Therefore, we recommend having the jacks on the left or right of the termination box.

7.1.5 Main Distribution Frame

The main distribution frame connects all the IDFs. There should always be plenty of spare cabling between the MDF and the IDFs, as new connections are often needed, and running new fiber or copper between floors is expensive and best done in batches. An MDF, like an IDF, is an extension of your data center and should have similar levels of physical security, power protection, and cooling.

It is not uncommon for part of the data center to be the MDF. In such cases, the MDF is often referred to as the **network row**, or **network racks**. Patch panels in these racks connect to a patch panel at the top of each rack in the data center, as shown in Figure 7.7. Data center layout is described in detail in Chapter 6. At sites with multiple smaller computer rooms, each one often has a built-in IDF.

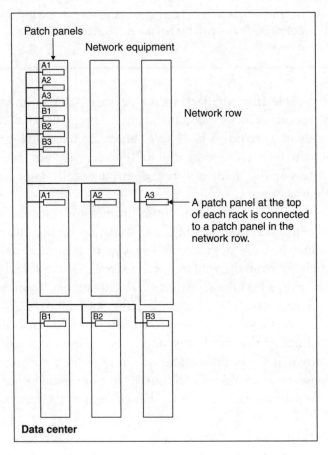

Figure 7.7 A patch panel in each data center rack connects back to a patch panel in the MDF or network row.

Multibuilding campuses tend to arrange their IDFs and MDFs in one of two ways. Smaller campuses connect each IDF to a single MDF in a central building. Alternatively, each building may have an MDF and a master MDF that connects all the MDFs. Hybrid solutions are common, whereby a smaller building is considered an annex to the nearest large building and connects its IDFs to the larger building's MDF.

7.1.6 Demarcation Points

A demarcation point is the boundary between your organization and a utility company, such as a telephone company or network provider. The demarcation point can be a fiber cabinet, a set of punch-down blocks, a board in a rack, a piece of network hardware, or a small plastic box[5] on the wall, with a jack or socket for plugging in a cable. The telephone company is responsible only for the wiring up to its demarcation point (demarc). If you have a fault with a line, you need to be able to point out where the correct demarc is so that the service engineer doesn't end up trying to test and fix another operational line. You also need to be able to test your cabling from the demarc all the way back to the network equipment. The main thing to know about your demarcation points is where they are. Make sure that they are properly labeled.

7.1.7 Documentation

Network documentation takes on many forms, the most fundamental of which is labeling. The need for documentation and the forms it should take are not likely to change with time.

Maps of both the physical and logical networks should be part of the network documentation. The physical-network map should show where the wires go and the end points or ranges of wireless links. If redundancy was part of the physical-network design, it should clearly indicate and document the physically diverse paths. The amount and type of connectivity available for each link should be indicated. For example, if 200 pairs of copper wires and 20 pairs of fiber-optic cables connect a pair of buildings, the documentation should specify how both sets are rated and terminated and the distances between the termination points.

The logical-network map should show the logical-network topology, with network numbers, names, and speeds. This map should also show any

---

5. Often termed a *brick*, or a *biscuit*.

routing protocols and administrative domains that vary across the network. Both the physical- and logical-network maps should reach to the perimeter of the organization's network and identify its outer boundaries.

Labeling is the single most important component of the network documentation. Clear, consistent labeling on patch panels and long-distance connections is particularly important. A patch panel should clearly indicate the physical location of the corresponding patch panel or jacks, and each of the connections on the patch panel should be clearly and consistently labeled at both ends. Long-distance connections should clearly indicate where the circuit goes, whom to report problems to, and what information will be required when reporting a problem, such as the circuit ID and where it terminates. Placing this label immediately beside the unit's fault-indicator light can be helpful. Doing so eliminates the need to trace cables to find the necessary information when a fault occurs. For example, one might otherwise have to trace cables from a channel service unit/data service unit to the punch-down block at the telephone company's demarcation point or to a jack on the wall.

Less permanent connections, such as the network connection for each host on the network, also should be labeled. Labeling on each wire is easier to maintain in a relatively static environment and more difficult to maintain in a highly dynamic one. You should attempt to do this level of labeling only if you can maintain it. Incorrect labels are worse than none at all.

A compromise between no labels and full cable labeling is to purchase cables with a unique serial number shown at each end. With a serial number, you can quite quickly trace exactly where a cable goes, if you have an approximate idea of the location of the other end. The serial number label can also indicate length and the way that the cable is wired. For example, the first two digits can indicate straight-through, crossover, twisted-pair, FDDI, or other wiring arrangements, followed by a dash, three digits indicating the cable length, another dash, and the serial number. Colored covers on the connectors can also be used to indicate cable type.

Network cables are often difficult to label. One of the most effective ways we have seen is to use a cable tie with a protruding flat tab to which standard sticky labels can be affixed. It is securely attached and can be easily altered.

The other key location for documentation is online, as part of the configuration of the network devices themselves. Wherever possible, comment fields and device names should be used to provide documentation for the network administrators. Naming standards for devices can go a long way toward making network administration easier and more intuitive.

Case Study: Naming Conventions

A midsize multinational software company used a multistar topology for its wide-area connectivity. One of the star centers was in Mountain View, California. The router at each remote site that connected to Mountain View was called `location2mtview`: for example, `denver2mtview` or `atlanta2mtview`. The router at the Mountain View end of the connection was called `location-router`: for example, `denver-router` or `atlanta-router`, in addition to any other names that it might have. When a remote site, suffered connectivity problems, everyone could immediately identify which routers served that site, without resorting to network maps or tracing cables. This standardization vastly improved the level of support that remote sites could expect from the average SA. All those capable of performing basic network debugging were given read-only access to the network equipment and were able to perform basic diagnostics before handing the problem to the network team.

Routers usually permit a text comment to be recorded with each interface. For WAN connections, this comment should include all the information a technician needs in an emergency involving the link going down: the name of the vendor providing the link, the vendor's phone number, the circuit identifier, and the maintenance contract number that the vendor needs to provide service. For LAN connections, include the name of the subnet and the contact information for the owner of the subnet, if it is not the main SA team. If your LAN equipment has a comment field for each port, use it to indicate the room number and jack at the other end of the cable.

7.1.8 Simple Host Routing

Leave routing to the routers; don't configure hosts to route. Hosts should be configured with a default gateway (route). Keep things simple. Routing within a site should be simple, deterministic, predictable, and easy to understand and diagnose.

UNIX systems can be configured to speak many of the same routing protocols as your router, such as Routing Information Protocol (RIP, RIPv2). In the old days, when all the hosts on a TCP/IP network ran some form of UNIX, it was common that every host spoke to RIP to determine where to send a packet. For the 99 percent of hosts that had only one network interface card (NIC), this was wasteful because a lot of CPU resources and network bandwidth would be used to generate a huge routing table that simply said to use the single NIC for any outgoing packets. This practice was also dangerous. Many LAN outages were caused by a customer misconfiguring a host, which would then broadcast incorrect routing information. All other hosts would listen to this information and abide by it, often losing their ability to communciate with the rest of the network.

If your router supports it, configure it to not send routing protocols on LANs that don't need it. This prevents hosts accidentally configured to speak routing protocols from doing so and prevents malicious users from injecting false or bad routing information.

A host that is single-homed—has a single network interface—should have a single default route and it should not listen to any dynamic routing information. A host that is multihomed should not route packets from other hosts but should accept only traffic addressed to it. This host should have a static routing table, not listen to dynamic routing information, and should be configured as simply as possible. A multihomed host that is connected to networks A, B, and C and needs to communicate with another host on network B should use its network interface that is connected to network B to communicate with that host. This path is the simplest, most obvious, and most direct. In the absence of compelling reasons to do otherwise, all traffic to networks that are not directly connected to the multihomed host—that is, to hosts that are not on networks A, B, or C—should be directed to a single static default router. This is the simplest routing configuration for a multihomed host. Occasionally, it may be necessary to have some additional static routes on the multihomed host to direct traffic along preferred paths. For example, the multihomed host may be configured to send traffic for network D via a router on network C and to send traffic for networks other than A, B, C, or D via a router on network A. However, it is best to avoid even this much complexity, when possible.

Simple host routing makes debugging network problems easier and more predictable because routing is more deterministic. When every host on a network is configured the same way, they should all behave the same way. When hosts listen to dynamic routing, the unexpected can happen. Worse yet, when hosts actively participate in dynamic routing, an environment can become completely unpredictable. If possible, enforce the policy that hosts cannot participate in your dynamic-routing infrastructure, using any security or authentication mechanisms that the protocol provides.

Case Study: Problems from Complex Host Routing

A large multinational computer manufacturer ran routing software on all the desktops and servers in the company at a time when basic routing protocols were still under development. Whenever any device on the network sent out incorrect or rogue information, every machine was affected. The company also had persistent problems with incompatibilities between its implementation and a network device vendor's implementation of some protocols. If the hosts on the network had used simple, static host routing, these problems would not have arisen.

Requiring hosts to perform routing also leads to a performance problem. As the number of routes in a network grows, the routing protocol updates become more difficult to process. We have seen large networks on which every host pauses every 300 seconds as RIP broadcasts are sent out and simultaneously processed by all hosts on a LAN. If a subnet contains exactly one router, it need not broadcast the routing protocol to that subnet; that is, it can use **passive mode**. In fact, if the routing protocol uses broadcasts, also known as **advertising,** a noticeable performance issue can arise even if the hosts are not configured to speak to any routing protocols. Not only do the broadcasts consume network bandwidth, but also every host on a subnet stops to process the broadcasts even if the processing is to simply throw the packet away.

7.1.9 Network Devices

The building blocks of any modern network should be dedicated network devices, such as routers and switches, rather than general-purpose hosts that have been configured to do routing. These network devices should be designed to perform only tasks directly related to pushing packets, managing the traffic, and the device itself. These devices should not be all-purpose devices that are configured to handle only network traffic, and they should most definitely not be devices that are also trying to perform other tasks or to provide additional services.

Before a network router device existed, sites configured a UNIX system with multiple Ethernets to perform routing functions. Later, Cisco and other companies started selling routers and other network devices based on custom hardware and firmware. Network devices are optimized to move packets as quickly as possible. They reduce packet delay, or latency; they integrate better into network-management tools; they provide better monitoring facilities;

and they are simpler devices, which means that they are less prone to failure, because they have fewer moving parts.

Packet routing is done in the kernel, which means that it gets higher priority over all other functions. If you have a file server that is also your router, you'll notice that the more network traffic it is processing, the slower the file service will be. The kernel time is often unaccounted for by system tools; we have seen performance problems that were undetectable by the usual profiling tools because CPU cycles were being quietly stolen by the kernel to route traffic.

Case Study: Central Host

One computer hardware manufacturer[6] had a network built around a single multi-homed host that primarily routed traffic. However, because it was a multipurpose machine and was conveniently multihomed on all key networks, other services were added to it over time. Sometimes, these other services had problems or became overloaded, resulting in loss of network connectivity or serious network performance problems.

When the time came to replace that machine with a different dedicated machine, the work was considerably more difficult than it should have been. The new hardware routed only packets. It was not a multipurpose machine. All the other services that ran on the old central machine had to be tracked down and rearchitected for an environment in which they would not be running on a single machine that touched every network.

Firewalls have gone through a similar evoluton. Originally, firewalls were servers or workstations with special software to add filtering functionality to the operating system. Only later did prebuilt firewall appliances reach the market. These appliances had the benefit of being able to handle larger amounts of traffic without slowing down and innovated by adding many features. OS-based firewalls then caught up, and the two have played feature leapfrog ever since. The downside of an OS-based approach is that it can be tempting to put additional services directly on the machine, which increases the possibility of introducing a security hole. We prefer a firewall to simply filter and not also be a file server, email server, and Swiss army knife. OS-based systems are often custom or home-brew solutions that are unmaintainable

---

6. A manufacturer who, ironically, designed and built boxes dedicated to providing a single service well across the network.

after the designer has left the company. On the other hand, OS-based solutions are usually more flexible and often have new features sooner than appliances. In general, we prefer dedicated firewall appliance devices.

Computers and network hardware have different upgrade regiments. Once a network device is working, one avoids software upgrades and configuration changes unless they are required. Application servers are more frequently upgraded, reconfigured, and rebooted. The tension between two competing regiments on one machine causes stress for everyone involved.

Even as the UNIX workstation community seems to have finally moved away from using workstations and servers as routers, we see a disturbing trend whereby such vendors as Microsoft, Novell, and Apple are encouraging the use of general-purpose machines as routers, firewalls, or RAS devices. We feel that this is a mistake that should not be repeated.

Too Many Eggs in a Basket

In 2004, a small business with offices around the world rolled out a new computing and network architecture that included putting at each office an Apple OS X server, which was used as the Internet router/firewall, as well as being the email server, file server, and web server for the division. A problem with any application on the server became a problem for all applications on the server. A bug in the file server software could be fixed only by an occasional reboot of the entire system. If the hard drive failed, the office was disconnected from the Internet and couldn't order a replacement. Urgent security patches and software upgrades were being delayed because of fear that they might break one of the other services. If too many people were surfing the web, the file service slowed down and caused domino effects that were difficult to trace.

Tom was brought in to bring stability to the network. It took months to migrate all offices to dedicated firewall devices, but soon, applications were decoupled from networking/firewalling. Although he changed little else, the improvement in stability was easy to measure.

❖ **Home Routers**   Configuring a Linux or FreeBSD system as a router for your home network is an excellent way to learn about networking and firewalls. However, outside of that one special case, we recommend a consumer-grade home router appliance for the home. For $50 to $100, you can purchase one that will be about as functional, and the power savings will pay for itself. It doesn't have a fan, and the lack of noise will be appreciated, too.

7.1.10 Overlay Networks

An overlay network is a logical topology that rides on top of a physical topology. Examples include VLAN, Frame Relay, and ATM. This lets us design simple physical architectures that can support whatever complexity we require in the logical overlay yet maintain simplicity on the physical layer.

You can build a very simple—and therefore stable—flat physical network and then construct overlay networks on top of the solid base to give the appearance of the more complicated connections that are needed. On the WAN level, this could mean that all sites have a single connection to the ATM or Frame Relay cloud. The Frame Relay or ATM switches are then configured to provide virtual connections—circuits—between sites. For example, each remote office might have a virtual circuit to the main office. If any two remote sites exchange a lot of traffic, it is then a simple matter of changing the switch configurations so that a virtual circuit is added between those two sites. In fact, a common configuration is called a **full mesh**, whereby each site has a virtual connection to all other sites. The benefit is that the main site is then not burdened with that traffic passing through it, and the company did not have to go to the delay and expense of having a new physical circuit installed. Another wide-area example is the use of encrypted tunnels—virtual private networks—across the Internet. A company can simply give each site a firewall, a VPN device, and an Internet connection and build its WAN over the Internet. An ISP can also use this approach to build and maintain one solid infrastructure that is literally sold time and time again to different customers.

On the LAN level, an overlay network usually means creating a simple, flat physical topology and using IEEE 802.1q VLAN protocols to overlay the subnetworks that the customers need. For example, each IDF can connect to the MDF, using high-speed redundant links, all mediated at layer 2 (Ethernet link layer), using the spanning tree protocol.

Case Study: Large LAN Using VLANs

The largest single-building LAN that Tom ever experienced included nearly 100 IDFs and supported 4,000 people throughout the building. All IDFs were connected exclusively to a single MDF. Even if two IDFs were on the same floor, the connection went from one IDF, up to the MDF, then back down to the other IDF. This simplicity meant that to connect two IDFs, the connection passed through the MDF. Although this sounds wasteful when the IDFs were sometimes only one floor away, it is much better than the nightmare that would have existed if they had chosen to create direct connections between all IDFs.

One aspect was, however, painful to maintain. Some customers needed their sub-networks to appear in a single IDF or a couple of IDFs; other customers needed theirs to appear in nearly every IDF. Every subnetwork was individually tied back to the MDF as needed. For example, if a jack was requested in a wing served by an IDF that didn't already include the necessary subnetwork, fiber was allocated between that IDF and the MDF, a hub in that IDF was allocated, and the new hub was connected to that subnet's hub in the MDF. This made the first request for a subnet in any part of the building take a long time. As the network grew to include hundreds of subnetworks, it became a nightmare to maintain. It was difficult even to track which subnets appeared in which IDFs, huge amounts of manual labor were required nearly every time a new jack was activated.

The replacement for this network maintained the same physical plant but replaced the individual fibers with overlays on a large flat network. A large Fast Ethernet switch was installed in each IDF. Each switch was connected to larger switches in the MDF. These connections were redundant Gigabit Ethernet connections. Although this was a huge flat network from a layer 1 perspective, VLANs were overlaid onto it at layer 2. Then, network change requests involved configuration changes on the switches, which were done without a walk to the closet. To bring a particular subnet to an IDF, an SA did not have to allocate and connect fiber pairs; instead he configured the appropriate VLAN to extend into that IDF and configured the switch in the IDF to provide that VLAN to the appropriate port. The result was a greatly reduced cost of maintenance and quicker response to requests for change.

This design is future-proofed. The links to the MDF can be replaced by faster technology (as long as future technologies work on the type of fiber that was installed and support VLANs). If new technology brings back ring topologies, the ring could follow the star-shaped pattern of the IDFs and the switches become nodes on the ring.

VLAN and overlay networks make it very difficult to draw network topology diagrams accurately. We recommend that you draw two diagrams: one depicting the physical topology and another depicting the logical networks.

7.1.11   Number of Vendors

Using equipment from many vendors can add unnecessary complexity to managing the network. The more vendors whose equipment is on the network, the more interoperability problems you are likely to experience, as well as extra overhead for the network administration staff to learn the configurations and quirks of the diverse equipment and to track software upgrades and bugs. Minimizing the number of vendors makes the network more reliable and easier to maintain. It also gets the company bigger discounts on the equipment, thanks to larger volume purchasing.

However, exclusive use of a single vendor has its own problems. A single vendor cannot possibly make the best product in every area. Exclusive use of a single vendor also leaves untested your protocol interoperability, which can lead to a surprise the first time a new vendor is introduced.

Somewhere between the extremes is a reasonable balance. Some sites find that choosing a single vendor for each protocol layer or each tier of the network works well. For example, one might consistently use a particular WAN router vendor, a different vendor for the core LAN switches, and yet another vendor for hubs and switches in offices.

7.1.12 Standards-Based Protocols

An organization's network should be built using standards-based protocols. This rule does not change over time. Vendor-proprietary protocols lock you in to a single vendor by making it difficult to integrate equipment from competing vendors. Being locked in to a single vendor makes it difficult to negotiate for better prices and prevents you from adopting another company's products to take advantage of its improvements. It also leaves you vulnerable to that vendor's business problems.

If you require features that are provided only by vendor-proprietary protocols, you should pressure the vendor to open the standard. Ideally, the standards should also be well established, rather than new, so that all hardware is likely to be fully compliant with the standard. Using established IETF standards means that any hardware or software that you choose should comply with that standard. Established IETF standards are stable and do not suffer from version interoperability problems. When a vendor brags about a new feature, it can be useful to ask which IETF Request for Comments number or IEEE document defines the standard. If the new feature is not standards based, the vendor should be questioned on how this equipment will interoperate with your other devices. See also Sections 5.1.3 and 23.1.6.

7.1.13 Monitoring

You need network monitoring to build a fast, reliable network; to scale the network in advance of growing demand; and to maintain its reliability.

You don't know how your network is performing or how reliable it is until you monitor it. There are two primary types of network monitoring. One is real-time availability monitoring and alerting. The other is gathering data to do trend analysis to predict future demand or for usage-based billing purposes. For companies that are providing a service across the Internet, whether they be ISPs, application service providers, or e-commerce sites, both types of monitoring are an essential part of running the business. Within a corporate environment, both types are good things to implement but usually are not business critical.

Real-time monitoring of the network should be incorporated into any existing trouble-ticket and alerting system used at your site. At a minimum, such monitoring should be able to alert you to network-interface state transitions. In other words, the monitoring should tell you when a network interface goes down and, preferably, when it comes back up again. Ideally, the monitoring should also inform you of routing problems, though exactly what form that monitoring takes is completely dependent on the routing protocol. You also can consider alerts based on unusual conditions, such as sudden, unexpected spikes or drops in traffic that may indicate a problem. Spikes can indicate a misconfigured computer, a new ill-behaved application, or a virus/worm. A drop can indicate a cable cut or lunch.

Lunch-Related Network Traffic

Tom once received a demo of a network monitoring system. The salesperson plugged it into his network and saw a huge quantity of traffic, virtually overloading every port, sustained for a few minutes. Then near silence.

The salesperson had gone from thinking that he had found the most badly overloaded network in the world to wondering whether there were any devices at all. It turned out that at this computer-aided design (CAD) shop, nearly everyone left for lunch at exactly noon. At 11:59 AM every day, everyone clicked Save on their huge CAD designs and then left for the cafeteria. The simultaneous writing of so much data flooded both the network and the file servers, but no customers were around to even notice. All the saves would complete eventually, and then the network would remain silent until the designers returned.

It was just a coincidence that the device was turned on shortly before noon. The rest of the day, the traffic was quite normal.

The most common and important use of historical data collection is to predict future needs. For most sites, it is sufficient to simply monitor all network interfaces that are of interest to see how much traffic is going over them and to perform trend analysis to predict when more bandwidth will be required. Other sites, particularly those in the Internet services industry, will want to gather data on the traffic flow within their network to determine whom they should establish direct connections to, what size those connections should be, and where they should be made geographically to optimize the traffic on the network.

Gathering historical data on faults, errors, and outages can also prove useful and informative, showing when problems start or deteriorate. Analysis of the historical data can also be used to detect behavioral anomalies that can indicate problems (Brutlag 2000) or to build availability statistics for management or customers. You know that historical monitoring is useful when you can point to a graph of network utilization, follow the growth trajectory, and have a good idea when that link will be overloaded and therefore upgraded to a faster technology.

Monitoring is discussed in greater detail in Chapter 22.

7.1.14 Single Administrative Domain

Properly designing networks, maintaining them, and debugging problems across multiple organizations are always difficult. A network should be a single organism that moves traffic around in a coherent, coordinated fashion. A network should be governed by a single set of policies and practices that are implemented consistently across the entire network. The more independent groups there are directing the movement of the traffic, the more likely that the network will become incoherent and uncoordinated. Having a single administrative domain means having a single, closely tied network administration team with a single management structure. When parts of the network team are managed by management structures that meet only at the CEO level, different parts of the company inevitably go in different directions, following their own sets of policies and practices.

Case Study: Problems from a Lack of a Single Administrative Group

A large multinational computer manufacturing company had different groups of people responsible for different parts of the network. The groups reported through different management structures. A closely tied group was responsible for the WANs, and a loosely tied group was responsible for LANs at each site. The different groups could not agree on a single routing protocol to use across the company. In part, the disagreement was aligned with the different management chains. Some of the site-specific networking groups reported through the engineering organization, which wanted the desktops—all of which used the company's own hardware and software—to participate in the routing. That desire severely limited the available network protocols, none of which were suitable for the other requirements that the wide-area group had to meet. Ultimately, both groups used different routing protocols and identified some redundant locations for exchanging routing information. However, because of the lack of cooperation between the groups, they could never quite get the configuration right and ended up with routing loops if both of the redundant hand-off points were connected at once. A single, coherent network administration group would not have had this problem.

Security issues are associated with not having a single administrative domain. When they have control over different parts of the network, different groups probably will also have different policies with respect to connecting other networks to their piece of network and the security that should surround those connections. This results in an unknown level of security for the network because it is a single entity and only as secure as the weakest link.

Having a single administrative domain does not exclude the possibility of having regional or divisional network teams that all report to the same management structure and are all governed by the same set of policies and practices. The network will still act as a single organism if multiple teams work closely together in a coordinated fashion (see Section 7.2.2).

7.2 The Icing

A few additional things beyond the basic tasks are involved to further improve your network. You must strike a balance between the risk of using cutting-edge, "hot" technologies and staying with older but more reliable equipment and technologies. Finally, if you find yourself in a situation that requires multiple administrative domains, you can follow our suggestions to mitigate the problems that occur.

7.2.1 Leading Edge versus Reliability

Typically, the most important quality that people seek in their networks is reliability. Older products that have gone through many firmware and hardware revisions tend to be more reliable. The bugs have been shaken out. On the other hand, newer features and faster connectivity are often available only in new products, which may not have been field tested. It is your job to find a balance.

You can manage this risk in various ways. You might perform your own certification of new products in a lab before they are put into production situations and then only slowly deploy them to establish confidence before beginning a major installation. Certification should also include documenting an installation procedure and configuration standards.

You might have separate customer groups that differ in the amount of risk they are willing to accept. Some may be willing to accept slightly lower reliability in exchange for having access to newer features. Even then, such equipment should be tested in the lab first. People who want cutting-edge performance still want reliability.

Sometimes, the customer groups that are willing to take the risks are in a different SA team's domain of control. That team may have customer groups with business requirements such that they must use some of the new technologies when they become available. Let *them* suffer through the teething problems, if you can, and take advantage of your chance to let others work out the bugs for you. Learn from their experiences.

If you use leading-edge gear, make sure that each person who is going to be affected by its early problems knows that outages are likely to occur because the technology is so new. If you don't do that in advance, your customers will be unhappy, and the reputation of your network as a whole will be adversely affected. If a high-level manager approves the risk, make sure that the end users and their direct managers are aware of this decision so that outages are not blamed on you. The equipment should still be configured and tested in a lab before deployment.

❖ **The Edges**

- *Leading edge*: being on the forefront of technology. You are leading the way into new technological territory.
- *Cutting edge*: adopting new innovations sooner than leading edge, a term named after the forward-most part of a blade.
- *Bleeding edge*: how users feel after they've suffered though too many cutting edges.

7.2.2 Multiple Administrative Domains

For political, practical, or security reasons, it is sometimes impossible to have a single administrative domain. If different organizations manage different parts of the network and are not governed by the same set of policies or managed by the same management chain, the network needs a different model. The various pieces of the network should have explicit borders between them, making use of border routing protocols, such as BGP, and security mechanisms, such as firewalls, to provide routing stability and known levels of security in each of the administrative domains, independent of the others.

A common division is to have one group for WAN connectivity and another for LAN connectivity. This is reasonable because they are different skill sets. The same with having a separate group to manage connections to the Internet or network security.

If you must have multiple administrative domains, you should do it the right way. The choices and actions of one network administration team should be completely independent of what the other teams are doing and unable to affect the operations or reliability of other networks. Agree to common standards at the meeting points, and establish committees with delegates from each group to set global standards.

7.3 Conclusion

In this chapter, we looked at the various aspects of designing and building a network. Because network technology changes rapidly, some of these areas change significantly over time. But other components of building a network are constants. In this chapter, we discussed ways that technology has changed networks, as well as the areas that always need to be considered.

So, although many of the key pieces that determine exactly how you are going to build your network continually change, you can use some solid building blocks as foundations for your network, making it easier to achieve a reliable network and to move with the times.

7.3.1 Constants in Networking
- The need for a clean architecture
- Reliability
- Good labeling and documentation
- IDFs and MDFs built to the highest standards of wiring available
- Protected power and cooling provided to the IDFs and MDF

- A consistent IDF layout across floors and buildings
- Demarcation points
- A single administrative domain, where possible; otherwise, a clean separation of responsibilities
- Open Internet (IETF and IEEE) standard protocols
- Simple host routing
- Dedicated network hardware for pushing packets
- A minimal number of vendors
- Avoidance of leading-edge gear whenever possible

7.3.2 Things That Change in Network Design

- The type of intrabuilding and interbuilding wiring required
- The physical- and logical-network topologies
- The network devices and protocols
- Wide-area connectivity options
- Internet connectivity architectures
- Strategies for redundancy
- Monitoring technologies

Exercises

1. Draw a physical-network map for your organization.

2. Draw a logical-network map for your organization.

3. How do hosts route packets in your environment? Where is there redundancy in the network? If there isn't any, how would you implement it?

4. If your organization were just moving into the campus that you now occupy and you had the opportunity to lay out the IDFs and MDF, how would you do it? How is this different from the current situation?

5. Where are your demarcation points? How are they documented and labeled?

6. What protocols do you use on your network, and what are the corresponding RFC numbers for those protocols? Are any of them proprietary protocols? If so, how could you avoid using those protocols?

7. What vendors' equipment do you use in your network? How could you reduce the number of vendors that you use? What would be the advantages and disadvantages of doing so?

8. What policy, informal or otherwise, does your organization have for using leading-edge hardware? How do you limit the impact of reliability problems with that hardware?

9. If your organization had multiple administrative domains, how would you implement the approach suggested in Section 7.2.2?

10. What do you monitor on your network? What would you like to monitor, and how would you go about it?

Chapter **8**

Namespaces

In this chapter, we explain principles of organizing and managing namespaces. A namespace is a set of unique keys and associated attributes. Examples of namespaces are the account names in use, the printers available, the names of hosts, Ethernet addresses, service name/port number lists, and home directory location maps. Every namespace has attributes for each element. Account names have UIDs (Unix) or SIDs (Windows), home directories, owners, and so on. Hostname attributes usually include IP addresses, hardware serial numbers, customer (owner) information, Ethernet MAC address, and so on.

The term *namespace* can be confusing because it can refer to either an abstract concept or a concrete thing. For example, usernames are a namespace. Every multiuser operating system has a namespace that is the list of identifiers for users. Therefore, a typical company has the abstract concept of a username namespace. However, the namespace used at one company is different from the one at another company (unless you've just hired all of my coworkers!). In that sense, companies have different username namespaces (your set of users and my set of users). Most of this chapter uses the term *namespace* to refer to a particular (concrete) namespace database. We are specific when we feel that it's worthwhile to differentiate the two.

Namespaces come in many shapes. Some namespaces are flat; that is, there are no duplicates. For example, in Windows, a **WINS** directory is a flat namespace. In Unix, the set of UIDs is a flat namespace. Other namespaces are hierarchical, like a directory tree. No two files in a particular directory can have the same name, but two different files called `example.txt` can be in different subdirectories.

The larger and more sophisticated an environment becomes, the more important it is that namespaces be managed formally. Smaller environments tend to need very little formality with their namespaces. They all might be controlled by one person who keeps certain information in her head. On the other hand, megacorporations must divide and delegate the responsibility among many divisions and people.

It is very powerful to simply acknowledge that your environment has namespaces in the first place. Until that happens, you just have piles of data. When each namespace is thought of independently, we lose the potential benefits that can be gained by linking them. New SAs tend to see each namespace as a separate item but over time learn to see a more global picture. They learn to see the whole forest rather than getting caught up with each tree. Seeing a particular namespace in the context of a larger vision, opens up new options.

In this chapter, we examine the basics of namespace management and then explore more advanced topics on the management and use of namespaces. This chapter should help you see the forest, not just the trees.

8.1 The Basics

The basics of namespaces are very simple.

- Namespaces need policies: naming, longevity, locality, and exposure.
- Namespaces need procedures: adding, changing, and deleting.
- Namespaces need centralized management.

8.1.1 Namespace Policies

Namespaces should be controlled by general policies rather than by any specific technological system. The larger your SA team is, the more important it is for policies to be actual documents, rather than oral traditions. As a team grows, these written policies become tools for communicating to SAs or training new SAs. You can't reprimand an SA for permitting a customer to name a new PC outside the permitted name rules if those rules are not in written form. Written policies should be the basis for the requirements specified when you create automation to maintain namespaces. Written policies also set expectations with customers.

8.1.1.1 Defining Names

The namespace's naming policy should answer these questions: What names are permitted in this namespace? What names are not permitted in this namespace? How are names selected? How are collisions resolved? When is renaming allowed?

One needs rules for what names can be part of a namespace. Some rules are dictated by the technology. For example, UNIX login IDs can only be alphanumeric characters plus a limited number of symbols. Other rules may emerge from corporate policy, such as restrictions on "offensive" login IDs. External standards bodies set rules too: Before RFC 1123 (Braden 1989, Section 2.1), DNS names couldn't begin with a digit, making it difficult for 3Com, Inc., to register its domain.

When selecting names, you can use multiple methods:

1. *Formulaic.* Names fit a strict formula. For example, some sites name all desktop workstations as "`pc-`" followed by a four-digit number. Login names might be strictly the first initial followed by the first six letters of the last name, followed by a random series of digits to make a unique name.

2. *Thematic.* All names fit a theme, such as naming all servers after planets, and using planet names from science fiction when you run out of real planet names.

3. *Functional.* Names have functions. Accounts for a specific role (`admin`, `secretary`, `guest`), hostnames that reflect the duties of the machine (`dns1`, `cpuserver22`, `web01`), or permission groups (webmasters, marketing).

4. *Descriptive.* Descriptive names usually communicate factual information, rather than rules. Good examples are disk partition labels that describe the customers or data for which the partition is intended (S:\Departments\Finance, test data), printer names that tell what type of printer or driver is used (laserjet, photo, 11 × 14), or their location (testlab, inkjet, CEO-desktop). Geographical names, usually by city or airport code, are heavily used by large organizations for permissions groups and email lists (sjc-all, chicago-execs, reston-eng).

5. *No method.* Sometimes, the formula is no formula. Everyone picks something. Conflicts and collisions are resolved by first-come, first-serve policies.

There is tension among these four methods. Once you use one scheme, it is difficult to change. Many organizations avoid making a specific choice by combining more than one method, but will usually pick one as primary and another as secondary in the combination. The most common choice is functional naming with descriptive naming when an organization has multiple geographical locations, e.g., "nyc-marketing"or "sjc-web-03." This is especially true for networking gear, which is commonly named so as to provide maximum debugging information, such as abbreviations for the network provider, the colocation facility, or even the rack location.

❖ **Merging Existing Namespaces**   When organizations merge operations, dealing with namespace conflicts can be a political issue as much as a technical issue. Many mergers are really an acquisition being called a merger to make the other group feel better about the changes that will be coming. Mutually deciding on a policy for handling namespace conflicts before they arise will help prevent bad feelings, especially if the policy is perceived as fair by both sides.

The chances for name collision are greater if both organizations are using the same method of assigning names. Whose server named gandalf has to be renamed? Which Susan has to change her login name from sue to something else? Where will mail to the sales alias go? The following sample policies have worked for us in the past:

- *Servers*. All servers with name conflicts are given a company-specific hostname alias in the directory or DNS. Thus, the two servers named gandalf are reachable as gandalf-CompanyA and gandalf-CompanyB until one can be retired or easily renamed.

- *Logins*. The customer who has been with his or her organization longest gets to keep the login name. In one merger that Strata assisted with, a high-ranking manager gave up his first-name login to an individual employee in the firm being acquired, even though he could have used his status in the company to make himself an exception to the policy. Word of this got around quickly and made a positive difference in moving forward.

- *Email*. First.last conflicts in email addresses can be very irksome. The policy that we've seen meet with most success is that both individuals change their email addresses. The mail gateways are then configured to route mail to these customers based on the domain to which it was addressed. Mail to susan.jones@companyA will be resent to susan.a.jones@Merged, and mail to susan.jones@companyB will be resent to susan.b.jones@Merged. Most firms choose to re-route mail rather than bounce it, but the same strategy can be used to bounce mail with a customized message: "Susan.Jones@companyA: Address has changed to Susan.A.Jones@companyA, please update your address books." When implementing an email routing policy such as this one, it is important to specify a time limit, if any, when the special routing will be disabled.

Functional names can make software configuration easier: Helpdesks can support software more easily if the mail server is called `mail` and the calendar server is called `calendar`. However, if such services ever move to different hosts, a confusing situation can arise. It is better to have functional aliases that point to such hosts. Aliases, such as DNS CNAMEs are great for noninteractive service machines like mail, web, DNS, and so on. Aliases don't work nearly as well for interactive compute servers, because users will notice the hostname and start to use it. It can be confusing when logs are generated with the real hostname rather than the functional alias, but it would be more confusing if they referred to the alias with no way to determine which specific machine was intended.

Sequential Names

Formulaic names give a false sense of completeness. A customer submitted a panicked trouble ticket when she noticed that hosts `software-build`-1, -4, -5, and -7 weren't pinging. Of course, only -2, -3, -6, and -8 still existed; the rest had been recycled for other uses. This situation is a problem only when a clear sequence is being used.

Theme names can be cute—sometimes too cute. One part of Bell Labs where Tom worked used coffee-related names—`latte`, `decaf`, `grande`, `froth`—for its printers. Although this approach was cute, it was much less frustrating to locate a printer in the divisions that named their printers after the printer's room number—plus the letter *c* if it was a color printer. Some naming conventions make a lot more sense than others. The coffee names were frustrating to new people, whereas the formulaic names meant less need for lists of where to find printers.

The method used for naming reflects the corporate culture. If one is trying to establish a progressive, fun, enlightened work atmosphere, `latte` is a great name for a printer. If one is trying to reflect a culture where work is boring, not fun, and painfully dull, require hosts to be named `pc` followed by a four-digit number. (Of course, in that case, one should start numbering them with `pc0011` so that nobody gets jealous of the special people with single-digit numbers. While you are at it, skip numbers ending with 00, primes, numbers with salacious connotations, and any of the "interesting" numbers discovered by the mathematician Ramanujan.)

Names have security implications. Intruders might find `sourcecodedb` a more interesting target than `server05`. Alternatively, intruders have long known that SAs usually break the naming rules for their own systems. The goal of an intruder is to work for as long as possible without being detected. Therefore, they avoid any host that might be closely watched, such as the desktop machines of the SA team. If they discover a network where all hostnames are strictly formulaic except for a few random machines named after Star Trek characters, the intruders will assume that the Star Trek hosts are the SAs' machines and will avoid those hosts to decrease their chances of being detected. It's even reasonable to assume that the lead SA's host is the one named `picard` and that the person in charge of security sits in front of `worf`. Although we don't encourage anyone to rely on security through obscurity, there are benefits in camouflaging the machines with unremarkable names.

RFC 1178 (Libes 1990) has excellent advice about selecting names for hosts. However, we'd like to interject that for desktop workstations, it can make an SA's life a lot easier if the host's name reflects the name of the customer. If one receives email from `ajay` reporting that "my machine is having a problem," it is very convenient to be able to rely on the fact that his host's name is `ajay`. Of course, some directory services don't permit hostnames to be the same as names in the user directory, in which case names such as `ajaypc` can be sufficient.

Difficult-to-Type Names

A site had an architecture in which every cluster had a file server and a number of compute servers. Customers were required to do their work on the compute servers and not `telnet` directly into the file server. To discourage people from logging in to the file servers, those servers were given names that were long or difficult to spell, and the compute servers were given easy-to-type names. One such cluster named its machines after famous mathematicians, naming the file server `ramanujan` and the compute server `boole`. It's much easier to type `boole`!

8.1.1.2   Access Controls

A namespace's access control policy should answer the following questions.

- What kind of protection or security does this namespace require?
- What are we trying to protect the names from and why?
- Do the names in the space need to be protected, or just their attributes?
- Who can add, change, or delete entire records?
- Can the owner of a record change certain fields within the record?

Whom should the contents of a namespace be protected from? It depends on the namespace. Everyone should be prevented from reading a namespace such as a list of passwords. Some namespaces are a secret held by a few people—customers in the cluster, all employees, anyone except the competition—or by nobody—who cares how many people know that Tom's UID is 27830?

The answer can be different for each namespace and may also depend on context. For example, the individual login IDs of a UNIX system can be safely exposed in the outbound email message, on business cards, in advertisements, and so on. However, the complete list of IDs shouldn't be exposed externally, because spammers will use the list for sending junk email. The passwords associated with the IDs shouldn't be exposed, obviously. Thus, on UNIX systems, the /etc/shadow file that stores the password has stricter protection than the /etc/passwd file that stores the UID, person's full name, home directory, and preferred shell. On the other hand, although we don't mind the exposure of the UID internally, we generally don't want to expose all the UIDs to the outside world.

Printing /etc/passwd

An SA was setting up a printer and kept printing /etc/passwd to generate test pages. In an environment that didn't have a namespace access control policy, he didn't realize that exposing the contents of /etc/passwd was a bad thing. (He didn't realize that intruders were sometimes found looking through corporate dumpsters for just that kind of thing.[1]) It was recommended that it would be safer for him to print /etc/motd or create his own test file. A more experienced SA would have had a greater appreciation for namespace protection issues and wouldn't have done this.

---

1. This practice is called *dumpster diving*.

Changes are a different matter. Customers should be able to change certain settings but not others, but only specific people should be able to create or delete accounts. On the other hand, ISPs often have a policy that the user can create an account, based on the person's ability to provide a credit card number; deleting an account also is customer initiated. Universities often have systems on which professors can create dozens of accounts at a time for the students taking a particular course that will require access to certain machines. However, non-SAs couldn't create a privileged account or delete other people's accounts. One major web-based email provider doesn't have a procedure to delete accounts on request. An account that is not used for a certain period is automatically deleted.

Another facet of protection includes change control and backup policies. Change control is discussed in Chapter 17; here, suffice it to say that it is important to be able to roll back a change. Namespaces that are stored in plaintext format can be checked into a revision-control system, such as SubVersion under UNIX or SourceSafe under Windows for network-based management. Backup policies should pay particular attention to namespaces. Backups are the ultimate insurance policy.

How a namespace is protected from modification is another issue. Sometimes, a namespace is maintained in a flat text file, and modifications are prevented by using the appropriate file-permission controls. In other instances, modifications are done through a database that has its own access controls. It is important to remember that a namespace is only as secure as the methods that can be used to modify it. The method used to update a namespace should be more secure than the systems that depend on that namespace for security. For example, is the method used to access and update the namespace encrypted? Is it authenticated through a secure mechanism? If only a password is required, you face a significant risk of someone making unauthorized changes.

8.1.1.3 Namespace Longevity

A namespace's longevity policy should answer the question, When are entries in this namespace removed? Some entries in a namespace need to expire on a certain date or after a certain amount of inactivity. You might prescribe that accounts for contractors be sponsored by a regular employee, who must renew the request once a year, and be removed if no renewal is performed. IP addresses can be scarce, and in a loosely controlled environment, you might expire the IP address that has been granted to a customer if a network-monitoring system shows that the IP address hasn't been used in a certain number of months.

Names, once exposed to customers, last longer than you would ever expect. Once a name is established in the minds of your customers, it is very difficult to change. You should plan for this. If an email address is printed on a business card, it is difficult to recall all those cards if you require a person to change an email address. Once a document repository is announced to be on fileserver `fred`, don't even think of moving it to `barney`.

Good technology lets you obscure names that shouldn't be interrelated. The UNIX automounter can be used so that customers refer to the repository as `/home/docs`, and the name of the fileserver is obscured. The location of the documents should not be tied to the name of the server. The fact that they are interrelated shouldn't matter to your customers. Aliases can be a good solution here, though some technologies, such as NFS, require clients to be rebooted for them to "see" the change. Never name a web server `www`. Give it a generic name, and make `www` an alias to it. Announce only the `www` name, and you can move the functionality to a different host without worry. If you consistently use aliases and other technologies that obscure names as appropriate, you can move functionality from one host to another with confidence.

A Machine Named `calendar`

For many years, the calendar server that Tom used was on a host named `calendar`. It seemed like a good idea at the time, because the host was purchased expressly for the job of being the calendar server. But eventually, it also became the main print server, and customers were confused that their print jobs were being spooled to a host named `calendar`. The hostname couldn't be changed, because the software license was locked to that hostname. This problem could have been avoided if the host had been called something else and `calendar` was an alias for the machine. In an ideal world, Tom could define "printer" as an alias for the host, and make the customers happy, or, at least, less confused.

8.1.1.4 Questions of Scope

A namespace's scope policy should answer the question, Where will this namespace be used? How global or local a particular namespace is can be measured on two axes: diameter (geographically, or how widely it is used) and thickness (how many services use it).

The **diameter** is how many systems use a particular namespace database: single host, cluster, division, enterprisewide, and so on. Although your entire enterprise might use Microsoft ActiveDirectory, a given namespace database—say, username/passwords—might be usable only for your department's machines. Other departments have different lists of users and passwords for their machines.

RADIUS (Rigney et al. 1997), an authentication protocol for modem pools, VPN servers, and other network devices, can be implemented so that devices all around a global enterprise access the same database: both username and password. People can log in with the same username/password no matter which modem pool they use when traveling around the world.

Sites that use the Network Information Service—often UNIX systems—tend to implement namespaces that have a diameter of a single cluster of UNIX hosts. Each cluster has its own namespace databases.

The **thickness** of a namespace is based on how many services use it. For example, a company might allocate a unique ID, such as `tal` or `chogan`, for each employee and use that for the person's email name, login ID, ID for logging into intranet services, name on modem pools, VPN services, and so on. Even though these are different databases and use different protocols—ActiveDirectory, NIS, RADIUS, and so on—the ID is used for all of them. In fact, even though each of those uses of the ID might involve a different password, it is still a measurement of the thickness.

The diameter of a namespace has a lot of implications. If each division has a different namespace for login IDs, what happens if a person has accounts in two namespace databases? For example, what if `tal` is Tom Limoncelli in one division and Terry Levine in another? This can be fine until Tom needs a login in Terry's division. Should Tom be `tal2` exclusively in Terry's division, or should Tom be required to change his account name everywhere? That would be very disruptive, especially if Tom needed an account on Terry's network for only a short time.

Case Study: Lucent's "Handles"

It can be useful to have a single, global namespace and to encourage all other namespaces to align themselves with it. Lucent gives each employee a "handle" that is a unique identifier. Employees can select their own handles, but the default is a person's first initial followed by his or her last name. This namespace is globally unique, a challenge considering that in 2000, Lucent had more than 160,000 employees. The database of handles can be accessed as a field in the online corporate directory. Each division is encouraged to create account names that are the same as the person's handle. All services run by the central chief information officer group—email, human resources, remote access, and so on—use the handle exclusively to model proper behavior. This system results in the best of both worlds. Locally run services can adopt login IDs that match the associate's Lucent handle; the services may deviate if they wish, but they would have to accept the risk that current and future collisions will cause confusion. The benefits of using the Lucent handle rather than letting customers select unique ones are obvious, and thus little enforcement is required. During corporate acquisitions, the company being acquired has to deal with namespace collisions that may occur.

Sometimes, one does not want a globally flat namespace. In some cases, the technology in use provides for a hierarchical namespace instead. For example, it is not required that hostnames be unique within an entire corporation, because DNS provides for zones and subzones. With departmental DNS zones, each department can have a www. machine—ideally, an alias to the actual server with a more unique name. A department could even name its desktop PCs pc followed by a number, and sites wouldn't have to coordinate with one another to ensure that no overlapping numbers were used.

Case Study: Wide and Thick E-Commerce Namespaces

E-commerce sites usually are able to have a username namespace that is extremely wide and thick. The customer establishes and uses one username and password for all the services at the site, whether they are on one machine or hundreds. Yahoo is well known for this. Once a customer establishes a profile, it applies to all the services offered. The customer might have to activate those additional services, but they are all tied to one username and password for the person to remember.

8.1.1.5 Consistency
A namespace's consistency policy should answer the question, where the same name is used in multiple namespaces, which attributes will be kept consistent also?

High consistency means that a name used in one place will have the same attributes in all the places it exists. For example, you might establish a policy that if someone has a UNIX account, the numeric UID must be the same everywhere the person has UNIX accounts. You might establish a policy that although the same ID is used to access email and to connect to the company's VPN server, the passwords are not kept in sync. In fact, it would be wise to require different passwords for both systems.

Case Study: A Simple Way to Set Naming Standards

Bell Labs Research has many different UNIX environments, or clusters, but amazingly few conflicting UIDs. This fact was discovered, much to our surprise, when some of these environments were merged. How this happened is an interesting story.

Many years ago, someone invited all the SAs from all the computing centers to lunch. At that lunch, the SAs divided up the UID space, allocating large ranges to each research center. Everyone agreed to stay within their allocated space except when creating accounts for people from other computing centers, in which case their UIDs from that center would be carried forward. No policy was created, no bureaucratic allocation czar was appointed, and no penalty scheme was implemented. Everyone agreed to follow the decisions because they knew it was the right thing to do. Shortly after the meeting, someone sent out email describing the ranges.

Years later, those UID ranges are still followed. When new SAs are hired, someone forwards them a copy of that email explaining what was agreed on many years ago. Each center has some kind of "create an account" script that embodies the guidelines in that email. This convention has worked very well all these years because it is truly the simplest solution for the problem.

One UID for an Account Everywhere

At Bell Labs, most people can log in to all the general-purpose machines with the same username and password and using the same UID. However, not everyone can access the special-purpose machines. Tom inherited ownership of a DNS server that was one such machine. Only people who needed to make updates to DNS had accounts, and their UIDs were allocated starting at 1,000 and incrementing upward. The previous SA had justified the situation by stating that the DNS server was considered too secure to ever speak NFS. Thus, the UIDs didn't have to be the same as everywhere else, and it would have taken an entire 10 seconds per account to identify their regular UIDs. That might have been a minute per year that he saved in the 3 years he ran the machine. As a result, when backups of this machine were restored to other hosts, the UIDs mismatched. To forestall future problems, Tom set a policy such that all new accounts were created using UIDs from their home system, and the legacy UIDs were realigned during an upgrade, when downtime was permitted.

8.1.1.6 Reuse

The namespace's reuse policy should answer this question, How soon after a name has been deleted or expired can it be reused? Usually, the name can be reused immediately. For example, you might want to reuse a printer name immediately so that PCs do not need to be reconfigured.

You might be more concerned with email addresses, however. You might have a policy that once an email address has been deleted, nobody else can reuse that address for 6 months, so that a new person is less likely to receive email intended for someone else. This policy prevents the following mischievous trick: Some companies have an automated procedure to allocate vanity email addresses to be forwarded to your mailbox. For example, you might allocate `foosupport@companyname.com` to be forwarded to yourself—the person who supports product `foo`. If your job function changes, the address can be forwarded to your replacement. However, if John Doe (`jdoe@companyname.com`) leaves the company, you could use this process to have `jdoe`'s email forwarded to you and to pick up his mail until all his correspondents learn his new email address. This would be particularly bad if it was the CEO who left the company. By requiring deleted email addresses to be invalid for 6 months, you can be fairly sure that allocating that address is safe again.

A reuse policy can be implemented in software. However, in small, infrequently changing namespaces, the SAs should simply be sensitive to the ramifications of reuse. For example, if you are asked to give a customer's PC a name that was recently used for a popular server, you might suggest a different name, to prevent confusion. The confusion will be particularly high if a lot of hardcopy documentation mentioning the server's name is still in the field.

8.1.1.7 Summary

Policies on naming, access control, longevity, scope, consistency, and reuse must be written, approved by management and technical staff, and available for reference to customers and SAs, thereby clearly establishing the rules of your namespaces. Much grief can be avoided by doing so. Small sites that run without such documentation and survive do so because the few SAs have to work closely together to have such policies as part of their culture. However, this informality doesn't scale. Such sites become large sites that suddenly find themselves with a larger group of SAs who have not been indoctrinated into the "standard" way of doing things. Many disagreements can be prevented by having these policies documented. That way, a new SA who disagrees with them can discuss any proposed changes. Without documentation, each SA is free to assume that his or her way is the right way. (More on documenting procedures is provided in Chapter 9.)

8.1.2 Namespace Change Procedures

All namespaces need procedures for additions, changes, and deletions. These procedures should be documented just as the policies are but the documents may not be available to customers. Again, a small group may be able to operate without these procedures being explicitly written down. The procedures are performed only by the people who invented the system and thus do not require documentation. However, as the system grows and new SAs are involved, confusion sets in. Documentation can serve the dual purposes of providing both a basis for training and step-by-step instruction when the task is being performed.

If something can be documented in a clear, concise manner, it can be automated. Not all automation needs to be complicated, as we will see in the next section.

8.1.3 Centralizing Namespace Management

Namespace management should be centralized as much as possible for any given environment. With centralization comes consistency. Otherwise, namespaces become scattered around various servers or even different directories on the same server. It is better to have a single host maintain your namespaces and have them distributed to all other hosts.

Case Study: A Namespace Cleanup

At one site, Tom found that some namespaces had their master copies on a particular host and were distributed to all hosts by the Unix `make` command. A couple of other hosts stored the master copies of other namespaces. For those namespaces, the file would be edited, and then a script would be run to push the data to other hosts. In fact, it wasn't only one script but a set of scripts with such names as `update_printcap`, `aliases_push`, and `push_stuff`. The scripts were named inconsistently because the environment was the merger of a few smaller environments. The directory that stored the files and scripts often were different on the various hosts.

Part of Tom's indoctrination at this site was to be taught, for every namespace, what directory it was stored in, on which machine, and which script to run to push any changes to the other machines. All this information was taught from memory by a senior SA, because none of it was documented. As SA's competence was judged not on how much UNIX knowledge one had but how well the person could memorize a list of oddly named scripts. By the end the week, Tom had assembled all this information into a large chart. Tom doesn't have a very good memory, so this complicated system concerned him greatly.

None of the files were stored under RCS or Source Code Control System (SCCS), so SAs had to rely on tape backups for any kind of change control. The SAs couldn't roll back any change without a lot of effort. Tom has his error-prone days, so this too concerned him.

After a month of effort, the master file for every namespace had been moved to a single directory on a single host. These files were maintained under RCS control so that changes could be rolled back. A new `Makefile` in that directory fired off the appropriate legacy script, depending on which file had been changed. After this transition was made, the system was not only easier to administer but also more consistent. This made it easier to train new SAs, who could then focus on more important technical tasks.

Once the new system was stable, it could be optimized. Some of the legacy scripts were brittle or slow. With the system consolidated, there was a focus on replacing the scripts one at a time with better ways of doing things.

This consolidation also made it easier to introduce new automated processes, such as creating new accounts. Rather than requiring SAs to remember the names of scripts to create an account, for example, `make newuser` would list a set of reminders. The scripts themselves were integrated into the `Makefile`. So, rather than remembering which script created an account, one simply issued the `make account` command and the script would ask the appropriate questions and complete the task.

Mark Burgess's GNU cfengine (Burgess 1995) is an excellent UNIX tool for maintaining master copies of namespaces and configuration files and distributing them to hosts. This tool has the benefit of being able to automatically maintain any kind of configuration on a UNIX host and can be programmed to know that certain hosts should have different configurations. Microsoft's ActiveDirectory and Apple Mac OS X's OpenDirectory take a different tack, having clients query LDAP servers that store namespace information centrally.

8.2 The Icing

Now we can take things to the next level by centralizing and automating further. Using namespaces can become a ubiquitous way of doing business.

8.2.1 One Huge Database

Centralization is a good trend, and centralizing all namespaces into a SQL database is even better. You can develop web-based or forms-based front ends that let operators make most changes. Programs can then feed the data into other systems, such as ActiveDirectory, LDAP, NIS, printer configurations, and so on. Jon Finke of Rensselaer Polytechnic Institute has written several papers on this topic (Finke 1994a, 1994b, 1995, 1996, 1997). Many organizations were unable to consider this option until recently. SQL-based open source database implementations such as Postgres and My SQL have dramatically lowered the financial burden to db-based centralization.

8.2.2 Further Automation

Once the fundamentals are completed, further automation is easier. If the primary automation is done properly, higher levels of automation can be interfaces to the primary automation and provide, for example, additional data validation or the ability to iterate over the process many times.

If you can iterate over the elements of a namespace, automation can be driven by namespaces. For example, a simple iteration over the `passwd` namespace can be the basis of a system that audits various security parameters, such as the contents of `.rhosts` files. Many sites have one mailing list per department, and these mailing lists can be automatically generated from a corporate directory.

An inventory of all systems can be one of your most powerful namespaces if it is kept up to date—a process which itself can be partially automated.

Automated Inventory

Tom once worked at a site that had an inventory database that could be easily queried from shell scripts. The site also had a program that would run the same command on a list of hosts. Putting them together made it easy to write a program that would make changes globally or on hosts with specific characteristics, such as OS, OS revision, amount of memory, and so on. When a new application was deployed, a query could quickly determine which hosts would need additional memory to support it. Driving maintenance processes off a database of hosts was very powerful.

8.2.3 Customer-Based Updating

Automation can also lean in another direction: making customers self-sufficient. Every environment has many opportunities for automating services. Review your request logs and workload periodically and also talk to customers about what they would like to have automated. Section 3.1.3.3 describes a DHCP system that makes allocating IP addresses self-service.

Case Study: Account Creation at Rutgers

At Rutgers University, many of the computer science classes required that accounts be created for every student on machines in the computer science cluster. Automation was provided for mass-producing accounts. Teaching assistants had access to a command that would create a large number of accounts for a class by querying the enrollment database. A similar command would delete all the accounts for a particular class when the course ended. As a result of this automation, the SAs didn't have to be involved in maintaining this aspect of the namespace anymore—a major win at an academic institution!

8.2.4 Leveraging Namespaces

Although pervasive namespaces are useful in your computing infrastructure, they also can be useful in other infrastructures. There is a trend to reduce the administrative burden of noncomputer infrastructure by tying it to the namespaces from the computing infrastructure. For example, PBXs, voice mail systems, card-key access, and cafeteria credit card systems are increasingly speaking LDAP. Imagine making an addition to your corporate LDAP database when new employees are hired and having their email accounts created, their external home page templates copied into place, their phone and voicemail boxes configured, and their card-key access configured to let them into appropriate parts of the building.

8.3 Conclusion

In this chapter, we established some rules for namespaces. First, we must acknowledge that namespaces exist. Then, it becomes obvious that all namespaces share certain qualities. Namespaces need policies for naming, access control, longevity, scope, consistency, and reuse. Once policies have been established, procedures can be established. The policies must be established before the procedures, because the policies should drive the procedures.

Establishing written policies and procedures about namespaces improves communication within the SA team and communicates expectations to customers. Namespaces can greatly benefit from central management and automation.

Namespaces are part of the fundamental infrastructure of a computing environment. Well-managed namespaces are one of the key systems that will make all other systems run smoothly. You could, for example, maintain an email system without a well-managed namespace, but it would be difficult, cumbersome, and confusing to the system's users.

Automation is required to do a good job of maintaining namespaces, and yet good namespaces can aid further automation if they provide standardized methods, or APIs. Moving all namespaces into a single large database system enables us to take this to an extreme.

Once the basics have been completed, new opportunities arise. Benefits can come from generating all namespaces from a single database system. Better automation can be created, including automation that permits customers to accomplish what they need without SA intervention. Finally, we like the trend of tying noncomputer infrastructure, such as human resources, PBXs, and card-key systems to centralized databases.

Exercises

1. What are the namespaces in your environment? How are they maintained?

2. One aspect of an environment's maturity can be measured by determining whether the basics listed in Section 8.1 are being observed for the namespaces in the environment. Evaluate your environment.

3. In your environment, what automation is in place for maintaining the namespaces? What automation should be created?

4. What namespace maintenance should be pushed down to your customers through automation?

5. Suppose that you moved to a new organization and your login ID was already in use. What would you do?

6. Who was Ramanujan, and which numbers did he find interesting?

Chapter 9

Documentation

In system administration terms, documentation means keeping records of where things are, explaining how to do things, and making useful information available to customers. In general, SAs dislike writing documentation: There's hardly enough time to do the work; why write documentation, too? The reason is that documentation helps in many ways, and a lack of documentation hurts SAs' ability to do a good job.

It can be difficult to decide what to document. We recommend being selfish: Use documentation as a tool to make your work easier. Is the helpdesk flooded with the same few questions over and over? Provide documentation so that customers can help themselves. Are there tasks that you dislike doing? Document them so it is easier to delegate them or to have a junior SA take them over. Do you find it difficult to relax while on vacation? Do you skip vacations altogether? Document the processes that only you can do. Do you spend days fixing mistakes that could have been prevented? Maintain checklists and hint sheets to improve repeatability.

Documentation is a way of creating an institutional memory that lets an SA team increase its knowledge and skill level. Think of documentation as RAID for the SA staff: It gives you redundancy in the group. Some SAs fear that documentation will make them more replaceable and therefore refuse to document what they do. As a result, they often eventually feel trapped, cornered, and unable to leave their position. They get stressed and, ironically, quit out of frustration. The truth is that, because it simultaneously retains and shares knowledge, documentation enables an organization to promote people from within.

This chapter offers advice about how to create documentation, how to store it and make it available, and how to manage larger and larger repositories. We stress techniques for making it easy to create documentation by

241

reducing the barriers, real and mental, that prevent people from maintaining documentation.

9.1 The Basics

The basics involve having some easy ways to create documentation, store it so that it's easily used, and make it available to everyone who might need it.

9.1.1 What to Document

The things that are most important to document tend to be either (1) complicated and unpleasant and (2) things that you explain all the time. Sometimes, an item is in both categories: for example, how to access the corporate intranet while traveling. We use the phrase *complicated or unpleasant* to refer to both individual processes and the consequences if you make a mistake. One good example is the process for setting up the IT presence of a new employee: setting up the new hire's computer; creating the accounts he needs, including any department-specific aspects; whom to notify; and so on.

Thus, if a process has a lot of steps, especially ones for which the order is significant—or messing up requires you to call your manager—it's a good idea to document it as soon as possible. You will be saving someone a lot of trouble, and that someone could be you.

Documenting Disliked Processes

Tom finds that he's bad at doing processes he dislikes. He gets distracted, forgets steps, and so on. By documenting them as a checklist, he is less likely to skip a step and less likely to make mistakes. It's also easier to delegate the process to someone else once the difficult work of creating the process is done.

Documenting the tasks that you disklike makes it easier to find someone else to do them. Often, the difficult part is to create the process itself. Doing the process then becomes easier. When we get permission to hire an additional system administrator for our team, we are often tempted to hire someone with the same skill set we have and to divide the work evenly. It can be difficult to hire someone so senior. If we have documented the tasks that we dislike doing, we can hire a junior person to do them and mentor the person over time and promote from within. A junior person is less expensive and will eventually be someone with the knowledge of how the company and your IT department works and the competency you've fostered.

A job description usually has two parts: the list of responsibilities and the list of required skills. Generate the list of responsibilities by enumerating the processes that you dislike and that have been documented. Generate the list of required skills by drilling down into each document and cataloging the skills and technologies an SA needs to be familiar with to understand the documents. The entire job description basically writes itself.

9.1.2 A Simple Template for Getting Started

The most difficult part of creating a document is getting started. Here's a simple formula: Identify the four basic elements of a piece of documentation: *title, metadata, what,* and *how.* Create a document template or outline, and then fill in the sections from start to end.

1. *Title:* A simple title that others will understand.
2. *Metadata:* The document's author—usually your—contact information, and revision date or history. People reading the document will be able to contact the author with questions and when you get promoted, and your successors will honor you as the person who gifted them with this document. The revision date and history will help people understand whether the document is still relevant.
3. *What:* A sentence describing the contents of the document or the goal that someone can achieve by following the directions. One or two sentences is fine.
4. *How:* The steps to take to accomplish the goal. For any step that seems mysterious or confusing, you might add a *why*, such as "Re-tension the tape (*Why?* Because we find that on a full backup, we get tape errors less often if we have done so, even with a new tape)."

Next, do some basic quality assurance (QA) on the document. Accuracy is important. A typo or a skipped step could result in someone's creating more problems than the document seeks to fix.

Follow the steps in the document yourself, typing each command, and so on. Next, have someone else use your document to accomplish the goal and to give you feedback on where he had any problems. Give the person a copy on paper, making it more likely that the person will take notes to give back to you.

Although it is possible to do this interactively, with you watching and writing down the person's feedback, it's easy to have the session turn into a conversation, with you helping the person along with the process, taking mental notes to write down when you get back to your desk. Be strict with yourself: If you don't let the person do the work, he is not testing your instructions. If the person is comfortable with you watching, sit out of view and watch, taking notes on what causes confusion.

After a few people have successfully used this documentation, use it to create a shorter "quick guide" that summarizes the steps. This guide simply helps the experienced SA not to forget anything. The SA should be able to cut and paste command lines from this document into a shell so that the process goes quickly.

Case Study: Two Sets of Documentation

At Bell Labs, Cliff Miller created a system for maintaining a software depot for homogeneous UNIX environments. An important part of the depot's design was the namespace used for the various packages, some of which would be visible only on certain platforms or certain individual hosts. The process for adding software packages into the namespace was a little tricky; although it was well documented, that documentation contained a lot of hand-holding verbiage. This was great the first time a package was added but was cumbersome after that. His solution was to create a brief "quick guide" that included only the commands to be entered, with brief reminders of what the person was doing and hypertext links to the appropriate section of the full documentation. Now, both new and experienced SAs could easily execute the process and receive the right amount of documentation.

9.1.3 Easy Sources for Documentation

One way to make documenting your tasks easy is to take notes the next time you do the task. Even if this slows down the process, it is easier than writing the document from memory.

9.1.3.1 Saving Screen Shots

Learn how to use a tool for capturing screen shots. The next time you are doing something that you'd like to have documented, take screen shots as you perform each step. If you create the document from the screen shots, all you need is a line or two of text for each picture, describing what is being done in that step. Suddenly, you have a multimedia document, complete with visual aids. It's another cross-check for correctness, since anyone using the document can compare the screen shot to the real monitor at each step and be satisfied that everything looks like it is supposed to before moving on.

9.1.3.2 Capturing the Command Line

If you are working on a command line rather than with a graphical interface, copy and paste the terminal or console window into the document. Some terminal or console window programs include a capture-to-file feature; the UNIX `script` command captures entire sessions to a file.

The UNIX command `history` lists the last commands that were executed. These saved commands can be the starting point for documenting a process, by converting them into an automated script. Documentation is the first step to automation: If you don't know exactly how you do something, you can't automate it.

The combination of `script` and `history` is a powerful tool. The `script` command gathers both what you type and what the computer puts out but can, however, get obscured with odd characters if you use various aspects of command line editing. The `history` command accurately shows the commands that were used and can be used to verify that they were recorded.

Whether you use a cut-and-paste ability or automatically capture output, it's better than retyping things from scratch. It is less work and more accurate.

9.1.3.3 Leveraging Email

How often do you have an email conversation with your coworkers about a given task? Here's a ready source of ad hoc documentation that can be gathered together with a little work.

The two large problems with simply using email for your documentation are that email is not easily shareable and is likely not well organized. Other people cannot access your email, and you probably can't always find what you want. You're unlikely to have a single piece of email that contains everything you want to have in a document. There is usually a larger message and some back-and-forth smaller messages in which something is solved or communicated. Combine those separate messages in one file, and put it where your coworkers can find it.

If you already save a copy of every email you send, congratulations! You have the material for a number of easy and helpful documents just waiting for you to cut and paste them into the template mentioned in Section 9.1.2.

You can look in your Sent Mail folder for messages that can be used to assemble a document on a topic. Use your email client's ability to sort by conversations or thread to find good potential emails to turn into documentation. If there were more than one or two exchanges on a topic, the conversation probably contains enough information to be worth turning into a document. Even if your email client does not support conversations, sort by the message subject.

9.1.3.4 Mining the Ticket System

Another good source of potential documentation is your organization's trouble-ticket or request-tracking system. Some of these systems include tools to create a *solutions database* or *solution documents* that can be sent out when new requests arrive that are similar to those already solved.

Many sites use software with a *solutions database* feature but never use it or even enable it. It gets easier to use after the first couple times, so enable it and use it now.

If you know that you'll be using your ticket system as a resource when writing documentation, you can make the process easier and the ticket information more useful. If your SAs note how they resolved an issue, including pasting commands and output, and include it in the ticket work log, it quickly improves the value of those logs with shared documentation.

You might customize your ticket system with a flag for "knowledge base" checkbox and a comment field where you can note the process that needs to be documented. You'll also want a way to get a summary of those flagged tickets—a weekly email report, for example. If your ticket system is not easily extensible in this way, you can create a separate ticket queue for adding things to the knowledge base and simply clone or duplicate tickets into that queue. The original customer-request ticket can be closed and the duplicate left in the separate queue until someone has a chance to turn it into a document. The ticket data enables SAs to quickly write formal documentation. Using these methods usually leads to more documentation being written and fewer complaints about writing documentation: a win-win situation!

9.1.4 The Power of Checklists

A good way to start creating documentation and to function more efficiently in general is to use **checklists,** or lists of things arranged so that each line or paragraph contains only one step. As each item is completed, it can be checked off by making a mark next to it.

Checklists let you complete complex tasks and then verify that you have completed the steps. It's very obvious that you skipped a step if you are marking them off as each one is completed. A checklist can be used by someone less experienced to ensure that every aspect of the process has been finished. Requiring junior staff to file completed checklists or simply to hand them to their manager is a good way to create accountability. For really important processes, especially those that may involve the cooperation of several people or departments to accomplish, a signed checklist can be a good way to document that all the steps have been performed by the appropriate parties. Many SAs use checklists in their own daily task management to keep track of all the steps in complex tasks and all the tasks that need to be done.

Some typical checklists include

- Tasks to be done for each new hire
- Tasks to be done for each employee termination
- Installation tasks for each operating system used at a location
- Process for archiving and for off-site storage of data as required by the legal department
- Process for securing the OS before deploying a machine

Add checklists to regular documentation, especially for tasks that are performed frequently. After having used the full document many times, the person will need only the checklist.

Automating entire processes can be difficult; automating the most error-prone steps from a checklist can be more manageable. If this process is repeated enough, the entire sequence will be eventually automated.

9.1.5 Documentation Storage

Creating a storage area for documents, or **document repository**, is an important step in the documentation process. A centralized location provides a starting point for organizing and updating the documents. Typically, each SA has personal source copies of documents and personal notes; having a central repository makes it easier for people to find the most recent version of a document.

Creating a document repository is also a great way to find out about documentation you didn't realize you had. If there is a central repository, people will bring odd pieces of documentation that they have written. Most SAs have one or more directories full of reminder documents and will gladly share them when there is a place to put them.

The simplest method for making a document repository is to create a documentation directory on a shared volume. Start it off with a `README` file that describes any rules or policies that should be followed in making the documentation for inclusion in this repository. You might want to add the template from Section 9.1.2. Create some starter subdirectories named after the kinds of topics you want to have, such as desktops or printers or Linux.

As the SA staff creates documents, add them to the appropriate subdirectory, creating one, if necessary, and use filenames that describe the document. Someone looking for something in particular can simply list the subdirectory contents and search for items of interest. For example, someone looking for a document on how to add printers could list the `printers` subdirectory or list all the subdirectories and filter on any filenames that include the word `print`.

Adding source code control to a document repository can be useful in recovering earlier versions of a document if someone makes changes that turn out to be incorrect or if a file is accidentally deleted. It is usually much less trouble to check out a duplicate version from a source code repository than to do a restore from backup media. Open source products, such as SubVersion, make it easy to set up a simple repository.

A web site can be an excellent document repository, but manually maintaining tables of contents and so on can be more work than you're saving by having the documents in the first place. One solution is to configure the web server to list the contents of directories. Many web servers' default directory listing code supports only filenames of a certain length, so long descriptive names may become truncated. Other web servers make it easy to control the filename width that is displayed in an index.

Setting up a Shared Directory

When Tom worked for Mentor Graphics, his group maintained a directory on a central server, `/home/adm/docs`, that contained informal instructions on various topics. Filenames were long and descriptive: `how-to-create-accounts.txt` or `reasons-why-printer-p32-fails.txt`. Searching was done with Unix command line tools, such as `ls` and `grep`. In a very primitive attempt to maintain accuracy, everyone always checked the date of the file as part of judging whether the information was out of date. Today, a version control system would be used instead.

Although unsophisticated, this system served its purpose well. It was easy to create a new document, easy to edit an old one, and easy to find needed information.

9.1.6 Wiki Systems

A **wiki** is a web-based publishing and collaboration tool that has revolutionized documentation repositories. The name is derived from *Wikiwiki*, colloquial Hawaiian for *quick*. The first wiki was software called WikiWikiWeb, which begat the generic term *wiki*.

A wiki is a web-based documentation repository that makes it easy for anyone with appropriate access to add and edit documents. Documents may contain plaintext, text with Hypertext Markup Language (HTML), or text with wiki-specific embedded formatting tags or commands. Often, the wiki has a built in source code control system to check document files in and out and to retain revision history. More advanced wiki environments include user authentication, automated tagging of updates (date, time, user), per user locking of files, access control by user or group, and various degrees of granularity of read/modify/publish on individual document directories or subdirectories.

The most powerful aspect of wikis is that anyone can update any page. If something is wrong or out of date, the person who spots the error can correct it or add a note asking for someone to verify and fix the information. Documents magically evolve and stay current. One might wonder what prevents someone from simply deleting random text and adding wrong information; all changes are tracked by user; therefore, someone doing mischief will be identified. In a corporate environment, social pressure will keep such events rare. If they do occur, pages can be reverted to a previous state, using the full revision histories. It is possible to protect pages so that only certain people can modify them, a good precaution for highly sensitive documents.

The wiki formatting commands are very easy to learn and are much easier for nontechnical people to use than HTML is. Many email conventions they already use are supported, such as `*this text would appear bold*` and `_this text underlined_`. URLs are automatically turned into hypertext links. Writing the name of another wiki page is detected and turned into links. Wiki pages are usually named in CamelCase—also known as WikiWords or StudlyCaps—so the software is able to detect them easily. Using a WikiWord that does not relate to a wiki page generates a link that will prompt the user to create the page.

The ability to create placeholder pages for things as you realize that you will need them is extremely useful. It's so useful that until you have experienced it, you might not think it's a big deal. You can create an index or table of contents for a document repository and fill in documents as they are created.

Together, these features create an ideal collaboration tool. It can be very satisfying to see how quickly documents take shape and the repository begins to look real and useful. This encourages other people to contribute and keeps the momentum up.

Using a Wiki

The ease with which documentation of various forms can be created with a wiki was made especially obvious to Strata when working at a small start-up in an old factory building in Seattle. A number of employees, including Strata, were from out of town and tended to travel frequently, taking meals in the office and keeping random schedules. Without any specific requests or directive, bits of useful information started showing up on the intranet wiki site, much as information often shows up on whiteboards in a shared office. The difference was that the out-of-town employees could participate as easily as those in the office, and the information ranged from contact info for the small company that shared the net connection to people's travel schedules to self-rescue advice on the rickety old service elevator that sometimes got stuck between floors. There was even a recipe page for the office rice cooker. The wiki site was an elegant testament to the power of technology to assist self-organizing systems rather than getting in the way.

❖ **Help Picking a Wiki**   WikiMatrix (www.wikimatrix.org) provides tools to help compare and select the package that's right for a given situation.

9.1.7 A Search Facility

A search facility is a must for a living documentation system. People are going to put stuff where it cannot be easily found by others. Fortunately, many drop-in search engine tools can be used with a web repository. These tools range from open source packages to hardware appliances that are designed to index data across an entire enterprise. When choosing a search engine, consider the level of search granularity and search options available, as well as what types of documents can be accessed for full-contents indexing.

It is preferable to be able to limit the search to specific areas or objects. One might specify to search only the titles of documents or the text on the pages where they are linked. Other searches might include the content of the documents themselves or the keywords or tags associated with the pages.

Not all search engines support sophisticated queries, such as requiring that specific words be present or absent, or allow one to query metadata about the documents. An example of the latter might be asking to find documents that include the phrase *software license* and were created before January 1.

9.1.8 Rollout Issues

A crucial aspect to delivering a new document repository is getting buy-in from the community that will be using it. The users are also the authors, and if a high percentage of folks dig in their heels, the efficacy of the entire project becomes questionable. Ironically, it's many of the old-guard techies who are the most resistant. They've lived in an email-centric world for ages and don't feel that having to go out on the web to participate is respectful of their time. There's certainly an argument to be made for having one inbox of new stuff to monitor! One way to solve this issue is to make certain that a Recent Changes area is automatically generated as part of the wiki. Some systems permit this page to be periodically emailed to a list of concerned people, or it can be configured to provide the information as an RSS[1] feed so that it can be read as a blog. Providing many ways to access the same information makes it easier for people to adopt.

Adopting Better Documentation Practices

The power of wikis is that there is so little hindrance to getting started that people are drawn in to using it. At one site, Tom hadn't gotten buy-in for a wiki-based system yet, so he installed one on a server and started using it to store his own documentation. Soon, when people asked him where to find certain information, the answer would include a link to the appropriate wiki page.

As people started seeing the wiki used more and more, they started asking for training so they too could use it. Tom would resist a little and then "give in." The more he resisted, the more people wanted to use the system. Soon, enough people were using it so that new people assumed that this was the official place for documentation. And then, it was.

9.1.9 Self-Management versus Explicit Management

It is good to decide in advance whether to have a site librarian or manager do the kinds of maintenance a documentation repository needs or whether the site will be self-managed. Most groups fall somewhere in between, with the team lead or manager periodically setting explicit examples by reformatting

---

1. RSS is a family of web feed formats, and stands for Really Simple Syndication, or Rich Site Summary, or RDF (Resource Description Framework) Site Summary.

areas or leaving comments on pages about how she would like to see things done.

If it is possible to have someone include site management as part of her job, a much more useful site can be created via successive refinements. An example is monitoring the search logs and referring-link logs to find out what kind of information people are having trouble finding, then making it more prominent on the site. Another example is working with one's ticket system to create documents to promote case studies or solution logs that can then be refined or added to FAQ areas.

If the role of site manager is created, it should be that of an enabler, not a gatekeeper. The site manager should not be controlling every addition to the repository or rolling back other contributors' edits, except when a clear error or abuse is occurring. The site manager is there to maintain and enhance the structure of the site, moving documents where needed and making it more usable.

9.2 The Icing

Having covered the basics of creating simple documents and document repositories, we now turn to creating larger repositories, being more formal, and managing content.

9.2.1 A Dynamic Documentation Repository

The idea of a "living documentation" site, or dynamic documentation repository, is simply that of a site or repository where documents are expected to be updated periodically to meet the needs of the environment. The Internet phenomenon known as Wikipedia (www.Wikipedia.org) is a wonderful example of this kind of system. Beginning with the original Wiki Encyclopedia, dozens of groups have created special-interest content repositories on this model. In contrast to a traditional document repository, a living documentation repository shifts the focus to the customer's interaction with the documents. Rather than being able to merely locate and read a document, the customer can annotate, edit, collect documents into views, send document references to colleagues, and so on.

Although we use a wiki as the primary example of a living documentation site, it is important to note that this does not mean that everything must be integrated into the wiki. It is sufficient to have a central point to organize information, including links to other information systems.

Using Different Wikis for Different Situations

Different software packages have different strong points. One site found that it was better to maintain DokuWiki for its customer-facing support documentation, Trac for documents and ticket tracking related to internally developed source code, and RT for the customer-facing request tracker. The site found that it was rare that documents cross-linked, and when they did, it was easy to copy and paste or hyperlink to bridge them.

9.2.2 A Content-Management System

A **content-management system** (CMS) is a publication system for web sites. For example, a newspaper CMS system might facilitate the process of reporters creating stories, which are then queued to editors, edited, and approved for publication. The CMS system releases the article at a specific time, placing it on the web site, updating tables of contents, and taking care of other details. For an IT site, CMS might permit plug-ins that give portal features, such as summaries of recent outages.

A number of features are required to implement a functional CMS. A content-management system specifically consists of three layers: repository, history, and presentation. The repository layer is generally a database but may also be a structured file system with metadata. The content is stored in this layer. The history layer implements version control, permissions, audit trails, and such functionality as assigning a global document identifier to new documents. The history layer may be a separate journal or database or may be stored in the repository. The presentation layer is the user interface. In addition to allowing document interaction, such as browsing or editing, the presentation layer may also implement document controls, such as read-only access or permissions.

Advanced wiki systems have many of the features of a full CMS. Many CMS systems now include wikilike features. Two popular open source CMS systems are Drupal and MediaWiki.

9.2.3 A Culture of Respect

A living documentation site needs a culture of respect; otherwise, people become hesitant to post or feel that they may post only "approved" stuff. Such trade-offs are inherent in implementing a moderated posting process. Not just anybody should be editing the standby-generator test instructions, for instance, yet the approved author may have missed or changed something in the original posting. This problem can be addressed in most cases by enabling comments to a page and promoting comments into content when they seem valid to the original author or to enough other commenters. When a genuine mistake is made, revision control can enable access to an unaltered version. When it is unclear which version is authoritative, at least revision control can show a list of changes and provide some context with which to make a judgment call or to request clarification via phone or email.

Expect to put in a bit of management time on the wiki until people get the hang of it and match it to your particular culture. There's a level of detail that will be "right" for your group, and, like any kind of writing, there'll be some bracketing on either side before things start looking as you feel they should look. Some groups have a documentation system that is merely pasted emails in no particular order under topics; other groups have elaborate runbook-style pages for each important piece of infrastructure. The lovely thing about using a wiki or similar living documentation system as an interim CMS is that you can transition from an ad hoc system to a more formalized system as documents mature. Pages and entries can be reorganized and cleaned up during slow days and perhaps promoted to new areas or exported to the more formal CMS.

9.2.4 Taxonomy and Structure

Wiki systems tend to impose very little structure. Some simply provide navigation.

At the outset, don't spend time worrying about structure. A major killer of wiki projects is the imposition of too much structure during the early stages. A notion of *low barrier to entry* spawned the wiki. Updating a page should be as easy as sending an email; otherwise, people won't use it. It's far better to have to clean up some pages for readability than to have the info sequestered in someone's mail folders where no one can find it when he is on vacation. If a particular type of document will be written many times by many people—for example, design proposals or feature requests—provide a template to keep those more formal documents in the same format.

Differentiate between writing documentation and organizing documentation. As your content grows, folks will increasingly use search rather than categories to look for things. You can always create structured categories and refactor the pages or their links as the wiki grows.

9.2.5 Additional Documentation Uses

Here are some more ways to use a living document system. Many wiki systems have templates or plug-ins specific to these applications.

9.2.5.1 Self-Help Desk

Customers can use the self-help desk area of the documentation site to interact directly with the site. Perhaps your current site has a `Create a new ticket` link that allows customers to make a request via the ticket system.

This area is a good place for such items as news on planned outages, updates on situations in progress, and prominent links to policies and how-to documents. Examples of the latter might be how to log in remotely via VPN, how to set up synchronization to your mobile device, and so on.

Another item that belongs in the self-help desk area is customer access to monitoring results, such as multirouter traffic graphics (MRTGs) or even scripted lists of free space on shared volumes. Sites that rely heavily on shared software licenses, such as those used by CAD tools, may find it very helpful to place a link to the license-monitoring utility on this page, to head off questions about who has what licenses checked out.

9.2.5.2 Internal Group–Specific Documents

SAs are early adopters, and many SA groups build out a living documentation site for their own benefit. Having information on how to perform complex tasks that only one or two people in the group routinely undertake can save the day when someone is out sick or called away. The creation of group-specific documents is the beginning of forming an institutional memory, a very important piece of continuity for any group.

Although the SA group might lead the way, any group or department can benefit from having its own area in the site. Some groups have a de facto living documents site in the form of a source code repository, which may be used for specifications, customer lists, and marketing materials, as well as code. Owing to the sensitive nature of some group-specific documentation, this area is likely to have restricted access, with only that group and administrative staff able to access the area.

9.2.5.3 How-To Docs

At many sites, a short, self-explanatory document called a How-To, or HOWTO, helps customers to help themselves when SAs are unavailable. HOWTO documents cover a single topic, generally the accomplishment of a specific task; are usually customized to the environment of the site; and generally include both customer input and program response, often with screen shots. A HOWTO document is designed to solve a particular problem rather than to serve as a conceptual tutorial. The streamlined format, tailored to the environment, serves to encourage buy-in from customers who would otherwise consider reading documentation to be too time consuming or difficult and would open a support call instead.

Typical examples of HOWTOs include setting up an email client, obtaining remote access to networks or file servers, accessing printers, and configuring software for use in the local environment. University sites, which often have a very large ratio of customers to SAs, benefit particularly from the self-help desk and How-To documents. Sites documenting helpdesk usage and support levels in their organizations might consider web server logs of HOWTO access as a metric to track and report.

9.2.5.4 Frequently Asked Questions

To most Internet users, the Frequently Asked Questions (FAQ) list is a familiar tool. The FAQ is simply a list of the most common queries about a particular topic, often organized into sections and subsections and usually evolving over time. Some wiki plug-ins automatically generate a table of contents or present the questions as hypertext links to the answers. (This approach has the downside of making it difficult to read all the questions and answers in order or to print or search the list.)

The FAQ list and a collection of HOWTO documents differ primarily in length and format. The HOWTO is a single topic; the FAQ, a collection of questions and answers. Often, an answer may point to a HOWTO document or to a choice of documents, based on aspects of the customer's request.

If you do not already have a FAQ list at your site, a good way to create one is to look at your ticket system and see what subjects are often raised as tickets. The types of questions will vary widely, depending on the type of organization you have and the degree to which customers are supported. A small engineering start-up company's FAQ might include such questions as, "Where do I download drivers for the video cards in our development lab systems?" A nonprofit organization's FAQ might have such questions as, "Where can our volunteers open free weblogs or start community web sites?"

9.2.5.5 Reference Lists

Reference lists are accumulated lists of things that are not accessed often but that serve a specific purpose. For example, a list of corporate acronyms is not something one needs every day, but when you see an acronym you've never seen before, you know to go to the list to look it up.

Here are more such lists:

- Vendors and their contact information
- Serial numbers and asset tag numbers of hardware
- License keys and number of users for software
- Compatibility lists: which optical mice are compatible with which hardware; which drives work with which controllers
- Employee directory: a manual or automatically generated from a corporate database
- Corporate acronyms
- List of local restaurants, taxi companies, and so on: one page per office
- For each office location, a list of tips for visitors: airport suggestions, hotel recommendations, whether normal badge access works, and so on
- Whom to notify for outages, suggestions, and comments about various products and/or issues

9.2.5.6 Procedures

Many organizations must comply with International Organization for Standardization (ISO) standards, Occupational Safety and Health Administration (OSHA) regulations, or Sarbanes-Oxley governing-practice regulations. Such sites benefit from having an easy way to create, maintain, and access procedures, checklists, and scripts relating to the relevant practices. Compile a runbook of procedures, and record compliance with the procedures.

Procedures or runbooks are useful whether or not you are obliged to create them. When it is time to shut down the generator after power is restored, a procedural list of how to do so cleanly will be more useful than a diagram showing all the electrical hookups in the data center.

9.2.5.7 Technical Library or Scrapbook

Storing documents that vendors, suppliers, and customers send to you; articles that you bought or saved from other sources; and possibly even a manual on fixing the kitchen sink can be a challenging area to organize. Some sites merely create alphabetical lists of the content; other sites appoint a document librarian who creates elaborate taxonomies of information. If overdone, such taxonomies can make documents more, not less, difficult, to find. (Will the instructions on how to wire up a connector for the Cisco console be found in the Vendor Docs area, the Cabling Area, or the Networking Area? The document can be in all those areas, but someone has to maintain those links.)

9.2.6 Off-Site Links

The Internet contains a wealth of useful information on technical and business topics, ranging from helpful blog articles to the Linux Documentation Project to online collaborative encyclopedias, such as Wikipedia. Much of this content cannot be duplicated on your own site owing to copyright restrictions or practical considerations, such as disk space and keeping pace with updates. Linking to this content, however, can be very helpful to your customer community. Examples of items to explicitly link into your site include tutorials and HOWTO articles on using tools or software, vendor support forums for commercial or open source products used at your organization, and online publications related to topics of technical interest.

It is important that an **anonymizing redirection service** be used for such links. When most browsers request a web page, they include a reference to the page that directed the browser to the page being requested. This lets sites track who is linking to them and calculate which of these links are the most successful. However, there is a privacy concern: If the referring page name is from an internal web site, the referral site will learn that this site exists. The referred-to site may learn the name of your internal web server, which shouldn't be a problem unless your security is based on simply hiding hostnames. However, the full URL might reveal secret project code names and other information.[2] For example, a site seeing referrals from that URL might give away the big surprise you are planning in May. Just a few calls to reporters, and suddenly, newspapers are reporting that your company has a project called "quickfox," and the big surprise is ruined. The solution is to make sure that the document repository redirects external links through a service that eliminates referral headers.

9.3 Conclusion

Documentation provides information to customers so they need to bother SAs less often and so saves them time. It helps SAs repeat processes without error and simplify processes so that they can be delegated easily.

---

2. For example, http//secret.example.com/project/quickfox/competitors-to-destroy-may27.html.

It is easier to create documentation by using a template you can use for screen shots, terminal session captures, email archives, and ticket system archives to help generate content for documents. Checklists are a good way to document multistep procedures to help you repeat them consistently, document what other groups expect from you, or provide a way for junior SAs to mark an assignment as complete and hand it in to a manager.

Documenting a process is difficult. However, once you have done the hard work of creating the process, the documentation can be used by less knowledgeable people. Thus, the process becomes easier to delegate. Having procedures documented makes it easier to create job descriptions when hiring new people.

Documents should be kept in a repository so they can be shared and maintained. Wikis are a very useful system for making repositories because they make it easy to create and update documents and do not require HTML knowledge. Plug-ins extend wikis to do more services.

It can be difficult to get people to start using a documentation repository. Providing help, training, and templates eases the barrier to entry.

Repositories can be useful for more than procedures. Repositories can become self-help desks and store HOWTO docs, FAQ managers, reference docs, and inventory lists.

High-functioning SA teams are generous about documenting processes and sharing information. A good repository can facilitate this. Documentation saves you and everyone time and leverages everyone's knowledge to make a better environment.

Exercises

1. What topics seem to come up most often in customer requests at your site? What percentage might be handled by a self-help desk with some HOWTO documents?

2. Describe how you share information with other team members. What works best about it? What would you change?

3. Which documents in your organization would most benefit from having a template? Design the template.

4. What items would go into a documentation template in your organization. Are any of them unusual or specific to your group?

5. On a scale of 1 to 10, with 10 being most important, how would you rate "ease of use" for a shared document system? Why? How would you rate "access control"?

6. If your site or group does not have a document repository, ask three people why they would resist using it. If your site or group has one but it is underutilized, ask three people what would make it easier to use. How would you mitigate these issues?

7. Of the solutions for shared-document systems discussed in this chapter, which ones best fit with your answers to the two previous questions?

Chapter 10

Disaster Recovery and Data Integrity

A disaster-recovery plan looks at what disasters could hit the company and lays out a plan for responding to those disasters. Disaster-recovery planning includes implementing ways to mitigate potential disasters and making preparations to enable quick restoration of key services. The plan identifies what those key services are and specifies how quickly they need to be restored.

All sites need to do some level of disaster-recovery (DR) planning. DR planners must consider what happens if something catastrophic occurs at any one of their organization's sites and how they can recover from it. We concentrate on the electronic data aspects of DR. However, this part of the plan should be built as part of a larger program in order to meet the company's legal and financial obligations. Several books are dedicated to disaster-recovery planning, and we recommend them for further reading: Fulmer (2000), Levitt (1997), and Schreider (1998).

Building a disaster-recovery plan involves understanding both the risks that your site faces and your company's legal and fiduciary responsibilities. From this basis, you can begin your preparations. This chapter describes what is involved in building a plan for your site.

10.1 The Basics

As with any project, building a disaster-recovery plan starts with understanding the requirements: determining what disasters could afflict your site, the likelihood that those disasters will strike, the cost to your company if they do strike, and how quickly the various parts of your business need to be revived. Once you and your management understand what can happen, you can get a budget allocated for the project and start looking at how to meet and, preferably, beat those requirements.

10.1.1 Definition of a Disaster

A disaster is a catastrophic event that causes a massive outage affecting an entire building or site. A disaster can be anything from a natural disaster, such as an earthquake, to the more common problem of stray backhoes cutting your cables by accident. A disaster is anything that has a significant impact on your company's ability to do business.

Lack of Planning Can Cause Risk-Taking

A computer equipment manufacturer had a facility in the west of Ireland. A fire started in the building, and the staff knew that the fire-protection system was inadequate and that the building would be very badly damaged. Several staff members went to the data center and started throwing equipment out the window because the equipment had a better chance of surviving the fall than the fire. Other staff members then carried the equipment up the hill to their neighboring building. The staff members in the burning building left when they judged that the fire hazard was too great.

All the equipment that they had thrown out the window actually survived, and the facility was operational again in record time. However, the lack of a disaster-recovery plan and adequate protection systems resulted in staff members' risking their lives. Fortunately, no one was badly injured in this incident. But their actions were in breach of fire safety codes and extremely risky because no one there was qualified to judge when the fire had become too hazardous.

10.1.2 Risk Analysis

The first step in building a disaster-recovery plan is to perform a risk analysis. Risk management is a good candidate for using external consultants because it is a specialized skill that is required periodically, not daily. A large company may hire specialists to perform the risk analysis while having an in-house person responsible for risk management.

A risk analysis involves determining what disasters the company is at risk of experiencing and what the chances are of those disasters occurring. The analyst determines the likely cost to the company if a disaster of each type occurred. The company then uses this information to decide approximately how much money is reasonable to spend on trying to mitigate the effects of each type of disaster.

The approximate budget for risk mitigation is determined by the formula

(Probable cost of disaster − Probable cost after mitigation)
× Risk of disaster

For example, if a company's premises has one chance in a million of being affected by flooding, and if a flood would cost the company $10 million, the budget for mitigating the effects of the flood would be in the range of $10. In other words, it's not even worth stocking up on sandbags in preparation for a flood. On the other hand, if a company has 1 chance in 3,000 of being within 10 miles of the epicenter of an earthquake measuring 5.0 on the Richter scale, which would cause a loss of $60 million, the budget for reducing or preventing that damage would be in the $20,000 range.

A simpler, smaller-scale example is a large site that has a single point of failure whereby all LANs are tied together by one large router. If it died, it would take one day to repair, and there is a 70 percent chance that failure will occur once every 24 months. The outage would cause 1,000 people to be unable to work for a day. The company estimates the loss of productivity to be $68,000. When the SAs go looking for redundancy for the router, the budget is approximately $23,800. The SAs also need to investigate the cost of reducing the outage time to 4 hours—for example, by increasing support contract level. If that costs a reasonable amount, it further reduces the amount the company would lose and therefore the amount it should spend on full redundancy.

This view of the process is somewhat simplified. Each disaster can occur to different degrees with different likelihoods and a wide range of cost implications. Damage prevention for one level of a particular disaster will probably have mitigating effects on the amount of damage sustained at a higher level of the same disaster. All this complexity is taken into account by a professional risk analyst when she recommends a budget for the various types of disaster preparedness.

10.1.3 Legal Obligations

Beyond the basic cost to the company, additional considerations need to be taken into account as part of the DR planning process. Commercial companies have legal obligations to their vendors, customers, and shareholders in terms of meeting contract obligations. Public companies have to abide by the laws of the stock markets on which they are traded. Universities have contractual obligations to their students. Building codes and work-safety regulations also must be followed.

The legal department should be able to elaborate on these obligations. Typically, they are of the form "The company must be able to resume shipping product within 1 week" or "The company can delay reporting quarterly results by at most 3 days under these circumstances." Those obligations translate into requirements for the DR plan. They define how quickly various pieces of the physical and electronic infrastructure must be restored to working order. Restoring individual parts of the company to working order before the entire infrastructure is operational requires an in-depth understanding of what pieces of infrastructure those parts rely on and a detailed plan of how to get them working. Meeting the time commitments also requires an understanding of how long restoring those components will take. We look at that further in Section 10.1.5.

10.1.4 Damage Limitation

Damage limitation is about reducing the cost of the disasters. Some damage limitation can come at little or no cost to the company through advance planning and good processes. Most damage limitation does involve additional cost to the company and is subject to the cost/benefit analysis that is performed by the risk analysts.

For little or no cost, there are ways to reduce the risk of a disaster's causing significant damage to the company or to limit the amount of damage that the disaster can inflict. For example, in an area prone to minor flooding, placing critical services above ground level may not significantly increase construction and move-in costs but avoids problems in the future. Choosing rack-mountable and reasonably sturdy racks to bolt it into rather than putting equipment on shelves can significantly reduce the impact of a minor earthquake for little or no extra cost. Using lightning rods in the construction of buildings in an area that is prone to lightning storms is also a cheap way of limiting damage. These steps are particularly economical because they fix the problem once, rather than requiring a recurring cost.

Limiting the damage caused by a major disaster is more costly and always should be subject to a cost/benefit analysis. For example, a data center could be built in an underground military-style bunker to protect against tornados and bombs. In an earthquake zone, expensive mechanisms allow racks to move independently in a constrained manner to reduce the risk of computer backplanes' shearing, the major issue with rigidly fixed racks during a strong earthquake. These mechanisms for limiting damage are so costly that only the largest companies are likely to be able to justify implementing them.

Most damage-limitation mechanisms fall somewhere between "almost free" and "outlandishly expensive." Fire-prevention systems typically fall into the latter category. It is wise to consider implementing a fire-protection system that is designed to limit damage to equipment in the data center when activated. Local laws and human-safety concerns limit what is possible in this area, but popular systems at the time of writing include inert gas systems and selective, limited-area, water-based systems with early-warning mechanisms that permit an operator to detect and resolve a problem, such as a disk or power supply catching fire, before the fire-protection system is activated. Systems for detecting moisture under raised data center floors or in rarely visited UPS or generator rooms are also moderately priced damage-limitation mechanisms.

Another area that often merits attention is loss of power to a building or campus. Short power outages, spikes, or brownouts can be handled by a UPS; longer interruptions will require a generator. The more equipment on protected power—freezers at biotech companies, call centers at customer-service companies—and the longer you need to be able to run them, the more it will cost. See Chapter 6 for building disaster-proof data centers, particularly Section 6.1.1 discusses issues related to picking a good location and Section 6.1.4 explains issues related to power.

10.1.5 Preparation

Even with a reasonable amount of damage control in place, your organization may still experience a disaster. Part of your disaster planning must be preparation for this eventuality. Being prepared for a disaster means being able to restore the essential systems to working order in a timely manner, as defined by your legal obligations.

Restoring services after a disaster can require rebuilding the necessary data and services on new equipment if the old equipment is not operational. Thus, you need to arrange a source of replacement hardware in advance from companies that provide this service. You also need to have another site to which this equipment can be sent if the primary site cannot be used because of safety reasons, lack of power, or lack of connectivity. Make sure that the company providing the standby equipment knows where to send it in an emergency. Make sure that you get turnaround time commitments from the provider and that you know what hardware the company will be able to provide on short notice. Don't forget to take the turnaround time on this equipment into account when calculating how long the entire process will take. If a disaster is large enough to require the company's services, chances are it will have other customers that also are affected. Find out how the company plans to handle the situation in which both you and your neighbor have the right to the only large Sun server that was stockpiled.

Once you have the machines, you need to recreate your system. Typically, you first rebuild the system and then restore the data. This requires that you have backups of the data stored off-site—usually at a commercial storage-and-retrieval service. You also need to be able to easily identify which tapes are required for restoring the essential services. This part of the basic preparation is built on infrastructure that your site should have already put in place. An ongoing part of disaster preparation is to try retrieving tapes from the off-site storage company on a regular basis to see how long it takes. This time is subtracted from the total amount of time available to completely restore the relevant systems to working order. If it takes too long to get the tapes, it may be impossible to complete the rebuild on time. For more on these issues, see Chapter 26, particularly Section 26.2.2.

A site usually will need to have important documents archived at a document repository for safekeeping. Such repositories specialize in DR scenarios. If your company has one, you may want to consider also using it to house the data tapes.

Remember that you may need power, telephone, and network connectivity as part of restoring the services. Work with the facilities group on these aspects. It may be advisable to arrange an emergency office location for the critical functions as part of the disaster plan.

Good Preparation for an Emergency Facility

A company had a California call center that was used by its customers, predominantly large financial institutions. The company had a well-rehearsed procedure to execute in case of a disaster that affected the call center building. The company had external outlets for providing power and the call center phone services and appropriate cables and equipment standing by, including tents and folding tables and chairs. When a strong earthquake struck in 1991, the call center was rapidly relocated outside and was operational again within minutes. Not long after it was set up, it received lots of calls from its customers in New York, who wanted to make sure that services were still available if they required them. The call center staff calmly reassured customers that all services were operating normally. Customers had no idea that they were talking to someone who was sitting on a chair in the grass outside the building. The call center had to remain outside for several days until the building was certified safe. But from the customers' perspectives, it remained operational the entire time.

The plan to relocate the call center outside in the case of emergency worked well because the most likely emergency was an earthquake and the weather was likely to be dry, at least long enough for the tents to be put up. The company had prepared well for its most likely disaster scenario.

10.1.6 Data Integrity

Data integrity means ensuring that data is not altered by external sources. Data can be corrupted maliciously by viruses or individuals. It can also be corrupted inadvertently by individuals, bugs in programs, and undetected hardware malfunctions. For important data, consider ways to ensure integrity as part of day-to-day operations or the backup or archival process. For example, data that should not change can be checked against a read-only checksum of the data. Databases that should experience small changes or should have only data added should be checked for unexpectedly large changes or deletions. Examples include source code control systems and databases of gene sequences. Exploit your knowledge of the data on your systems to automate integrity checking.

Disaster planning also involves ensuring that a complete and correct copy of the corporate data can be produced and restored to the systems. For disaster recovery, it must be a recent, coherent copy of the data with all databases in sync. Data integrity meshes well with disaster recovery.

Industrial espionage and theft of intellectual property are not uncommon, and a company may find itself needing to fight for its intellectual property rights in a court of law. The ability to accurately restore data as it existed on a certain date can also be used to prove ownership of intellectual property. To be used as evidence, the date of the information retrieved must be accurately known, and the data must be in a consistent state. For both disaster-recovery purposes and use of the data as evidence in a court, the SAs need to know that the data has not been tampered with.

It is important to make sure that the implementers put in place the data-integrity mechanisms that the system designers recommend. It is inadvisable to wait for corruption to occur before recognizing the value of these systems.

10.2 The Icing

The ultimate preparation for a disaster is to have fully redundant versions of everything that can take over when the primary version fails. In other words, have a redundant site with redundant systems. In this section, we look at having a redundant site and some ways a company might be able to make that site more cost-effective.

Although this sounds expensive, in large companies, especially banks, having a redundant site is a minimum. In fact, large companies have stopped using the term *disaster recovery* and instead use the term *contingency planning* or business *continuity planning*.

10.2.1 Redundant Site

For companies requiring high availability, the next level of disaster planning is to have a fully redundant second site in a location that will not be affected by the same disaster. For most companies, this is an expensive dream. However, if a company has two locations with data centers, it may be possible to duplicate some of the critical services across both data centers so that the only problem that remains to be solved is how the people who use those services get access to the redundant site.

Rather than permanently having live redundant equipment at the second site, it can instead be used as an alternative location for rebuilding the services. If the company has a contract for an emergency supply of equipment, that equipment could be sent to the alternative data center site. If the site that was affected by the disaster is badly damaged, this may be the fastest way to have the services up and running. Another option is to designate some services at each site as less critical and to use the equipment from those services to rebuild the critical services from the damaged site. Sometimes, you are lucky enough to have a design that compartmentalizes various pieces, making it easy to design a redundant site.

10.2.2 Security Disasters

A growing concern is security disasters. Someone breaks into the corporate web site and changes the logo to be obscene. Someone steals the database of credit card numbers from your e-commerce site. A virus deletes all the files it can access. Unlike with natural disasters, no physical harm occurs, and the attack may not be from a physically local phenomenon.

A similar risk analysis can be performed to determine the kinds of measures required to protect data. Architecture decisions have a risk component. One can manage the risk in many ways—by building barriers around the system or by monitoring the system so that it can be shut down quickly in the event of an attack.

We continually see sites that purchase large, canned systems without asking for an explanation of the security risks of such systems. Although no system is perfectly secure, a vendor should be able to explain the product's security structure, the risk factors, and how recovery would occur in the event of data loss. Chapter 11 covers constructing security policies and procedures that take into account DR plans.

10.2.3 Media Relations

When a disaster occurs, the media will probably want to know what happened, what effect it is having on the company, and when services will be restored. Sadly, the answer to all three questions is usually, "We aren't sure." This can be the worst answer you can give a reporter. Handling the media badly during a disaster can cause bigger problems than the original disaster.

We have two simple recommendations on this topic. First, have a public relations (PR) firm on retainer before a disaster so that you aren't trying to hire one as the disaster is happening. Some PR firms specialize in disaster management, and some are proficient at handling security-related disasters. Second, plan ahead of time how you will deal with the media. This plan should include who will talk to the media, what kinds of things will and will not be said, and what the chain of command is if the designated decision makers aren't available. Anyone who talks to the media should receive training from your PR firm.

Note that these recommendations have one thing in common: They both require planning ahead of time. Never be in a disaster without a media plan. Don't try to write one during a disaster.

10.3 Conclusion

The most important aspect of disaster planning is understanding what services are the most critical to the business and what the time constraints are for restoring those services. The disaster planner also needs to know what disasters are likely to happen and how costly they would be before he can complete a risk analysis and determine the company's budget for limiting the damage.

A disaster plan should be built with consideration of those criteria. It should account for the time to get new equipment, retrieve the off-site backups, and rebuild the critical systems from scratch. Doing so requires advance planning for getting the correct equipment and being able to quickly determine which backup tapes are needed for rebuilding the critical systems.

The disaster planner must look for simple ways to limit damage, as well as more complex and expensive ways. Preparations that are automatic and become part of the infrastructure are most effective. Fire containment, water detection, earthquake bracing, and proper rack-mount equipment fall into this category. The disaster planner also must prepare a plan for a team of people to execute in case of emergency. Simple plans are often the most effective. The team members must be familiar with their individual roles and should practice a few times a year.

Full redundancy, including a redundant site, is an ideal that is beyond the budget of most companies. If a company has a second data center site, however, there are ways to incorporate it into the disaster plan at reasonable expense.

Exercises

1. Which business units in your company would need to be up and running first after a disaster, and how quickly would they need to be operational?

2. What commitments does your company have to its customers, and how do those commitments influence your disaster planning?

3. What disasters are most likely to hit each of your sites? How big an area might that disaster affect, and how many of your company's buildings could be affected?

4. What would the cost be to your company if a moderate disaster hit one of its locations?

5. What forms of disaster limitation do you have in place now?

6. What forms of disaster limitation would you like to implement? How much would each of them cost?

7. If you lost use of a data center facility because of a disaster, how would you restore service?

8. What are your plans for dealing with the media in the event of a disaster? What is the name of the PR firm you retain to help you?

Chapter 11

Security Policy

Security entails much more than firewalls, intrusion detection, and authentication schemes. Although all are key components of a security program, security administrators also have to take on many different roles, and the skills for those roles are quite diverse. In this chapter, we look at all aspects of security and describe the basic building blocks that a company needs for a successful security program, some guiding principles, and some common security needs. We also briefly discuss how the approaches described here apply in various-size companies and mention some ways in which the approach you take to security may differ in an academic environment.

Security is a huge topic, with many fine books written on it. Zwicky, Chapman, and Cooper (2000) and Bellovin, Cheswick, and Rubin (2003) are excellent books about firewalls. The books by Garfinkel and Spafford (1996, 1997) discuss UNIX and Internet security, along with web security and commerce. Norberg and Russell (2000) and Sheldon and Cox (2000) provide details on Windows security. The book by Miller and Davis (2000) covers the area of intellectual property. Wood (1999) is well known for his sample security policies. Kovacich (1998) deals with the topic of establishing a program for information protection. Neumann (1997) and Denning (1999) cover the topics of risks and information warfare.

Security should be everyone's job. However, it is important to have individuals who specialize in and focus on the organization's security needs. Security is a huge, rapidly changing field, and to keep current, SAs working in security must focus all their attention on the security arena. Senior SAs with the right mind-set for security are good candidates for being trained by security specialists to join the security team.

Data security requires more negotiating skills and better contacts throughout the company than does any other area of system administration. People in many companies perceive computer security as being an obstacle to getting work done. To succeed, you must dispel that notion and be involved as early as possible in any projects that affect the electronic security of the company.

If you learn one thing from this chapter, we hope it is this: The policy that gets adhered to is the one that is the most convenient for the customer. If you want people to follow a policy, make sure that it is their easiest option. For example, if you want people to use encrypted email, make sure that the application you provide makes it as easy as sending regular email, or they won't do it. Refining a policy or technology to the point that it is easier than all the alternatives is a lot of work for you. However, it is better than spending your time fighting security problems.

Over time, computer use has evolved from requiring physical proximity to remote access from around the world. Security trends have evolved in tandem. How will the computer and network access models change in the future, and what impact will such change have on security? The trend so far has been a decreasing ability to rely on physical security or on trust, with more use of encryption and strong authentication. Each new access model has required an increased need for planning, education, testing, and new technology.

11.1 The Basics

Two basic patterns in security policy are *perimeter security* and *defense in depth*.

1. **Perimeter security** is like a castle with a high wall around it. Make a good wall, and you are free to do what you want inside. Put a good firewall at the entry to your network, and you don't have to worry about what's inside. Bellovin, Cheswick, and Rubin (2003) refer to this as the crunchy candy shell with the soft gooey center, or a policy of putting all your eggs in one basket and then making sure that you have a really good basket. The problem with perimeter security is that the crunchy candy shell is disappearing as wireless networks become common and as organizations cross-connect networks with partners.

2. **Defense in depth** refers to placing security measures at all points in a network. For example, a firewall protects the organization from attacks via the Internet, an antivirus system scans each email message, antimalware software runs on each individual PC, and encryption is used between computers to ensure privacy and authentication.

As with the design of other infrastructure components, the design of a security system should be based on simplicity, usability, and minimalism. Complexity obscures errors or chinks in your armor. An overly complex system will prove to be inflexible and difficult to use and maintain and will ultimately be weakened or circumvented for people to be able to work effectively. In addition, a successful security architecture has security built into the system, not simply bolted on at the end. Good security involves an in-depth approach with security hooks at all levels of the system. If those hooks are not there from the beginning, they can be very difficult to add and integrate later.

Some consider security and convenience to be inversely proportional. That is, to make something more secure makes it more difficult to use. This certainly has been true for a number of security products. We believe that when security is done correctly, it takes into account the customer's ease of use. The problem is that often, it takes several years for technology to advance to this point. For example, passwords are a good start, but putting a password on every application becomes a pain for people who use a lot of applications in a day's work. However, making things even more secure by deploying a secure single-sign-on system maximizes security and convenience by being much more secure yet nearly eliminating the users' need to type passwords.

When security is inconvenient, your customers will find ways around it. When security technology advances sufficiently, however, the system becomes more secure *and* easier to use.

> ❖ **Security and Reliability**   Reliability and security go hand in hand. An insecure system is open to attacks that make it unreliable. Attackers can bring down an unreliable system by triggering the weaknesses, which is a denial-of-service (DoS) attack. If management is unconcerned with security, find out whether it is concerned with reliability. If so, address all security issues as realiability issues instead.

11.1.1   Ask the Right Questions

Before you can implement a successful security program, you must find out what you are trying to protect, from whom it must be protected, what the risks are, and what it is worth to the company. These business decisions should be made through informed discussion with the executive management of the company. Document the decisions that are made during this process, and review the final document with management. The document will need to evolve with the company but should not change too dramatically or frequently.

11.1.1.1 Information Protection

Corporate security is about protecting assets. Most often, information is the asset that a company is most concerned about. The information to be protected can fall into several categories. A mature security program defines a set of categories and classifies information within those categories.

The classification of the information determines what level of security is applied to it. For example, information could be categorized as public, company confidential, and strictly confidential. Public information might include marketing literature, user manuals, and publications in journals or conferences. Company-confidential information might include organization charts, phone lists, internal newsletters with financial results, business direction, articles on a product under development, source code, or security policies. Strictly confidential information would be very closely tracked and available on a need-to-know basis only. It could include contract negotiations, employee information, top-secret product-development details, or a customer's intellectual property.

Another aspect of information protection includes protecting against malicious alteration, deliberate and accidental release of information, and theft or destruction.

Case Study: Protect Against Malicious Alteration

Staff members from a major New York newspaper revealed to a security consultant that although they were concerned with information being stolen, their primary concern was with someone modifying information without detection. What if a report about a company was changed to say something false? What if the headline was replaced with foul language? The phrase "Today, the [insert your favorite major newspaper] reported . . ." has a lot of value, which would be diminished if intruders were able to change the paper's content.

11.1.1.2 Service Availability

In most cases, a company wants to protect service availability. If a company relies on the availability of certain electronic resources to conduct its business, part of the mission of the security team will be to prevent malicious DoS attacks against those resources. Often, companies do not start thinking about this until they provide Internet-based services, because employees generally tend not to launch such attacks against their own company.

11.1.1.3 Theft of Resources

Sometimes, the company wants to protect against theft of resources. For example, if a production line is operated by computer equipment at less than full capacity because the computer has cycles being used for other purposes, the company will want to reduce the chance that compute cycles are used by intruders on that machine. The same applies to computer-controlled hospital equipment, where lives may depend on computing resources being available as needed. E-commerce sites are also concerned with theft of resources. Their systems can be slowed down by bandwidth pirates hiding FTP or chat servers in the infrastructure, resulting in lost business for the e-commerce company.

11.1.1.4 Summary

In cooperation with your management team, decide what you need to protect and from whom, how much that is worth to the company, and what the risks are. Define information categories and the levels of protection afforded to them. Document those decisions, and use this document as a basis for your security program. As the company evolves, remember to periodically reevaluate the decisions in that document with the management team.

Case Study: Decide What Is Important; Then Protect It

As a consultant, one gets to hear various answers to the question "What are you trying to protect?" The answer often, but not always, is predictable.

A midsize electronic design automation (EDA) company that had a cross-functional information-protection committee regarded customers' and business partners' intellectual property, followed by their own intellectual property, as the most important things to be protected. Customers would send this company their chip designs if they were having problems with the tools or if they had a collaborative agreement for optimizing the software for the customers' designs. The company also worked with business partners on collaborative projects that involved a two-way exchange of information. This third-party information always came with contractual agreements about security measures and restrictive access. The company recognized that if customers or business partners lost trust in its security, particularly by inadvertently giving others access to that information, the company would no longer have access to the information that had made this company the leader in its field, and ultimately, customers would go elsewhere. If someone gained access to the company's own intellectual property, it would not be as damaging as the loss of customer confidence.

A company based entirely on e-commerce, availability of the company's e-commerce site was most important, with protecting access to customers' credit cards coming in second. The company was not nearly as worried about access to its own intellectual property.

A hardware manufacturing division of a large multinational electronics company had a different priority. In this case, availability of and access to the manufacturing control systems was of the utmost importance.

A large networking hardware and software company, the crown jewels were identified as the financial and order-processing systems. Surprisingly, neither their intellectual property nor that of their customers was mentioned.

11.1.2 Document the Company's Security Policies

Policies are the foundation for everything that a security team does. Formal policies must be created in cooperation with people from many other departments. The human resources department needs to be involved in certain policies, especially in determining acceptable-use policies, monitoring and privacy policies, and creating and implementing the remedies for any policy breach. The legal department should be involved in such policies as determining whether to track and prosecute intruders and deciding how and when to involve law enforcement when break-ins occur. Clearly, all policies need the support of upper management.

The decisions the security team makes must be backed by policy to ensure that the direction set by the management team is being followed in this very sensitive area. These policies must be documented and formally approved by the appropriate people. The security team will be asked to justify its decisions in many areas and must be able to make decisions with the confidence it is doing so in the best interests of the company, as determined by the management of the company, not by the security, engineering, or any other group.

Different places need different sets of policies, and, to some degree, that set of policies will continually evolve and be added to as new situations arise. However, the following common policies are a good place to start in building your repertoire.

- An **acceptable use policy** (AUP) identifies the legitimate users of the computer and network resources and what they are permitted to use those resources for. The AUP may also include some explicit examples of unacceptable use. The legitimate users of the computer and network resources are required to sign a copy of this policy, acknowledging that they have read and agreed to it before being given access to those resources. Multiple AUPs may be in place when a company has multiple security zones.

- The **monitoring and privacy policy** describes the company's monitoring of its computer and network resources, including activity on individual computers, network traffic, email, web browsing, audit trails, and log monitoring. Because monitoring may be considered an invasion of privacy, this policy should explicitly state what, if any, expectations of privacy an individual has while using these resources. Especially in Europe, local laws may restrict what can and can not be in this policy. Again, each individual should read and sign a copy of this policy before getting access to the resources.

- The **remote access policy** should explain the risks associated with unauthorized people gaining access to the network, describe proper precautions for the individual's "secret" information—password, personal identification number (PIN), and so on—and provide a way to report lost or stolen remote access tokens so that they can be disabled quickly. This policy should also ask for some personal information—for example, shoe size and favorite color—through which people can be identified over the telephone. Everyone should complete and sign a copy of this policy before being granted remote access.

- The **network connectivity policy** describes how the company sets up network connections to another entity or some shared resources for access by a third party. Every company will at some point want to establish a business relationship with another company that requires closer network access and perhaps some shared resources: an extranet. You should prepare in advance for this eventuality. The policy should be distributed to all levels of management and stipulate that the security team be involved as early as possible. The policy should list the various forms of connectivity and shared resources that are supported, which offices can support third-party connections, and what types of connections they can support.

- The **log-retention policy** describes what is logged and for how long. Logs are useful for tracking security incidents after the event but take up large amounts of space if retained indefinitely. It is also important to know whether logs for a certain date still exist if subpoenaed for a criminal case.

Case Study: Use Better Technology Means Less Policy

The easiest policy to follow is one that has been radically simplified. For example, password policies often include guidelines for creating acceptable passwords and specifying how often they need to be changed on various classes of machines. These details can be reduced or removed with better technology. Bell Labs' infrastructure includes a secure handheld authenticator (HHA) system, which eliminates passwords altogether. What could be simpler?

❖ **Handheld Authenticators**   An HHA, a device the size of a small calculator or a fat credit card, is used to prove that people are who they say they are. An HHA generates a one-time password (OTP) to identify the user. One brand of HHA displays a new 7-digit number every 30 seconds. Clocks are synchronized such that the host knows what digits should be displayed at a given time for a particular user. The user enters the digits instead of a password. (The HHA is protected with a PIN.) Therefore, the computer can know that the user is who she claims to be or at least is holding the right HHA and knows the PIN for that person. This is more secure than a password that never, or rarely, changes.

HHAs can be used to log in to hosts, gain secure access—UNIX su command—and even gain access to web sites. With this infrastructure in place, password policies, become much simpler. Hosts outside the firewall no longer require password policies, because they don't use plain passwords. Gaining root access securely on UNIX systems, previously difficult because of paranoia over password sniffing, is made more feasible by virtue of HHAs combined with encryption.[1] This is an example of how increased security, done correctly, made the system more convenient.

Lack of Policy Hampers the Security Team

Christine was once brought in as a consultant to a large multinational computer manufacturer that had no formal, approved written security policy. In particular, the company had no network connectivity policy. As a result, many offices had connections to third

---

1. SSH provides an encrypted rsh/telnet-like system. (Yben 1996. See also Farrow 1997 and Thorpe 1998b.)

parties that were not secure; in many cases, the corporate IT department and the security group did not even know that the connections existed, because the remote offices were not under any obligation to report those connections.

Christine was asked to work on centralizing third-party access to the corporate network into three U.S. sites, two European sites, one Australian site, and one Asian site. On the process of discovering where all the existing connections were, the estimated number of third-party connections increased from 50+ to 80+.

The security team spoke to the people responsible for the connections and described the new architecture and its benefits to the company. The team then discussed with the customers what services they would need in this new architecture. Having assured themselves and the customers that all the services would be available, the team then discussed the transition to the new architecture. In most cases, this is where the process began to fail. Because the new architecture centered on multiple hub sites, connections to a small sales office closest to the third party would need to be moved farther away, and so the costs would increase. Lacking not only a policy stating the permissible ways to connect third parties to the network but also money allocated to pay the extra connectivity costs, the security group had no recourse when customers refused to pay the extra cost of moving the connection or adding security to the existing connection.

Despite having been built at the main office, the initial third-party connection infrastructure saw very little adoption; as a result, the other connection centers were not deployed. If there had been a network connectivity policy that was reasonable and supported by upper management, the result would have been very different. Management needed to support the project both financially and by instituting a formal policy with which the groups had to comply.

In contrast, Christine also worked at a security-conscious site that had policies and an information-protection team. At that site, she set up a similar centralized area for third-party connectivity, which included access for people from other companies who were working on-site. That area was used by the majority of third-party connections. The other third-party connections had their own security infrastructure, as was permitted by the network connectivity policy. There were no issues surrounding costs, because this arrangement was required by company policy, and everyone understood and accepted the reasons.

Reigning in Partner Network Connections

The U.S. Federal Aviation Administration (FAA) has a network connection to the equivalent organization of nearly every government in the world, as well as to many airlines, vendors, and partners. However, the FAA did not have a uniform policy on how these connections would be secured and managed. In fact, the FAA had no inventory of the connections. Without an inventory, these connections could not be audited. Without auditing, there was no security.

The FAA was very smart in how it went about building the inventory so that securing and auditing could begin. First, it built the inventory from all the information it did have and any it could gain from analyzing its network with various tools.

Once the network group felt that it had done the best it could on its own, it was time to announce the new auditing policy to all the IT organizations within the FAA. The group's first thought was to announce that any network connections not on its list and therefore not secured and audited would result in trouble for the people responsible for the network connection. However, the group realized that this would simply make people increase their effort to hide such connections. It would, in fact, encourage people with unreported connections to go "underground."

Instead, the group announced an amnesty program. For a certain number of months, anyone could report unofficial network connections and receive no punishment but instead help in securing and auditing the connection. However, anyone who didn't come forward by a certain deadline: Well, that would be a bad thing.

People confessed in droves, sometimes via email, sometimes by a very scared person entering the office of the director to confess in person. But the program worked. Many people came to the group for help; nobody was punished. In fact, even after the amnesty program ended, one person who came to the director nearly in tears confessed and received no punishment. The goal was to secure the network, not to get people fired; being as open and forgiving as possible was the best policy.

At the same time, the network team had many of its own undocumented connections that required analysis to determine where they connected to. Sometimes, billing records were consulted to help identify lines. Sometimes, the jack was labeled, and a little research could identify the network carrier, which led to more research that identified the line. Other times, the team wasn't as lucky.

In the end, a few connections could not be identified. After all other attempts failed, the team simply picked a date and time that had the fewest flights in the air and disconnected them. In some cases, it was months later before the country that was disconnected noticed and complained. The remaining were never identified and remain disconnected. We're not sure which is more disconcerting: the connections that were never identified or the fact that some countries flew for months without complaint.

11.1.2.1 Get High-Level Management Support

For a security program to succeed, it must have high-level management support. The management of the company must be involved in setting the policies and ground rules for the security program so that the right decisions are made for the business and so that management understands what decisions were made and why. You will need to be able to clearly explain the possibilities, risks, and benefits if you are to successfully represent the security group, and you will need to do so in business language, not technical jargon.

In some cases, the security staff may disagree with the decisions that are made by the management of the company. If you find that you disagree with those decisions, try to understand why they were made. Remember that you may not have access to the same information or business expertise as the management team. Business decisions take into account both technical and nontechnical needs. If you represent the security group well, you must believe that the management team is making the decisions that it believes are best for the company and accept them.[2] Security people tend to want to build a system so secure that it wouldn't be completed until the business had missed a market opportunity or would be so secure that it would be unusable. It is important to seek balance between building the perfect system and keeping the business running.

Once the corporate direction on security has been agreed on, it must be documented and approved by the management team and then be made available and publicized within the company. Ideally, a security officer who is not a part of the IT division of the company should be at a high level of the management hierarchy. This person should have both business skills and experience in the area of information protection. The security officer should head up a cross-functional information-protection team with representatives from the legal, human resources, IT, engineering, support, and sales divisions, or whatever the appropriate divisions may be in the company. The security officer would be responsible for ensuring that appropriate polices are developed, approved, and enforced in a timely manner and that the security and information-protection team are taking the appropriate actions for the company.

No Management Support

When Christine arrived at the computer company described in an earlier anecdote, she asked about the company's security policy. Two years earlier, a cross-functional group had written a policy in the spirit of the company's informal policy and had submitted it to management for formal approval. The policy got stalled at various levels within the IT management hierarchy for months at a time. No one in senior management was interested in pushing for it. The manager of the security team periodically tried to push it from below but had limited success.

---

2.   If you think that you didn't represent the security group well, figure out what you failed to communicate and how best to express it, and then try to get one more chance to discuss it. But it is best to get it right the first time!

> This lack of success was indicative of the company's overall lack of interest in security. As a result, the company's security staff had a very high turnover because of the lack of support, which is why the company now outsourced security to a consulting company.

If the security team cannot rely on high-level management support, the security program inevitably will fail. There will be large turnover in the security group, and money spent on security will be wasted. High-level management support is vital.

Training Your Boss

Having a boss who understands your job can be quite a luxury. Sometimes, however, it can be useful to be able to train your boss.

In one financial services company, the person responsible for security found himself reporting to a senior VP with with little or no computer background. Should be a nightmare, right? No.

They created a partnership. The security person promised to meet the company's security goals and keep to the technical aspects as long as the VP got him the resources (budget) required. The partnership was successful: The VP provided the funding needed every step of the way; the security person fed the VP talking points before any budget meetings and otherwise was left alone to build the company's security system.

Together they were a great success.

11.1.2.2 Centralize Authority

Questions come up. New situations arise. Having one place for these issues to be resolved keeps the security program united and efficient. There must be a **security policy council**, or central authority, for decisions that relate to security: business decisions, policy making, architecture, implementation, incident response, and auditing.

It is impossible to implement security standards and have effective incident response without a central authority that implements and audits security. Some companies have a central authority for each autonomous business unit and a higher-level central authority to establish common standards. Other times, we have seen a corporatewide security authority with one rogue division outside of its control, owing to a recent acquistion or merger. If the company feels that certain autonomous business units should have control over their own policy making, architecture, and so on, the computer and network resources of these units should be clearly divided from those of the rest of the company. Interconnects should be treated as connections to a third party, with each side applying its own policies and architectural standards to those connections.

Multiple autonomous networks for the same company can be very difficult to manage. If two parts of a company have different monitoring policies, for example, with no clear division between the two business units' resources, one security team could inadvertently end up monitoring traffic from an employee of the other business unit in contravention of that employee's expectation of privacy. This could lead to a court case and lots of bad publicity, as well as alienation of staff.

On a technical level, your security is only as good as the weakest link. If you have open access to your network from another network whose security you have no control over, you don't know what your weakest link is, and you have no control over it. You may also have trouble tracing an intruder who comes across such an open link.

Case Study: No Central Authority

At a large company, each site effectively decided on its own (unwritten) policies but had one unified network. Many sites connected third parties to the network without any security. As a result, a security scare occurred every few weeks at one of the offices, and the security team had to spend a few days tracking down the people responsible for the site to determine what, if anything, had happened. On a few occasions, the security team was called in the middle of the night to deal with a security incident but had no access to the site that was believed to be compromised and was unable to get a response from the people responsible for that site until the next day. By contrast, at the site that did have central authority and policies, there were no such scares or incidents.

11.1.3 Basics for the Technical Staff

As a technical member of the security team, you need to bear in mind a few other basics, the most important of which is to meet the daily working needs of the people who will be using the systems you design. These people must be able to do their work. You must also stay current with what is happening in the area of vulnerabilities and attacks so that when new vulnerabilities and attack appear, your site will be adequately protected. A critical part of the infrastructure that you will need, and that you should be responsible for selecting, is an authentication and authorization system. We provide some guidelines on how to select the right products for security-sensitive applications.

> ❖ **State of Security**   Although this chapter is about helping you build the right policy for your organization and building a good security infrastructure based on that policy, the following technology "must haves" apply to *all* sites:
>
> - *Firewalls.* The organization's network should be separated from the Internet via a firewall.
>
> - *Email filtering.* Email entering your organization should pass through a filter that protects against spam—unwanted commercial email—and viruses.
>
> - *Malware protection.* Every PC should have software that detects and removes malware, which includes viruses,[3] spyware,[4] and worms.[5] This protective software always requires updated signature databases. The software should automatically download these updates, and there should be a way to monitor which PCs in your organization have not updated recently so this situation can be rectified.
>
> - *VPNs.* If office networks within your organization connect to each other over the Internet, or if remote users connect to your organization's network over the Internet, these connections should be authenticated and encrypted using some form of VPN technology.
>
> We are surprised at how many of the sites we visit do not have these four basic technologies in use. "Who would want to attack us?" Simply put: If you have computers, you are a target. If the intruders don't want your data, they want your bandwidth to spread spam. We find PCs using virus-scanning products that don't automatically update their signature databases. We wonder why such products are still on the market. We often find piecemeal approaches to email filtering; ad hoc use of email

---

3. A virus is a piece of software that spreads computer-to-computer and causes some kind of malfunction or damage.

4. Spyware is software that monitors user activity and reacts to it, for example by inserting paid advertisements when websites are viewed.

5. A worm is software that spreads to many computers and enables an outsider to remotely program the computer for nefarious purposes.

filtering software on some but not all desktops rather than doing it in a centralized, pervasive, manner on the server. We have audited many sites where site-to-site VPNs are thought to be in use, but simple testing demonstrates that packets are not actually being encrypted. We call these "VPNs without the V or the P."

While your organization's security program should be based on good policy and process, lacking the time for that, having the above four technologies in place is a minimum starting point.

11.1.3.1 Meet the Business Needs

When designing a security system, you must always find out what the business needs are and meet them. Remember that there is no point in securing a company to the point that it cannot conduct its business. Also remember that the other people in the company are smart. If they cannot work effectively while using your security system, they will find a way to defeat it or find a way around it. This issue cannot be overstated: *The way around it that they find will be less secure than the system you've put in place.* Therefore, it is better to use a slightly less secure system than one that will be evaded.

To effectively meet the security needs of the business, you need to understand what the employees are trying to do, how they are trying to do it, and what their workflow looks like. Before you can pick the right solution, you will also have to find out what all the reasonable technological solutions are and understand in great detail how they work. The right solution

- Enables people to work effectively
- Provides a reasonable level of security
- Is as simple and clean as possible
- Can be implemented within a reasonable time scale

Case Study: Enable People to Work Effectively

At one e-commerce site, the security group decided that it needed to reduce the number of people having superuser access to machines and that the SA groups would no longer be permitted to have superuser access on one another's machines. Although defining clean boundaries between the groups' areas of responsibility sounded fine in principle, it did not take into account shared responsibilities for machines that needed to run, for example, databases and complex email configurations. Under the new policy, the database SAs and the mail SAs were in different groups and couldn't both have superuser access to the same machine. The outcome was that about 10 to 15 percent of their trouble tickets now took two to three times as long because multiple groups had to be paged and one group had to direct the other verbally over the phone on how to fix the problem.

Both the SAs and the security team had a common desire for a policy that removed superuser access from approximately 100 developers who didn't need that access to get their work done and who were inadvertently causing problems when they did things as the superuser. However, the policy that was implemented prevented the SAs from working effectively and promoted an adversarial relationship between the SAs and the security team.

Preventing people from working effectively is not in the best interests of the company. Any policy that does so is not a good policy. The security team should have consulted the SAs and the engineers to understand how they worked and what they needed the superuser access for and implemented an appropriate policy.

Case Study: Design a Shared Development Environment

Christine was once part of a team that needed to design a software development environment in which a division of one company would be collaborating with a division of another company to develop a software product. The two companies competed with each other in other areas, so they needed to isolate the codevelopment effort from other development work.

The first question the team asked was, "What will the engineers need to do?" The answer was they would need to check code and designs into and out of a shared source code control system, build and run the code, access the web, send and receive email, and access internal resources at their own company. Some of the engineers would also have to be able to work on software that was not shared with the other company. Engineers from one company would be spending time at the other company, working there for weeks or months at a time. There needed to be a way for the release engineering group to retrieve a completed version of the software when it was ready for release. The support engineers also would need access to the shared code for customer support.

The next question that the team asked was, "Would two desktops, one on the shared network and one on the company's private network, provide an acceptable working model for the software developers?" After a reasonable amount of discussion with various engineers, it became apparent that this simple solution would not work from a workflow point of view. Most likely, if the security team had continued down this path, some of the engineers would have ended up connecting their computers to both networks in order to work effectively, thus circumventing any security the security team thought it had. The engineers needed to be able to do everything from a single desktop.

Based on what the security team had learned, it came up with a few possible technological solutions. Each had a different impact in terms of implementation speed, performance for the users, and differences in workflow for each group. In the end, they implemented a short-term solution that was in place as close as possible to the date the companies wanted to start working together, but didn't have the performance that the team wanted. They set the expectations correctly for the environment and started working on another solution that would have acceptable performance, but could not be ready for a few months because of some outside dependencies.

It was extra work and the first solution was not ideal, but it met the business need for enabling people to get started with the project on time and incorporated a plan for improving the performance and working environment so that the engineers would be able to work more effectively in the future.

11.1.3.2 Build Security Using a Solid Infrastructure

Building an effective security program requires a solid computer and network infrastructure that is built with security in mind. Deploying security effectively requires that you have known, standard configurations; can build and rebuild secured systems quickly and cheaply; can deploy new software and patches quickly; and can track patch levels and versions well. A repeatable process for deploying and upgrading machines means being able to consistently raise the bar against attacks.

Another piece of infrastructure required for a good security program is a process for someone leaving the company. The exit process typically involves notifying the human resources department, which notifies other appropriate departments, such as payroll, facilities, and information technology. The most useful tool in the exit process is a checklist for the manager of the person who is leaving. It should remind the manager to ask for keys, access badge(s), identity badge(s), authentication token(s), home equipment, company phone card, company credit card, mobile phone, pager, radio, and any other equipment that the person might have. The checklist should also remind the manager to contact the IT department at the appropriate time. The IT department must have an efficient process, which should be automated as much as possible, for disabling a person's access. Efficiently disabling access is particularly important for adverse terminations. This process is described in more detail in Chapter 36.

Case Study: Security Through Good Infrastructure

This story is the one we tell the most often when trying to explain how the techniques presented in the earlier chapters can be leveraged time and time again and how skipping those basics make things like security either very expensive or impossible.

A small team of security consultants was brought into a successful Internet commerce site that had experienced a break-in. The consultants started fixing machines one at a time. However, the commerce site was growing so quickly that new machines were being deployed all around them. Each was getting broken into faster than the team could fix and block the new intruders. The situation was becoming unwinnable.

After some analysis, the consultants realized that the fundamental problem was that the site had no system for automating OS loading, upgrading, or patching. Everything was done by hand, one host at a time, without even a written procedure or checklist. Naturally, nothing was being done consistently across all the machines.

To make this site secure, the consultants would have to take an entirely different strategy: Stop fixing individual problems; instead, build the infrastructure that the company should have had all along for automatically loading the operating system, upgrading, and applying patches. Although these systems are not usually considered the domain of a security team, the consultants realized that if they didn't build it, nobody would. When that infrastructure was in place, the company could reload all the machines that were part of its Internet commerce site, thus removing the intruders and ensuring that all machines had properly secure configurations and that new intruders would be blocked.

The company was also lacking other pieces of infrastructure—including a centralized logging system, time synchronization, and console servers—which hampered the quick deployment of a security infrastructure. In many ways, the security consultants became the infrastructure team because they could not deploy security systems without a complete infrastructure.

When the security team left, the company had an almost entirely new, secure, and reliable commerce infrastructure. While this made the cost of the original request ("secure the site") seem very expensive, the large gains in efficiency and reliability greatly benefited the company.

Implementing the new security policies would not have been so expensive if the company already had the basic site infrastructure in place.

It is important to build the basic system and network infrastructure and to get it right, because other things, such as security, depend on it.

The earlier chapters of this book detail the basic infrastructure that makes it easier to maintain higher-level maintainability, repeatability, and efficiency. They give you leverage. Without them, you will find yourself wasting time and effort repeatedly solving the same problems.

11.1.3.3 Know the Latest Attacks

A security professional must be able to deal with the current types of attacks and the ways to protect the company's systems from those attacks. This means tracking several mailing lists and websites daily. The sorts of things that you need to track are security bulletins from vendors and advisories from organizations that track security issues, such as

- *Bugtraq:* http://www.securityfocus.com (Levy n.d.)
- *CERT/CC:*[6] http://www.cert.org
- *Computer Incident Advisory Capability (CIAC):* http://www.ciac.org
- *Australian Computer Emergency Response Team (AUSCERT):* http://www.auscert.org.au

Full-disclosure mailing lists generally provide exploits that you can test on your own systems to see whether they are vulnerable. These lists often publicize a new vulnerability more quickly than the other lists do because they do not need to develop and test a patch before releasing the news. A security professional should try to find out about new vulnerabilities as soon as possible to evaluate how best to protect the company's systems and how to check for attacks that take advantage of this vulnerability.

Mean Time to Attack

Since the late 1990s, tools for scanning hosts or entire networks for known and possible vulnerabilities have been in widespread use by potential intruders. A newly connected host on the Internet will be scanned and attacked within minutes. Gone are the days when attackers would scan a network one day and return weeks later to attack it.

In 1998, a friend of Christine's got a new DSL connection to his house, and he watched to see how long it would take before his small network was scanned. It took less than 2 hours. Fortunately, he had secured his machines before he brought up the connection and, because he read lots of security lists, he had up-to-date patches in place.

Now machines are attacked within minutes. Considering how long it takes to install security packs, a newly installed machine will be attacked before they have been downloaded.

New machines should be loaded on networks firewalled off from the Internet and, possibly, large corporate networks too. Never use an unsecured network to install a new machine.

---

6. The organization formerly known as the Computer Emergency Response Team/Coordination Center, is now known as CERT/CC, a registered service mark of Carnegie Mellon University.

Secure Hosts Before Going Live

A publishing company that produced both paper and online editions of its weekly magazine was working on a new web site. The security consultant was expected the next day to secure the machines to be used for the web servers. A member of the implementation team was impatient and connected the machines directly to the Internet without waiting. Within a few hours, she noticed something strange happening on one of the machines and realized that it had been broken into. She couldn't understand how anyone had found the machine, because it didn't have a name in the company's external DNS yet. The machine had been scanned, and vulnerabilities in its OS and configuration had been identified and exploited within hours of being connected. The vulnerabilities that were exploited were all well known and avoidable. Because she wasn't a security person and didn't receive or pay attention to security bulletins, she had no idea what vulnerabilities existed, how dangerous they were, or that so much automated scanning took place with break-in kits being used once vulnerabilities were identified.

11.1.3.4 Use Authentication and Authorization

One of the fundamental building blocks of a security system is a strong authentication system with a unique identity for each person and no accounts used by multiple people. Along with the authentication system goes an authorization system that specifies the level of access that each person is authorized to have. **Authentication** gives the person's identity, and **authorization** determines what that person can do.

A **role account** is one that gives people privileges to perform one or more functions they cannot perform with their normal account privileges. Typical examples include the SA role, the database administrator role, and the website administrator role. Shared accounts, even shared role accounts, should be avoided. For example, a role account might be called `dbadmin`, and any person who needs to administer the database logs in to this account to do so. The password is known by all the people who need access. Shared accounts make it difficult, if not impossible, to have accountability. If something goes wrong, there may be no way to tell who did what. It also makes it a lot more difficult to disable someone's access completely when he or she leaves the company. The SAs have to know what role accounts the person had access to and cause inconvenience to others by changing the passwords on those accounts. The SAs need to make sure that the person who has left no longer knows any valid username and password combinations.

Most OSs have other mechanisms for providing the same level of access to multiple people who authenticate as separate entities. Check into the possibilities on your system before deciding to use a shared account. For example, people who need access to the `dbadmin` account could instead be added to a `dbadmin` group, which lets them act as the database administrator. The UNIX concept of a `root` account is a role account, as is the Windows concept of the `Administrator` account. It is better to give someone Windows `PowerUser` permissions on the machines they need or `Domain Admins` if the person needs highly privileged access on all machines. Strong authentication systems generally make it difficult to have shared accounts.

A strong authentication system gives you a high degree of confidence that the person the computer believes it has authenticated is in fact that person and not someone using that person's credentials (password). For example, a strong authentication system may be a biometric mechanism, such as a fingerprint or eye scan, or it may be a handheld token-based system in which the person needs to have a physical device (the token), as well as a secret, such as a PIN that he or she remembers. A person who gives the physical device to someone else no longer has access, which is often a sufficient deterrent against sharing. If the device is stolen, the thief would not automatically know the secret PIN. In other words, a handheld token system requires something you have and something you know.

A handheld authenticator token is less cumbersome to carry around if it has multiple uses. In other words, if it is also a keychain, people will carry it with them because they find it useful beyond simply logging in to computers. This also ties it to something they personally care about, their home or car, and are thus less likely to casually loan it to someone.

Case Study: Stronger Security Spotlights Bad Behavior

When it switched from fixed passwords to HHAs, one company received complaints from the sales team. Many of those people were unhappy that they could no longer give their username and password information to customers and potential customers to try out the company's products on the corporate network before deciding to buy them. Anyone loaning out an HHA couldn't send and receive email until it was returned.

The security team had to educate people about the problems with giving others access to the corporate network and help them to establish better ways for customer trials, such as loaning equipment or special restricted VPN access for customers.

Strong authentication systems are typically inflexible. But sometimes, a little flexibility is needed for emergencies. At times, something will go wrong with the strong authentication mechanism, and you will need a way to authenticate people over the telephone, particularly if they are traveling. For example, someone could lose or break the physical device—HHA or portable biometric device—needed for authentication. You have to prepare for this eventuality when you initially set up the strong authentication system.

When creating an account, have the person fill out a form asking for information that can be used for authentication over the phone. For example, the person could supply his or her shoe size, favorite fruit, the shop where a particular purchase was made, where he or she was for the Y2K New Year, favorite subject in high school, or something that can be checked within the company, such as who sits in the next office/cubicle. For a person who can provide successful authentication over the phone in this way, another mechanism should be able to grant that person temporary access to the systems until the problem can be fixed. For example, many systems permit normal password use on a temporary basis for 24 hours, or long enough to issue a replacement HHA.

Shared Voicemail

At one fast-growing customer site, a group of people shared one telephone and voicemail box. One day, a new person started using that telephone and voicemail box and asked what the password for the voicemail was. In reply, one of the other people in that group lifted up the handset and pointed to the number taped to the underside of the handset. Thus, anyone could find the password and listen to potentially confidential information left in the voicemail box. Many sites consider voicemail a secure way to deliver sensitive information, such as news of a potential new customer, initial passwords, staff announcements, product direction, and other information potentially damaging to the company if the wrong people hear it.

The same site used shared accounts for administrative access rather than associating authorization levels with authenticated individuals. The end result was a book with administrative account name and password pairs associated with each host. Someone who had authority to access the password for one host could easily obtain the password for others at the same time and then anonymously access the other machines, using the administrative accounts. Lack of accountability because of shared accounts is a bad thing, as is having a book of passwords from which people can easily obtain a greater level of access than they are entitled to.

> This site suffered several break-ins, and the use of shared role accounts made it more difficult to identify and track the intruder. This system was also not as easy to use as one that granted increased access based on each person's unique personal authentication token, because everyone had to make periodic trips to check the book of passwords. Authorization based on individuals' authentication would have been easier to use and more secure.

Shared Role Accounts Make Identification Difficult

A site that used a shared superuser role account suffered several break-ins while the primary SA was away for an extended period and an inexperienced SA was standing in for her. The primary SA was minimally available through remote access, and the site enlisted the help of an experienced SA who was working at the site in a different role.

At one point, the primary SA became afraid that the superuser account had been compromised when she saw logs of SSH access to that account from an unknown machine. It turned out that the helpful SA had been the one accessing that superuser account from the unknown machine. If the SA group had been much larger, it would have been difficult, if not impossible, to notice suspicious accesses and trace them to their sources. Failing to notice suspicious accesses could lead to machines remaining compromised when the problem was thought to be solved. Failing to trace those accesses to their (innocent) sources could lead to a huge amount of wasted effort and unnecessary outages rebuilding key machines that were not compromised. It is best to avoid this scenario by not using shared role accounts.

In these examples, using shared accounts was done because it seemed easier at the time. Yet the result was a system that was less secure and more difficult to use, especially since people had to specifically log in to their role accounts to perform many procedures. With very little effort, individual accounts could have been granted access to the resources as needed, making the system more secure and accountable and making access less cumbersome to the SAs who needed access. More secure and easier to use: all for a little extra effort up front.

11.1.3.5 Authorization Matrix

Authentication proves who someone is. Authorization is what that person is allowed to do. For example, a typical customer should be able to read his or her own email but not that of other people. Certain people should be able to

Table 11.1 Authorization Matrix

Group	Machines							
	Dev	RE	Fin	Res	HR	Ops	Inf	Sec
Developers	W	R		R				
Release Engineers	R	W		R				
Finance			W	R				
Human Resources				R	W			
Operations		R		R		W		
System Administration	A	A	A	A	A	A	A	
Security	A	A	A	A	A	A	A	A

Dev, developer; RE, release engineering; Fin, finance; Res, corporate resource (intranet, etc.);
HR, human resources; Ops, operations/manufacturing; Inf, infrastructure (mail servers, auth servers,
etc.); Sec, security (firewalls, intrusion detection, strong auth, etc.); Access: administrative;
R, read; W, write

read a particular database, with a smaller set allowed to update the data, and only a few administrators able to make changes to the database schema.

More useful than setting these policies in paragraph form is to use an **authorization matrix** based on roles within the company, categories of system, and classes of access, such as the one shown in Table 11.1. The authorization matrix describes the level of access that a given group of people has on a certain class of machines. Such a policy should be developed in cooperation with management and representatives from all parts of the company. Once that is done, an authorization system should be linked to the authentication system that implements the policy. The set of identities and information stored in the authentication and authorization systems is one of the namespaces at a site. Managing this and other namespaces is discussed further in Chapter 8.

Authorization Matrix Saves the Day

Tom entered a site that was having a long debate about improving the security of certain networks. For the previous 2 months, the site hadn't been able to reach a decision on which networks would be able to access which services.

Up until then, the debate had all been done verbally, never getting closer to a conclusion. Tom listened to people's views and thought he was hearing a lot of overlap, but since the debate was evolving and positions were changing, he wasn't sure where the agreement was and where the disagreements were.

In one meeting, Tom said, "Oh, I have a tool that will solve this problem." People thought he might be reaching for a baseball bat. Instead, he opened up a spreadsheet program and drew a grid.

He listed the networks in a column on the left and the various services across the top. He started filling out the individual boxes where he thought he heard agreement. He then confirmed with the group that he was capturing things properly. The group suggested a few more boxes that could be filled in. It turned out that only a few boxes couldn't be filled, because they were yet unresolved.

Tom suggested that rather than let the very expensive firewall hardware sit in boxes for another 2 months, the group set it up with the policy in the grid as a start. The unfinished boxes would be assumed to be "no access" until the grid was complete.

During the week it took to install the hardware, management was shown the grid and given an opportunity to set the policy. These people weren't very technical, but the matrix let them make the decision without having to understand the technology, and they were able to break the tie where the SAs disagreed.

By the time the hardware was ready, the grid was complete. The engineer installing the firewall only had to make sure that the configuration accurately reflected the grid. A different SA could then audit the firewall by comparing the configuration to the grid.

After 2 months of debate, the entire project was completed in 1 week because the right tool was used.

11.1.3.6 Select the Right Products and Vendors

When selecting a product for any security-sensitive purpose, you need to select the right one. Evaluating a product from a security point of view is different from evaluating a product for which security is not a priority.

A **security-sensitive product** is one that has one or more of these qualities:

- Is used by any third party having a restricted level of access to that system or the network(s) that it is connected to
- Is part of the authentication, authorization, or access control system
- Is accessible from the Internet or any untrusted network
- Has access to the Internet or any untrusted network
- Provides authenticated access to sensitive data or systems, such as payroll data

When evaluating a security-sensitive product, you also need to consider several additional things. For example, you need some degree of confidence in the security of the product. You should consider several usability criteria that affect security. You also need to think about ongoing maintenance issues and the vendor's direction, along with some of the more usual concerns, such as functionality and integration issues.

- *Simplicity:* Simple systems tend to be more reliable and more secure than complex ones. For example, an email system that sends and receives email is not as complex as one that also stores address books and notes and perhaps has a built-in calendar service. The more basic email system can be augmented by other pieces of software that provide the extra functionality, if required. Several small, simple components that interact are likely to have fewer security problems than a single large, complex system. The more complex a system, the more difficult it is to test in detail, and the more likely it is to have unforeseen problems that can be exploited by an attacker.

- *Security:* Why do you believe that the product is reasonably secure? Research the product and find out who the principal designers and programmers are. Do you know (of) them? Are they well respected in the industry? What else have they done? How well have their previous products worked, and how secure are those products? How does the product address some known problem areas? For example, you might ask how a firewall addresses mail delivery, which is an area that has traditionally had many security problems. FTP is another service traditionally fraught with security problems: not only FTP server implementations but also how firewalls handle the protocol. Look through a couple of years of security advisories, and pick a recurring problem area to investigate.

- *Open source:* Is this an open source product? In a nutshell, the open source debate is as follows: If the source is available, intruders can find problems and exploit them, but on the other hand, it also gets reviewed by many people, problems are found more quickly, patches are available more quickly, and you can always fix it yourself, if necessary. Closed source leads to suspicions of security through obscurity: the mentality that keeping a method secret makes it secure even when it's fundamentally not secure. Security through obscurity does not work; the attackers find the problems, anyway.

- *Usability:* Is it easy to understand and verify the configuration? How easy is it to accidentally configure the application in a way that is not secure? How do the components interact? How does a configuration change in one area affect other areas? For example, in a firewall that has both proxies and packet filters, if some separate configuration rules try to control something at both the network (packet filter) layer and the application (proxy) layer, which layer's rules are applied first, and what happens? Does the application notice configuration conflicts? How long does it take to train new people on the product?

- *Functionality:* The product should provide only the features that you need. Superfluous functionality may be a source of problems, especially if it can't be disabled.

- *Vendor issues:* Maintenance patches and updates are very important for a security-sensitive product. In most cases, you will also want to be able to report problems to a vendor and have a reasonable expectation of getting a quick fix or workaround for the problem. If a vendor has a free version and a commercial product, you will probably get better service on the commercial one. How security-conscious is the vendor? Does the vendor release security patches for its products? What is the vendor's mechanism for notifying customers of security problems?

- *Integration:* How well will this product integrate with the rest of your network infrastructure?
  - Will it use your existing authentication system?
  - What kind of load does it put on the network and other key systems?
  - If it has to talk to other systems or people through a firewall, are the protocols it uses supported adequately by the firewall? Open protocols usually are; proprietary ones often are not.
  - Does the product embed communications into another protocol, such as riding an instant message (IM) protocol over HTTP? Doing so can make it difficult or impossible to control access to the new application independently from real use of that protocol.[7] New services should have their own ports.
  - Can its logs be sent to a central log host?
  - What network services does it expect, and do you provide them already?
  - Does it run on an OS that is already supported and understood at the site?

---

7. A product that is web based or has a web interface should, obviously, use HTTP for the web-based communication. However, a product that is sending information back and forth between a client that is not a web browser and a server that is not a web server should not use HTTP; nor should it use port 80.

- *Cost of ownership:* How long does it take to configure this software? Does it have autoload options that can help to standardize configurations and speed the set-up time? How much day-to-day maintenance is there on this system; does it need lots of tuning? Are people in your organization already familiar with it? Are people you hire likely to be familiar with it, or are you going to have to train them? How difficult will it be to make a new person comfortable with your configuration?

- *Futures:* How well does this product scale, and what are the scaling options when it reaches capacity? What direction is the vendor taking the product, and does it match your company's direction? For example, if you are in a UNIX-based company that does little with Windows and is not likely to move in that direction, a product from a company focused primarily on Windows for the future is not a good choice. Is the product likely to die soon or stop being developed? How long are versions supported? How often do new releases come out? What is the market acceptance of this product? Is it likely to survive market pressures? Market acceptance also implies that you will have an easier time hiring people who know the product.

11.1.3.7 Internal Audits

Auditing performed by a group internal to the company is called **internal auditing**. We believe that internal and external auditing groups should both be used; we discuss the external audit function further in Section 11.1.4.3.

We define **auditing** in a very broad sense to cover all of the following:

- Checking whether security environments are in compliance with policies and design criteria
- Checking employee and contractor lists against authentication and authorization databases
- Making physical checks on machine rooms, wiring, and telecom closets for foreign devices
- Checking that relevant machines have up-to-date security patches
- Scanning relevant networks to verify what services are offered
- Launching sophisticated, in-depth attacks against particular areas of the infrastructure, with clearly specified success criteria and limitations

We recommend that the internal audit team perform those tasks that can be more thoroughly and easily performed using inside knowledge of the site:

- *Logging and log processing.* Logs, especially those from security-sensitive machines and applications, are an important source of security information. Logs can help the security team trace what has happened in an attack. Logs can be analyzed to help detect attacks and gauge the seriousness of an attack. From a security standpoint, you can never have too many logs. From a practical standpoint, infinite logs consume an infinite amount of space and are impossible to search for important information. Logs should be processed by a computer to extract useful information and archived for a predefined period to be available for reexamination if an incident is discovered. All security-sensitive logs should go to one central place so that they can be processed together and information from different machines correlated. Security-sensitive logs should not remain on security-sensitive machines, because the logs can be erased or modified by an attacker who compromises those machines. The central log host must be very well secured to protect the integrity of the logs.

- *Internal verification.* Consider ways that you can check for anomalies on your network and important systems. Do you see any strange routes on the network, routes going in strange directions, or traffic from unexpected sources, for example? Try war-dialing all the phone numbers assigned to your company to see whether any modems answer on unexpected numbers.[8] Check what machines and services are visible on public networks to make sure that nothing new or unexpected has appeared. Does someone who is in the office also appear to be actively accessing the network, using a remote access system? Intrusion detection systems (IDS) should make some of this type of anomaly detection easier, as well as other kinds of attack detection.

- *Per project verification.* Periodically check on each security project that has been implemented to make sure that the configuration has not been materially changed. Make sure that it still matches the design specifications and conforms to all appropriate policies. Use this occasion to also check with the people who are using this security system to see whether it serves their needs adequately and whether any new requirements may arise.

---

8. *War-dialing* refers to having a program that dials all the numbers in a given list, which may include entire exchanges, and having it log which numbers respond with a modem sound. War dialing can also include logging what greeting the machine at the other end gives or trying certain combinations of usernames and passwords and logging the results.

- *Physical checks.* Check on areas that are key points in the computing, networking, or communications infrastructure. Look for additional
devices, perhaps concealed, that may be monitoring and recording or
transmitting data. Such areas include data centers, networking closets,
telecommunications closets, videoconferencing rooms, wiring between
such rooms, and wired/wireless connections between buildings.

Physical Security Breaches Do Happen

The security team in a large multinational corporation did not perform regular physical
checks of the data centers and communications closets. One day, someone from the
company that supplied and maintained the telephone switch came to do some maintenance on the switch and discovered a device attached to it. Further investigation revealed
that the device was monitoring all telephone communications within the building and
across the outside lines and transmitting them off site. It turned out that someone dressed
in the uniform of the telephone company had come to the building, saying that he needed
to bring in some new lines to the telephone closet. No one had checked with the telecom
and networking groups to see whether the phone company was expected. After this
incident, the security group reemphasized its policy that no one should be allowed into
those rooms without the consent and supervision of the telecom or networking group
and instituted regular physical checks of all computer and communications rooms and
the wiring between them.

11.1.4 Management and Organizational Issues

There are several areas in which the security team particularly needs management support. Maintaining reasonable staffing levels for the size of the
company, with the appropriate roles within the group, is one such area. The
manager of the security team can also help with coordinating with the rest of
the SA managers to establish an incident-response team that is prepared for
emergencies. Setting up a relationship with an outside auditing company and
scheduling its work to fit in with the needs of the rest of the company is another task that typically falls to the security team manager. We discuss some
approaches for successfully selling security to other groups in the company.

11.1.4.1 Resources

The security team needs access to various resources. One key to a successful
security program is to have lots of contacts in the industry, thereby getting to
know what other companies are doing and what others consider to be state of

the art. Through their contacts, security professionals also hear what attacks are happening before they become generally known, which enable the security people to be one step ahead and as prepared as possible. It also enables them to benchmark how the company is doing compared with other companies. Is the company spending too much on security or too little? Does it lack some important policies? The security team can also find out what experiences others have had in trying to implement some new technology and what the return on investment has been. Has anyone had any particularly positive or negative experiences with a new product that the security team is considering?

Contacts are made by attending conferences regularly and becoming a part of some select intercompany security focus groups. Security people need to become known and trusted by other security professionals in order to stay in touch with the industry.

The security team needs people with a variety of skills. In a small company, one person may need to take on all the roles, perhaps with some management assistance. In a larger company, however, the manager of the security team should look at hiring people for a number of roles within the security team. Some of these roles require particular skill sets and personalities. The various roles include policy writer, architect, implementer, operations, auditor, risk manger, and incident response.

- The *policy writer* is responsible for writing corporate policies and therefore needs to have contacts in key areas of the company and to be a part of some cross-functional teams in order to discuss policy with managers, the legal department, and the human resources department. The policy writer needs to be able to identify what policies the company needs and to get support for those policies within the company, particularly at upper management levels. The policy writer should be aware of what other companies, especially those in the same industry, have in the way of policies and should know what is standard and what is considered state of the art with respect to policies. The policy writer should be able to judge the business environment and spirit of the company to know what is appropriate to that company.

- The *security architect* represents the security group to the rest of the company and should be on cross-functional teams within the company. This person is responsible for staying in touch with what is happening within the company, finding out which upcoming projects the group will need to incorporate, and finding out each project's requirements, business needs, and key people. The security architect also designs the security environment and takes an overview of what is happening with security within the company, including what infrastructure would help the group and the company. This person should be involved with vendor relations, tracking technologies, products, and futures and should decide when or whether the company should move toward a new technology.

- The *implementer* puts the architect's designs into practice and works with the architect on product evaluations. The implementer becomes part of the cross-functional project teams when identified as the person who will be building that particular environment. The implementer should also understand what the business requirements are, bring up issues, and suggest alternative solutions. This person documents the setup and operational aspects of the systems implemented and trains the operations staff on how to run them. The implementer acts as a level of escalation for the security operations staff and should discuss future directions, technologies, and products with the architect and bring up any requirements that may arise in the future.

- The *security operations staff* runs the security infrastructure on a day-to-day basis. These people are trained by and consult the implementer on problems they can't resolve. In large companies, an operations staff that provides 24/7 coverage can serve double duty by also being the security operations staff, responding to alerts or reports from the log-monitoring system or other IDSs. The operations people deal with the day-to-day issues that arise from the authentication and authorization system, such as lost or broken tokens, new employees or contractors, and departures from the company, and are the people whom the rest of the SA staff talk to when they suspect that a piece of the security infrastructure may have a problem. Where possible, operations staff should help the implementer to build the infrastructure.

- An *auditor* may be internal to the company or from an external consulting group. One company may use both kinds of auditors in different roles. The auditor builds a program[9] for verifying that the security of the company matches expectations, working closely with the security team and management to determine whether these particular areas should be tested in depth. Such testing may include social engineering, which is

---

9. The term *program* here refers to a system of projects and services intended to meet a need, not a software program.

typically the weakest part of any company's defenses. The role of auditors, especially external auditors, is discussed later in this section.

- A *risk manager* is a technical management role from the business side. The risk manager evaluates technical requests to assess the risk to the company of allowing a deviance from policy standards, determines whether to allow it or require the solution to be reengineered to avoid this deviance, and then justifies any risk acceptances to the auditors (internal or external). For example, a request might be to enable anonymous FTP on a server, enabling outside providers to access a particular internal resource via a particular method, or setting a weaker password policy on a particular device. Large companies may have many risk managers, aligned to the divisions of the company, with a large risk-management structure supporting them.

❖ **Social Engineering**   Social engineering is the art of persuading people to give you access to something you are not entitled to, normally by using a small piece of information you have ferreted out. An example might be finding out the name of a new sales engineer at a company, calling up the helpdesk, pretending to be that engineer and saying that you need to dial in, and asking for the phone number. Then later, you call the helpdesk, pretending to be the same or a different person and say that you have lost your HHA but need access and get the helpdesk to give you some other way of authenticating, such as a password. Most people do their best to be helpful; social engineering exploits their helpfulness.

- The *incident-response team* springs into action when a real or suspected intrusion occurs. This team also meets on a regular basis to go over incident-response procedures. Depending on the size of the company and the security team, the team probably will be composed of people from across the SA organization, as well as the security team. The rest of the time, this team has another role within the SA organization, sometimes within and sometimes outside the security group.

11.1.4.2 Incident Response

In this section, we discuss establishing a process for handling security incidents preparing for effective incident response, and exploring how various company policies relating to incident response affect how the team works.

To handle an incident well, one must be prepared. One shouldn't be forming the team during a crisis. Ironically, the best time to form the team and the processes is when you feel you don't need them.

❖ **"Above the Fold"**   The larger a company grows, the more likely it is to be concerned with the embarrassment of having an incident rather than the data or productivity that would be lost as a result of an incident. Embarrassment comes from not handling an incident well. Handle something properly, and it becomes a minor article in the newspaper. Handle something badly, and you become one of the headlines that is "above the fold" on the front page. That can affect the company's share price and the confidence of customers.

When setting up an incident-response team, you first need to establish how reports of possible incidents are going to get to the team. To do so, you need to look at your problem-reporting mechanisms (see Section 14.1.2). To whom does a person report a potential incident, and how is it handled? Do any electronic devices report a potential incident, and, if so, where do those reports go, and how are they handled? During what hours are you willing to respond to potential security incidents, and how does this affect the reporting mechanisms? For example, if you provide internal-customer support only during business hours but want to be able to respond to security incidents around the clock, how can someone report a potential security incident outside of business hours?

This first stage of the process must be integrated into your standard problem-reporting procedures. Customers cannot be expected to know in the heat of the moment that network or system failures should be handled one way but potential security incidents should be handled another way. Customers are not usually qualified to determine whether something is a security incident.

The person who receives the report needs to have a process for handling a call relating to a potential security incident and for determining whether this call should be escalated to an incident-response team member. The team should have one or more points of contact to whom calls are initially escalated; these contacts must be capable of deciding whether it is a full-blown incident that needs the team to respond. The points of contact should be members of the security team. The person who initially receives the report should be able to determine whether a call is a true potential security incident but should err on the side of caution and escalate any calls he or she is unsure about to the appropriate contact on the incident-response team. Failing to escalate a security incident to the appropriate people is a bad thing.

Have an Incident-Reporting Mechanism

A computer manufacturer had no formal incident-response team; instead, a security group also responded to incidents and had a reasonably well-established set of procedures for doing so. The company also had 24/7 internal computer support coverage.

An engineer in the web group was working late and noticed something strange on one of the machines in the web cluster. He looked closer and discovered that the machine had been broken into and that the attacker was actively defacing web pages at that moment. The engineer did his best to get the attacker off the machine and keep him off but realized that he was not up to the challenge because he did not know exactly how the attacker was getting onto the machine. He called the 24/7 internal support group at about 2 AM and explained what was happening.

Lacking procedures for dealing with this and not having helpdesk outside-hours contact information for the security group, he simply opened a trouble ticket and assigned it to someone in the security group. When that security administrator came in at 8 AM, he found the trouble ticket in his email and set the incident-response processes into motion. At this stage, both the engineer and the attacker had grown tired and gone to bed, making it more difficult to get complete details to track down the attacker. The engineer felt let down by the SA organization because he had rightly expected that someone would come to his aid to deal with an attack in progress.

The SA organization and the security organization both failed but in different ways. The security organization failed because it didn't give clear instructions to the internal support group on how to escalate a security incident. The SA organization failed because no attempts at escalation were made for something that merited at least escalation within the organization if an outside escalation path was unknown.

After this incident, the security team made sure that the SA organization knew the escalation path for security incidents. (Incidentally, the intruder was eventually tracked down and successfully prosecuted for a number of incidents of breaking into and defacing web sites, including government sites.)

Once you have figured out how reports of potential security incidents will reach the incident-response team contacts, you need to determine what course of action the team should take. That depends on preparation and corporate decisions made well in advance of an incident.

- The *response policy* determines what incidents you respond to and at what level. For example, the entire incident-response team is activated for a large-scale attack on many machines. However, a smaller group of people may be activated for a small-scale attack on only one machine.

How do you respond if your network is being scanned? You may choose to log that and ignore it or to try to track down the attacker. Based on the various ways that incidents are reported and the level of filtering that happens before an incident is passed on to the incident-response team contact, you should build a list of general scenarios and determine how to respond to each of them. Regardless of whether you plan on pursuing attackers, detailed and timestamped logs of events, actions, and findings should be kept by the security team. You should also document how your response will be different if the incident appears to be of internal origin. How you respond will be determined partly by the company's prosecution policy, disconnection policy, and communication policies, as described next.

- The *prosecution policy* should be created by upper management and the legal department. At what point does the company prosecute attackers? The answer can range from "never" to "only when significant damage has been done" to "only in successful break-ins" to "always, even for scanning." The company may choose "never" because of the associated bad press and risks of gathering evidence. Once you have determined the criteria for prosecution, you also need to determine at what point law enforcement will be contacted. Training for all incident-response team members on how and when to gather evidence that is admissible in court will be necessary for any prosecution to be successful.

- The *disconnection policy* determines when, if ever, you sever connectivity between the machines that are being attacked—and possibly, other company networks—and the attacker. In some cases, this may mean severing network connections, possibly Internet connectivity, possibly some form of remote access; perhaps powering down one or more machines; perhaps terminating some TCP sessions; perhaps stopping a particular service; or adding some firewall filtering rules to a perimeter security device. You need to consider in advance what forms of connectivity you may wish to sever, how you would do it, and what the impact would be on the operations of the company. You also need to define the risks of not severing that connection in various scenarios. Remember to include the possibility that your site may then be used to launch an attack against another site. When this data is clear and well organized, the management of the company needs to decide in what cases connectivity must be severed and how, when it should not be severed, when it may or may not be severed, and who gets to make that call. It also needs to state when the connection can be restored and who can make that decision.

> ❖ **Your Site Used to Launch New Attacks**   If your site is used as a launchpad for attacks against other sites, the company may well become involved in a court case against the attacker; even if your company decides not to prosecute, in order to avoid adverse publicity, the next company to be attacked may have a different policy. To protect your site from being used as a launchpad for attacks against others, it is important to use egress filtering to restrict what traffic can leave your network.

- Senior management needs to decide the *communication* policy for within and outside the company for the various sorts of security incidents. Depending on what is decided here, this policy may involve having marketing or press relations department contacts who need to be kept informed from the outset about what is happening. A company may choose to keep as many incidents as possible as quiet as possible in order to avoid bad press. This policy may include no internal communications about the incident, for fear that it will accidentally reach the ears of the press. The communication policy will affect the structure of the team. Does someone need to act as the communication contact? Does the team try to be unnoticed? Does it limit how many people respond to the incident?

The communication policy may affect the disconnection policy, because a disconnection may draw attention to the incident. The prosecution policy also affects the disconnection policy, because disconnecting may make it more difficult to trace the attacker or may trigger an automated cleanup of a compromised system, thus destroying evidence. On the other hand, an attacker left connected may be able to erase evidence.

Responding to a security incident is a very detail-oriented process that is well described in the SANS *Computer Security Incident Handling: Step-by-Step* booklet (Northcutt 1999). The process is divided into six phases: preparation, identification, containment, eradication, recovery, and follow-up. These phases comprise 90 actions in 31 steps, with most of the actions being part of the preparation phase. Being prepared is the most critical part of responding to an incident effectively.

11.1.4.3 External Audits

We recommend employing outside security consultants in an auditing role. They should be people the technical team can recommend and work with, or the company will not get the most out of the arrangement. Using external auditors has several benefits. It gives the security team independent feedback on how it is doing and provides extra pairs of eyes examining the company's security. The consultants have the advantage of distance from the work that is going on, and their approach will be unaffected by expectations and inside knowledge. Ideally, the auditing group should not be involved in the design or maintenance of the company's security systems. Senior management will usually value getting an outside view of the company's security; if the security consultants are experienced in this area, they may well have more data to present to senior management on the existing state of the art in the industry, the resources that similar companies assign to security, and the risks associated with any shortcomings they have found or have been told about by the security team. The external group may be able to help the internal security team to get more resources, if that is appropriate, and may have good ideas on approaches to take or advice on what software or hardware to use.

This external auditing role does not replace the internal auditing function. We recommend different roles and tasks for the internal and external auditing groups. The role of the external group is discussed here; the role of the internal group, in Section 11.1.3.7. Briefly, we recommend splitting the auditing function, with the internal auditing team tracking things on an ongoing basis and the external group being brought in periodically for larger-scale audits and for the benefits associated with its external viewpoint.

We believe that the external auditing team should examine the security of the company from the outside, which would cover in-depth attacks against particular areas and scanning of exposed networks and remote access points. What do we mean by "in-depth attacks" against a particular area? We mean giving the external auditing team a task, such as getting access to the company's financials or customer database, rather than a task such as "breaking through the firewall," which focuses on a particular security mechanism. The in-depth attack takes a more holistic approach to checking site security. The external auditing team may think of ways to get in that the security team did not consider. Specifying the security infrastructure to attack limits the consultants' scope in ways that a real attacker will not be limited. An in-depth attack is a more realistic test of how site security will hold up against a determined attacker.

For some of these tests, the security team may wish to deliberately exclude social engineering. Social engineering involves an attacker's convincing people to reveal certain information or provide access, usually by pretending to be someone else, such as a new employee or a contractor. Social engineering is typically the weakest link. It is important to have an awareness program that addresses it. The success of the program can be periodically checked by permitting social engineering attacks. When social engineering is no longer a problem, it should no longer be restricted as a method.

Scanning exposed networks and remote access points is another area that lends itself to being delegated to an external auditing group. It may be a good source of statistics to use when talking to upper management about what the security team is doing. It is also a tedious task, and the consultants will often have better tools for it. In addition, the external group will be performing its work from a network or a location that will not be assigned an extra level of privilege, because it belongs to the company or an employee.

External auditing should include penetration testing, if that is appropriate for your company. If consultants are doing penetration testing for you, there should be a written schedule of areas to be tested and bounds placed on the extent of the testing. Make sure that you are very clear on the goals, restrictions, and limitations for the group. For example, you may specify that the group should stop as soon as it gets inside your security perimeter, obtains access to a certain database, gets superuser privileges on any of the target machines, or has shown that a denial-of-service attack works on one or two machines. During the testing, the consultants should coordinate carefully with one or two points of company contact who would be able to tell them to stop at any point if they are causing unexpected damage. Be sure that you have approval from the highest level of management to conduct such audits.

Penetration Testing Must Be Coordinated

A consultant was employed to perform penetration testing on a large multinational networking company. A very clear contract and statement of work described the dates, extent, and limits of testing. Part of the penetration testing was checking for DoS vulnerabilities. The consultant came across a cascading DoS vulnerability that disabled all the European connections before he could stop it. Such a large network failure naturally caused a great deal of high-level management interest. Fortunately, the consultant had carefully followed the contract and statement of work, so the incident cost a lot less than it would have if a malicious attacker had come across the vulnerability first or if the company had not been able to quickly figure out what was happening. Once the high-level managers found out what had happened and why, they were understanding and happy to accept the cost of finding that vulnerability before it could be used against them.

11.1.4.4 Cross-Functional Teams

The security group cannot work in isolation. It needs to learn as quickly as possible any new business developments that may affect security. The group needs to be in touch with the company ethos and the key players when developing security policies. The group needs to have a strong relationship with the rest of the SA team to make sure that what it implements is understood and maintainable and must know that other SAs will not, on their own, do anything that will compromise security. The group needs to be aware of the working models of other people in the company and how security changes will affect those people, especially in the field offices.

- A strong alliance with the *legal department* of the company provides many benefits. The right person, or people, within that department typically will be glad to have a strong relationship with the security group because they will have questions and concerns that the security group can address. The right person in that group is usually the person who is responsible for intellectual property, often known as the intellectual property manager, or simply IP manager (not to be confused with Internet Protocol).

The IP manager is a good person to lead an information-protection team that regularly brings together representatives from all over the company to discuss how best to protect intellectual property within the company and how the proposed changes will affect each group. This team needs representatives from the following departments: legal, risk management and disaster planning, facilities, (data) security, system administration, human resources, marketing and communications, engineering, and sales.

The IP manager within the legal department is interested in electronic security because how the company protects its information relates to how well it can defend the company's right to that information in court. The IP manager will also typically be involved in, or at least aware of, any partnership negotiations with other companies, mergers, and acquisitions because there will be intellectual property issues to be discussed. If you have a good relationship with this person, she can make you aware of upcoming projects that you will need to plan for and get you involved with the project team from the outset. She will also be able to give you the basis for your security model, based on the contractual agreement between the two companies, and will be able to help with the policies that need to surround the agreement and with providing training to the people who will be working with the other party to the agreement.

Case Study: Importance of a Relationship with the Legal Department

One division of a multinational EDA company formed an alliance with a group within the EDA division of IBM. The alliance involved codevelopment of a software product, which meant that both groups were to have complete access to the source for that product and needed a workable development environment. However, other groups within the EDA division of IBM competed directly with other groups within the EDA company, and other parts of IBM competed with customers of the EDA company. The EDA company often received from its customers confidential information that typically related to the next generation of chips that the customer was designing. It was very sensitive and very valuable information. Therefore, the EDA company needed to carefully limit the information that it shared with IBM.

The security group's contact in the legal department at the EDA company ensured that a design team for the shared development environment was formed long before the contract was signed and that the security group was a part of that team. Other members included the people responsible for the development tools, the release management team, the development manager for the product, technical support, and the equivalent people from IBM. Several other groups were formed to deal with other aspects of the agreement, and progress was tracked and coordinated by the people responsible for the deal. The IP manager also directed the group that developed training materials for the engineers who would be working on the codeveloped product. The training included a guide to the contractual obligations and limitations, the policies that were being implemented with respect to this project, and a technical overview on how to use the codevelopment area. The same training materials was given to both sides.

With a project of this magnitude, involving so many different departments of the company, the security group would have failed if it had not been involved from the outset. It would also have failed without clear direction from the legal department on what was to be shared and what was to be protected. The other vital component for the success of the security group in this project was a spirit of cooperation within the cross-functional team that was designing the environment.

This may sound like the obvious thing to do, but time and time again we hear of business alliances established in secret with the IT group being the last to know.

- Security needs to be a cooperative effort within the company in general and within the system administration team in particular. The SAs often will know what is happening or going to happen within their business units before they think to get the security team involved. The SAs can help to get the security team involved at the outset, which will give the projects much better success rates. The SA team can also help by keeping an eye open for unusual activity that might indicate an attack, knowing what to do when they see such activity, and possibly by being involved in the incident-response team.

In some companies, the business applications support team (sometimes referred to as *MIS*) is considered part of the SA teams, in others, it is not. The people on this team are responsible for a specific set of business applications: human resource systems, payroll, order tracking, and financials. It is very important that the security team also has support from this group and knowledge of what is happening within this group. If the applications support team does not understand the security model and policies, it may select and deploy a software system that comes with dial-in support from the vendor or connectivity to the vendor and not arrange for an appropriate security model for this setup. Or the team may deploy a security-sensitive application without realizing it or using the appropriate security guidelines for selecting it. If the security team works well with this group, these pitfalls can be avoided.

- The *product-development group* is the main profit center for the company. In a consulting company, this group is the consultants; in a university, it is the academics and the students; in a nonprofit organization, it is the people who perform the primary functions of that organization. If these people cannot perform their jobs efficiently, the whole company will be adversely affected, so it is very important to work closely with them so that you understand their requirements. The product-development group is also the group most likely to need connectivity to business partners and to have complex security requirements. Getting to know them well and learning of the new projects before they become official allows the security team to be better prepared. The product-development group is most likely to be using the security environments on a regular basis. Therefore, the group's feedback on how usable the environment is, what its work model looks like, and what it sees as future requirements is very important.

- The security function is normally based in one or more major *field offices* of a company. The smaller field offices often feel that their needs are ignored or neglected because they often have different sets of requirements from people in the larger offices and do not have much, if any, direct contact with the security group. Field offices typically house sales and support staff who frequently travel to customers and may need to access corporate information while on the road or at customer sites. A customer site will usually restrict the types of access available to connect to the company, because of the customer's policies and facilities. If the offices cannot use one of the officially sanctioned methods, they may set up something for themselves at their own office in order to get their work done. It may prove very difficult to discover that such access has been opened up at a remote office, because of the lack of SA and security team contact with that office. It is vital that the people in these offices know that their voice is heard and that their needs are met by the security team. It is also important that they understand what the security team is doing and why going around the security team is a bad thing for the company.

11.1.4.5 Sell Security Effectively

Selling security is like selling insurance. There is no immediately obvious benefit in spending the money, except peace of mind. But with insurance, at least customers can see from year to year, or decade to decade, how they are doing and can see the potential costs if they do not have the insurance, even if the risks are difficult for the average person to visualize. For security, it is less easy to see the benefits unless the security team can provide more data on failed attacks, trends in attacks on a global scale, and potential losses to the company.

You need to sell security to senior management, to the people who will be using the systems, and to the SAs who will have to install, maintain, and support users on those systems. Each of these groups cares about different things, and all their concerns must be taken into account when designing and implementing a security system.

To sell security to senior management, you need to show how your security helps the company meet its obligation to its shareholders and its customers and ways in which security could be considered a competitive advantage. All organizations have an equivalent of customers and shareholders. In a university, the customers are the students and the funding bodies; in a non-profit or government organization, the customers are the constituents that they serve.

When trying to sell something to others, it is important to show them how buying it is in their best interest, not your own. The legal team should be able to help with information on legal obligations. If the company receives confidential information from customers, good security is an asset that may increase business. Universities may be able to get more lucrative industrial sponsorship if they can show that they can keep confidential information safe. Companies selling services or support can also gain customer confidence from demonstrating their security consciousness. Think about what you, a security-conscious person, would want from your company if you were a customer. If you can provide it and market it, that is a competitive advantage.

Also gather data on what the company's competitors are doing in terms of investing in security or at least data on other similar-size companies in reasonably similar industries. Senior management will want to be able to gauge whether what is being spent on security is too much, too little, or about the right amount. If possible, produce metrics on the work that the security team is doing. Metrics are discussed further in Section 11.2.3. Also consider having an outside group perform a formal risk analysis for your company. Senior management likes to have solid data on which to base its decisions.

Case Study: Use Security as a Competitive Advantage

An EDA company received chip designs from its customers on a regular basis for a variety of reasons. The company had to be very careful with this extremely valuable third-party intellectual property. The company was very security aware, with good security measures in place and an information-protection team, which considered its security program to be a competitive advantage and marketed it as such to its customers and to the management team. This helped to maintain the high level of support for security within the company.

To sell security, you need to ensure that the people who will be using the systems will be able to work effectively in an environment that is comfortable for them. You also need to show them that it is in their best interests or the best interest of the company. If you can provide them with a system that does not interfere with their work but provides extra security, customers will be happy to use it. However, you do need to be particularly careful not to lose the trust of these customers. If you provide slow, cumbersome, or invasive systems, customers will lose faith in your ability to provide a security system that does not adversely affect them and will be unwilling to try future security systems. Credibility is very important for a successful sale.

To sell security to the SAs who will be maintaining the systems, looking after the people who use those systems, and potentially installing the systems, you need to make sure that the systems you design are easy to use and implement; have simple, straightforward setups; and are reliable and do not cause problems for their customers. You also will need to provide them with tools or access for debugging problems. Supporting a security system ideally should not put any more overhead on them than supporting any other system.

11.2 The Icing

This section discusses ideals for your security program. To be able to achieve these goals, you will need to have a solid infrastructure and security program already in place. One of the ideals of the security team and the information-protection team should be to make security awareness pervasive throughout the company. The security team should also, ideally, stay up to date with the industry, which means maintaining contacts within the industry and tracking new technologies and directions. Another ideal for the security team is to be able to produce metrics to describe how the team is performing and the benefits of the security program.

11.2.1 Make Security Pervasive

A good information-protection program will make everyone aware of security and intellectual property issues. For example, at a company where Christine worked, the information-protection team and the marketing group ran an awareness campaign that included a series of cartoon posters of some common ways that information was stolen and raising awareness of laptop theft at airports.

If you can make security a part of the way that people work and think, the job of the security team will become much easier. People will automatically get the security team involved early in projects, will notice strange system behavior that may indicate a break-in, and will be careful with sensitive information.

Case Study: Make Security Pervasive

At IBM, the Clean Desk Policy said that all paperwork, confidential or not, was to be locked inside your desk every night and that confidential documents had to be locked away at all times. In general, infractions caused a note to be left on your desk by security, IT, or facilities, depending on who was responsible for checking that particular office. Multiple infractions were dealt with differently, depending on the site, but a specific set of punishment criteria existed. At least one person was fired for leaving highly confidential information out on her desk.

IBM had entire blocks of offices and conference rooms without windows because of the possibility of people spying through the windows with telescopes. Security is pervasive and very much a part of the corporate culture.

Case Study: Raise Security Awareness

Motorola instituted a Protection of Proprietary Information (POPI) program. This security-awareness program included informational posters reminding people to be careful of proprietary information, even within the company's buildings. Reminders at the printers stated that all printouts would be cleared away at a certain time in the evening, so that people didn't print something and leave it there for anyone to see or pick up. Little table tents reminded people: "Please don't leave proprietary information on my desk while I am out." Each group had "POPI cops" who periodically went around and checked desks and whiteboards for sensitive information. The cops left either a green "Well done!" note or a red "You did the following things wrong ..." note on each desk after it had been checked.

People generally want to do the right thing. If you keep reminding them what it is and they keep trying, it becomes second nature. It is important to be respectful and to make sure that the reminders do not cause them to feel nagged, mothered, or otherwise less than intelligent adults. Condescension and nagging engender resentment and are not conducive to building good security habits.

11.2.2 Stay Current: Contacts and Technologies

Contacts within the security industry can be a good source of information on current attacks and vulnerabilities, varying product experiences, and emerging technologies. Going to security conferences is a good way to build these contacts and keeps you several months ahead of the rest of the industry. Security professionals are typically more paranoid about disclosing their experiences to people they do not know well, so it is important to attend lots of conferences, get involved and recognized, and build a good rapport with others at the conferences.

You should also aim to keep up with all the new technologies being developed, their supposed benefits, how they work, and their deployment and operational needs. In doing this, you will need to develop a skill for distinguishing snake oil from a useful product. Advice can be found in Matt Curtin's *Snake Oil Warning Signs: Encryption Software to Avoid* (Curtin 1999a, b).

For any new product idea, vendors typically take several fundamentally various approaches, and it is often difficult to tell how successful any of them will be. However, watching the development of the various approaches, understanding the operational implications, and knowing the people behind various products helps you to predict which products and technologies might succeed.

11.2.3 Produce Metrics

Metrics for security are very difficult. As mentioned earlier, selling security is like selling insurance. If you can produce some form of metrics that makes sense, describing at some level how the security team is performing and what value it is giving the company for its money, it will be easier to convince management to fund security infrastructure projects.

Having an external auditing team, may be a useful source of metrics. For example, you could describe the area that was audited or attacked, the level of success, and the possible cost of a breach in security of that area. If problems were found with an area, you can provide information on what it would cost to fix it and then track your improvements over time.

If you have a clear security perimeter, you may be able—for example, using an intrusion-detection system—to gather data on the number of attacks or possible attacks seen outside and inside the security perimeter, thus enabling you to graph the level of protection provided by your security perimeter. You may be able to start with simple graphs of the number of machines that are visible to people outside the company, statistics on the number of services that each of those is making available, and the number of vulnerabilities. You could also graph the number of security patches that the team needed to make overall by OS and by application.

Good metrics should help management and other nonsecurity people within the company understand, at some level, what you are doing and how well you are doing it. Good metrics help build confidence in the security team for the rest of the company. At the least, they demonstrate what work is done and what areas are the most-repeated issues.

11.3 Organization Profiles

In this section, we present a brief overview of the stages of development of a reasonable company security program, depending on the size and function of the company. This section is meant as a guideline only, to give you a sense of whether you are behind the curve or ahead of it and how your security program should develop as your company grows.

We describe a sample security program at a small, medium, and large company; an e-commerce site; and a university. For these examples, a small company typically has between 20 and 100 employees; a medium-size company, between 1,000 and 3,000 employees; and a large company, more than 20,000 employees.

11.3.1 Small Company

In a small company with one or two SAs, security will be a fairly small component of one SA's job. The company should have an acceptable-use policy and should be thinking about a monitoring and privacy policy. The SAs will probably know just about everything that is going on and so will probably not need to form or participate in any formal cross-functional teams. The company will be concerned primarily with perimeter security, particularly if it is a young company. The SAs should be considering a strong authentication mechanism, making management aware of it, and deciding when it is appropriate for the company to invest in one.

If the small company is a start-up, particularly in the computer industry, engineering may need open access to the Internet for immediate access to new technologies as they become available. In this case, the company should look at whether a lab environment will work for that and, if not, how to protect engineering as best possible without interfering with their work and how to protect the rest of the company from engineering.

11.3.2 Medium-Size Company

A medium-size company should have a small staff of full-time SAs. The primary role of one of these SAs should be security architect. Some other SAs should be primarily implementers, with secondary roles in security. The responsibilities of the security function should be centralized, even if SAs in remote locations take on some security work as all or part of their jobs. Remote SAs who have security responsibilities should report to the security group for that aspect of their work.

The security architect will do quite a lot of implementation, and the implementers will also take on the operations responsibilities. Policies will be the responsibility of the architect and possibly the manager of the group. Auditing may be taken on by an implementer or the architect, or they may work with some external consultants to build an auditing program. The company should have all the basic policies mentioned in Section 11.1.2 and at least a rudimentary auditing program. There should be an information-protection group with representatives from the legal, facilities, human resources, IT, sales departments, and core business groups. The company should have a security-awareness program driven by the information-protection group.

The company should have significant security infrastructure and a strong authentication system that is centralized, robust, and thoroughly deployed. The company will probably have many remote access mechanisms that should all be linked to the authentication system. The company will almost certainly have connections to third parties for a variety of business reasons. These connections should make use of standard security mechanisms and share infrastructure where possible and appropriate. The company may have areas that require a higher level of security and have additional protection from the rest of the company. It may also have lab environments that are more exposed but from which the rest of the company is protected.

11.3.3 Large Company

The biggest problems that large companies face are related to size. Incident response, policy conformance, and tracking changes all become more difficult.

A large company should have several dedicated staff for each security role. The company will probably be split across administrative business units, each with its own policies and security perimeter, with clear methods of exchanging information between the business units. Each business unit should have all the policies described in Section 11.1.2 and more, as appropriate.

The company should have a large security infrastructure with a comprehensive auditing program. Many interdepartmental groups should focus on security and security-awareness programs in each of the business units.

Many areas will have much higher physical and electronic security requirements than others. Large companies typically have less de facto trust of all employees. There is simply more opportunity for accidental or malicious disclosure of sensitive information.

There will certainly be many third-party connections, with many restrictions and contracts relating to their use. There may also be lab environments in which research networks are more exposed to external networks.

Mergers and acquisitions bring new challenges. Resolving differences in security policies, culture and attitudes, and integrating network inventories (network discovery) become major endeavors for large companies.

11.3.4 E-Commerce Site

A company that conducts a significant amount of business over the Internet has special requirements, in addition to those already mentioned. In particular, an e-commerce company must have a clear division between "corporate" machines and "online service" machines. The latter machines are used for conducting business over the Internet; corporate machines are used for anything other than providing online services to customers.

No matter what its size, the e-commerce company must have at least one full-time security professional on staff. The company will need to scale its security staff a lot more quickly than other companies of similar size because of the nature of the business. The company will also need to develop policies, for example, regarding protecting customer information, more quickly than other companies of similar size.

E-commerce companies need separate policies governing access to corporate machines and online service machines. No matter what its size, the company must have an authorization matrix that defines the level of access to each type of online service machine. In addition, the company must pay special attention to customer billing information, including credit card information, addresses, and telephone numbers. An e-commerce company has a business-critical need to focus on trying to prevent DoS attacks against its online service infrastructure.

11.3.5 University

The university environment is typically very different from that of a business. In a business, the people who have legitimate access to the network are typically quite trusted by definition.[10] The company is normally willing to assume that the employees are working toward the best interests of the company.[11] In a university, however, the people who have access to the network are typically not trusted by default, in part because physical access is quite open.

A university typically has administrative networks and computers that have restricted access and tight security controls, as well as academic networks that are quite open. Frequently, a university will have open access to and from the Internet because it is a research environment, where openness and learning are considered to go hand-in-hand.

Universities usually have less money to spend on their computing environment in general and security in particular and so are in some ways similar to a small company. A university must have an acceptable-use policy and a

---

10.   There often are different levels of access and protection even within a company, but usually everybody in a company has access to all but the most sensitive information, unless it is a very large company divided into smaller subcompanies.

11.   This may not be wise from a security point of view, but it is a pragmatic business compromise that most executives make.

monitoring and privacy policy that every computer user signs before getting access to the computing systems.

Recall that the first questions you need to ask involve what you are trying to protect, from whom it must be protected, and what it is worth. Universities typically share and publish their research, and thus the value of that research is not as high as the design of the next computer microprocessor or the details about a new drug. For academic networks, the university management may determine that it is interested in preventing large-scale loss of service or data and may also determine that some people who have legitimate access to the systems should be considered a threat.

In a university environment, you will need to have in-depth security on key servers and additional security around the administrative networks. For the open-access machines in labs, you need to have a good autoinstall and autopatch system, as described in Chapter 3, and you need to find the balance among security, research, and teaching needs.

11.4 Conclusion

Security is a large, complex area that requires even more communication skills than other areas of system administration and must be a cooperative effort that crosses administrative divisions. Security should be built on solid foundations in policies that are approved and supported by senior management. Building security systems relies on the other systems infrastructure.

There are some areas that the technical staff should concentrate on and others with which management can help. The technical staff must consider business needs, convenience for customers, staying up to date with attacks and vulnerabilities, building a solid authentication and authorization system, and selecting good security software. Ideally, the technical staff should also build good contacts within the industry and keep an eye on new technologies to do its best to keep up to date with what is happening in the security world.

The security group's management can help with resources and staffing, establishing an incident-response team, engaging external auditors, and selling security to other groups within the company. Ideally, security should be a pervasive part of the company culture. This sort of company culture takes a lot of time and effort to build and will succeed only if it comes from senior management. One of the best ways to gain management support is to produce meaningful metrics on the work that the security team is doing.

Exercises

1. What security polices do you have? Which of them need to be updated? Which policies listed in this chapter are missing? What problems is this causing?

2. Why do you think we recommend that the network connectivity policy stipulate the various forms of third-party connectivity that are supported?

3. What third-party connections does your institution have? Do you know beyond all doubt that those are the only ones? What about small remote offices? Can you categorize those connections into types of access?

4. Do you have infrastructure to support bringing up a new third-party connection easily? If not, try designing such an infrastructure; afterward, see whether you can fit your existing third-party connections into that infrastructure.

5. What three changes in security would you recommend right now to your management?

6. In Section 11.1.3.6, page 295, a definition is provided for "security-sensitive products." Classify devices in your network that are and are not security-sensitive.

Chapter 12

Ethics

What policies related to ethics should a site have? What are the additional ethical responsibilities of SAs and others with privileged technical access? This chapter discusses both of these issues.

Ethics, the principles of conduct that govern a group of people, are different from morals. **Morals** are a proclamation of what is right and good, a discussion that is beyond the scope of this book.

Whether your organization involves you in drafting the ethics guidelines for all network users or only the SAs, bring this chapter along. We hope to provide you with the tools you need to get the job done.

12.1 The Basics

Organizations usually have various ethics-related policies for their employees and other affiliates. Ethics policies concerning network use fall into two categories: policies applying to all users and those applying only to privileged users, such as managers, SAs, and database administrators. In general, an SA needs to carefully follow company policies, as well as to set a higher standard. You have access to confidential information that most other employees cannot see; as a result, you have special responsibilities.

Recently, a flurry of U.S. and European Union (EU) legislation has mandated enhanced corporate responsibility for ethical policies and controls with respect to IT. Laws such as Sarbanes-Oxley Act, the Family Educational Rights and Privacy Act, and the Health Insurance Portability and Accountability Act (HIPAA) have changed the way companies think about these issues. The occupation of system administration has been directly affected.

12.1.1 Informed Consent

The principle of **informed consent**, originally formulated by medical ethicists, applies to SAs as well as to doctors. In medical ethics, informed consent has two parts. First, the patient should be fully educated, or informed, as to all the treatment options, all the possible benefits and drawbacks of those options, and the various probabilities of success. The information should be explained in whatever way the person is competent to understand, and the patient must be given the opportunity to permit the treatment or refuse it, without coercion of any sort: the consent part.

Consent is not possible if someone is legally incompetent—unable to understand the ramifications—or unable to give consent—for example, the person is in a coma and has no next of kin. In these cases, the generally accepted standard is to fully satisfy all three of the following conditions. First, the procedure must have a high likelihood of success. Second, it must be in the *patient's* best interest, such that if the procedure is successful, the person would likely be thankful in retrospect. Third, all other avenues must have been attempted first. In other words, violating informed consent must be a last resort.

These principles can be applied to many SA tasks. People should understand the rules under which they are living. For example, an SLA should specify that maintenance will be done only in certain hours, and your customers should be aware of those hours. For instance, a compute server may be designated for long-term jobs, such as simulations. If the simulation software doesn't have a checkpointing feature, a reboot might lose days or weeks of work. If a reboot is absolutely unavoidable, the SLA might specify that the current users of the machine will be notified: informed consent. On the other hand, compute servers for shorter jobs might have a blanket SLA that specifies only a 15-minute warning. The SLA informs your customers how you will be operating in various situations.

12.1.2 Professional Code of Conduct

SAGE, the System Administrators' Guild, and LOPSA, League of Professional System Administrators have granted us permission to print the revised System Administrators Code of Ethics.[1] We are doing so because we feel that

---

1. SAGE (www.sage.org). LOPSA http://www.lopsa.org.

it does an excellent job of putting into words our feelings regarding the need for SAs to maintain an extremely high level of professionalism. It's a useful starting point for writing your own corporate code of conduct. It is intentionally *not* a set of enforceable laws, an enumeration of procedures, proposed responses to situations, all-encompassing, or an enumeration of sanctions and punishments.

The System Administrator's Code of Ethics

Professionalism

- I will maintain professional conduct in the workplace and will not allow personal feelings or beliefs to cause me to treat people unfairly or unprofessionally.

Personal Integrity

- I will be honest in my professional dealings and forthcoming about my competence and the impact of my mistakes. I will seek assistance from others when required.
- I will avoid conflicts of interest and biases whenever possible. When my advice is sought, if I have a conflict of interest or bias, I will declare it if appropriate, and recuse myself if necessary.

Privacy

- I will access private information on computer systems only when it is necessary in the course of my technical duties. I will maintain and protect the confidentiality of any information to which I may have access, regardless of the method by which I came into knowledge of it.

Laws and Policies

- I will educate myself and others on relevant laws, regulations, and policies regarding the performance of my duties.

Communication

- I will communicate with management, users, and colleagues about computer matters of mutual interest.
- I will strive to listen to and understand the needs of all parties.

System Integrity

- I will strive to ensure the necessary integrity, reliability, and availability of the systems for which I am responsible.

- I will design and maintain each system in a manner to support the purpose of the system to the organization.

Education
- I will continue to update and enhance my technical knowledge and other work-related skills.
- I will share my knowledge and experience with others.

Responsibility to Computing Community
- I will cooperate with the larger computing community to maintain the integrity of network and computing resources.

Social Responsibility
- As an informed professional, I will encourage the writing and adoption of relevant policies and laws consistent with these ethical principles.

Ethical Responsibility
- I will strive to build and maintain a safe, healthy, and productive workplace.
- I will do my best to make decisions consistent with the safety, privacy, and well-being of my community and the public, and to disclose promptly factors that might pose unexamined risks or dangers.
- I will accept and offer honest criticism of technical work as appropriate and will credit properly the contributions of others.
- I will lead by example, maintaining a high ethical standard and degree of professionalism in the performance of all my duties. I will support colleagues and co-workers in following this code of ethics.

12.1.3 Customer Usage Guidelines

Every organization needs a set of guidelines for acceptable uses of an organization's computers.[2] The guidelines might address some of the following points. Under what circumstances is personal use of employer equipment permitted? What types of personal use are forbidden? Can an employee run a fledgling dot-com out of his or her cubicle? Can an employee post to a blog from work? How about using the organization's computer for surfing "adult" web sites? How do the rules change if an employee is using company equipment at home?

---

2. Internet service providers often refer to these agreements as an acceptable use policy, or AUP; colleges often call them a user code of conduct, or UCC. The terms are interchangeable.

A code of conduct should define and forbid threatening or harassing communications, explain how to report them, and explain how reports are processed. Sometimes, these guidelines are part of the acceptable-use policy mentioned in Chapter 11.

Codes of conduct at academic institutions are usually very different from codes of conduct in industry. The differences stem from the requirements for academic freedom and the fact that, for many students, the campus *is* home.

You can find sample policies through various industry and academic consortia, which often have a web site with a collection of policies from various organizations. Dijker (1999) is one such archive. The best way to write a policy is to use an archive to find a policy whose philosophy is close to your own and to use it as a base document.

12.1.4 Privileged-Access Code of Conduct

Some users need privileged access to do their jobs. The ability to write and debug device drivers, install software for other people, and perform many other tasks all require root, or Administrator, access. Organizations need special codes of conduct for these people; as we all know, privileges can be abused. This code of conduct should include the following points.

- The individual acknowledges that privileged access comes with a responsibility to use it properly.
- The individual promises to use elevated access privileges solely for necessary work-related uses. Management should explicitly describe these uses.
- The company acknowledges that mistakes happen and encourages procedures for minimizing the damage a mistake may cause. For example, SAs should make backups before making any changes.
- Procedures should be defined for what to do if privileged access gives someone information about something that wouldn't have otherwise been made public. For example, suppose that an SA fixing a problem with a mail server and she accidentally sees a message implying that someone is running a gambling operation from his or her cubicle. What should the SA do? The policy should describe what the organization expects the SA to do.

In another scenario, say a privileged user learns about something that is less nefarious but just as important such as a message about a pending merger. What should that the SA do? Again, the code of conduct should be explicit and should explain what an employee coming across privileged company information should do.

- Consequences making a mistake should be specified. We believe that the best policy here is to state that there will be no punishment for making an honest mistake as long as it is reported quickly and honestly. The sooner a mistake is reported, the sooner it can be fixed and the less domino-effect damage will result.

- A warning should be made about the possible penalties, including termination, for violating the policy.

People with privileged access should sign a statement saying that they have read the code of conduct for privileged users. The original should be filed with the person's manager or HR department, whichever is customary at the organization. Both the individual and that person's manager should be given a copy of it for their files.

As a good security measure, the SA team should track who has privileged access to which systems. This practice is especially useful for alerting the SAs to remove access privileges when a privileged user leaves the organization. Some organizations have a policy that privileged access expires every 12 months unless the form is re-signed. This practice encourages regular policy reviews. Automatic reminders are another good tool.

Tom gives these instructions to junior SAs that he hires:

Tom's Three Rules of Privileged Access

(1) Be careful. (2) Respect privacy. (3) If you mess up, tell me right away.

Rule 1: Be careful.

You can do a lot of damage when you are root/Administrator, data base admin, etc, so be careful. Make backups. Pause before you press ENTER. Make backups. Test wildcards before you use them. Make backups. Pay attention to what you are doing. Make backups. Don't drink and compute. Make backups.

Rule 2: Respect privacy.

Don't look at anything that isn't required for a task. Don't "browse." Don't look at something if you wouldn't want someone looking at yours.

Rule 3: If you mess up, tell me right away.

You will make mistakes. That's OK. You will never be punished for an honest mistake if you tell me as soon as you realize it's beyond what you can fix. It's most likely my job to fix your mistake, and you will have to watch as I do so. The sooner you tell me, the happier I will be because the less I will have to fix. However, if you hide a mistake and I have to fix it without knowing that the mistake was made, I will figure out what the mistake was, who made it, and there will be negative consequences.

❖ **The Right Reminder at the Right Time** The popular program sudo (Snyder et al. 1986) enables limited privileged access to UNIX systems. Certain versions of sudo print this message:

```
We trust you have received the usual lecture from the local
System Administrator. It usually boils down to these two things:
#1) Respect the privacy of others.
#2) Think before you type.
```

The program does an excellent job of reminding people about a policy at the right time.

Have a Witness

A company's buggy email server was mangling people's mailboxes. While waiting for a software patch, the SAs discovered that the mailboxes could be fixed with a text editor. However, an SA could see someone's messages while fixing the mailbox. When the CEO's mailbox was mangled, the SAs faced a challenge. The industry was experiencing a high level of merger activity, and the SAs didn't want the responsibility that would come with accidentally seeing a critical email message in the CEO's mailbox. They decided that the CEO's assistant would watch the SA while he fixed the CEO's mailbox. That way, the assistant would see that the SA wasn't nosing around for confidential information and would also understand how much exposure the CEO's confidential email had received. This protected the CEO and the SA alike.

Sometimes, these policies are governed by federal law. For example, the Securities and Exchange Commission (SEC) has rules against monitoring networks used to trade stock, which can make debugging a network problem on Wall Street very difficult. Also, the Federal Communications Commission (FCC) has rules about how telephone operators and technicians can use information accidentally obtained while doing their jobs. These people can discuss the information only with its source and can't use it for personal gain.

Finally, network users have to understand that monitoring may happen as part of running the network. A monitoring and privacy policy should be in place, as discussed in Section 11.1.2.

12.1.5 Copyright Adherence

Organizations should have policies stating that their members abide by copyright laws. For example, software piracy is pervasive, and many people don't realize that "borrowing" software that is not freely redistributable is in fact *stealing* it.[3]

Companies are very concerned about being caught using pirated software. The financial liabilities and bad publicity don't make executives or shareholders very happy. Add this fact to the highly publicized raids conducted by anti-software-piracy organizations, and you get a recipe for disaster. The bottom line: Don't use pirated software on company equipment, and don't let users sneak it past you.

Telling people not to pirate software isn't all that effective, they're always convinced that what they're doing is not software piracy. Many people don't understand what constitutes software piracy. Even if they do, they will try to plead ignorance when caught. "I thought we had a site license." "I didn't know it was also installed on another machine." "Someone told me it was OK."

To solve this problem, a copyright-adherence policy should give three or four examples of the most common violations. It might, for example, state that individually licensed PC software packages should be purchased for individual PCs and that a single-use installation disk should not be used on multiple machines. The policy could also require that manuals and media for software be stored in the room with the PC using the software.

---

3. Pirated software is also a vector for spreading computer viruses and therefore a security concern. Nowadays, because Internet email is a much larger vector, viruses introduced via pirated software are barely noticed. However, we would be remiss if we didn't point out that in a couple of famous cases, commercial, shrink-wrapped software was a vector!

Some companies bar employees from installing *any* software without explicit management approval. Alternatively, and for the sake of simplicity, a policy statement might specify software that employees may download at will, such as new versions of Adobe Acrobat Reader or new versions of web browsers. Installing software not on the list would require management approval.

Finally, a statement along the following lines might be useful: "We are always striving to reduce overhead costs, and we appreciate your efforts in this area. That said, software piracy is a recipe for trouble, and we do not consider it to be a valid cost-saving measure. No one at this company is authorized to pirate software; if anyone pirates software or asks you to do so, please follow this procedure."

The easiest way to ensure policy compliance is to mold your policy into the path of least resistance: Bulk-license popular packages for all workstations. You can't be out of compliance if you have a site license. Install it as part of the standard set of software delivered with all workstations. People are less likely to seek out alternative software packages if there is no effort required to use the one you have licensed. If this is not feasible, another approach is to require that new workstation or server requests also include necessary OS and application software or licenses.

One major benefit of free and open source software is that the licenses permit, if not actively encourage, copying. There is still a license that must be adhered to, but normal use rarely creates a problem. If employees are modifying the source code or using the source code as part of a product, the license should be carefully studied. Some large companies have a designated group to globally manage their free/open source compliance and to look for ways to better leverage their involvement in the open source community.

It is important to inform people of this sad bit of reality: When faced with a copyright-violation lawsuit, companies rarely accept the blame. Instead, they implicate whoever let the violation happen and relay the damages to that person. Document this in the policy, and make sure that the policy is communicated to all.

It is especially important for SAs to realize this. It is much more likely that the person to be blamed will be the hapless SA who used a development OS license to get new workstations running than the manager who refused to sign the purchase order for new licenses in a timely manner. If your management tells you to break the law, refuse politely, in writing/email.

Simple License Management Using Paper

Administrating bulk licenses need not be complicated. Tom once ordered 50 right-to-use licenses of a software package and one copy of the documentation and media. He then numbered 50 lines on a piece of paper, and, when someone requested the software, he wrote the person's name on a line. He taped the paper inside the installation manual. This solution worked extremely well and required very little effort—there was no database to maintain and no overhead.

Simple License Tracking Using Groups

There's a really simple way to track software licences on a network. Suppose that you've licensed 50 copies of a software package to be given out to people as they request it. Create a group in Microsoft ActiveDirectory or LDAP named after the software package (or maybe lic.NameOfPackage). When you install the software package on a person's computer, add the person to this group. You can now count the number of people in the group to determine how many licenses have been handed out. Best of all, when someone is terminated and his or her account is deleted, the person will be removed from the group, and the license will be freed up.

12.1.6 Working with Law Enforcement

Organizations should have a policy on working with law enforcement agencies so that SAs know what to do if one contacts them. Law enforcement officials sometimes contact SAs to help with investigations in areas of computer-related crime, as well as with harassment issues or other instances in which evidence is needed. Panicking can be a natural response in these situations; for this reason, and to avoid violating the law or company policy, SAs need a procedure to guide them. Generally speaking, working with these agencies through a manager is a good idea. One company had the following procedure:

If Contacted by Law Enforcement

1. Relax. Be calm.
2. Be polite. *(SAs often have problems with authority and need to be reminded that being rude to an investigator is A Bad Thing.)*

3. Refer the issue to your manager. Suggested words are, "As a policy, we gladly cooperate with law enforcement. I need to refer this matter to my boss. Can I take your phone number and have her call you?" *(Law enforcement will always give a phone number. Pranksters and scam artists will not.)*

4. If you are a manager, contact the legal department for advice.

5. Keep a log of all requests, all related phone calls, and any commands typed.

6. The SA who collects evidence should give it to the legal department, which will give it to law enforcement unless the manager directs otherwise. *(This policy protects the SA.)*

7. If the law enforcement agency is the internal corporate security department, the evidence should be given to the SA's manager, who will give it to corporate security. Again, be polite when explaining this policy to corporate security: "We always comply with requests from your group. However, it is department policy for me to collect these logs and give them to my boss, who will then give them to you. My boss can be contacted as follows...."

An organization *must* verify the identity of a person claiming to be from a law enforcement agency before telling him or her *anything*, including your manager's name and contact information. Perform this verification even before you admit that you are an SA. The best way to do this is to tell the person that you need to verify his or her identity. Ask for the person's phone number and agency's switchboard number, and then call the switchboard and ask for the person. If you question whether the switchboard number is real, look up the number in the phone book. (Yes, the FBI, CIA, and even the NSA are all listed!)

Failing to verify the identity of someone claiming to be a law enforcement official can turn out to be a disaster. Unfortunately, some of society's seamier characters pretend to be officials when they steal company information, using a tactic termed *social engineering*. It works like this.

1. Start with a small piece of information.

2. Make telephone calls while pretending to be an official or a new employee.

3. Leverage the piece of information into more useful information. Repeat with the new piece of information.

4. Repeat the previous steps until there is sufficient information to wreak havoc.

A Failed Experiment in Social Engineering

A naive young SA once received a phone call from someone claiming to be from the local police. The guy claimed that he was trying to understand how local companies secured their computer networks as part of a community assistance program. He asked several pointed questions, which the SA happily answered.

Over the next few days, other people at the company received phone calls from the same guy, this time claiming that he was a new member of their computer security group. He certainly sounded knowledgeable about the system. Luckily, one woman tried to verify his identity; when she couldn't, she alerted the SA team's manager. As a result, an executive warned everyone in the company that a scam was afoot, that no one should reveal sensitive information over the phone, and that any unusual requests for sensitive information should be reported to a manager. These actions stopped the guy in his tracks.

If the guy had continued, he might have used his techniques to gain access to the corporate network. For example, when he claimed to be from the security group, he sounded authentic because he had learned so much about the company's security system from the naive SA. If he had continued, he could have collected enough small bits of information to leverage them into full system access.

Real law enforcement personnel and real employees will provide information to verify their identities, and they will not be offended when you ask them for this information.

Sometimes, would-be social engineers hatch their plans by starting with the information they find by rooting through dumpsters and rubbish bags: dumpster diving. They look for anything that might help them harm your company: names, phone numbers, or project information.

Suppose that while a malicious person finds a memo on company letterhead dumpster diving about a mysterious Project Zed in the R&D department. Attached to it is a list of people involved in the project and their phone numbers. The person will use this starting material and the telephone tactics described to get as much as possible out of unsuspecting employees. These people can sound *very* smooth on the phone and can succeed if employees aren't on their toes. The person may start by claiming to be new on Project Zed, working with [insert the name of someone listed on the memo], and trying to find out how to have an account created, get details for remote access, and so on. Once the account is created, the person can walk right into your systems. The moral of this story is to tell people to be careful about what they say on the phone, and to shred documents that may contain sensitive information—even if they feel silly doing it!

If you run your organization's Internet gateway, you are much more likely to be contacted by law enforcement. If law enforcement agencies contact you regularly, it's time to consider streamlining your procedures for dealing with them to avoid making mistakes or becoming a target. You might get training from the legal department and establish a procedure that lets you handle a standard police inquiry yourself and simply notify the legal department about the existence of the inquiry. This way, the legal department won't need to hold your hand every step of the way. Of course, exceptional cases should still be referred to the legal department. In the best case, a problem is quickly fixed, and no future reports are generated. However Internet service providers and web-hosting companies may have a continual stream of problems.

Don't Be Too Accommodating

Once upon a time, a company offered a demo of a web-based service that let people surf the web anonymously. Crackers used this service to harass other sites. This activity, unfortunately, was traced back to the anonymizer service. This was *not* good. Whenever the problem arose, law enforcement contacted the SA, who passed the message along to the people running the service. He would never hear of it again and assumed that appropriate action was being taken. Many services shared his Internet connection and, being a typically overworked SA, it took him a while to notice the trend: multiple requests from law enforcement all concerning the same service.

The SA was worried about the negative effects of the service but also wanted to be accomodating to his customer. He advised the group how to change the service to make it less susceptible to abuse, but the group ignored him. Soon the requests from law enforcement started taking up more of his time, as he was being listed on subpoenas. Not surprisingly, he became extremely frustrated and burned out.

Eventually, he realized that he was trying to fix this problem at the wrong level. He brought the issue to his manager, and they agreed that he shouldn't take on the responsibility of problems caused by one of his customers, especially since he had made valid suggestions on how to fix the service. At the manager's level, he could require the customer to fix its software or be cut off in 30 days. The manager also decided that it was more appropriate for the requests from law enforcement to be forwarded to the company's legal department, to make sure that they were handled properly.

The corporate legal department shut down the service within minutes of being told that the situation existed, not waiting the entire 30 days. Legal was shocked that the problem had been permitted to persist at all.

In hindsight, the SA should have been tougher with the customer from the beginning. If he didn't have the backbone or the authority to shut the customer down, he should have turned the problem over to the legal department, which would have been much firmer. The moral of this story is to be firm with people who are harming your company, even if they're customers. If they turn into bullies, it's better to find a bigger bully to fight for you.

No matter how you feel about a policy, your duty is to follow the requests from corporate security. If you feel uncomfortable with those requests, take the issue to your manager; don't take the situation into your own hands.

> **Printer Log Panic**
>
> A young SA who ran the print system for a large company was contacted by corporate security. As part of a sexual harassment investigation, security wanted logs related to what had been printed on a particular color printer. This printer was in the SA's building, which meant that he might know the suspect. The SA panicked. He collected all the logs from that printer and copied them to his own computer at home. Next, he deleted the logs at work. Finally, he sought advice from two friends. "Someone could be fired! What should I do?" They both gave him the same advice: To avoid getting fired himself, he should restore the logs and give corporate security what had been requested. By hiding evidence, he had endangered his own position and made himself look like an accomplice to the accused.

12.2 The Icing

This section discusses setting expectations and some example situations one might encounter.

12.2.1 Setting Expectations on Privacy and Monitoring

Establishing a policy on privacy and monitoring is a fundamental ethical issue. This section emphasizes the need to remind the customers time and time again about this policy and its implications.

Setting employee expectations on privacy is important because putting people in situations in which they don't know the laws governing them is unfair. Punishing people for violating a rule they've never been told about is abusive.

There are many ways to set expectations. When hired, employees should be required to sign a statement that they have read the privacy and monitoring guidelines. Companies can also require employees to sign these statements annually. Companies should occasionally reprint privacy statements in newsletters or bulletins.[4] Having a summary of the policy, or even the

---

4. To avoid confusion about whether a policy has changed or is merely being reprinted as a reminder insist on version numbers, as well as dates, on policies.

sentence "All sessions are open to monitoring" displayed at every login screen can be more effective than having a long policy stored on a web server that nobody visits.

Allowing employees to remain uninformed about privacy policies can be dangerous for business reasons. System users who do not realize what risks their actions involve cannot manage those risks. Suppose that customers discuss proprietary business details via email, which they think is secure. If it is not, the information could be leaked. Because they were uninformed, they exposed the company to unnecessary risk.

In the financial community, email is regularly monitored for SEC violations, such as insider trading. The threat of monitoring may be enough to prevent illegal exchanges of insider information via email. Of course, it also could simply push insider trading back to channels that are more difficult to monitor, such as the telephone. However, that decision is for the SEC to make, not you.

E-commerce sites, and any site doing international business, must be concerned with privacy laws as they vary from country to country. For example, if you do business with EU citizens, there are strict regulations on how you must protect private information. U.S. laws add similar responsibilities (see Section 12.1).

Setting expectations also protects the reputations of SAs because a lack of information will result in customers' assuming the worst. Tom once had a customer who had previously been at a site that fired its SA for reading other people's email. The customer now assumed that all SAs read other people's email. However, some customers believe that email is somehow magically private in all situations and will take unreasonable risks, such as sending salary data via email. Companies that understand the realities of networked computing environments keep their most critical data on removable media— such as USB "thumb" drives, or writeable CDs or DVDs—rather than putting it on network file and email servers.

Since removable media represent an easy way for data to leave company premises, or be lost or stolen during legitimate transport, policies should address these issues as well. For example, it is common practice for salespeople to copy their email address book & contacts list onto removable media as an extra backup. It is also common for those backups to stay with them when they leave, despite policies prohibiting retention of confidential data, because "that's how everyone does it." If your policy sets different expectations, make sure that management is willing to stand behind their enforcement.

> **Case Study: Email Forwarding**
>
> A company had a liberal policy permitting email to ex-employees to be forwarded to their new email addresses for a year. The policy created problems because proprietary business information was often bulk emailed to lists that hadn't been updated to remove terminated employees. It was assumed that email within the company was private, even if it was sent to an entire department. Until everyone in the company was told about the problem, current employees weren't aware that they were risking security breaches by sending bulk emails.
>
> A better policy is to set up autoreply systems that reply with a message that includes the person's new email address and an explicit statement that the sender's message has not been forwarded. Sadly, owing to email addresses harvesting by spammers, it is now preferable to simply state that the account has been disabled and to omit any new email address.
>
> It is customary these days for individuals to maintain personal email addresses outside of work, such notification is no longer necessary.

12.2.2 Being Told to Do Something Illegal/Unethical

No chapter on ethics would be complete without a discussion of what to do if your manager tells you to do something illegal, unethical, or against company rules. We hope that you won't ever need the information in this section, but it is better to be prepared with an understanding of the issues than to be facing them cold.

The most important thing to remember in this situation is to maintain a record of events. Keep logs of when such requests are made, when related phone calls happen, what commands you type to execute such requests, and so on. Logs are your friend.

We recommend a simple process: Verify the request—maybe you didn't hear it right—verify that it's illegal or against company policy—check the written policy or ask someone for advice—and, if the request is against policy, assert yourself politely and reject the request explicitly.

If the manager persists, you can go along with it, go to a higher authority, or both. Many companies have an ombudsperson with whom you can confidentially discuss these situations. Highly regulated industries, such as financial institutions, have clearly established guidelines for what to do next. Even in a small firm, you have the option of approaching the HR or legal department and letting them know that you have a situation where you require guidance.

A useful technique is to ask that the request be made in writing or email. That gives you a paper trail and requires the person to restate the request. If the request was an innocent request that was misinterpreted, seeing the request in email may clarify.

Someone who is requesting something unethical and knows it won't put it in writing. This can put an end to the request. However, asking that a request be put writing without sounding confrontational is difficult. Asking for a request to be repeated in writing or email sounds a lot like insubordination to most managers. Instead, you can ask, "Can you email me a reminder so I'll see the request after lunch?" If the person doesn't, you can say that you need the email to be sure that you understand the request. Finally, you have to put your cards on the table: "Either I'm misunderstanding the request, or you are asking me to do something that I'm uncomfortable doing." Then suggest that you add someone to the conversation, such as your manager, your manger's manager, or someone else directly involved.

Asked to Read Someone Else's Email

Let's follow this through in a fictional example: Department head Bob asks you to read Alice's department head email to see whether her department is planning on canceling a project on which Bob's department relies. A good response would be to ask, in person, if you heard the request correctly. "What did you want me to do?"

If the request is confirmed, verify that it's against company policy, by finding the appropriate paragraph in your organization's privacy and monitoring guidelines. Gently verify that the person realizes that what is being asked is unethical by stating, "I'm not sure I heard you correctly.[5] You mean I should..." and point out that this is against policy.

Use the policy to provide a gentle reminder to Bob. Bob might rationalize his request, explaining that Alice has canceled other commitments and that he's only trying to help you because he knows that you too rely on this project.

At this point, you have a decision to make. You can stall and use the time to talk with an ombudsperson, corporate security, or Bob's manager. You could go along with the request, but doing so would make you an accessory. Might Bob make more requests of you, possibly pointing out that if you don't comply, he'll reveal the previous incident, claiming that you did it on your own initiative. He might also claim that if you do not comply, he'll simply

---

5. Or, if the request was via email, "I think I must be confused or misunderstanding your request ..."

find someone else who will do it. This tactic is a very threatening way for someone to convince a person to do something.

Obviously, we cannot make this decision for you. However, we can give you this advice: When you aren't sure whether you should do something, get the request in writing and keep a log of exactly what you do. Never act on verbal instructions that you find questionable. Even if you think that it might be OK, get it in writing. This is critical not only to cover yourself but also to assist the person making the request to be sure that he or she really wants it done. Someone who is not willing to put a request in writing is not willing to take responsibility for the action. Your log should note the time, the request, who made it, why it was done, and what was done. Also note anything unusual about the request. Not creating a log is something that people regret when it is too late. Automatically timestamped logs provide better accountability and take the tedium out of record keeping.

12.3 Conclusion

Ethics are the principles of conduct that govern what people's actions. Many people find the word *ethics* to be scary and vague. We hope to have laid down some guiding principles for you to consider and to have left things open-ended enough so that you can make your own choices.

The System Administrator's Code of Ethics seeks to enhance the professionalism and image of SAs by establishing a standard for conduct. The policies an organization should create include a network/computer user code of conduct, privileged-access code of conduct, copyright-adherence policy, and a policy on working with law enforcement. Informed consent decrees that we have a monitoring and privacy policy that is clearly communicated to all customers. Unless all these policies include a penalty for violations and are enforced consistently, they have no teeth.

Having thought about potential situations greatly prepares you for the situations when they arise. Try to think about potential ethical dilemmas you might encounter and what you would do in those instances. This might be a good thing to discuss occasionally at staff meetings or at lunch. This should be done with your manager present so that you can develop an understanding of the official policy.

If you learned one thing in this chapter, we hope it was that when you are in a gray area, the best way to protect yourself is to keep logs. Ask for the request in writing to create a log of the request, log when you receive phone calls, log what you are asked to do, and log what you do. Log everything!

Exercises

1. Describe an experience in which the System Administrator's Code of Ethics or the informed-consent rule would (or did) affect your actions.

2. Give examples of where you or your team enforced policies that customers were not aware of. In particular, consider the areas of conditions of acceptable use, sharing and availability of common resources, and system monitoring. How would you improve your performance in this area?

3. Think of an incident in which you or another SA were not acting in a fully professional manner. How would you have handled the incident with the SA Code of Ethics in mind?

4. Of the policies discussed in this chapter, which does your site have? If you are at a large site with corporate policies, do you have policies specific to your division?

5. Describe the policies detailed in the previous question as being easygoing or strict. Give examples. How would you change things, and why?

6. Ask three customers whether they know where to find any of the policy documents mentioned in this chapter.

7. Suppose that you were debugging a problem and as a result accidentally heard or read that a coworker was dealing drugs from the office. What would you do? What if the person was instead planning on sabotaging the company? Stealing office supplies? Stealing pieces of equipment for resale on an Internet auction site? Having an affair with the boss? What if the person was not your coworker but a high-level executive?

8. How long do you keep various logs on your system (printer, login/logout, and so on)? If you had been involved in the printing log anecdote in Section 12.1.6, how long would you now retain such logs? Why?

9. Suppose that you work at a web-based e-commerce site. An engineer who doesn't have the skill or patience to properly test his code in the development environment asks you to let him look at his logs on a production machine, then let him quickly change a logging parameter so he gets more information. Before you know it, you have an engineer doing development on the live production hosts. How would you handled this situation? Realistically, how could you have prevented it?

10. An executive asks you to allocate additional disk space for someone. You respond that you don't have the space but are told, "Make space, this person is important." Soon the same request is made for another person.

You are told, "You did it for the last person. This guy is just as important." How would you handled this situation? Realistically, how could
you have prevented it?

11. A person who is not an SA has privileged access to her workstation because the software she uses requires it. Friends ask for accounts on her
system. It's against policy, but she does it anyway. One of her friends
starts engaging in illegal activity on the workstation. How would you
have handled this situation? What if the employee who violated policy
was above you in management? A peer? Realistically, how could you
have prevented the problem?

Chapter 13

Helpdesks

This chapter is a macro view of helpdesks: what they are, how to organize them, how to manage them, and so on. Handling a call to the helpdesk is covered in the next chapter.

A helpdesk is a place, real or virtual, where people can get answers to their computing questions, report problems, and request new services. It may be a physical desk that people walk to, or it may be a virtual helpdesk that people access electronically.

Nothing is more important than your helpdesk; it is the face of your organization. The helpdesk staff make the first impression on your customers and maintain your relationship, good or bad, with them. The helpdesk staff fix the daily problems that are part of living with modern computers and are the heroes who are called when customers have an emergency. A good helpdesk reflects well on your organization. The typical customer sees only the helpdesk portion of your organization and often assumes that this is your entire organization. Customers have no idea what back-office operations and infrastructure are also performed. In short, a helpdesk is for helping the customers. Don't forget the *help* in helpdesk.

13.1 The Basics

The basics of running a helpdesk are first to simply have one and to ensure that it has a friendly face. The helpdesk should have enough staff to support the traffic, a defined scope of coverage, processes for staff, an escalation process for when things go badly, and call-tracking software.

13.1.1 Have a Helpdesk

Every organization has a helpdesk. It may be, physical, such as a walk-up counter, or virtual, such as by phone or email. Sometimes, the helpdesk is unofficial, as the portion of each day spent directly helping customers.

Small SA teams, with just one or two people, frequently have no official helpdesk, but that isn't sustainable. As the organization grows, small SA teams, become big SA teams, and big SA teams become enterprise organizations. Organizations don't realize that they need to institute a formal helpdesk until it is too late.

We believe that earlier is better when it comes to setting up a formal helpdesk. The best time to do this is 9 months before you realize that you should have done this 6 months ago. Organizations without access to time-travel devices need other techniques. Organizations grow through planning, and adopting a formal helpdesk should be part of that planning. If growth is slow, you can simply look for warning signs. One warning sign is when SAs start to notice that their group has grown to the point that communication problems are occurring. Alternatively, SAs might notice that they aren't able to get project work done because they are continually being interrupted by customer requests. Typically, the SAs might decide that it would be better if, for example, one SA could be interrupted in the morning and focus on project work in the afternoon, and the other SA could do the opposite. If you are considering such a structure, you are in the formative stage of adopting a formal helpdesk.

The transition from ad hoc to formal helpdesk can be uncomfortable to customers. SAs should expect this and do their best to ease the transition. Communicating the new helpdesk procedures clearly is important.

Tell People About Changes

When establishing a formal helpdesk, whether physical or virtual, people must be told that this is being done. When Lumeta had fewer than ten people, most of them did their own computer support, and Tom intervened for more difficult problems. Eventually, the company grew and had three SAs, including one who was dedicated to PC-related problems and other employees. For all intents and purposes, this person was the helpdesk. The customers didn't understand that the various SAs had specializations. This frustrated both the SAs, who felt pestered with inappropriate questions, and the customers, who were confused because every SA wasn't able to help in every situation. The problem was fixed when email went out explaining which SAs to contact for what kinds of problems; the message was repeated at weekly staff meetings two meetings in a row. You can prevent this confusion by making such announcements as the change happens.

Ease Transitions

A 75-person department had a network decoupled from the centralized, corporate IT department. People who were more knowledgeable about the systems did more of the SA duties, and others did less. One semitechnical clerk on staff, named Karen—not her real name—took care of backups and was trained to do most installations and other semiautomated tasks. Nearly every bit of user documentation included the instruction, "Email Karen to get started." As a result of business changes, the department was eventually required to use the centralized support that other departments in that building used. Customers were frustrated that instead of sending email to Karen, they had to send email to "help." The personal touch had been lost. Rather than deal with the emotional issue head-on, management simply kept pushing people to use the new process.

Karen held a lot of political weight in the department because everyone knew her, and she could spread pessimism effectively if she chose to do so. Because she was not made part of the process but was shoe-horned into it, she felt that she was being pushed out. She eventually quit, and it took a couple of years for the new helpdesk system to be fully accepted by the customers.

The problems could have been prevented if the transition had been handled better, first by understanding what the customers were used to and then by integrating that culture into the new process.

Helpdesks do not need to be purely physical objects but instead can be virtual. Problems can be reported and replies returned via email. Text-based and audio chat systems that enable people to interact with a human without using a phone can also be used.

Self-help systems are also popular but should not be considered replacement for systems that involve human interaction. With the pervasiveness of the web, there is no excuse not to have at least a simple repository of documentation for customers on such topics as how to get help or request service activation and solutions to common problems. A simple single-page web site with links to important documents, a wiki, or even a searchable blog (one post per FAQ) can be used. web-based systems let customers help themselves by offering documentation, lists of frequently asked questions and their answers, and just-in-time help. These systems can reduce the workload of helpdesk attendants but cannot provide the interactive debugging and workflow issues that require real-time interaction. There should be a phone number to call to report that the self-help system is down.

13.1.2 Offer a Friendly Face

A helpdesk should have a friendly face. For a physical helpdesk, the interior design should be pleasant and welcoming. A virtual helpdesk should be equally welcoming, which often means a design that uses soothing colors and readable fonts with the most commonly selected items at the top left of the first page.

The faces of the staff members also should be welcoming and friendly, as should their personalities. Some people have personalities that are suited for customer service; others don't. That should be a consideration when hiring people for your staff. The tone set by the staff will reflect that set by the supervisor. A supervisor who yells at the staff will find staff yelling at customers. A good-natured supervisor who can laugh and is always friendly will attract similar staff, who will reflect such an attitude with customers. It is easier to build a reputation for being friendly initially than to restore a bad reputation. In short, if you are the supervisor, be the friendly person you want your staff to be. Be a role model.

13.1.3 Reflect Corporate Culture

The look and feel of your helpdesk should reflect corporate culture. Often, we find that a helpdesk doesn't garner respect in a company when people working at the helpdesk buck the corporate culture. For example, a company that is very strict and formal may reflect this with strict dress codes and ways of conducting business, but the people at the helpdesk wear logo T-shirts and jeans, and the sound of a video game being played is in the background. A little asking around will find that the helpdesk has a reputation of being a bunch of slackers, no matter how hard they work or the quality of the service they provide.

The opposite happens too. When Tom was at Bell Labs, he worked in an area with very creative, free-thinking people. The dress code was simply, "You must be dressed," and protocol was very relaxed. Tom's SA team was tasked with being a buffer between these researchers and corporate IT. Any time these two groups of people interacted directly, it was like a bad sitcom episode.

Take time to consider the culture and "look" of your helpdesk as compared to that of the customers they serve. Try to evolve to a culture that suits the customers served.

13.1.4 Have Enough Staff

A helpdesk can be helpful only if it has enough people to serve customers in a timely manner. Otherwise, people will look elsewhere for their support.

Sizing a helpdesk staff is very difficult because it changes from situation to situation. Universities often have thousands of students per helpdesk attendant. Corporate helpdesks sometimes have a higher ratio or sometimes a lower ratio. In a commercial computer science research environment, the ratio is often 40:1, and the first-tier SAs have a similar skill level as second-tier SAs at other helpdesks, to meet the more highly technical level of questions. E-commerce sites usually have a separate helpdesk for internal questions and a "customer-facing" helpdesk to help resolve issues reported by paying customers. Depending on the services being offered, the ratio can be 10,000:1 or 1,000,000:1.

Ratios are a no-win situation. Management will always push to have a higher ratio; customers will always demand a lower ratio. You can always increase the ratio by providing less service to the customers, which usually costs the organization more because the customers spend time doing their own SA work inefficiently.

Rather than focus on customer-to-attendant ratios, it is better to focus on call-volume ratios and time-to-call completion. For example, you can monitor the rate at which customers receive busy signals or how long they wait to receive a response to their email or the number of minutes issues take to be resolved—minus, of course, time spent in "customer wait," as described in Section 16.2.6.

These metrics focus on issues that are more important to the customer. Customer-to-attendant ratios are an indirect measurement of benefit to the customers. In metric-based management, direct metrics are better.

Managing resources based on call volume also presents a more diverse set of potential solutions. Instead of one solution—headcount management—companies can invest in processes that let customers help themselves without need for human intervention. For example, new automation can be created that empowers customers to do tasks that previously required privileged access, online documentation can be provided, new services can be provisioned automatically via web interfaces, and so on.

You need to have appropriate metrics to make decisions about improving processes. Metrics can reveal good candidates for new automation, documentation, or training for both SAs and customers. Metrics can reveal which processes are more effective, which are used heavily, or which are not used at all.

Case Study: Human Web Browsers

Making the customers more self-sufficient can backfire if not done correctly. One company established a web site to give easy access to all the documentation and FAQs that previously had been the domain of the helpdesk staff. By monitoring the logs of the web site, the management saw an interesting trend. At first, the web site was wildly successful. The hits to the site were coming from the customers. The volume of phone calls was reduced, and everything was happening as planned. However, by the third month, the logs indicated a new trend: The web site was seeing an increasing number of hits from the helpdesk itself. Investigation showed that people had returned to calling the helpdesk and that the helpdesk attendants were reading answers off the web site. The helpdesk was acting as a human web browser! The situation was rectified when the helpdesk attendants were instructed to try to refer people to the appropriate web page rather than give answers directly. Customers were reminded to visit the web site before calling the helpdesk.

13.1.5 Define Scope of Support

A helpdesk should have a policy defining the scope of support. This document explains what an SA group is and isn't responsible for. The components of scope are *what*, *who*, *where*, *when*, and *how long*.

- *What* is being supported: only the PCs or the LAN itself? All PCs no matter what OS is being used, or only certain OSs and certain revisions? Which applications are being supported? How are unsupported platforms handled?

- *Who* will be supported: a particular department, building, division, enterprise, university? What if a person has offices in multiple buildings, each with its own helpdesk? Only people who pay? Only people of a certain management level and higher (or lower)?

- *Where* are the customers? This question is similar to *who* if one is supporting, for example, everyone in a particular building or location. However, *where* also includes support of traveling customers, customers visiting external customer sites, customers performing demos at trade shows, and people working from home.

- *When* is support provided? Are the hours of operation 8 AM to 6 PM, Monday through Friday? How are things handled outside of these hours? Do people have to wait until the helpdesk reopens, or is there a mechanism to reach SAs at home? If there is no support in the off hours, what should facilities management do if environmental alarms sound or if there is a fire?

- *How long* should the average request take to complete? Certain categories of requests should be instant; others should take longer. Establishing these goals sets expectations for the staff and customers. Customers expect everything to be immediate if they aren't told that certain tasks should be expected to take longer (see Section 31.1.3). A tiered structure might list certain things that are to be fast (5 minutes), slow (1 hour), and long (requests for new service creation).

Having a written scope-of-support policy is one of the best gifts management can give to a SA group. Without it, the group either will become overworked from trying to do everything for customers, or will infuriate customers by saying no when inappropriate. If you are a manager, it is your responsibility to clearly communicate when it is OK to say no and when it isn't, in writing, communicated to all people who work for you. This policy should also be publically accessible on the internal IT web site to set expectations with customers.

When we counsel overworked SAs, we often find that they do not have a written scope-of-support policy. We encourage the SA to create a written log of what they worked on for a week and to write down all their open tasks. Showing this list to their managers often makes them realize that their staff people are spread too thin or are working on tasks that are not department priorities. Often, managers are surprised to find that their SAs are, in essence, doing their customers' jobs for them. Writing a policy defining the scope of support empowers the staff to clearly communicate priorities to the group.

When we investigate SA teams that have gained reputations for being unhelpful curmudgeons, we often see the root problem to be a lack of written scope policy. Here, having a written policy sets a higher expectation for what the team's responsibilities are.

Without a written policy, the SAs are simply going on the accumulation of verbal edicts, and newer SAs simply follow the folklore they hear from their team members. New SAs, trying to be helpful, can undo a precedent without realizing it when they try to be helpful but instead go against the ad hoc policy. Or worse, they break something that shouldn't have been touched or step on a different department's toes.

Case Study: Wide Scope, Narrow Responsibility

Scope of support also means scope of responsibility. The New Jersey engineering division of a computer-aided design company was entirely in one building. The helpdesk's policy was that no question was inappropriate, but the SAs had a sharply defined scope of responsibility. This worked because they understood where their responsibility ended. They had complete responsibility for certain issues: If someone reported a workstation problem, the SAs would fix it. For other issues, they would advocate on behalf of the customer: If the problem was with a WAN link that they didn't control, they would take responsibility for contacting the corporate network operations center and seeing that it got fixed. With other issues, they acted as a referral service: Someone reporting a burned-out light in the office was referred to facilities management, and they would not take responsibility for seeing the issue to completion. They became a clearing house for requests and information.

To save money, the regional sales office was in the same building. The helpdesk was funded by the engineering division, not the sales office, and therefore the scope of responsibility for the sales staff was different. The helpdesk could refer the sales engineers to the proper documentation or suggest where they could get more training, but they could not be involved in helping to set up machines for demos or presentations. The sales staff used the central email server that was run by the engineering group, so email support was complete only if the salesperson was using the email client supported by the engineering group. However, because the support of the sales staff was free, there usually was a limit to how far the helpdesk staff would go to support their requests.

Having a clearly defined scope of responsibility prevented the helpdesk from taking on more work than it could handle, yet let it provide an extremely friendly referral service. It also prevented the sales group from abusing its service by giving the helpdesk the ability to say "no" in a way that had management support.

A helpdesk must have a good process for dealing with requests about technologies that are out of scope. The helpdesk can simply state that the request is out of scope and refuse to help, but that is an unfriendly response. It is much better to clearly state the scope of what the helpdesk can and can't do for the person and then offer a little help but give a time limit before you begin. For example, you might say, "We don't support systems with that video card, but I'll try my best for 30 minutes. If I can't fix it, you are on your own." You might spend 45 minutes on the problem and then politely tell the customer that you've reached your limit. The customer will appreciate your effort.

> **Set Expectations When Working Outside of Job Scope**
>
> One of Jay Stiles's favorite stories takes place before DHCP made network configuration automatic. At one point, he worked in a place that had one set of technicians who installed network jacks in offices and a different set of technicians who configured the PC to connect it to the network. The customers often asked the first group of technicians to configure their PCs. The technicians weren't trained on how to do this but sometimes felt pressured and tried. Rarely were they successful, and more often than not, they corrupted some other configuration while trying to configure the PC. When they made this kind of mistake, their boss would be called and put in a difficult position: How do you answer a complaint about an employee who wasn't supposed to do a particular task and didn't do it correctly?
>
> Later, the technicians learned that if they were asked to configure a PC, they should stop what they were doing, back away from the machine, and explain, "Well, that really isn't my job, but I happen to know a little about these PC computers, and I can give it a try. However, if I can't figure it out, I'm going to ask you to wait for the people who are supposed to do that kind of thing. OK?" If they said those magic words, the result was very different. If they were successful, the customer was very happy, knowing that the technician had gone above the call of duty. If they weren't successful, the customer was ecstatic because the technician had tried.
>
> The boss started receiving calls that were compliments: "The technician tried to configure my PC and couldn't, but I want to thank him for trying so hard!"
>
> It's all in how you sell it.

13.1.6 Specify How to Get Help

The companion to the scope of support is one specifying how to get help. This document tells customers what to do to get help: by phone, email, a ticket system, and so on. Certain types of requests may be directed to certain departments, or a unified helpdesk might be the single point of contact that forwards requests as appropriate to individual departments.

Such a document should be a few hundred words at most. Ideally, a shorter version that can fit on a sticker should be put on every new PC deployed. The same image can appear on default Windows background wallpaper images: "CompanyName IT helpdesk: [phone number] [email address] [web site]."

This is one of the most important things IT management can do to help the staff in time management. If customers have not been given clear direction on the proper way to get help, they will contact SAs directly, interrupting them at inappropriate times, making it impossible to get larger projects done. Or worse, SAs will be contacted at home!

13.1.7 Define Processes for Staff

Helpdesk staff should have well-defined processes to follow. In a smaller environment, this is not as important, because the processes are more ad hoc or are undocumented because they are being used by the people who built them. However, for a large organization, the processes must be well documented.

Very large helpdesks use *scripts* as part of their training. Every service supported has an associated flow of dialogue to follow to support that service. For example, the script for someone calling to request remote access service captures the appropriate information and tells the operator what to do, be it enable remote access directly or forward the request to the appropriate service organization. The script for a request to reset a password would, for security reasons, require callers to prove who they are possibly by knowing a unique piece of personal information, before a new password would be set.

Chapter 14 discusses a formal process that helpdesk attendants can use to process individual trouble reports.

13.1.8 Establish an Escalation Process

Escalation is a process by which an issue is moved from the current staff person to someone with more expertise. The first line of operators should be able to handle 80 percent to 90 percent of all calls and escalate the remaining calls to a second tier of support. The people at this second tier may have more experience, more training, and, possibly, other responsibilities. Larger organizations may have up to four or more tiers; the higher tiers may include the people who built or currently maintain the service in question.

It is common to have a policy that the first tier of support should escalate all calls that get to the 15-minute mark. This has a carryover effect in that the second-tier people, who may be responsible for project-oriented work, now have less time for projects. This situation can be alleviated by designating one second-tier person to sit with the first-tier people each week, that is, to make the helpdesk his or her project for the week. Although upper-tier staff people usually dislike this policy, a sizable organization will require this of people only once every 6 weeks or so. A side benefit to this strategy is that the first-tier staff will learn from the second-tier person. The second-tier person will also get a better understanding of the kinds of issues coming in to the helpdesk, which will help determine which new projects will be the most help to the first tier and the customers.

The escalation process is also what customers use when they are dissatisfied with the support they are receiving. One hopes that this happens as little as possible, but inevitably, someone will want to talk to a manager. The helpdesk should be prepared for this. Large numbers of calls being escalated to the second tier is a warning sign of a larger, systemic problem. Usually, this indicates that the first-tier staff people need more training or do not have the tools to do their job properly. If large numbers of calls are escalated to management, there may be systemic problems with the support the helpdesk is providing.

Escalate for Results

Escalation should not exist simply to pacify angry customers. One small ISP's helpdesk often receives calls from angry individuals who demand to speak to a manager. In that case, the person hands the phone to the person on his or her left, who then claims to be the manager. Although this works in the short term or when business growth is exploding, we do not feel that this is a sustainable way of maintaining a helpdesk.

13.1.9 Define "Emergency" in Writing

It may sound simple, but writing a definition of what constitutes an emergency can become a political battle. It may be part of a larger SLA document, or a stand-alone policy written to help helpdesk personnel make the right decision. This definition is often included in an escalation policy.

Often, we find that SAs are overloaded because every customer claims to have an emergency that requires immediate attention. SAs who feel that customers are using this claim to boss them around lessens morale and increases stress levels. Having a written policy empowers SAs to know when to push back and gives them something physical to point to when they need it. If the customer still disagrees with this assessment, the SA can pass the issue up to someone in management who can make the decision. This lets the SA focus on technical duties and lets management focus on setting priorities and providing resources.

Every company should be able to define what constitutes an emergency. At a factory, an emergency is anything that stops the assembly line. At a web-based service or ISP, an emergency might be anything that will prevent the service from meeting an SLA. A sales organization might define an emergency as anything that will prevent a demo from happening, end-of-quarter revenues from being booked, or commissions from being processed. At a teaching institution, which has tightly scheduled lecture times that cannot be simply moved or delayed owing to a system outage, an emergency might be anything that would disrupt scheduled technology-dependent lectures, as well as other matters related to the seasons of the school year: new-student arrival, exam deadlines, grade publication, graduation, new-student recruitment deadlines, and so on.

Plan Well

When Tom was in college, the business office put up a poster that said, "Bad planning on your part does not constitute an emergency." The students were offended, but the sign stayed. The truth is that this statement could be one of the most important lessons the university could teach its students before they hit the real world.

13.1.10 Supply Request-Tracking Software

Every helpdesk needs some kind of software to help it manage requests. The alternative is a collection of notes written on scraps of paper. Although it is simple in the beginning and sufficient for environments with one or two SAs, this solution doesn't scale. Requests get lost, and management has no ability to oversee the process to better allocate resources. Those are the first qualities that you need in helpdesk software. As a helpdesk grows, software can help in other areas. The scripts mentioned in Section 13.1.7 can be displayed automatically and can be "smart" by being part of the information-gathering process rather than simply a static screen.

Helpdesk software should permit some kind of priority to be assigned to tickets. This not only helps meet customer expectations but also helps SAs manage their time. An SA should be able to easily list the top-priority issues that have been assigned to him or her.

Another important aspect of helpdesk software is that it collects logs about what kinds of requests are made and by whom. Statistical analysis of such logs can be useful in managing the helpdesk. However, if the software doesn't capture that information, one can't gain the benefits of such statistics. This often happens when there is a lot of walk-up and phone traffic. In such cases, it can be useful for the software to have a one-click way to log common questions or issues. Caller ID can be used to populate fields with the caller's information.

Helpdesk software can also automate the collection of data on customer satisfaction. Every day, the software can select a random sample of yesterday's customers and survey them about the service they received.

Case Study: From Good to Bad

A software company of about 1,500 people was using an enhanced version of a freely available call-tracking system. It was very simple to use, with a few different interfaces, the most popular of which was the email interface. The system tracked customer, department, category, status, who the call was assigned to, how much time had been spent on it and by whom, priority, due date, and so on. Custom scripts produced metrics that management could use to track how things were going. Customers could use a web interface to see the history of their calls and all the other associated fields. Customers could also look at the call queue for the person the call was assigned to and see where it was in the person's priority list. Although the system wasn't glitzy, everyone was comfortable with it and could get the needed information out of it.

The management information systems (MIS) group, which provided support for databases and the applications that ran on top of them and was not a part of the SA group, was commissioned to build a new call-tracking system for the customer-support center. The management chain of that group expanded the scope of the project to make this into one unified call-tracking system that would also be used by the operations group, MIS, and the SA group. Neither the operations group nor MIS had a call-tracking system, so they were designing a system without knowing what a good one was like. No one in the SA group was told of the project, so its needs and those of its customers were not taken into consideration in the design.

The graphical user interface (GUI) system that resulted had no email interface and no command line interface. Creating a new call involved bringing up ten different windows, each a pop-up that was slow to appear and required mouse movements to chase to the right place on the screen. Updating a call required five or six different pop-ups. It was impossibly slow for many SAs who dialed in over modems to use the system from home. The system didn't work for anyone with a Mac or UNIX system since the client was only made for Microsoft Windows. It frequently took longer to open a trouble ticket than it took to solve the problem, so the numerous small calls were no longer tracked. What was once a quick email process had become a ten-minute endeavor. Several SAs went back to tracking projects on pieces of paper or in their heads.

Customers complained because they could no longer see the status of their calls or where those calls were in the priority queues. They also complained because they

> couldn't open a ticket via email any more and because the new system sent them far too much email whenever a small field in the call was changed. All of these complaints were predicted by the SA group when they were suddenly presented with the new system that they were going to have to start using, but it was too late to change anything.
>
> The system was supposed to provide better tools for producing metrics. However, because a lot of the data was no longer entered into the system, it clearly didn't, even though the tools it provided for metrics may have been better.

It is critical that helpdesk software match the workflow of the people who use it. If one ticket is opened per week, it is reasonable for the creation of a ticket to take a long time. However, if you expect hundreds of tickets per day, initiating the new ticket should be almost instantaneous, such as sending email. Do not use helpdesk software to introduce radical new workflow concepts.

Choosing helpdesk software is not an easy process. Most software will need a lot of customizing to your environment. When you decide to invest in helpdesk software, you need to be prepared to invest in the customizations also, so that the SAs can use it effectively. If it is a burden to use, they will not use it or will use it only for large projects.

13.2 The Icing

Now that we have a solid helpdesk, the icing helps us expand it on many different axes: quality, coverage, clarity of policy, and scaling.

13.2.1 Statistical Improvements

More sophisticated statistics can be gathered about a helpdesk. You can monitor the rate of escalations to determine where more training is needed. However, when dealing with upper management for budgeting and planning purposes, historical statistics become much more valuable. You can make a better case for your budget if you can show multiyear trends of customer growth, call volume, types of calls, technologies, services provided, and customer satisfaction. When being asked to support a new technology or service, you can use past data to predict what the support costs may be.

The value of statistics increases as the organization grows, because the management becomes less directly involved in the work being done. It is often difficult to collect statistics in small organizations, because practices are often less automated and can't be instrumented to collect data. As an organization grows, statistics are easier to collect, and it becomes more important that they be collected.

Identify the Percent Top 10 Requesters

SAs are usually detail people. Statistics gloss over the details to find general trends. So SAs are often not the best people to generate statistics about helpdesk requests.

When asked to generate statistics from a helpdesk request system, Tom was stymied. How could useful statistics be generated if they didn't first change the software to ask SAs how many minutes of work a ticket had required, a classification of the type of work, and what department the work was for? Then, after a year of collecting this data, he could produce excellent charts and graphs for a complete analysis.

The problem was that his boss wanted an answer in 24 hours. His boss suggested a very different tack: The entire process could be simplified if one assumed that all requests took the same amount of time. Tom was horrified but was eventually convinced that, on average, all their requests took an average amount of time.

His boss then suggested a database query that would determine who generated the most request tickets. It turned out that three customers had created 10 percent of all tickets in the past year.

Rather than meticulously classifying all tickets, Tom and his boss looked at a few from each of the three top customers and spoke with the SAs who had helped them the most. They learned that one person was continually requesting help with a product that was out of scope; the SAs were nicely helping the person anyway. The manager put his foot down and told the SAs that the product was intentionally not supported because it was too difficult to do so. Future requests for help were to be denied. The manager visited the customer to explain that he had to either become self-sufficient or permit the helpdesk to help him convert to the corporate standard product. The helpdesk didn't usually provide this kind of conversion service but would be willing to in this case.

The second-top customer was asking a lot of basic questions. Tom's manager spoke to the customer's manager about getting the person more training. The person's manager was aghast at the level of help this person had needed, and took care of the issue.

The third-top customer was, to put it politely, getting an SA to do the person's job. This issue was raised to the person's manager, who took care of it.

In the absence of any statistics, some basic rough estimates were still extremely useful. This one technique was able to eliminate approximately 10 percent of all the tickets entered into the system. That's a a big improvement!

13.2.2 Out-of-Hours and 24/7 Coverage

As computers become critical to an ever-expanding list of business processes, customers are asking for 24/7 coverage more often. Although full three-shift coverage may be required in some organizations, some very simple ways to provide 24/7 coverage are not as expensive.

You can set up a voicemail box that alerts a pager when new messages arrive. The pager can be passed to various staff members on a rotation basis. The responsibility of the staff person may not be to fix the problem but to simply alert the appropriate person or keep calling various people until someone is found. This requires all staff to have a list of everyone's home phone number.

A variation on this technique is to have all managers of the customer groups know the home phone number of the helpdesk's supervisor, who then takes responsibility for calling SAs in turn until one is found. This has the benefit of spreading personal information around to fewer people but can wear down a helpdesk supervisor and doesn't take into account the supervisor's vacations. However, local solutions can be found, such as rotating this duty among a couple of supervisors.

You can also treat the issue the same way other industries treat fire and other alarms, because the modern equivalent of a researcher's laboratory catching fire at night is a major file server being down. Always having a call list in case of alarms, fires, and so on, security personnel at factories start at the top of the list and keep calling numbers until they find someone. Depending on the issue, that person may tell the security guard whom to call.

Out-of-Hour Coverage at T. J. Watson

In the late 1990s, IBM's T. J. Watson facility extended the process for handling fire and other alarms to the major computer systems. If a major computer was down, customers could call the security desk and report the issue. The security guards had a separate list of people to call for a computer-related problem.

No matter how SAs are contacted out of hours, the person must be compensated, or there is no incentive to fix the problem. Some organizations have a salary incentive for on-call time, equivalent to a fraction of the employee's salary and time and a half if the person is called. Other organizations issue comp time[1] either officially or unofficially.

13.2.3 Better Advertising for the Helpdesk

Having your policies defined and announcements available for all to see on a web site is nice. However, rarely will anyone seek them out to read them.

---

1. Compensation time allows the employee to take off that much time—or 1.5 times that amount, in some cases—without claiming it against vacation time.

In this section, we talk about getting your policies and announcements "out there" and understood.

Since the introduction of the web, it is easy to make all policies accessible to all customers. There is no excuse for not doing this. However, you must get customers to that web site. Some SA organizations choose to have a portal web site that is the gateway to all their services, policies, and documentation. By making it the way customers receive information that is important to them, they also will know where to go for information that is important to you.

Pick the right message. Talk with customers to find out what is important to them. It's difficult to get people to read something that isn't important to them. They may not care that server3 will be down during the weekend, but knowing that the database stored on server3 won't be accessible all weekend will draw their attention.

New policies can be emailed to customers or sent via paper memo if they are particularly critical. Portals can highlight a "policy of the month." If the message will benefit from repetition, put posters in appropriate places. A physical helpdesk should have its hours posted at all entrances. People spend a lot of time staring at the wall while waiting for their turn; fill those blank walls with the message you want them to remember. Posters that say "Change your password every 30 days!" or "Server3 is being decommissioned on May 1" give good advice and warn of upcoming changes.

Messages are most effective when received at the right time. If server3 is being decommissioned in a month, tell people that every time they use server3.

13.2.4 Different Helpdesks for Service Provision and Problem Resolution

When an organization grows, it may make sense to have two separate helpdesks: one for requesting new services and another for reporting problems that arise after the service has been successfully enabled. Often, a third group deals with installing the new service, especially if it requires physical work. This third group may be an internal helpdesk that installers all over the organization can call to escalate installation problems. It is not uncommon, though, for this third group to be the second tier of one of the other helpdesks.

The benefit of dividing the helpdesk this way is that the three or four groups can be under different supervisors. A supervisor can effectively manage only a certain number of people. This division of labor makes it clear where to place various supervisors. They should all report to the same manager to make sure that communication happens and finger-pointing doesn't.

Another benefit is that the different groups can be separately trained for the different skills required for their task. This tends to be less expensive than hiring people who are experienced enough to be able to do all the tasks.

Provisioning service is a process that should be the same for all customers. The initial collection of data can be done by someone trained to ask the right questions. This person may have more sales experience than the other staff. Solving installation problems is a highly technical issue but has a narrow focus, and training can be customized to those issues. The separate helpdesk for reporting problems requires people with wider technical experience and background. This division of labor is critical to scaling the organization to very large sizes.

Having a web-based request system for provisioning new services can save a lot of data entry and prevent mistakes. Having the customer enter the data reduces the number of typos that can come from having a third party entering data. The system can check for common errors and reject inconsistent or conflicting requests. Phone requests can be replaced by phone assistance for people who need help filling out the web form.

One does not need to create an entirely new software system to support this kind of functionality. The form data can simply be submitted into the regular request-tracking system, which can then handle the workflow.

13.3 Conclusion

To your customers, the helpdesk is how they see you, how they get service, and how they have their problems fixed. It is the number-one component to your reputation. To you, a helpdesk is a tool to create once your organization has grown to a certain size and a tool for creating a division of labor as you grow. A helpdesk is not needed for small organizations, but there is a particular growth point at which it becomes useful and, later, critical.

The helpdesk is the "face" of your organization, so make it a happy, friendly one, no matter whether it is physical or virtual. Properly sizing the helpdesk is important and affects not only your budget but also customer satisfaction. In planning your helpdesk, you must define what is supported, who is supported, where they are, when you provide support, and how long customers should expect an average call to last. Constructing accurate budget and staffing plans is made easier by collecting the statistics mentioned in Section 13.1.10.

Processes should be defined for staff to follow regarding how they provide support for various services and how issues are escalated. Software must be used to collect statistics on all calls and to track issues that last longer than a single call.

Once those things are established, a helpdesk can grow in other areas. Out-of-hours coverage can be instituted; policies can be better advertised; and, with high growth, the helpdesk can be split into separate groups for new-service provisioning and trouble reporting.

We discussed much in this chapter, and every issue in some way touched on communication. The helpdesk is how customers communicate with your organization, yet it is often the role of the helpdesk to communicate to customers how, when, and why things are done. Such communicate can determine whether you are perceived as friendly or unfriendly. The statistics that are collected help communicate to management the needs of the organization during planning cycles. Escalation procedures keep the communication flowing when things stall. Having a written out-of-hours support policy sets expectations with customers and prevents the frustration of unexpected calls late at night.

Exercises

1. Describe your helpdesk staff structure.

2. How many attendants does your helpdesk have at any given moment? How is that number selected?

3. Which helpdesk attendant in your organization is perceived as the least friendly by the customers? How would you know? How would you help that person improve?

4. How hands-on are you with your helpdesk? What statistics do you use to manage it, or what statistics are given to your management? If you were one step less hands on, what new statistics would you need then?

5. Figure out what customers generate the top 10 percent—or 1 percent for larger sites—of all requests. What trends do you see in those requests, and how can this information be used to improve your helpdesk?

6. Report a problem tonight at 10 PM. Describe how well it went.

Chapter 14

Customer Care

At the close of World War II, the United States found itself with a huge excess of manufacturing capacity. As a result, companies started producing hundreds of new products, giving households and businesses unprecedented choices. Thousands of returning service people found jobs selling these new products. All these factors combined to produce a new era for the U.S. economy.

Along with choices came competition. Companies found that it was no longer sufficient merely to have a large sales force; a *good* sales force was needed. They started to ask what makes high-performing salespeople different from the others.

Industry encouraged business schools to increase their study of the sales process. Research showed that the better salespeople—whether or not they realized it—used a specific, structured method involving specific phases or steps. Mediocre salespeople deviated from these phases in varying ways or performed certain phases badly. The low performers had little or no consistency in their methods.

The methods, now identified, could be taught. Thus, sales skills went from an intuitive process to a formal process with well-defined parts. Previous sales training had consisted mostly of explaining the product's features and qualities. Subsequently, training included exploration of the selling process itself.

This deconstruction of the process into individual steps permitted further examination and therefore further improvement. Each step could be studied, measured, taught, practiced, and so on. Focus was improved because a single step could be studied in isolation. Also, the entire flow of steps could be studied: a holistic approach.

We imagine that if anyone explained the structured process to the high-performing salespeople, it would sound strange. To them, it comes naturally.

To the beginners, however, this framework gives structure to a process they are learning. After they master it, they may modify or customize it for their situation. Without first learning one structured system, it is difficult to get to the place where you need to be to invent your own.

In the 1990s, system administration began a similar journey. Previously, it was a craft or an art practiced by few people. With the explosive growth of corporate computing and intranet/Internet applications, the demand for SAs was similarly explosive. A flood of new SAs arrived to meet the need. The quality of their work varied. Training often took the form of teaching particular product features. Other training methods included exploring manuals and documentation, trial by fire, and training by social and professional institutions.

System administration needed to mature in ways similar to how the sales process matured. The late 1990s saw an increase in the academic study of system administration (Burgess 2000). In fact, this book's inspiration comes from that same need to provide training founded on non-platform-specific themes, principles, and theoretical models rather than on specific details about particular technologies, vendors, and products (Limoncelli and Hogan 2001).

14.1 The Basics

SAs spend much of their time responding to requests from customers. In this chapter, we present a structured process defining how customer requests are gathered, evaluated, fixed, and verified.[1] Responding to customer requests is a more specific task than the general issues that surround running a helpdesk.

Customer requests are the trouble tickets, calls, problem reports, or whatever your site calls them. These requests may take the form "I can't print," "The network is slow," or "A program that compiled yesterday won't compile anymore."

SAs do many tasks, but often, customers see only the parts that involve responding to their requests, not all the back-office work, and shouldn't have to see it. Therefore, how well you respond to customer requests is critical to maintaining an organization's reputation.

---

1.   This process is based on a paper by Tom (Limoncelli 1999).

The method for processing these customer requests has nine steps, which can be grouped into four phases:

- Phase A: The greeting ("Hello.")
  - Step 1: The greeting
- Phase B: Problem identification ("What's wrong?")
  - Step 2: Problem classification
  - Step 3: Problem statement
  - Step 4: Problem verification
- Phase C: Planning and execution ("Fix it.")
  - Step 5: Solution proposals
  - Step 6: Solution selection
  - Step 7: Execution
- Phase D: Verification ("Verify it.")
  - Step 8: Craft verification
  - Step 9: Customer verification/closing

This method gives structure to what is, for newer SAs, a more haphazard process. The method helps you solve problems more efficiently by keeping you focused and helps you avoid mistakes. It introduces a common set of terminology that, when used by the entire SA team, increases the ability to communicate within the group.

This tool does not bestow any additional technical expertise on the people using it, but it may help the junior people gain insight into how the senior SAs approach problem solving. Creativity, experience, the right resources, tools, and personal and external management are still important.

If customers understand this model, they become more skilled in getting the help they desire. They will be prepared with the right information and can nudge the SA through the process, if necessary.

As Figure 14.1 shows, the phases deal with

- Reporting the problem
- Identifying the problem
- Planning and executing a solution
- Verifying that the problem resolution is complete

Sometimes, certain steps are iterated as required. For example, during step 4 (problem verification), the SA may realize that the issue has been

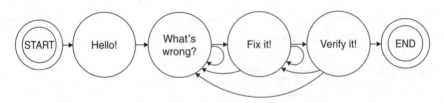

Figure 14.1 General flow of problem solving

misclassified and must return to step 2 (problem classification). This can happen at any step and requires returning to any previous step.

❖ **Trouble-Tracking Software**   We cannot overemphasize the importance of using a software package to track problem reports. In the 1980s and early 1990s, SAs rarely used software to track such requests. Today, however, installing such software is profoundly transformational, affecting your ability to manage your time and to deliver consistent results to customers. If you find a site that has no trouble-tracking software, simply install whatever you were comfortable with at a previous site or software that has an Internet mailing list of active supporters.

14.1.1 Phase A/Step 1: The Greeting

The first phase only has one deceptively simple step (Figure 14.2). Issues are solicited from the customers. This step includes everything related to how the customer's request is solicited. This step may range from someone saying, "How may I help you?" on the phone to a web site that collects problem reports. Step 1 should welcome the customer to the system and start the process on a positive, friendly, helpful note.

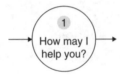

Figure 14.2 Greeting phase

The person or system that responds to the requests is called a **greeter**. Greeters may be people in a physical helpdesk, on the phone, or accessible via email or other instant technology; a phone-response system; even a web form that takes the data. Multiple ways to collect reports are needed for easy and reliable access, ensuring that the customer can report the problem.

Sometimes, problems are reported by automated means rather than by humans. For example, network-monitoring tools, a such as Big Brother (Peacock and Giuffrida 1988) HP OpenView, and Tivoli, can notify SAs that a problem is occurring. The process is the same, although some of the steps may be expedited by the tool.

Every site and every customer is different. What is an appropriate way to report issues is different for every part of every organization. Is the customer local or remote? Is the customer experienced or new? Is the technology being supported complicated or simple? These questions can help when you select which greeters to use.

How do customers know how to find help? Advertise the available greeters by signs in hallways, newsletters, stickers on computers or phones, and even banner advertisements on internal web pages. The best place is where customers' eyes are already looking: on a sticker on their PC, in an error message, and so on.

Although this list certainly isn't complete, the greeters we have seen include email, phone, walk-up helpdesk, visiting the SA's office, submission via web, submission via custom application, and report by automated monitoring system.

14.1.2 Phase B: Problem Identification

The second phase is focused on classifying the problem and recording and verifying it (Figure 14.3).

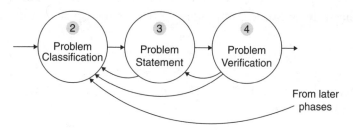

Figure 14.3 What's wrong?

14.1.2.1 Step 2: Problem Classification

In step 2, the request is classified to determine who should handle it. This **classifier** role may be performed by a human or may be automated. For example, at a walk-up helpdesk, staff might listen to the problem description to determine its classification. A phone-response system may ask the user to press 1 for PC problems, 2 for network problems, and so on. If certain SAs help certain customer groups, their requests may be automatically forwarded, based on the requester's email address, manually entered employee ID number, or the phone caller's caller ID information.

When the process is manual, a human must have the responsibility of classifying the problem from the description or asking the customer more questions. A formal decision tree may be used to determine the right classification.

You need to ask more questions when you aren't as familiar with the customer's environment. This is often the case at the helpdesk of e-commerce sites or extremely large corporate helpdesks.

No matter how the classification is performed, the customer should be told how the request is classified, creating a feedback loop that can detect mistakes. For example, if a classifier tells a customer, "This sounds like a printing problem. I'm assigning this issue to someone from our printer support group," the customer stays involved in the process. The customer may point out that the problem is more pervasive than simply printing, leading to classification as a network problem.

If a phone-response system is used, the customer has classified the request already. However, a customer may not be the best person to make this decision. The next person who speaks with the customer should be prepared to validate the customer's choice in a way that is not insulting. If the customer had misclassified the request, it should be remedied in a polite manner. We feel that the best way to do so is for the customer to be told the correct phone number to call or button to press, and then the SA should transfer the call to the right number. Some companies do one or the other, but doing both is better.

When asking a customer to classify the problem, the choices presented must be carefully constructed and revised over time. You should gather statistics to detect mismatches between customers' perceptions of what the classifications mean and what you intended them to mean, or at least you should monitor for customer complaints.

Marketing-Driven Customer Support

Phone menus should use terminology that the customers expect to hear. A large network equipment manufacturer once had its phone menu based on the marketing terminology that segments its product lines rather than on the technical terminology that most of its customers used. This caused no end of confusion because the marketing terminology had little basis in reality from the typical technician's point of view. It was particularly confusing for customers of any company that was acquired by this company, because the acquired company's products were reclassified into marketing terms unfamiliar to the acquired company's customers.

Many requests may be transferred or eliminated at this stage. A customer requesting a new feature should be transferred to the appropriate group that handles requests for features. If the request is outside the domain of work done by the support group, the customer might be referred to another department. If the request is against policy and therefore must be denied, the issue may be escalated to management if the customer disagrees with the decision. For this reason, it is important to have a well-defined scope of service and a process for requesting new services.

At very large sites, you are more likely to find yourself acting on behalf of your customer, coordinating between departments or even the helpdesks of different departments! Complicated problems that involve network, application, and server issues can require the helpdesk attendant to juggle conversations with three or more organizations. Navigating such a twisty maze of passages for the customer is a valuable service you can provide.

14.1.2.2 Step 3: Problem Statement

In step 3, the customer states the problem in full detail, and the **recorder** takes this information down. Often, the recorder is also the classifier. The skill required by the recorder in this step is the ability to listen and to ask the right questions to draw out the necessary information from the customer. The recorder extracts the relevant details and records them.

A problem statement describes the problem being reported and records enough clues to reproduce and fix the problem. A bad problem statement is vague or incomplete. A good problem statement is complete and identifies all hardware and software involved, as well as their location, the last time it worked, and so on. Sometimes, not all that information is appropriate or available.

An example of a good problem statement is this: "PC `talpc.example.com` (a PC running Windows Vista) located in room 301 cannot print from MS-Word 2006 to printer "rainbow," the color printer located in room 314. It worked fine yesterday. It can print to other printers. The customer does not know whether other computers are having this problem."

Certain classes of problems can be completely stated in simple ways. Internet routing problems can best be reported by listing two IP addresses that cannot ping each other but that both can communicate to other hosts; including a traceroute from each host to the other, if possible, helps considerably.

More information is usually better than less. However, customers may be annoyed when required to provide information that is obviously superfluous, such as what OS they are using, when the issue is a smoking monitor. Yet we continually see web-based trouble-reporting systems requiring that no fields be left blank.

It is unreasonable to expect problem statements from customers to be complete. Customers require assistance. The problem statement cited earlier comes from a real example in which a customer sent an SA email that simply stated, "Help! I can't print." That is about as ambiguous and incomplete as a request can be. A reply was sent asking, "To which printer? Which PC? What application?"

The customer's reply included a statement of frustration. "I need to print these slides by 3 PM. I'm flying to a conference!" At that point, the SA abandoned email and used the telephone. This permitted a faster back-and-forth between the customer and the classifier. No matter the medium, it is important that this dialogue take place and that the final result be reported to the customer.

Sometimes, the recorder can perform a fast loop through the next steps to accelerate the process. The recorder might find out whether the device is plugged in, whether the person has checked the manual, and so on. However, such questions as, "Is it plugged in?" and "Have you checked the manual?" make customers defensive. They have only two possible answers and only one clearly right answer. Avoid making customers feel compelled to lie. Instead, ask what outlet it's plugged into; ask for confirmation, while you're on the phone, that the cable is firmly seated at both ends. Tell the customer that you've checked the manual and that, for future reference, the answer is on page 9, if the problem comes up again.

You also should make sure to never make the customer feel like an idiot. We cringed when we heard that a helpdesk attendant informed a customer that "an eight-year-old would understand" what he was explaining. Instead, reassure customers that they'll get better at using computers as they gain experience.

Help the Customer Save Face

Finding ways to let customers save face can be very beneficial. An SA in London once took a call from a person who was in a panic about not being able to print his monthly reports on a printer used almost exclusively for this purpose. After a series of tests, the SA found that the printer was unplugged. He explained to the customer that the cleaning staff must have unplugged the printer when needing an outlet for the vacuum.

A month later, the same person called the SA with the same problem pointed out that this time, he has checked to make sure that the printer was plugged in. Investigation showed that it had been turned off at the switch. The customer felt so embarrassed that he'd missed such obvious faults both times that he bought the SA a beer. After that, the problem never occurred again.

By not criticizing the person and by keeping him in the loop about what the problem was, the customer learned to solve his own problems, the two remained on friendly terms, and the SA got a free beer.

Flexibility is important. In the previous example, the customer indicated that there was an urgent need to have a monthly report printed. Here, it might be appropriate to suggest using a different printer that is known to be working rather than fixing the problem right now. This accelerates the process, which is important for an urgent problem.

Large sites often have different people recording requests and executing them. This added handoff introduces a challenge because the recorder may not have the direct experience required to know exactly what to record. In that case, it is prudent to have preplanned sets of data to gather for various situations. For example, if the customer is reporting a network problem, the problem statement must include an IP address, the room number of the machine that is not working, and what particular thing the person is trying to do over the network that is not working. If the problem relates to printing, you should record the name of the printer, the computer being used, and the application generating the print job.

It can be useful if your trouble-ticket software records different information, depending on how the problem has been classified.

14.1.2.3 Step 4: Problem Verification

In step 4, the SA tries to reproduce the problem: the **reproducer** role. If the problem cannot be reproduced, perhaps it is not being properly communicated, and you must return to step 3. If the problem is intermittent, this process becomes more complicated but not impossible.

Nothing gives you a better understanding of the problem than seeing it in action. This is the single most important reason for doing problem verification. Yet we see naive SAs skip it all the time. If you do not verify the problem, you may work on it for hours before realizing that you aren't even working on the right issue. Often, the customer's description is misleading. A customer who doesn't have the technical knowledge to accurately describe the problem can send you on a wild goose chase. Just think about all the times you've tried to help someone over the phone, failed, and then visited the person. One look at the person's screen and you say, "Oh! That's a totally different problem!" And a few keystrokes later, the problem is fixed. What happened was that you weren't able to reproduce the problem locally, so you couldn't see the whole problem and therefore couldn't figure out the real solution.

It is critical that the method used to reproduce the problem be recorded for later repetition in step 8. Encapsulating the test in a script or a batch file will make verification easier. One of the benefits of command-driven systems, such as UNIX, is the ease with which such a sequence of steps can be automated. GUIs make this phase more difficult when there is no way to automate or encapsulate the test.

The scope of the verification procedure must not be too narrowly focused or too wide or misdirected. If the tests are too narrow, the entire problem may not be fixed. If the tests are too wide, the SA may waste time chasing nonissues.

It is possible that the focus is misdirected. Another, unrelated problem in the environment may be discovered while trying to repeat the customer's reported problem. Some problems can exist in an environment without being reported or without affecting users. It can be frustrating for both the SA and the customer if many unrelated problems are discovered and fixed along the way to resolving an issue. Discovery of an unrelated problem that is not in the critical path should be recorded so that it can be fixed in the future. On the other hand, determining whether it is in the critical path is difficult, so fixing it may be valuable. Alternatively, it may be a distraction or may change the system enough to make debugging difficult.

Sometimes, direct verification is not possible or even required. If a customer reports that a printer is broken, the verifier may not have to reproduce the problem by attempting to print something. It may be good enough to verify that new print jobs are queuing and not being printed. Such superficial verification is fine in that situation.

However, at other times, exact duplication *is* required. The verifier might fail to reproduce the problem on his or her own desktop PC and may need to duplicate the problem on the customer's PC. Once the problem is duplicated in the customer's environment, it can be useful to try to duplicate it elsewhere to determine whether the problem is local or global. When supporting a complicated product, you must have a lab of equipment ready to reproduce reported problems.

Verification at E-Commerce Sites

E-commerce sites have a particularly difficult time duplicating the customer's environment. Although Java and other systems promise that you can "write once, run anywhere," the reality is that you must be able to duplicate the customer's environment for a variety of web browsers, web browser versions, and even firewalls. One company needed to test access to its site with and without a firewall. The company's QA effort had a PC that was live on the Internet for such testing. Because the PC was unprotected, it was isolated physically from other machines, and the OS was reloaded regularly.

14.1.3 Phase C: Planning and Execution

In this phase, the problem is fixed. Doing so involves planning possible solutions, selecting one, and executing it (Figure 14.4).

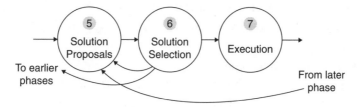

Figure 14.4 Flow of repair

14.1.3.1 Step 5: Solution Proposals

This is the point at which the subject matter expert (SME) enumerates possible solutions. Depending on the problem, this list may be large or small. For some problems, the solution may be obvious, with only one proposed solution. Other times, many are solutions possible. Often, verifying the problem in the previous step helps to identify possible solutions.

The "best" solution varies, depending on context. At a financial institution, the helpdesk's solution to a client-side NFS problem was to reboot. It was faster than trying to fix it, and it got the customer up and running quickly. However, in a research environment, it would make sense to try to find the source of the problem, perhaps unmounting and remounting the NFS mount that reported the problem.

Case Study: Radical Print Solutions

In our earlier printing example, because the customer indicated that he needed to leave for the airport soon, it might have been appropriate to suggest alternative solutions, such as recommending a different printer known to be working. If the customer is an executive flying from New Jersey to Japan with a stop-over in San Jose, it might be reasonable to transfer the file to an office in San Jose, where it can be printed while the customer is in flight. A clerk could hand the printout to the executive while he waits for his connecting flight at the San Jose airport. Tom witnessed such a solution being used. The printer, in this case, was a very expensive plotter. Only one such plotter was at each company location.

Some solutions are more expensive than others. Any solution that requires a desk-side visit is generally going to be more expensive than one that can be handled without such a visit. This kind of feedback can be useful in making purchasing decisions. Lack of remote-support capability affects the total cost of ownership of a product. Both commercial and noncommercial tools are available that add remote support to such products.

An SA, who does not know any possible solutions should escalate the issue to other, more experienced SAs.

14.1.3.2 Step 6: Solution Selection

Once the possible solutions have been enumerated, one of them is selected to be attempted first—or next, if we are looping through these steps. This role too is performed by the SME.

Selecting the best solution tends to be either extremely easy or extremely difficult. However, solutions often cannot and should not be done simultaneously, so possible solutions must be prioritized.

The customer should be included in this prioritization. Customers have a better understanding of their own time pressures. A customer who is a commodities trader, will be much more sensitive to downtime during the trading day than, say, a technical writer or even a developer, provided that he or she is not on deadline. If solution A fixes the problem forever but requires downtime and solution B is a short-term fix, the customer should be consulted as to whether A or B is "right" for the situation. The SME has responsibility for explaining the possibilities, but the SA should know some of this, based on the environment. There may be predetermined service goals for downtime during the day. SAs on Wall Street know that downtime during the day can cost millions, so short-term fixes may be selected and a long-term solution scheduled for the next maintenance window. In a research environment, the rules about downtime are more relaxed, and the long-term solution may be selected immediately.[2]

When dealing with more experienced customers, it can be useful to let them participate in this phase. They may have useful feedback. In the case of inexperienced customers, it can be intimidating or confusing to hear all these details. It may even unnecessarily scare them. For example, listing every possibility from a simple configuration error to a dead hard disk may cause the customer to panic and is a generally bad idea, especially when the problem turns out to be a simple typo in `CONFIG.SYS`.

Even though customers may be inexperienced, they should be encouraged to participate in determining and choosing the solution. This can help educate them so future problem reports can flow more smoothly and even enable them to solve their own problems. It can also give customers a sense of ownership—the warm fuzzy feeling of being part of the team/company, not simply "users." This approach can help break down the us-versus-them mentality common in industry today.

14.1.3.3 Step 7: Execution
The solution is attempted in step 7. The skill, accuracy, and speed at which this step is completed depends on the skill and experience of the person executing the solution.

---

2. Some sites centralize their helpdesks to a bizarre extreme that results in SAs' no longer knowing into which category their customers fall. This is rarely a good thing.

The term **craft worker** refers to the SA, operator, or laborer who performs the technical tasks involved. This term comes from other industries, such as telecommunications, in which one person may receive the order and plan the provisioning of the service but the craft workers run the cables, connect circuits, and so on, to provide the service. In a computer network environment, the network architect might be responsible for planning the products and procedures used to give service to customers, but when a new Ethernet interface needs to be added to a router, the craft worker installs the card and configures it.

Sometimes, the customer becomes the craft worker. This scenario is particularly common when the customer is remote and using a system with little or no remote control. In that case, the success or failure of this step is shared with the customer. A dialogue is required between the SA and the customer to make the solution work. Has the customer executed the solution properly? If not, is the customer causing more harm than good?

Adjust the dialogue based on the skill of the customer. It can be insulting to spell out each command, space, and special character to an expert customer. It can be intimidating to a novice customer if the SA rattles off a complex sequence of commands. Asking, "What did it say when you typed that?" is better than "Did it work?" in these situations. Be careful, however, not to assume too much; some customers are good at sounding as though they are more experienced than they are.

This kind of communication is not an innate skill but rather must be learned. Training is available. Workshops that focus on this area often have titles that include the buzzwords *active listening, interpersonal communication, interpersonal effectiveness*, or simply *advanced communication*.

At this point, it is tempting to think that we have finished. However, we haven't finished until the work has been checked and the customer is satisfied. That brings us to the final phase.

14.1.4 Phase D: Verification

At this point, the problem *should* have been remedied, but we need to verify that. This phase isn't over until the customer agrees that the problem has been fixed (Figure 14.5).

14.1.4.1 Step 8: Craft Verification

In step 8, the craft worker who executed step 7 verifies that the actions taken to fix the problem were successful. If the process used to reproduce

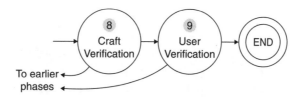

Figure 14.5 Verification flow

the problem in step 4 is not recorded properly or not repeated exactly, the verification will not happen correctly. If the problem still exists, return to step 5 or, possibly, an earlier step.

❖ **The Unix `diff` Program**   The UNIX command `diff` can be useful in this situation; this program displays the difference between two text files. Capture the output generated when the problem is reproduced. As attempts are made to fix the problem, run the program again, capturing the output to a new file. Run `diff` against the two captures to see whether there is any difference. Alternatively, you might copy the output that demonstrates the problem to a new file and edit it the way it should be on a working system. (You might have a working system to generate sample "good" output.) The `diff` program can then be used to compare the current output with the corrected output. You'll know you've made the right changes when `diff` claims that the files are the same. Some systems do not generate output that is well suited to `diff`, but Perl and other tools can pare down the output to make it more palatable to `diff`.

Case Study: TEX Installation Problem

A customer was once able to provide Tom with a sample TEX file that processed fine in his previous department's TEX installation but not on the local one. Because Tom had an account on the computers of the customer's previous department, he could establish a basis for comparison. This was extremely useful. Eventually, he was able to fix the TEX installation through successive refinement of the problem and comparison on both systems.

14.1.4.2 Step 9: Customer Verification/Closing

The final step is for the customer to verify that the issue has been resolved. If the customer isn't satisfied, the job isn't done. This role is performed by the customer.

Presumably, if the craft worker verified that the solution worked (step 8), this step should not be needed. However, customers often report at this point that the problem still exists. This is such a critical problem that we emphasize it by making it a separate step.

Customer verification reveals mistakes made in previous phases. Perhaps the customer did not properly express the problem, the SA did not understand the customer, or the SA did not properly record the problem—all communication problems. Errors may have crept into the planning phase. The problem that was verified in step 4 may have been a different problem that also exists, or the method that verified the problem may have been incomplete. The solution may not have fixed the entire problem or may have turned the problem into an intermittent one.

In either case, if the customer does not feel that the problem has been fixed, there are many possible actions. Obviously, step 4 should be repeated to find a more accurate method to reproduce the problem. However, at this point, it may be appropriate to return to other steps. For example, the problem could be reclassified (step 2), or restated (step 3), or escalated to more experienced SAs (step 5). If all else fails, you may have to escalate the problem to management.

It is important to note that "verification" isn't to verify that the customer is happy but that the customer's request has been satisfied. Customer satisfaction is a metric to be measured elsewhere.

Once customer verification is complete, the issue is "closed."

14.1.5 Perils of Skipping a Step

Each step is important. If any step in this process is performed badly, the process can break down. Many SAs skip a step, either because of lack of training or an honest mistake. Many stereotypes about bad SAs are the result of SAs' skipping a particular step. We assigned Seinfeldesque names to each of these stereotypes and list possible ways of improving the SAs process.

- *The Ogre:* Grumpy, caustic SAs are trying to scare customers away from step 1 and are preventing the greeting from happening. *Suggestion*: Management must set expectations for friendliness. The scope of responsibility must be a written policy communicated to both SAs and customers.

- *The Misdelegator:* If you've called a large company's technical support line and the person who answered the phone refused to direct your call to the proper department (step 2), you know what it's like to deal with a misdelegator. *Suggestion*: Design a formal decision tree of what issues are delegated where.

- *The Assumer:* Step 3 usually isn't skipped; these SAs simply assume that they understand what the problem is when they really don't. *Suggestion*: Coach the person on active listening; if that fails, send the person to a class on the topic.

- *The Nonverifier:* An SA who skips problem verification (step 4) is usually busy fixing the wrong problem. One day, Tom was panicked by the news that "the network is down." In reality, a nontechnical customer couldn't read his email and reported that "the network is down." This claim hadn't been verified by the newly hired SA, who hadn't yet learned that certain novice customers report all problems that way. The customer's email client was misconfigured. *Suggestion*: Teach SAs to replicate problems, especially before escalating them. Remind them that it isn't nice to panic Tom.

- *The Wrong Fixer:* Inexperienced SAs sometimes are not creative or are too creative in proposing and selecting solutions (steps 5 and 6). But skipping these steps entirely results in a different issue. After being taught how to use an Ethernet monitor (a network sniffer), an inexperienced but enthusiastic SA was found dragging out the sniffer no matter what problem was being reported. He was a Wrong Fixer. *Suggestion*: Provide mentoring or training. Increase the breadth of solutions with which the SA is familiar.

- *The Deexecutioner:* Incompetent SAs sometimes cause more harm than good when they execute incorrectly. It is quite embarrassing to apply a fix to the wrong machine; however, it happens. *Suggestion*: Train the SA to check what has been typed before pressing ENTER or clicking OK. It can be vital to include the host name in your shell prompt.

- *The Hit-and-Run Sysadmin:* This SA walks into a customer's office, types a couple of keystrokes, and waves goodbye while walking out the door and saying, "That should fix it." The customers are frustrated to discover that the problem was not fixed. In all fairness, what was typed really should have fixed the problem, but it didn't. *Suggestion*: Management needs to set expectations on verification.

- *The Closer:* Some SAs are obsessed with "closing the ticket." Often, SAs are judged on how quickly they close tickets. In that case, the SAs are pressured to skip the final step. We borrow this name from the term used to describe high-pressure salespeople focused on "closing the deal." *Suggestion*: Management should not measure performance based on how quickly issues are resolved but on a mixture of metrics that drive the preferred behavior. Metrics should not include time waiting for customers when calculating how long it took to complete the request. Tracking systems should permit a request to be put into a "customer wait" state while waiting for them to complete actions, and that time should be subtracted from the time-to-completion metrics.

14.1.6 Team of One

The solo SA can still benefit from using the model to make sure that customers have a well-defined way to report problems; that problems are recorded and verified; that solutions are proposed, selected, and executed; and that both the SA and the customer have verified that the problem has been resolved. When one is the solo SA in an organization, problems with specific applications can be escalated to that vendor's support lines.

14.2 The Icing

Once the basic process is understood, there are ways to improve it. On the micro level, you can look into improving each step; on the macro level, you can look at how the steps fit together.

14.2.1 Model-Based Training

Internal training should be based on this model so that the SA staff members consistently use it. After the initial training, more experienced staff should mentor newer SAs to help them retain what they have learned. Certain steps can be helped by specific kinds of training.

Improvements can be made by focusing on each step. Entire books could be written on each step. This has happened in other professions that have similar models, such as nursing, sales, and so on.

A lack of training hurts the process. For example, an ill-defined delineation of responsibilities makes it difficult for a classifier to delegate the issue to the right person. Inexperienced recorders don't gather the right information in step 3, which makes further steps difficult and may require contacting the customer unnecessarily. A written chart of who is responsible for what, as well as a list of standard information to be collected for each classification, will reduce these problems.

14.2.2 Holistic Improvement

In addition to focusing on improving each step, you may also focus on improving the entire process. Transitioning to each new step should be fluid. If the customer sees an abrupt, staccato handoff between steps, the process can appear amateurish or disjointed.

Every handoff is an opportunity for mistakes and miscommunication. The fewer handoffs, the fewer opportunities there are for mistakes.

A site small enough to have a single SA has zero opportunities for this class of error. However, as systems and networks grow and become more complicated, it becomes impossible for a single person to understand, maintain, and run the entire network. As a system grows, handoffs become a necessary evil. This explains a common perception that larger SA groups are not as effective as smaller ones. Therefore, when growing an SA group, you should focus on maintaining high-quality handoffs. Or, you might choose to develop a single point of contact or customer advocate for an issue. That results in the customers' seeing a single face for the duration of a problem.

14.2.3 Increased Customer Familiarity

If a customer talks to the same person whenever calling for support, the SA will likely become familiar with the customer's particular needs and be able to provide better service. There are ways to improve the chance of this happening. For example, SA staff subteams may be assigned to particular groups of customers rather than to the technology they support. Or, if the answering phone-staff is extremely large, the group may be using a telephone call center system, whereby customers call a single number and the call center routes the call to an available operator. Modern call center systems can route calls based on caller ID, using this functionality, for example, to route the call to the same operator the caller spoke to last time, if that person is available. This means there will be a tendency for customers to be speaking to the same person each time. It can be very comforting to speak to someone who recognizes your voice.

14.2.4 Special Announcements for Major Outages

During a major network outage, many customers may be trying to report problems. If customers report problems through an automatic phone response system ("Press 1 for ..., press 2 for ..."), such a system can usually be programmed to announce the network outage before listing the options. "Please note the network connection to Denver is currently experiencing trouble. Our service provider expects it to be fixed by 3 PM. Press 1 for ... press 2 for...."

14.2.5 Trend Analysis

Spend some time each month looking for trends, and take action based on them. This does not have to be a complicated analysis, as this case study describes.

Case Study: Who Generates the Most Tickets?

At one site, we simply looked at which customers opened the most tickets in the last year. We found that 3 of the 600 people opened 10 percent of all tickets. That's a lot! It was easy to visit each person's manager to discuss how we could provide better service; if the person was generating so many tickets, we obviously weren't matching the person's needs.

One person opened so many tickets because he was pestering the SAs for workarounds to the bugs in the old version of the LATEX typesetting package that he was using and refused to upgrade to the latest version, which fixed most of the problems he was reporting. This person's manager agreed that the best solution would be for him to require his employee to adopt the latest LATEX and took responsibility for seeing to it that the change was made.

The next manager felt that his employee was asking basic questions and decided to send the customer for training to make him more self-sufficient.

The last manager felt that his employee was justified in making so many requests. However, the manager did appreciate knowing how much the employee relied on us to get his job done. The employee did become more self-sufficient in future months.

Here are some other trends to look for:

- *Does a customer report the same issue over and over?* Why is it recurring? Does the customer need training, or is that system really that broken?

- *Are there many questions in a particular category?* Is that system difficult to use? Could it be redesigned or replaced, or could the documentation be improved?

- *Are many customers reporting the same issue?* Can they all be notified at once? Should such problems receive higher priority?

- *Can some categories of requests become self-service?* Often, a customer request is that an SA is needed because something requires privileged access, such as superuser or administrator access. Look for ways to empower customers to help themselves. Many of these requests can become self-service with a little bit of web programming. The UNIX world has the concept of set user ID (SUID) programs, which, when properly administered, permit regular users to run a program that performs privileged tasks but then lose the privileged access once the program is finished executing. Individual SUID programs can give users the ability to perform a particular function, and SUID wrapper programs can be constructed that gain the enhanced privilege level, run a third-party program, and then reduce the privileges back to normal levels. Writing SUID programs is very tricky, and mistakes can turn into security holes. Systems such as `sudo` (Snyder, Miller et al. 1986) let you manage SUID privilege on a per user and per command basis and have been analyzed by enough security experts to be considered a relatively safe way to provide SUID access to regular users.

- *Who are your most frequent customers?* Calculate which department generates the most tickets or who has the highest average tickets per member. Calculate which customers make up your top 20 percent of requests. Do these ratios match your funding model, or are certain customer groups more "expensive" than others?

- *Is a particular time-consuming request one of your frequent requests?* If customers often accidentally delete files and you waste a lot of time each week restoring files from tape, you can invest time in helping the user learn about `rm -i` or use other safe-delete programs. Or, maybe it would be appropriate to advocate for the purchase of a system that supports snapshots or lets users do their own restores. If you can generate a report of the number and frequency of restore requests, management can make a more informed decision or decide to talk to certain users about being more careful.

This chapter does not discuss metrics, but a system of metrics grounded in this model might be the best way to detect areas needing improvement. The nine-step process can be instrumented easily to collect metrics. Developing metrics that drive the right behaviors is difficult. For example, if SAs are rated by how quickly they close tickets, one might accidentally encourage the closer behavior described earlier. As SAs proactively prevent problems, reported problems will become more serious and time consuming. If average time to completion grows, does that mean that minor problems were eliminated or that SAs are slower at fixing all problems?[3]

14.2.6 Customers Who Know the Process

A better-educated customer is a better customer. Customers who understand the nine steps that will be followed can be better prepared when reporting the problem. These customers can provide more complete information when they call, because they understand the importance of complete information in solving the problem. In gathering this information, they will have narrowed the focus of the problem report. They might have specific suggestions on how to reproduce the problem. They may have narrowed the problem down to a specific machine or situation. Their additional preparation may even lead them to solve the problem on their own! Training for customers should include explaining the nine-step process to facilitate interaction between customers and SAs.

Preparing Customers at the Department of Motor Vehicles

Tom noticed that the New Jersey Department of Motor Vehicles had recently changed its "on hold" message to include what four documents should be on hand if the person was calling to renew a vehicle registration. Now, rather than waiting to speak to a person only to find out that you didn't have, say, your insurance ID number, there was a better chance that once connected, you had everything needed to complete the transaction.

14.2.7 Architectural Decisions That Match the Process

Architectural decisions may impede or aid the classification process. The more complicated a system is, the more difficult it can be to identify and duplicate the problem. Sadly, some well-accepted software design concepts, such as delineating a system into layers, are at odds with the nine-step process. For example, a printing problem in a large UNIX network could be a problem

---

3. Strata advocates SA-generated tickets for proactive fixes and planned projects, to make the SA contributions clearer.

with DNS, the server software, the client software, misconfigured user environment, the network, DHCP, the printer's configuration, or even the printing hardware itself. Typically, many of those layers are maintained by separate groups of people. To diagnose the problem accurately requires the SAs to be experts in all those technologies or that the layers do cross-checking.

You should keep in mind how a product will be supported when you are designing a system. The electronics industry has the concept of "design for manufacture"; we should think in terms of "design for support."

14.3 Conclusion

This chapter is about communication. The process helps us think about how we communicate with customers, and it gives us a base of terminology to use when discussing our work. All professionals have a base of terminology to use to effectively communicate with one an another.

This chapter presents a formal, structured model for handling requests from customers. The process has four phases: greeting, problem identification, planning and execution, and fix and verify. Each phase has distinct steps, summarized in Table 14.1.

Following this model makes the process more structured and formalized. Once it is in place, it exposes areas for improvement within your organization.

Table 14.1 Overview of Phases for Problem Solution

Phase	Step	Role
Phase A: "Hello!"	1. The greeting	Greeter
Phase B: "What's wrong?"	2. Problem classification	Classifier
	3. Problem statement	Recorder
	4. Problem verification	Reproducer
Phase C: "Fix it"	5. Solution proposals	Subject matter expert
	6. Solution selection	
	7. Execution	Craft worker
Phase D: "Verify it"	8. Craft verification	
	9. Customer verification	Customer

You can integrate the model into training plans for SAs, as well as educate customers about the model so they can be better advocates for themselves. The model can be applied for the gathering of metrics. It enables trend analysis, even if only in simple, ad hoc ways, which is better than nothing.

We cannot stress enough the importance of using helpdesk issue-tracking software rather than trying to remember the requests in your head, using scraps of paper, or relying on email boxes. Automation reduces the tedium of managing incoming requests and collecting statistics. Software that tracks tickets for you saves time in real ways. Tom once measured that a group of three SAs was spending an hour a day per person to track issues. That is a loss of 2 staff days per week!

The process described in this chapter brings clarity to the issue of customer support by defining what steps must be followed for a single successful call for help. We show why these steps are to be followed and how each step prepares you for future steps.

Although knowledge of the model can improve an SA's effectiveness by leveling the playing field, it is not a panacea; nor is it a replacement for creativity, experience, or having the right resources. The model does not replace the right training, the right tools, and the right support from management, but it must be part of a well-constructed helpdesk.

Many SAs are naturally good at customer care and react negatively to structured techniques like this one. We're happy for those who have found their own structure and use it with consistently great results. We're sure it has many of the rudiments discussed here. Do what works for you. To grow the number of SAs in the field, more direct instruction will be required. For the millions of SAs who have not found the perfect structure for themselves, consider this structure a good starting point.

Exercises

1. Are there times when you should not use the nine-step model?

2. What are the tools used in your environment for processing customer requests, and how do they fit into the nine-step model? Are there ways they could fit better?

3. What are all the ways to greet customers in your environment? What ways could you use but don't? Why?

4. In your environment, you greet customers by various methods. How do the methods compare by cost, speed (faster completion), and customers'

preference? Is the most expensive method the one that customers prefer the most?

5. Some problem statements can be stated concisely, such as the routing problem example in step 3. Dig into your trouble tracking system to find five typically reported problems. What is the shortest problem statement that completely describes the issue?

6. Query your ticket-tracking software and determine who were your top ten ticket creators overall in the last 12 months; then sort by customer group or department. Then determine what customer groups have the highest per customer ticket count. Which customers make up your top 20 percent? Now that you have this knowledge, what will you do? Examine other queries from Section 14.2.5.

7. Which is the most important of the nine steps? Justify your answer.

Part III

Change Processes

Chapter 15

Debugging

In this chapter, we dig deeply into what is involved in debugging problems. In Chapter 14, we put debugging into the larger context of customer care. This chapter, on the other hand, is about *you* and what you do when faced with a single technical problem.

Debugging is not simply making a change that fixes a problem. That's the easy part. Debugging begins by understanding the problem, finding its cause, and then making the change that makes the problem disappear for good. Temporary or superficial fixes, such as rebooting, that do not fix the cause of the problem only guarantee more work for *you* in the future. We continue that theme in Chapter 16.

Since anyone reading this book has a certain amount of smarts and a level of experience,[1] we do not need to be pedantic about this topic. You've debugged problems; you know what it's like. We're going to make you conscious of the finer points of the process and then discuss some ways of making it even smoother. We encourage you to be systematic. It's better than randomly poking about.

15.1 The Basics

This section offers advice for correctly defining the problem, introduces two models for finding the problem, and ends with some philosophy about the qualities of the best tools.

---

1. And while we're at it, you're good looking and a sharp dresser.

15.1.1 Learn the Customer's Problem

The first step in fixing a problem is to understand, at a high level, what the customer is trying to do and what part of it is failing. In other words, the customer is doing something and expecting a particular result, but something else is happening instead.

For example, customers may be trying to read their email and aren't able to. They may report this in many ways: "My mail program is broken" or "I can't reach the mail server" or "My mailbox disappeared!" Any of those statements may be true, but the problem also could be a network problem, a power failure in the server room, or a DNS problem. These issues may be beyond the scope of what the customer understands or should need to understand. Therefore, it is important for you to gain a high-level understanding of what the customer is trying to do.

Sometimes, customers aren't good at expressing themselves, so care and understanding must prevail. "Can you help me understand what the document should look like?"

It's common for customers to use jargon but in an incorrect way. They believe that's what the SA wants to hear. They're trying to be helpful. It's very valid for the SA to respond along the lines of, "Let's back up a little; what exactly is it you're trying to do? Just describe it without being technical."

The complaint is usually not the problem. A customer might complain that the printer is broken. This sounds like a request to have the printer repaired. However, an SA who takes time to understand the entire situation might learn that the customer needs to have a document printed before a shipping deadline. In that case, it becomes clear that the customer's complaint isn't about the hardware but about needing to print a document. Printing to a different printer becomes a better solution.

Some customers provide a valuable service by digging into the problem before reporting it. A senior SA partners with these customers but understands that there are limits. It can be nice to get a report such as, "I can't print; I think there is a DNS problem." However, we do not believe in taking such reports at face value. You understand the system architecture better than the customers do, so you still need to verify the DNS portion of the report, as well as the printing problem. Maybe it is best to interpret the report as two possibly related reports: Printing isn't working for a particular customer, and a certain DNS test failed. For example, a printer's name may not be in DNS, depending on the print system architecture. Often, customers will ping a host's name to demonstrate a routing problem but overlook the error message and the fact that the DNS lookup of the host's name failed.

Find the Real Problem

One of Tom's customers was reporting that he couldn't ping a particular server located about 1,000 miles away in a different division. He provided traceroutes, ping information, and a lot of detailed evidence. Rather than investigating potential DNS, routing, and networking issues, Tom stopped to ask, "Why do you require the ability to ping that host?" It turned out that pinging that host wasn't part of the person's job; instead, the customer was trying to use that host as an authentication server. The problem to be debugged should have been, "Why can't I authenticate off this host?" or even better, "Why can't I use service A, which relies on the authentication server on host B?"

By contacting the owner of the server, Tom found the very simple answer: Host B had been decommissioned, and properly configured clients should have automatically started authenticating off a new server. This wasn't a networking issue at all but a matter of client configuration. The customer had hard-coded the IP address into his configuration but shouldn't have. A lot of time would have been wasted if the problem had been pursued as originally reported.

In short, a reported problem is about an expected outcome not happening. Now let's look at the cause.

15.1.2 Fix the Cause, Not the Symptom

To build sustainable reliability, you must find and fix the cause of the problem, not simply work around the problem or find a way to recover from it quickly. Although workarounds and quick recovery times are good things, fixing the root cause of a problem is better.

Often, we find ourselves in a situation like this: A coworker reports that there was a problem and that he fixed it. "What was the problem?" we inquire.

"The host needed to be rebooted."

"What was the problem?"

"I told you! The host needed to be rebooted."

A day later, the host needs to be rebooted again.

A host needing to be rebooted isn't a problem but rather a solution. The problem might have been that the system froze, buggy device drivers were malfunctioning, a kernel process wasn't freeing memory and the only choice was to reboot, and so on. If the SA had determined what the true problem was, it could have been fixed for good and would not have returned.

The same goes for "I had to exit and restart an application or service" and other mysteries. Many times, we've seen someone fix a "full-disk" situation by deleting old log files. However, the problem returns as the log files grow again. Deleting the log files fixes the symptoms, but activating a script that would rotate and automatically delete the logs would fix the problem.

Even large companies get pulled into fixing symptoms instead of root causes. For example, Microsoft got a lot of bad press when it reported that a major feature of Windows 2000 would be to make it reboot faster. In fact, users would prefer that it didn't need to be rebooted so often in the first place.

15.1.3 Be Systematic

It is important to be methodical, or systematic, about finding the cause and fixing it. To be systematic, you must form hypotheses, test them, note the results, and make changes based on those results. Anything else is simply making random changes until the problem goes away.

The process of elimination and successive refinement are commonly used in debugging. The **process of elimination** entails removing different parts of the system until the problem disappears. The problem must have existed in the last portion removed. **Successive refinement** involves adding components to the system and verifying at each step that the desired change happens.

The process of elimination is often used when debugging a hardware problem, such as replacing memory chips until a memory error is eliminated or pulling out cards until a machine is able to boot. Elimination is used with software applications, such as eliminating potentially conflicting drivers or applications until a failure disappears. Some OSs have tools that search for possible conflicts and provide test modes to help narrow the search.

Successive refinement is an additive process. To diagnose an IP routing problem, `traceroute` reports connectivity one network hop away and then reports connectivity two hops away, then three, four, and so on. When the probes no longer return a result, we know that the router at that hop wasn't able to return packets. The problem is at that last router. When connectivity exists but there is packet loss, a similar methodology can be used. You can send many packets to the next router and verify that there is no packet loss. You can successively refine the test by including more distant routers until the packet loss is detected. You can then assert that the loss is on the most recently added segment.

Sometimes, successive refinement can be thought of as **follow-the-path** debugging. To do this, you must follow the path of the data or the problem, reviewing the output of each process to make sure that it is the proper input to the next stage. It is common on Unix systems to have an assembly-line approach to processing. One task generates data, the others modify or process the data in sequence, and the final task stores it. Some of these processes may happen on different machines, but the data can be checked at each step. For example, if each step generates a log file, you can monitor the logs at each step. When debugging an email problem that involves a message going from one server to a gateway and then to the destination server, you can watch the logs on all three machines to see that the proper processing has happened at each place. When tracing a network problem, you can use tools that let you snoop packets as they pass through a link to monitor each step. Cisco routers have the ability to collect packets on a link that match a particular set of qualifications, Unix systems have `tcpdump`, and Windows systems have Ethereal. When dealing with Unix software that uses the shell | (pipe) facility to send data through a series of programs, the `tee` command can save a copy at each step.

Shortcuts and optimizations can be used with these techniques. Based on past experience, you might skip a step or two. However, this is often a mistake, because you may be jumping to a conclusion.

We'd like to point out that if you *are* going to jump to a conclusion, the problem is often related to the most recent change made to the host, network, or whatever is having a problem. This usually indicates a lack of testing. Therefore, before you begin debugging a problem, ponder for a moment what changes were made recently: Was a new device plugged into the network? What was the last configuration change to a host? Was anything changed on a router or a firewall? Often, the answers direct your search for the cause.

15.1.4 Have the Right Tools

Debugging requires the right diagnostic tools. Some tools are physical devices; others, software tools that are either purchased or downloaded; and still others, homegrown. However, knowledge is the most important tool.

Diagnostic tools let you see into a device or system to see its inner workings. However, if you don't know how to interpret what you see, all the data in the world won't help you solve the problem.

Training usually involves learning how the system works, how to view its inner workings, and how to interpret what you see. For example, when training someone how to use an Ethernet monitor (sniffer), teaching the person how to capture packets is easy. Most of the training time is spent explaining how various protocols work so that you understand what you see. Learning the tool is easy. Getting a deeper understanding of what the tool lets you see takes considerably longer.

UNIX systems have a reputation for being very easy to debug, most likely because so many experienced UNIX SAs have in-depth knowledge of the inner workings of the system. Such knowledge is easily gained. UNIX systems come with documentation about their internals; early users had access to the source code itself. Many books dissect the source code of UNIX kernels (Lions 1996; McKusick, Bostic, and Karels 1996; Mauro and McDougall 2000) for educational purposes. Much of the system is driven by scripts that can be read easily to gain an understanding of what is going on behind the scenes.

Microsoft Windows developed an early reputation for being a difficult system to debug when problems arose. Rhetoric from the UNIX community claimed that it was a black box with no way to get the information you needed to debug problems on Windows systems. In reality, there were mechanisms, but the only way to learn about them was through vendor-supplied training. From the perspective of a culture that is very open about information, this was difficult to adjust to. It took many years to disseminate the information about how to access Windows' internals and how to interpret what was found.

Know Why a Tool Draws a Conclusion

It is important to understand not only the system being debugged but also the tools being used to debug it. Once, Tom was helping a network technician with a problem: A PC couldn't talk to any servers, even though the link light was illuminated. The technician disconnected the PC from its network jack and plugged in a new handheld device that could test and diagnose a large list of LAN problems. However, the output of the device was a list of conclusions without information about how it was arriving at them. The technician was basing his decisions on the output of this device without question. Tom kept asking, "The device claims it is on network B, but how did it determine that?" The technician didn't know or care. Tom stated, "I don't think it is really on network B! Network B and C are bridged right now, so if the network jack were working, it should claim to be on network B and C at the same time." The technician disagreed, because the very expensive tool couldn't possibly be wrong, and the problem must be with the PC.

It turned out that the tool was guessing the IP network after finding a single host on the LAN segment. This jack was connected to a hub, which had another workstation connected to it in a different office. The uplink from the hub had become disconnected from the rest of the network. Without knowing how the tool performed its tests, there was no way to determine why a tool would report such a claim, and further debugging would have been a wild goose chase. Luckily, there was a hint that something was suspicious—it didn't mention network C. The process of questioning the conclusion drew them to the problem's real cause.

What makes a good tool? We prefer minimal tools over large, complicated tools. The best tool is one that provides the simplest solution to the problem at hand. The more sophisticated a tool is, the more likely it will get in its own way or simply be too big to carry to the problem.

NFS mounting problems can be debugged with three simple tools: `ping`, `traceroute`, and `rpcinfo`. Each does one thing and does that one thing well. If the client can't mount from a particular server, make sure that they can ping each other. If they can't, it's a network problem, and `traceroute` can isolate the problem. If `ping` succeeded, connectivity is good, and there must be a protocol problem. From the client, the elements of the NFS protocol can be tested with `rpcinfo`.[2] You can test the `portmap traceroute` function, then `mountd`, `nfs`, `nlockmgr`, and `status`. If any of them fail, you can deduce that the appropriate service isn't working. If all of them succeed, you can deduce that it is an export permission problem, which usually means that the name of the host listed in the export list is not exactly what the server sees when it performs a reverse DNS lookup. These are extremely powerful diagnostics that are done with extremely simple tools. You can use `rpcinfo` for all Sun RPC-based protocols (Stern 1991).

Protocols based on TCP often can be debugged with a different triad of tools: `ping`, `traceroute/tracert`, and `telnet`. These tools are available on

---

2. For example, `rpcinfo -T udp servername portmap` in Solaris or `rpcinfo -u servername portmap` in Linux.

every platform that supports TCP/IP (Windows, UNIX, and others). Again, `ping` and `traceroute` can diagnose connectivity problems. Then `telnet` can be used to manually simulate many TCP-based protocols. For example, email administrators know enough of SMTP (Crocker 1982) to TELNET to port 25 of a host and type the SMTP commands as if they were the client; you can diagnose many problems by watching the results. Similar techniques work for NNTP (Kantor and Lapsley 1986), FTP (Postel and Reynolds 1985), and other TCP-based protocols. *TCP/IP Illustrated, Volume 1*, by W. Richard Stevens (Stevens 1994) provides an excellent view into how the protocols work.

Sometimes, the best tools are simple homegrown tools or the combination of other small tools and applications, as the following anecdote shows.

Find the Latency Problem

Once, Tom was tracking reports of high latency on a network link. The problem happened only occasionally. He set up a continuous (once per second) ping between two machines that should demonstrate the problem and recorded this output for several hours. He observed consistently good (low) latency, except that occasionally, there seemed to be trouble. A small `perl` program was written to analyze the logs and extract pings with high latency—latency more than three times the average of the first 20 pings—and highlight missed pings. He noticed that no pings were being missed but that every so often, a series of pings took much longer to arrive. He used a spreadsheet to graph the latency over time. Visualizing the results helped him notice that the problem occurred every 5 minutes, within a second or two. It also happened at other times, but every 5 minutes, he was assured of seeing the problem. He realized that some protocols do certain operations every 5 minutes. Could a route table refresh be overloading the CPU of a router? Was a protocol overloading a link?

By process of elimination, he isolated the problem to a particular router. Its CPU was being overloaded by routing table calculations, which happened every time there was a real change to the network plus every 5 minutes during the usual route table refresh. This agreed with the previously collected data. The fact that it was an overloaded CPU and not an overloaded network link explained why latency increased but no packets were lost. The router had enough buffering to ensure that no packets were dropped. Once he fixed the problem with the router, the ping test and log analysis were used again to demonstrate that the problem had been fixed.

The customer who had reported the problem was a scientist with a particularly condescending attitude toward SAs. After confirming with him that the problem had been resolved, the scientist was shown the methodology, including the graphs of timing data. His attitude improved significantly once he found respect for their methods.

Regard Tuning as Debugging

Six classes of bugs limit network performance:

1. Packet losses, corruption, congestion, bad hardware
2. IP routing, long round-trip times
3. Packet reordering
4. Inappropriate buffer space
5. Inappropriate packet sizes
6. Inefficient applications

Any one of these problems can hide all other problems. This is why solving performance problems requires a high level of expertise. Because debugging tools are rarely very good, it is "akin to finding the weakest link of an invisible chain" (Mathis 2003). Therefore, if you are debugging any of these problems and are not getting anywhere, pause a moment and consider that it might be one of the other problems.

15.2 The Icing

The icing really improves those basics: better tools, better knowledge about how to use the tools, and better understanding about the system being debugged.

15.2.1 Better Tools

Better tools are, well, better! There is always room for new tools that improve on the old ones. Keeping up to date on the latest tools can be difficult, preventing you from being an early adopter of new technology. Several forums, such as USENIX and SAGE conferences, as well as web sites and mailing lists, can help you learn of these new tools as they are announced.

We are advocates for simple tools. Improved tools need not be more complex. In fact, a new tool sometimes brings innovation through its simplicity.

When evaluating new tools, assess them based on what problems they can solve. Try to ignore the aspects that are flashy, buzzword-compliant, and full of hype. **Buzzword-compliant** is a humorous term meaning that the product applies to all the current industry buzzwords one might see in the headlines of trade magazines, whether or not such compliance has any benefit.

Ask, "What real-life problem will this solve?" It is easy for salespeople to focus you on flashy, colorful output, but does the flash add anything to the utility of the product? Is the color used intelligently to direct the eye at important details, or does it simply make the product pretty? Are any of the buzzwords relevant? Sure, it supports SNMP, but will you integrate it into your SNMP monitoring system? Or is SNMP simply used for configuring the device?

Ask for an evaluation copy of the tool, and make sure that you have time to use the tool during the evaluation. Don't be afraid to send it back if you didn't find it useful. Salespeople have thick skins, and the feedback you give will help them make the product better in future releases.

15.2.2 Formal Training on the Tools

Although manuals are great, formal training can be the icing that sets you apart from others. Formal training has a number of benefits.

- Off-site training is usually provided, which takes you away from the interruptions of your job and lets you focus on learning new skills.

- Formal training usually covers all the features, not only the ones with which you've had time to experiment.

- Instructors often will reveal bugs or features that the vendor may not want revealed in print.

- Often, you have access to a lab of machines where you can try things that, because of production requirements, you couldn't otherwise try.

- You can list the training on your resume; this can be more impressive to prospective employers than actual experience, especially if you receive certification.

15.2.3 End-to-End Understanding of the System

Finally, the ultimate debugging icing is to have at least one person who understands, end to end, how the system works. On a small system, that's easy. As systems grow larger and more complex, however, people specialize and end up knowing only their part of the system. Having someone who knows the entire system is invaluable when there is a major outage. In a big emergency, it can be best to assemble a team of experts, each representing one layer of the stack.

Case Study: Architects

How do you retain employees who have this kind of end-to-end knowledge? One way is to promote them.

Synopsys had "architect" positions in each technology area who were this kind of end-to-end person. The architects knew more than simply their technology area in depth, and they were good crossover people. Their official role was to track the industry direction: predict needs and technologies 2 to 5 years out and start preparing for them (prototyping, getting involved with vendors as alpha/beta customers, and helping to steer the direction of the vendors' products); architecting new services; watching what was happening in the group; steering people toward smarter, more scalable solutions; and so on. This role ensured that such people were around when end-to-end knowledge was required for debugging major issues.

Mystery File Deletes

Here's an example of a situation in which end-to-end knowledge was required to fix a problem. A customer revealed that some of his files were disappearing. To be more specific, he had about 100MB of data in his home directory, and all but 2MB had disappeared. He had restored his files. The environment had a system that let users restore files from backups without SA intervention. However, a couple of days later, the same thing happened; this time, a different set of files remained. Again, the files remaining totaled 2MB. He then sheepishly revealed that this had been going on for a couple of weeks, but he found it convenient to restore his own files and felt embarrassed to bother the SAs with such an odd problem.

The SA's first theory was that there was a virus, but virus scans revealed nothing. The next theory was that someone was playing pranks on him or that there was a badly written cron job. He was given pager numbers to call the moment his files disappeared again. Meanwhile, network sniffers were put in place to monitor who was deleting files on that server. The next day, the customer alerted the SAs that his files were disappearing. "What was the last thing you did?" Well, he had simply logged in to a machine in a lab to surf the web. The SAs were baffled. The network-monitoring tools showed that the deletions were not coming from the customer's PC or from a rogue machine or misprogrammed server. The SAs had done their best to debug the problem using their knowledge of their part of the system, yet the problem remained unsolved.

Suddenly, one of the senior SAs with end-to-end knowledge of the system, including both Windows and UNIX and all the various protocols involved, realized that web browsers keep a cache that gets pruned to stay lower than a certain limit, often 2MB. Could the browser on this machine be deleting the files? Investigation revealed that the lab machine was running a web browser configured with an odd location for its cache. The location was fine for some users, but when this user logged in, the location was equivalent to his home directory because of a bug (or feature?) related to how Windows parsed directory paths that involved nonexistent subdirectories. The browser was finding a cache with 100MB of data and deleting files until the space used was less than 2MB. That explained why every time the problem appeared, a different set of files remained. After the browser's configuration was fixed, the problem disappeared.

The initial attempts at solving the problem—virus scans, checking for cron jobs, watching protocols—had proved fruitless because they were testing the parts. The problem was solved only by someone having end-to-end understanding of the system.

Knowledge of Physics Sometimes Helps

Sometimes, even having end-to-end knowledge of a system is insufficient. In two famous cases, knowledge of physics was required to track down the root cause of a problem.

The Cuckoo's Egg (Stoll 1989) documents the true story of how Cliff Stoll tracked down an intruder who was using his computer system. By monitoring network delay and applying some physics calculations, Stoll was able to accurately predict where in the world the intruder was located. The book reads like a spy novel but is all real!

The famous story "The Case of the 500-Mile Email" and associated FAQ (Harris 2002) documents Trey Harris's effort to debug a problem that began with a call from the chairman of his university's statistics department, claiming, "We can't send mail more than 500 miles." After explaining that "email really doesn't work that way," Harris began a journey that discovered that, amazingly enough, this in fact was the problem. A timeout was set too low, which was causing problems if the system was connecting to servers that were far away enough that the round-trip delay was more than a very small number. The distance that light would travel in that time was 3 millilightseconds, or about 558 miles.

15.3 Conclusion

Every SA debugs problems and typically develops a mental catalog of standard solutions to common problems. However, debugging should be a systematic, or methodical, process that involves understanding what the customer is trying to do and fixing the root cause of the problem, rather than smoothing over the symptoms. Some debugging techniques are subtractive—process of elimination—and others are additive—successive refinement. Fixing the root cause is important because if the root problem isn't repaired, the problem will recur, thus generating more work for the SA.

Although this chapter strongly stresses fixing the root problem as soon as possible, you must sometimes provide a workaround quickly and return later to fix the root problem (see Chapter 14). For example, you might prefer quick fixes during production hours and have a maintenance window (Chapter 20) reserved for more permanent and disruptive fixes.

Better tools let you solve problems more efficiently without adding undue complexity. Formal training on a tool provides knowledge and experience that you cannot get from a manual. Finally, in a major outage or when a problem seems peculiar, nothing beats one or more people who together have end-to-end knowledge of the system.

Simple tools can solve big problems. Complicated tools sometimes obscure how they draw conclusions.

Debugging is often a communication process between you and your customers. You must gain an understanding of the problem in terms of what the customer is trying to accomplish, as well as the symptoms discovered so far.

Exercises

1. Pick a technology that you deal with as part of your job function. Name the debugging tools you use for that technology. For each tool, is it homegrown, commercial, or free? Is it simple? Can it be combined with other tools? What formal or informal training have you received on this tool?

2. Describe a recent technical problem that you debugged and how you resolved it.

3. In an anecdote in Section 15.1.4, the customer was impressed by the methodology used to fix his problem. How would the situation be different if the customer were a nontechnical manager rather than a scientist?

4. What tools do you not have that you wish you did? Why?

5. Pick a tool you use often. In technical terms, how does it do its job?

Chapter 16

Fixing Things Once

Fixing something once is better than fixing it over and over again. Although this sounds obvious, it sometimes isn't possible, given other constraints; or, you find yourself fixing something over and over without realizing it, or the quick fix is simply emotionally easier. By being conscious of these things, you can achieve several goals. First, you can manage your time better. Second, you can become better SAs. Third, if necessary, you can explain better to the customer why you are taking longer than expected to fix something.

Chapter 15 described a systematic process for debugging a problem. This chapter is about a general day-to-day philosophy.

16.1 The Basics

One of our favorite mantras is "fix things once." If something is broken, it should be fixed once, such that it won't return. If a problem is likely to appear on other machines, it should be tested for and repaired on all other machines.

16.1.1 Don't Waste Time

Sometimes, particularly for something that seems trivial or that affects you only for the time being, it can seem easier to do a quick fix that doesn't fix the problem permanently. It may not even cross your mind that you are fixing multiple times a problem that you could have fixed once with a little more effort.

Fix It Once

Once, Tom was helping an SA reconfigure two large Sun Solaris servers. The configuration required many reboots to test each step of the process. After each reboot, the SA would log in again. The root account on this host didn't have `tty` TERM, PATH, and other environment variables set properly. This usually wouldn't burn him. For example, it didn't matter that his TERM variable was unset, for he wasn't using any curses-based tools. However, this meant that his shell wouldn't support command line editing. Without that, he was doing much more typing and retyping than would normally be required. He was on a console, so he didn't even have a mouse with which to cut and paste. Eventually, he would need to edit a file, using a screen-based editor (`vi` or `emacs`), and he would set his TERM variable so that the program would be usable.

It pained Tom to see this guy manually setting these variables time and time again. In the SA's mind, however, he was being very efficient because he spent time setting a variable only right before it was required, the first time it was required. Occasionally, he would log in, type one command, and reboot, a big win, considering that none of the variables needed to be set that time. However, for longer sessions, Tom felt that the SA was distracted by having to keep track of which variables hadn't been set yet, in addition to focusing on the problem at hand. Often, the SA would do something that failed because of unset variables; then he would set the required variables and retype the failed command.

Finally, Tom politely suggested that if the SA had a `/.profile` that set those variables, he could focus more on the problem rather than on his environment. *Fix the problem once, Corollary A: Fix the problem permanently.*

The SA agreed and started creating the host's `/.profile` from scratch. Tom stopped him and reminded him that rather than inventing a `/.profile` from scratch, he should copy one from another Solaris host. *Fix the problem once, Corollary B: Leverage what others have done; don't reinvent the wheel.* By copying the generic `/.profile` that was on most other hosts in that lab, the SA was leveraging the effort put into the previous hosts. He was also reversing the entropy of the system, taking one machine that was dissimilar from the others and making it the same again.

As the SA copied the `/.profile` from another machine, Tom questioned why they were doing this at all. Shouldn't Solaris JumpStart have already installed the fine `/.profile` that all the other machines have? In Chapter 3, we saw the benefits of automating the three big deployment issues: loading the OS, patching the OS, and network configuration. This environment had a JumpStart server; why hadn't it been used?

It turned out that this machine came from another site, and the owner simply configured its IP address; he didn't use JumpStart. (The security risk of doing this is an entirely different issue.) This was to save time, because it was unlikely that the host would stay there for more than a couple of days. A year later, it was still there. Tom and the SA were paying the price for customers who wanted to save their own time. The customer saved time but cost Tom and the SA time.

Then Tom realized a couple more issues. If the machine hadn't been JumpStarted, it was very unlikely that it got added to the list of hosts that were automatically patched. This host had not been patched since it arrived. It was insecurely configured, had none of the recent security patches installed, and was missed by the Y2K scans: It was sure to have problems on January 1, 2000.

Fix the problem once, Corollary C: Fix a problem for all hosts at the same time. The original problem was that Solaris includes a painfully minimalist /.profile file. The site's solution was to install a better one at install time via JumpStart. The problem was fixed for all hosts at the same time by making the fix part of the install procedure. If the file needed to be changed, the site could use the patch system to distribute a new version to all machines.

All in all, the procedure that Tom and his coworker were there to do took twice as long because the host hadn't been JumpStarted. Some of the delays were caused because this system lacked the standard, mature, and SA-friendly configuration. Other delays came from the fact that the OS was a minefield of half-configured or misconfigured features.

This was another reminder about how getting the basics right makes things so good that you forget how bad things were when you didn't have the basics done right. Tom was accustomed to the luxury of an environment in which hosts are configured properly. He had been taking it for granted.

16.1.2 Avoid Temporary Fixes

The previous section is fairly optimistic about being able to make the best fix possible in every situation. However, that is not realistic. Sometimes, constraints on time or resources require a quick fix until a complete fix can be scheduled. Sometimes, a complete fix can require an unacceptable interruption of service in certain situations, and a temporary fix will have to suffice until a maintenance window can be scheduled. Sometimes, temporary fixes are required because of resource issues. Maybe software will have to be written or hardware installed to fix the problem. Those things will take time. If a disk is being filled by logs, a permanent fix might be to add software that would rotate logs. It may take time to install such software, but in the meanwhile, old logs can be manually deleted.

It is important that temporary fixes be followed by permanent fixes. To do this, some mechanism is needed so that problems don't fall through the cracks. Returning to our example of the full log disk, it can be tempting on a busy day to manually delete the older logs and move on to the next task without recording the fact that the issue needs to be revisited to implement a permanent fix. Recording such action items can be difficult. Scribbled notes on paper get lost. One might not always have one's Day Runner to-do book on hand. It is much easier to email a reminder to oneself. Even better is to have a helpdesk application that permits new tickets to be created via email. If you can create a ticket via email, it becomes possible to create a ticket wherever you are so you don't have to remember later. Typically, you can send email from your cellphone, a two-way pager, handheld or PDA.

UNIX systems can generally be configured to send email from the command line. No need to wait for an email client to start up. Simply type a sentence or two as a reminder, and work the ticket later, when you have more time.[1] It should be noted, however, that many sites configure their UNIX systems to properly deliver email only if they are part of the email food chain. As a result, email sent from the command line on other machines does not get delivered. It is very easy to define a simple "null client" or "route all email to a server" configuration that is deployed as part of the default configuration. Anything else is amateurish and leads to confusion as email gets lost.

Temporary fixes are emotionally easier than permanent fixes. We feel as though we've accomplished something in a small amount of time. That's a lot easier on our ego than beginning a large project to permanently fix a problem or adding something to our never-ending to-do list.

Fixing the same small things time after time is habit forming. With Pavlovian accuracy, we execute the same small fix every time our monitoring systems warn us of the problem. When we are done, we admonish ourselves to make the fix; "Next time I'll have the time to do the permanent fix!" Soon, we are so efficient at the quick fix that we forget that there is a permanent fix. We get the feeling that we are busy all day but don't feel as though we are accomplishing anything. We ask our boss or coworker to look at our day with new eyes. When the boss or coworker does so, her or she sees that our days are spent mopping the floor rather than turning off the faucet.

We have grown so accustomed to the quick fix that we are now the experts at it. In shame, we discover that we have grown so efficient at it that we take pride in our efficiency, pointing out the keyboard macros we have written and other time-saving techniques we have discovered.

Such a situation is common. To prevent it, we must break the cycle.

---

1. At Bell Labs, Tom had a reputation for having nearly as many self-created tickets as tickets from customers.

Case Study: Bounced Email

Tom used to run many mailing lists using Majordomo, a very simple mailing list manager that is driven by email messages to a command processor to request that subscriptions be started and discontinued. At first, he diligently researched the occasional bounce message, finding that an email address on a particular list was no longer valid. If it remained invalid for a week, he removed the person from the mailing list. He became more efficient by using an email filtering program to send the bounces to a particular folder, which he analyzed in batches every couple of days. Soon, he had shell scripts that helped hunt down the problem, track who was bouncing and if the problem had persisted for an entire week, and macros that efficiently removed people from mailing lists.

Eventually, he found himself spending more than an hour every day with this work. It was affecting his other project deadlines. He knew that other software (Viega, Warsaw, and Memheimer 1998) would manage the bounces better or would delegate the work to the owners of the individual mailing lists, but he never had time to install such software. He was mopping the floor instead of turning off the faucet.

The only way for Tom to break this cycle was to ignore bounces for a week and stay late a couple of nights to install the new software without interruption and without affecting his other project deadlines. Even then, a project would have to slip at least a little. Once he finally made this decision, the software was installed and tested in about 5 hours total. The new software reduced his manual intervention to about 1 hour a week, for a 4 hour/week saving, the equivalent of gaining a half day every week. Tom would still be losing nearly a month of workdays every year if he hadn't stopped his quick fixes to make the permanent fix.

Let's dig deeper into Corollary A: Fix the problem permanently. It certainly sounds simple; however, we often see someone fix a problem only to find that it reappears after the next reboot. Sometimes, knowing which fixes are permanent and which need to be repeated on reboot is the difference between a new SA and a wizard.

Many OSs run scripts, or programs, to bring the machine up. The scripts involved in booting a machine must be edited from time to time. Sometimes, a new daemon—for example, an Apache HTTP server—must be started. Sometimes, a configuration change must be made, such as setting a flag on a new network interface. Rather than running these commands manually every time a machine reboots, they should be added to the start-up scripts. Be careful writing such scripts. If they contain an error, the system may no longer boot. We always reboot a machine shortly after modifying any start-up scripts; that way, we detect problems now, not months later when the machine is rebooted for another reason.

Case Study: Permanent Configuration Settings

The Microsoft Windows registry solves many of these problems. The registry contents are permanent and survive reboots. Every well-written program has its settings and configuration stored in the registry. No need for every program to reinvent the wheel. Each service, or what UNIX calls daemons, can fail to start without interrupting the entire boot process.

In a way, Microsoft has attempted to fix it once by providing software developers with the registry and the Services Control Panel and the Devices Control Panel rather than requiring each to reinvent something similar for each product.

16.1.3 Learn from Carpenters

SAs have a lot to learn from carpenters. They've been building and fixing things for a lot longer than we have.

Carpenters say, "Measure twice; cut once." Measuring a second time prevents a lot of errors. Wood is expensive. A little extra care is a small cost compared with wasted wood.

Carpenters also understand how to copy things. A carpenter who needs to cut many pieces of wood all the same size cuts the first one to the proper length and uses that first piece over and over to measure the others. This is much more accurate than using the second piece to measure the third piece, the third piece to measure the fourth piece, and so on. The latter technique easily accumulates errors.

SAs can learn a lot from these techniques. Copying something is an opportunity to get something right once and then replicate it many times. Measuring things twice is a good habit to develop. Double-check your work before you make any changes. Reread that configuration file, have someone else view the command before you execute it, load-test the capacity of the system before you recommend growing, and so on. Test, test, and test again.

❖ **Be Careful Deleting Files** UNIX shells make it easy to accidentally delete files. This is illustrated by the classic UNIX example of trying to delete all files that end with .o but accidentally typing `rm * .o`—note the space accidentally inserted after the *—and deleting all the files in the directory. Luckily, UNIX shells also make it easy to "measure twice." You can change `rm` to `echo` to simply list which files will be deleted.

If the right files are listed, you can use command line editing to change the `echo` to `rm` to really delete the files.

This technique is an excellent way to "measure twice," by performing a quick check to prevent mistakes. The use of command line editing is like using the first block of wood to measure the next one. We've seen SAs who use this technique but manually retype the command after seeing the `echo` came out right, which defeats the purpose of the technique. Retyping a command opens one up to an accumulation of errors. Invest time in learning command line editing for the shell you use.

Case Study: Copy Exact

Intel has a philosophy called Copy Exact. Once something is done right, it is copied exactly at other sites. For example, if a factory is built, additional capacity is created by copying it exactly at other locations. No need to reinvent the wheel. The SAs adopt the policy also. Useful scripts that are distributed to other sites are used without change, rather than ending up with every site having a mess of slightly different systems. This forces all SAs to maintain similar environments, develop code that works at all sites without customization, and feed back improvements to the original author for release to the world, thus not leaving any site behind.

Case Study: France Nuclear Power

After experimenting with various designs of nuclear power plants, France settled on one design, which is used at 56 power plants. Because the plants were all the same, they were cheaper to build than their U.S. equivalents. More important, safety management is easier. "The lessons from any incident at one plant could be quickly learned by managers of the other 55 plants."[2] This is not possible in the United States, with its many different utility companies with many different designs.

System administrators can learn from this when designing remote office networks, server infrastructures, and so on. Repetition makes things easier to manage.

You'll never hear a carpenter say, "I've cut this board three times, and it's still too short!" Cutting the same board won't make it any longer. SAs often find themselves trying the same thing over and over, frustrated that

---

2. http://www.pbs.org/wgbh/pages/frontline/shows/reaction/readings/french.html.

they keep getting the same failed results. Instead, they should try something different. SAs complain about security problems and bugs yet put their trust into software from companies without sufficient QA systems. SAs run critical systems without firewalls on the Internet. SAs fix problems by rebooting systems rather than by fixing the root cause.

> ❖ **Excellent Advice**   In the famous UNIX Room at Bell Labs, a small sign on the wall simply states: "Stop Doing Things That Don't Work."

16.2 The Icing

The icing for this chapter is about not having to perform the fix for yourself, through automation. One type of automation fixes symptoms and alerts an SA so that he or she can fix it permanently. The other type of automation fixes things permanently, on its own.

Automation that fixes problems can be worrisome. We've seen too much bad science fiction in which the robot "fixes" a problem by killing innocent people or blowing up Earth. Therefore, automation should be extremely careful in what it does and should keep logs so that its work can be audited.

Automation often fixes symptoms without fixing the root cause. In that situation, it is critical that the automation provide an alert that it has done something so that a human can implement a permanent fix. We have seen automation that reacts to a full-disk situation by deleting old log files. This works fine until the consumers of disk space outpace the log files, and suddenly, there are very few logs to delete. Then the automation requests immediate human intervention, and the human finds an extremely difficult problem. If the automation had alerted the human that it was making temporary fixes, it would have given the human time to make a more permanent fix.

However, now we risk the "boy-who-cried-wolf" situation. It is very easy to ignore warnings that a robot has implemented a temporary fix and that a longer-term fix is needed. If the temporary fix worked this time, it should work the next time, too. It's usually safe to ignore such an alert the first time. It's only the time after that that the permanent fix is done. Because an SA's workload is virtually always more than the person has time for, it is too easy to hope that the time after that won't be soon. In a large environment, it is likely that different SAs will see the alerts each time. If all of them assume they are the first to ignore the alert, the situation will degenerate into a big problem.

Fixing the real problem is rarely something that can be automated. Automation can dig you out of a small hole but can't fix buggy software. For example, it can kill a runaway process but not the bug in the software that makes it run away.

Sometimes, automation can fix the root problem. Large systems with virtual machines can allocate additional CPUs to overloaded computations, grow a full-disk partition, or automatically move data to an other disk. Some types of file systems let you grow a virtual file system in an automated fashion, usually by allocating a spare disk and merging it into the volume. That doesn't help much if the disk was running out of space as a result of a runaway process generating an infinite amount of data, because the new disk also will fill. However, it does fix the daily operational issue of disks filling. You can add spares to a system, and automation can take care of attaching them to the next virtual volume that is nearly full. This is no substitute for good capacity planning, but it would be a good tool as part of your capacity-management system.

The solution is policy and discipline, possibly enforced by software. It takes discipline to fix things rather than to ignore them.

Sometimes, the automation can take a long time to create. However, sometimes, it can be done a little bit at a time. The essentials of a 5-minute task can be integrated into a script. Later, more of the task can be added. It may seem as though 5-minute tasks are taking an hour to automate, but you will be saving time in the long run.

Case Study: Makefiles

A makefile is a series of recipes that instruct the system how to rebuild one file if the files that were used to create it got modified. For example, if a program is made up of five C++ files, it is easy to specify that if any one of those files is updated, the program must be recompiled to make a new object file. If any of the object files are changed, they must be relinked to remake the program. Thus, one can focus on editing the source files, not on remembering how to recompile and make the program.

System administrators often forget that this developer tool can be a great boon to them. For example, you can create a makefile that specifies that if `/etc/aliases` has been changed, the `newaliases` program must be run to update the indexed version of the file. If that file has to be copied to other servers, the makefile recipes can include the command to do that copy. Now you can focus on editing the files you want, and the updates that follow are automated.

This is a great way to record the institutional knowledge about processes so that other people don't have to learn them.

16.3 Conclusion

Fixing something once is better than fixing something many times over. Ultimately, fixes should be permanent, not temporary. You should not reinvent the wheel and should, when possible, copy solutions that are known to work. It is best to be proactive; if you find a problem in one place, fix it on all similar hosts or places. It is easy for an SA to get into a situation and not realize that things should be fixed the right way. Sometimes, however, limited resources leave an SA no choice other than to implement a quick fix and to schedule the permanent fix for later. On the other hand, SAs must avoid developing a habit of delaying such fixes and the emotionally easier path of repeating small fixes rather than investing time in producing a complete solution. In the end, it is best to fix things the right way at the right time.

This chapter was a bit more philosophical than the others. In the first anecdote, we saw how critical it is to get the basics right early on. If automating the initial OS load and configuration had been done, many of the other problems would not have happened. Many times, the permanent fix is to introduce automation. However, automation has its own problems. It can take a long time to automate a solution; while waiting for the automation to be completed, SAs can develop bad habits or an emotional immunity to repeatedly fixing a problem. Nevertheless, good automation can dramatically lessen your workload and improve the reliability of your systems.

Exercises

1. What things do you fix often rather than implement a permanent fix? Why hasn't a permanent fix been implemented?

2. In what ways do you use the carpenters' techniques described in Section 16.1.3?

3. Describe a situation in which you had to delay a permanent fix because of limited resources.

4. Does your monitoring system emulate "the boy who cried wolf"?

Chapter 17

Change Management

Change management is the process that ensures effective planning, implementation, and post-event analysis of changes made to a system. It means that changes are well documented, have a back-out plan, and are reproducible. Change management is about managing risk. Changes that SAs make risk outages for their customers. Change management assesses the risks and manages them with risk mitigation strategies. There is forward planning for changes, communication, scheduling, a test plan, a back-out plan, and a set of conditions that determine whether and when to implement the back-out plan. This chapter looks at the underlying process; and the following chapters show how change management applies in various SA scenarios.

Change management yields an audit trail that can be used to determine what was done, when, and why. Part of change management is communicating with customers and other SA teams about the project before implementation. Revision control, another component of change management, is a low-level process for controlling the changes to a single configuration file.

Change management is one of the core processes of a mature SA team. It is a mechanism through which a group of people can make sure that changes that may have an impact on other changes do not occur simultaneously. It is a mechanism for reducing outages or problems by making SAs think through various aspects of a change before they implement it. It is a communication tool that makes sure that everyone is on the same page when changes are made. In other words, it means having a lower "oops" quotient and being able to deal more quickly with an oops when it happens. Change management is crucial in e-commerce companies whose revenue stream relies on 24/7 availability.

17.1 The Basics

In this section, we discuss how change management is linked to risk management and look at four primary components of change management for SAs:

1. *Communication and scheduling.* Communicate with the customers and other SAs so that they know what is happening, and schedule changes to cause the least impact.

2. *Planning and testing.* Plan how and when to do the change, how to test whether everything is working, and how and when to back out the change if there are problems.

3. *Process and documentation.* Changes must follow standard processes and be well planned, with all eventualities covered. The changes must be documented and approved before they are implemented.

4. *Revision control and automation.* Use revision control to track changes and to facilitate backing out problem updates. Automate changes wherever possible to ensure that the processes are performed accurately and repeatably.

We show how, together, these components can lead to smooth systems updates, with minimal problems.

Change management should take into account various categories of systems that are changed, types of changes that are made, and the specific procedures for each combination. For example, the machine categories may include desktops, departmental servers, corporate infrastructure systems, business-critical systems, Internet presence, and production e-commerce systems. Categories of changes may include account and access management, directory updating, new service or software package installation, upgrade of an existing service or software package, hardware changes, security policy changes, or a configuration change.

Minor changes can, and frequently will, fall outside of a company's process for change control; having too cumbersome a process for minor changes will prevent the SAs from working efficiently. But significant changes should be subject to the complete change-control process. Having this process means that SAs can't make a significant change without following the correct procedure, which involves communicating with the right people and scheduling the change for an appropriate time. On critical systems, this may involve writing up a small project plan, with test procedures and a back-out plan, which is reviewed by peers or more senior SAs, and it may also involve appointing a "buddy" to observe and help out with the change. Sections 17.1.2 and 17.1.3 discuss the communications structure and scheduling of changes in more detail.

Each company must decide what level of change-management process to have for each point in the machine category/type of change matrix. Systems critical to the business obviously should be controlled tightly. Changes to a single desktop may not need such control. Changes to every desktop in the company probably should. Having enough process and review for changes on more critical systems will result in fewer, potentially costly, mistakes. The IT Infrastructure Library (ITIL) is a valuable resource for further reading in the area of change management and SA processes. ITIL best-practice processes are becoming widely recognized as standards.

17.1.1 Risk Management

Part of being an SA is managing risk. The main risks that we are concerned with boil down to loss of service, a subset of which is loss of data. One of the most basic ways that all SAs manage risk is by making backups. Backups are part of a risk-mitigation strategy, protecting against loss of data and service. In Chapter 25 we look in more detail at how various technologies, such as RAID, help us to mitigate the risk of data service loss.

The first steps in risk management are risk discovery and risk quantification. What systems and services can a change impact? What are the worst-case scenarios? How many of your customers could these scenarios affect? It helps to categorize machines by usage profile, such as infrastructure machines, departmental servers, business-critical, or desktops and to quantify the number of machines that the change impacts.

After assessing the risk of a change, the next step is to figure out how to mitigate the risk. Mitigation has five core components. The first is to institute a change advisory board: Does this change request meet a business need; does it impact other events or changes; when should it be implemented? The second is a test plan: How do you assess whether the change has been successful? The third is a back-out plan: If the change is not successful, how do you revert to the old service or system? The fourth component is a decision point: How and when should you decide to implement a back-out plan? The final part is preparation: What can you do and test in advance to make sure that the change goes smoothly and takes the minimum amount of time?

It is important to decide in advance what the absolute cutoff conditions are for making the system update work. The cutoff has to give sufficient time for the back-out plan to be implemented before the service must be up and running again. The time by which the service must be up again may be based on a committment to customers, a business need or may be because this change is part of a larger sequence of changes that will all be impacted if this service is not restored on time.

The decision point is often the most difficult component for the SA making the change. We often feel that if we could spend "just 5 more minutes," we could get it working. It is often helpful to have another SA or a manager to keep you honest and make sure that the back-out plan is implemented on schedule, if the change is unsuccessful.

Ideally, it is best to perform and verify the change in advance in a test lab. It may also be possible to make the change in advance on an extra machine that can be swapped in to replace the original machine. However, test labs and extra machines are luxuries that are not available at all sites, and some changes are not well suited to being tested in a lab environment.

17.1.2 Communications Structure

Communication of change has two aspects: making sure that the whole SA team knows what is happening and making sure that your customers know what is going on. When everyone on a team is well informed about changes, all the SAs can all keep their eyes and ears open for problems that may have resulted from the change. Any problems will be spotted sooner and can be fixed more quickly.

You also need to develop a communications structure for informing your customers about the changes you are making. If the changes involve a hard cutover, after which the old service, system, or software will not be available, you must make sure that all your customers who use the old version will be able to continue to work with the new version. If a soft cutover is involved, with the old version available for a time, you should ensure that everyone knows in advance when it is happening, how they use the older version if they need to, and when or whether the old version will no longer be available. If you are adding a service, you need to ensure that the people who requested it, and those who might find it useful, know how to use it when it is available. In all three cases, let your customers know when the work has been successfully completed and how to report any problems that occur.

Although it is necessary and good practice to inform customers whose work may be affected about changes and the schedule for implementation, you must take care not to flood your customers with too many messages. If you do, the customers will ignore them, thinking them irrelevant. Targeting the correct groups for each service requires understanding your customer base and your services in order to make appropriate mappings. For example, if you know that group A uses services A to K and that group B uses services B, D, and L to P, you need to let only group A know about changes to service A, but you should let both groups, A and B, know about modifications to service B. This task may seem tedious, but when it is done well, it makes a huge difference to your customers.

The most effective communication method will vary from company to company and depends on the company culture. For example, in some companies, a newsgroup that people choose to subscribe to, whereby they can quickly scan the subjects of the messages for relevance, may be the most effective tool. However, other companies may not use newsgroups, so email may work more effectively. For significant changes, we recommend that you send a message out to people ("push") rather than require your customers to check a certain web page every couple of days ("pull"). A significant change is one that is either sensitive or major, as defined in Section 17.1.3.

Case Study: Bell Labs' Demo Schedule

The Bell Labs research area had a very relaxed computing environment that did not require too much in the way of change management. However, there was a need for an extremely stable environment during demos. Therefore, the research area maintained a simple calendar of the demo schedule, using the UNIX `calendar` command. Researchers notified the SAs of demos via the usual helpdesk procedure, and the SAs paid attention to this calendar when scheduling downtime. They also avoided risky changes on those days and avoided any kind of group lunch that might take too many SAs away from the building. If the demo included CEOs or heads of state, an SA stood ready outside the door.

17.1.3 Scheduling

A key component of change management is timing. When you make the change can be a significant factor in how much it affects your customers. We briefly discuss the scheduling of three types of changes: routine updates, sensitive updates, and major updates.

A **routine update** can happen at any time and is basically invisible to most of the customer base. These changes happen all the time: updating the contents of a directory server or an authentication database, helping an individual customer to customize his or her environment, debugging a problem with a desktop or a printer, or altering a script that processes log files to produce statistics. You do not need to schedule a routine update; the scope of the problem that an error would cause is very limited because of the nature of the task.

Major updates affect many systems or require a significant system, network, or service outage or touch a large number of systems. What is considered large varies from site to site. For most sites, anything that affects 30 percent or more of the systems is a large update. Major updates include upgrading the authentication system, changing the email or printer infrastructure, or upgrading the core network infrastructure. These updates must be carefully scheduled with the customer base, using a "push" mechanism, such as email. Major updates should not be happening all the time. If they are, consider whether you should change the way you are classifying some updates. Some companies may want them performed at off-peak times, and others may want all the major updates to happen in one concentrated maintenance window (see Chapter 20).

A **sensitive update** may not seem to be a large update or even one that will be particularly visible to your customers but could cause a significant outage if there is a problem with it. Sensitive updates include altering router configurations, global access policies, firewall configurations, or making alterations to a critical server. You should have some form of communication with your customers about a sensitive update before it takes place, in case there are problems. These updates will happen reasonably often and you do not want to overcommunicate them, so a "pull" mechanism, such as a web page or a newsgroup, is appropriate. The helpdesk should be told of the change, the problems that it might cause, when work starts and finishes, and whom to contact in the event of a problem.

Sensitive updates should happen outside of peak usage times, to minimize the potential impact and to give you time to discover and rectify any problems before they affect your customers. Peak usage times may vary, depending on who your customers are. If you work at an e-commerce site that is used primarily by the public in the evenings and on the weekends, the best time for making changes may be at 9 AM. Sensitive updates also should not be immediately followed by the person who made the change going home for the evening or the weekend. If you make a sensitive change, stay around for a couple of hours to make sure that you are there to fix any problems that you may have caused.

Case Study: No Changes on Friday

One of Tom's customers did a lot of SA tasks, and Tom was affected by his customer's changes and schedule, rather than the other way around. When his customer made a mistake, Tom was blamed because some of the group's systems depended on the customer's systems. The customer and Tom had the following debate.

Within his own area, Tom instituted the rule that no changes should be made on Friday, because if mistakes were discovered over the weekend, response times would be slower, increasing the risk of adversely affecting his customer's work. Tom also didn't want his weekend ruined, and he thought that the customer too should abide by this guideline.

The customer believed that no matter what day Tom's group made changes, the SAs should check their work more thoroughly and then wouldn't have to be concerned about making changes the day before a weekend or vacation. Even though the customer's own changes often caused problems, he refused to acknowledge that even when changes are carefully checked before they are made, the unexpected may happen or an error may occur. He also refused to acknowledge the increased risk to other customers and that lowering that risk was in everyone's best interest.

The customer also felt that the SAs should make their changes during the day, because there's no better test of a change than having live users try to work on the system. He felt that if changes were made during off-hours, the SAs wouldn't find the problem until people who used the system returned in the morning or after the weekend. He preferred to make changes during lunch, so that there was a half day of testing before he went home. There was no lunch hour at that company. The cafeteria was open from 11:15 to 1:30, and at least a third of their customers were active on the network at any time.

Both Tom and this customer had valid points, and no one rule will do for all situations. However, ignoring the risks to other customers is not appropriate, and saying that more careful checking is sufficient is not a valid point. More careful checking is always good, but it is not a sufficient reason to ignore a higher risk to the customers.

Many sites like to make some changes during the working day for the same reason that they don't like to make them on a Friday: They want people to be around when the change happens to notice and fix any problems. However, many sites like to wait until no one, or almost no one, is around to make changes that require an outage.

You need to figure out what is right for your situation. However, you should try to avoid situations in which people outside the SA organization can make changes that may have an adverse impact on important systems.

Different people have different philosophies on performing sensitive updates. More senior SAs typically are more cautious than junior SAs, understanding the potential impact better and having been burned by lack of caution in the past. In a mature SA organization, everyone will have been made aware of a documented, consistent set of guidelines to follow. These guidelines will include acceptable times to make certain kinds of changes.

When trying to classify updates as routine, sensitive, or major, take into account that some changes may be considered to be routine updates at some sites and sensitive updates at other sites or even in different areas at the same site. For example, at an e-commerce company, attaching a new host to the corporate network may be considered a routine update, but attaching a new host to the customer-visible service network may be considered a sensitive update. Consider how various sorts of updates should be categorized in the various areas of your site, and institute a scheduling practice that reflects your decision.

It is useful to institute **change-freeze** times when only minor updates can be performed. Change freezes typically occur at the end of a quarter and the end of the fiscal year. Figure 17.1 is an example of one company's change-freeze announcement that is sent out to all SA staff and department heads. It includes a change-control form that is part of the change-management process. Some companies call this "network quiet time," as in Figure 17.1.

17.1.4 Process and Documentation

Process and documentation are important parts of change management. Following the processes and producing the documentation force SAs to prepare thoroughly for significant changes. The SAs have to fill out *change-control*, or *change-proposal*, forms that detail the changes they will make, the systems and services affected, the reasons for the change, the risks, the test procedure, the back-out plan, how long the change will take to implement, and how long the back-out plan takes to implement. Sometimes, SAs are required to list all the commands they will type. The level of detail required varies from site to site and usually is dependent on how critical the affected machine or service is. For very critical machines, the SA cannot type anything that is not listed on the change-control form that was approved. However, the process and documentation requirements for less critical machines should be less stringent, or

```
Subject: FYI - QUIET TIME IS COMING   09/25 - 10/06

Team
Just a reminder for you all that QUIET TIME will be here in three weeks.
It is scheduled to begin on 9/25 and go to 10/06.
Change control 96739 is below:

              CHANGE SUMMARY DISPLAY           CHANGE: 00096739
    Assignee Class/Queue... GNSC              Change Status/Type OR/INF
    Assignee Name........  _____ IPL/Service Disrpt N/N
    Requester Name........ FRED/ADDAMS         Risk/Chg Reason... 1/QT
    Enterer's Name........ FRED/ADDAMS         Proc Ctr/Cntl Ctr. NET/GNS
    Enterer's Phone....... (555)555-8765       Problem Fixed..... _____
    Enterer's Class/Queue.. GNSC               Business Unit..... ALL
    Plan Start Date/Time... 09/25/2000  00:01  Location Code..... GLOBAL
    Plan End Date/Time..... 10/06/2000  24:00  COI.............. ALL
    Date/Time Entered...... 04/10/2000  14:26  Approval Status... PENDING
    Date/Time Last Altered  06/22/2000  16:02  User Last Altered. NCCOFHA
    Date Closed.......... _____            Associated Doc.... N/A
    System.............. _____
    Component/Application.. FISCAL-PROCESS&NTWK-QUIET-TIME
    Description.......... 4Q00/1Q01 FISCAL EXTENDED AVAILABILITY
    System edited........ _____ Loc added.... _____

Fiscal processing, email, and network quiet time to support
quarterly book close/open activities.
Changes that may impact access to or data movement
between server/mainframe applications or email should be
rescheduled. Only emergency changes to prevent or
fix outages will be  reviewed for possible implementation.
All changes will require a change exception form be
submitted to the CMRB.
See URL for Quiet Time Guidelines and contact information:
   http://wwwin.foo.com/gnsc/quiet-time.html

   Customer Impact: None
   Test plan: None
   Contact and Phone/Pager Numbers:
      JOHN SMITH..........(555)555-1234
      JANE JONES..........(555)555-4321
      ALICE WALTER........(555)555-7890   800-555-5555 pin 123456

   Backout Plan: None
   *** BOTTOM OF DATA ***
```

Figure 17.1 Sample change-freeze, or network quiet time announcement

SAs will find that their hands are tied by change-management red tape and they are unable to work effectively.

If a site can readily identify one or two machines that are absolutely critical to the running of the business, those machines should be covered by stringent change-management processes. For example, the main database machines and credit card processing machines at an e-commerce site could fall into this category. At a drug-development company, machines involved in that process often are required by law to comply to very strict change-management controls. Machines in this category usually are not servers that provide such important services as email, printing, DNS, or authentication. Machines that provide those services should be covered by less stringent change-management policies to strike a balance between the benefits of change management and the benefits of SAs' being able to quickly respond to customers' needs. However, significant changes to these servers or services do need to follow good change-management process so that they happen smoothly, with few surprises.

Later chapters cover in detail the processes associated with various types of changes. In particular, Chapter 18 covers server upgrades, Chapter 19 covers service conversions, and Chapter 20 covers maintenance windows.

17.1.5 Technical Aspects

You need to have a documented procedure that everyone in the SA team follows for updating system configuration files. This procedure should be consistently used everywhere that configuration files are updated. It should be documented clearly in a step-by-step manner, including the procedure to follow if any of the steps fail, and given to all SAs as they join the team. The procedure should include creating revision histories, locking the configuration files so that only one person at a time can edit them, running automated checks on the format of or information in the files, and, if appropriate, notifying other systems or applications that an update has occurred. It is a fundamentally good practice that should be followed at all times by everyone. It is simple and surprisingly often can save the day.

17.1.5.1 Revision History and Locking

A revision history lets anyone with appropriate access review the changes that have been made to a file, step by step, and enables you to return quickly to a previous version of the file, which is very useful if the current version becomes corrupt. Typically, a revision history also will record who made the change and when, and it can add an optional comment along with the change. Revision-control software usually also provides a locking mechanism, which should be used to prevent two people from trying to modify the same configuration file at once.

Having each person's identity attached to his or her changes is useful. If a junior SA makes a mistake, the more senior person who discovers it can take the person aside and use the opportunity to do some mentoring on that area of the system.

Source code control systems that are used by software developers are the sorts of tools that you should look at for this functionality. Under UNIX, such tools are SubVersion, Revision Control System and Source Code Control System (Bolinger 1995), and Concurrent Versions System (Berliner 1990), which store the differences from version to version, along with identity and a comment, and also provide locking. SourceSafe is an example of such a system under Windows. Many commercial systems also are available and may already be in use by developers at a given site.

❖ **Maintaining Revision History in** UNIX   It's easy to get started maintaining revision history of a file in UNIX with Revision Control System (RCS). Start doing this the next time you edit any file and, before you know it, you'll have simple but efficient revision history on all your important configuration files.

Suppose that the file is `/etc/named.conf`. Create a directory named `/etc/RCS`. Start the revision history with the command `ci -l named.conf`. The revision history of the file will now be stored in `/etc/RCS/named.conf,v`. (Note the `,v` at the end of the file.) To edit the file, check it out with `co -l named.conf`, and then edit it with your favorite editor. When you are satisfied with your changes, check in the revision with `ci -u named.conf`. This three-step process is traditionally put into a shell script named `xed` or `vir`. It is always advisable to run `rcsdiff named.conf` before running `co`. That way, if someone has made changes but forgotten to use RCS, you will see the changes and can commit them to RCS before you proceed. To commit someone else's changes, use `rcs -l named.conf`, followed by the usual command to check in changes: `ci -u named.conf`. Taking the extra time to ensure that you don't clobber someone else's changes can save much heartache and debugging later.

> RCS has other useful commands: `rlog named.conf` will show you the history of the file's changes, and `rcsdiff -r1.1 -r1.2 named.conf` will show you the changes between revision 1.1 and 1.2. You can see what version 1.2 looked like explicitly with a command such as `co -p -r1.2 named.conf`.

A good reference, such as Bolinger (1995), will explain more complicated issues, such as backing out of changes. Create a simple text file to experiment with while reviewing the manual pages. You'll be an expert in no time.

Revision History Saves the Day

A midsize software company had a script that automated the process of account creation. One day, the disk that contained the account database filled up while the program was rewriting the database. Because it did almost no error checking, the script failed to notice. It proceeded to push out the new account database to all the authentication servers, even though it was missing most of the accounts. The SAs quickly realized what had happened and were able to immediately clear some space and go back to the old account database as it existed immediately before the script was run. If they had not had a revision history, they would have had to restore the file from backup tape, which would have taken much longer and meant that any password changes customers had made since the backup would have been lost. The automated program had identified itself in the optional comment field, and thus it was easy to track down the entity responsible for the truncation. The script was subsequently changed to do a lot more error checking.

17.1.5.2 Automated Checks

The final steps in updating a file or a set of files are to verify that each file is syntactically correct and then to ensure that the applications using these files start to use the new information. These steps should be performed by an automated program, which also should tell various servers that their configuration files have changed or push files to other locations, as necessary.

Sometimes, you may need to separate these two steps. If getting the applications to use the new configuration information will cause a small service outage, and if the update can wait until a time that will cause less, or no, disruption, the syntax should be checked immediately but the update process scheduled for a later time.

Some system configurations are difficult to check with an automated program and ideally should be generated by a program so that they are at least syntactically correct. Establish a practice of testing these components in some other way that gives you a high level of confidence that they are working correctly. For example, under UNIX, the system boot scripts are often modified by hand to change the set of services that are started at boot time or perhaps to configure the behavior of the network interfaces. It is important that these scripts be tested carefully, because an error may prevent the system from completing the reboot cycle. In most commercial UNIX systems, the start scripts are split into many small pieces, one for each service, that can be individually tested so that you can be reasonably confident that changes and additions are correct.

If the start scripts are not tested in advance, problems with them will not be found until the next reboot. Therefore, it is critical to make boot scripts completely reliable. Machines seem to reboot at the most inconvenient times. Systems crash late at night, when you are on vacation, and so on. If you find out only at the next reboot that a script you wrote has a typo, you are making this discovery at a very bad time. To make matters even worse, good systems stay up for months on end. It is extremely difficult to remember what changes have been made since the last reboot, particularly when it happened months ago. Even if the site has a policy of logging changes in a log book or a trouble-ticket system, it can be difficult to find the relevant change if months have gone by.

The Reboot Test

Before distributed computing, most sites—or sometimes entire colleges—had only one big computer that everyone accessed through terminals or modems. Tom's one big computer was a VAX 11/750 running Digital's VMS operating system. Now, before you young whippersnappers yawn at the antique 1980s technology and skip to the next section, there is a lesson here that is still valuable today, so keep reading. The script that executed on boot-up was rarely changed. The SAs had a rule that if you changed the start-up script at all, you had to reboot the VAX soon after.

They usually rebooted the machine once a month, as part of their stand-alone backup procedure. First, they would reboot the VAX to make sure that it could come up on its own. In theory, that step should be unnecessary. Then they would make changes to the system files that were needed. Another reboot would test their changes; any bugs found were fixed and also reboot tested. After that, the SAs would do the reboot that was required for the tape backup procedure. The benefit of this technique was that mistakes were discovered soon after they were made, when the change was still fresh in the SA's mind. With distributed computing, it is more likely that a reboot is not such a terrible thing. Machines also reboot more quickly now. However, it is even more important today to reboot a machine or to perform some kind of rigorous testing of changes to such critical code. In the old days, a typo would have meant that the VAX would be down until the morning, when the SAs arrived to fix it. In today's world, business comes to a halt when a computer is down, and such an outage would result in you, the SA, being awakened in the middle of the night or pulled out of vacation to fix the problem *right now*. An extra reboot is a strategic investment in your sleep!

If your customers have been notified that a certain host will not be available at a certain time, take the opportunity to give it an extra reboot after you think you are done.

17.2 The Icing

Once you have in place basic change management that describes a process for configuration updates, the communication methods that are used, and how to schedule a change, you can use some other change-management techniques to improve stability at your site. In particular, you can create automated front ends for common configuration updates that perform all the locking, revision history, checking, and updating for the SAs. You should also institute formal change-management meetings with cross-functional change councils to review change proposals.

17.2.1 Automated Front Ends

Automatically checking system files for format and syntax errors before bringing an update live brings greater stability to your systems. The next step along that path is to provide to those system files a front-end interface that asks the appropriate questions, checks the answers for errors, looks for omissions, and then updates the file correctly, using the information supplied. If everyone uses this front end, there is only one place to check for errors and to test for correctness.

17.2.2 Change-Management Meetings

Change-management meetings for reviewing, discussing, and scheduling proposed changes, if approved, are a valuable tool for increasing the stability of the systems. This formal process asks the SAs what they plan to do and when, how long it will take, what can go wrong, how they will test it, how to back out the change, and how long that will take. It forces the SAs to think about the implications of what they are doing, as well as to prepare for problems that might arise.

It also makes other people aware of changes that are being made so that they can recognize the potential source of problems. The people who approve, refuse, or reschedule proposed changes should be drawn from across the company, so that representatives from each area that might be affected can alert everyone as to how it will affect their groups and prepare their groups for the changes that will be made. The attendees of such a meeting are called **stakeholders**.

These meetings give the stakeholders an overall view of what is happening at the site. It provides an opportunity for senior SAs or managers to spot a change that will cause problems before it happens and prevent it from happening. It reduces entropy and leads to a more stable environment. Typically, a change-management meeting occurs once a week or once a month, as appropriate for the rate of change at the site.

Having all stakeholders sign off on each change not only improves stability of the system but also provides a cover-your-butt opportunity for the SA staff. We don't mean this to be cynical. If customer groups are complaining that things are out of control and outages happen at bad times, a good solution is to create a change-review board to increase their involvement and get their approval for changes.

Case Study: Daily Change-Management Meetings

At a popular e-commerce site that handles a large and ever-increasing volume of traffic, the service network is continually being updated to handle the increased demand. The site's unusual change-management process involves daily change-management meetings. Change proposals are submitted before the cutoff time each day. The SAs who have proposed changes, all the SA managers, and some representatives from the engineering and operations groups attend the meetings, where the change proposals are discussed, approved, postponed, or refused with an alternative approach suggested. Each change proposal includes a proposed date and time for making the change. If it is approved, the change should be made at the approved time; otherwise, it needs to be discussed in another change-management meeting.

This company's service is used primarily by the consumer market in the United States. Because the company is on the west coast of the United States, its peak usage times are after 2 PM on Monday to Friday—that is, after 5 PM on the east coast of the United States—and all day during the weekend. The time specified in a change proposal is typically the following morning, before peak time. Another thing decided at the change-management meeting is whether the change should go ahead regardless of "the weather" or wait until there is "good weather": the operating status of the service. In other words, some changes are approved on the condition that the service is operating normally at the time the SA or engineer wants to make the change. Other changes are considered so critical that they are made regardless of how well or badly the service is functioning.

This approach is unusual for a couple of reasons. It is certainly a step better than having no change-management, because there is at least a minimal review process, a defined off-peak time in which changes are performed, and a process for postponing some tasks to avoid possibly introducing extra problems when the system is unstable. However, the frequency of the meetings and the changes to the service network mean that it is difficult to look at the big picture of what is going on with the service network, that entropy and lots of small instabilities that may interact with each other are constantly introduced, and that the SAs and the engineers are not encouraged to plan ahead. Changes may be made quickly, without being properly thought out. It is also unusual that changes are permitted to happen while the service network that is the company's revenue stream is unstable. Changes at such a time can make debugging existing problems much more difficult, particularly if the instabilities take a few days to debug. The formal process of checking with the operations group before making a change and giving them the ability to prevent at least some changes from happening is valuable, however.

Although the site was often successful in handling a large number of transactions, for a while it was known for having stability problems and large, costly outages, the source of which was hard to trace because of the rapidly changing nature of the network. It was not possible to draw a line in time and say "the problems started after this set of changes, which were approved in that change-management meeting." That would have enabled them to narrow their search and perhaps find the problem more quickly.

A mature change-management process can also take on overtones of project management, with a proposed change being carefully considered for its impact on not only other systems but also other deadlines the group must meet. If making the change will cause other, more important deadlines to slip, it will be refused.

Case Study: IBM's Nagano Olympics

IBM built and operated the computer infrastructure to support the 1996 Summer Olympics in Atlanta and the 1998 Winter Olympics in Nagano. In the 1996 Atlanta Games, IBM did not have a change-management review process, and many changes were made by programmers who were unaware of the impact their "small" changes would have on the rest of the system. Some systems were completed "just in time," with no time for testing. Some were still being developed after the Games had started. There were many problems, all heavily reported by the press, much to IBM's embarrassment. The outages prevented getting out information about the athletic events and left the press little to write about except the fact that IBM's computer system wasn't working. It was a public relations nightmare for IBM.

A root-cause analysis was performed to make sure that these problems were not repeated at the 1998 Winter Olympics. It was determined that better change management was required. IBM implemented change-management boards that had up to ten representatives from various areas of the project to review change proposals. Through this mechanism, IBM successfully managed to prevent several similar "small" changes from occurring, and all the hardware and software was completed and fully tested before the events, with many problems discovered and fixed in advance. The final result was that the information system for the 1998 Winter Olympics ran smoothly when the events started (Guth and Radosevich 1998).

Case Study: Change Management Makes Large-Scale Events Succeed

When it ran the first NetAid event in 1999, Cisco had roughly 4 weeks to build and run a distributed network that had to handle 125,000 simultaneous video streams across 50 ISPs. Cisco had to develop mechanisms that scaled across the planet. In the end, Cisco had nearly 1,000 pieces of hardware to manage and occasionally change. The company did this with a full-time staff of about five people and many volunteers.

Nobody had ever scaled to the size Cisco was engineering toward. Thus, the staff knew operational challenges would require changing the router and server configurations. With lots of people and a volatile environment, it was important for the staff to maintain configuration control, particularly because the reasoning behind certain routing configurations was not intuitively obvious—for example, why did Paul put in that particular route filter? In addition, the staff used an intrusion-detection system to guard its e-commerce site. Any time such a system is configured, it must be tailored to the environment in which it will run, a process that usually takes about 4 weeks. It was important to keep track of the changes made so that they knew the reasons for those filters. The change-management process provided a documentation trail that enabled everyone working on the system to understand what had been done before, why it had been done, and how their changes fit in with the others' work. Without this documentation, it would have been impossible to get the system working correctly in time. Such processes all contributed to the project's success.

17.2.3 Streamline the Process

Ultimately, when you think you have everything in place, you should look at your process to see whether you can streamline it. Are any questions on your change-proposal form not used? Could any paper-based parts of the process be done more efficiently? If the forms are online, is there a way for each person to save defaults for some of the fields, such as name and contact information? What problems do the people who use the system have with the current setup?

17.3 Conclusion

Change management is a valuable tool that mature sites use to increase the reliability of the site, both through restricting when certain changes can happen and by having a process for reviewing changes in advance to catch any adverse effects the SA may have missed or interactions that the SA might not have known about. Change management also helps with debugging problems, because changes are tracked and can be reviewed when a problem arises.

The frequency with which you have change-management meetings depends on their scope and how rapidly the environment that they cover changes. Instituting a mechanism through which SAs check that the site is operating normally before they make their changes reduces the risk that a change made during debugging of an existing problem complicates the debugging process or makes the site even less stable.

Exercises

1. Describe the change-management process in your organization.
2. How would you define the off-peak times for your site?
3. Look at the sorts of tasks you perform in your job, and categorize them as routine, sensitive, or major updates.
4. What kind of communication process would work best for your company? Would you have both a "push" and a "pull" mechanism? Why? What would you use each of them for?
5. How would you organize change-management meetings in your company? Who do you think should attend? How often would you have them?
6. To what extent would change management affect the way that you do your job?

7. Consider how various sorts of updates should be categorized in the various areas of your site, and institute a scheduling practice that reflects your decision.

8. What problems do the people who use the system have with the current setup?

9. In reference to the case study in Section 17.1.3, about making big changes on Friday or before a vacation, pick a side, and defend your decision.

Chapter 18

Server Upgrades

This chapter has a very specific focus: upgrading the operating system of a single host. This task is deceptively simple, requiring a lot of preparation beforehand and a lot of testing afterward. The upgrade itself can be performed in many ways. The more critical the host is, the more important it is to do the upgrade correctly. This technique is a building block. Once mastered, you can move on to larger upgrade projects, such as those described in Chapter 20.

A single tool is required to do this task successfully, no matter what OS is involved. This tool is a piece of paper that will be used to maintain a checklist. There is no excuse for not using this tool. Our publisher, Addison-Wesley, has graciously agreed to include a blank piece of paper in the back of this book for your convenience.[1]

Some people choose to simulate a piece of paper by using a web page, a wiki, or a spreadsheet. These high-tech solutions have many benefits, which are described later. However, the fundamental issue is the same: There is no excuse for upgrading a server without using a checklist to guide you. Grab a pencil. Let's begin.

18.1 The Basics

The fundamental goal of any OS upgrade is that, at minimum, all the services provided *before* the upgrade will be working *after* the upgrade. While an upgrade may be performed to *add* functionality or reliability, it should not reduce these attributes. With this in mind, the process is as follows.

---

1. If you desire additional blank paper, we highly recommend purchasing additional copies of this book.

1. Develop a service checklist:
   a. What services are provided by the server?
   b. Who are the customers of each service?
   c. What software package(s) provide which service?
2. Verify that each software package will work with the new OS, or plan a software upgrade path.
3. For each service, develop a test to verify that it is working.
4. Write a back-out plan, with specific triggers.
5. Select a maintenance window.
6. Announce the upgrade as appropriate.
7. Execute the tests developed earlier to make sure that they are still valid.
8. Lock out users.
9. Do the upgrade with someone watching/helping (mentoring).
10. Repeat all the tests developed earlier. Follow the usual debugging process.
11. If tests fail, or other events occur that trigger the back-out plan, execute the back-out plan.
12. Let users back in.
13. Communicate completion/back-out to the customers.
14. Analyze what went right and what didn't; modify the checklist to reflect the experience.

And you thought it was all about using an install disc, didn't you? Let's look a little more closely at each step.

18.1.1 Step 1: Develop a Service Checklist

The **service checklist** is a tool that you use to drive the entire process. The list should record *what* services are provided by the host, *who* the customers of each service are, and *which* software package provides each service.

Spreadsheets are an excellent way to maintain such information. The biggest benefit of maintaining this information in electronic form is that it can be easily shared both within the team and with customers. Making the file accessible via the web is better than mailing it to individuals, because the web version can be rapidly updated. People will always see the latest updates.[2] However, the web is a pull mechanism. People won't seek it out on their own. You can include the URL in every email about the project, but that will not guarantee that it gets read. It's a good idea to announce any significant updates.

Double-check your plans by having a review meeting with key representatives of the affected community. Walk them through the plan, step by step, asking for people to verify your assumptions. It is most effective to begin the process with a meeting and then use email for updates, possibly having another face-to-face meeting only at key points in the process.

Customer Dependency Check

An SA once had a meeting of ten experienced SAs, all of whom looked at a plan and agreed right away that it looked fine to them. When the SA started stepping through it, asking such specific questions as, "What's going to happen when we turn this off?" they started saying, "Oops, no, if you do that, the billing system won't work any more. I guess we need to add a step where we move the billing information." The result was a completely different plan with three times as many steps. If they hadn't had an in-person meeting to carefully go through each step specifically, the original plan would have created a major disaster.

Including the customers as part of the decision and planning processes gives them a feeling of participation and control. Customers are invested in the outcome and become part of the team, which generally leads to a more positive experience for them and a better relationship between the SA and business units. Sharing dependency and status information with customers on the web and via email helps to maintain the working relationship.

A machine may be dedicated to providing a single service, or it may provide many services. Either way, many software packages may be involved in providing the complete service.

❖ **What's on a Machine?**   Sometimes, you know what a machine is being used for, and it is easy to create the initial upgrade checklist. However, over time, additional services, features, and software are added to a machine (Evard 1997). We can cross-check ourselves by analyzing

---

2. Be sure that there is a prominent version number and date on the checklist, so that anyone can easily see if they have a current version.

the host itself. You can review the software that is installed on UNIX by looking in `/opt`, `/usr/local` and various places that are common on such systems. Microsoft OSs usually put programs in a directory named `Program Files`, though some sites adopt local conventions, such as installing them in `C:\apps`. You can look at which processes are running on the system. UNIX and NT systems will list all the TCP/IP and UDP/IP ports being listened to with the command `netstat -an`. UNIX has various boot-time scripts that can be analyzed. NT has the Services console. UNIX has `crontab` files to browse through. Every OS has at least one way to list all the software packages that have been installed. Some of examples are `pkginfo` (Solaris and SVR4), `swlist` (HP-UX 10 and up), and 'rpm-qa'(Linux).

Usually, each service is directly related to a single software package. Sometimes a service is related to multiple packages, such as a calendar server that relies on an LDAP server. Document all of these interdependencies in the checklist.

It is also important to determine the key customers relying on various services. These customers may be directly relying on a service, using the service itself, or they may indirectly rely on the service, interacting with services that rely on another service for data or input. If they are people, they should be included in the process or at least notified that the process is happening. If other machines are dependent on the services, users of those machines should be included.

Often, you will find a service with no direct or indirect customers, and the service can be eliminated. These are always happy moments, but be careful: You might find the dependency after the service no longer exists. Consider having the service in a ready-to-run but dormant state so that it is easy to bring up, if necessary. Make sure that you document why the service is there but not running, so that it gets cleaned up next time through, if it has not been reenabled by then. The best place for this documentation is in one of the configuration files that will be edited to reenable the service.

18.1.2 Step 2: Verify Software Compatibility

The next step is to verify that each software package will work with the new OS and to plan an upgrade path for those that don't. Using the list developed earlier, contact the vendor and find out whether the software release in use will work after the upgrade. Vendors often list such information on their web sites.

You may wish to test the reliability of the information yourself or find another customer who has already performed the upgrade. Vendors' ideas about what it means for a version to work often don't include the features your site needs or the exact configuration you're going to use. Doing the tests yourself can be expensive but possibly cheaper than a failed upgrade, and reduces the risk of failure. The point of this is risk management. If only one system is being upgraded and if the application is not critical, personally testing it might be a waste of time. If the upgrade is going to be repeated thousands of times, in an automated fashion and in a way that failure would be highly visible, testing is a requirement.

If the software release being used will work on the new OS release, document where you found this information for future reference. If the software isn't supported on the new OS, you have several options.

- *Upgrade to a release that is supported on both OSs.* If you are lucky, the software can be upgraded to a release that works on both the current system and the future system. If so, schedule an upgrade to that release before the OS upgrade. The tests developed in step 3 can be useful here.

- *An upgrade is available but works only on the new OS.* In this case, you must schedule the software upgrade after the OS upgrade is complete. Depending on the customer requirements, this upgrade may be required as part of the OS upgrade, or a service gap may be negotiated if the customers do not require uninterrupted access. For example, if a host is a busy web server, the customers may request that the new web server software be installed immediately because it is a major function of the host. However, if a little-used compiler requires an upgrade, the customers may simply request that it be upgraded in the next week or before a certain development cycle is complete. This is especially true if some other host can be used for compilation in the meantime.

- *The product is no longer supported.* Sometimes, it is only when we are upgrading an OS that we learn that a product is no longer being supported by the vendor. This may block the upgrade, or customers may be willing to change vendors or go without this product.

18.1.3 Step 3: Verification Tests

As each service is identified, a test should be developed that will be used to verify that the service is working properly after the upgrade. The best scenario is to have all the tests recorded as scripts that can be run unattended.

A master script can be written that outputs an OK or a FAIL message for each test. Tests can then be run individually as specific problems are debugged. For more complicated services, customers may write the tests or at least review them or offer to be on call to execute their own set of manual tests. Some software packages have an installation test suite that can be run, for verification. Sometimes these test suites are not commonly available to customers, but may be acquired through a vendor representative.

Software Verification Procedures

All software packages should have such verification procedures, but they rarely do. Sometimes, it is best to write your own. The tests can be simple, such as testing a compiler by compiling a Hello, World program. One test is infinitely better than no testing at all.

Sometimes, a verification procedure is provided, but doesn't actually work. One supercomputer vendor was notorious for having bad verify databases, especially in the beta OS releases.

The software world uses the term **regression testing** to describe a particular way of doing verification. You capture the output of the old system, make a change, and then capture the output of the new system. The output should match exactly. If the new output is expected to be slightly different, you might edit the baseline output by hand to reflect expected changes, or use a *fuzzy match* algorithm. Simple tools, can be used to compare the outputs. For example, Unix diff is an extremely useful program that compares two text files and points out the differences between them.[3] The diff tool has a limited fuzzy-match capability; the -w option makes all whitespace the same. More sophisticated regression-testing software can be programmed to ignore certain specific changes, usually based on a system of regular expressions. However, such complexity is not required. You can manually change the old output—Make a backup first!—to reflect the differences that are expected in the new output. For example, you might change the version numbers in the output to match the new software. Excellent examples of regression testing are included in Kernighan and Pike's *The Practice of Programming* (1999), as well as the installation procedure for perl. (Look how make tests is implemented.)

Sometimes, the tests can be as simple as a Hello, world! program that is compiled and run to verify that a compiler works. It may be a particular

---

3. Although diff first appeared in Unix, there are ports to nearly every OS in existence.

sequence of commands or mouse clicks to see whether an expected result is displayed. However, be careful to make sure that the tests are not superficial.

Hello, World!

Tom was once responsible for maintaining a large range of compilers for many operating systems. He maintained a library of simple programs; most only printed `Hello, world!` and then exited. He could always verify that a new compiler installation was at least fundamentally correct if the appropriate program(s) compiled and ran. When new languages were added to the mix, he would often recruit the programmers to write the test program. The programmers enjoyed being asked to help out!

You must subject the tests to the same level of scrutiny as any other service. When the tests are put into use, you don't want there to be any doubt whether a test failed because of the upgrade or if the test itself was flawed.

It is tempting to perform these tests manually. However, remember that each test will be done a minimum of three times, and more if there are problems. There will be benefits to automating the tests. If they are general enough, they can be reused during future upgrades. Ultimately, they can be reused on a regular basis simply to debug problems, or as monitoring tools to notice outages before your customers do.

Scripted tests work fine for programs that produce predictable text output, but they're much more difficult for graphical programs, for network services like NFS, or for such physical issues as printing. For NFS, you can try to access a file rather than test the protocol itself. Testing of network services that have simple text-based protocols, such as email (SMTP, POP, IMAP) or web HTTP services, can be automated with simple scripts using a tool such as `netcat` to send and receive protocol text on the appropriate network port.

For other programs and services, you can find specialized test systems, but those are usually extremely expensive. In these cases, you will simply end up testing by hand, documenting a few key features to test or a sequence of operations to perform. Everyone is in this situation at one time or another, and we should all complain to vendors until they instrument their products so that such testing can be automated.

Although it is preferable to automate all tests, it is not always possible. Some tests are too difficult to automate or require physical observation. Even if you have automated all tests, if you get a hunch that an additional manual test might be useful, go for it. Sometimes, the human eyeball catches things that the best automation can't.

> ❖ **Test-Driven Development (TDD)**   TDD is a relatively new trend in the industry. Previously, developers wrote code and then wrote tests to verify the code. (Well, not really; rarely did anyone have time to write the tests.) TDD is the reverse. The tests are written first and then the code. This ensures that the tests get written for all new code. Since the tests are executed in an automated fashion, you build up a body of tests that stay with the project. As code evolves, there is less risk that a change will break functionality without being noticed. Developers are free to rewrite, or *refactor*, big or small parts of the code, knowing that if they break something, it will be noticed right away. As a result, software has fewer bugs.
>
> Tests are better than comments in code (documentation) because comments often become out of date without anyone noticing. Tests that cover all the edge cases are more thorough than documentation could ever be. Tests do not get out of date, because they can be triggered as part of the build process to alert developers of bugs when they are introduced into the code.
>
> We would like to see the field of system administration learn from TDD and adopt these practices.

Keeping Tests Around for Later

A large business their wanted to test 400 UNIX servers just after midnight of Y2K to ensure that the core functionality of the operating system and associated infrastructure were working correctly. A series of noninvasive tests was created, each with a PASS/FAIL response: Is the box up, can we log in, can it see the NIS servers, is the time correct, can it resolve DNS, can it mount from the NFS servers and read a file, is the auto-mounter working, and so on. Using a central administration point, the tests could be fired off on multiple boxes at a time and the results collected centrally. All 400 boxes were tested within 20 minutes, and the team was able to report their PASS to the Y2K tracking-management team well in advance of other, smaller, units. So popular did the tests become with the SA team that they became part of the daily monitoring of the environment.

The tests found other uses. An obscure bug in the Solaris 2.5.1 and 2.6 automounters could be triggered after a major network outage but only on a few random machines. By running this test suite, the affected machines were quickly identified after any outage.

18.1.4 Step 4: Write a Back-Out Plan

If something goes wrong during the upgrade, how will you revert to the former state? How will you "undo"? How long will that take? Obviously, if something small goes wrong, the usual debugging process will try to fix it. However, you can use up the entire maintenance window—time allocated for the outage—trying just one more thing to make an upgrade work. It is therefore important to have a particular time at which the back-out plan will be activated. Take the agreed on end time and subtract the back-out time, as well as the time it would take to test that the back-out is complete. When you reach that time, you must either declare success or begin your back-out plan. It is useful to have the clock watcher be someone outside the group directly performing the upgrade, such as a manager. The back-out plan might also be triggered by one or more key tests failing, or by unexpected behavior related to the upgrade.

Small-to medium-size systems can be backed up completely before an upgrade begins. It can be even easier to clone the disks and perform the upgrade on the clones. If there are serious problems, the original disks can be reinstalled. Larger systems are more difficult to replicate. Replicating the system disks and doing incremental backups of the data disks may be sufficient in this case.

❖ **Upgrade the Clone** Q: If you are going to clone a hard disk before the server is upgraded, should you perform the upgrade on the clone or on the original?

A: Upgrade the clone. If the upgrade fails you don't want to discover that the clone wasn't properly made. You've just destroyed the original. We've seen this happen many times.

Cloning a disk is easy to get wrong. Sometimes, the data was copied but the boot block has a problem and the disk was not bootable; sometimes, the data wasn't copied completely; sometimes, the data wasn't copied at all.

To avoid this situation, boot up on the clone. Make sure that the clone works. Then perform the upgrade on the clone.

18.1.5 Step 5: Select a Maintenance Window

The next step is a test of your technical and nontechnical skills. You must come to agreement with your customers on a maintenance window, that is, when the upgrade will happen. To do that, you must know how long the process will take and have a plan if the upgrade fails. That is more of a technical issue.

- *When?* Your SLA should include provisions for when maintenance can be done. Customers usually have a good idea of when they can withstand an outage. Most business systems are not needed at night or on the weekend. However, SAs might not want to work those hours, and the vendor support might not be available at certain times. A balance must be found. Sites that are required to be up 24/7 have a maintenance plan engineered into the entire operation, perhaps including fall-back systems.

- *How long?* The length of the maintenance window equals the time the upgrade should take, plus the time testing should take, plus the time it will take to fix problems, plus the time it takes to execute the back-out plan, plus the time it takes to ensure that the back-out worked. Initially, it is best to double or triple your estimates to adjust for hubris. As time goes on, your estimates will become more accurate.

    Whatever length of time you have calculated, announce the window to be much longer. Sometimes, you may get started late. Sometimes, things take longer than you expect for technical reasons (hardware, software, or unrelated or unexpected events) or nontechnical reasons (weather or car problems). The flip side to calling a longer time window is that if you complete the upgrade and testing early, you should always notify the customers.

- *What time is the back-out plan initiated?* It is a good idea to clearly document the exact time that the back-out plan will be initiated for reasons described in step 4.

❖ **Scotty Always Exaggerated**   In the *Star Trek: The Next Generation* episode "Relics," James Doohan made a cameo appearance as Scotty from the original series. Among Scotty's interesting revelations was that he always exaggerated when giving estimates to Captain James T. Kirk. Thus, he always looked like a miracle worker when problems were solved more quickly than expected. Now we know why the warp drive was always working sooner than predicted and the environmental systems lasted longer than were indicated. Follow Scotty's advice! Exaggerate your estimates! But also follow Scotty's practice of letting people know as soon as the work is tested and complete.

Case Study: The Monday Night Carte Blanche

When Tom worked at a division of Mentor Graphics, the SA staff had the luxury of a weekly maintenance window. Monday night was SA Carte Blanche Night. Users were expected to be logged out at 6 PM, and the SA staff could use that evening to perform any kind of major upgrades that would require bringing down services. Every Monday by 4 PM, the customers were informed of what changes would be happening and when the systems should be usable again. Customers eventually developed a habit of planning non-work-related activities on Monday nights. Rumor has it that some spent the time with their family.

   Although it required a big political investment to get the practice approved through management, it was an important factor in creating high reliability in the division's network. There was rarely a reason to put off timely system upgrades. Problems during the week could be taken care of with quick fixes, but long-term fixes were done efficiently on Monday night. Unlike some environments in which the long-term fixes were never implemented, those were always put in relatively soon.

   When there wasn't much to be done, one supervisor believed it was important to reboot some critical servers at 6 PM to "encourage" users to go home for the night. He believed that this helped the users maintain their habit of not planning anything critical for Monday night. Of course, the SAs were flexible. When the customers were up against a critical deadline and would be working around the clock, the SAs would cancel the Monday night maintenance or collaborate with the customers to determine which outages could happen without interfering with their work.

18.1.6 Step 6: Announce the Upgrade as Appropriate

Now announce the upgrade to the customers. Use the same format for all announcements so that customers get used to them. Depending on the culture of your environment, the message may best be distributed by email, voicemail, desk-to-desk paper memo, newsgroup posting, web page, note on door, or smoke signals. No matter what format, the message should be brief and to the point. Many people read only the Subject line, so make it a good one, as shown in Figure 18.1.

   It is better to have a blank template that is filled out each time than to edit previous announcements to include new information. This prevents the form from mutating over time. It also prevents the common problem of forgetting to change some parts. For example, when creating Figure 18.1, we initially used a real announcement that referred to a router reboot. We changed it to be about servers instead but forgot to change the Subject: line. The example went four rounds of proofreading before anyone noticed this. This wouldn't have happened if we had started with a blank template instead.

```
To: all-users
Subject: SERVER REBOOT: 6 PM TODAY
From: System Administration Group <help@example.com>
Reply-To: tom@example.com
Date: Thu, 16 Jun 2001 10:32:13 -0500


WHO IS AFFECTED:

        All hosts on DEVELOPER-NET, TOWNVILLE-NET, and BROCCOLI-NET.


WHAT WILL HAPPEN:

        All servers will be rebooted.


WHEN?

        Today between 6-8 PM (should take 1 hour)


WHY?

            We are in the process of rolling out new kernel tuning
            parameters to all servers. This requires a reboot. The
            risk is minimal. For more information please visit:
                    http://portal.example.com/sa/news0005


I OBJECT!

            Send mail to "help" and we will try to reschedule. Please
            name the server you want us to keep up today.
```

Figure 18.1 Sample upgrade message

18.1.7 Step 7: Execute the Tests

Right before the upgrade begins, perform the tests. This last-minute check ensures you that you won't be chasing problems after the upgrade that existed before the upgrade. Imagine the horror of executing the back-out plan, only to discover that the failing test is still failing.

18.1.8 Step 8: Lock out Customers

It is generally better to let customers log out gracefully than to let them be kicked out by a reboot or disconnection of service. Different services have different ways to do this. Use the facilities available in the OS to prevent new logins from occurring during the maintenance window. Many customers use an attempt to log in or to access a resource as their own test of an upgrade. If the attempt succeeds, the customer believes that the system is available for normal use, even if no announcement has been made. Thus it is important to lock out customers during a maintenance window.

18.1.9 Step 9: Do the Upgrade with Someone Watching

This is where most SA books begin. Aren't you glad you bought this book instead?

Now, the moment you've all been waiting for: Perform the upgrade as your local procedures dictate. Insert the DVD, reboot, whatever.

System upgrades are too critical to do alone. First of all, we all make mistakes, and a second set of eyes is always useful. Upgrades aren't done every day, so everyone is always a little out of practice. Second, a unique kind of mentoring goes on when two people do a system upgrade together. System upgrades often involve extremes of our technical knowledge. We use commands, knowledge, and possibly parts of our brains that aren't used at other times. You can learn a lot by watching and understanding the techniques that someone else uses at these times. The increasingly popular practice of co-development or so-called peer programming has developers working in pairs and taking turns being the one typing. This is another development practice that SAs can benefit from using.

If the upgrade isn't going well, it is rarely too early to escalate to a colleague or senior member of your team. A second set of eyes often does wonders, and no one should feel ashamed about asking for help.

18.1.10 Step 10: Test Your Work

Now repeat all the tests developed earlier. Follow the usual debugging process if they fail. The tests can be repeated time and time again as the problem is debugged. It is natural to run a failing test over again each time a fix is attempted. However, since many server processes are interrelated, be sure to run the full suite before declaring the upgrade a success. The fix for the test that failed may have broken a previously successful test!

Customers should be involved here. As with the helpdesk model in Chapter 14, the job isn't done until customers have verified that everything is complete. This may mean having the customer called at a prearranged time, or the customer may agree to report back the next day, after the maintenance window has elapsed. In that case, getting the automated tests right is even more critical.

18.1.11 Step 11: If All Else Fails, Rely on the Back-Out Plan

If the clock watcher announces that it is time to begin the back-out plan, you have to begin the back-out plan. This may happen if the upgrade is taking longer than expected or if it is complete but the tests continue to fail. The decision is driven entirely by the clock—it is not about you or the team. Its can be disappointing and frustrating to back out of a complex upgrade but maintaining the integrity of the server is the priority.

Reverting the system back to its previous state should not be the only component of the back-out plan. Customers might agree that if only certain tests fail, they may be able to survive without that service for a day or two while it is repaired. Decide in advance the action plan for each potential failure.

After the back-out plan is executed, the services should be tested again. At this point it is important to record in your checklist the results of your changes. This is useful in reporting status back to management, record keeping for improving the process next time, or recalling what happened during a postmortem. Record specifics such as "implemented according to plan," "implemented but exceeded change window," "partial implementation; more work to be done," "failed; change backed out," "failed; service unusable; end of world predicted." If possible, capture the output of the test suite and archive it along with the status information. This will help immensely in trying to remember what happened next week, month, or year.

18.1.12 Step 12: Restore Access to Customers

Now it is safe to let customers start using the system again. Different services have different ways to permit this. However, it is often difficult to do testing without letting all users in.

There are some ways to do this, however. For example, when upgrading an email server, you can configure other email servers to not relay email to the server being upgraded. While those servers are holding email, you can manually test the upgraded server and then enable the surrounding servers one at a time, keeping a mindful eye on the newly upgraded server.

18.1.13 Step 13: Communicate Completion/Back-Out

At this point, the customers are notified that the upgrade is complete or, if the back-out plan was initiated, what was accomplished, what didn't get accomplished, and the fact that the systems are usable again. This has three goals. First, it tells people that the services they have been denied access to are now usable. Second, it reminds the customers what has changed. Finally, if they find problems that were not discovered during your own testing, it lets them know how to report problems they have found. If the back-out plan was initiated, customers should be informed that the system should be operating as it had before the upgrade attempt.

Just as there are many ways to announce the maintenance window, there are many ways to communicate the completion. There is a catch-22 here. Customers cannot read an email announcement if the email service is affected by the outage. However, if you keep to your maintenance window, then email, for example, will be working and customers can read the email announcement. If customers hear nothing, they will assume that at the end of the announced maintenance window, everything is complete.

Announcements should be short. Simply list which systems or service, are functioning again, and provide a URL that people can refer to for more information and a phone number to call if a failed return to service might prevent people from being able to send email. One or two sentences should be fine.

The easiest way to keep the message short is to forward the original email that said that services were going down, and add a sentence to the top, saying that services are re-enabled and how to report problems. This gives people the context for what is being announced in a very efficient way.

Big Red Signs

Customers tend to ignore messages from SAs. Josh Simon reports that at one client site, he tried leaving notes—black text on bright red paper taped to the monitors—saying "DO NOT LOG IN—CONTACT YOUR SYSTEM ADMINISTRATOR AT [phone number] FIRST!" in huge type. More than 75 percent of the customers ripped the paper off and proceeded to log in rather than call the phone number. The lesson to be learned here is that it is often better to actually disable a service than to ask customers not to use it.

18.2 The Icing

Once you have mastered the basics of upgrading a server, what can you do to expand on the process?

18.2.1 Add and Remove Services at the Same Time

During an upgrade, you must sometimes add or remove services simulta-neously. This complicates matters because more than one change is being made at a time. Debugging a system with two changes is much more difficult because it affects the tests that are being executed. Adding services has all the same problems as bringing up a new service on a new host, but you are now in a new and possibly unstable environment and cannot prepare by creating appropriate tests. However, if the new service is also available on a different host, tests can be developed and run against that host.

Removing a service can be both easy and difficult at the same time. It can be easy for the same reason that it is easier to tear down a building than to build one. However, you must make sure that all the residents are out of the building first. Sometimes, we set up a network sniffer to watch for packets, which indicates that someone is trying to receive that service from the host. That information can be useful to find stragglers.

We prefer to disable a service in a way that makes it easy to reenable quickly if forgotten dependencies are discovered later. For example, the service can be halted without removing the software. It is usually safe to assume that if no forgotten dependencies are discovered in the next month or year, it is safe to remove the software. Some services may be used only once a quarter or once a year, especially certain financial reports. Don't forget to come back to clean up! Create a ticket in your helpdesk system, send yourself email, or create an `at` job that emails you a reminder sometime in the future. If multiple SA groups or privileged customers have access to the box, it can be a good idea to add a comment to the configuration file, or rename it to include 'OFF' or 'DISABLED'. Otherwise, another SA might assume the service is supposed to be up and turn it back on.

18.2.2 Fresh Installs

Sometimes, it is much better to do a fresh install than an upgrade. Doing upgrade after upgrade can lead to a system with a lot of damage. It can result in files left over from old patches, fragmented file systems, and a lot of "history" from years of entropy.

Earlier, we mentioned the luxury of cloning the appropriate disks and doing the upgrade on the clone. An even more luxurious method is to perform the upgrade as a fresh install on a different system because it doesn't require an outage of the old system. You can do the fresh install on a temporary machine at a leisurely pace, make sure that all services are working, and then move the disks into the upgrade machine and adjust network configuration settings as appropriate. Note that the machine on which the rebuild takes place must be almost identical to the machine that is to be upgraded, to ensure that the new OS disks have all the appropriate hardware support and configurations.

18.2.3 Reuse of Tests

If the tests are properly scripted, they can be integrated into a real-time monitoring system. In fact, if your monitoring system is already doing all the right tests, you shouldn't need anything else during your upgrade. (See Chapter 22 for more discussion about service monitoring.)

It is rare that all tests can be automated and added to the monitoring system. For example, load testing—determining how the system performs under simulated amounts of work—often cannot be done on a live system. However, being able to run these tests during otherwise low-usage hours or on demand when debugging a problem can make it easy to track down problems.

18.2.4 Logging System Changes

Building the service checklist is much easier if you've kept a log of what's been added to the machine as it was added. For example, on a UNIX system, simply keep a record of changes in a file called /var/adm/CHANGES. The easier it is to edit the file, the more likely people are to update it, so consider creating a shell alias or short script that simply brings up that file in a text editor.

Of course, if the machine goes down, the change log may be inaccessible. Keeping the change log on a wiki or shared file server solves that problem, but may lead to confusion if someone tries to start a new change log on the host. Set a policy on where the change log will be kept and follow it.

18.2.5 A Dress Rehearsal

Take a lesson from the theater world: Practice makes perfect. Why not perform a dress rehearsal on a different machine before you perform the upgrade? Doing so might reveal unexpected roadblocks, as well as give you an indication of how long the process will take. A dress rehearsal requires a lot of resources. However, if you are about to perform the first upgrade of many, this can be a valuable tool to estimate the time the upgrades will require. An absolutely complete dress rehearsal results in a new machine that can simply replace the old machine. If you have those resources, why not do just that?

The theater also has what's referred to as the *tech rehearsal*, a rehearsal for the lighting and sound people more than for the actors. The actors run through their lines with the right blocking as the lighting and sound directions are put through their paces. The SA equivalent is to have all the involved parties walk through the tasks.

We also borrow from theater the fine art of pantomime. Sometimes, a major system change involves a lot of physical cables to be changed. Why not walk though all the steps, looking for such problem areas as cable lengths, crossover/straight-through mismatches, male/female connector mismatches, incorrect connectors, and conflicting plans? Pantomime the change exactly how it will be done. It can be helpful to have someone else with you and explain the tasks as you act them out. Verify to the other person that each connector is correct, and so on. It may seem silly and embarrassing at first, but the problems you prevent will be worth it.

18.2.6 Installation of Old and New Versions on the Same Machine

Sometimes, one is simply upgrading a single service on a machine, not the entire OS. In that situation, it is helpful if the vendor permits the old versions of the software to remain on the machine in a dormant state while the new software is installed and certified.

The web server Apache on UNIX is one such product. We usually install it in `/opt/apache-x.y.z`, where `x.y.z` is the version number, but place a symbolic link from `/opt/apache` to the release we want to be using. All configurations and scripts refer to `/opt/apache` exclusively. When the new version is loaded, the `/opt/apache` link is changed to point to the new version. If we find problems with the new release, we revert the symbolic link and restart the daemon. It is a very simple back-out plan. (Using symbolic links in a software depot is discussed in Section 28.1.6).

In some situations, the old and new software can run simultaneously. If a lot of debugging is required, we can run the new version of Apache on a different port while retaining the old version.

18.2.7 Minimal Changes from the Base

Upgrades become easier when there is little work to do. With a little planning, all add-on packages for UNIX can be loaded in a separate partition, thus leaving the system partitions as generic as possible. Such additions to the system can be documented in a CHANGELOG file. Most changes will be in /etc, which is small enough to be copied before any upgrades begin and used as a reference. That is preferable to the laborious process of restoring files from tape.

In a dataless UNIX environment—all machines have an OS local but otherwise get all data from a server—usually only /var needs to be preserved between upgrades and then only the crontabs and at jobs, the mail spool, and, for systems such as Solaris, the calendar manager files. A version control system, such as RCS, is good for tracking changes to configuration files.

Case Study: Upgrading a Critical DNS Server

This case study combines many of the techniques discussed in this chapter. During the rush to fix Y2K bugs before January 1, 2000, Tom found a critical DNS server that was running on non-Y2K-compliant hardware and that the vendor had announced would not be fixed. Also, the OS was not Y2K compliant. This was an excellent opportunity to perform a fresh load of the OS on entirely new hardware.

Tom developed a service checklist. Although he thought that the host provided only two services, using netstat -a and listing all the running processes he found many other services running on the machine. He discovered that some of those extra services were no longer in use and found one service that nobody could identify!

People knew that most of the software packages involved would work on the new OS because they were in use on other machines with the newer OS. However, many of the services were homegrown, and there was panic when it was thought that the author of a homegrown package was no longer at the company and the source code couldn't be found immediately. Luckily, the code was found.

Tom built the new machine and replicated all the services onto it. The original host had many configuration files that were edited on a regular basis. He needed to copy these data files to the new system to verify that the scripts that processed them worked properly on the new machine. However, because the upgrade was going to take a couple of weeks, those files would be modified many times before the new host would be ready. The tests were be done on aging data. When the new system was cut in, Tom stopped all changes on the old host, recopied the files to the new system, and verified that the new system accepted the new files.

The tests that were developed were not run only once before the cutover but were run over and over as various services on the new system became usable. However, Tom did leave most services disabled when they weren't being tested because of concern that the old and new machines might conflict with each other.

The cut-over worked as follows: The old machine was disconnected from the network but left running. The new machine's IP address was changed to that of the old one. After five minutes, the ARP caches on the local network timed out, and the new host was recognized. If problems appeared, he could unplug the new machine from the network and reconnect the network cable of the legacy machine. The legacy machine was left running so that not even a reboot would be required to bring it back into service: Just halt the new server and plug in the old server's network cable.

The actual maintenance window could have been quite short—a minimum of five minutes if everything went right and the machine could be reconnected instantly. However, a 30-minute window was announced.

Tom decided to have two people looking over his shoulder during the upgrade because he wasn't as familiar with this version of UNIX as he is with others and didn't get much sleep the night before. It turned out that having an extra pair of hands helped with unplugging and plugging wires.

The group pantomimed the upgrade hours before the maintenance window. Without changing anything, they walked through exactly what was planned. They made sure that every cable would be long enough and that all the connectors were the right type. This process cleared up any confusion that anyone on the team might have had.

The upgrade went well. Some tests failed, but the group was soon able to fix the problems. One unexpected problem resulted in certain database updates not happening until a script could be fixed. The customers who depended on that data being updated were willing to live with slightly stale data until the script could be rewritten the next day.

18.3 Conclusion

We have described a fairly complete process for upgrading the OS of a computer, yet we have not mentioned a particular vendor's OS, particular commands to type, or buttons to click. The important parts of the process are not the technology, which is a matter of reading manuals, but rather communication, attention to detail, and testing.

The basic tool we used is a checklist. We began by developing the checklist, which we then used to determine which services required upgrading, how long the upgrade would take, and when we could do it. The checklist drives what tests we develop, and those tests are used over and over again. We use the tests before and after the upgrade to ensure quality. If the upgrade fails, we activate the back-out plans included in the checklist. When the process is complete, we announce this to the list of concerned customers on the checklist.

A checklist is a simple tool. It is a single place where all the information is maintained. Whether you use paper, a spreadsheet, or a web page, the checklist is the focal point. It keeps the team on the same page, figuratively speaking, keeps the individuals focused, lets the customers understand the process, helps management understand the status, and brings new team members up to speed quickly.

Like many SA processes, this requires communication skills. Negotiation is a communication process, and we use it to determine when the upgrade will happen, what needs to happen, and what the priorities are if things go wrong. We give the customers a feeling of closure by communicating to them when we are finished. This helps the customer/SA relationship. We cannot stress enough the importance of putting the checklist on a web page. The more eyes that can review the information, the better.

When the tests are automated, we can repeat them with accuracy and ensure completeness. These tests should be general enough that they can be reused not only for future upgrades on the same host but also on other similar hosts. In fact, the tests should be integrated into your real-time monitoring system. Why perform these tests only after upgrades?

This simple process can be easily understood and practiced. This is one of the basic processes that an SA must master before moving on to more complicated upgrades. The real-world examples we used all required some kind of deviation from the basic process yet still encompassed the essential points.

Some OS distributions make upgrading almost risk-free and painless, and some are much more risky. Although there are no guarantees, it is much better when an operating system has a way to do upgrades reliably, repeatably, and with the ability to easily revert. The minimum number of commands or mouse clicks reduces the possibility of human error. Being able to upgrade many machines in a repeatable way has many benefits; especially important is that it helps maintain consistent systems. Any ability to revert to a previous state gives a level of undo that is like an insurance policy: You hope you never need it but are glad it exists when you do.

Exercises

1. Select a server in your environment and figure out what services it provides. If you maintain a documented list of services, what system commands would you use to cross-check the list? If you do not have the services documented, what are all the resources you might use to build a complete list?

2. In your environment, how do you know who depends on which services?

3. Select a location that should be easy to walk to from your machine room or office, such as a nearby store, bank, or someplace at the other end of your building, if it is very large. Have three or four fellow students, coworkers, or friends estimate how long it will take to walk there and back. Now, all of you should walk there and back as a group, recording how long it takes. (Do this right now, before you read the rest of the question. Really!) How long did it take? Did you start walking right away, or were you delayed? How many unexpected events along the way—runing into customers, people who wanted to know what you were doing, and so on—extended your trip's time? Calculate how close each of you was to being accurate, the average of these, and the standard deviation. What did you learn from this exercise? If you repeat it, how much better do you think your estimate will be if you select the same location? A different location? Would bringing more people have affected the time? Relate what you learned to the process of planning a maintenance window.

4. In Section 18.1.3, the claim is made that the tests that are developed will be executed at least three times; more if there are problems. What are the three minimum times? What are some additional times the tests may be run?

5. Section 18.2.7 includes a case study in which the source code to a home-grown service almost couldn't be found. What would you do in that situation if the source code couldn't be found?

6. How do you announce planned outages and maintenance windows in your environment? What are the benefits and problems with this method? What percentage of your customers ignore these announcements?

7. Customers often ignore announcements from SAs. What can be done to improve this situation?

8. Select a host in your environment and upgrade it. (Ask permission first!)

9. What steps would you take if you had to replace the only restroom in your building?

Chapter 19

Service Conversions

Sometimes, you need to convert your customer base from an existing service to a new replacement service. The existing system may not be able to scale or may have been declared "end of life" by the vendor, requiring you to evaluate new systems. Or, your company may have merged with a company that uses different products, and both parts of the new company need to integrate their services with each other. Perhaps your company is spinning off a division into a new, separate company, and you need to replicate and split the services and networks so that each part is fully self-sufficient. Whatever the reason, converting customers from one service to another is a task that SAs often face.

Like many things in system and network administration, your goal should be for the conversion to go smoothly and be completely invisible to your customers. To achieve or even approach that goal, you need to plan the project very carefully. This chapter describes some of the areas to consider in that planning process.

An Invisible Change

When AT&T split off Lucent Technologies, the Bell Labs research division was split in two. The SAs who looked after that division had to split the Bell Labs network so that the people who were to be part of Lucent would not be able to access any AT&T services and vice versa. Some time after the split had been completed, one of the researchers asked when it was going to happen. He was very surprised when he was told that it had been completed already, because he had not noticed that anything had changed. The project was successful in causing minimal disruption to the customers.

19.1 The Basics

As with many high-level system administration tasks, a successful conversion depends on having a solid infrastructure in place. Rolling out a change to the whole company can be a very visible project, particularly if there are problems. You can decrease the risk and visibility of problems by rolling out the change slowly, starting with the SAs and then the most suitable customers. With any change you make, be sure that you have a back-out plan and can revert quickly and easily to the preconversion state, if necessary.

We have seen how an automated patching system can be used to roll out software updates (Chapter 3) and how to build a service, including some of the ways to make it easier to upgrade and maintain (Chapter 5). These techniques can be instrumental parts of your roll-out plan.

Communication plays a key role in performing a successful conversion. It is never wise to change something without making sure that your customers know what is happening and have told you of their concerns and timing constraints.

In this section, we touch on each of those areas, along with ways to minimize the intrusiveness of the conversion for the customer, and discuss two approaches to conversions. You need to plan every step of a conversion well in advance to pull it off with minimum impact on your customers. This section should shape your thinking in that planning process.

19.1.1 Minimize Intrusiveness

When planning the conversion rollout, pay close attention to the impact on the customer. Aim for the conversion to have as little impact on the customer as possible. Try to make it seamless.

Does the conversion require a service interruption? If so, how can you minimize the time that the service is unavailable? When is the best time to schedule the interruption in service so that is has the least impact?

Does the conversion require changes on each customer's workstation or in the office? If so, how many, how long will they take, and can you organize the conversion so that the customer is disturbed only once?

Does the conversion require that the customers change their work methods in any way, for example, by using new client software? Can you avoid changing the client software? If not, do the customers need training? Sometimes, training is a larger project than the conversion itself. Are the customers comfortable with the new software? Are their SAs and the helpdesk familiar enough with the new and the old software that they can help with any questions the customers might have? Have the helpdesk scripts (Section 13.1.7) been updated?

Look for ways to perform the change without service interruption, without visiting each customer, and without changing the workflow or user interface. Make sure that the support organization is ready to provide full support for the new product or service before you roll it out. Remember, your goal is for the conversion to be so smooth that your customers may not even realize that it has happened. If you can't minimize intrusiveness, at least you can make the intrusion fast and well organized.

The Rioting Mob Technique

When AT&T was splitting into AT&T, Lucent, and NCR, Tom's SA team was responsible for splitting the Bell Labs networks in Holmdel, New Jersey (Limoncelli et al., 1997). At one point, every host needed to be visited to perform several changes, including changing its IP address. A schedule was announced that listed which hallways would be converted on which day. Mondays and Wednesdays were used for conversions; Tuesdays and Thursdays, for fixing problems that arose; Fridays, unscheduled, in the hope that the changes wouldn't cause any problems that would make the SAs lose sleep on the weekends.

On conversion days, the team used what they called the Rioting Mob Technique. At 9 AM, the SAs would stand at one end of the hallway. They'd psych themselves up, often by chanting, and move down the hallways in pairs. Two pairs were PC technicians, and two pairs were UNIX technicians, one set for the left side of the hallway and another for the right side. As the technicians went from office to office, they shoved out the inhabitants and went machine to machine, making the needed changes. Sometimes, machines were particularly difficult or had problems. Rather than trying to fix the issue themselves, the technicians called on a senior team member to solve the problem as the technicians moved on to the next machine. Meanwhile, a final pair of people stayed at command central, where SAs could phone in requests for IP addresses and provide updates to the host, inventory, and other databases.

The next day was spent cleaning up anything that had broken and then discussing the issues in order to refine the process. A brainstorming session revealed what had gone well and what needed improvement. The technicians decided that it would be better to make one pass through the hallway, calling in requests for IP addresses, giving customers a chance to log out, and identifying nonstandard machines for the senior SAs to focus on. On the second pass through the hallway, everyone had the IP addresses needed, and things went more smoothly. Soon, they could do two hallways in the morning and all the cleanup in the afternoon.

The brainstorming session between each conversion day was critical. What the technicians learned in the first session inspired radical changes in the process. Eventually, the brainstorming sessions were not gathering any new information; the breather days became planning sessions for the next day. Many times, a conversion day went smoothly and was completed by lunchtime, and the problems resolved by the afternoon. The breather day became a normal workday.

Consolidating all of the customer disruption to a single day for any given customer was a big success. Customers were expecting some kind of outage but would have found it unacceptable if the outage had been prolonged or split up over many instances. One group of customers used their conversion day to have an all-day picnic.

19.1.2 Layers versus Pillars

A conversion project, as with any project, is divided into discrete tasks, some of which have to be performed for every customer. For example, with a conversion to new calendar software, the new client software must be rolled out to all the desktops, accounts will need to be created on the server, and existing schedules must be converted to the new system. As part of the project planning for the conversion, you need to decide whether to perform these tasks in layers or in pillars.

With the *layers* approach, you perform one task for all the customers before moving on to the next task and doing that for all of the customers.

With the *pillars* approach, you perform all the required tasks for each customer at once, before moving on to the next customer.[1]

Tasks that are not intrusive to the customer, such as creating the accounts in the calendar server, can be safely performed in layers. However, tasks that are intrusive for a customer, such as installing the new client software, freezing the customer's schedule and converting it to the new system, and getting the customer to connect for the first time and initialize his or her password, should be performed in pillars.

With the pillars approach, you need to schedule with each customer only one period rather than many small ones. By performing all the tasks at once, you disturb each customer only once. Even if it is for a slightly longer time, a single intrusion is typically less disruptive to your customer's work than many small intrusions.

A hybrid approach achieves the best of both worlds. Group all the customer-visible interruptions into as few periods as possible. Make all other changes silently.

---

1. Think of baking a large cake for a dozen people versus baking 12 cupcakes, one at a time. You'd want to bake one big cake. But suppose instead you were making omelets. People would want different things in their omelets—it wouldn't make sense to make just one big one.

Case Study: Pillars versus Layers at Bell Labs

When AT&T split off Lucent Technologies and Bell Labs was divided in two, many changes needed to be made to each desktop to convert it from a Bell Labs machine to either a Lucent Bell Labs machine or an AT&T Labs machine. Very early on, the SA team responsible for implementing the split realized that a pillars approach would be used for most changes but that sometimes, the layers approach would be best. For example, the layers approach was used when building a new web proxy. The new web proxies were constructed and tested, and then customers were switched to their new proxies. However, more than 30 changes had to be made to every UNIX desktop, and it was determined that they should all be made in one visit, with one reboot, to minimize the disruption to the customer.

There was great risk in that approach. What if the last desktop was converted and then the SAs realized that one of those changes was made incorrectly on every machine? To reduce this risk, sample machines with the new configuration were placed in public areas, and customers were invited to try them out. This way, the SAs were able to find and fix many problems before the big changes were implemented on each customer workstation. This approach also helped the customers become comfortable with the changes. Some customers were particularly fearful because they lacked confidence in the SA team. These customers were physically walked to the public machines and asked to log in, and problems were debugged in real time. This calmed customers' fears and increased their confidence. The network-split project is described in detail in Limoncelli et al. (1997).

E-commerce sites, while looking monolithic from the outside, can think about their conversions in terms of layers and pillars. A small change or even a new software release can be rolled out in pillars, one host at a time, if the change interoperates with the older systems. Changes that are easy to do in batches, such as imports of customer data, can be implemented in layers. This is especially true of non-destructive changes, such as copying data to new servers.

19.1.3 Communication

Although the guiding principle for a conversion is that it be invisible to the customer, you still have to communicate the conversion plan to your customers. Indeed, communicating a conversion far in advance is critical.

By communicating with the customers about the conversion, you will find people who use the service in ways you did not know about. You will need to support them and their uses on the new system. Any customers who use the system extensively should be involved early in the project to make sure that their needs will be met. You should find out about any important deadline dates that your customers have or any other times when the system needs to be absolutely stable.

Customers need to know what is taking place and how the change is going to affect them. They need to be able to ask questions about how they will perform their tasks in the new system and need to have all their concerns addressed. Customers need to know in advance whether the conversion will require service outages, changes to their machines, or visits to their offices.

Even if the conversion should go seamlessly, with no interruption or visible change for the customers, they still need to know that it is happening. Use the information you've gained to schedule it for minimum impact, just in case something goes wrong.

Have the high-level goals for the conversion planned and written out in advance; it is common for customers to try to add new functionality or new services as requirements during an upgrade planning process. Adding new items increases the complexity of the conversion. Strike a balance between the need to maintain functionality and the desire to improve services.

19.1.4 Training

Related to communication is training. If any aspect of the user experience is going to change, training should be provided. This is true whether the menus are going to be slightly different or entirely new workflows will be required.

Most changes are small and can be brought to people's attention via email. However, for rollouts of large, new systems, we see time and time again that training is critical to the success of introducing new systems to an organization. The less technical the customers, the more important that training be included in your rollout plans.

Creating and providing the actual training is usually out of scope for the SA team doing the service conversion, but SAs may need to support outside or vendor training efforts. Work closely with the customers and management driving the conversion to discover any plans for training support well in advance. Non-technical customers may not realize the level of response required by SAs to set up a 5–15 workstation training room with special firewall settings for the instructor's laptop computer.[2]

---

2. Strata has heard a request like this given with only 3 business days notice, which the requester seemed to think was "plenty of time."

19.1.5 Small Groups First

When performing a rollout, whether it is a conversion, a new service, or an update to an existing service, you should do so gradually to minimize the potential impact of any failures. Start by converting your own system to the new service. Test and perfect the conversion process, and test and perfect the new service before converting any other systems. When you cannot find any more problems, convert a few of your coworkers' desktops; debug and fix any problems that arise from that process and their testing of the new system. Expand the test group to cover all the SAs before starting on your customers. When you have successfully converted the SAs, start with customers who are better able to cope with problems that might arise and who have agreed to be on the cutting edge, and gradually move toward more conservative customers. This "one, some, many" technique for rolling out new revisions and patches applies more globally across rollouts of any kind, including conversions (see Section 3.1.2).

Upgrading Google Servers

Google's web farm includes thousands of computers; the real number is an industry secret. When upgrading thousands of redundant servers, Google has massive amounts of automation that first upgrades a single host, then 1 percent of the hosts, then batches of hosts, until all are upgraded. Between each set of upgrades, testing is performed, and an operator has the opportunity to halt and revert the changes if problems are found. Sometimes, the gap of time between batches is hours; at other times, days.

19.1.6 Flash-Cuts: Doing It All at Once

Wherever possible, avoid converting everyone simultaneously from one system to another. The conversion will go much more smoothly if you can convert a few willing test subjects to the new system first. Avoiding a flash-cut may mean budgeting in advance for duplication of hardware, so when you prepare your budget request, remember to think about how you will perform the conversion rollout.

In other cases, you may be able to use features of your existing technology to slowly roll out the conversion. For example, if you are renumbering a network or splitting a network, you might use an IP multinetting network, secondary IP addresses, in conjunction with DHCP (see Section 3.1.3) to initially convert a few hosts without using additional hardware.

Alternatively, you may be able to make both old and new services available simultaneously and encourage people to switch during the overlap period. That way, they can try out the new service, get used to it, report problems with it, and switch back to the old service if they prefer. It gives your customers an "adoption" period. This approach is commonly used in the telephone industry when a change in phone number or area code is introduced. For a few months, both the old and new numbers work. In the following few months, the old number gives an error message that refers the caller to the new number. Then the old number stops working, and some time later, it becomes available for reallocation.

Physical-Network Conversion

When a midsize company converted its network wiring from thin Ethernet to 10Base-T, it divided the problem into two main preparatory components and had a different group attack each part of the project planning. The first group had to get the new physical-wiring layer installed in the wiring closets and cubicles. The second group had to make sure that every machine in the building was capable of supporting 10Base-T, by adding a card or upgrading the machine, if necessary.

The first group ran all the wires through the ceiling and terminated them in the wiring closets. Next, the group members went through the building and pulled the wires down from the ceiling, terminated them in the cubicles and offices, and tested them, visiting each cubicle or office only once.

When both groups had finished their preparatory work, they gradually went through the building, moving people to the new wiring but leaving the old cabling in place so that they could switch back if there were problems.

This conversion was done well from the point of view of avoiding a flash-cut and converting people over gradually. However, the customers found it too intrusive because they were interrupted three times: once for wiring to their work areas, once for the new network hardware in their machines, and finally for the actual conversion. Although it would have been very difficult to coordinate, and would have required extensive planning, the teams could have visited each cubicle together and performed all the work at once. Realistically, though, this would have complicated and delayed the project too much. It would have been simpler to have better communication initially, letting the customers know all the benefits of the new wiring, apologizing in advance for the need to disturb them three times, (one of which would require a reboot) and scheduling the disturbances. Customers find interruptions less of an annoyance if they understand what is going on, have some control over the scheduling, and know what they are going to get out of it ultimately.

Sometimes, a conversion or a part of a conversion must be performed simultaneously for everyone. For example, if you are converting from one corporatewide calendar server to another, where the two systems cannot communicate and exchange information, you may need to convert everyone at once; otherwise, people on the old system will not be able to schedule meetings with people on the new system, and vice versa.

Performing a successful flash-cut requires a lot of careful planning and some comprehensive testing, including load testing. Persuade a few key users of that system to test the new system with their daily tasks before making the switch. If you get the people who use the system the most heavily to test the new one, you are more likely to find any problems with it before it goes live, and the people who rely on it the most will have become comfortable with it before they have to start using it in earnest. People use the same tools in different ways, so more testers will gain you better feature-test coverage.

For a flash-cut, two-way communication is particularly critical. Make sure that all your customers know what is happening and when, and that you know and have addressed their concerns in advance of the cutover. Also, be prepared with a back-out plan, as discussed in the next section.

Phone Number Conversion

In 2000, British Telecom converted the city of London from two area codes to one and lengthened the phone numbers from seven digits to eight, in one large number change. Numbers that were of the form (171) xxx-xxxx became (20) 7xxx-xxxx, and numbers that were of the form (181) xxx-xxxx became (20) 8xxx-xxxx. More than six months before the designated cutover date, the company started advertising the change; also, the new area code and new phone number combination started working. For a few months after the designated cutover date, the old area codes in combination with the old phone numbers continued to work, as is usual with telephone number changes.

However, local calls to London numbers beginning with a 7 or an 8 went from seven to eight digits overnight. Because this sudden change was certain to cause confusion, British Telecom telephoned every single customer who would be affected by the change to explain, person to person, what the change meant and to answer any questions that their customers might have. Now that's customer service!

19.1.7 Back-Out Plan

When rolling out a conversion, it is critical to have a back-out plan. A *conversion*, by definition, means removing one service and replacing it with another. If the new service does not work correctly, the customer has been deprived of one of the tools that he or she uses to do the job, which may seriously affect the person's productivity.

If a conversion fails, you need to be able to restore the customer's service quickly to the state it was in before you made any changes and then go away, figure out why it failed, and fix it. In practical terms, this means that you should leave both services running simultaneously, if possible, and have a simple, automated way of switching someone between the two services.

Bear in mind that the failure may not be instantaneous or may not be discovered for a while. It could be as a result of reliability problems in the software, it could be caused by capacity limitations, or it may be a feature that the customer uses infrequently or only at certain times of the year or month. So you should leave your back-out mechanism in place for a while, until you are certain that the conversion has been completed successfully. How long? For critical services, we suggest one significant reckoning period, such as a fiscal quarter for a company, or a semester for a university.

A major difficulty with back-out plans is deciding when to execute them. When a conversion goes wrong, the technicians tend to promise that things will work with "one more change," but management tends to push toward starting the back-out plan. It is essential to have decided in advance the point at which the back-out plan will be put into use. For example, one might decide ahead of time that if the conversion isn't completed within 2 hours of the start of the next business day, then the back-out plan must be executed. Obviously, if in the first minutes of the conversion, one meets insurmountable problems, it can be better to back out of what's been done so far and reschedule the conversion. However, getting a second opinion can be useful. What is insurmountable to you may be an easy task for someone else on your team.

When an upgrade has failed, there is a big temptation to keep trying more and more things to fix it. We know we have a back-out plan, we know we promised to start reverting if the upgrade wasn't complete by a certain time, but we keep on saying "just 5 more minutes" and "I just want to try one more thing." Is it ego? Hubris? Desperation? We don't know. However, we do know that it is a natural thing to want to keep trying. It's a good thing, actually. Most likely, we got where we are today by not giving up in the face of insurmountable problems. However, when a maintenance window is ending and we need to revert, we need to revert. Often, our egos won't let us, which is why it can be useful to designate someone outside the process, such as our manager, to watch the clock and make us stop when we said we would stop.

Revert. There will be more time to try again later.

19.2 The Icing

When you have become adept at rolling out conversions with minimal impact for your customers, there are two refinements that you should consider to further reduce the impact of conversions on your customers. The first of these is to have a back-out plan that allows for instant rollback, so that no time is lost in converting your customers back to the old system the moment that a problem with the new one is discovered. The other is to try to avoid doing conversions altogether. We discuss some ways of reducing the number of conversion projects that might arise.

19.2.1 Instant Rollback

When performing a conversion, it is nice to be able to instantly roll everything back to a known working state if a problem is discovered. That way, any customer disruption resulting from a problem with the new system can be minimized.

How you provide instant rollback depends on the conversion that you are performing. One component of providing instant rollback might be to leave the old systems in place. If you are simply pointing customers' clients to a new server, you can switch back and forth by changing a single DNS record. To make DNS updates happen more rapidly, set the *time to live* (TTL) field to a lower value—5 minutes, perhaps—well in advance of making the switch. Then, when things are stable, set the TTL back to whatever value is usually in place. The **refresh period** of the domain's SOA record tells the DNS secondary servers how often they should check whether the master DNS server has been updated. If both of these fields are left set low, DNS updates should reach the clients quickly, and therefore rollback can happen quickly and simply. *Note*: Many DNS client libraries ignore the TTL field and cache it forever. Be sure that connections to the old machine are handled gracefully or are rejected.

Another approach that achieves instant rollback is to perform the conversion by stopping one service and starting another. In some cases, you may have two client applications on the customers' machines, one of which uses the old system and another that uses the new one. This approach works especially well when the new service has been running for tests on a different port than the existing service.

Sometimes, the change being made is an upgrade of a software package to a newer release. If the old software can exist dormant on the server while the new software is in use, you can instantly perform a rollback by switching to the old software. Vendors can do a lot to make this difficult, but some are very good about making it easy. For example, if versions 1.2 and 1.3 of a server get installed in /opt/example-1.2 and /opt/example-1.3, respectively, but a symbolic link /opt/example points to the version that is in use, you can rollback by simply repointing the single symbolic link. (An example software repository that uses this technique is described in Section 28.1.6.)

These simple methods either violate the principle of doing a slow rollout or make the change more visible to the customer. Providing instant rollback with minimal customer impact and using a gradual rollout method are more complex and require careful planning and configuration. You can set up extra DNS servers that provide the information for the new servers and all the common information to clients that use them and then use your automated client network configuration tool, described in Chapter 3, to selectively convert a few hosts at a time to the alternative DNS servers. At any stage, you can roll those hosts back to the original configuration by changing their network configuration back to its original state.

19.2.2 Avoiding Conversions

Advanced planning can reduce the need for upgrades and conversions. For example, upgrades are often required to scale the service to more simultaneous users. Such upgrades can be avoided by starting with a system that has more capacity.

Some conversions can be avoided in other ways. Before purchasing, talk to the vendor about future directions for the product and how it scales from your current usage patterns along your own predicted growth curve. If you select a product that scales well and integrates with other components of your network, even if you don't see the need for such integration at purchase time, you minimize the chances that you will need to switch to another one in the future because of new feature requirements, scaling problems, or the end of the product's life cycle.

Where possible, select products that use standard protocols to communicate between the client on the desktop and the server that is providing the service. If the client and the server use a proprietary protocol and you want to change the server, you will also have to change the client software. However, if the products use standard protocols, you should be able to select another server that uses the same protocol and avoid converting your customers to new client software.

You should also be able to avoid laboriously converting customers' configurations by using methods that are part of building a good infrastructure. For example, using automatic network configuration (Chapter 3) with good documentation as to which service is located on which host (Chapter 8) makes it much easier to split the network without bothering the customers. Using names that are service-based aliases for your machines (Chapter 5) enables you to move a service to a new machine or set of machines without having to change client configurations.

19.2.3   Web Service Conversions

More and more services are web based. In these situations, an upgrade of the server rarely requires upgrading the client software also, because the service works with any web browser. On the other hand, we are still dismayed by how many web-based services refuse to work with anything other than Microsoft Internet Explorer. The point of HTML is that the client is decoupled from the server. What if I want to connect with the browser on my cellphone, game console, or smart panel of my refrigerator? The service shouldn't care.

Services that test for particular web browser software and refuse to work with anything but a specific browser show bad form at best and lazy programming at worst. We can't expect a vendor to test its service with every version of every browser. However, it is perfectly reasonable for a vendor to have a list of browsers that are fully supported (quality assurance includes testing with these browsers and bugs submitted will be taken seriously), a list of browsers that are best-effort (the service works but bugs submitted related to this browser will be fixed on a "best-effort" basis, no promises), and a declaration that all other browsers may work, but perfect functionality is not guaranteed. When possible, a service should gracefully reduce functionality when an unsupported browser is in use. For example, animated menus stop working, but there is some other way to select choices.

The service should not detect which browser is in use and refuse to work, as casual users may be willing to suffer though formatting problems rather than buy a computer simply to use the vendor's browser of choice. This is particularly true for cellphone-based browsers; customers do not expect flawless formatting. Refusing to work except when specific browsers are in use is rude and potentially dangerous. Many vendors have been burned when the new release of their supported browser is misidentified, and suddenly, no customers are able to use the service.

19.2.4 Vendor Support

When doing large conversions, make sure that you have vendor support. Contact the vendor to find out if there are any pitfalls. This can prevent major problems. If you have a good relationship with a vendor, that vendor should be willing to be involved in the planning process, sometimes even lending personnel. If not, the vendor may be willing to make sure that its technical support hotline is properly staffed on your conversion day or that someone particularly knowledgeable about your environment is available.

Don't be afraid to reveal your plans to a vendor. There is rarely a reason to keep such plans secret. Don't be afraid to ask the vendor to suggest which days of the week are best for receiving support. It can't hurt to ask the vendor to assign a particular person from its support desk to review the plans as they are being made so that the vendor will be better prepared if you do call during the upgrade with a problem. Good vendors would rather review your plans early than discover that a customer has a problem halfway through an upgrade that involves unsupported practices.

19.3 Conclusion

A successful conversion project is based on lots of advance planning and a solid infrastructure. The success of a conversion project is measured in how little adverse impact it had on the customers. The conversion should intrude as little as possible into their work routines.

The principles for rollouts of any kind, updates, new services, or conversions are the same. Start with lots of planning, deploy slowly with lots of testing, and be ready to back the changes out if you need to.

Exercises

1. What conversions can you foresee in your network's future? Choose one, and build a plan for performing it with minimum customer impact.

2. Now try to add an instant roll-back option to that plan.

3. If you had to split your network, what services would you need to replicate, and how would you convert people from one network and set of services to the other? Consider each service in detail.

4. Can you think of any conversions that you could have avoided? How could you have avoided them?

5. Think about a service conversion that really needs to be done in your environment. Would you do a phased roll-out or a flash-cut? Why?

6. If your IT group were converting everyone from using an office phone system to Voice over IP (VoIP), create an outline of the process using the pillar method. Now create one with the layer method.

7. In the previous question, was a hybrid approach more useful than a strict layer or pillar model? If so, please describe how, exactly.

Chapter 20

Maintenance Windows

If you found out you had to power off an entire data center, do a lot of maintenance, then bring it all back up, would you know how to manage the event? Some companies are lucky enough to be able to do this every quarter or once a year. SAs delay tasks that require interruption of service, such as hardware upgrades, parts replacement, or network changes, until this window. Sometimes a weekly timeslot is allocated for major and risky changes to consolidate downtime to a specific time when customers will be least affected. Other times we are forced to do this because of physical maintenance such as construction, power or cooling upgrades, or office moves. Other times we need to do this for emergency reasons, such as a failing cooling system. This chapter describes as a technique for managing such major planned outages. Along the way will be tips useful in less dramatic settings. Projects like this require more planning, more orderly execution, and considerably more testing. We call this the **flight director** technique, named after the role of the flight director in NASA space launches.[1]

Although most people clean their houses or apartments on a weekly or monthly basis, an annual spring cleaning is certainly useful. Similarly, networks sometimes need massive, disruptive cleaning. Cooling systems must be powered off, drained, cleaned, and refilled. Messy nests of wires become impediments to working effectively and sometimes must be tidied. Large volumes of data must be moved between file servers to optimize performance for users or simply to provide room for growth. Improvements that involve many changes can be done much more efficiently if all users agree to a large window of downtime. The flight director technique guides the

---

1. The origin of this chapter's techniques and terminology was Paul Evans, an avid observer of the space program. The first flight directors wore a vest, like the one worn by the flight director in *Apollo 13*. The terminology helped everyone remember that the role of SA in the vest was different from normal.

Table 20.1 Three Stages of a Maintenance Window

Stage	Activity
Preparation	• Schedule the window. • Pick a flight director. • Prepare change proposals. • Build a master plan.
Execution	• Disable access. • Determine shut-down sequence. • Execute plan. • Perform testing.
Resolution	• Announce completion. • Enable access. • Have a visible presence. • Be prepared for problems.

activities before the window, during execution, and after execution (see Table 20.1).

Some companies are willing to schedule regular maintenance windows for major systems and networking work in return for better availability during normal operations. Depending on the size of the site, this could be one evening and night per month or perhaps from Friday evening to Monday morning once a quarter. These maintenance windows are necessarily very intense, so consider the capacity and well-being of the system administration staff, as well as the impact on the company, when deciding to schedule them.

SAs often like to have a maintenance window during which they can take down any and all systems and stop all services because it reduces complexity and makes testing easier. It's difficult to change the tires while the car is driving down the highway. For example, in cutting email services over to a new system, you need to transfer existing mailboxes, as well as switch the incoming mail feed to the new system. Trying to transfer the existing mailboxes while new email arrives and yet ensure consistency is a very tricky problem. However, if you can bring email services down while you do the transfer, it becomes a lot easier. In addition, it is a lot easier to check that the system is working correctly before you turn the mail feed and the read access on again than it is to deal with having dropped or bounced mail if something didn't work quite right with the live cutover.

However, you will have to sell the concept in terms of a benefit to the company, not in terms of it making the SA's life easier. You need to be able to promise better service availability the rest of the time. You need to plan in advance: If you have one maintenance window per quarter, you need to make sure that the work you do this quarter will hold you through the end of the next quarter, so that you won't need to bring the system down again. All members of the team must commit to high availability for their systems for this to work. You should also be prepared to provide metrics to back up your claims of higher availability from before and after you have succeeded in getting scheduled maintenance windows. (Monitoring to verify availability levels is covered more in Chapter 22.)

Many companies will not agree to a large scheduled outage for maintenance. In that case, an alternative plan must be presented, explaining what would be entailed if the outage were granted, demonstrating that customers, not the SAs, are the real beneficiaries. A single large outage can be much less annoying to customers than many little outages (Limoncelli et al. 1997).

Other companies are unable to have a large outage for business reasons. E-commerce sites and ISPs fall into this category. Those sites need to provide high availability to their customers, who typically are off-site and not easily contacted. They do, however, still need maintenance windows. The end of this chapter looks at how the principles learned in this chapter apply in a high-availability site.

These techniques also ring true for single, major, planned outages, such as moving the company to a new building.

20.1 The Basics

A **maintenance window,** by definition a short period in which a lot of systems work must be performed, is disruptive to the rest of the company, and so the scheduling must be done in cooperation with the customers. A group of SAs must perform various tasks, and that work must be coordinated by the flight director.

Some of the basics needed for success in this type of major undertaking are coordinating scheduling of the maintenance window, creating the grand plan for the entire change, organizing the preparatory work, communicating with any affected customers, and performing complete system testing afterward. In this chapter, we discuss the role and activities of the flight director and the mechanics of running a maintenance window as it relates to these elements.

20.1.1 Scheduling

In scheduling periodic maintenance windows, you must work with the rest of the company to coordinate dates. In particular, you will almost certainly need to avoid the end-of-month, end-of-quarter, and end-of-fiscal-year dates so that the sales team can enter rush orders and the accounting group can produce financial reports for that period. You also will need to avoid product release dates, if that is relevant to your business. Universities have different constraints around the academic year. Some businesses, such as toy and greeting card manufacturers, may have seasonal constraints. You must set and publicize the schedule far in advance, preferably more than a year ahead, so that the rest of the company can plan around those times. If you are involved at the start of a new company, make a regularly scheduled maintenance window a part of the new company's culture.

Case Study: Maintenance Window Scheduling

In a midsize software development company, the quarterly maintenance windows had to avoid various dates immediately before and after scheduled release dates, which typically occurred three times a year, as the engineering and operations divisions required the systems to be operational to make the release. Dates leading up to and during the major trade show for the company's products had to be avoided because engineering typically produced new alpha versions for the show, and demos at the trade show might rely on equipment at the office. End-of-month, end-of-quarter, and end-of-year dates, when the sales support and finance departments relied on full availability to enter figures, had to be avoided. Events likely to cause a spike in customer-support calls, such as a special product promotion, needed to be coordinated with outages, although they were typically scheduled after the maintenance windows were set.

As you can see, finding empty windows was a tricky business. However, maintenance schedules were set at least a year in advance and were well advertised so that the rest of the company could plan around them.

Once the dates were set, weekly reminders were posted beginning 6 weeks in advance of each window, with additional notices the final week. At the end of each notice, the schedule for all the following maintenance windows was attached, as far ahead as they had been scheduled.

The maintenance notice highlighted a major item from those that were scheduled, to advertise as the benefit to the company of the outage period, such as bringing a new data center online or upgrading the mail infrastructure. This helped the customers understand the benefit they received in return for the interruption of service.

Unfortunately for the SA group, the rest of the company saw the maintenance weekends as the perfect times to schedule company picnics and other events, because no one would feel compelled to work—except for the SAs, of course.

That's life.

Lumeta's Weekly Maintenance Windows

It can be difficult to get permission to have periodic scheduled downtime. Therefore it was important to Tom to start such a tradition at the creation of Lumeta rather than try to fight for it later. He sold the idea by explaining that while the company was young, the churn and growth of the infrastructure would be extreme. Rather than annoy everyone with constant requests for downtime, he promised to restrict all planned outages for Wednesday evening after 5 PM. Explained that way the reaction was extremely positive. Because he used terms such as, "while the company is young" rather than a specific time limit, he was able to continue this Wednesday night tradition for years.

For the first few months Tom made sure there was always a reason to have downtime on Wednesday night so that it would become part of the corporate culture. Rebooting an important server was good enough to encourage people to go home even though it only look a few minutes. Departments planned their schedule around Wednesday night, knowing it was not a good time for late-night crunches or deadlines. Yet he also established a reputation for flexibility by postponing the maintenance window at the tiniest request. People got into the habit of spending Wednesday night with their families.

Once the infrastructure was stable the need for such maintenance windows became rare. People complained mostly when an announcement of "no maintenance this week" came late on Wednesday. Tom established a policy that any maintenance that would have a visible outage had to be announced by Monday evening and that no announcement meant no outage. While not required, sending an email to announce that there would be no user-visible outage each week prevented his team from becoming invisible and kept the notion of potential outages on Wednesday nights alive in people's minds. Formatting these announcements differently trained people to pay attention when there really would be an outage.

20.1.2 Planning

As with all planned maintenance on important systems, the tasks need to be planned by the individuals performing them, so that no original thought or problem solving should be involved in performing the task during the window. There should be no unforeseen events but only planned contingencies.

Planning for a maintenance window also has another dimension, however. Because maintenance windows occur only occasionally, the SAs need to plan far enough in advance to allow time to get quotes, submit purchase orders and get them approved, and have any new equipment arrive a week or so before the maintenance window. The lead time on some equipment can be 6 weeks or more, so this means starting to plan for the next maintenance window almost immediately after the preceding one has ended.

20.1.3 Directing

The flight director is responsible for crafting the announcement notices, making sure that they go out on time, scheduling the submitted work proposals based on the interactions between them and the staff required, deciding on any cuts for that maintenance window, monitoring the progress of the tasks during the maintenance window, ensuring that the testing occurs correctly, and communicating status to the rest of the company at the end of the maintenance window. The person who fills the role of flight director must be a senior SA who is capable of assessing work proposals from other members of the SA team and spotting dependencies and effects that may have been overlooked. The flight director also must be capable of making judgment calls on the level of risk versus need for some of the more critical tasks that affect the infrastructure. This person must have a good overview of the site and understand the implications of all the work—and look good in a vest.

In addition, the flight director cannot perform any technical work during that maintenance window. Typically, the flight director is a member of a multiperson team, and the other members of the team take on the work that would normally have been the responsibility of that individual. The flight director is not normally a manager, unless the manager was recently promoted from a senior SA position, because of the skill requirements.

Depending on the structure of the SA group, there may be an obvious group of people from which the flight director is selected each time. In the midsize software company discussed earlier, most of the 60 SAs took care of a division of the company. About 10 SAs formed the core services unit and were responsible for central services and infrastructure that were shared by the whole company, such as security, networking, email, printing, and naming services. The SAs in this unit provided services to each of the other business units and thus had a good overview of the corporate infrastructure and how the business units relied on it. The flight director was typically a member of that unit and had been with the company for a while.

Other factors also had to be taken into account, such as how the person interacted with the rest of the SAs, whether she would be reasonably strict about the deadlines but show good judgment where an exception should be made, and how the person would react under pressure and when tired. In our experience with this technique, we found that some excellent senior SAs performed flight director duties once and never wanted to do it again. In the future, we had to be careful to make sure that the flight director we selected was a willing victim.

20.1.4 Managing Change Proposals

One week before the maintenance window, all change proposals should have been submitted. A good way of managing this process is to have all the change proposals online in a revision-controlled area. Each SA edits documents in a directory with his name on it. The documents supply all the required information. One week before the change, this revision-controlled area is frozen, and all subsequent requests to make changes to the documents have to be made through the flight director. A change proposal form should answer at least the following questions.

- What changes are going to be made?
- What machines will you be working on?
- What are the premaintenance window dependencies and due dates?
- What needs to be up for the change to happen?
- What will be affected by the change?
- Who is performing the work?
- How long will the change take in active time and elapsed time, including testing and how many additional helpers will be needed?
- What are the test procedures? What equipment do they require?
- What is the back-out procedure, and how long will it take?

20.1.4.1 Change Proposal: Sample 1

- *What change are you going to make?*
  Upgrade the SecurID authentication server software from v1.4 to v2.1.
- *What machines are you working on?*
  `tsunayoshi` **and** `shingen`.
- *Prewindow dependencies and due dates?*
  The v2.1 software and license keys are to be delivered by the vendor and should arrive on September 14. Perform backups the night before the window.
- *Dependencies on other systems?*
  The network, console service, and internal authentication services (NIS).
- *What will be affected by the change?*
  All remote access and access to secured areas that require token authentication.

- *How long will the change take?*
  Time: 3 hours active; 3 hours elapsed.

- *Who is performing the work?*
  Jane Smith.

- *Additional helpers?*
  None.

- *Test procedure?*
  Try to dial in, establish a VPN in, connect over ISDN, and access each secured area. Test creating a new user, deleting a user, and modifying a user's attributes; check that each change has taken effect.

- *Equipment required?*
  Laptop with modem and VPN software, analog line, external ISP account, ISDN modem, and BRI.

- *Back-out procedure?*
  Installing new software in a parallel directory and copying the database into a new location. Don't delete old software and database until after a week of successful running. To back out (takes 5 minutes, plus testing), change links to point back to the old software.

20.1.4.2   Change Proposal: Sample 2

- *What change are you going to make?*
  Move `/home/de105` and `/db/gene237` from `anaconda` to `anachronism`.

- *What machines are you working on?*
  `anaconda`, `anachronism`, and `shingen`.

- *Prewindow dependencies and due dates?*
  Extra disk shelves for `anachronism` need to be delivered and installed; due to arrive September 17 and installed by September 21. Perform backups the night before the window.

- *Dependencies on other systems?*
  The network, console service, and internal authentication services (NIS).

- *What will be affected by the change?*
  Network traffic on 172.29.100.x network, all accounts with home directories on `/home/de105`, and database access to `/db/gene237`.

- *How long will the change take?*
  Time: 1 hour active; 12 hours elapsed.

- *Who is performing the work?*
  Greg Jones.

- *Additional helpers?*
  None.

- *Test procedure?*
  Try to mount those directories from some appropriate hosts; log in to a desktop account with a home directory on `/home/de105`, check that it is working; start the gene database, check for errors, run test database access script in `/usr/local/tests/gene/access-test`.

- *Equipment required?*
  Access to a non-SA desktop.

- *Back-out procedure?*
  Old data gets deleted after successful testing; change advertised locations of directories back to the old ones and rebuild tables. Takes 10 minutes to back out.

20.1.5 Developing the Master Plan

One week before the maintenance window, the flight director freezes the change proposals and starts working on a master plan, which takes into account all the dependencies and elapsed and active times for the change proposals. The result is a series of tables, one for each person, showing what task each person will perform during which time interval and identifying the coordinator for that task. A master chart shows all the tasks that are being performed over the entire time, who is performing them, the team lead, and what the dependencies are. The master plan also takes into account complete systemwide testing after all work has been completed.

If there are too many change proposals, the flight director will find that scheduling all of them produces too many conflicts, in terms of either machine availability or the people required. You need to have slack in the schedule to allow for things to go wrong. The difficult decisions about which projects should go ahead and which ones must wait should be made beforehand rather than in the heat of the moment when something is taking too long and blowing the schedule, and everyone is tired and stressed. The flight director makes the call on when some change proposals must be cut and assists the parties involved to choose the best course for the company.

Case Study: Template for a Master Plan

Once we had run a few maintenance windows, we discovered a formula that worked well for us. The systems on which most people were dependent for their work were operated on Friday evening. The first thing to be upgraded or changed was the network. Next on the list was console service, then the authentication servers. While these were in progress, all the other SAs helped out with hardware tasks, such as memory, disk, or CPU upgrades; replacing broken hardware; or moving equipment within or between data centers. Last thing on Friday night, large data moves were started so that they could run overnight.

The remaining tasks were then scheduled into Saturday, with some people being scheduled to help others in between their own tasks. Sunday was reserved for comprehensive systemwide testing and debugging, because of the high importance placed on testing.

20.1.6 Disabling Access

The very first task in the maintenance window is to disable or discourage system access and provide reminders that it is a maintenance window. Depending on what the site looks like and what facilities are available, this process may involve

- Placing on all doors into the campus buildings notices with the maintenance window times clearly visible
- Disabling all remote access to the site, whether by VPN, dial-in, dedicated lines, or wireless
- Making an announcement over the public address system in the campus buildings to remind everyone that systems are about to go down
- Changing the helpdesk voicemail message to announce that this is a maintenance window and stating when normal service should be restored

These steps reduce the chance that people will try to use the systems during the maintenance window, which could cause inconsistencies in, damage to, or accidental loss of their work. It also reduces the chance that the person carrying the on-call pager will have to respond to urgent helpdesk voicemails saying that the network is down.

Before the maintenance window opens, we recommend that you test console servers and other tools that will be used during the maintenance window. Some of these facilities are used infrequently enough that they may be nonfunctional without anyone noticing. Make sure to give yourself enough time to fix anything that is nonfunctional before the maintenance is due to start.

20.1.7 Ensuring Mechanics and Coordination

Some key pieces of technology enable the maintenance window process described here to proceed smoothly. These aspects are not useful solely for maintenance windows but are critical to their success.

20.1.7.1 Shutdown/Boot Sequence

In most sites, some systems or sets of systems must be available for other systems to shut down or to boot cleanly. A machine that tries to boot when machines and services that it relies on are not available will fail to boot properly. Typically, the machine will boot but will fail to run some of the programs that it usually runs on start-up. These programs might be services that others rely on or programs that run locally on someone's desktop. In either case, the machine will not work properly, and it may not be apparent why. When shutting down a machine, it may need to contact file servers, license servers, or database servers that are in use in order to properly terminate the link. If the machine cannot contact those servers, it may hang for a long time or indefinitely, trying to contact those servers before completing the shutdown process. It is important to understand and track machine dependencies during boot-up and shutdown. You do not want to have to figure it out for the first time when a machine room unexpectedly loses power.

The most critical systems, such as console servers, authentication servers, name-service machines, license servers, application servers, and data servers, typically need to be booted before compute servers and desktops. There also will be dependencies between the critical servers. It is vital to maintain a boot-sequence list for all data center machines, with one or more machines at each stage, as appropriate. Typically, the first couple of stages will have few machines, maybe only one machine in them, but later stages will have many machines. All data center machines should be booted before any non-data-center machines, because no machine in a data center should rely on any machine outside that data center (see Section 5.1.7).

One site created the shutdown/boot list as shown in Table 20.2. The shutdown sequence is typically very close to, if not exactly the same as, the reverse of the boot sequence. There may be one or two minor differences.

The shutdown sequence is a vital component to starting work at the beginning of the maintenance window. The machines operated on at the start of the maintenance window typically have the most dependencies on them, so

Table 20.2 Template for a Boot Sequence

Stage	Function	Reason
1	Console server	So that SAs could monitor other servers during boot.
2	Master authentication server	Secondary authentication servers contact the master on boot.
	Master name server	Secondary name servers contact the master on boot.
3	Secondary authentication servers	• So that SAs could log in to other servers as they booted. • UNIX hosts contact NIS servers when they boot. • Rely on nothing but the master authentication server.
	Secondary name servers	• Almost all services rely on name service. • Rely on nothing but the master name server.
4	Data servers	• Applications and home directories reside on data servers. • Most other machines rely on data servers. • Rely on name service.
	Network config servers	Rely on name service.
	Log servers	Rely on name service.
	Directory servers	Rely on name service.
5	Print servers	Rely on name service and log servers.
	License servers	Rely on name service, data servers, and log servers.
	Firewalls	Rely on log servers.
	Remote access	Relies on authentication service, name service, log service.
	Email service	Relies on name, log, and directory services and data servers.
6	All other servers	Rely on servers previously booted and not on each other.
7	Desktops	Rely on servers.

any machine that needs to be shut down for hardware maintenance/upgrades or moving has to be shut down before the work on the critical machines starts. It is important to shut down the machines in the right order, to avoid wasting time bringing machines back up so that other machines can be shut down cleanly. The boot sequence is also critical to the comprehensive system testing performed at the end of the maintenance window.

The shutdown sequence can be used as part of a larger emergency power off (EPO) procedure. An EPO is a decision and action plan for emergency issues that require fast action. In particular, action is required more quickly than one could get management approval. Think of it as precompiling decisions for later execution. An EPO should include what situations require its activation—fire, flood, overheating conditions with no response from facilities—and instructions on how to verify these issues. A decision tree is the best way to record this information. The EPO should then give instructions on how to migrate services to other data centers, whom to notify, and so on. Document a process for situations where there is time to copy critical data out of the data center and a process for when there is not. Finally, it should use the shutdown sequence to power off machines. In the case of overheating, one might document ways to shut down some machines or put machines into low-power mode so they generate less heat by running slower but still provide services. The steps should be documented such that they can be performed by any SA on the team. Having such a plan can save hardware, services, and revenue.

Emergency Use of the Shutdown Sequence

One company found that its shutdown sequence was helpful even for an unplanned outage. The data center had a raised floor, with the usual mess of air conditioning conduits, power distribution points, and network cables hiding out of sight. One Friday, one of the SAs was installing a new machine and needed to run cable under the floor. He got the tile puller, lifted a few tiles, and discovered water under the floor, surrounding some of the power distribution points. The SA who discovered the water notified his management—over the radio—and after a quick decision, radio notification to the SA staff, and a quick companywide broadcast, out came the shutdown list, and the flight director for the upcoming maintenance window did a live rehearsal of shutting everything in the machine room down. It went flawlessly because of the shutdown list.

In fact, management chose an orderly shutdown over tripping the emergency power cutoff to the room, knowing that there was an up-to-date shutdown list and having an assessment of how long before water and electricity would meet. Without the list, management would have had to cut power to the room, with potentially disastrous consequences.

20.1.7.2 KVM and Console Service

Two data center elements that make management easier are KVM switches and serial console servers. Both can be instrumental in making maintenance windows easier to run by making it possible to remotely access the console of a machine.

A KVM switch permits multiple computers to all share the same keyboard, video display, and mouse. A KVM switch saves space in a data center—monitors and keyboards take up a lot of space—and makes access more convenient; indeed, more sophisticated console access systems can be accessed from anywhere in the network.

A serial console server connects devices with serial consoles—systems without video output, such as network routers, switches, and many UNIX servers—to one central device with many serial inputs. By connecting to the console server, a user can then connect to the serial console of the other devices. All the computer room equipment that is capable of supporting a serial console should have its serial console connected to some kind of console concentrator, such as a networked terminal server.

Much work during a maintenance window requires direct console access. Using console access devices permits people to work from their own desks rather than having to try to coordinate access for many people to the very limited number of monitors in the computer room or having to waste computer room space, power, and cooling with more monitors. It is also more convenient for the individual SAs to work in their own workspace with their preparatory notes and reference materials around them.

20.1.7.3 Radios

Because the maintenance window is tightly scheduled, the high number of dependencies, and the occasional unpredictability of system administration work, all the SAs have to let the flight director know when they are finished with a task, and before they start a new task, to make sure that the prerequisite tasks have all been completed. We recommend using handheld radios to communicate within the group. Rather than seeking out the flight director, an SA can simply call over the radio. Likewise, the flight director can contact the SAs to find out status, and team members and team leaders can find one another and coordinate over the radio. If SAs need extra help, they can also ask for it over the radio. There are multiple radio channels, and long conversations can move to another channel to keep the primary one free. The radios are also essential for systemwide testing at the end of the maintenance window (see Section 20.1.9).

It is useful to use radios, cellphones, or some other effective form of two-way communication for campuswide instant communication between SAs. We recommend radios because they are not billed by the minute and typically work better in data center environments than do cellphones. Remember, anything transmitted on the airwaves can be overheard by others, so sensitive information, such as passwords, should not be communicated over radios, cellphones, or pagers.

Several options exist for selecting the radios, and what you choose depends on the coverage area that you need, the type of terrain in that area, availability, and your skill level. It is useful to have multiple channels, or frequencies, available on the handheld radios, so that long conversations can switch to another channel and leave the primary hailing channel open for others (see Table 20.3).

Line-of-sight radio communications are the most common and typically have a range of around 15 miles, depending on the surrounding terrain and buildings. Your retailer should be able to set you up with one or more frequencies and a set of radios that use those frequencies. Make sure that the retailer knows that you need the radios to work through buildings and the coverage that you need.

Table 20.3 Comparison of Radio Technologies

Type	Requirements	Advantages	Disadvantages
Line of sight	• Frequency license • Transmits through walls	Simple	• Limited range • Doesn't transmit through mountains
Repeater	• Frequency license • Radio operator license	• Better range • Repeater on mountain enables communication over mountain	• More complex to run • Skill qualifications
Cellular	Service availability	• Simple • Wide range • Unaffected by terrain • Less to carry	• Higher cost • Available only in cellphone providers' coverage area • Company contracts may limit options • Multiple channels may not be available

Repeaters can be used to extend the range of a radio signal and are particularly useful if a mountain between campus buildings would block line-of-sight communication. It can be useful to have a repeater and an antenna on top of one of the campus buildings in any case, for additional range, with at least the primary hailing channel using the repeater. This configuration usually requires that someone with a ham radio license set up and operate the equipment. Check your local laws.

Some cellphone companies offer push-to-talk features on cellphones so that phones work more like walk-talkies. This option will work wherever the telephones operate. The provider should be able to provide maps of the coverage areas. The company should supply all SAs with a cellphone with this service. This has the advantage that the SAs have to carry only the phone, not a phone and radio. This can be a quick and convenient way to get a new group established with radios but may not be feasible if it requires everyone to change to the same cellphone provider.

If radios won't work or work badly in your data center because of radio frequency (RF) shielding, put an internal phone extension with a long cord at the end of every row, as shown in Figure 6.14. That way, SAs in the data center can still communicate with other SAs while working in the data center. At worst, they can go outside the data center, contact someone on the radio, and arrange to talk to that person on a specific telephone inside the data center.

Setting up a conference call bridge for everyone to dial in to can have the benefits of radio communication with the benefit that people can dial in globally to participate. Having a permanent bridge number assigned to the group makes it easier to memorize and can save critical minutes when needed for emergencies.

Communication During an Emergency

A major news web site was flooded by users during the attacks of September 11, 2001. It took a long time to request and receive a conference call bridge and even longer for all the key players to receive dialing instructions.

20.1.8 Deadlines for Change Completion

A critical role of the flight director is tracking how the various tasks are progressing and deciding when a particular change should be aborted and the back-out plan for that change executed. For a general task with no other dependencies and for which those involved had no other remaining tasks, that time would be 11 PM on Saturday evening, minus the time required to implement the back-out plan, in the case of a weekend maintenance window. The flight director should also consider the performance level of the SA team. If the members are exhausted and frustrated, the flight director may decide to tell them to take a break or to start the back-out process early if they won't be able to implement it as efficiently as they would when they were fresh.

If other tasks depend on that system or service being operational, it is particularly critical to predefine a cut-off point for task completion. For example, if a console server upgrade is going badly, it can run into the time regularly allotted for moving large data files. Once you have overrun one time boundary, the dependencies can cascade into a full catastrophe, which can be fixed only at the next scheduled downtime, perhaps another week away. Make note of what other tasks are regularly scheduled near or during your maintenance window, so you can plan when to start backing out of a problem.

20.1.9 Comprehensive System Testing

The final stage of a maintenance window is comprehensive system testing. If the window has been short, you may need to test only the few components that you worked on. However, if you have spent your weekend-long maintenance window taking apart various complicated pieces of machinery and then putting them back together and all under a time constraint, you should plan on spending all day Sunday doing system testing.

Sunday system testing begins with shutting down all of the machines in the data center, so that you can then step through your ordered boot sequence. Assign an individual to each machine on the reboot list. The flight director announces the stages of the shutdown sequence over the radio, and each individual responds when the machine under their responsibility has completely shut down. When all the machines at the current stage have shut down, the flight director announces the next stage. When everything is down, the order is reversed, and the flight director steps everyone through the boot stages. If any problems occur with any machine at any stage, the entire sequence is halted until they are debugged and fixed. Each person assigned to a machine is responsible for ensuring that it shut down completely before responding and that all services have started correctly before calling it in as booted and operational.

Finally, when all the machines in the data center have been successfully booted in the correct order, the flight director splits the SA team into groups. Each group has a team leader and is assigned an area in one of the campus buildings. The teams are given instructions about which machines they are responsible for and which tests to perform on them. The instructions always include rebooting every desktop machine to make sure that it comes up cleanly. The tests could also include logging in, checking for a particular service, or trying to run a particular application, for example. Each person in the group has a stack of colored sticky tabs used for marking offices and cubicles that have been completed and verified as working. The SAs also have a stack of sticky tabs of a different color to mark cubicles that have a problem. When SAs run across a problem, they spend a short time trying to fix it before calling it in to the central core of people assigned to stay in the main building to help debug problems. As it finishes its area, a team is assigned to a new area or to help another team to complete an area, until the whole campus has been covered.

Meanwhile, the flight director and the senior SA troubleshooters keep track of problems on a whiteboard and decide who should tackle each problem, based on the likely cause and who is available. By the end of testing, all offices and cubicles should have tags, preferably all indicating success. If any offices or cubicles still have tags indicating a problem, a note should be left for that customer, explaining the problem; someone should be assigned to meet with that person to try to resolve it first thing in the morning.

This systematic approach helps to find problems before people come in to work the next day. If there is a bad network segment connection, a failed software depot push, or problems with a service, you'll have a good chance to fix it before anyone else is inconvenienced. Be warned, however, that some machines may not have been working in the first place. The reboot teams should always make sure to note when a machine did not look operational before they rebooted it. They can still take time to try to fix it, but it is lower on the priority list and does not have to happen before the end of the maintenance window.

Ideally, the system testing and sitewide rebooting should be completed sometime on Sunday afternoon. This gives the SA team time to rest after a stressful weekend before coming into work the next day.

20.1.10 Post-maintenance Communication

Once the maintenance work and system testing have been completed, the flight director sends out a message to the company, informing everyone that service should now be fully restored. The message briefly outlines the main successes of the maintenance window and briefly lists any services that are known not to be functioning and when they will be fixed.

This message should be in a fixed format and written largely in advance, because the flight director will be too tired to be very coherent or upbeat to write the message at the end of a long weekend. There is also little chance that anyone who proofreads the message at that point is going to be able to help, either.

Hidden Infrastructure

Sometimes, customers depend on a server or a service but neglect to inform us, perhaps because they implemented it on their own. This is what we call hidden infrastructure.

A site had a planned outage, and all power to the building was shut off. Servers were taken down in an orderly manner and brought back successfully. The following morning, the following email exchange took place:

```
From: IT
To: Everyone in the company
All servers in the Burlington office are up and running. Should you have
any issues accessing servers, please open a helpweb ticket.

From: A Developer
To: IT
Devwin8 is down.

From: IT
To: Everyone in the company
Whoever has devwin8 under their desk, turn it on, please.
```

20.1.11 Re-enable Remote Access

The final act before leaving the building should be to reenable remote access and restore the voicemail on the helpdesk phone to normal. Make sure that this appears on the master plan and the individual plans of those responsible. It can be very easily forgotten after an exhausting weekend, but it is a very visible, inconvenient, and embarrassing thing to forget, especially because it can't be fixed remotely if all remote access was turned off successfully.

20.1.12 Be Visible the Next Morning

It is very important for the entire SA group to be in early and to be visible to the company the morning after a maintenance window, no matter how hard they have worked during the outage. If everyone has company or group shirts, coordinate in advance of the maintenance window so that all the SAs wear those shirts on the day after the outage. Have the people who look after particular departments roam the corridors of those departments, keeping eyes and ears open for problems.

Have the flight director and some of the senior SAs from the central core-services group, if there is one, sit in the helpdesk area to monitor incoming calls and listen for problems that may be related to the maintenance window. These people should be able to detect and fix them sooner than the regular helpdesk staff, who won't have such an extensive overview of what has happened.

A large visible presence when the company returns to work sends the message: "We care, and we are here to make sure that nothing we did disrupts your working hours." It also means that any undetected problems can be handled quickly and efficiently, with all the relevant staff on-site and not having to be paged out of their beds. Both of these factors are important in the overall satisfaction of the company with the maintenance window. If the company is not satisfied with how the maintenance windows are handled, the windows will be discontinued, which will make preventive maintenance more difficult.

20.1.13 Postmortem

By about lunchtime of the day after the maintenance window, most of the remaining problems should have been found. At that point, if it is sufficiently quiet, the flight director and some of the senior SAs should sit down and talk about what went wrong, why, and what can be done differently. That should all be noted and discussed with the whole group later in the week. Over time, with the postmortem process, the maintenance windows will become smoother and easier. Common mistakes early on are taking on too much, not doing enough work ahead of time, and underestimating how long something will take.

20.2 The Icing

Although a lot of basics must be implemented for a successful large-scale maintenance window, a few more things are nice to have. After completion of some successful maintenance windows, you should start thinking about the icing that will make your maintenance windows more successful.

20.2.1 Mentoring a New Flight Director

It can be useful to mentor new flight directors for future maintenance windows. Therefore, flight directors must be selected far enough in advance so that the one for the next maintenance window can work with the current flight director.

The trainee flight director can produce the first draft of the master plan, using the change requests that were submitted, adding in any dependencies that are missing, and tagging those additions. The flight director then goes over the plan with the trainee, adds or subtracts dependencies, and reorganizes the tasks and personnel assignments as appropriate, explaining why. Alternatively, the flight director can create the first draft along with the trainee, explaining the process while doing so. The trainee flight director can also help out during the maintenance window, time permitting, by coordinating with the flight director to track status of certain projects and suggesting reallocation of resources where appropriate. The trainee can also help out before the downtime by discussing projects with some of the SAs if the flight director has questions about the project and by ensuring that the prerequisites listed in the change proposal are met in advance of the maintenance window.

20.2.2 Trending of Historical Data

It is useful to track how long particular tasks take and then analyze the data later and improve on the estimates in the task submission and planning process. For example, if you find that moving a certain amount of data between two machines took 8 hours and you have a large data move between two similar machines on similar networks another time, you can more accurately predict how long it will take. If a particular software package is always difficult to upgrade and takes far longer than anticipated, that will be tracked, anticipated, allowed for in the schedule, and watched closely during the maintenance interval.

Trending is particularly useful in passing along historical knowledge. When someone who used to perform a particular function has left the group, the person who takes over that function can look back at data from previous maintenance windows to see what sorts of tasks are typically performed in this area and how long they take. This data can give people new to the group and to planning a maintenance window a valuable head start so that they don't waste a maintenance opportunity and fall behind.

For each change request, record actual time to completion for use when calculating time estimates next time around. Also record any other notes that will help improve the process next time.

20.2.3 Providing Limited Availability

It is highly likely that at some point, you will be asked to keep service available for a particular group during a maintenance window. It may be something unforeseen, such as a newly discovered bug that engineering needs to work on all weekend, or it may be a new mode of operation for a division, such as customer support switching to 24/7 service and needing continuous access to its systems to meet its contracts. Internet services, remote access, global networks, and new-business pressure reduce the likelihood that a full and complete outage will be permitted.

Planning for this requirement could involve rearchitecting some services or introducing added layers of redundancy to the system. It may involve making groups more autonomous or distinct from one another. Making these changes to your network can be significant tasks by themselves, likely requiring their own maintenance window; it is best to be prepared for these requests before they arrive, or you may be left without time to prepare.

To approach this task, find out what the customers will need to be able to do during the maintenance window. Ask a lot of questions, and use your knowledge of the systems to translate these needs into a set of service-availability requirements. For example, customers will almost certainly need name service and authentication service. They may need to be able to print to specific printers and to exchange email within the company or with customers. They may require access to services across wide-area connections or across the Internet. They may need to use particular databases; find out what those machines depend on. Look at ways to make the database machines redundant so that they can also be properly maintained without loss of service. Make sure that the services they depend on are redundant. Identify what pieces of the network must be available for the services to work. Look at ways to reduce the number of networks that must be available by reducing the number of networks that the group uses and locating redundant name servers, authentication servers, and print servers on the group's networks. Find out whether small outages are acceptable, such as a couple of 10-minute outages for reloading network equipment. If not, the company needs to invest in redundant network equipment.

Devise a detailed availability plan that describes exactly what services and components must be available to that group. Try to simplify it by consolidating the network topology and introducing redundant systems for those networks. Incorporate availability planning into the master plan by ensuring that redundant servers are not down simultaneously.

20.2.4 High-Availability Sites

By the very nature of their business, high-availability sites cannot afford to have large planned outages.[2] This also means that they cannot afford *not* to make the large investment necessary to provide high availability. Sites that have high-availability requirements need to have lots of hot redundant systems that continue providing service when any one component fails. The higher the availability requirement, the more redundant systems that are required to achieve it.[3]

These sites still need to perform maintenance on the systems in service. Although the availability guarantees that these sites make to their customers typically exclude maintenance windows, they will lose customers if they have large planned outages.

20.2.4.1 The Similarities

Most of the principles described here for maintenance windows at a corporate site apply at high-availability sites.

- They need to schedule the maintenance window so that it has the least impact on their customers. For example, ISPs often choose 2 AM (local time) midweek; e-commerce sites need to choose a time when they do the least business. These windows will typically be quite frequent, such as once a week, and shorter, perhaps 4 to 6 hours in duration.

- They need to let their customers know when maintenance windows are scheduled. For ISPs, this means sending an email to the customers. For an e-commerce site, this means having a banner on the site. In both cases, it should be sent only to those customers who may be affected and should contain a warning that small outages or degraded service may occur during the maintenance window and give the times of that window. There should be only a single message about the window.

---

2. High availability is anything above 99.9 percent. Typically, sites will be aiming for three nines (99.9 percent) (9 hours downtime per year), four nines (99.99 percent) (1 hour per year), or five nines (99.999 percent) (5 minutes per year). Six nines (99.9999 percent) (less than 1 minute a year) is more expensive than most sites can afford.

3. Recall that $n + 1$ redundancy is used for services such that any one component can fail without bringing the service down, $n + 2$ means any two components can fail, and so on.

- Planning and doing as much as possible beforehand is critical because the maintenance windows should be as short as possible.

- There must be a flight director who coordinates the scheduling and tracks the progress of the tasks. If the windows are weekly, this may be a quarter-time or half-time job.

- Each item should have a change proposal. The change proposal should list the redundant systems and include a test to verify that the redundant systems have kicked in and that service is still available.

- They need to tightly plan the maintenance window. Maintenance windows are typically smaller in scope and shorter in time. Items scheduled by different people for a given window should not have dependencies on each other. There must be a small master plan that shows who has what tasks and their completion times.

- The flight director must be very strict about the deadlines for change completion.

- Everything must be fully tested before it is declared complete.

- Remote KVM and console access benefit all sites.

- The SAs need to have a strong presence when the site approaches and enters its busy time. They need to be prepared to deal quickly with any problems that may arise as a result of the maintenance.

- A brief postmortem the next day to discuss any remaining problems or issues that arose is useful.

20.2.4.2 The Differences

There also are several differences in maintenance windows for high-availability sites.

- A prerequisite is that the site must have redundancy if it is to have high availability.

- It is not necessary to disable access. Services should remain available.

- It is not necessary to have a full shutdown/boot list, because a full shutdown/reboot does not happen. However, there should be a dependency list if there are any dependencies between machines.[4]

---

4. Usually, high-availability sites avoid dependencies between machines as much as possible.

- Because ISPs and e-commerce sites do not have on-site customers, being physically visible the morning after is irrelevant. However, being available and responsive is still important. Find ways to increase your visibility and ensure excellent responsiveness. Advertise what the change was, how to report problems, and so on. Maintain a blog, or put banner advertisements on your internal web sites advertising the newest features.

- A post-maintenance communication is usually not required, unless customers must be informed about remaining problems. Customers don't want to be bombarded with email from their service providers.

- The most important difference is that the redundant architecture of the site must be taken into account during the maintenance window planning. The flight director needs to make sure that none of the scheduled work can take the service down. The SAs need to make sure that they know how long failover takes to happen. For example, how long does the routing system take to reach convergence when one of the routers goes down or comes back up? If redundancy is implemented within a single machine, the SA needs to know how to work on one part of the machine while keeping the system operating normally.

- Availability of the service as a whole must be closely monitored during the maintenance window. There should be a plan for how to deal with any failure that causes an outage as a result of temporary lack of redundancy.

20.3 Conclusion

The basics for successfully executing a planned maintenance window fall into three categories: preparation, execution, and post-maintenance customer care. The advance preparation for a maintenance window has the most effect on whether it will run smoothly. Planning and doing as much as possible in advance are key. The group needs to appoint an appropriate flight director for each maintenance window. Change proposals should be submitted to the flight director, who uses them to build a master plan and set completion deadlines for each task.

During the maintenance window, remote access should be disabled, and infrastructure, such as console servers and radios, should be in place. The plan needs to be executed with as few hiccups as possible. The timetable must be adhered to rigidly; it must finish with complete system testing.

Good customer care after the maintenance window is important to its success. Communication about the window and a visible presence the morning after are key.

Integrating a mentoring process, saving historical data and doing trend analysis for better estimates, providing continuity, and providing limited availability to groups that request it can be incorporated at a later date. Proper planning, good back-out plans, strict adherence to deadlines for change completion, and comprehensive testing should avert all but some minor disasters. Some tasks may not be completed, and those changes will need to be backed out. In our experience, a well-planned, properly executed maintenance window never leads to a complete disaster. A badly planned or poorly executed one could, however. These kinds of massive outages are difficult and risky. We hope that you will find the planning techniques in this chapter useful.

Exercises

1. Read the paper on how the AT&T/Lucent network was split (Limoncelli et al. 1997), and consider how having a weekend maintenance window would have changed the process. What parts of that project would have been performed in advance as preparatory work, what parts would have been easier, and what parts would have been more difficult? Evaluate the risks in your approach.

2. A case study in Section 20.1.1 describes the scheduling process for a particular software company. What are the dates and events that you would need to avoid for a maintenance window in your company? Try to derive a list of dates, approximately 3 months apart, that would work for your company.

3. Consider the SAs in your company. Who do you think would make good flight directors and why?

4. What tasks or projects can you think of at your site that would be appropriate for a maintenance window? Create and fill in a change-request form. What preparation could you do for this change in advance of the maintenance window?

5. Section 20.1.6 discusses disabling access to the site. What specific tasks would need to be performed at your site, and how would you re-enable that access?

6. Section 20.1.7.1 discusses the shutdown and reboot sequence. Build an appropriate list for your site. If you have permission, test it.

7. Section 20.2.3 discusses providing limited availability for some people to be able to continue working. What groups are likely to require 24/7 availability? What changes would you need to make to your network and services infrastructure to keep services available to each of those groups?

8. Research the flight operations methodologies used at NASA. Relate what you learned to the practice of system administration.

Chapter 21

Centralization and Decentralization

This chapter seeks to help an SA decide how much centralization is appropriate, for a particular site or service, and how to transition between more and less centralization.

Centralization means having one focus of control. One might have two DNS servers in every department of a company, but they all might be controlled by a single entity. Alternatively, **decentralized** systems distribute control to many parts. In our DNS example, each of those departments might maintain and control its own DNS server, being responsible for maintaining the skill set to stay on top of the technology as it changes, to architect the systems as it sees fit, and to monitor the service. Centralization refers to nontechnical control also. Companies can structure IT in a centralized or decentralized manner.

Centralization is an attempt to improve efficiency by taking advantage of potential economies of scale: improving the average; it may also improve reliability by minimizing opportunities for error. Decentralization is an attempt to improve speed and flexibility by reorganizing to increase local control and execution of a service: improving the best case. Neither is always better, and neither is always possible in the purest sense. When each is done well, it can also realize the benefits of the other: odd paradox, isn't it?

Decentralization means breaking away from the prevailing hegemony, revolting against the frustrating bureaucratic ways of old. Traditionally, it means someone has become so frustrated with a centralized service that "do it yourself" has the potential of being better. In the modern environment decentralization is often a deliberate response to the faster pace of business and to customer expectations of increased autonomy.

Centralization means pulling groups together to create order and enforce process. It is cooperation for the greater good. It is a leveling process. It seeks to remove the frustrating waste of money on duplicate systems, extra work, and manual processes. New technology paradigms often bring opportunities for centralization. For example, although it may make sense for each department to have slightly different processes for handling paper forms, no one department could fund building a pervasive web-based forms system. Therefore, a disruptive technology, such as the web, creates an opportunity to replace many old systems with a single, more efficient, centralized system. Conversely, standards-based web technology can enable a high degree of local autonomy under the aegis of a centralized system, such as delegated administration.

21.1 The Basics

At large companies in particular, it seems as if every couple of years, management decides to centralize everything that is decentralized and vice versa. Smaller organizations encounter similar changes driven by mergers or opening of new campuses or field offices. In this section, we discuss guiding principles you should consider before making such broad changes. We then discuss some services that are good candidates for centralization and decentralization.

21.1.1 Guiding Principles

There are several guiding principles related to centralization and decentralization. They are similar to what anyone making large, structural changes should consider.

- **Problem-Solving:** *Know what specific problem you are trying to solve.* Clearly define what problem you are trying to fix. "Reliability is inconsistent because each division has different brands of hardware." "Services break when network connections to sales offices are down." Again, write down the specific problem or problems and communicate these to your team. Use this list as a reality check later in the project to make sure that you haven't lost sight of the goal. If you are not solving a specific problem, or responding to a direct management request, stop right here. Why are you about to make these changes? Are you sure this is a real priority?

- **Motivation:** *Understand your motivation for making the change.* Maybe you are seeking to save money, increase speed or become more flexible.

Maybe your reasons are political: You are protecting your empire or your boss, making your group look good, or putting someone's personal business philosophy into action. Maybe you are doing it simply to make your own life easier; that's valid too. Write down your motivation and remind yourself of it from time to time to verify that you haven't strayed.

- **Experience Counts:** *Use your best judgment.* Sometimes, you must use experience and a hunch rather than specific scientific measurements. For example, we've found that when centralizing email servers, our experience has developed these rules of thumb: Small companies—five departments with 100 people—tend to need one email server. Larger companies can survive with an email server per thousands of people, especially if there is one large headquarters and many smaller sales offices. When the company grows to the point of having more than one site, each site tends to require its own email server but is unlikely to require its own Internet gateway. Extremely large or geographically diverse companies start to require multiple Internet gateways at different locations.

- **Involvement:** *Listen to the customers' concerns.* Consult with customers to understand their expectations: Retain the good aspects and fix the bad ones. Focus on the qualities that they mention, not the implementation. People might say that they like the fact that "Karen was always right there when we needed new desktop PCs installed." That is an implementation. The new system might not include on-site personnel. What should be retained is that the new service has to be responsive—as responsive as having Karen standing right there. That may mean the use of overnight delivery services or preconfigured and "ready to eat" systems[1] stashed in the building, or whatever it takes to meet that expectation. Alternatively, you must do expectation setting if the new system is not going to deliver on old expectations. Maybe people will have to plan ahead and ask for workstations a day in advance.

- **Be Realistic:** *Be circumspect about unrealistic promises.* You should thoroughly investigate any claims that you will save money by decentralizing, add flexibility by centralization, or have an entirely new system without pain: The opposite is usually the case. If a vendor promises that a new product will perform miracles but requires you to centralize

---

1. Do not attempt to eat a computer. "Ready to eat" systems are hot spares that will be fully functional when powered up: absolutely no configuration files to modify and so on.

(or decentralize) how something is currently organized, maybe the benefits come from the organizational change, not the product!

- **Balance:** *Centralize as much as makes sense for today, with an eye toward the future.* You must find the balance between centralization and decentralization. There are time considerations: Building the perfect system will take forever. You must set realistic goals yet keep an eye to future needs. For example, in 6 months, the new system will be complete and then will be expected to process a million widgets per day. However, a different architecture will be required to process 2 million widgets per day, the rate that will be needed a year later, and will require considerably more development time. You must balance the advantage of having a new system in 6 months—with the problem of needing to start building the next-generation system immediately—versus the advantage of waiting longer for a system that will not need to be replaced so soon.

- **Access:** *The more centralized something is, the more likely it is that some customers will need a special feature or some kind of customization.* An old business proverb is: "All of our customers are the same: They each have unique requirements." One size never fits all. You can't do a reasonable job of centralizing without being flexible; you'll doom the project if you try. Instead, look for a small number of models. Some customers require autonomy. Some may require performing their own updates, which means creating a system of access control so that customers can modify their own segments without affecting others.

- **No Pressure:** *It's like rolling out any new service.* Although more emotional impact may be involved than with other changes, both centralization and decentralization projects have issues similar to building a new service. That said, new services require careful coordination, planning, and understanding of customer needs to succeed.

- **110 Percent:** *You have only one chance to make a good first impression.* A new system is never trusted until proven a success, and the first experience with the new system will set the mood for all future customer interactions. Get it right the first time, even if it means spending more money up front or taking extra time for testing. Choose test customers carefully, making sure they trust you to fix any bugs found while testing, and won't gossip about it at the coffee machine. Provide superior service the first month, and people will forgive later mistakes. Mess up right at the start, and rebuilding a reputation is nearly impossible.

- **Veto Power:** *Listen to the customers, but remember that management has the control.* The organizational structure can influence the level of centralization that is appropriate or possible. The largest impediment to centralization often is management decisions or politics. Lack of trust makes it difficult to centralize. If the SA team has not proved itself, management may be unwilling to support the large change. Management may not be willing to fund the changes, which usually indicates that the change is not important to them. For example, if the company hasn't funded a central infrastructure group, SAs will end up decentralized. It may be better to have a central infrastructure group; lacking management support, however, the fallback is to have each group make the best subinfrastructure it can—ideally, coordinating formally or informally to set standards, purchase in bulk, and so on. Either way, the end goal is to provide excellent service to your customers.

21.1.2 Candidates for Centralization

SAs continually find new opportunities to centralize processes and services. Centralization does not innately improve efficiency. It brings about the opportunity to introduce new economies of scale to a process. What improves efficiency is standardization, which is usually a by-product of centralization. The two go hand in hand.

The cost savings of centralization come from the presumption that there will be less overhead than the sum of the individual overheads of each decentralized item. Centralization can create a simpler, easier-to-manage architecture. One SA can manage a lot more machines if the processes for each are the same.

To the previous owners of the service being centralized, centralization is about giving up control. Divisions that previously provided their own service now have to rely on a centralized group for service. SAs who previously did tasks themselves, their own way, now have to make requests of someone else who has his or her own way to do things. The SAs will want to know whether the new service provider can do things better.

Before taking control away from a previous SA or customer, ask yourself what the customer's psychological response will be. Will there be attempts to sabotage the effort? How can you convince people that the new system will be better than the old system? How will damage control and rumor control be accomplished? What's the best way to make a good first impression?

The best way to succeed in a centralization program is to pick the right services for centralization. Here are some good candidates.

- **Distributed Systems:** *Management of distributed systems.* Historically, each department of an organization configured and ran its own web servers. As the technology got more sophisticated, less customization of each web server was required. Eventually, there was no reason not to have each web server configured exactly the same way, and the need for rapid updates of new binaries was becoming a security issue. The motivation was to save money by not requiring each department to have a high level of web server expertise. The problem being fixed was the lack of similar configurations on each server. A system was designed to maintain a central configuration repository that would update each of the servers in a controlled and secure manner. The customers affected were the departmental SAs, who were eager to give up a task that they didn't always understand. By centralizing web services, the organization could also afford to have one or more SAs become better-trained in that particular service, to provide better in-house customer support.

- **Consolidation:** *Consolidate services onto fewer hosts.* In the past, for reliability's sake, one service was put on each physical host. However, as technology progresses, it can be beneficial to have many services on one machine. The motivation is to decrease cost. The problem being fixed is that every host has overhead costs, such as power, cooling, administration, machine room space, and maintenance contracts. Usually, a single, a more powerful machine costs less to operate than several smaller hosts. As services are consolidated, care must be taken to group customers with similar needs.

  Since the late 1990s, **storage consolidation** has been a big buzzword. By building one large storage-area network that each server accesses, there is less "stranded storage"—partially-full disks—on each server. Often, storage consolidation involves decommissioning older, slower, or soon-to-fail disks and moving the data onto the SAN, providing better performance and reliability.

  Server virtualization, a more recent trend, involves using virtual hosts to save hardware and license costs. For example, financial institutions used to have expensive servers and multiple backup machines to run a calculation at a particular time of the day, such as making end-of-day transactions after the stock market closes. Instead, a virtual machine can be spun up shortly before the market closes; the machine runs its tasks, then spins down. Once it is done, the server is free to run other virtual machines that do other periodic tasks.

By using a global file system, such as a SAN, a **virtualization cluster** can be built. Since the virtual machine images—the data stored on disk that defines the state of a virtual machine—can be accessed from many hardware servers, advanced virtualization management software can migrate virtual machines between physical machines with almost unnoticable switch-over time. Many times, sites realize that they need many machines, each performing a particular function, none of which requires enough CPU horsepower to justify the cost of dedicated hardware. Instead, the virtual machines can share a farm, or cluster, of physical machines, as needed. Since virtual machines can migrate between different hardware nodes, workload can be rebalanced. Virtual machines can be moved off an overloaded physical machine. Maintenance becomes easier too. If one physical machine is showing signs of hardware problems, virtual machines can be migrated off it onto a spare machine with no loss of service; the physical machine can then be repaired or upgraded.

- **Administration:** *System administration.* When redesigning your organization (see Chapter 30), your motivation may be to reduce cost, improve speed, or provide services consistently throughout the enterprise. The problem may be the extra cost of having technical management for each team or that the distributed model resulted in some divisions' having poorer service than others. Centralizing the SA team can fix these problems.

  To provide customization and the "warm fuzzies" of personal attention, subteams might focus on particular customer segments. An excellent example of this is a large hardware company's team of "CAD ambassadors," an SA group that specializes in cross-departmental support of CAD/CAM tools throughout the company. However, a common mistake is to take this to an extreme. We've seen at least one amazingly huge company that centralized to the point that "customer liaisons" were hired to maintain a relationship with the customer groups, and the customers hired liaisons to the centralized SA staff. Soon, these liaisons numbered more than 100. At that point, the savings in reduced overhead were surely diminished. A regular reminder and dedication to the original motivation may have prevented that problem.

- **Specialization:** *Expertise.* In decentralized organizations, a few of the groups are likely to have more expertise in particular areas than other groups do. This is fine if they maintain casual relationships and help one another. However, certain expertise can become critical to business, and therefore an informal arrangement becomes an unacceptable business risk. In that case, it may make sense to consolidate that expertise into one group. The motivation is to ensure that all divisions have access to a minimum level of expertise in one specific area or areas. The problem is that the lack of this expertise causes uneven service levels, for example, if one division had unreliable DNS but others didn't or if one division had superior Internet email service, whereas others were still using UUCP-style addresses. (If you are too young to remember UUCP-style addresses, just count your blessings.) That would be intolerable!

  Establishing a centralized group for one particular service can bring uniformity and improve the average across the entire company. Some examples of this include such highly specialized skills as maintaining an Internet gateway, a software depot, various security issues—VPN service, intrusion detection, security-hole scanning, and so on—DNS, and email service. A common pattern at larger firms is to create a "Care Services" or "Infrastructure" team to consolidate expertise in these areas and provide infrastructure across the organization.

- **Left Hand, Right Hand:** *Infrastructure decisions.* The creation of infrastructure and platform standards can be done centrally. This is a subcase of centralizing expertise. The motivation at one company was that that infrastructure costs were high and interoperability between divisions was low. There were many specific problems to be solved. Every division had a team of people researching new technologies and making decisions independently. Each team's research duplicated the effort of the others. Volume-purchasing contracts could not be signed, because each individual division was too small to qualify. Repair costs were high because so many different spare parts had to be purchased. When divisions did make compatible purchasing decisions, multiple spare parts were still being purchased because there was no coordination or cooperation. The solution was to reduce the duplication in effort by having one standards committee for infrastructure and platform standards. Previously, new technology was often adopted in pockets around the company because some divisions were less averse to risk; these became the divisions that performed product trials or became early adopters of new technology.

This last example brings up another benefit of centralization. The increased purchasing power should mean that better equipment can be purchased for the same cost. Vendors may provide better service, as well as preferred pricing, when they deal with a centralized purchasing group that reflects the true volume of orders from that one source. Sometimes, money can be saved through centralization. Other times, it is better to use the savings to invest in better equipment.

- **Commodity:** *If it has become a commodity, consider centralization.* A good time to consider centralizing something is when the technology path it has taken has made it a commodity. Network printing, file service, email servers, and even workstation maintenance used to be unique, rare technologies. However, now these things are commodities and excellent candidates for centralization.

Case Study: Big, Honkin' File Servers

Tom's customers and even fellow SAs fought long and hard against the concept of large, centralized file servers. The customers complained about the loss of control and produced, in Tom's opinion, ill-conceived pricing models that demonstrated that the old Unix-based file servers were the better way to go. What they were really fighting was the notion that network file service was no longer very special; it had become a commodity and therefore an excellent candidate for centralization. Eventually, an apples-to-apples comparison was done. This included a total cost-of-ownership model that included the SA time and energy to maintain the old-style systems. The value of some unique features of the dedicated file servers, such as file system snapshot, was difficult to quantify. However, even when the cost model showed the systems to cost about the same per gigabyte of usable storage, the dedicated file servers had an advantage over the old systems: consistency and support. The old systems were a mishmash of various manufacturers for the host; for the RAID controllers; and for the disk drives, cables, network interfaces, and, in some cases, even the racks they sat in! Each of these items usually required a level of expertise and training to maintain efficiently, and no single vendor would support these Frankenstein monsters. Usually, when the SA who purchased a particular RAID device left the group, the expertise left with the person. Standardizing on a particular product resulted in a higher level of service because the savings were used to purchase top-of-the line systems that had fewer problems than inexpensive competitors. Also, having a single phone number to call for support was a blessing.

Printing is another commodity service that has many opportunities for centralization, both in the design of the service itself and when purchasing supplies. Section 24.1.1 provides more examples.

21.1.3 Candidates for Decentralization

Decentralization does not automatically improve response times. When done correctly, it creates an opportunity to do so. Even when the new process is less efficient or is inefficient in different ways, people may be satisfied simply to be in control. We've found that people are more tolerant of a mediocre process if they feel they control it.

Decentralization often trades cost efficiency for something even more valuable. In these examples, we decentralize to democratize control, gain fault tolerance, acquire the ability to have a customized solution, or remove ourselves from clue-lacking central authorities. ("They're idiots, but they're *our* division's idiots.") One must seek to retain what was good about the old system while fixing what was bad.

Decentralization democratizes control. The new people gaining control may require training; this includes both the customers and the SAs. The goal may be autonomy, the ability to control one's own destiny, or the ability to be functional when disconnected from the network. This latter feature is also referred to as **compartmentalization,** the ability to achieve different reliability levels for different segments of the community. Here are some good candidates for decentralization.

- *Fault tolerance.* The duplication of effort that happens with decentralization can remove single points of failure. A company with growing field offices required all employees to read email off servers located in the headquarters. There were numerous complaints that during network outages, people couldn't read or even compose email, because composition required access to directory servers that were also at the headquarters. Divisions in other time zones were particularly upset that maintenance times at the headquarters were their prime working hours. The motivation was to increase reliability, in particular access during outages. The problem was that people couldn't use email when WAN links were down. The solution was to install local LDAP caches and email servers in each of the major locations. (It was convenient and effective to also use this host for DNS, authentication, and other services.) Although mail would not be transmitted site to site during an outage, customers could access their email store, local email could be delivered, and messages that needed to be relayed to other sites would transparently queue until the WAN link recovered. This could have been a management disaster if each site was expected to have the expertise required to configure and maintain such systems or if different sites created different standards. Instead, it was a big success because management was centralized. Each site received preconfigured hardware and software that simply needed to be plugged in. Updates were done via a centralized system. Even backups could be performed remotely, if required.

- *Customization.* Sometimes, certain customer groups have a business requirement to be on the bleeding edge of technology, whereas others require stability. A research group required early access to technology, usually before it was approved by corporate infrastructure standards committees. The motivation was largely political because the group maintained a certain status by being ahead of others within the company, as well as in the industry. There was also business motivation: The group's projects were far-reaching and futuristic, and the group needed to "live in the future" if it was going to build systems that would work well in the networks of the future. The problem was that the group was being prevented from deviating from corporate standards. The solution was to establish a group-specific SA team. The team members participated in the committees that created the corporate standards and were able to provide valuable feedback because they had experience with technologies that the remainder of the committee was just considering. Providing this advice also maintained the groups elite status. Their participation also guaranteed that they would be able to establish interoperability guidelines between their "rogue" systems and the corporate standards. This local SA team was able to meet the local requirements that were different from those of the rest of the company. They could provide special features and select a different balance of stability versus cutting-edge features.

- *Meeting your customers' needs.* Sometimes, the centralized services group may be unable to meet the demands placed on it by some of the departments in the company. Before abandoning the centralized service, try to understand the reason for the failures of the central group to meet your customers' needs. Try to work with the customers to find a solution that works for both SAs and customers, such as the one described earlier. Your ultimate responsibility is to meet your customers' needs and to make them successful. If you cannot make the relationship with the central group work, your company may have to decentralize the necessary services so that you can meet your group's needs. Make sure that you have management support to make this move; be aware of the pitfalls of decentralization, and try to avoid them. Remember why you moved to a centralized model, and periodically reevaluate whether it still makes sense.

Advocates of decentralization sometimes argue that centralized services are single points of failure. However, when centralization is done right, the savings can be reinvested into technology that increases fault tolerance. Often, the result of decentralization is many single points of failure spread all over the company; redundancy is reduced. For example, when individual groups build their own LANs, they might have the training only to set up a very basic, simple LAN infrastructure. The people doing the work have other responsibilities that keep them from being able to become experts in modern LAN technology. When LAN deployment is centralized, people who specialize in networking and do it full-time are in charge. They have the time to deploy redundancy protocols and proactive monitoring that will enable them to fix problems within a defined SLA. The savings from volume discounts often will pay for much of the redundancy. The increased reliability from a professional SLA-driven design and operation process benefits the company in many ways.

Another point in support of decentralization is that there are benefits to having diversity in your systems. For example, different OSs have different security problems. It can be beneficial to have only a fraction of your systems taken out by a virus. A major software company had a highly publicized DNS outage because all of its DNS servers were running the same OS and the same release of DNS software. If the company had used a variety of OSs and DNS software, one of them might not have been susceptible to the security hole that was being leveraged. If you are the centralized provider, accept that this may sometimes be necessary.

21.2 The Icing

Centralization and decentralization can be major overhauls. If you are asking people to accept the pain of converting to a new system, you should be proposing a system that is not only cheaper but also better for them.

There is an old adage that often appears on buttons and bumper stickers: "Cheap, fast, good. Pick two." This pointed statement reveals a time-tested truism. In general, you must sacrifice one of those three items to achieve the other two. In fact, if someone tries to claim that they provide all three simultaneously, look under the tablecloth of their slick demo and check for hidden wires. This section describes some examples that achieved or promised to achieve all three. Some, like the purchasing example in 21.2.1, were a great overall success. Others had mixed results.

21.2.1 Consolidate Purchasing

In this example, centralization resulted in better products more quickly delivered for less money. An SA group was able to position itself to approve all computer-related purchasing for its division. In fact, the group was able to have the purchasing agent who handled such purchases moved into its group so they could work closely on contracts, maintenance agreements, and so on. As a result, the group was able to monitor what was being purchased. Particular purchases, such as servers, would alert the SAs to contact customers to find out what special requirements the server would create: Did it need machine room space, special networking, or configuration? This solved a problem whereby customers would blindside the SAs with requests for major projects. Now the SAs could contact them and schedule these large projects.

As a side benefit, the group was able to do a better job of asset management. Because all purchasing was done through one system, there was one place where serial numbers of new equipment were captured. Previous attempts at tracking assets had failed because it depended on such data to be collected by individuals who had other priorities.

Centralized purchasing's biggest benefit was the fact that the SAs now had knowledge of what was being purchased. They noticed certain products being purchased often and arranged volume purchasing deals for them. Certain software packages were preordered in bulk. Imagine the customers' surprise when they tried to purchase a particular package and instead received a note saying that their department would be billed for one-fiftieth of a 50-license package purchased earlier that year and were given a password they could use to download the software package and manuals. That certainly beat waiting for it to be delivered!

The most pervasive savings came from centralizing the PC purchasing process. Previously, customers had ordered their own PCs and spent days looking through catalogs, selecting each individual component to their particular needs. The result was that the PC repair center had to handle many types of motherboards, cards, and software drivers. Although a customer might take pride in saving the $10 by selecting a nonstandard video card, he or she would not appreciate the cost of a technician at the PC repair department spending half a day to get it working. With the repair group unable to stock such a wide variety of spare parts, the customers were extremely unhappy with having to wait weeks for replacement parts to arrive.

The average time for a PC to be delivered under the old system had been 6 weeks. It would take a week to determine what was to be ordered and push it through the purchasing process. The vendor would spend a couple of weeks building the PC to the specifications and delivering it. Finally, another week would pass before the SAs had time to load the OS, with possibly an additional week if there were difficulties. A company cannot be fast paced if every PC requires more than a month to be delivered. To make matters worse, new employees had to wait weeks before they had a PC. This was a morale killer and reflected badly on the company. The temporary solution was that management would beg the SAs to cobble together a PC out of spare parts to be used until the person's real PC was delivered. Thus, twice as much work was being done because two complete PC deliveries were required.

The centralized purchasing group was able to solve these problems. The group found that by standardizing the PC configuration, a volume discount could be used to reduce cost. In fact, the group was able to negotiate a good price even though it had negotiated four configurations: server, desktop, ultralight laptop, and ultrapowerful laptop. Fearing that people would still opt for a custom configuration, the group used some of the savings to ensure that the standard configuration would be more powerful, with better audio and video than any previously purchased custom PC. Even if the group matched the old price, the savings to the PC repair department would be considerable. The ability to stock spare parts would be a reduction in lost productivity by customers waiting for repairs.

The purchasing group realized that it wouldn't be able to push a standard on the customers, who could simply opt for a fully custom solution if the standard configuration wasn't to their liking. Therefore, purchasing made sure to pull people to their standard by making it amazingly good. With the volume discounts, the price was so low and quality so high that most of the remaining customization options would result in a less powerful machine for more money. How could anyone not choose the standard? Using pull instead of push is using the carrot, not the stick, get a mule to move forward.

One more benefit was achieved. Because the flow of new machines being purchased was relatively constant, the purchasing group was able to pre-order batches of machines that would be preloaded with their OS by the SAs. New employees would have a top-notch PC installed on their desk the day before they arrived. They would be productive starting on the very first day.

Ordering time for PCs was reduced from 6 weeks to 6 minutes. When faced with the choice between ordering the exact PC they wanted and waiting 6 weeks or waiting 6 minutes and getting a PC that was often more powerful than they required, for less money, it was difficult to reject the offer.

Any company that is rapidly growing, purchasing a lot of computer-related items, or deploying PCs should consider these techniques. Other advice on rapid PC deployment can be found in Chapter 3. More information about how PC vendors price their product lines is in Section 4.1.3.

21.2.2 Outsourcing

Outsourcing is often a form of centralization. **Outsourcing** is a process by which an external company is paid to provide certain technical functions for a company. Some commonly outsourced tasks are running the corporate PC helpdesk, remote access, WAN and LAN services, and computer deployment operations. Some specific tasks, such as building the infrastructure to support a particular application—web site, e-commerce site, enterprise resource planning (ERP) system—are outsourced, though probably vendors refer to that process "professional services" instead.

The process of outsourcing usually involves centralization to reduce redundant services and to standardize processes. Outsourcing can save money by eliminating the political battles that were preventing such efficiencies. When executives are unable to overcome politics through good management, outsourcing can be a beneficial distraction.

Advocates emphasize that outsourcing lets a company focus on its core competency rather than on all the technological infrastructure required to support that core. Some companies become bogged down in supporting their infrastructure, to the detriment of their business goals. In that situation, outsourcing can be an appealing solution.

The key in outsourcing is to know what you want and to make sure that it is specified in the contract. The outsourcing company isn't required to do anything that isn't in the contract. Although the salespeople may paint an exciting picture, once the contract is signed, you should expect only what is specified in ink. This can be a particular problem when the outsourced services had been provided previously in-house.

We've seen three related problems with signing an outsourcing contract. Together, they create an interesting paradox. Outsourcing to gain new technical competence means that the people you are negotiating with have more technical competence than you do. This gives the outsourcing firm the power seat in the negotiations. Second, to accurately state your requirements in the contract, you must have a good understanding of your technical needs; however, if your executive management had a good handle on what was needed and was skilled at communicating this, you wouldn't need outsourcing. Finally, companies sometimes don't decide to outsource until their computing infrastructure has deteriorated to the point that outsourcing is being done as an emergency measure and are thus too rushed or desperate to keep the upper hand in negotiations. These companies don't know what they want or how to ask for it and are in too much of a panicked rush to do adequate research. As you can imagine, this spells trouble. It is worth noting that none of these situations that specifically allow for technology knowledge refer to the buying company.

You should research the outsourcing process, discuss the process with peers at other companies, and talk with customer references. Make sure that the contract specifies the entire life cycle of services—design, installation, maintenance and support, decommissioning, data integrity, and disaster recovery—SLAs penalties for not meeting performance metrics, and a process for adding and removing services from the contract. Negotiating an outsourcing contract is extremely difficult, requiring skills far more sophisticated than our introduction to negotiating (Section 32.2.1).

Some outsourcing contracts are priced below cost in order for the vendor to be considered a preferred bidder on project work; it's on this project work that outsourcing deals make money for the supplier. Contracts usually specify what is "in scope" of the contract and casually mention a standard rate for all other "out-of-scope" work. The standard rate is often very high, and the outsource organization hopes to identify as much out-of-scope work as possible. Clients don't usually think to send such work out to bid to receive a better rate.

There are outsourcing consultants who will lead you through the negotiating process. Be sure to retain one who has no financial ties to the outsourcing firms that you are considering.

Don't Hide Negotiations

When one Fortune 500 company outsourced its computing support infrastructure, the executive management feared a large backlash by both the computing professionals within the company and the office workers being supported. Therefore, the deal was done quickly and without consulting the people who were providing the support. As a result, the company was missing key elements, such as data backups, quality metrics, and a clear service-level specification. The company had no way to renegotiate the contract without incurring severe penalties. When it added backups after the fact, the out-of-scope charges in the contract were huge.

Don't negotiate an outsource contract in secret; get buy-in from the affected customers.

When you outsource anything, your job becomes quality assurance. Some people think that after outsourcing, the contract will simply take care of itself. In reality, you must now learn now to monitor SLAs to make sure that you get all the value out of the contract. It is common for items such as documentation or service/network architecture diagrams to be specified on the contract, but not delivered until explicitly requested.

Critically Examine Metrics

Executives at one company were very proud of their decision to outsource when, after a year of service, the metrics indicated that calls to the helpdesk were completed, on average, in 5 minutes. This sounded good, but why were employees still complaining about the service they received? Someone thought to ask how this statistic could be true when so many calls included sending a technician to the person's desk. A moderate percentage of calls like that would destroy such an excellent average. It turned out that the desk-side support technicians had their own queue of requests, which had their own time-to-completion metrics. A call to the helpdesk was considered closed when a ticket was passed on to the desk-side technician's queue, thus artificially improving the helpdesk's metrics. Always ask for a detailed explanation of any metrics you receive from a vendor, so that you can clearly relate them to SLAs.

While you are trying to get the most out of your contract, the outsourcing company is trying to do the same. If the contract is for "up to $5 million over 5 years," you can be assured that the account executive is not going to let you spend only $4.5 million. Most outsourcing companies hold weekly meetings to determine whether they are on schedule for using the entire value of the contract as quickly as possible; they penalize their sales team for coming in "under contract." Does the contract charge $1,000 per server per month? "How can we convince them that a new service they've requested needs a dedicated host rather than loading it onto an existing machine?" will be asked at every turn. Here's the best part: If they can get you to spend all $5 million of a 5-year contract in only 4.5 years, those last 6 months usually won't be at the discounted rate you negotiated. How can anyone predict what their IT needs will be that far out? This is the most dangerous aspect of long-term outsourcing contracts.

Make sure that your contract specifies an exit strategy. When starting a long-term contract, the outsourcing company usually retains the right to hire your current computing staff. However, the contract never says that you get them back if you decide that outsourcing isn't for you. Many contracts fail to guarantee that your former staff will remain on-site for the duration of the contract. The company may decide to use their skills at another site! Even switching to a different outsourcing company is difficult, because the old company certainly isn't going to hand over its employees to the competition. Make sure that the contract specifies what will happen in these situations so that you do not get trapped. Switching back to in-house service is extremely difficult. Eliminate any noncompete clauses that would prevent you from hiring back people.

Our coverage of outsourcing is admittedly centric to our experiences as SAs. Many books give other points of view. Some are general books about outsourcing (Gay and Essinger 2000, Rothery and Robertson 1995); by contrast, Williams (1998) gives a CIO's view of the process. Mylott (1995) discusses the outsourcing process with a focus on managing the transfer of MIS duties. Group Staff Outsource (1996) has a general overview of outsourcing. Kuong (2000) discusses the specific issue of provisioning outsourced web application service provider services. Jennings and Passaro (1999) is an interesting read if you want to go into the outsourcing business yourself. Finally, Chapman and Andrade (1997) discuss how to get out of an outsourcing contract and offer an excellent sample of outsourcing horror stories. We pick up the topic of outsourcing again in Section 30.1.8.

The first edition of this book was written during the outsourcing craze of the late 1990s. We had numerous warnings about the negative prospects of outsourcing, many of which came true. Now the craze is over, but **off-shoring** is the new craze. Everything old is new again.

21.3 Conclusion

Centralization and decentralization are complicated topics. Neither is always the right solution. Technical issues, such as server administration, as well as nontechnical issues, such as organizational structure, can be centralized or decentralized.

Both topics are about making changes. When making such pervasive changes, we recommend that you consider these guiding principles: know what specific problem you are solving; understand your motivation for making the change; centralize as much as makes sense for today; recognize that as in rolling out any new service, it requires careful planning; and, most important, listen to the customers.

It is useful to learn from other people's experiences. The USENIX LISA conference has published many case studies (Epp and Baines 1992; Ondishko 1989; Schafer 1992b; and Schwartz, Cottrell, and Dart 1994). Harlander (1994) and Miller and Morris (1996) describe useful tools and the lessons learned from using them.

Centralizing purchasing can be an excellent way to control costs, and our example showed that it can be done not by preventing people from getting what they want, but by helping them make purchases in a more cost-effective manner.

We ended with a discussion of outsourcing. Outsourcing can be a major force for centralization and will be a large part of system administration for a very long time, even under different names.

> ❖ **Centralization Rules of Thumb**   Every site is different, but we have found that, as an informal rule of thumb, centralization of the following services is preferred once a company grows large enough to have multiple divisions:
>
> * Network security
> * Internet connectivity
> * WAN services
> * LAN deployment and operations
> * Email services
> * ActiveDirectory/LDAP
> * Desktop deployment and life-cycle management

- Storage within a data center
- Web services with external access
- IP address allocation and DNS management

Exercises

1. How centralized or decentralized is your current environment? Give examples.

2. Give an example of a service or an aspect of your organization that should be centralized. Relate guiding principles in Section 21.1.1 to such a project.

3. Give an example of a service or an aspect of your organization that should be decentralized. Relate guiding principles in Section 21.1.1 to such a project.

4. In Section 21.1.3, we describe decentralizing email servers to achieve better reliability. How would you construct a similar architecture for print servers?

5. Describe a small centralization project that would improve your current system.

6. Share your favorite outsourcing horror story.

Part IV

Providing Services

Chapter 22

Service Monitoring

Monitoring is an important component of providing a reliable, professional service. The two primary types of monitoring are real-time monitoring and historical monitoring. Each has a very different purpose. As discussed in Section 5.1.13, monitoring is a basic component of building a service and meeting its expected or required service levels.

"If you can't measure it, you can't manage it." In the field of system administration, that useful business axiom becomes: "If you aren't monitoring it, you aren't managing it."

Monitoring is essential for any well-run site but is a project that can keep increasing in scope. This chapter should help you anticipate and prepare for that. We look at what the basics of a monitoring system are and then discuss the numerous ways that you can improve your monitoring system.

For some sites, such as sites providing a service over the Internet, comprehensive monitoring is a business requirement. These sites need to monitor everything to make sure that they don't lose revenue because of an outage that goes unnoticed. E-commerce sites will probably need to implement everything presented in this chapter.

22.1 The Basics

Systems monitoring can be used to detect and fix problems, identify the source of problems, predict and avoid future problems, and provide data on SAs' achievements. The two primary ways to monitor systems are to (1) gather historical data related to availability and usage and (2) perform real-time monitoring to ensure that SAs are notified of failures.

Historical monitoring is used for recording long-term uptime, usage, and performance statistics. This has two components: collecting the data and viewing the data. The results of historical monitoring are conclusions: "The web service was up 99.99 percent of the time last year, up from the previous year's 99.9 percent statistic." Utilization data is used for capacity planning. For example, you might view a graph of bandwidth utilization gathered for the past year for an Internet connection. The graph might visually depict a growth rate indicating that the pipe will be full in 4 months. Cricket and Orca are commonly used historical monitoring tools.

Real-time monitoring alerts the SA team of a failure as soon as it happens and has two components: a monitoring component that notices failures and an alerting component that alerts someone to the failure. There is no point in a system's knowing that something has gone down unless it alerts someone to the problem. The goal is for the SA team to notice outages before customers do. This results in shorter outages and problems being fixed before customers notice, along with building the team's reputation for maintaining high-quality service. Nagios and Big Brother are commonly used real-time monitoring systems.

Typically, the two types of monitoring are performed by different systems. The tasks involved in each type of monitoring are very different. After reading this chapter, you should have a good idea of how they differ and know what to look for in the software that you choose for each task.

But first, a few words of warning. Monitoring uses network bandwidth, so make sure that it doesn't use too much. Monitoring uses CPU and memory resources, so you don't want your monitoring to make your service worse. Security is important for monitoring systems.

- Within a local area network, *network bandwidth* is not usually a significant percentage. However, over low-bandwidth—usually long-distance—connections, monitoring can choke links, causing performance to suffer for other applications. Make sure that you know how much bandwidth your monitoring is using. A rule of thumb is that it should not exceed 1 percent of the available bandwidth. Try to optimize your monitoring system so that it is easy on low-bandwidth connections. Consider putting monitoring stations at the remote locations with a small amount of communication back to the main site or using primarily a trap-based system, whereby the devices notify the monitoring system when there is a failure, rather than a polling-based system, whereby the monitoring system checks status periodically.

- Under normal circumstances, a reasonable monitoring system will not consume enough *CPU and memory* to be noticed. However, you should test for failure modes. What happens if the monitoring server[1] is down or nonfunctional? What happens if there is a network outage? Also be careful of transitions from one monitoring system to another: Remember to turn off the old service when the new one is fully operational.

- *Security* is a factor in that monitoring systems may have access to machines or data that can be abused by an attacker. Or, it may be possible for an attacker to spoof a real-time monitoring system by sending messages that indicate a problem with a server or a service. Strong authentication between the server and the client is best. Older monitoring protocols, such as SNMPv1, have weak authentication.

22.1.1 Historical Monitoring

Polling systems at predefined intervals can be used to gather utilization or other statistical data from various components of the system and to check how well services that the system provides are working. The information gathered through such historical data collection is stored and typically used to produce graphs of the system's performance over time or to detect or isolate a minor problem that occurred in the past. In an environment with written SLA policies, historical monitoring is the method used to monitor SLA conformance.

Historical data collection is often introduced at a site because the SAs wonder whether they need to upgrade a network, add more memory to a server, or get more CPU power. They might be wondering when they will need to order more disks for a group that consumes space rapidly or when they will need to add capacity to the backup system. To answer these questions, the SAs realize that they need to monitor the systems in question and gather utilization data over a period of time in order to see the trends and the peaks in usage. There are many other uses for historical data, such as usage-based billing, anomaly detection (see Section 11.1.3.7) and presenting data to the customer base or management (see Chapter 31).

Historical data can consume a lot of disk space. This can be mitigated by condensing or expiring data. **Condensing data** means replacing detailed data with averages. For example, one might collect bandwidth utilization data for a link every 5 minutes. However, retaining only hourly averages requires about 90 percent less storage. It is common to store the full detail for the past week but to reduce down to hourly averages for older data.

---

1. The machine that all the servers report to.

Expiring data means deleting it. One might decide that data older than 2 years does not need to be retained at all. Alternatively, one might archive such data to removable media—DVD or tape—in case it is ever needed.

Limiting disk space consumption by condensing the data or expiring it affects the level of detail or historical perspective you can provide. Bear this trade-off in mind as you look for a system for your historical data collection.

How you intend to use the data that you gather from the historical monitoring will help to determine what level of detail you need to keep and for how long. For example, if you are using the data for usage-based billing and you bill monthly, you will want to keep complete details for a few years, in case there is a customer complaint. You may then archive the data and expire the online detailed data but save the graphs to provide online access for your customers to reference. Alternatively, if you are simply using the graphs internally for observing trends and predicting capacity needs, you might want a system that keeps complete data for the past 48 hours, reasonably detailed information for the past 2 weeks, somewhat less detailed information for the past 2 months, and very condensed data for the previous 2 years, with everything older than 2 years being discarded. Consider what you are going to use the data for and how much space you can use when deciding on how much to condense the data. Ideally, the amount of condensing that the system does and the expiration time of the data should be configurable.

You also need to consider how the monitoring system gathers its data. Typically, a system that performs historical data collection will want to poll the systems that it monitors at regular intervals. Ideally, the polling interval should be configurable. The polling mechanism should be able to use a standard form of communication, such as SNMPv2, as well as the usual IP mechanisms, such as Internet control message protocol (ICMP) echoes (pings) and opening TCP connections on any port, sending some specific data down that connection and checking the response received by using pattern matching. It is also useful to have a monitoring system that records latency information, or how long a transaction took. The latency correlates well to the end users' experiences. Having a service that responds very slowly is practically the same as having one that doesn't respond at all. The monitoring system should support as many other polling mechanisms as possible, preferably incorporating a mechanism to feed in data from any source and parse the results from that query. The ability to add your own tests is important, especially in highly customized environments. On the other hand, a multitude of predefined tests is also valuable, so that you do not need to write everything from scratch.

The output that you generally want from this type of monitoring system is graphs that have clear units along each axis. You can use the graphs to see what the usage trends are or to notice problems, such as sudden, unexpected peaks or drops in usage. You can use the graphs to predict when you need to add capacity of any sort and as an aid in the budget process, which is discussed in more detail in Chapter 34. A graph is also a convenient form of documentation to pass up the management chain. A graph clearly illustrates your point, and your managers will appreciate your having solid data to support your request for more bandwidth, memory, disk space, or whatever it is that you need.

22.1.2   Real-Time Monitoring

A real-time monitoring system tells you that a host is down, a service is not responding, or some other problem has arisen. A real-time monitoring system should be able to monitor everything you can think of that can indicate a problem. The system should be able both to poll systems and applications for status and to receive alerts directly from those systems if they detect a problem at any time. As with historical monitoring, the system should be able to use standard mechanisms, such as SNMPv2 polling, SNMPv2 traps, ICMP pings, and TCP, as well as to provide a mechanism for incorporating other forms of monitoring.

The system also should be capable of sending alerts to multiple recipients, using a variety of mechanisms, such as email, paging, telephone, and opening trouble tickets. Alerts should go to multiple recipients because an alert sent to one person could fail if that person's pager or phone has died or if the person is busy or distracted with something else.

The storage requirements of a real-time monitoring system are minimal. Usually, it stores the previous result of each query and the length of time since the last status change. Sometimes, the system stores running averages or high and low watermarks, but it rarely stores more than that. Unlike historical monitoring, which is used for proactive system administration, real-time monitoring is used to improve reactive system administration.

When evaluating a monitoring system, look at the things that it can monitor natively to see how well it matches your needs. You should be considering monitoring both availability and capacity. **Availability monitoring** means detecting failures of hosts, applications, network devices, other devices, network interfaces, or connections of any kind. **Capacity monitoring** means detecting when some component of your infrastructure becomes, or is about to become, overloaded. For example, that component could be CPU, memory, disk space, swap, backup device, network or other data connection, remote access device, number of processes, available ports, application limitations, or the number of users on a system. As with historical monitoring systems, the system needs to be flexible and to permit the creation of your own test modules. Preferably, a system should be able to use the same modules for both real-time and historical monitoring.

The most important components of a real-time monitoring system are the notification mechanism and the processes your site puts in place for dealing with the notifications or alerts.

22.1.2.1 SNMP

SNMP stands for Simple Network Monitoring Protocol. Nobody is sure whether the *simple* refers to *networks* or to *protocol*. Problems with SNMP make it difficult to use on larger-than-simple networks. Although it attempted to be simple, the protocol itself is rather complex.

In SNMP's most basic form, a packet is sent to a network device, such as a router, with a question called a `GET`. For example, one might ask, "What is the value of `IF-MIB::ifOutOctets.1`?" That variable is in the group of interface-related (`IF`) variables, the one that records how many bytes (octets) were sent out of the interface (`ifOutOctets`), on interface number 1. The router replies with a packet containing the value.

There are variables for just about everything and every kind of technology. A group of related variables is called a MIB. There are standard MIBs for Ethernet devices, DSL devices, ATM devices, SONET devices, T1/E1 devices, and even non-network technologies: disks, printers, CPUs, processes, and so on.

Other packet types can be used to change a variable (`PUT`), and even a special packet that means, "Reply to this packet when a particular variable changes above/below a particular value." These are called *traps*.

SNMP's simplicity is also its downfall. One variable is requested in each packet. If you'd like to monitor five variables for each interface, and if a system has dozens of interfaces and hundreds of devices, you are soon sending a lot of packets! SNMP-based monitoring systems use complicated schemes to gather all the information they are trying to gather in a timely basis. When some devices are far away and latency is high, waiting for each reply before sending the next request drags down performance. Later versions of SMNP support requesting multiple variables in one packet, but this feature is not always supported.

SNMP is also associated with security problems. Devices that support SNMP require a password, called *community string*, for some reason, in the packet to prevent just anyone from gathering data. GET defaults to the password public, and PUT defaults to the password private. Luckily, most vendors do not provide sensitive data in variables that GET can read, and they disable PUT completely. SNMP versions 2 and 3 encrypt the password, which is an improvement. However, having the same password for many devices is not very secure. If you had to change the SNMP password on every router in your enterprise every time an SA leaves the company, a large company would always be changing the passwords.

Most devices can be configured to permit SNMP requests to come only from specific IP addresses. We encourage sites to designate one or two specific ranges of IP addresses that will house any SNMP clients and to configure all SNMP-capable devices to respond only to devices in those ranges.

The data in an SNMP packet is encoded in a format called ANS.1. The format is very complicated and difficult to implement. In 2002, there was a big scare when it was discovered that many of the routers on the Internet had a security flaw in their ANS.1 decoding software. In some cases, the security flaw could be triggered as part of the password verification, so it didn't matter whether an attacker knew your SNMP community strings.

The situation has improved greatly. However, we make the following five recommendations for all SNMP-capable equipment.

1. Configure network equipment to process SNMP packets only from particular IP ranges. Two ranges, one for each redundant network monitoring center, is reasonable.

2. Use SNMPv3 when the vendor supports it. Encrypt all community strings.

3. Change SNMP community strings once a year. Have a transition period during which the old and new community strings are accepted.

4. Automate a weekly audit of all network devices. From one of the approved network ranges, attempt to use all the previous SNMP community strings that should have been eliminated. Also attempt to use public, private, and other default passwords. A few web searches, and you'll find a list of default vendor network device passwords. Try them all. Now repeat this test from outside the designated network ranges.

5. Track vendor security bulletins related to SNMP closely. New vulnerabilities appear a few times a year.

22.1.2.2 Alerting Mechanism

The monitoring system has an alerting mechanism to make you aware that something requires human attention. There is no point in software knowing that something has failed or is overloaded unless it tells a human about it or does something about it and makes a note of it for a human to look at later.

A monitoring system's alerting mechanism should not depend on any components of the system that is being monitored. If any given failure causes the monitoring system to be unable to report the failure, it needs to be re-designed. Email is a popular alerting mechanism, but it should not be the only one. Email can fail and can have long delays. Alerting needs to happen quickly. Also consider whether the alerting mechanism can be monitored by third parties. Wireless communication, such as paging, is susceptible to third-party spying. At a minimum, do not send sensitive information, such as passwords, over these channels, and consider whether such information as `backbone-router is down for 45 minutes` is proprietary.

Whatever monitoring system you use, you need to have a policy that describes how the alerts are handled. The policy needs to answer some fundamental questions before you can implement real-time monitoring. How many people do the alerts go to? Do alerts go to the helpdesk or to the individuals who look after the components that are having problems, or some combination of the two? How do the recipients of the alerts coordinate their work so that everyone knows who is handling each problem and they don't get in one another's way? If problems persist beyond some predetermined length of time, do you want to escalate the problem? If so, what is the escalation path? How often do you want to be informed of a problem, and does that depend on what the problem is? How do you want to be informed of the problem? What is the severity of each problem? Can the severity be used as a way to determine the policy on how the problem is handled? Your monitoring and alerting system must be able to implement your policy.

When choosing a real-time monitoring system, look at what your policy says about how you want it to alert you of problems and how often. For example, if you implement an early-warning mechanism for capacity problems, you may want it to open a trouble ticket with an appropriate priority in your existing helpdesk system. You probably also want it to do so only when the value being monitored changes from acceptable to unacceptable, as opposed to every time it registers as unacceptable, which could be every few minutes, though you may want it to update the existing ticket when it detects that the problem still exists after some configurable interval. On the other hand, if the monitoring system detects an outage, particularly of a critical component, you probably want it to actively page someone who is on call. You may even want it to continue paging that person every time it detects that the error condition still exists, with information on how long the condition has existed. You may want the notifications to become more frequent or less frequent as the problem persists. Your monitoring system should be flexible in the forms of alerting that it uses, and it should allow you to use different alerting mechanisms for different types of problems.

The error messages that the system delivers must be clear and easy to understand. If recipients of an alert need to look up information or call another person to translate the error message into something they understand, the message is not clear enough. For example, the error message `SNMP query to 10.10.10.1 for 1.2.3.4.5.6.7.8.9.10 failed` is not as clear as `Interface Hssi4/0/0 on wan-router-1 is down`. Equally, `Connect to port 80 on 10.10.20.20 failed` is not as clear as `web server on www-20 is not responding`.

However, the message must not make assumptions that may be wrong. For example, if the message said `web server on www-20 is not running` rather than that it was not responding, an SA might check whether it was running and assume that it was a false alert rather than checking whether it might be hung or failing to respond for some other reason.

I'm Hot! I'm Wet!

One night, very early in the morning, a couple's phone rang. The wife woke up and answered, to hear a sultry female voice saying, "I'm hot. I'm wet." Putting it down as a prank call, the wife hung up. Thirty minutes later, the same call repeated. After the fourth call, the husband finally woke up and took the call and bolted from his bed.

It was the alarm system in his machine room. The HVAC had broken down, spilling water under the floor. The alerting system was calling him. The vendor hadn't told him how the alert sounded, just that he should put his phone number in a particular configuration file. Test your alerting system, and inform those who might encounter it in your stead.

22.1.2.3 Escalation

Another component of the policy and procedures that your monitoring and alerting system should implement is the escalation policy describing how long each problem should be permitted to persist before it is escalated to another person, typically a manager. The escalation policy ensures that even if the person receiving the alert is on vacation or doesn't respond, the issue will be passed on to someone else. The escalation policy needs to describe various escalation paths for various categories of alerts.

Case Study: Escalation Procedure

One homegrown system had a particularly sophisticated escalation procedure. The system could be configured with a responsibility grid that mapped services to responsible entities. The entities could be a person or a group of people. The system could be configured with vacation schedules, so it knew whom not to alert. If a problem persisted, the system could walk up a responsibility chain, paging increasingly senior staff. Each type of service—email, web, DNS, and so on—had its own configuration, and particular systems—the CEO's web proxy, the e-commerce web site, and so on—could be marked as critical, in which case the escalations happened more quickly. Each service had a default responsible entity, but this could be overridden for particular systems that had special requirements. All this led to an extremely effective alerting service.

You may also want to be able to acknowledge an urgent alarm so that it stops sending alerts for a given period, until it is manually cleared, until the problem clears, or some combination of those, depending on the policy. This is similar to the snooze button on an alarm clock. The acknowledgment is an indication that you are actively working on the problem and relieves you of the annoyance of continual paging while you are trying to fix the problem. Without this feature, it is tempting to turn off an alarm, which leads to forgetting to fix the problem or, worse, forgetting to reset the alarm.

22.1.2.4 Active Monitoring Systems

An active monitoring system processes the problems it detects and actively fixes the ones that it knows how to deal with. For example, an active monitoring system might reset a modem port that it detects is in a strange state or might remove a modem from a modem pool if it could not be fixed by a reset.

Active monitoring systems can be useful up to a point. Although they respond more quickly than a human can, they have limitations. In general, an active monitoring system can implement only a temporary fix. The system won't detect and permanently fix the root of a problem, which is what really needs to happen (see Chapter 16). An active monitoring system also needs to make sure that it reports what it is doing and opens a trouble ticket for the permanent fix. However, it may be more difficult for the SAs to diagnose the real source of the problem when a temporary fix has been applied. The SAs also need to make sure that they don't get lazy and not bother to permanently fix the problems that the active monitoring system has identified. If the SAs simply automate temporary fixes through an active monitoring system, entropy will set in, and the system as a whole will become less reliable.

Case Study: Active Monitoring and the Wrong "Fix"

An active monitoring system at one company monitored /var and rotated log files if the disk filled up too much. This deleted the oldest log file and thus reclaimed space. One day, the log files were being rotated each time the monitoring system checked the disk, and the /var partition was 100 percent unable to look at the log files for clues, because they were all zero length by then.

It turned out that a developer had turned on debugging for one of his processes that was run from cron once a minute. And so, once a minute, the cron job sent out an email. The mailbox (in /var/mail) filled up the disk!

Active monitoring systems also have a limit to the problems they can solve, even temporarily. Some problems that the system may detect but cannot fix are caused by a physical failure, such as a printer running out of ink or paper or being switched off or disconnected. If it doesn't accurately diagnose the source of the problem and tries to fix it through software commands, the system may cause more problems than it solves. Other problems may require complex debugging, and it is not feasible to expect an automated system to be able to correctly diagnose all such problems. In particular, problems that require debugging on multiple hosts and pieces of networking equipment, such as slow file transfers between two hosts on a quiescent network, are beyond the abilities of all the automated systems we know.

It is a good idea to limit what an automated system can do, in any case. From a security point of view, an automated system that has privileged access to all or most machines is very vulnerable to exploitation. The focus in writing such a system is always utility rather than security, and active monitoring systems are large, complex programs that have privileged access to some machines; thus, there will be security holes to exploit. Such systems are also interesting targets because of the level of networkwide privileged access they have. An active monitoring system is not something that you want to have on an unprotected network. From a reliability perspective, the more this program is permitted to do on your network, the greater the calamity that can befall you if it goes awry.

22.2 The Icing

Once you have basic monitoring in place and start scaling it up to monitor more devices, you will want to make the monitoring system more accessible to other SAs, so that all the SAs in the company are able to maintain their own device lists. You will also start noticing the things that it doesn't catch and want to start monitoring entire transactions from beginning to end. In other words, instead of simply checking that the mail machine is up and accepting SMTP connections, you might want to check that it can deliver a mail message. You also may want to see how long the transactions take to complete.

You, your team, and your management ultimately will want to monitor more and more items until you are monitoring, essentially, everything. We look at ways to ease scaling. Another enhancement that you may want to add in the future is device discovery, so that you know when new devices are added to the network.

22.2.1 Accessibility

Typically, a monitoring system is set up by one or two SAs, who become familiar with every detail of it. They are the only ones who know how to add things to monitor, so they also become the ones to do all the additions and changes. Initially, this may not involve much work, but with time, the monitoring system will become more popular, and the workload will increase.

As the monitoring system becomes more established and stable, it is important to make it accessible to the group as a whole. Any of the SAs should be able to add something to the list of things monitored rather than having to submit a request to a particular SA who will be busy with other tasks.

Making the monitoring system accessible requires good documentation. Some forms of monitoring may require finding a piece of information that is not normally used in the course of day-to-day administration, such as the SNMP MIB for a component of the system. The documentation should tell the SA what information he will need and how to find it, as well as how to put that information into the monitoring configuration. If there are choices, such as how often the item should be queried, what values correspond to what alert state, problem prioritization, what graphs to draw, or how to define an escalation path, those options must all be clearly documented as well. In this situation, documenting the preferred defaults is key.

It is frustrating for both the SAs who set up the system and the rest of the SAs in the group if all requests for additional monitoring have to go through one or two people. A system that is not accessible to the whole group will not be used as extensively, and the group will not benefit as much from it.

22.2.2 Pervasive Monitoring

Ultimately, it is nice to be able to monitor everything, or at least everything beyond the desktops. This is particularly important for sites that depend on extremely high availability, such as e-commerce sites. If adding systems and services to be monitored is a task that is performed manually, it will be forgotten or omitted on occasion. To make monitoring pervasive throughout your service, it should be incorporated into the installation process.

For example, if you build many identical machines to provide a service, you should be using an automated installation process, as described in Chapter 3. If you are building machines this way, you could incorporate adding the machine to the monitoring system as part of that build process. Alternatively, you could install on the machine something that detects when it has been deployed in its final location—if you stage the machines through a protected build network—and provide a way for it to notify the monitoring system that it is alive and what it needs to have monitored. Being sure that you are in fact monitoring everything requires some degree of automation. If such things can't be automated, the installation process can at least automatically generate a help ticket requesting that it be added to the monitoring system.

22.2.3 Device Discovery

It can also be useful to have a monitoring system that detects when devices are added to the network. Such a system is useful at sites that need pervasive monitoring, because it should detect any devices that fell through the cracks and failed to be added to the monitoring system through some other means. It can also be useful simply to know that a device was added and when that happened. If the device is causing a problem on the network, for example, that knowledge can save hours of debugging time.

22.2.4 End-to-End Tests

End-to-end testing means testing entire transactions, with the monitoring system acting as a customer of the service and checking whether its entire transaction completes successfully. An end-to-end test might be relatively simple, such as sending email through a mail server or requesting particular web pages that cause database queries and checking the content that is returned. It might be a more complex test that simulates all the steps that a customer would make to purchase something on your e-commerce site.

Case Study: Mailping

At AT&T and later Lucent, John Bagley and Jim Witthoff developed the mailping facility. It relays email messages, or mailpings, off mail servers and measures the time it takes to find its way back to the mailping machine. At one point, it monitored more than 80 email servers, including both Unix and MS-Exchange SMTP gateways. It provides several web tools to display the delivery time data for a given day or for a given server over a specified period. In addition to historical data collection, it includes a mechanism for generating alerts if a particular message has not been delivered after a certain threshold. The ability to have end-to-end monitoring of the mail transport within their company permitted them to not only respond to problems quickly but also develop metrics that let them improve the service over time. Some commercial monitoring systems now offer this kind of feature.

Once you start monitoring extensively, you will see problems that your monitoring system fails to catch. For example, if you are providing an e-commerce service over the Internet, a sequence of events has to complete successfully for your customer to be able to complete a transaction. Your monitoring system may show that everything is up and working, but an end user may still experience a problem in executing a complete transaction.

The transaction may rely on things that you haven't thought of monitoring or that are very difficult to monitor. For example, if the transaction relies on sending email, something may be wrong with your mail server configuration, preventing the message from being delivered properly, even though the email server accepted the email for delivery. Or, a bug in the application could cause it to loop, fail, or generate garbage at some point in the process. Or the database could be missing some tables. Any number of things could go wrong without being detected by your monitoring system.

The best way to ensure that the service your customers want to use is up and functioning properly is to emulate a customer and check whether the transaction completes successfully. In the example of an e-commerce site, build a test case that requests pages in the order that a customer would, and check the content of the page returned at each stage to make sure that the appropriate data and links are there. Check the database to ensure that the transaction has been recorded in the appropriate place. Perform a credit card authorization check, and make sure that it completes successfully. Send email and make sure that it arrives. Step through every part of the process as the customer would do, and make sure that everything is as expected at each step.

This end-to-end testing can uncover problems that might otherwise go unnoticed until a customer calls to complain. In an e-commerce environment, failing to notice a problem for a while can be very costly. There is a large and growing market of commercial monitoring systems, many of which are focused on the particular needs of e-commerce customer space.

22.2.5 Application Response Time Monitoring

The other sort of extended monitoring that can be very useful in both corporate and e-commerce environments is application response time. Every component of a system can be operational, but if the system is too slow, your customers will not be happy. In an e-commerce environment, this means that you will lose business. In a corporate environment, it will lead to a loss of productivity and numerous calls about the slow network or perhaps a slow system or application. In either case, unless you are monitoring the application response time, it will probably take quite a while to figure out why your customers are unhappy, by which time your reputation may have suffered heavy damage.

It is much better to devise a way to monitor the application response time as it appears to the end user of the application. It is then useful to have both a historical chart and some sort of a threshold alert for the response time. Application response time is typically an extension of the end-to-end testing discussed previously. Where appropriate, this information can be fed to the application developers to help them scale and optimize their product.

22.2.6 Scaling

Once you start monitoring some things and see how useful the monitoring is, you will want to monitor more aspects of your site. Increasing the number of things to be monitored introduces scaling problems. All monitoring systems have problems as you scale them. Simply gathering all the data that needs to be checked every 5 minutes is time consuming. It can reach a point where the monitoring system is still trying to collect and process the data from one run when the next round of data collection begins.

Systems doing historical monitoring usually need to do extra processing to condense the data they store. Some devices may take a while to respond to the information requested, and the system usually can handle only a limited number of open requests at a time. All this can lead to scaling problems as the system monitors more objects.

Case Study: Scaling Problems

WebTV Networks used MRTG (Oetiker 1998a) to monitor its network equipment and provide historical graphs. As the network grew, it ran into performance problems: Each monitoring run required so much processing that it was still running when the next one started. The network operations staff ended up writing a new application, called Cricket (Allen 1999), which is more efficient.

When scaling a monitoring system to thousands of entities around a large network, network links can become clogged simply from the monitoring traffic. To solve this problem, some monitoring systems have remote probes that collect data and send only summaries back to the master station. If these probes are strategically placed around the network, they can greatly reduce the amount of network traffic generated. The master station stores the data and makes it available to the SAs. The master station also holds the master configuration and distributes that to the remote monitoring stations. This model scales much farther than a single monitoring station or multiple unrelated monitoring stations.

Real-time monitoring systems also have scaling problems. When such a system is watching many aspects of many devices, there will always be some things that are "red," indicating some form of outage requiring attention. To scale the system appropriately, the SAs must be able to tell at a glance which of the "red" issues is the "reddest" and having the most impact. Essentially, the problem is that a monitoring system typically has only a few states to indicate the condition of the monitored item. Often, there are only three: "green," "yellow," and "red." Monitoring many things requires a finer granularity. For example, a very granular priority system could be built in, and the reporting system could display the problems in a priority-ordered list.

Another problem often experienced is that an outage of a nonredundant network component between the monitoring system and objects that are being monitored can cause a huge flood of failures to show up in the monitoring system, when there is in fact only one failure. The flood of alerts can hide the real cause of the problem and cause the people receiving the alerts to panic. Ideally, a monitoring system should have a concept of dependency chains. The dependency chain for an object that the system is watching lists the other outages that will cause this object to show up as experiencing an outage as well. The monitoring system should then use the dependency chain to alter its alerting. For example, rather than sending 50 pager alerts, it could send one that says "multiple failures: root cause . . ." and list only the highest outage in the chain, not the outages that are downstream. On a graphical display, it should show the outages along with their dependency chains in an appropriate tree structure so that the root is clearly visible. This is not a trivial feature to implement or maintain, and it is unlikely to be available in every monitoring system. If you do not have an error roll-up feature like this in your monitoring system, you may be able to implement something similar by having multiple remote monitoring stations, particularly in a WAN environment, with the central monitoring system alerting the SAs when it fails to receive a report from the remote monitoring systems, and otherwise alerting them of the problems that the remote systems found. Alternatively, you should train your staff on the situation and keep up-to-date dependency maps available for them to reference when flooded with alerts.

Another problem with scaling a real-time monitoring system relates to how the problems are handled. If multiple people all try to solve the same problem in an uncoordinated way, not knowing that others are working on it, they may make the problem worse. At the very least, some time will be wasted. In addition, they will get in one another's way and confuse one another as to what is happening on the system. The monitoring system should have some way to enable an SA to "claim" a problem, so that other SAs know that someone is working on it and whom to go to if they want to help out. This may be done through the trouble-ticket system and procedures surrounding the assignment of a problem before an SA begins work on it.

22.2.7 Metamonitoring

Metamonitoring is monitoring your monitoring system. That is, how do you know that your monitoring system hasn't died? If you haven't received an alert in 3 days, is everything fine, or did someone power off the machine that processes the alerts? Sites often forget to monitor their monitoring system; when an outage occurs, they simply don't get notified.

The most simple form of metamonitoring is to have the monitoring system monitor a few simple things about itself, such as its own disk becoming full. These alerts should trigger long before the condition would prevent the monitoring system from working.

If monitoring a larger number of devices or if uptime is extremely critical, a second monitoring system that monitors only the primary monitoring system is warranted.

Metamonitoring should be based on an SLA, just like any other monitoring system. For example, if you expect the primary monitoring system to be able to do all its probes every 10 minutes, metamonitoring should generate an alert if a probe has not executed for more than 10 minutes.

If a system was able to perform a full rotation of probes within the SLA for weeks and now suddenly it can't, this situation should be investigated. If this condition persists, perhaps a hard drive is starting to fail, the network is misconfigured, or a process has gone out of control. It may also indicate that someone has accidentally messed up the configuration.

Historical metamonitoring can record how the system responds to growing numbers of probes. As more services are monitored, the system needs more time to probe them all. Collecting historical data can help predict the point at which the monitoring system will no longer be able to meet the SLA. Scaling techniques can be invoked to prevent the monitoring system from becoming overloaded.

22.3 Conclusion

In this chapter, we discussed monitoring in its two incarnations: historical data gathering and real-time monitoring and alerting. The two forms are quite different in what each involves and what each is useful for, yet you need to consider some of the same problems with both.

Historical availability monitoring and data collection means tracking availability and usage of systems in order to graph and analyze the data later. It involves gathering, storing, and condensing lots of data. Historical data collection requires lots of disk space, databases, and processing. It is useful for capacity planning, budget justification, customer billing, providing an overview of what is happening at a site when a problem is detected, and anomaly detection.

Real-time monitoring involves polling systems to check their state and watching for problem notifications from built-in system monitors. Real-time monitoring is generally combined with an alerting system. This combination is used to detect problems and notify the SAs of them (almost) as soon as they happen. It is a tool for providing better service and for detecting the root of a problem. It gives more precise information than a customer-oriented problem report, such as "I can't download my mail."

Both types of monitoring are required tools at an e-commerce site because the customers are so much more distant and fickle—they don't really care whether you know about or fix the problem, because they can simply go to another site. Monitoring is a useful tool in both its forms in any well-run site.

Both forms of monitoring have problems when it comes to scaling, and splitting the monitoring system into several data gatherers and one central master is the best method in both cases. Real-time monitoring has scaling problems involving prioritization and response to alerts in an appropriate, timely, and coordinated manner.

As your monitoring system becomes more sophisticated, you will want to consider implementing end-to-end testing and application response time testing so that you know exactly what the end user is experiencing and whether that is acceptable. You also may want to consider ways to ensure that everything is monitored appropriately, particularly in a service provider environment. To do so, you can look at ways to add a system to the monitoring list when it is built. You may also look at ways to detect when devices have been added to the network but not to the monitoring system.

Monitoring is a very useful tool. It is also a project that will increase in scope as it is implemented. Knowing the ways that the system will need to grow will help you select the right monitoring systems at the beginning of the project, scale them, and add functionality to them as needed during their lifetime.

Exercises

1. How do you monitor systems for which you are responsible? If you do not have a formal monitoring system, have you automated any of your ad hoc monitoring?

2. Have you implemented active monitoring for anything in your environment? If so, how well does it work? Does it ever prevent you from finding the root cause of a problem? Explain why or why not.

3. What systems would you add to a monitoring system if you had it, and why? What aspects of those systems would you monitor?

4. If you already have a monitoring system, in what ways could you improve it?

5. What features discussed in this chapter are most important to you in selecting a monitoring system for your site, and why?

6. What, if any, other features not discussed are important to you, and why?

7. Investigate freely available historical data monitoring systems. Which one do you think would suit your environment best, and why?

8. Investigate commercial historical data monitoring systems. Which one do you think would suit your environment best, and why?

9. If you had to choose between the free and commercial historical data monitoring systems that you selected in the previous questions, which would you pick for your site, and why? What, if any, features do you feel it lacks?

10. Investigate freely available real-time monitoring systems. Which one do you think would suit your environment best, and why?

11. Investigate commercial real-time monitoring systems. Which one do you think would suit your environment best, and why?

12. If you had to choose between the free and commercial real-time monitoring systems that you selected in the previous questions, which would you pick for your site, and why? What, if any, features do you feel it is lacking?

13. How many items—machines, network devices, applications, and so on—do you think a monitoring system at your site would need to scale to in the next 3 years? What would you need to meet that demand?

14. Are there any advantages or disadvantages to using the same package for both types of monitoring, if that is possible?

Chapter 23

Email Service

Email is a service that companies rely on to conduct business. Everyone expects email to simply work, and outages are unacceptable. It is often the only application that your CEO uses. Your CEO's impression of the reliability of email can have far-ranging effects on other aspects of the SA team, such as budget and reputation.

Nearly 45 percent of business-critical information is housed in email message storage (Osterman 2000). For many companies, it is one of the primary ways for existing and for potential customers to contact the sales and support staff. Reliability should be the focal point of the email service, with scalability a close second.

If you are to build a successful email system, you must also have good namespaces (Chapter 8), security architecture (Chapter 11), service monitoring (Chapter 22), and backups (Chapter 26).

23.1 The Basics

A reliable, scalable email service must be built on strong foundations. An SA who is designing and building an email service must put the basics first, before trying to add features or scale the service to deal with high traffic volumes.

A simple, clear, well-documented architecture for the email system is fundamental to building a reliable service. It also is important to use open protocols and standards throughout the email system to ensure maximum interoperability with other sites and other applications within the site. In particular, one key piece of infrastructure that the email system needs to interact with is the namespace management system, which implements the organizational structure of the corporate namespaces that relate to email. Recall from Chapter 5 that nothing can be called a service until it is monitored.

Email is a method of communicating with the rest of the world, so some parts of the service will always be a target for potential attackers. Security must therefore be considered during the design and implementation of the email system.

Finally, because email contains so much vital information, email privacy, retention, and storage must be examined and brought in to compliance with company policy and with any legal requirements.

23.1.1 Privacy Policy

Every site must have an email privacy policy that is communicated to and acknowledged by every employee. The privacy policy must explain under what circumstances a person's email may be read and by whom. The policy must also explain that email may be inadvertently seen by administrative staff during the course of their work, usually when performing diagnostics. The policy should also state that email that crosses over other networks, such as the Internet, cannot be considered private and that company-confidential information that has not been encrypted should not be emailed to an address on or across another entity's network.

At many companies, email that arrives on or crosses over corporate servers is not considered private. Other companies state that corporate machines should not be used for personal communication, which typically amounts to the same thing. Some companies automatically monitor incoming and outgoing mail for certain keywords; a few go so far as to examine attached files for potentially confidential information. Others state that people using the corporate email system have a reasonable expectation of privacy and outline the circumstances when an expectation of privacy may no longer hold.

Whatever the policy decided by the upper management of the company, the SAs must implement it. The SA management team should ensure that everybody who uses the company's email service is aware of the policy and has acknowledged it.

23.1.2 Namespaces

Namespaces are discussed in Chapter 8; we here, focus on the email namespace. The email address namespace at a site is the most visible one both externally, to the company's customers and business partners, and internally, to the employees who use it daily. It is crucial to get it right.

The most fundamental part of getting the email namespace right is to use the same email addresses for internal and external email. If one address is used for internal mail and a different one for mail coming from outside the company, people will inevitably give the wrong email address to customers and business partners, which can lead to lost business. Don't expect people to remember that they have two email addresses and which one they should give to whom. It is far simpler for all concerned, including the SAs debugging problems, if everyone only has one email address for both internal and external email.

Standardizing email addresses by using a `first.last`-style email address, such as `John.Smith@foo.com`, is popular, particularly with management. However, we generally discourage `first.last`-style email addresses. There is too much of a chance that your company will employ two people with the same name, or even same first, last, and middle initial. When your second John Smith is hired, `John.Smith` becomes `John.A.Smith` to avoid being confused with the new hire, `John.Z.Smith`. At that point, the first person's business cards become invalid. Business cards, once distributed, are difficult to update.

Some email systems deal with ambiguous `first.last`-style addresses by generating an automatic reply that tries to help the sender figure out which "John Smith" he was trying to reach, possibly listing the first ten matches in the corporate directory. Although this sounds nice, it is not a perfect solution. The replies are useful only if a human receives them. If the person was on any email mailing lists, those messages will now bounce.

Eric Allman, who developed Sendmail in 1985, explains why this kind of formatting is problematic in this quote from Sendmail's `cf/README` file (Shapiro and Allman 1999):

> As a general rule, I am adamantly opposed to using full names as email addresses, since they are not in any sense unique. For example, the UNIX software-development community has two Andy Tannenbaums, at least two well-known Peter Deutsches, and at one time Bell Labs had two Stephen R. Bournes with offices along the same hallway. Which one will be forced to suffer the indignity of being Stephen.R.Bourne.2? The less famous of the two, or the one that was hired later?

Instead, we prefer making a namespace that is unique corporation-wide, using name tokens, such as `chogan`, `tal`, `jsmith`, and so on. A directory service can be provided to help people look up the email address of the person they want to contact. Customers should be able to select their own token, though an initial default should be preselected, based on an algorithm that combines initials and first or last names. It should be relatively difficult to change once it has been set, to discourage people from making gratuitous changes. Tokens should not be reused for a couple of months, to prevent someone from hijacking the token of a recently removed employee to see what residual email he receives.

23.1.3 Reliability

Email is a utility service. People expect to be able to send and receive email at all times, just as they expect to always have a dial tone when they lift the phone and power when they turn on a light. As with other utilities, people don't realize how much they rely on it until it is no longer working.

A failure of the email system is a very stressful event and results in lots of support calls over a short period. It will inevitably occur when someone has to urgently send important documents, because that is happening all the time, unseen by the SAs. Because the email system is so critical, failures will be emotional times for both the SAs and the customers. The email service is not a service with which SAs should experiment. New systems and architectures should be deployed into the email service only after extensive testing.

More important, costs are associated with a malfunctioning email system. Missed email can cause business panic. Contractual obligations are missed, customers turn to other vendors, and time is lost as people revert to older, slower forms of communication.

Case Study: The Email Service Beta Test

A major technology company was promoting the concept of centrally located server farms for business applications such as email. As a proof of concept, the company quickly moved all 100,000 employees off their local, department-based servers to a single, global server farm. The network connections into the server farm were overloaded to the point of being unusable. As a result, the entire company was unable to communicate for nearly a month until more network capacity was added. Not one to learn from mistakes, the company then decided to use this server farm to demonstrate a new release of its email software. This may have been the single largest beta test ever attempted. It was also a disaster. Eventually, the company learned to not take such risks with such a critical application. It was, however, too late. By this time, many organizations had created rogue email servers for their local members, making the situation worse. Your corporate email system is simply too critical to use as a playground or experimenter's lab.

The national power grids and telephone networks of all developed countries are highly redundant systems, designed and built with reliability in mind. The design of an email system should have a similar focus on reliability, if on a smaller scale.

Start with a clear, simple design. Select hardware and software for their reliability and interoperability. Data should be stored on RAID systems to reduce outages.

Having hot spares for all the email machines is ideal. Many companies cannot justify that expense, however. If you do not have the luxury of hot spares, have a plan that you can execute rapidly to restore service if anything fails.

23.1.4 Simplicity

The email system should be simple. Complexity decreases reliability and makes the system more difficult to support.

Limit the number of machines involved in the email service. That limits the number of machines that have to be reliable and the number of places SAs must look to debug a problem. Above all, do not involve desktop machines in the mail-delivery process. While UNIX desktops can be configured as email servers, they should not be. They usually do not have reliable backups, power, or other things that a server should have.

An email service has five main aspects: mail transport, mail delivery, access, list processing, and filtering. The mail transport agent (MTA) gets email from place to place, usually from server to server; *mail delivery agents* (MDA) receive email messages and store them at the destination server; *email access servers* provide the access protocols (POP3, IMAP4) that allow a mail user agent (MUA) on a customer workstation to access individual emails; *list processing* is how one message gets delivered to a group of people on a list; *filtering* refers to anti-spam and anti-virus filtering.

For small sites, a simple architecture typically means having all these functions provided by the same machine, possibly with an additional Internet-facing mail-relay system being the interface between the company and the rest of the world. For larger sites, simplicity often involves separating mail transport, mail delivery, and list processing out onto different systems or groups of systems. Several dedicated mail relays will deliver mail to either the list processing machines or the delivery machines. The list processing machines also use mail relays to deliver messages to the individual recipients on each list.

At a large site, several machines may be involved in email service, but ideally all of the systems are of the same type. Avoid delivering mail to people's desktops, and make sure that their mail clients are configured to send email by contacting a mail relay rather than routing mail themselves. Disable the simple mail transport protocol (SMTP) service on machines that are not officially part of the email service. If email is required, such as the ability to email a developer when her software compile is done, create a relay-only SMTP configuration to send the mail via the email service. Doing so means that the SAs always know where all the mail for a particular account is being delivered. A configuration that can lead to email being delivered in several possible places for a single account inevitably leads to confusion and "lost" mail.[1]

Speaking of confusion, servers that are configured to send all email to the centralized email service should also be configured to label the sender as being specifically from that server, and the central email system should not rewrite the sender's address unless it is a customer's account. If you have a 500-server web applications cluster, and periodically get email from `dbadmin` about a database access error, it would be good to know immediately which server had the problem. Yes, there are other ways to find out,[2] but simpler is usually better for email.

Case Study: Bad Mail-Delivery Scheme

A computer manufacturer's mail scheme permitted email delivery on any UNIX machine on which the recipient had an account. This scheme also exposed the full hostname of the machine from which the person sent the email. For example, email sent from `server5.example.com` had a `From:` line of `user123@server5.example.com`. Whenever someone replied to one of these emails, the reply was addressed to the person at the machine from which the mail had been sent, so it was delivered there rather than to the person's primary email box. Thus, when someone sent an email from a machine that he did not normally use, the reply went to that machine and was "lost." If that address made it into someone's address book and the machine was decommissioned, email would start bouncing. The helpdesk frequently received complaints about lost email, but because the email system was so unstructured, the staff had a difficult time finding out what had happened.

---

1. The mail is lost in the sense that the intended recipient is unaware of it and doesn't see it because it has arrived in an unexpected place; such mail doesn't bounce back to the sender, because it was successfully delivered, albeit to the wrong recipient.

2. Such as the Received-From headers, or comparing the message-id with email logs.

> The SAs should have implemented an email system that passed all mail to a central relay that rewrote the sender's email address so that it did not contain the name of the machine that it came from—known as hostname masquerading. That way, all replies would automatically go through the central mail relay, which would direct email to each person's primary email box.

Simplicity also means avoiding gateways and other email translation devices. Use the same standards throughout the network and for communication with other sites. Gateways translate email between two or more different formats, often between a proprietary, or nonstandard format or protocol, and a standard one. Gateways add complexity and are typically the source of endless problems at sites that use them. Gateways also typically strip off delivery-history information because it is in a different format, and this makes it more difficult to trace problems. See Section 5.1.3 for anecdotes that should sway you against gateways.

We recommend providing a single mechanism for implementing and managing email lists. There are many different ways of doing it, and sites that have been around for a few years are typically using more than one. This lack of standardization makes it more difficult to maintain the lists and much more difficult to implement automated list maintenance and pruning mechanisms. Forcing customers to learn and remember multiple email procedures is unacceptable.

Large sites with multiple servers need to be able to shift people's email boxes between servers to compensate for load. That is, if a server becomes overloaded, some of the mailboxes are moved to a less-loaded machine. When this happens, each person's email client has to be reconfigured to point to the new machine. One way to avoid that is to set up DNS entries for each user in the form of `username.pobox.example.com`, which is an alias to the username's current email server. If their mailbox moves to a different machine, the DNS data is changed and their client does not need to be reconfigured. (If you provide web-based email readers, use the same DNS name to redirect HTTP requests to the proper web server.) Another way is to use an MDA that supports file locking with your MUA clients. These multiple mail access servers can be used to access the same account without having to move mailboxes.

23.1.5 Spam and Virus Blocking

Electronic junk mail is also known as spam, or unsolicited commercial email (UCE). It is common for more than 50 percent of email coming from the

Internet to a mail server to be UCE. Since the late 1990s, email has also been a dominant way for computer viruses and other malware to copy itself from computer to computer.

Both spam and malware can be blocked at either the email client or the server. We believe that it is best to block them at the server. It is easier to upgrade the server than to upgrade hundreds of email clients. We also find that customers tend to easily get tricked into disabling the protection software on their clients. Some customers simply disable it, thinking that the system will run faster.

There is no perfect antispam software. How can a computer know that you don't want a particular piece of email? There are rare cases in which an incoming email messages matches, bit for bit, a known spam message. However, that technique doesn't work on spam that hasn't been seen before. The same is true of anti-virus software. Further, although it is possible to detect email that contains a known virus, it's nearly impossible to detect a newly unleashed one. Thus, blocking bad email has become an arms race situation: spammers and virus spreaders figure out a way to get through traditional detection software; then detection-software vendors improve their software, and the attackers improve their techniques, and on it goes.

We believe that centralizing this function to a particular set of machines is important. In fact, there are now services that will do spam analysis for you. One directs email to their service, using the DNS MX record, where it is processed and then delivered to your server. There are privacy concerns with such a service, however. On the other hand, if the email was secret, it shouldn't have been sent unencrypted over the Internet.

23.1.6 Generality

One of the fundamental reasons for the existence of an email system is to open communication paths within and outside the company. To successfully communicate with the maximum number of people, the email system should be built around open protocols that are universally accepted and implemented.

For mail transport, this means using an SMTP-based protocol. Because mail transport involves communicating with many other sites, the well-established Internet-standard will continue to be supported for a long time to come. SMTP is extremely pervasive on the Internet. It is more likely that a new email protocol would be an extension of SMTP such as the widely used ESMTP, or extended SMTP, rather than a completely new and incompatible protocol. All sites must support SMTP as a transport protocol; for simplicity and generality, it should be the only transport protocol that a site uses.

Generality is also about communications within the company and mail user agents. It applies to the methods that are available for people to read their email. The number of protocols in this area is a little larger and changes more easily with time because it is usually easy to add support for an additional email client/server protocol without affecting the existing ones. Most sites support one or two of the most popular email client protocols, thereby supporting almost all mail readers. A site can trivially support lots of mail clients on lots of different OSs if the mail delivery and relay systems use Internet-standard protocols. Supporting the maximum number of clients by supporting a small number of standard protocols means that people who have a strong preference for one client over another are able to use that client. Typically, email clients also support multiple protocols, and it is not difficult to find a protocol in common between the client and the mail delivery server. On the other hand, a site using a proprietary protocol locks the customers into a vendor's one or two clients that may not have the features they need or want.

Nonstandard Protocols Are Expensive

A small, successful Silicon Valley Internet start-up company was bought by a large, well-established Washington company. The Internet start-up used standard protocols for its email service. The clients were primarily UNIX machines but also included a significant number of Macintoshes and a handful of Windows PCs. Its email system worked well and was accessible to everyone in the company. When the company was bought and integrated into the parent company, the employees of the start-up had to switch to the parent company's email service, based on Microsoft proprietary standards rather than on Internet standards.[3] No clients were available for the UNIX machines or the Macintoshes. The company had to buy a PC running Windows for each of the UNIX and Macintosh users—almost everyone—just so that they could continue to send and receive email. It was an outrageously expensive solution!

More philosophy and anecdotes on this subject can be found in Section 5.1.3.

---

3. Even though Microsoft Exchange now supports open protocols, such as POP3 and IMAP4, one loses many features related to calendaring and address books. Lotus Notes has similar issues.

23.1.7 Automation

As with everything that SAs do, automation can simplify common tasks and ensure that they are performed reliably and accurately. Many areas of email administration should be automated as part of the process of building the service or should be incorporated into existing email services.

In particular, setting up an email account should be automated as part of the account creation process. The automation should include putting the person onto any relevant companywide and group-specific email lists. Equally, removing the email account should be an automated part of account deletion.

Earlier, we discussed the need to occasionally move email accounts between machines for the purpose of balancing load. Automating this process is important, as it is often a complicated process.

We have found that it is best not to provide automatic email forwarding for people who have left the company, because sensitive information may be inadvertently sent by someone who does not realize that person he has left. Implementing a redirect message that automatically replies with the new email address and a message stating that the person has left the company is preferred.

Another useful form of email service automation is automating mailing list administration so that the lists can be created, deleted, and administered directly by the customers who need them rather than by the SAs. This provides a better, more responsive service for the list owners as well as relieving the SAs of a recurring duty.

A departing employee should be removed from all internal mailing lists. Periodic automatic checks of active email accounts against the personnel database should also be implemented, along with checks to ensure that email to local accounts is not forwarded outside the company and that disabled accounts are not on any internal mailing lists. A site can also automate examining sensitive internal mailing lists for unauthorized members.

23.1.8 Basic Monitoring

Chapter 5 introduced the notion that a service isn't properly implemented until it is monitored. Email is no exception to that rule. A basic level of monitoring must be performed on an email service: every machine that is part of the service should be up and on the network (responds to ping), and it is responding to requests on the relevant TCP ports (SMTP on port 25, POP3 on port 110, IMAP4 on port 143, and so on).

All email servers should also be monitored for disk space, disk activity, and CPU utilization. Monitoring disk space helps plan for increases in demand and alert SAs when disk space is nearing capacity. Email service has huge demands on disk and CPU utilization. Monitoring those elements permits one to detect service-level variability caused by large influxes in email, email loops, and other problems. In those situations, having a baseline of what is normal—past history—helps to identify problems when they happen.

Email to the `postmaster` also must be monitored. The `postmaster` address at every site receives email messages showing mail delivery errors or bounces. By monitoring the email sent to this address, the person in charge of the email service will notice when failures occur and be able to address them. The bounces sent to `postmaster` contain all the headers from the failed email and the error message indicating why it failed. This information is vital for debugging email problems and often is not supplied when end users report problems. Finally, the logs on the email machines should be monitored to track the message-flow rate, which can help with historical predictions, noticing when mail delivery has stopped for some reason, and debugging problems that can arise when the message-flow rate increases unexpectedly.

These are the basics of monitoring an email system. Advanced monitoring techniques are covered, in Section 23.2.3. See also Chapter 22.

23.1.9 Redundancy

Because email service is central to the operation of all modern companies, sites should introduce redundancy into the email system as soon as realistically possible. Section 5.1.9 describes some general ways of building reliability into a service. This chapter concentrates on email-specific issues.

When there is no redundant hardware for the email systems, there must be a recovery plan that can be implemented quickly in case of failure. It is easy to introduce redundancy for mail relay hosts and list on processing hosts using DNS Mail eXchanger (MX) records and multiple servers with the same configuration.

Redundancy of mail delivery hosts is different because entire hosts cannot easily be redundant for each other. Instead, you can make the server internally redundant with RAID and other techniques. You can replicate the host that accesses a shared message storage facility using network attached storage or storage area network technology (Katcher 1999). However, in that case, you must be extremely careful to ensure that proper locking and access control are performed.

The client access must be made redundant with transparent failover. To do so, you must understand how the client works. Clients typically cache the result of the initial DNS query that occurs when they try to contact the mail-delivery server to download email; therefore, simple DNS tricks will not suffice. Redundancy for the client must happen at the IP level. Several technologies are available for permitting a host to take over answering requests directed to a specific IP address when the original machine at that address dies. Two common techniques are the use of load balancers (layer 4) (Black 1999) and the Virtual Router Redundancy Protocol (VRRP) (Knight et al. 1998).

Consider all components of the system and how they function when deciding on a redundancy strategy. As part of the decision-making process, consider how the various mechanisms work, what impact they will have on the rest of your environment, and how other machines will interact with them.

23.1.10 Scaling

All aspects of the mail system need to scale in advance of demand. Mail transport systems, mail delivery systems must be prepared to deal with higher volumes of traffic; mail access servers must deal with more people picking up their email; and list processing systems must handle spikes in traffic and membership of these. All need to scale in advance of new technologies that significantly increase message sizes.

Mail transport systems need to scale to meet increased traffic levels. Three independent variables govern email traffic levels: the size of the messages, the number of messages per person, and the number of people using the email system. The more people using the email service, the more email messages it will need to handle. The number of messages per person typically increases gradually over time, with spikes around holidays. The size of individual messages tends to increase in jumps with new technologies.

The email service also needs to scale to cope with large bursts of traffic that might be triggered by promotional events or significant, unexpected problems. Sudden increases in traffic volume through mail transport systems are not unheard of. The mail transport system should be designed to deal with unexpectedly high traffic peaks. Mail transport systems should also be prepared to store the large quantities of email that might accumulate if there are problems passing the messages downstream.

Mail delivery systems need to scale predictably as the number of people served by the delivery system increases. The mail delivery server will have to scale with time even if there is no increase in the number of people that it serves, because of increases in the number and size of messages that people receive. If customers store their email on the delivery server for a long time after they have read it, the delivery server will also have to scale to meet that demand. Mail delivery systems should always have plenty of extra mail spool capacity; the usual rule of thumb for peak use is twice the size of regular use. Sudden, unexpected bursts of large messages can occur.

The Wrong Way to Scale

A university department had its own email delivery server. When it became overloaded, it sometimes refused POP3 (Myers and Rose 1996) client-connection requests. To fix the problem, the SA sent an email around the department, publicly berating customers who were using email clients that automatically checked for new email at a predefined interval, such as every 10 minutes. It was the default configuration for the email clients, not a deliberate, selfish choice as her message had implied. However, several customers did take the time to figure out how to turn the feature off in their email clients, and the problem was resolved, at least temporarily. However, the problem kept reccurring as new people arrived and the traffic volume increased. As we saw in Chapter 16, it is better to fix things once than to partially fix them many times. It provides better service to the customers and ultimately less work for the SAs.

  Instead of trying to embarrass and blame her customers, the SA should have been monitoring the mail server to figure out what lack of resources was causing the refused connections. She could then have fixed the problem at its root and scaled the server to deal with the increased demand. Alternatively, some mail server products optimize a client checking for new email by quickly replying that there are no new messages if the client has queried in the last 10 minutes. This requires fewer resources than checking whether new mail has arrived for that user.

As new technologies emerge, message sizes typically increase significantly. In the early days, email was simple text and was transmitted over slow modem connections. When people started sharing basic images and large programs, the larger files were turned into text and broken into small chunks that were sent in separate messages so that they could still be transmitted over modems. Early images were of low resolution and black and white. Higher-resolution monitors and color monitors resulted in significant increases in the size of images that were emailed. When email became common on PC and Macintosh systems, people started sharing documents and slide presentations, which were large files with the potential to be huge. More document formats and documents, including more higher-resolution images, continue to increase message sizes. The introduction of standard video and audio file formats and the subsequent sharing of those files also increased the volume of data sent in email.

Always have plenty of spare mail spool space. Watch for emerging technologies, and be prepared to scale rapidly when they emerge. Most mail systems let the SAs set message size limits, which can help with size problems, if handled well. However, if they get in the way of people's work, people will find a way around the limitation, such as by splitting the email into several smaller chunks that will pass the size limit or by complaining to the CEO. We recommend using size limits only as a temporary stopgap measure to deal with an overload problem while you find a permanent solution or with a really huge limit to prevent people accidentally sending something enormous.

Organizations moving from POP3 to IMAP4 need to consider special scaling issues, since IMAP4 requires more resources on the server than POP3. POP3 is primarily used for moving email off a server and on to someone's laptop or desktop client. Disk space requirements are minimal because the server is used mostly as a holding area until the next connection from the client. Once the transfer is complete, the server can delete its copy of the mailbox. The connections from the client are short-lived. Clients connect, download the mailbox, and disconnect. They do not return until it is time to check for new mail, which may be hours or days. IMAP4, however, maintains the mailbox and all folders on the server and simply provides access to it from the client. Therefore, disk space requirements are much greater, and servers experience long connection times. Having the email on the server has the benefit of more centrally controlled and predictable backups. Because of the various network usage pattern, servers must be tuned for many simultaneous network connections that are long-lived. This can require extra effort, as many operating systems are not configured, by default, to properly handle thousands of open TCP/IP connections.

List processing systems have the same volume concerns as delivery and relay systems do but also have to deal with an increased and more diverse list membership. When a list processing machine has to deliver messages to a large number of other machines, a number of them will likely be unavailable for some reason. The list processing system needs to deal gracefully with this situation without delaying the delivery of the message to other systems that are available. Some parts of scaling a list processing system are related to software configuration (Chalup et al. 1998). Usage of disk space network bandwidth, CPU, and memory should all be monitored and scaled appropriately, too.

23.1.11 Security Issues

Mail relay hosts that communicate with places outside the company are traditionally targets for attackers because such communication inherently requires exposure to the Internet or other extranets. These high-value targets for attacks have access to both the outside world and the internal corporate network and often have special access to internal naming and authentication services. Mail delivery is a complex process and therefore prone to bugs that, historically, have been leveraged as security holes. Consider security issues starting with the initial design; security is difficult to add later.

The mail system is also a conduit through which undesirable content, such as viruses, can get into the company. Several vendors offer products that scan email content for viruses and other undesirable or destructive content before it is accepted and delivered to the recipient. Consider whether your site should implement such content scanning and whether it conflicts with the site's privacy policy. If content scanning is implemented, try to make sure that the application understands the maximum number of possible data formats so that it can examine all the files in, for example, a `zip` archive attachment. Be aware that some things will slip through the net, however, and that similar scanning should also take place on your customers' desktop machines. When processing thousands or millions of email messages a day, such virus scanning can be a big bottleneck. If you use such systems, plan for high disk I/O rates.

Also consider how the email system fits into the security architecture. For example, if the site has a perimeter security model, what protection does the firewall system provide for email? Does the system have a facility to prevent transmission of messages with suspicious headers that might be trying to exploit security holes? If not, where can that function best be implemented? Can the external mail relay systems be used by unauthorized persons to relay email not destined for the company? How can unauthorized mail relaying be prevented? How do customers access their email when they are on the road or at home? Many of the easiest and most common ways of providing people with access to their email when they are traveling involve transmitting passwords and potentially confidential email unencrypted across public, unsecured networks. The system's design should include a secure mechanism for remote email access, such as described in Chapter 27.

23.1.12 Communication

An important part of building any service is communication, particularly telling people what its features are and how to use it. Another important component of communication about a service is the documentation of the system for SAs.

For the customers of an email service, it is important to ensure that everybody who uses the system understands the policies associated with the system: regarding privacy, forwarding email off-site, email backups and schedule, any content filtering and its implications, and how the company defines acceptable-use and applies that definition to email (see Section 11.1.2). Customers should be made aware of the risks associated with email: potential forwarding of anything to inappropriate recipients, viruses, and the fact that any program they are asked to run is most likely a virus. Customers should be made aware of chain letters so that they recognize them and do not propagate them.

Customers should also be made aware of useful features that may be available to them, such as encryption mechanisms and mailing list administration tools.

Sadly, handing a person a stack of policies is not very effective. It can be easier to brief new hires verbally or with a brief slide presentation and make the complete policies available online. Some firms are creating a series of web forms, requiring customers to acknowledge and agree to each policy.

Documenting the email system for other SAs is important. Failover and recovery procedures should be clear and well documented, as should the design of the system, including diagrams that show the flow of mail and what processing happens on what systems. SAs who do not work directly with the email system should be able to perform some preliminary debugging before reporting a problem, and that process should also be well documented. It is particularly important that SAs who may be in different time zones at remote sites understand the mail system architecture be able to perform basic debugging tasks on their own.

23.2 The Icing

A site can do several things to improve its email service after covering all the basics. In the interest of protecting people's privacy and company-confidential information, a site can look at making email encryption a simple, easy-to-use option, particularly for the senior management. Also, the legal departments at many sites may want the SAs to implement an email-specific backup policy that discards email backups more quickly than others. A site that has an email service that is very visible to customers will want to implement more advanced monitoring. Some sites, such as ISPs or e-commerce sites, may need to scale the list processing system to handle high-volume, high-membership lists. We look at all of these in more detail.

23.2.1 Encryption

One enhancement to the basic email system is the addition of an easy-to-use encryption mechanism. Encryption is especially useful for senior managers, who are continually working with highly confidential information. Encryption must be quick and easy so that it does not take extra time to encrypt the message before sending it. The encryption needs to be fully integrated into the email client, so that managers can simply click the ENCRYPT WHEN SENDING button, configure automatic encryption for certain recipients, or turn encryption on by default for all messages. Most importantly, it must be equally easy for the intended recipient to decrypt the message. Difficulties with installing or configuring email clients to decrypt messages can foil even the best strategic encryption plans.

Available commercial encryption packages are integrated with email clients to varying degrees of transparency. When looking at the various products, consider both the user-interface issues and key-management issues. An encryption system needs a repository for everyone's encryption keys and a way for those keys to be rescinded if they are compromised. Consider also the issue of what to do in a disaster scenario in which something catastrophic happens to a key staff member and important emails are encrypted so that only that person can read them. Some systems have key-recovery mechanisms, but those mechanisms should have adequate controls to ensure that the keys cannot be compromised.

Encryption systems and key management are complex topics and should be researched in detail before being implemented at a site. A well-implemented encryption service is an asset to any company. However, many cryptography vendors are selling problems rather than solutions and should be avoided. Advice on detecting them can be found in Matt Curtin's *Snake Oil Warning Signs: Encryption Software to Avoid* (Curtin 1999a, b). For more information on email encryption standards, see Garfinkel (1994) and Oppliger (2000).

Consider the Sarbanes-Oxley implications to using encryption. If you allow encryption of email, the company must be able to recover the private key so as to make message contents available, if demanded by the appropriate authorities.

23.2.2 Email Retention Policy

Although backups are an essential part of good system administration practice, they also can be harmful to the company in an unexpected way. Many companies have a policy of not performing backups on email or of discarding those backups after a predefined short period of time.

The problem is that if the company becomes involved in a legal battle of any sort, such as defending its patent or intellectual property rights, all documents relating to the case are likely to be subpoenaed, which means searching through all backup tapes for relevant documents. Typically, formal documents relating to the topic will have been kept in well-known places. However, informal documents, such as emails, can be in any mailbox, and all email then has to be searched for potentially relevant documents. Whether on backup tapes or disk, emails that match the search criteria then have to be individually examined by someone who is able to determine whether the document is relevant and should be turned over to the court. This is a very expensive and time-consuming process that the legal department would rather avoid, regardless of whether it turns up documents in the company's favor. The process of having to search through years' worth of old email on backup tapes is simply too expensive.

Medium-size and large companies usually have a document retention policy that specifies how long certain types of documents should be kept. This policy is in place to limit the amount of document storage space that is needed and to make it easier to find relevant documents. The document retention policy is typically extended to cover email at some point, often in relation to attaining Sarbanes-Oxley conformance. At that point, the legal department will request that the SAs implement the policy. If email is distributed across many machines and in some nonstandard places, implementing the policy becomes difficult. In particular, if the email is stored on the laptops and desktops of people who use POP3 servers, the policy needs to cover the laptop and desktop backups and somehow separate the email backup from the system backup, so that the former can be discarded sooner. When designing your email service, it is best to bear in mind that you may be asked to implement this policy and to consider how you will do so.

23.2.3 Advanced Monitoring

For companies in which email is tied quite closely into the revenue stream, it is advisable to implement some more advanced monitoring methods for the email system. Because email transmission and delivery comprise a complex series of events, SAs can easily overlook some small aspect of the system if they try to perform only basic monitoring on each component. Although basic monitoring is very useful and necessary, a more complex end-to-end model must be implemented at sites where email is truly mission-critical.

End-to-end monitoring means building a test that emulates someone sending email to someone served by this email system. The test should emulate a customer or revenue-generating transaction as closely as possible to detect all possible problems, including those that are visible only from outside the site network. Chapter 22 covers monitoring in detail. In particular, Section 22.2.4 discusses end-to-end monitoring in general and includes an example that applies directly to email.

23.2.4 High-Volume List Processing

Most sites have mailing lists, and many have mailing lists that serve paying customers. For example, a company might have a mailing list that announces product upgrades or new products to its customers. It might have a mailing list that keeps customers up to date with events at the company or one that announces serious bugs with its products. Other companies have mailing lists for people who are beta testing a product. A nonprofit organization may have one or more mailing lists to keep its members up to date with what is happening and what events are being organized. A university may have mailing lists for the students in each class. A service provider will almost certainly have mailing lists for its customers to let them know of outages that might affect them.

Mailing lists are handled centrally on mail servers rather than as an alias in one person's mail client. Everyone can send email to the same address to reach the same list of people. Mailing lists can be protected so that only a few authorized people can send to them or so that messages have to be approved by an authorized person before they are sent or so that only people who are members of the list can send messages to it. The lists can also be open so that anyone can send email to all the list recipients. Most list management software gives the SAs the ability to delegate control of list membership, posting restrictions and message approval to the person who manages the list from a business perspective. The list management software should also be able to permit customers to create and delete their own mailing lists without SA involvement. For example, if a company starts a beta-test program for a particular product, the manager in charge of the beta test should be able to set up the mailing list for the beta users, add and remove them from the list, control who sends messages to the list, and delete the list when the beta test is over. When unsupervised creation of mailing lists is allowed, however, a policy and monitoring mechanism should be in place governing the rules for work-related and non-work-related lists. The list policy should clearly indicate what types of lists are appropriate and who can join them. A carpool list for employees in a particular region? Very likely. A carpool list for employees going to baseball games? Less clear. What about a fan list for a particular team? What happens when someone leaves the company? Can they still be on the baseball list with a new email address? And so on.

Relatively few companies will have high-volume, high-membership lists that require special scaling. Often, such sites are providing external services for others. The requirements for the average site's list-processing service can be met using basic, freely available software. However, high-volume lists often exceed the capabilities of those systems. In those situations, we recommend investing in commercial software or services that are capable of handling those large volumes or using open source software and hiring a consultant who has designed such systems previously. High-volume list services should also be built across several redundant systems to avoid cascading outages caused by the list server's getting swamped with work as soon as it recovers from an outage. On a high-volume list server, it is important to monitor the total length of elapsed time from when it starts sending a message to the first person on the list to when it finishes sending it to the last person on the list, excluding sites that it has problems contacting. It is important to the list members not to suffer from a large time lag. If people at the end of the list receive the message a day after people at the beginning of this list, it is difficult for them to participate in the conversation in a meaningful way, because they are so far behind the other people on the list. Conversely, some large lists have been known to throttle traffic to prevent "flame wars." Matching the responsiveness of the list servers to the goals of the list is key.

The USENIX LISA conference and the IETF have published many useful papers on the subject of list servers (Chapman 1992, Houle 1996) and list management (Bernstein 1997, Chalup et al. 1998). Email list server technology has changed dramatically over the years as the demands placed on it have increased. As with many areas of system administration, it is important to keep up with technology improvements in this area.

23.3 Conclusion

Email is an important service to get right. People rely on it even more than they realize. In many ways, it is like a utility, such as power or water. Scaling the system to meet increasing demand, monitoring the service, and building redundancy should not be an afterthought. Security should be considered from the outset, too, because email servers are a common target for attackers, and email is a common vector for viruses.

Before building an email system, you must consider several policies. Companies should carefully consider the email namespace policy and make sure that the same namespace is used internally and externally to the company. In addition, a privacy policy should be defined and communicated to people who use the service.

Some companies may want to consider integrating encryption into the email service to provide extra protection for sensitive information. Larger companies may want to implement a policy for reducing how long backups of email are retained and to protect themselves from the expense of searching through old email to find messages of relevance to a court case. Sites where the email service is linked to the revenue stream should consider implementing end-to-end monitoring of the email service. Those sites that run high-volume list servers have special needs that must be addressed and should invest in a commercial package.

Exercises

1. What is the email privacy policy at your site? How many people know about it?

2. How many email namespaces are at your site? Who controls them?

3. Identify your mail relay machines. Do they have other functions?

4. Identify your mail delivery machines. Do they have other functions?

5. Where does list processing happen at your site?

6. When do you anticipate having to scale up your existing email system? What aspect do you expect to scale, and why? How do you predict when it will run out of capacity?

7. How do you monitor your email system at the moment? Is there anything you would like to change or add?

8. How reliable is email service at your site? How did you arrive at that figure?

9. If your site has multiple delivery machines, explain why each one exists. Could you reduce the number?

10. If your company has remote offices, can people in those offices access their email when the connection to the main site is down?

11. How is email security handled at your site?

12. How does email flow from the Internet into your enterprise? How does it flow out to the Internet? What security risks and exposures are involved, and how does your design mitigate them? What improvements can be made?

13. How would you implement a 6-month retention schedule for email backups? Would you need to include desktops in this policy? How would you implement that component?

Chapter 24

Print Service

Printing is about getting a paper[1] copy of the information you want when you want it. Printing is a critical business function. In our experience, customers tend to rank it as one of the most critical services that is provided, second only to email.

Oddly, many SAs have disdain for printing or even anyone who prints a lot. "What happened to the paperless office?" laments the antiprinter crowd. Many SAs pride themselves on how little they print, refusing to work with paper when an electronic version is available. Therefore, many SAs who do not appreciate how important printing is to their customers will not provide good printing support. The priorities of the SAs must align with those of the customers.[2]

Printing is important to customers because, like it or not, business still runs on paper. Contracts need to be signed in ink. Diagrams need to be posted on walls. Paper can go places that computers can't. When you are driving, it is easier to read directions on paper than on a laptop. People find different mistakes when proofreading from paper than on the screen, possibly as a result of the human ability to take the document to new environments. Even technocrats use paper: Although it may shock you, dear reader, every chapter of this book was proofread on white, bond, laser printer–compatible . . . paper.

When a contract must absolutely, positively get there overnight, missing the overnight delivery truck because of a printer jam is an unacceptable excuse. Printing is a utility; it should always work. However, printing technology has radically changed many times during our careers. We therefore

---

1. You can print on a lot of things besides paper, but for the sake of simplicity, we refer to paper in this chapter. Transparencies are simply paper that didn't come from trees.

2. We, however, are still chagrined when we discover people who print every interesting web page they see.

choose not to discuss the pros and cons of various print technologies—those choices may not even be available by the time the ink on these pages is dry. Instead, we discuss the invariants of printing: making sure that the ink gets to the page, printing policies, and designing print servers. Finally, we discuss ways to encourage environmentally friendly printer use. All these things are important, regardless of the evolution of the technology used to actually print anything.

24.1 The Basics

A successful print system begins with an understanding of the requirements for a good policy, followed by solid design. Without proper policy, the design will be without direction. Without design, printing functions will be unstable and more difficult to use.

24.1.1 Level of Centralization

What would the perfect print environment look like? Some people want their own printers attached to their own computers. In their perfect world, every machine would have its own high-speed, high-quality printer. This is extremely expensive but very convenient for the customers. For others, the key issue is that no matter how many printers exist, they should be able to print from any host to any printer. This has the benefit of being able to "borrow" someone's high-quality (possibly color) printer as needed and is certainly a flexible configuration. Finance people look at the high cost of printers and printer maintenance and would prefer to centralize printing, possibly recommending that each building have one high-speed printer, one high-quality printer, and one color printer.[3] To others, it doesn't matter how many printers there are or who can access them, as long as every penny of cost is recouped via a charge-back system. Somewhere, there is a middle ground.

The primary requirement of a print system is that people can print to any printer they have permission to use, which might encompass all printers or only a well-defined set of printers. Costs are recouped either in per page increments, as part of a "tax," or by having each group—center, department, division—fund its own. If your life is not complicated enough, try using

---

3. We have nightmares of a CFO requesting one printer for an entire multinational company and arranging for printouts to be distributed by next-day delivery. However, Internet-based services that do specialty printing that way are popping up all over.

completely different cost-recovery methods for the hardware, supplies, and maintenance.

A typical office arrangement is to have one printer per section of a building, be it hallway, wing, or floor. These printers can be accessed either by anyone in the company or in the same cost center. Some individuals may have private printers because of confidentiality issues (they need to print documents containing confidential information), ego (they're important and demonstrate this by having their own printers), or some other business reason. In addition, high-speed, photographic-quality, wide-format plotters, and special printers other may have special-access control because of their special cost or operating requirements.

There is a trade-off between cost and convenience. More printers usually means more convenience: a shorter walk to the printer or increased variety of types of printers available. However, having more printers costs more in a variety of ways.

On the other hand, a shared, centralized printer can be so much less expensive that you can use some of the savings to purchase a significantly higher-quality printer. Suppose that inexpensive desktop printers cost $100 each. If ten people share a network printer, the break-even point is $1,000. At the time of this writing, $1,000 can purchase a nice network printer and still have room for a few years of maintenance. If 20 people share that printer, they now have a better printer at half the price of individual desktop printers; in addition, they get a little exercise walking to get their printouts.

Case Study: No Standards for Printers

Where there is little or no control over spending, costs will get out of control. One company had few restrictions on spending for items less than $600. When the cost of desktop laser printers dropped below that limit, droves of employees started purchasing them, introducing dozens of new models to the support load of the SA team, which often had to install the printer, maintain printer drivers, and debug problems. Without maintenance contracts, people were throwing away printers rather than repairing them. Management began to crack down on this problem and in an informal audit found that many of the printers that had been purchased were now attached to the employee's home computer. Cost controls were put into place, and soon the problem was halted. Most of the printers purchased were slow and had low-quality output compared with the centrally purchased printers located in each hallway. However, employees hated the policy. They were more concerned that a printer be within inches of their desk than be of higher quality or more cost-effective.

24.1.2 Print Architecture Policy

Every site should have certain written architecture policies related to printing. The first policy is a *general printer architecture policy* about how centralized printing will be. The goal of this document is to indicate how many people will share a printer for general printing—that is, one printer per desktop, one per hallway, one per building, one per floor—who qualifies for personal printers, and how the printers will be networked.

For reasonable reliability, networking printers requires a central print spool, the device that receives jobs for a printer and holds them until the printer is ready to receive them. The spooler is often part of the access control system because it decides who can print to which printer. Spoolers also can reroute print jobs around broken printers and permit such intelligent decisions as "print this on letterhead to any printer on the fourth floor."[4] Modern printers have a built-in spooler, but their memory may be limited, so a separate spooling host may still be required. The policy should indicate the level of redundancy required. One spooler often can handle dozens or hundreds of printers, but that creates a single point of failure. Some print spoolers can have hot standbys, or redundant spool hosts can be configured. Some OSs cannot spool to a machine that runs a different OS without losing features. You may choose to have such machines spool to a central host that uses the same OS but has gateway software that can spool to the main print system, which talks directly to the printer (Limoncelli 1998).

This policy also should detail how maintenance is handled: in-house, time and materials, or service contract. The policy should indicate the point at which maintenance costs, including labor, time, and downtime or other impact, become high enough that replacing the printer is more cost-effective.

A site should also have an *accounting policy* that determine whether printers are purchased by the department that uses the printer, from a central budget, or via an ad hoc source. Similar decisions must be made regarding paying for maintenance and repairs. Paying for supplies—media, toner—can be a contentious issue if printers are not obviously dedicated to particular financial units of the organization. Photocopiers and laser printers use the same paper, and thus it can be confusing if they are covered by different budgets. The simplest method is to have everything paid for out of a central budget.

---

4.   Of course, they must be able to notify the customer which printer was eventually selected!

Since more and more photocopiers connect to networks and double as laser printers, this becomes a natural evolution.

On the other hand, billing on a finer granularity may discourage wasting resources. Universities often bill per page, with different cost schedules for different kinds of printers. Students may receive a certain number of "free" pages every semester. There is no perfect solution, but the money has to come from somewhere. The objective is to create the least-objectionable solution.

The issue of who orders supplies and who resupplies the printers should also be part of the written policy. Some offices simply have the department secretary order the supplies, but sometimes the ordering is centralized. At some sites, the users of a particular printer are expected to refill the paper and change toner; at others, operators monitor printers and perform these tasks. We recommend against permitting customers to handle toner cartridges themselves. Sometimes, this procedure is complicated and error prone, not something that should be left to the typical customer. Moreover, it is our experience that customers will change toner at the slightest sign of quality problems, whereas a trained operator can take other steps, such as shaking the toner cartridge to get another couple hundred pages out of it. Changing toner cartridges needlessly is a waste of money and has environmental implications.

There should be a documented *printer equipment standard*. This policy should have two parts. The first part should change rarely and should specify long-term standards, such as whether PostScript or PCL will be used, whether duplexing units, when available, should be purchased, what protocol printers must speak—Line Printer Daemon Protocol (LPD) over TCP/IP (McLaughlin 1990), NT's Server Message Block (SMB) print protocol (Epps et al. 1999), AppleTalk, or parallel/USB cable connection—how they are connected to the network, and so on. The second part should be a list of currently recommended printers and configurations. For example, you might list an approved configuration or two for someone purchasing a color printer, a color printer for transparencies, and a couple of black-and-white printers of two or three price ranges. This part should be updated on a regular basis. These standards can also save money because they may qualify your company for volume discounts. Problems can be avoided by having all equipment orders filtered through the SA team or other knowledgeable people, as described in Section 21.2.1, to verify the completeness of orders and schedule installations so SAs are not caught unprepared when the devices arrive. Limiting the number of models in use also reduces the number and types of supplies you have to inventory, which saves money and confusion.

Case Study: Recommended Configurations Save SA Time

Recommended configurations should include all the items that customers might forget but that SAs will need to complete the installation. A site had a centralized printing system and provided a printer in each part of the building. These printers were always the same model. A group wanting a printer for its own, dedicated use often made the valiant effort of purchasing the same model as the others around the building. However, the group didn't know to purchase the optional duplexing unit, cable, and network connectivity package. When the SAs were asked to install such printers, they had to give the customer the sad news that there would be a delay while the proper add-ons were purchased so that the device would be usable. This problem continued until a printer standards document was written.

A *printer access policy* should determine who can access which printers and how that will be enforced. For example, people may be permitted to print to all printers, only to printers that their department paid for, or somewhere in between. This policy should also specify who can cancel print jobs on printers: For example, people other than administrators should be able to cancel only their own print jobs, with administrators being able to cancel any print job on the spoolers they control. Universities may have to meticulously control this because students may be prone to having "cancel wars."

We take an optimistic stance for the office environment. In business, inside a firewall, it is reasonable to permit everyone within the company to print to every printer and cancel any job on any printer. Being able to print to any printer in the company makes it possible for people to replace faxing with printing. A designer in San Jose can print to the printer in Japan over the corporate WAN, saving the cost of the international phone call. Can this be abused? Absolutely. However, this is extremely rare and will be even rarer if the cover page names the perpetrator. If employees have a private printer that they don't want others to print to, they can lock their doors. If someone has to ask for a printout, this can be an opportunity to tell the person not to print to the private printer. If people can print to any printer, it needs to be clear to them where the printers are located. You don't want people to print to the wrong country by mistake.

Case Study: An "Open" Cancellation Policy

Permitting anyone to cancel other people's printouts seems like asking for trouble. However, this policy was used successfully when Tom was at Bell Labs. Peer pressure prevented canceling any job but one's own. However, during the common event of a print job going out of control—most commonly PostScript code rather than PostScript output, being printed by mistake—paper waste was prevented because the first person to notice the problem could cancel the print job. This won't be as successful in less cooperative environments or where camaraderie among employees is not as good. Considering that jobs can be canceled from the front panel of most printers, this has become the de facto standard in most offices.

A *printer naming policy* should be established. We prefer printers to be named geographically; that is, the name indicates where the printer is located. Nothing is more frustrating than having printers named with a theme that is not helpful in locating the printer. Although it may be creative and cool to have printers named decaf, latte, mocha, and froth, it makes it difficult for people to find their printouts. Naming a printer after the room number it is in or near makes it easier for customers to find the printer.

One major pitfall to naming a printer after its location is that if the location changes, everyone must update their printer configuration. Otherwise, people will be frustrated to learn that they couldn't find printer fl2rm203 because it is now across the hall in room 206. This is less likely to happen if floorplans have designated printer areas that are unlikely to move or are the wrong shape to be used for anything else.

If the printer is likely to move, or in a small office, a more general name might be more appropriate, such as a name that indicates what floor it is on, possibly concatenated with the word *north*, *east*, *south*, or *west*.

Printers owned and managed centrally should not be named after the group that uses the printer. If that group moves to another part of the building, the group will want to take its printer. People left behind will lose their printer or have to change their printer configuration, which is like being punished for not doing anything. Printers owned by particular groups should not be named after the group that uses the printer so that when you decide to centralize the service, people will have an easier time letting go.

UNIX printers often have a two-part name. The first part indicates the printer's common name, and the second part may be a code for what kind of printout will be produced. For example, printer 2t408-d may send the job to the printer in room 2t408 in duplex (double-sided) mode, and 2t408-s may be an alias that prints to the same printer but in single-sided mode.

24.1.3 System Design

Once the policies have been defined, you can design and implement the print system architecture. Some print systems give very little flexibility; others, too much.

- A *peer-to-peer* print architecture is very decentralized: All hosts spool jobs directly to the destination printer over a network. This is the simplest to set up because often, you need to know only the IP address or name of the printer in order to send print jobs to it. However, this configuration can be the most difficult to administer. Any printer change that requires host-side (client) changes must be propagated to all clients. For example, if the printer is replaced by a newer model, all hosts may require a new printer driver.

- The *central funnel* is more centralized architecture that gives a higher level of control. In the simplest version of this architecture, all hosts send their print jobs to a central server, which then distributes the jobs to the various printers under its control. This server acts as a funnel that collects the print jobs and can then make intelligent decisions. For example, the server can convert various print formats—PostScript to PCL or vice versa—collect per page billing information, and so on, and can do intelligent printer selection. For example, customers could submit jobs to "the first available printer on the fourth floor" or "any color printer" or "the highest-quality color transparency printer." Only this one host needs the particular printer drivers and utilities that require maintenance, so there is only one place for upgrades to be done.

These two architectures have several variations. One problem with peer-to-peer architectures is that they become more complex and chaotic as they grow larger. This problem can be mitigated by either adopting a more centralized approach or using some kind of automated client-update mechanism. For example, you might use whatever automated software-deployment mechanism is used to distribute a patch that updates a printer driver or changes a printer setting. UNIX systems can distribute printcap information via various mechanisms: NIS, cfengine, and so on. Although most UNIX print clients cannot read their configuration directly from NIS, replacements, such as Line

Printer Remote, next generation (LPRng) [Powell and Mason 1995] can. Alternatively, a simple script can turn information stored in an NIS database into the local configuration file.

The problem with the centralized funnel is that it creates a single point of failure. However, because you can save money through centralization, some of those savings can be used to build in redundancy. The funnel can be two redundant print spoolers that can either manually or automatically fail over. This also makes server upgrades cleaner because one server can be taken out of service for upgrading without a reduction in service. Sometimes, automatic failover can be difficult to achieve. Considering how rare a hardware failure is, you can choose manual failover if the process is well documented and something that all SAs can be trained to do.

Other variations on these architectures include per group spoolers, multiply-redundant spoolers, one spooler per building, and so on. Some sites have two spoolers, each serving half of their customers, possibly divided between two buildings, but the spoolers have the ability to fail over to each other. Every spooler in the print system increases the work the administrators must do to maintain the service. Much of this work can be mitigated through automation, but be aware that not everything can be automated.

Peer to peer is becoming more common lately because modern network printers have reliable built-in spooling software. Such a thing used to be rare, and when it did exist, it was often buggy. Configuring contemporary operating systems to speak to a printer is much easier and usually can be done by customers without any SA help required.

A problem with peer-to-peer printing is that it becomes difficult to know how to cancel a rogue print job if you can't find the machine spooling to the printer. However, more and more printers permit jobs to be canceled directly from the printer console.

24.1.4 Documentation

It goes without saying that the architecture, operations procedures, and software used in your print system should be documented. Documentation is a critical part of any well-run system. SAs must provide three kinds of printing documentation to their customers.

1. *The how-to print* document should include which menus and buttons to click on to connect to the printer of the customer's choosing and explain which commands must be executed. For example, a UNIX

574　　Chapter 24　Print Service

environment might explain the environment variables that must be set, whether `lpr` or `lp` is used, and what options to use to get simplex, duplex, letterhead, or other specialty output. This document shouldn't need to change very often. It should be made available as part of the getting-started manual or web site that new customers are given.

2. *The list of printers* should be a catalog of all the printers available, where they are located, and what special features they have, such as color, quality, and so on. This document should tell customers where they can find the how-to-print document. This catalog needs to be updated every time a new printer is added or removed from the system. This document should be posted on the wall near every printer it lists, in addition to being part of the getting-started manual or web site that new customers are given.

3. A *printer label* should be on every printer, indicating its name or names. Trays should be labeled if they are intended for transparencies, letterhead, and so on.[5] Labeling printers is such a simple thing, yet we have seen many environments in which SAs forget to do it. The printer users will feel that this is the most important documentation you can provide. The rest can usually be figured out!

Printer Maps

At Google, one can go to http://print to view a web site that lists all the printers by location and floorplan maps to help customers find them. Clicking on the name of a printer brings up a menu of choices, including links for configuring your desktop to print to this printer—it detects your OS and gives those instructions first—a link to a description of the printer's capabilities, a link that displays the print queue for that printer, and a link that opens a ticket at the helpdesk about that printer.

24.1.5 Monitoring

As we said in Chapter 5, nothing deserves the name *service* until it is monitored. Two aspects need this attention. The first is the spooling and printing service itself. The SAs need to monitor each spooler to make sure that the

---

5. We recommend a consistent tray scheme. For example, transparencies are always tray 2. This will help prevent the situation in which documents are accidentally printed on transparencies or slides are printed on paper.

queue hasn't stalled, the spool disk hasn't filled, logs are being recycled, the CPU is not overloaded, the spool disk hasn't died, and so on. This should be a part of the normal monitoring system.

The second aspect that needs to be monitored is the status of each printer. Toner and paper trays need to be refilled. Shelves of paper need to be restocked. Most network printers speak SNMP and can alert your monitoring system that they are jammed, low on toner, or out of paper. Printers monitor exactly how much paper they have remaining, so that SAs can be alerted when they are nearly out of paper, though we prefer to let customers load the paper themselves.

Although there are automated means to tell whether a printer is out of paper, there is no automated way to tell whether a good supply of paper is sitting near the printer. SAs can either visit the printers on a regular basis or deputize customers to alert them when paper supplies are running low.

Case Study: Print Tests

Newer printers indicate when they are low on toner, but older printers require a test print. One site used a program to generate a test print on every printer each Monday morning. The page included a time, date, a warning to customers not to throw it out, and a large test pattern. An operator was assigned to retrieve these printouts and add toner if the test pattern was unreadable. The operator pulled a cart of paper along and restocked the supply cabinets under each printer. This very simple system maintained a high level of service.

24.1.6 Environmental Issues

As SAs, we must take responsibility for the environmental aspects of printing. Toner is toxic. Printing kills trees, and disposing of printouts fills up landfills. A page that is not printed has a lower impact than a page that is printed and then recycled; however, there also is a cost and environmental impact to recycling. Print systems must be designed to minimize waste. Toner cartridges should be recycled. SAs should be sensitive to the environmental impact of the chemicals used in the printing process. Wasteful printing should be discouraged and paperless solutions encouraged, when possible. Considerable cost savings are also gained by the reduction in paper and toner to be purchased. Waste-disposal charges usually are lowered if recyclable paper is separated.

Customers will recycle when it is easy and not when it is impossible. If there are no recycling bins, people won't recycle. Putting a recycling bin next to each trash can and near every printer makes it easy for customers to recycle. As SAs, it is our responsibility to institute such a program if one doesn't exist, but creation of such a system may be the direct responsibility of others. We should all take responsibility for coordinating with the facilities department to create such a system or, if one is in place, to make sure that proper paper-only wastebaskets are located near each printer, instructions are posted, and so on. The same can be said for recycling used toner cartridges. This is an opportunity to collaborate with the people in charge of the photocopying equipment in your organization because many of the issues overlap.

Some issues are the responsibility of the customers, but SAs can facilitate them by giving customers the right tools. SAs must also avoid becoming roadblocks that encourage their customers to adopt bad habits. For example, making sure that preview tools for common formats, such as PostScript, are available to all customers helps them print less. Printers and printing utilities should default to duplex (double-sided) printing. Don't print a burst page before each printout. Replacing paper forms with web-based, paperless processes also saves paper, though making them as easy to use is a challenge.

Case Study: Creating a Recycling Program

A large company didn't recycle toner cartridges, even though new ones came with shipping tags and instructions on how to return old ones. The vendor even included a financial incentive for returning old cartridges. The company's excuse for not taking advantage of this system was simply that nobody had created a procedure within the company to do it! Years of missed cost savings went by until someone finally decided to take the initiative to create a process. Once the new system was in place, the company saved thousands of dollars per year.

   Lesson learned: These things don't create themselves. Take the initiative. Everyone will use the process if someone else creates it.

24.2 The Icing

SAs can build some interesting add-ons into their print service to make it more of a Rolls-Royce quality of service.

24.2.1 Automatic Failover and Load Balancing

We discussed redundant print servers; often, the failover for such systems is manual. SAs can build automatic failover systems to reduce the downtime associated with printer problems.

If the printing service deals with high volumes, the SAs might consider using the redundant systems to provide load balancing. For example, there may be two print spoolers, with each handling half of the printers to balance the load and substituting for each other if one dies, to mitigate downtime.

Automated failover has two components: detection of a problem and the cutover to the other spooler. Detecting that a service is down is difficult to do properly. A spooler may be unable to print even if it responds to pings, accepts new connections, answers requests for status, and permits new jobs to be submitted. It is best if the server can give a more detailed diagnostic without generating printout. If no jobs are in the queue, you can make sure that the server is accepting new jobs. If jobs are in the queue, you can make sure that the current job has not been in the process of being printed for an inordinate amount of time, which may indicate a problem. You must be careful, because small PostScript jobs can generate many pages or can run for a long time without generating any pages.

It is important to devise a way to avoid false positives. You must also differentiate between the server being out of service and the printer being out of service.

Outside of server problems, we find most printing problems to be on the PC side, particularly the drivers and the application software. At least having reliable print servers to print documents to can reduce the chance of multiple simultaneous failures.

Outsourced Printing

If you need a fancy print feature only occasionally, such as binding, three-hole punch, high-volume printing, or extra-wide formats, many print shops accept PDF files. Walking a PDF file to a store once in a while is much more cost-effective than buying a fancy printer that is rarely used.

Nearly all print shops will accept PDFs via email or on their web site. Print shop chains have created printer drivers that "print to the web." These drivers submit the printout to their printing facility directly from applications. You can then log in to their web site to preview the output, change options, and pay. Most will ship the resulting output to you, which means that you never have to leave your office.

24.2.2 Dedicated Clerical Support

Printers are mechanical devices, and often their reliability can be increased by keeping untrained people away from their maintenance tasks. We don't mean to disparage our customers' technical abilities, but we've seen otherwise brilliant people break printers by trying to change the toner cartridge.

Therefore, it can be advantageous to have a dedicated clerk or operator service them. Many sites have enough printers that it can be a part-time job for someone to simply visit every printer every few days to verify that it is printing properly, has enough paper, and so on. This person can also be responsible for getting printers repaired. Although a company may have a service contract to "take care of that kind of thing," someone still has to contact, schedule, and babysit the repair person. Arranging service and describing the problem can be very time consuming, and it's less expensive to have a clerk do this task than an SA. Often, one can recruit a secretary or office manager to do this.

Ordering supplies can often be delegated to secretaries or office clerks if you first get their manager's permission. Write up a document with the exact order codes for toner cartridges so there is no guesswork involved.

24.2.3 Shredding

People print the darnedest things: private email, confidential corporate information, credit card numbers, and so on. We've even met someone who tested printers by printing UNIX's /etc/passwd file, not knowing that the encrypted second field could be cracked. Some sites shred very little, some have specific shredding policies, and others shred just about everything.

We don't have much to say about shredding except to note that it is good to shred anything that you wouldn't want on the front page of the *New York Times* and that you should err on the side of caution about what you wouldn't want to see there. Something that isn't printed is even more secure than something shredded.

The other thing to note is that on-site shredding services bring a huge shredder on a truck to your site to perform the shredding services, and off-site shredding services take your papers back to their shredding station for treatment. Now and then, we hear stories that an off-site shredding service was found to not actually shred the paper as they had promised. We aren't sure whether these are true or merely urban legends, but we highly recommend regular spot-checks of your off-site shredding service if you choose one. Shredding services are typically quite expensive, so you should make sure that you are getting what you pay for.

We prefer on-site shredding, and we designate a person to watch the process to make sure that it is done properly.

24.2.4 Dealing with Printer Abuse

According to an old Usenet saying, "You can't solve social problems using technology," and this applies to printing as well. You can't write a program to detect nonbusiness use of printers, and you can't write a program to detect wasteful printing. However, the right peer pressure and policy enforcement can go a long way. Your acceptable-use policy (Section 11.1.2) should include what constitutes printer abuse.

Billing on a per page basis can create a business reason for conserving paper. If the goal is to control printing costs rather than to recover funds spent by the SA team on supplies, you might give each person a certain amount of "free" printing per month or let departments pool their "free" allotment. A lot of psychology is involved in a scheme like that. You wouldn't want to create a situation in which people waste time doing other things because they fear that the boss will punish them for going over their allotment.

One site simply announced the top-ten page generators each month as a way to shame people into printing less. The theory was that people would print less if they learned that they were one of the largest consumers of printing services. However, a certain set of employees took this as a challenge and competed to appear in the listing for the most consecutive months. This technique might have been more effective if the list had been shown only to management or if an SA had personally visited the people and politely let them know of their status. Shame can work in certain situations and not in others.

We suggest a balanced, nontechnical, approach. Place the printer in a very visible, public place. This will discourage more personal use than any policy or accounting system. If someone does something particularly wasteful, address the person. Don't get petty about every incident; it's insulting.

The 500-Page Printout

SAs were perturbed to find a 500-page printout of "game cheats" tricks for winning various computer games at the printer one day. When this was brought to the attention of the director, he dealt with it in a very smart way. Rather than scolding anyone, he sent email to all employees, saying that he had found this printout by the printer without a cover page to indicate who made the printout. He reminded people that a small amount of nonbusiness printing was reasonable and that he didn't want this obviously valuable document to accidentally go to the wrong person. Therefore, he asked the owner of the document to stop by his office to pick it up. After a week, the printout was recycled, unclaimed. Nothing more needed to be said.

24.3 Conclusion

Printing is a utility. Customers expect it to always work. The basis of a solid print system is well-defined policies on where printers will be deployed—desktop, centralized, or both—what kinds of printers will be used, how they will be named, and what protocols and standards will be used to communicate with them. Print system architectures can run from very decentralized—peer to peer—to very centralized. It is important to include redundancy and failover provisions in the architecture. The system must be monitored to ensure quality of service.

Users of the print system require a certain amount of documentation. How to print and the location of the printers they have access to should be documented. The printers themselves must be labeled.

Printing has an environmental impact; therefore, SAs have a responsibility to not only work with other departments to create and sustain a recycling program but also provide the right tools so that customers can avoid printing whenever possible.

The best print systems also have automated failover and load balancing rather than manual failover. They have clerks who do maintenance and refill supplies rather than SAs spending time with these tasks or inflicting untrained users on the printers' delicate components. The best print systems provide shredding services for sensitive documents and recognize that many printing issues are social problems and therefore can't be solved purely with technology.

Exercises

1. Describe the nontechnical print policies in your environment.
2. Describe the print architecture in your environment. Is it centralized, decentralized, or a mixture?
3. How reliable is your print system? How do you quantify that?

4. When there is an outage in your print system, what happens, and who is notified?

5. When new users arrive, how do they know how to print? How do they know your policies about acceptable use?

6. How do you deal with the environmental issues associated with printing at your location? List both policies and processes you have, in addition to the social controls and incentives.

7. What methods to avoid printing are provided to your customers?

Chapter 25

Data Storage

The systems we manage store information. The capacity for computers to store information has doubled every year or two. The first home computers could store 120 kilobytes on a floppy disk. Now petabytes—millions of millions of kilobytes—are commonly bandied about. Every evolutionary jump in capacity has required a radical shift in techniques to manage the data.

You need to know two things about storage. The first is that it keeps getting cheaper—unbelievably so. The second is that it keeps getting more expensive—unbelievably so.

This paradox will become very clear to you after you have been involved in data storage for even a short time. The price of an individual disk keeps getting lower. The *price per megabyte* has become so low that people now talk about *price per gigabyte*. When systems are low on disk space, customers complain that they can go to the local computer store and buy a disk for next to nothing. Why would anyone ever be short on space?

Unfortunately, the cost of connecting and managing all these disks seems to grow without bound. Previously, disks were connected with a ribbon cable or two, which cost a dollar each. Now fiber-optic cables connected to massive storage array controllers cost thousands. Data is stored multiple times, and complicated protocols are used to access the data from multiple simultaneous hosts. Massive growth requires radical shifts in disaster-recovery systems, or *backups*. Compared to what it takes to manage data, the disks themselves are essentially free.

The shift in emphasis from having storage to managing the data through its life cycle is enormous. Now the discussion is no longer about price per gigabyte but *price per gigabyte-month*. A study published in early 2006 by a major IT research firm illustrated the variability of storage costs. For array-based simple mirrored storage, the report found two orders of magnitude difference between low-end and high-end offerings.

Storage is a huge topic, with many fine books written on it. Therefore, we focus on basic terminology, some storage-management philosophy, and key techniques. Each of these is a tool in your toolbox, ready to be pulled out as needed.

25.1 The Basics

Rather than storage being a war between consumers and providers, we promote the radical notion that storage should be managed as a community resource. This reframes storage management in a way that lets everyone work toward common goals for space, uptime, performance, and cost. Storage should be managed like any other service, and we have advice in this area. Performance, troubleshooting, and evaluating new technologies are all responsibilities of a storage service team.

But first, we begin with a whirlwind tour of common storage terminology and technology.

25.1.1 Terminology

As a system administrator, you may already be familiar with a lot of storage terminology. Therefore, we briefly highlight the terminology and key concepts used later in the chapter.

25.1.1.1 Key Individual Disk Components

In order to understand the performance issues of various storage systems, it is best to have an understanding of the underlying media and how basic disk operations work. Understanding the bottlenecks of the individual components gives a basis for understanding the bottlenecks and improvements that appear in the more complex systems.

- *Spindle, platters, and heads:* A disk is made up of several platters on which data is stored. The platters are all mounted on a single spindle and rotate as a unit. Data is stored on the platters in tracks. Each track is a circle with the spindle as its center, and each track is at a different radius from the center. A cylinder is all the tracks at a given radius on all the platters. Data is stored in sectors, or blocks, within the track, and tracks have different numbers of blocks based on how far from the center they are. Tracks farther from the center are longer and therefore have more blocks. The heads read and write the data on the disk by hovering over the appropriate track. There is one head per platter, but they are all mounted on the same robotic arm and move as a unit. Generally, an entire track or an entire cylinder will be read at once, and the data cached, as the time it takes to move the heads to the right place (seek time) is longer than it takes for the disk to rotate 360 degrees.

- *Drive controller:* The electronics on the hard drive, the drive controller implements the drive protocol, such as SCSI or ATA. The drive controller communicates with the host to which the disk is attached. Drive controllers are important for their level of standards compliance and for any performance enhancements that they implement, such as buffering and caching.

- *Host bus adapter (HBA):* The HBA is in the host and manages communication between the disk drive(s) and the server. The HBA uses the data access protocol to communicate with the drive controller. A smart HBA can also be a source of performance enhancements. It is usually on the motherboard of the computer or an add-on card.

25.1.1.2 RAID: A Redundant Array of Independent Disks

RAID is an umbrella category for techniques that use multiple independent hard drives to provide storage that is larger, more reliable, or faster than a single drive can provide. Each RAID technique is called a *level* (see Table 25.1).

- *RAID 0*, also known as striping, spreads data across multiple disks in such a way that they can still act as one large disk. A RAID 0 virtual disk is faster than a single disk; multiple read and write operations can be executed in parallel on different disks in the RAID set. RAID 0 is less reliable than a single disk, because the whole set is useless if a single disk fails. With more disks, failures are statistically more likely to happen.

- *RAID 1*, also known as mirroring, uses two or more disks to store the same data. The disks should be chosen with identical specifications.

Table 25.1 Commonly Used RAID Levels

Raid Level	Methods	Characteristics
0	Stripes	Faster reads and writes; poor reliability
1	Mirrors	Faster reads; good reliability; very expensive
5	Distributed parity	Faster reads; slower writes; more economical
10	Mirrored stripes	Faster reads; best reliability; most expensive

Each write operation is done to both (or all) disks, and the data is stored identically on both (all). Read operations can be shared between the disks, speeding up read access. Writes are as slow as the slowest disk. RAID 1 increases reliability. If one disk fails, the system keeps working.

Remembering RAID 0

RAID 0 and RAID 1 are two of the most commonly used RAID strategies. People often find it difficult to remember which is which. Here's our mnemonic: "RAID 0 provides zero help when a disk dies."

- *RAID 2 and 3* are rarely used strategies that are similar enough to RAID 5 that we explain the general concept there. However, it should be noted that RAID 3 gives particularly good performance for sequential reads. Therefore, large graphics files, streaming media, and video applications often use RAID 3. If your organization is hosting such files, you may wish to consider a RAID 3 implementation for that particular storage server, especially if files tend to be archived and are not changed frequently.

- *RAID 4* is also similar to RAID 5 but used rarely because it is usually slower. RAID 4 is faster than RAID 5 only when a file system is specifically designed for it. One example is Network Appliance's file server, with its highly tuned WAFL file system.

- *RAID 5*, also known as distributed parity, seeks to gain reliability, like mirroring, with lower cost. RAID 5 is like RAID 0—striping, to get a larger volume—but with a single additional disk used to store recovery information. If a single disk fails, the RAID 5 set continues to work. When the failed disk is replaced, the data on that disk is rebuilt, using the recovery disk. Performance is reduced during the rebuild. RAID 5 gives increased read speed, as with RAID 0. However, writes can take longer, as creating and writing the recovery information requires reading information on all the other disks.

- *RAIDs 6–9*, either don't exist or are marketing hype for variations on the preceding. Really.

- *RAID 10*, originally called *RAID 1 + 0*, uses striping for increased size and speed and mirroring for reliability. RAID 10 is a RAID 0 group that has been mirrored onto another group. Each individual disk in the RAID 0 group is mirrored. Since mirroring is RAID 1, the joke is that this is 1 + 0, or 10. Rebuilds on a RAID 10 system are not as disruptive to performance as rebuilds on a RAID 5 system. As with RAID 1, multiple mirrors are possible and are commonly used.

RAID systems often allow for a *hot spare*, an extra unused disk in the chassis. When a disk fails, the system automatically rebuilds the data onto a hot spare. (This is not applicable to RAID 0, where the lost data cannot be rebuilt.) Some RAID systems can have multiple RAID sets but a single hot spare. The first RAID set to require a new disk takes the spare, which saves the cost of multiple spares.

25.1.1.3 Volumes and Filesystems

A *volume* is a chunk of storage as seen by the server. Originally, a volume was a disk, and every disk was one volume. However, with partitioning, RAID systems, and other techniques, a volume can be any kind of storage provided to the server as a whole. The server sees a volume as one logical disk; even if behind the scenes, it is made up of more complicated parts.

Each volume is formatted with a filesystem. Each of the many file system types was invented for a different purpose or to solve a different performance problem. Some common Windows filesystems are FAT, DOS FAT32, and NTFS. UNIX/Linux systems have UFS, UFS2, EXT2/EXT3, ReiserFS, and many experimental ones. Some filesystems do *journaling*, or simply keeping a list of changes requested to the filesystem and applying them in batch. This improves write speed and makes recovery faster after a system crash.

25.1.1.4 DAS: Directly Attached Storage

DAS is simply the conventional hard disk connected to the server. DAS describes any storage solution whereby the storage is connected to the server with cabling rather than with a network. This includes a RAID array that is directly attached to a server.

25.1.1.5 NAS: Network-Attached Storage

NAS is a new term for something that's been around for quite a while: clients accessing the storage attached to a server. For example, UNIX clients that use NFS to access files on a server, or Microsoft Windows systems that use CIFS to access files on a Windows server. Many vendors package turnkey network file servers that work out of the box with several file-sharing protocols. Network Appliance and EMC make such systems for large storage needs;

Linksys and other companies make smaller systems for consumers and small business.

25.1.1.6 SANs: Storage-Area Networks

A SAN is a system in which disk subsystems and servers both plug into a dedicated network, a special low-latency, high-speed network optimized for storage protocols. Any server can attach to any storage system—at least as access controls permit. What servers can attach to is a storage volume that has been defined and is referred to by its logical unit number (LUN). A LUN might be a disk, a slice of a RAID 5 group, an entire storage chassis, or anything the storage systems make available. Servers access LUNs on the block level, not the file system level. Normally, only one server can attach to a particular LUN at a time; otherwise, servers will get confused as one system updates blocks without the others realizing it. Some SAN systems provide **cluster file systems**, which elect one server to arbitrate access so that multiple servers can access the same volume simultaneously. Tape backup units can also be attached to the network and shared, with the benefit that many servers share a single expensive tape drive. Another benefit of SANs is that they reduce isolated storage. With DAS, some servers may be lacking free disk space while others have plenty. The free space is not available to servers that need it. With SAN technology, each server can be allocated volumes as big as they need, and no disk space is isolated from being used.

25.1.2 Managing Storage

Management techniques for storage rely on a combination of process and technology. The most successful solutions enlist the customer as an ally, instead of making the SA into the "storage police."

It is not uncommon for customers to come to an SA with an urgent request for more storage for a particular application. There is no magic answer, but applying these principles can greatly reduce the number of so-called emergency storage requests that you receive. It is always best to be proactive rather than reactive, and that is certainly the case for storage.

25.1.2.1 Reframe Storage as a Community Resource

Storage allocation becomes less political and customers become more self-managing when storage servers are allocated on a group-by-group basis. It is particularly effective if the cost of the storage service comes from a given group's own budget. That way, the customers and their management chain feel that they have more control and responsibility.

Studies show that roughly 80 percent of the cost of storage is spent on overhead—primarily support and backups—rather than in the price of the hard drives. It should be possible to work with management to also pass on at least some of the overhead costs to each group. This approach is best for the company because the managers whose budgets are affected by increasing storage needs are also the ones who can ask their groups to clean up obsolete work and save space.

However, it is sometimes not possible to dedicate a storage server to a single group. When a storage server must serve many groups, it is always best to start with a storage-needs assessment with your customer base; when the assessment is complete, you will know how much storage a group needs currently, whether the existing storage is meeting that need, and how much future capacity that group anticipates.

By combining data from various groups' needs assessments, you will be able to build an overall picture of the storage needs of the organization. In many cases, reshuffling some existing storage may suffice to meet the needs identified. In other cases, an acquisition plan must be created to bring in additional storage.

Doing a storage assessment of departments and groups begins the process of creating a storage community. As part of the assessment, groups will be considering their storage needs from a business and work-oriented perspective rather than simply saying, "The more, the better!"

One great benefit of bringing this change in attitude to your customers is that the SAs are no longer "the bad guy" and instead become people who are helping the customers implement their desired goals. Customers feel empowered to pursue their storage agendas within their groups, and a whole set of common customer complaints disappear from the support staff radar.

❖ **Raw versus Usable Disk Capacity**   When purchasing storage, it is important to remember that raw storage is significantly different from usable storage.

A site needed a networked storage array to hold 4 terabytes of existing data, projected to grow to 8 terabytes within 2 years. The customer told the vendor, who cheerfully sent an 8 terabyte array system. The customer began configuring the array, and a significant amount of space was consumed for file system overhead plus disks used for RAID redundancy, snapshots, and hot spares. Soon, the customer discovered that current usage amounted to 100 percent of what was remaining. The system would not support any growth.

Luckily, the customer was able to work with the vendor to replace the disks with ones twice as large. Because this was done before the customer took official delivery, the disks were not considered "used."

Although the site's future capacity problem was now solved, the problems continued. More disk required more CPU overhead. The application was extremely sluggish for almost 2 weeks while an emergency upgrade to the array processor controller was arranged. The finance people were not very happy about this, having approved the original system, then the drive upgrades, and, finally needing to write a big check to upgrade the processor.

25.1.2.2 Conduct a Storage-Needs Assessment

You might think that the first step in storage-needs assessment is to find out who is using what storage systems. That is actually the *second* step. The first step is to talk to the departments and groups you support to find out their needs. Starting with a discovery process based on current usage will often make people worry that you are going to be taking resources away from them or redistributing resources without their input.

By going directly to your customers and asking what does and doesn't work about their current storage environment, you will be building a bridge and establishing trust. If you can show graphs of their individual storage grown over the last year and use it to educate them rather than scold them, it can help understand their real needs.

You may be surprised at what you discover, both positive and negative. Some groups may be misrepresenting their needs, for fear of being affected by scarcity. Other groups may be struggling with too few resources but not complaining because they assumed that everyone is in the same situation.

What kinds of questions should you ask in the storage assessment? Ask about total disk usage, both current and projected, for the next 6 to 18 months. It's a good idea to use familiar units, if applicable, rather than simply "months." It may be easier for customers to specify growth in percentages rather than gigabytes. Ask about the next 2 to 6 quarters, for instance, in a company environment, and the upcoming terms in an academic environment. You should also inquire about what kinds of applications are being run and any problems that are being encountered in day-to-day usage. You may feel that you are adequately monitoring a group's usage and seeing a pattern emerge, such that you are comfortable predicting the group's needs, but some aspects of your storage infrastructure may already be stressed in ways that are not readily visible from simple metrics. These can become evident when customers provide clues.

Can't Get There from Here

A midsize chip development firm working closely with a new partner ordered high-end vendor equipment for a new cluster that would be compatible with the partner's requirements. Performance, affordability, reliability, and similar were analyzed and hotly debated. After the new hardware showed up on the dock, however, it was discovered that one small detail had been overlooked. The site ordering the new hardware was working with different data sets than the partner site, and the storage solution ordered was not scalable using the same hardware. Over half of the more expensive components (chassis, controller) would have to be replaced in order to make a larger cluster. Instead of serving the company's storage needs for all its engineering group for a year, it would work for one department for about 6 months.

It is also possible that upcoming events outside the current norm may affect storage needs. For example, the department you support may be planning to host a visiting scholar next term, someone who might be bringing a large quantity of research data. Or the engineering group could be working on adding another product to its release schedule or additional use cases to its automated testing: each of these, of course, requiring a significant increase in storage allocation. Often, the systems staff are the last to know about these things, as your customers may not be thinking of their plans in terms of the IS requirements needed to implement them. Thus, it is very useful to maintain good communication and explicitly ask about customers' plans.

Work Together to Balance System Stress

At one of Strata's sites, the build engineers were becoming frustrated trying to track down issues in automated late-night builds. Some builds would fail mysteriously on missing files, but the problem was not reproducible by hand. When the engineers brought their problem to the systems staff, the SAs were able to check the server logs and load graphs for the affected hosts. It turned out that a change in the build schedule, combined with new tests implemented in the build, had caused the build and the backups to overlap in time. Even though they were running on different servers, this simultaneous load from the build and the nightly backups was causing the load on one file server to skyrocket to several times normal, resulting in some remote file requests timing out. The missing files would cause sections of the build to fail, thus affecting the entire build at the end of its run when it tried to merge everything.

Since this build generally required 12–18 hours to run, the failures were seriously affecting engineering's schedule. Since backups are also critical, they couldn't be shut off during engineering's crunch time. A compromise was negotiated, involving changing the times at which both the builds and the backups were done, to minimize the chances of overlap. This solved the immediate problem. A storage reorganization, to solve the underlying problem, was begun so that the next production builds would not encounter similar problems.

25.1.2.3 Map Groups onto Storage Infrastructure

Having gleaned the necessary information about your customers' current and projected storage needs, the next step is to map groups and subgroups onto the storage infrastructure. At this point, you may have to decide whether to group customers with similar needs by their application usage or by their reporting structure and work group.

If at all possible, arrange customers by department or group rather than by usage. Most storage-resource difficulties are political and/or financial. Restricting customers of a particular server or storage volume to one work group provides a natural path of escalation entirely within that work group for any disagreements about resource usage. Use group-write permissions to enforce the prohibition against nongroup members using that storage.

Some customers scattered across multiple departments or work groups may have similar but unusual requirements. In that case, a shared storage solution matching those requirements may be necessary. That storage server should be partitioned to isolate each work group on its own volume. This removes at least one element of possible resource contention. The need for the systems staff to become involved in mediating storage-space contention is also removed, as each group can self-manage its allocated volume.

If your environment supports quotas and your customers are not resistant to using them, individual quotas within a group can be set up on that group's storage areas. When trying to retrofit this type of storage arrangement on an existing set of storage systems, it may be helpful to temporarily impose group quotas while rearranging storage allocations.

Many people will resist the use of quotas, and with good reason. Quotas can hamper productivity at critical times. An engineer who is trying to build or test part of a new product but runs into the quota limit either has to spend time trying to find or free up enough space or has to get in touch with an SA and argue for a quota increase. If the engineer is near a deadline, this time loss could result in the whole product schedule slipping. If your customers are resistant to quotas, listen to their rationale, and see whether there is a common ground that you can both feel comfortable with, such as emergency increase requests with a guaranteed turnaround time. Although you need to understand each individual's needs, you also need to look at the big picture. Implementing quotas on a server in a way that prevents another person from doing her job is not a good idea.

25.1.2.4 Develop an Inventory and Spares Policy
Most sites have some kind of inventory of common parts. We discuss spares in general in Section 4.1.4, but storage deserves a bit of extra attention.

There used to be large differences between the types of drives used in storage systems and the ones in desktop systems. This meant that it was much easier for SAs to dedicate a particular pool of spare drives to infrastructure use. Now that many storage arrays and workgroup servers are built from off-the-shelf parts, those drives on the shelf might be spares that could be used in either a desktop workstation or a workgroup storage array. A common spares pool is usually considered a good thing. However, it may seem arbitrary to a customer who is denied a new disk but sees one sitting on a shelf unused, reserved for the next server failure. How can SAs make sure to reserve enough drives as spares for vital shared storage while not hoarding drives that are also needed for new desktop systems or individual customer needs? It is something of a balancing act, and an important component is a policy that addresses how spares will be distributed. Few SAs are able to stock as many spares as they would like to have around, so having a system for allocating them is crucial.

It's best to separate general storage spares from infrastructure storage spares. You can make projections for either type, based on failures observed in the past on similar equipment. If you are tracking shared storage usage—and you should be, to avoid surprises—you can make some estimates on how often drives fail, so that you have adequate spares.

For storage growth, include not only the number of drives required to extend your existing storage but also whatever server upgrades, such as CPU and memory, might also be needed. If you have planned to expand by acquiring whole new systems, such as stand-alone network storage arrays, be sure to include spares for those systems through the end of the fiscal year when they will be acquired.

25.1.2.5 Plan for Future Storage
The particularly tricky aspect of storage spares is that a customer asking for a drive almost every time needs something more than simply a drive. A customer whose system disk has failed really needs a new drive, along with a standardized OS install. A customer who is running out of shared disk space

and wants to install a private drive really needs more shared space or a drive, along with plus backup services. And so on.

We don't encourage SAs to have a prove-that-you-need-this mentality. SAs strive to be enablers, not gatekeepers. That said, you should be aware that every time a drive goes out the door of your storage closet, it is likely that something more is required. Another way to think of it is that a problem you know how to solve is happening now, or a problem that you might have to diagnose later is being created. Which one would you rather deal with?

Fortunately, as we show in many places in this book, it's possible to structure the environment so that such problems are more easily solved by default. If your site chooses to back up individual desktops, some backup software lets you configure it to automatically detect a new, local partition and begin backing it up unless specifically prevented. Make network boot disks available for customers, along with instructions on how to use them to load your site's default supported installation onto the new drive. This approach lets customers replace their own drives and still get a standardized OS image. Have a planned quarterly maintenance window to give you the opportunity to upgrade shared storage to meet projected demands before customers start becoming impacted by lack of space. Thinking about storage services can be a good way to become aware of the features of your environment and the places where you can improve service for your customers.

25.1.2.6 Establish Storage Standards

Standards help you to say no when someone shows up with random equipment and says, "Please install this for me." If you set storage standards, people are less likely to be able to push a purchase order for nonstandard gear through accounting and then expect you to support whatever they got.

The wide range of maturity of various storage solutions means that finding one that works for you is a much better strategy than trying to support any and everything out there. Having a standard in place helps to keep one-off equipment out of your shop.

A standard can be as simple as a note from a manager saying, "We buy only IBM" or as complex as a lengthy document detailing requirements that a vendor and that vendor's solution must meet to be considered for purchase. The goal of standards is to ensure consistency by specifying a process, a set of characteristics, or both.

Standardization has many benefits, ranging from keeping a common spares pool to minimizing the number of different systems that an SA must cope with during systems integration. As you progress to having a storage plan that accounts for both current and future storage needs, it is important to address standardization. Some organizations can be very difficult places to implement standards control, but it is always worth the attempt. Since the life cycle of many systems is relatively short, a heterogeneous shop full of differing systems can become a unified environment in a relatively short period of time by setting a standard and bringing in only equipment that is consistent with the standard.

If your organization already has a standards process in place for some kinds of requests or purchases, start by learning that system and how to add standards to it. There may be sets of procedures that must be followed, such as meetings with potential stakeholders, creation of written specifications, and so on.

If your organization does not have a standards process, you may be able to get the ball rolling for your department. Often, you will find allies in the purchasing or finance departments, as standards tend to make their jobs easier. Having a standard in place gives them something to refer to when unfamiliar items show up on purchase orders. It also gives them a way to redirect people who start to argue with them about purchasing equipment, namely, to refer those people to either the standard itself or the people who created it.

Start by discussing, in the general case, the need for standards and a unified spares pool with your manager and/or the folks in finance. Request that they route all purchase orders for new types of equipment through the IT department before placing orders with the vendor. Be proactive in working with department stakeholders to establish hardware standards for storage and file servers. Make yourself available to recommend systems and to work with your customers to identify potential candidates for standards.

This strategy can prevent the frustration of dealing with a one-off storage array that won't interoperate with your storage network switch, or some new interface card that turns out to be unsupported under the version of Linux that your developers are using. The worst way to deal with attempts to bring in unsupported systems is to ignore customers and become a bottleneck for requests. Your customers will become frustrated and feel the need to route around you to try to address their storage needs directly.

Upgrading to a larger server often results in old disks or storage subsystems that are no longer used. If they are old enough to be discarded, we highly recommend fully erasing them. Often, we hear stories of used disks purchased on eBay and then found to be full of credit card numbers or proprietary company information.

Financial decision makers usually prefer to see the equipment reused internally. Here are some suggested uses.

- Use the equipment as spares for the new storage array or for building new servers.
- Configure the old disks as local scratch disks for write-intensive applications, such as software compilation.
- Increase reliability of key servers by installing a duplicate OS to reboot from if the system drive fails.
- Convert some portion to swap space, if your OS uses swap space.
- Create a build-it-yourself RAID for nonessential applications or temporary data storage.
- Create a global temp space, accessible to everyone, called `/home/ not_backed_up`. People will find many productivity-enhancing uses for such a service. The name is important: People need a constant reminder if they are using disk space that has no reliability guarantee.

25.1.3 Storage as a Service

Rather than considering storage an object, think of it as one of the many services. Then, you can apply all the standard service basics. To consider something a service, it needs to have an SLA and to be monitored to see that the availability adheres to that SLA.

25.1.3.1 A Storage SLA

What should go into a storage SLA? An engineering group might need certain amounts of storage to ensure that automated release builds have enough space to run daily. A finance division might have minimal day-to-day storage needs but require a certain amount of storage quarterly for generating reports. A QA group or a group administering timed exams to students might express its needs in response time as well as raw disk space.

SLAs are typically expressed in terms of availability and response time. Availability for storage could be thought of as both reachability and usable space. Response time is usually measured as latency—the time it takes to complete a response—at a given load. An SLA should also specify MTTR expectations.

Use standard benchmarking tools to measure these metrics. This has the advantage of repeatability as you change platforms. The system should still be tested in your own environment with your own applications to make sure that the system will behave as advertised, but at least you can insist on a particular minimum benchmark result to consider the system for an in-house evaluation that will involve more work and commitment on the part of you and the vendor.

25.1.3.2 Reliability

Everything fails eventually. You can't prevent a hard drive from failing. You can give it perfect, vendor-recommended cooling and power, and it will still fail eventually. You can't stop an HBA from failing. Now and then, a bit being transmitted down a cable gets hit by a gamma ray and is reversed. If you have eight hard drives, the likelihood that one will fail tomorrow is eight times more likely than if you had only one. The more hardware you have, the more likely a failure. Sounds depressing, but there is good news. There are techniques to manage failures to bring about any reliability level required.

The key is to decouple a component failure from an outage. If you have one hard drive, its failure results in an outage: a 1:1 ratio of failures to outages. However, if you have eight hard drives in a RAID 5 configuration, a single failure does not result in an outage. Two failures, one happening faster than a hot spare can be activated, is required to cause an outage. We have successfully decoupled component failure from service outages. (Similar strategy can be applied to networks, computing, and other aspects of system administration.)

The configuration of a storage service can increase its reliability. In particular, certain RAID levels increase reliability, and NASs can also be configured to increase overall reliability.

The benefit of centralized storage (NAS or SAN) is that the extra cost of reliability is amortized over all users of the service.

- *RAID and reliability:* All RAID levels except for RAID 0 increase reliability. The data on a redundant RAID set continues to be available even when a disk fails. In combination with an available hot spare, a redundant RAID configuration can greatly improve reliability.

  It is important to monitor the RAID system for disk failures, however, and to keep in stock some replacement disks that can be quickly swapped in to replace the failed disk. Every experienced SA can tell a horror story of a RAID system that was unmonitored and had a failed disk go unreplaced for days. Finally, a second disk dies, and all data on the system is lost. Many RAID systems can be configured to shut down after 24 hours of running in degraded mode. It can be safer to have a system halt safely than to go unmonitored for days.

- *NAS and reliability:* NAS servers generally support some form of RAID to protect data, but NAS reliability also depends on network reliability. Most NAS systems have multiple network interfaces. For even better reliability, connect each interface to a different network switch.

- *Choose how much reliability to afford:* When asked, most customers ask for 100 percent reliability. Realistically, however, few managers want to spend what it takes to get the kind of reliability that their employees say they would like. Additional reliability is exponentially more expensive. A little extra reliability costs a bit, and perfect reliability is more than most people can imagine. The result is sticker shock when researching various storage uptime requirements.

  Providers of large-scale reliability solutions stress the uptime and ease of recovery when using their systems and encourage you to calculate the cost of every minute of downtime that their systems could potentially prevent. Although their points are generally correct, these savings must be weighed against the level of duplicated resources and their attendant cost. That single important disk or partition will have a solution requiring multiple sets of disks. In an industry application involving live service databases, such as financial, health, or e-commerce, one typically finds at least two mirrors: one local to the data center and another at a remote data center. Continuous data protection (CDP), discussed later, is the most expensive way to protect data and is therefore used only in extreme situations.

  High-availability data service is expensive. It is the SA's job to make management aware of the costs associated with storage uptime requirements, work it into return on investment (ROI) calculations, and leave the business decision to management. Requirements may be altered or refocused in order to get the best-possible trade-off between expense and reliability.

25.1.3.3 Backups

One of the most fundamental components of a storage service is the backup strategy. Chapter 26 is dedicated to backups; here, we simply point out some important issues related to RAID, NAS, and SAN systems.

- *RAID is not a backup strategy:* RAID can be used to improve reliability, it is important to realize that RAID is not a substitute for a backup strategy. For most RAID configurations, if two disks fail, all the data is lost. Fires, earthquakes, floods, and other disasters will result in all data being lost. A brownout can damage multiple disks or even the RAID controller. Buggy vendor implementations and hardware problems could also result in complete data loss.

Your customers can, and will, delete critical files. When they do, their mistake will be copied to the mirror or parity disk. Some RAID systems include the abilty to have file snapshots, that is, the ability to view the filesystem as it was days ago. This is also not a backup solution. It is simply an improvement to the customer-support process of customers needing to request individual file restores when they accidentally delete a file. If those snapshots are stored on the same RAID system as the rest of the data, a fire or double-disk failure will wipe out all data.

Backups to some other medium, be it tape or even another disk, are still required when you have a RAID system, even if it provides snapshot capabilities. A snapshot will not help recover a RAID set after a fire in your data center.

It is a very common mistake to believe that acquiring a RAID system means that you no longer have to follow basic principles for data protection. Don't let it happen to you!

Whither Backups?

Once, Strata sourced a RAID system for a client without explicitly checking how backups would be done. She was shocked and dismayed to find that the vendor claimed that backups were unnecessary! The vendor did plan—eventually—to support a tape device for the system, but that would not be for at least a year. Adding a high-speed interface card to the box—to keep backups off the main computing network—was an acceptable workaround for the client. When purchasing a storage system, ask about backup and restore options.

• *RAID mirrors as backups:* Rather than using a mirror to protect data all the time, some systems **break**, or disconnect, the mirrored disks so they have a static, unchanging copy of the data to perform backups on. This is done in coordination with database systems and the OS to make sure that the data mirror is in a consistent state from an application point of view. Once the backups are complete, the mirror set is **reattached** and rebuilt to provide protection until the next backup process begins. The benefit is that backups do not slow down normal data use, since they affect only disks that are otherwise unused. The downside is that the data is not protected during the backup operation, and the production system runs much slower when the mirror is being rebuilt.

Many SAs use such mirroring capabilities to make an occasional backup of an important disk, such as a server boot disk, in case of drive failure, OS corruption, security compromise, or other issues. Since any error or compromise would be faithfully mirrored onto the other disk, the system is not run in true RAID 1 mirror mode. The mirror is established and then broken so that updates will not occur to it. After configuration changes, such as OS patches, are made and tested, the mirror can be refreshed and then broken again to preserve the new copy. This is better than restoring from a tape, because it is faster. It is also more accurate, since some tape backup systems are unable to properly restore boot blocks and other metadata.

- *RAID mirrors to speed backups:* A RAID set with two mirrors can be used to make backups faster. Initially, the system has identical data on three sets of disks, known as a **triple-mirror** configuration. When it is time to do backups, one mirror set is broken off, again in coordination with database systems and the OS to make sure that the data mirror is in a consistent state. Now the backup can be done on the mirror that has been separated. Done this way, backups will not slow down the system. When the backup is complete, the mirror is reattached, the rebuild happens, and the system is soon back to its normal state. The rebuild does not affect performance of the production system as much, because the read requests can be distributed between the two primary mirrors.

- *NAS and backups:* In a NAS configuration, it is typical that no unique data is stored on client machines; if data is stored there, it is well advertised that it is not backed up. This introduces simplicity and clarity into that site, especially in the area of backups. It is clear where all the shared customer data is located, and as such, the backup process is simpler.

  In addition, by placing shared customer data onto NAS servers, the load for backing up this data is shared primarily by the NAS server itself and the server responsible for backups and is thus isolated from application servers and departmental servers. In this configuration, clients become interchangable. If someone's desktop PC dies, the person should be able to use any other PC instead.

- *SANs and backups:* As mentioned previously, SANs make backups easier in two ways. First, a tape drive can be a SAN-attached device. Thus, all servers can share a single, expensive tape library solution. Second, by having a dedicated network for file traffic, backups do not interfere with normal network traffic.

SAN systems often have features that generate snapshots of LUNs. By coordinating the creation of those snapshots with database and other applications, the backup can be done offline, during the day, without interfering with normal operations.

25.1.3.4 Monitoring

If it isn't monitored, it isn't a service. Although we cover monitoring extensively in Chapter 22, it's worth noting here some special requirements for monitoring storage service.

A large part of being able to respond to your customers' needs is building an accurate model of the state of your storage systems. For each storage server, you need to know how much space is used, how much is available, and how much more the customer anticipates using in the next planning time frame. Set up historical monitoring so that you can see the level of change in usage over time, and get in the habit of tracking it regularly. Monitor storage-access traffic, such as local read/write operations or network file access packets, to build up a model that lets you evaluate performance. You can use this information proactively to prevent problems and to plan for future upgrades and changes.

Seeing monitoring data on a per volume basis is typical and most easily supported by many monitoring tools. Seeing the same data by customer group allows SAs to do a better job of giving each group individualized attention and allows customers to monitor their own usage.

❖ **Comparing Customers**   It can be good to let customers see their per group statistics in comparison to other groups. However, in a highly political environment, it may be interpreted as an attempt to embarass one group over another. Never use per group statistics to intentionally embarass or guilt-trip people to change behavior.

In addition to notifications about outages or system/service errors, you should be alerted to such events as a storage volume reaching a certain percentage of utilization or spikes or troughs in data transfers or in network response. Monitoring CPU usage on a dedicated file server can be extremely useful, as one sign of file services problems or out-of-control clients is an ever-climbing CPU usage. With per group statistics, notifications can be sent directly to the affected customers, who can then do a better job of self-managing their usage. Some people prefer to be nagged over strictly enforced space quotas.

By implementing notification scripts with different recipients, you can emulate having hard and soft quotas. When the volume reaches, for instance, 70 percent full, the script could notify the group or department email alias containing the customers of that volume. If the volume continues to fill up and reaches 80 percent full, perhaps the next notification goes to the group's manager, to enforce the cleanup request. It might also be copied to the helpdesk or ticket alias so that the site's administrators know that there might be a request for more storage in the near future.

To summarize, we recommend you monitor the following list of storage-related items:

- *Disk failures.* With redundant RAID systems, a single disk failure will not cause the service to stop working, but the failed disk must be replaced quickly, or a subsequent failure may cause loss of service.

- *Other outages.* Monitor access to every network interface on a NAS, for example.

- *Space used/space free.* This is the most frequently asked customer question. By providing this information to customers on demand on the internal web, you will be spared many tickets!

- *Rate of change.* This data is particularly helpful in predicting future needs. By calculating the rate of usage change during a typical busy period, such as quarterly product releases or the first semester of a new academic year, you can gradually arrive at metrics that will allow you to predict storage needs with some confidence.

- *I/O local usage.* Monitoring this value will let you see when a particular storage device or array is starting to become fully saturated. If failures occur, comparing the timing with low-level I/O statistics can be invaluable in tracking down the problem.

- *Network local interface.* If a storage solution begins to be slow to respond, comparing its local I/O metrics with the network interface metrics and network bandwidth used provides a clue as to where the scaling failure may be occurring.

- *Networking bandwidth usage.* Comparing the overall network statistics with local interface items, such as network fragmentation and reassembly, can provide valuable clues toward optimizing performance. It is usually valuable to specifically monitor storage-to-server networks and aggregate the data in such a way as to make it viewable easily outside the main network statistics area.

- *File service operations.* Providing storage services via a protocol such as NFS or CIFS requires monitoring the service-level statistics as well, such as NFS *badcall* operations.

- *Lack of usage.* When a popular file system has not processed any file service operations recently, it often indicates some other problem, such as an outage between the file server and the clients.

- *Individual resource usage.* This item can be a blessing or a slippery slope, depending on the culture of your organization. If customer groups self-police their resources, it is almost mandatory. First, they care greatly about the data, so it's a way of honoring their priorities. Second, they will attempt to independently generate the data anyway, which loads the machines. Third, it is one less reason to give `root` privilege to non-SAs. Using `root` for disk-usage discovery is a common reason cited why engineers and group leads "need" `root` access on shared servers.

25.1.3.5 SAN Caveats

Since SAN technologies are always changing, it can be difficult to make components from different vendors interoperate. We recommend sticking with one or two vendors and testing extensively. When vendors offer to show you their latest and greatest products, kick them out. Tell such vendors that you want to see only the stuff that has been used in the field for a while. Let other people work through the initial product bugs.[1] This is your data, the most precious asset your company has. Not a playground.

Sticking with a small number of vendors helps to establish a rapport. Those sales folks and engineers will have more motivation to support you, as a regular customer.

That said, it's best to subject new models to significant testing before you integrate them into your infrastructure, even if they are from the same vendor. Vendors acquire outside technologies, change implementation subsystems, and do the same things any other manufacturer does. Vendors' goals are generally to improve their product offerings, but sometimes, the new offerings are not considered improvements by folks like us.

---

1. This excellent advice comes from the LISA 2003 keynote presentation by Paul Kilmartin, Director, Availability and Performance Engineering, at eBay.

Create a set of tests that you consider significant for your environment. A typical set might include industry-standard benchmark tests, application-specific tests obtained from application vendors, and attempts to run extremely site-specific operations, along with similar operations at much higher loads.

25.1.4 Performance

Performance means how long it takes for your customers to read and write their data. If the storage service you provide is too slow, your customers will find a way to work around it, perhaps by attaching extra disks to their own desktops or by complaining to management.

The most important rule of optimization is to measure first, optimize based on what was observed, and then measure again. Often, we see SAs optimize based on guesses of what is slowing a system down. Measuring means using operating system tools to collect data, such as which disks are the most busy or the percentage of reads versus writes. Some SAs do not measure but simply try various techniques until they find one that solves the performance problem. These SAs waste a lot of time with solutions that do not produce results. We call this technique **blind guessing** and do not recommend it. Watching the disk lights during peak load times is a better measurement than nothing.

The primary tools that a SA has to optimize performance are RAM and spindles. RAM is faster than disk. With more RAM, one can cache more and use the disk less. With more spindles (independent disks), the load can be spread out over more disks working in parallel.

❖ **General Rules for Performance**

1. Never hit the network if you can stay on disk.
2. Never hit the disk if you can stay in memory.
3. Never hit memory if you can stay on chip.
4. Have enough money, and don't be afraid to spend it.

25.1.4.1 RAID and Performance

RAID 0 gives increased performance for both reads and writes, as compared to a single disk, because the reads and writes are distributed over multiple disks that can perform several operations simultaneously. However, as we have seen, this performance increase comes at the cost of reliability. Since any one disk failing destroys the entire RAID 0 set, more disks means more risk of failure.

RAID 1 can give increased read performance, if the reads are spread over both or all disks. Write performance is as slow as the slowest disk in the mirrored RAID set.

RAID 3, as we mentioned, gives particularly good performance for sequential reads. RAID 3 is recommended for storage of large graphics files, streaming media, and video applications, especially if files tend to be archived and are not changed frequently.

RAID 4—with a tuned filesystem—and RAID 5 give increased read performance, but write performance is worse. Read performance is improved because the disks can perform reads in parallel. However, when there is extensive writing to the RAID set, read performance is impaired because all the disks are involved in the write operation. The parity disk is always written to, in addition to the disk where the data resides, and all the other disks must be read before the write occurs on the parity disk. The write is not complete until the parity disk has also been written to.

RAID 10 gives increased read and write performance, like RAID 0, but without the lack of reliability that RAID 0 suffers from. In fact, read performance is further improved, as the mirrored disks are also available for satisfying the read requests. Writes will be as slow as the slowest mirror disk that has to be written to, as the write is not reported to the system as complete until both or all of the mirrors have been successfully written.

25.1.4.2 NAS and Performance

NAS-based storage allows SAs to isolate the file service workload away from other servers, making it easy for SAs to consolidate customer data onto a few large servers rather than have it distributed all over the network. In addition, applying consistent backup, usage, and security policies to the file servers is easier.

Many sites grow their infrastructures somewhat organically, over time. It is very common to see servers shared between a department or particular user group, with the server providing both computing and file-sharing services. Moving file-sharing services to a NAS box can significantly reduce the workload on the server, improving performance for the customers. File-sharing overhead is not completely eliminated, as the server will now be running a client protocol to access the NAS storage. In most cases, however, there are clear benefits.

25.1.4.3 SANs and Performance

SANs benefit from the ability to move file traffic off the main network. The network can be tuned for the file service's particular needs: low latency and high speed. The SAs is isolated from other networks, which gives it a security advantage.

Sites were building their own versions of SANs long before anyone knew to call them that, using multiple fiber-optic interfaces on key fileservers and routing all traffic via the high-speed interfaces dedicated to storage. Christine and Strata were coworkers at a site that was an early adopter of this concept. The server configurations had to be done by hand, with a bit of magic in the automount maps and in the local host and DNS entries, but the performance was worth it.

SANs have been so useful that people have started to consider other ways in which storage devices might be networked. One way is to treat other networks as if they were direct cabling. Each SCSI command is encapsulated in a packet and sent over a network. Fibre channel (FC) does this using copper or fiber-optic networks. The fibre channel becomes an extended SCSI bus, and devices on it must follow normal SCSI protocol rules. The success of fibre channel and the availability of cheap, fast TCP/IP network equipment has led to creation of **iSCSI**, sending basically the same packet over an IP network. This allows SCSI devices, such as tape libraries, to be part of a SAN directly. ATA over Ethernet (AoE) does something similar for ATA-based disks.

With advances in high-speed networking and the affordability of the equipment, protocol encapsulations requiring a responsive network are now feasible in many cases. We expect to see the use of layered network storage protocols, along with many other types of protocols, increase in the future.

Since a SAN is essentially a network with storage, SANs are not limited to one facility or data center. Using high-speed networking technologies, such as ATM or SONET, a SAN can be "local" to multiple data centers at different sites.

25.1.4.4 Pipeline Optimization

An important part of understanding the performance of advanced storage arrays is to look at how they manage a **data pipeline**. The term refers to preloading into memory items that might be needed next so that access times are minimized. CPU chip sets that are advertised as including **L2 cache** include extra memory to pipeline data and instructions, which is why, for some

CPU-intensive jobs, a Pentium III with a large L2 cache could outperform a Pentium IV, all other things being equal.

Pipelining algorithms are extensively implemented in many components of modern storage hardware, especially the HBA but also in the drive controller. These algorithms may be *dumb* or *smart*. A so-called dumb algorithm has the controller simply read blocks physically located near the requested blocks, on the assumption that the next set of blocks that are part of the same request will be those blocks. This tends to be a good assumption, unless a disk is badly fragmented. A smart pipelining algorithm may be able to access the filesystem information and preread blocks that make up the next part of the file, whether they are nearby or not. Note that for some storage systems, "nearby" may not mean *physically near* the other blocks on the disk but rather *logically near* them. Blocks in the same cylinder are not physically nearby, but are logically nearby for example.

Although the combination of OS-level caching and pipelining is excellent for reading data, writing data is a more complex process. Operating systems are generally designed to ensure that data writes are **atomic**, or at least as much as possible, given the actual hardware constraints. Atomic, in this case means "in one piece." Atoms were named that before people understood that there were such things as subatomic physics, with protons, electrons, neutrons, and such. People thought of an atom as the smallest bit of matter, which could not be subdivided further.

This analogy may seem odd, but in fact it's quite relevant. Just as atoms are made up of protons, neutrons, and electrons, a single write operation can involve a lot of steps. It's important that the operating system not record the write operation as complete until all the steps have completed. This means waiting until the physical hardware sends an acknowledgment, or ACK, that the write occurred.

One optimization is to ACK the write immediately, even though the data hasn't been safely stored on disk. That's risky, but there are some ways to make it safer. One is to do this only for data blocks, not for directory information and other blocks that would corrupt the file system. (We don't recommend this, but it is an option on some systems.) Another way is to keep the data to be written in RAM that, with the help of a battery, survives reboots. Then the ACK can be done as soon as the write is safely stored in that special RAM. In that case, it is important that the pending blocks be written before the RAM is removed. Tom moved such a device to a different computer, not realizing that it was full of pending writes. Once the new computer booted up, the pending writes wrote onto the unsuspecting disk of the new system, which was then corrupted badly. Another type of failure might involve the hardware itself. A failed battery that goes undetected can be a disaster after the next power failure.

`sync` **Three Times Before** `halt`

Extremely early versions of Unix did not automatically sync the write buffers to disk before halting the system. The operators would be trained to kick all the users off the system to acquiesce any write activity, then manually type the `sync` command three times before issuing or `shutdown` command. The `sync` command is guaranteed to schedule only the unwritten blocks for writing; there can be a short delay before all the blocks are finally written to disk. The second and third `sync` weren't needed but were done to pass the time before shutting down the system. If you were a fast typist, you would simply intentionally pause.

25.1.5 Evaluating New Storage Solutions

Whether a particular storage solution makes sense for your organization depends on how you are planning to use it. Study your usage model to make an intelligent, informed decision. Consider the throughput and configuration of the various subsystems and components of the proposed solution.

Look especially for hidden gotcha items. Some solutions billed as being affordable get that way by using your server's memory and CPU resources to do much of the work. If your small office or workgroup server is being used for applications as well as for attaching storage, obviously a solution of that type would be likely to prove unsatisfactory.

❖ **Test All Parts of a New System**   Early SATA-based storage solutions sometimes received a bad reputation because they were not used and deployed carefully. An example cited on a professional mailing list mentioned that a popular controller used in SATA arrays sent malformed email alerts, which their email system silently discarded. If a site administrator had not tested the notification system, the problem would not have been discovered until the array failed to the point where data was lost.

Another common problem is finding that an attractively priced system is using very slow drives and that the vendor did not guarantee a specific drive speed. It's not uncommon for some small vendors that assemble their own boxes to use whatever is on hand and then give you a surprise discount, based on the less-desirable hardware. That lower price is buying you a less-useful system.

Although the vendor may insist that most customers don't care, that is not your problem. Insist on specific standards for components, and check the system before accepting delivery of it. The likelihood of mistakes increases when nonstandard parts are used, complicating the vendor's in-house assembly process. Be polite but firm in your insistence on getting what you ordered.

25.1.6 Common Problems

Modern storage systems use a combination of layered subsystems and per layer optimizations to provide fast, efficient, low-maintenance storage—most of the time. Here, we look at common ways in which storage solutions can turn into storage problems.

Many of the layers in the chain of disk platter to operating system to client are implemented with an assumption that the next layer called will Do the Right Thing and somehow recover from an error by requesting the data again.

The most common overall type of problem is that some boundary condition has not been taken into account. A cascading failure chain begins, usually in the normal layer-to-layer interoperation but sometimes, as in the case of power or temperature problems, at a hardware level.

25.1.6.1 Physical Infrastructure

Modern storage solutions tend to pack a significant amount of equipment into a comparatively small space. Many machine rooms and data centers were designed based on older computer systems, which occupied more physical space. When the same space is filled with multiple storage stacks, the power and cooling demands can be much higher than the machine room design specifications. We have seen a number of mysterious failures traced ultimately to temperature or power issues.

When experiencing mysterious failures involving corruption of arrays or scrambled data, it can make sense to check the stability of your power infrastructure to the affected machine. We recommend including power readings in your storage monitoring for just this reason. We've been both exasperated and relieved to find that an unstable NAS unit became reliable once it was moved to a rack where it could draw sufficient power—more power than it was rated to draw, in fact.

A wattage monitor, which records real power use, can be handy to use to evaluate the requirements of storage units. Drives often use more power to start up than to run. A dozen drives starting at once can drain a shared PDU enough to generate mysterious faults on other equipment.

25.1.6.2 Timeouts

Timeouts can be a particular problem, especially in heavily optimized systems that are implemented primarily for speed rather than for robustness. NAS and SAN solutions can be particularly sensitive to changes in the configuration of the underlying networks.

A change in network configuration, such as a network topology change that now puts an extra router hop in the storage path, may seem to have no effect when implemented and tested. However, under heavy load, that slight delay might be just enough to trigger TCP timeout mischief in the network stack of the NAS device.

Sometimes, the timeout may be at the client end. With a journaling filesystem served over the network from a heavily loaded shared server, Strata saw a conservative NFS client lose writes because the network stack timed out while waiting for the filesystem to journal them. When the application on the client side requested the file again, the file received did not match; the client application would crash.

25.1.6.3 Saturation Behavior

Saturation of the data transfer path, at any point on the chain, is often the culprit in mysterious self-healing delays and intermittent slow responses, even triggering the timeouts mentioned previously. Take care when doing capacity planning not to confuse the theoretical potential of the storage system with the probable usage speeds.

A common problem, especially with inexpensive and/or poorly implemented storage devices, is that of confusing the speed of the fastest component with the speed of the device itself. Some vendors may accidentally or deliberately foster this confusion.

Examples of statistics that are only a portion of the bigger picture include

- Burst I/O speed of drives versus sustained I/O speeds—most applications rarely burst
- Bus speed of the chassis
- Shared backplane speed

- Controller and/or HBA speed
- Memory speed of caching or pipelining memory
- Network speed

Your scaling plans should consider all these elements. The only reliable figures on which to base performance expectations are those obtained by benchmarking the storage unit under realistic load conditions.

A storage system that is running near saturation is more likely to experience unplanned interactions between delayed acknowledgments implemented in different levels of hardware and software. Since multiple layers might be performing in-layer caching, buffering, and pipelining, the saturation conditions increase the likelihood of encountering boundary conditions, among them overflowing buffers and updating caches before their contents can be written. As mentioned earlier, implementers are likely to be relying on the unlikelihood of encountering such boundary condition; how these types of events are handled is usually specific to a particular vendor's firmware implementation.

25.2 The Icing

Now that we've explored storage as a managed service and all the requirements that arise from that, let's discuss some of the ways to take your reliable, backed-up, well-performing storage service and make it better.

25.2.1 Optimizing RAID Usage by Applications

Since the various RAID levels each give different amounts of performance and reliability, RAID systems can be tuned for specific applications. In this section, we see examples for various applications.

Since striping in most modern RAID is done at the block level, there are strong performance advantages to matching the stripe size to the data block size used by your application. Database storage is where this principle most commonly comes into play, but it can also be used for application servers, such as web servers, which are pushing content through a network with a well-defined maximum package size.

25.2.1.1 Customizing Striping

For a database that requires a dedicated partition, such as Oracle, tuning the block size used by the database to the storage stripe block size, or vice versa, can provide a very noticeable performance improvement. Factor in block-level parity operations, as well as the size of the array. An application using 32K blocks, served by a five-drive array using RAID 5 would be well matched by a stripe size of 8K blocks: four data drives plus one parity drive ($4 \times 8K = 32K$). Greater performance can be achieved through more spindles, such as a nine-drive array with use of 4K blocks. Not all applications will need this level of tuning, but it's good to know that such techniques are available.

This type of tuning is a good reason not to share storage between differing applications when performance is critical. Applications often have access patterns and preferred block sizes that differ markedly. For this technique to be the most effective, the entire I/O path has to support the block size. If your operating system uses 4K blocks to build pages, for instance, setting the RAID stripes to 8K might cause a page fault on every I/O operation, and performance would be terrible.

25.2.1.2 Streamlining the Write Path

Some applications use for their routine operations multiple writes to independent data streams; the interactions of the two streams causes a performance problem. We have seen many applications that were having performance problems caused by another process writing large amounts of data to a log file. The two processes were both putting a heavy load on the same disk. By moving the log file to a different disk, the system ran much faster. Similar problems, with similar solutions, happen with databases maintaining a transaction log, large software build processes writing large output files, and journaled file systems maintaining their transaction log. In all these cases, moving the write-intensive portion to a different disk improves performance.

Sometimes, the write streams can be written to disks of different quality. In the compilation example, the output file can be easily reproduced, so the output disk might be a RAM disk or a fast local drive.

In the case of a database, individual table indices, or views, are often updated frequently but can be recreated easily. They take up large amounts of storage, as they are essentially frozen copies of database table data. It makes sense to put the table data on a reliable but slower RAID array and to put the index and view data on a fast but not necessarily reliable array mirror. If the fast array is subdivided further into individual sets of views or indices, and if spare drives are included in the physical array, even the loss of a drive can cause minimal downtime with quick recovery, as only a portion of the dynamic data will need to be regenerated and rewritten.

25.2.2 Storage Limits: Disk Access Density Gap

The density of modern disks is quite astounding. The space once occupied by a 500M MicroVAX disk can now house several terabytes. However, the performance is not improving as quickly.

Improvements in surface technology are increasing the size of hard disks 40 percent to 60 percent annually. Drive performance, however, is growing by only 10 percent to 20 percent. The gap between the increase in how much a disk can hold and how quickly you can get data on and off the disk is widening. This gap is known as **disk access density** (DAD) and is a measurement of I/O operations per second per gigabyte of capacity (OPS/second/GB).

In a market where price/performance is so important, many disk buyers are mistaking pure capacity for the actual performance, completely ignoring DAD. DAD is important when choosing storage for a particular application. Ultra-high-capacity drives are wonderful for relatively low-demand resources. Applications that are very I/O intensive, especially on writes, require a better DAD ratio.

As you plan your storage infrastructure, you will find that you will want to allocate storage servers to particular applications in order to provide optimal performance. It can be tempting to purchase the largest hard disk on the market, but two smaller disks will get better performance. This is especially disappointing when one considers the additional power, chassis space, and cooling that are required.

A frequently updated database may be able to be structured so that the busiest tables are assigned to a storage partition made up of many smaller, higher-throughput drives. Engineering filesystems subject to a great deal of compilation but also having huge data models, such as a chip-design firm, may require thoughtful integration with other parts of the infrastructure.

When supporting customers who seem to need both intensive I/O and high-capacity data storage, you will have to look at your file system performance closely and try to meet the needs cleverly.

25.2.2.1 Fragmentation

Moving the disk arm to a new place on the disk is extremely slow compared to reading data from the track where the arm is. Therefore, operating systems make a huge effort to store all the blocks for a given file in the same track of a disk. Since most files are read sequentially, this can result in the data's being quickly streamed off the disk.

However, as a disk fills, it can become difficult to find contiguous sets of blocks to write a file. File systems become fragmented. Previously, SAs spent a lot of time defragmenting drives by running software that moved files around, opening up holes of free space and moving large, fragmented files to the newly created contiguous space.

This is not worthwhile on modern operating systems. Modern systems are much better at not creating fragmented files in the first place. Hard drive performance is much less affected by occasional fragments. Defragmenting a disk puts it at huge risk owing to potential bugs in the software and problems that can come from power outages while critical writes are being performed.

We doubt vendor claims of major performance boosts through the use of their defragmenting software. The risk of destroying data is too great. As we said before, this is important data, not a playground.

Fragmentation is a moot point on multiuser systems. Consider an NFS or CIFS server. If one user is requesting block after block of the same file, fragmentation might have a slight effect on the performance received, with network delays and other factors being much more important. A more typical workload would be dozens or hundreds of concurrent clients. Since each client is requesting individual blocks, the stream of requests sends the disk arm flying all over the disk to collect the requested blocks. If the disk is heavily fragmented or perfectly unfragmented, the amount of movement is about the same. Operating systems optimize for this situation by performing disk requests sorted by track number rather than in the order received. Since operating systems are already optimized for this case, the additional risk incurred by rewriting files to be less fragmented is unnecessary.

25.2.3 Continuous Data Protection

CDP is the process of copying data changes in a specified time window to one or more secondary storage locations. That is, by recording every change made to a volume, one can roll forward and back in time by replaying and undoing the changes. In the event of data loss, one can restore the last backup and then replay the CDP log to the moment one wants. The CDP log may be stored on another machine, maybe even in another building.

Increasingly, CDP is used not in the context of data protection but of service protection. The data protection is a key element of CDP, but many implementations also include multiple servers running applications that are tied to the protected data.

Any CDP solution is a process as much as a product. Vendor offerings usually consist of management software, often installed with the assistance of their professional services division, to automate the process. Several large hardware vendors offer CDP solutions that package their own hardware and software with modules from other vendors to provide vendor-specific CDP solutions supporting third-party applications, such as database transaction processing.

CDP is commonly used to minimize recovery time and reduce the probability of data loss. CDP is generally quite expensive to implement reliably, so a site tends to require compelling reasons to implement it. There are two main reasons that sites implement CDP. One reason is to become compliant with industry-specific regulations. Another is to prevent revenue losses and/or liability arising from outages.

CDP is new and expensive and therefore generally used to solve only problems that cannot be solved any other way. One market for CDP is where the data is extremely critical, such as financial information. Another is where the data changes at an extremely high rate. If losing a few hours of data means trillions of updates, CDP can be easier to justify.

25.3 Conclusion

In this chapter, we discussed the most common types of storage and the benefits and appropriate applications associated with them. The basic principles of managing storage remain constant: Match your storage solution to a specific usage pattern of applications or customers, and build up layers of redundancy while sacrificing as little performance as possible at each layer.

Although disks grow cheaper, managing them becomes more expensive. Considering storage as a service allows you to put a framework around storage costs and agree on standards with your customers. In order to do that, you must have customer groups with which to negotiate those standards and, as in any service, perform monitoring to ensure the quality level of the service.

The options for providing data storage to your customers have increased dramatically, allowing you to choose the level of reliability and performance required for specific applications. Understanding the basic relationship of storage devices to the operating system and to the file system gives you a richer understanding of the way that large storage solutions are built up out of smaller subsystems. Concepts such as RAID can be leveraged to build storage solutions that appear to a server as a simple, directly attached disk but whose properties are highly tunable to optimize for the customer applications being served.

We also discussed the serious pending problem of disk density versus the bandwidth of disk I/O, an issue that will become more and more critical in the coming years.

Exercises

1. What kinds of storage have you seen in use during your own lifetime? How many of them were "the next big thing" when introduced? Do you still have some systems at home?

2. Search for on-demand storage pricing. How do the features of the lowest-priced storage compare to those of the highest-priced? What price points do you find for various features?

3. How would you characterize your organization's main storage systems, based on the taxonomy we introduced in this chapter? Do you think that the current storage system used is a good match for your needs, or would another type be more useful?

4. Do you have a list of the common kinds of storage dataflow in your organization? What's the ratio of reads to writes?

5. RAID 1 and higher use multiple drives to increase reliability. Eight drives are eight times more likely to have a single failure in a given time period. If a RAID 5 set had eight drives, do these two factors cancel each other out? Why or why not?

6. A hard drive is ten times faster than RAM. Suppose that you had a huge database that required access that was as fast as RAM. How many disk spindles would be required to make 1,000 database queries per second as fast as keeping the database entirely in RAM? (Assume that the RAM would be on multiple computers that could each perform a share of the queries in parallel.) Look up current prices for disks and RAM, and calculate which would be less expensive if the database were 10 gigabytes, 1 terabyte, and 100 terabytes.

7. Which of the performance rules in the sidebar Rules for Performance are addressed by the use of HBAs with storage? Explain.

8. Do you keep metrics on disk performance? If you had to improve the performance of your local storage solution, what are some places you

might be able to make a difference without ripping the whole thing out and starting over?

9. What RAID characteristics would you want for an array supporting real-time data collection from environmental sensors or factory monitoring, and why?

10. Are the storage services in your organization set up for optimum usage? What kinds of changes would you make to improve the storage environment?

Chapter 26

Backup and Restore

Everyone hates backups. They are inconvenient. They are costly. Services run slower—or not at all—when servers are being backed up. On the other hand, customers *love* restores. Restores are why SAs perform backups.

Being able to restore lost data is a critical part of any environment. Data gets lost. Equipment fails. Humans delete it by mistake and on purpose. Judges impound all lawsuit-related documents that were stored on your computers on a certain date. Shareholders require the peace of mind that comes with the knowledge that a natural or other disaster will not make their investment worthless. Data also gets corrupted by mistake, on purpose, or by gamma rays from space. Backups are like insurance: You pay for it even though you hope to never need it. In reality, you need it.

Although the goal is to be able to restore lost data in a timely manner, it is easy to get caught up in the daily operational work of doing backups and to forget that restoration is the goal. As evidence, the collective name typically used for all the equipment and software related to this process is "backup system." It should really be called "backup and restore systems" or, possibly more fittingly, simply the "data restoration system."

This book is different in the way it addresses backups and restores. Readers of this book should already know what commands their OSs use to back up and restore data. We do not cover that information. Instead, we discuss the theory of how to plan your backups and restores in a way that should be useful no matter what backup products are available.

After discussing the theory of planning the backups and restores, we focus on the three key components of modern backup systems: automation, centralization, and inventory management. These three aspects should help guide your purchasing decision. Once the fundamentals are established, we discuss how to maintain well into the future the system you've designed.

The topic of backups and restores is so broad that we cannot cover the entire topic in detail. We have chosen to cover the key components. Books such as Preston's UNIX *Backup and Recovery* (Preston 1999) and Leber's *Windows NT Backup and Restore* (Leber 1998) cover the details for UNIX and Microsoft environments in great detail.

Backup and restore service is part of any data storage system. One study found that the purchase price of the disk is merely 20 percent of the total cost of ownership, with backups being nearly the entire remaining cost. Buying a raw disk and slapping it into a system is easy. Providing data storage as a complete service is difficult. The price of disks has been decreasing, but the total cost of ownership has risen mostly because of the increasing cost of backups. Therefore, an efficient backup and restore system is your key to cost-effective data storage.

With regard to terminology, we use **full backup** to mean a complete backup of all files on a partition; UNIX users call this a "level 0 backup." The term **incremental backup** refers to copying all files that have changed since the previous full backup; UNIX users call this a "level 1 backup." Incremental backups grow over time. That is, if a full backup is performed on Sunday and an incremental backup each day of the week that follows, the amount of data being backed up should grow each day because Tuesday's incremental backup includes all the files from Monday's backup, as well as what changed since then. Friday's incremental backup should include all the files that were part of Monday's, Tuesday's, Wednesday's, and Thursday's backups, in addition to what changed since Thursday's backup. Some systems perform an incremental backup that collects all files changed since a particular incremental backup rather than the last full backup. We borrow the UNIX terminology and call those *level 2 incremental backups* if they contain files changed since the last level 1, or *level 3* if they contain files changed since the last level 2, and so on.

26.1 The Basics

Engineering your backup and restore system should begin by determining the desired end result and working backward from there. The end result is the desired restore capability of the system. Restores are requested for various reasons, and the reasons that apply to your environment affect further decisions, such as creating a policy and a schedule.

We start by defining corporate guidelines, which drive your SLA for restores based on your site's needs, which becomes your backup policy, which dictates your backup schedule.

- The *corporate guidelines* define terminology and dictate minimums and requirements for data-recovery systems.
- The *SLA* defines the requirements for a particular site or application and is guided by the corporate guidelines.
- The *policy* documents the implementation of the SLA in general terms, written in English.
- The *procedure* outlines how the policy is to be implemented.
- The detailed *schedule* shows which disk will be backed up when. This may be static or dynamic. This usually is the policy translated from English into the backup software's configuration.

Beyond policies and schedules are operational issues. Consumables can be expensive and should be included in the budget. Time and capacity planning are required to ensure that we meet our SLA during both restores and backups. The backup and restore policies and procedures should be documented from both the customer and the SA perspectives.

Only after all that is defined can we build the system. Modern backup systems have three key components: automation, centralization, and inventory management. Each of these is discussed in turn.

26.1.1 Reasons for Restores

Restores are requested for three reasons. If you do not understand them, the backup and restore system may miss the target. Each reason has its own requirements. The reasons are as follows:

1. *Accidental file deletion.* A customer has accidentally erased one or more files and needs to have them restored.
2. *Disk failure.* A hard drive has failed, and all data needs to be restored.
3. *Archival.* For business reasons, a snapshot of the entire "world" needs to be made on a regular basis for disaster-recovery, legal, or fiduciary reasons.

26.1.1.1 Accidental File Deletion

In the first case, customers would prefer to quickly restore any file as it existed at any instant. However, that usually isn't possible. In an office environment, you can typically expect to be able to restore a file to what it looked like at any 1-day granularity and that it will take 3 to 5 hours to have the restore completed. Obviously, special cases, such as those found in the financial and e-commerce worlds, are much more demanding. Making the restores convenient is easier now that modern software (Moran and Lyon 1993) permits customers to do their own restores either instantly—if the tape[1] is still in the jukebox—or after waiting for some operator intervention—if the customers must wait for a tape to be loaded.

Self-service restores are not a new feature. Systems dating back to the 1980s provided this feature.

- In the early 1980s, the VAX/VMS operating system from DEC (now HP via Compaq) retained previous versions of files, which could be accessed by specifying the version number as part of the filename.

- In 1988 (Hume 1988), Bell Labs invented the File Motel, a system that stored incremental backups on optical platters permanently. AT&T's CommVault[2] offered this infinite-backup system as one of its products.

- In the 1990s, NetApp introduced the world to its Filer line of file server appliances that have a built-in snapshot feature. Hourly, daily, and weekly snapshots of a filesystem are stored on disk in an efficient manner. Data blocks that haven't changed are stored only once. Filers serve their file systems to UNIX hosts via the NFS protocol, as well as to other OSs using Microsoft's CIFS file protocol, making them the darling of SAs in multi-OS shops. Customers like the way snapshots permit them to "cd back in time." Other vendors have added snapshot and snapshot-like features with varying levels of storage efficiency.

Systems such as these are becoming more commonplace as technology becomes cheaper and as information's value increases.

To an SA, the value of snapshots is that they reduce workload because the most common type of request becomes self-service. To customers, the value of snapshots is that they give them new options for managing their work better. Customers' work habits change as they learn they can rely on snapshots. If the snapshots are there forever, as is possible with CommVault, customers manage their disk utilization differently, knowing that they can always get back what they delete. Even if snapshots are available going back only a

---

1. We refer to the backup media as *tape* in this chapter, even though we recognize that there are many alternatives.
2. CommVault is now a separate company.

fixed amount of time, customers develop creative, new, and more efficient workflows.

Snapshots also increase customer productivity by reducing the amount of manually reconstructed lost data. When they accidentally delete data, customers may reconstruct it rather than wait for the restore, which may take hours or even days. Everyone has made a change to a file and later regretted making the change. Reconstructing the file manually is an error-prone process, but it would be silly to wait hours for a restore request to be completed. With snapshots, customers are less likely to attempt to manually reconstruct lost data.

The most common reason for requesting a restore is to recover from accidental file deletion. Modern software coupled with jukeboxes can make this kind of restore a self-service function. Even better, fancy systems that provide snapshots not only take care of this without requiring the SA to be involved for each restore but also can positively affect the customer's work environment.

26.1.1.2 Disk Failure

The second kind of restore is related to disk failure—or any hardware or software failure resulting in total filesystem loss. A disk failure causes two problems: loss of service and loss of data. On critical systems, such as e-commerce and financial systems, RAID should be deployed so that disk failures do not affect service, with the possible exception of a loss in performance. However, in noncritical systems, customers can typically[3] expect the restore to be completed in a day, and although they do not like losing data, they usually find a single day of lost work to be an acceptable risk. Sometimes, the outage is between these two extremes: A critical system is still able to run, but data on a particular disk is unavailable. In that case, there may be less urgency.

This kind of restore often takes a long time to complete. Restore speed is slow because gigabytes of data are being restored, and the entire volume of data is unavailable until the last byte is written. To make matters worse, a two-step process is involved: First, the most recent full backup must be read, and then the most recent incremental(s) are read.

---

3. Again, *typical* refers to a common office environment.

26.1.1.3 Archival

The third kind of restore request is archival. Corporate policies may require you to be able to reproduce the entire environment with a granularity of a quarter, half, or full year in case of disasters or lawsuits. The work that needs to be done to create an archive is similar to the full backups required for other purposes, with four differences.

1. Archives are full backups. In environments that usually mix full and incremental backups on the same tapes, archive tapes should not be so mixed.

2. Some sites require archive tapes to be separate from the other backups. This may mean that archive tapes are created by generating a second, redundant set of full backups. Alternatively, archival copies may be generated by copying the full backups off previously made backup tapes. Although this alternative is more complicated, it can, if it is automated, be performed unattended when the jukebox is otherwise unused.

3. Archives are usually stored off-site.

4. Archive tapes age more than other tapes. They may be written on media that will become obsolete and eventually unavailable. You might consider storing a compatible tape drive or two with your archives, as well as appropriate software for reading the tapes.

5. If the archives are part of a disaster-recovery plan, special policies or laws may apply.

When making archival backups, do not forget to include the tools that go with the data. Tools get upgraded frequently, and if the archival backup is used to back up the environment, the tools, along with their specific set of bugs and features, should be included. Make sure that the tools required to restore the archive and the required documentation are stored with the archive.

Although there are some types of specialized backup and restore scenarios, most of them fit into one of three categories.

26.1.2 Types of Restores

It is interesting to note that the three types of restore requests typically serve three types of customers. Individual file restores serve customers who accidentally deleted the data, the direct users of the data. Archival backups serve the needs of the legal and financial departments that require them, people who are usually far detached from the data itself.[4] Complete restores after a disk failure serve the SAs who committed to providing a particular SLA. Backups for complete restores are therefore part of the corporate infrastructure.

In an environment that bills for services with a fine granularity, these kinds of backups can be billed for differently. If possible, these customer groups should be individually billed for these special requirements, just as they would be billed for any service. Different software may be required, and there may be different physical storage requirements and different requirements for who "owns" the tapes.

Passing the Cost to the Right Customer

During a corporate merger, the U.S. Department of Justice required the companies involved to preserve any backup tapes until the deal was approved. This meant that old tapes could not be recycled. The cost of purchasing new tapes was billed to the company's legal department. It required the special service, so it had to pay.

26.1.3 Corporate Guidelines

Organizations need a corporatewide document that defines terminology and dictates requirements for data-recovery systems. Global corporate policymakers should strive to establish minimums based on legal requirements rather than list every specific implementation detail of the items that are discussed later in this chapter.

The guideline should begin by defining why backups are required, what constitutes a backup, and what kind of data should be backed up. A set of retention guidelines should be clearly spelled out. There should be different SLAs for each type of data: finance, mission critical, project, general home directory data, email, experimental, and so on.

The guidelines should list a series of issues that each site needs to consider, so that they are not overlooked. For example, the guidelines should require sites to carefully plan when backups are done, not simply do them at the default "midnight until they complete" time frame. It wouldn't be appropriate to dictate the same window for all systems. Backups usually have a performance impact and thus should be done during off-peak times. E-commerce sites with a global customer base will have a very different backup window than offices with normal business schedules.

---

4. Increasingly, the legal requirement is to *not* back up data or to recycle tapes in increasingly short cycles. Judges can't subpoena documents that aren't backed up.

> **Backups Slow Down Services**
>
> In 1999, a telecom company got some bad press for mistimed backups. The company had outsourced its backup planning to a third party, which ran them at peak hours. This adversely affected the performance of the web server, annoying a technology columnist, who wrote a long article about how big companies in the bandwidth business didn't "get it." He assumed that the poor performance was owing to a lack of bandwidth. Although your backup-related performance problems might not make the news, they can still be embarrassing.
>
> People remember the bad PR, not the remediation (Dodge 1999).

If you are the person writing the global corporate requirements document, you should begin by surveying various groups for requirements: Consult your legal department, your executive management, the SAs, and your customers. It becomes your job to reach consensus among them all. Use the three major types of restores as a way of framing the subject.

For example, the legal department might need archival backups to prove copyright ownership or intellectual property rights. Insurance might require general backups that are retained for at least 6 months. The accounting department might need to have tax-related data kept for 7 years but recorded only on a quarterly basis. Increasingly, legal departments are requiring a short retention policy for email, especially in light of the fact that key evidence in the Microsoft lawsuit was gained by reviewing Microsoft's email archives. Most companies insist that email archives be destroyed after 6 months.

It is important to balance all these concerns. You might have to go through several rounds of surveys, revising the requirements, until they are acceptable to all involved.

Some companies, especially start-ups, may be too small to have guidelines beyond "there will be backups." As the company grows, consider adopting corporate guidelines, based on the requirements of your investors and legal counsel.

26.1.4 A Data-Recovery SLA and Policy

The next step is to determine the service level that's right for your particular site. An SLA is a written document that specifies what kind of service and performance that service providers commit to providing. This policy should be written in dialogue with your customers. Once the SLA is determined, it can be turned into a policy specifying how the SLA will be achieved.

To establish an SLA, list the three types of restores, along with the desired time to restoration, the granularity and retention period for such backups—how often the backups should be performed and how long the tapes should be retained—and the window of time during which the backups may be performed—for example, midnight to 8 AM.

For most SAs, a corporate standard already exists, with vague, high-level parameters that they must follow. Make sure that your customers are aware of these guidelines. From there, building the policy is usually very straightforward.

The example SLA we use in the remainder of this chapter is as follows: Customers should be able to get back any file with a granularity of 1 business day for the past 6 months and with a granularity of 1 month for the last 3 years. Disk failures should be restored in 4 hours, with no more than 2 business days of lost data. Archives should be full backups on separate tapes generated quarterly and kept forever. Critical data will be stored on a system that retains user-accessible snapshots made every hour from 7 AM until 7 PM, with midnight snapshots held for 1 week. Databases and financial systems should have higher requirements that should be determined by the application's requirements and therefore are not within the scope of this example policy.

The policy based on this SLA would indicate that there will be daily backups and that the tapes will be retained as specified. The policy can determine how often full versus incremental backups will be performed.

26.1.5 The Backup Schedule

Now that we have an SLA and policy, we can set the schedule, which is specific and lists details down to which partitions of which hosts are backed up when. Although an SLA should change rarely, the schedule changes often, tracking changes in the environment. Many SAs choose to specify the schedule by means of the backup software's configuration.

Following our example, backups should be performed every business day. Even if the company experiences a nonredundant disk failure and the last day's backups failed, we will not lose more than 2 days worth of data. Since full backups take significantly longer than incrementals, we schedule them for Friday night and let them run all weekend. Sunday through Thursday nights, incremental backups are performed.

You may have to decide how often full backups run. In our example, the requirement is for full backups once a month. We could, in theory, perform one-quarter of our full backups each weekend. This leisurely rate would meet the requirements of our policy, but it would be unwise. As we noted earlier, incremental backups grow over time until the next full backup is completed. The incrementals would be huge if each partition received a full backup only once a month. It would save tape to perform a full backup more often.

However, backup software has become increasingly automated over the years. It is common to simply list all partitions that need to be backed up and to have the software generate a schedule based on the requirements. The backups are performed automatically, and email notification is generated when tapes must be changed.

Let's look at an example. Suppose that a partition with 4GB of data is scheduled to have a full backup every 4 weeks (28 days) and an incremental all other days. Let's also assume that the size of our incremental backup grows by 5 percent every day. On the first day of the month, 4GB of tape capacity is used to complete the full backup. On the second day, 200MB; the third day, 400MB; the fourth day, 600MB; and so on. The tape capacity used on the eleventh and twelfth days is 2GB and 2.2GB, respectively, which total more than a full backup. This means that on the eleventh day, it would have been wiser to do a full backup.

Table 26.1 shows this hypothetical situation in detail with daily, 7-day, 14-day, 21-day, 28-day, and 35-day cycles. We assume zero growth after day 20 (80 percent) in the longer cycles because the growth of incrementals is not infinite.

The worst case would be doing daily full backup, or 168GB of data written to tape. This would waste tape and time. Most environments have more data than could be backed up in full every day. Compared with the best case, daily full backups use 341 percent tape. This chart shows that the longer the cycle, the closer we get to that worst case.

The best case in this example is the 7-day cycle, or 49.2GB of data written to tape. The jump to a 14-day cycle is about a one-third increase in tape usage, with the same amount to the 21-day cycle. Longer cycles have insignificant increases because of our assumption that incrementals never grow beyond 80 percent of the size of a full backup. If this example were our actual environment, it would be relatively efficient to have a 7-day or 14-day cycle or anything in between.

Figure 26.1 graphs the accumulated tape used with those cycles over 41 days, a running total for each strategy. The "daily" line shows a linear growth of tape use. The other cycles start out the same but branch off, each at its own cycle.

Table 26.1 Tape Usage 4GB Data, 5 Percent Change Daily

Day Number	Cycle					
	Daily	7-Day	14-Day	21-Day	28-Day	35-Day
1	4.0	4.0	4.0	4.0	4.0	4.0
2	4.0	0.2	0.2	0.2	0.2	0.2
3	4.0	0.4	0.4	0.4	0.4	0.4
4	4.0	0.6	0.6	0.6	0.6	0.6
5	4.0	0.8	0.8	0.8	0.8	0.8
6	4.0	1.0	1.0	1.0	1.0	1.0
7	4.0	1.2	1.2	1.2	1.2	1.2
8	4.0	4.0	1.4	1.4	1.4	1.4
9	4.0	0.2	1.6	1.6	1.6	1.6
10	4.0	0.4	1.8	1.8	1.8	1.8
11	4.0	0.6	2.0	2.0	2.0	2.0
12	4.0	0.8	2.2	2.2	2.2	2.2
13	4.0	1.0	2.4	2.4	2.4	2.4
14	4.0	1.2	2.6	2.6	2.6	2.6
15	4.0	4.0	4.0	2.8	2.8	2.8
16	4.0	0.2	0.2	3.0	3.0	3.0
17	4.0	0.4	0.4	3.2	3.2	3.2
18	4.0	0.6	0.6	3.4	3.4	3.4
19	4.0	0.8	0.8	3.6	3.6	3.6
20	4.0	1.0	1.0	3.8	3.8	3.8
21	4.0	1.2	1.2	3.8	3.8	3.8
	...	...	...	...	...	...
42-day total	**168**	**49.2**	66.6	91.6	94.6	107.2
Worst case	100%	29%	40%	55%	56%	64%
Best case	341%	100%	135%	186%	192%	218%

The first example illustrates the fundamentals in a simple scenario. A more complex and realistic model addresses the fact that most data access is a relatively low proportion of the data on disk. Our rule of thumb that 80 percent of accesses is generally to the same 20 percent of data and that customers modify about half the data they access. Although we still can't tell in advance which data will change, we can predict that the first incremental backup will be 10 percent data size and that each subsequent increment will grow by 1 percent until the next full backup resets the cycle (Table 26.2).

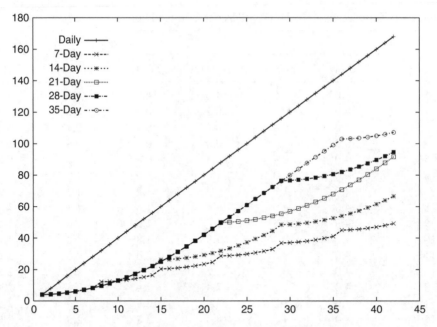

Figure 26.1 Accumulation of tape use by the cycles in Table 26.1

In this case, the 14-day cycle is the best case, with the 21-day cycle a close second. The 7-day cycle, which had been the most efficient cycle in our previous example, comes in third place because it does too many costly full backups. Again, the worst case would be doing daily full backups. Compared with the best case, daily full backups use 455 percent of tape. We can also observe that the 7- through 28-day cycles are all more similar to each other, (between 6 percent and 15 percent of the best case, whereas in our previous example, they varied wildly.

When we graph accumulations as before, we see how similar the cycles are. The graph in Figure 26.2 shows this. *Note:* This graph omits the daily full backups so as to expose greater detail for the other cycles.

The best length of a cycle is different for every environment. So far, we have seen an example in which a 7-day cycle was the obvious best choice and another in which it was obviously not the best. Careful tuning is required to determine what is best for your environment. If you are starting from scratch and have no past data on which to base your decision, it is reasonable to start with a 14-day cycle and tune it from there. By reviewing utilization reports and doing a little math, you can determine whether a longer or shorter cycle

Table 26.2 Tape Usage for 4GB Data, 10 Percent Change on Day 1, 1 Percent Change Thereafter

Day Number	Cycle					
	Daily	7-Day	14-Day	21-Day	28-Day	35-Day
1	4.00	4.00	4.00	4.00	4.00	4.00
2	4.00	0.40	0.40	0.40	0.40	0.40
3	4.00	0.44	0.44	0.44	0.44	0.44
4	4.00	0.48	0.48	0.48	0.48	0.48
5	4.00	0.52	0.52	0.52	0.52	0.52
6	4.00	0.56	0.56	0.56	0.56	0.56
7	4.00	0.60	0.60	0.60	0.60	0.60
8	4.00	4.00	0.64	0.64	0.64	0.64
9	4.00	0.40	0.68	0.68	0.68	0.68
10	4.00	0.44	0.72	0.72	0.72	0.72
11	4.00	0.48	0.76	0.76	0.76	0.76
12	4.00	0.52	0.80	0.80	0.80	0.80
13	4.00	0.56	0.84	0.84	0.84	0.84
14	4.00	0.60	0.88	0.88	0.88	0.88
15	4.00	4.00	4.00	0.92	0.92	0.92
16	4.00	0.40	0.40	0.96	0.96	0.96
17	4.00	0.44	0.44	1.00	1.00	1.00
18	4.00	0.48	0.48	1.04	1.04	1.04
19	4.00	0.52	0.52	1.08	1.08	1.08
20	4.00	0.56	0.56	1.12	1.12	1.12
21	4.00	0.60	0.60	1.16	1.16	1.16
	...	...	...	...	...	...
42-day total	**168**	42	**36.96**	39.2	41.16	47.04
Worst case	100%	25%	22%	23%	25%	28%
Best case	455%	114%	100%	106%	111%	127%

would use less tape. Obviously, these decisions should be in compliance with the SLA and policy.

Recent development has given the backup software the ability to tune itself. Although it can be difficult for a human (or even an SA) to keep track of the growing needs of hundreds of disk volumes, it is simple bookkeeping to a computer. We feel that eventually, all commercial backup software will provide some kind of dynamic schedule.

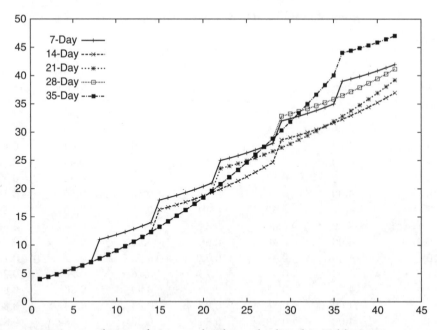

Figure 26.2 Accumulation of tape use by the cycles listed in Table 26.2

Case Study: The Bubble-Up Dynamic Backup Schedule

Dynamic schedules do not need to be complicated. Tom once created a simple dynamic schedule as follows. The SLA was that every partition on every server was to have a backup done each night, whether it was incremental or full, and full backups should be done every seven to ten days.

The list of partitions was sorted by backup date, putting the least recently backed up partitions at the front of the list. The first partitions were designated for full backups that night on a separate set of tape drives. The remainder of the partitions received incremental backups.

As a result, any failed backups tended to bubble up toward the top of the list and be the first priority the next night. Backups typically failed because of a down host or, more likely, because the tape ran out of space. The software wasn't capable of continuing a backup onto a second tape. (This was in the days before affordable jukeboxes.)

The system could be tuned in two ways. If the partitions weren't receiving full backups often enough, additional tape units were allocated to that function. If the incremental tapes were filling, more tape drives could be allocated for that function. In this case, the SAs had to watch whether the incrementals were not simply getting dangerously full but also whether they were taking longer than their backup window permitted.

Some systems have only a single level of incremental backup. Others have incremental backups that record all the changed files since the last backup of the same level—sometimes called *true incrementals*, or differentials.[5]

Another way to conserve tape is to perform two levels of incrementals, if your system supports it. For example, a full backup (level 0) is run on the first day of the month, followed by nightly incremental backups that capture any files modified since the original full backup: level 1 incrementals. The size of these incrementals grows to an excessive size by the middle of the month. On the fifteenth of the month, level 2 incrementals are begun; they record any file that has changed since the last level 1 backup. The midmonth incremental should return to being fairly small. This saves tape in the same way that doing incrementals instead of full backups saves tape.

However, there are two downsides. First, it is much more complicated to keep track of, although this is not a problem if the system is fully automated and maintains a good inventory. Second, it makes restores more difficult and error prone: You must now read the level 0, the level 1, and the level 2 tapes to make sure that all the files have been restored. This takes more time and, if the process is manual, the extra complication means that it is more prone to error. There is also a reliability factor: If there is a 1:1,000 chance that a tape is bad, having to rely on three tapes instead of two is an increased risk.

26.1.6 Time and Capacity Planning

Restores and backups are constrained by time. Restores need to happen within the time permitted by the SLA of the service, which may be disabled until the restore is complete. Backups can be done only during certain time windows. Most systems slow down considerably when backups are being performed.

The speed of a backup is limited by the slowest of the following factors: read performance of the disk, write performance of the backup medium, bandwidth, and latency of the network between the disk and the backup medium. Restore time is affected by the reverse of those factors. Tape units frequently write to the tape at a much slower speed than they read from it.

---

5. It is important to understand what your vendor means by *incremental*. Be safe rather than sorry, and take the time to test the system yourself to make sure that you understand how your vendor's backup system operates.

Many new SAs believe that vendors' statements about tape drive speeds and capacities bear some relationship to performance. They are gravely mistaken. The difference can be huge; we've seen a difference of up to 1,500 percent. Vendors continually tune and refine their backup algorithms for speed but often ignore restore speed; most of their customers don't think to demand fast restores, and the ones who need it are willing to pay extra for it.

The slowest link in the chain will determine the speed at which the backup will happen. The process is also affected by mechanical issues. Most tape drives write at a high speed if they are being fed data as quickly as they can write (streaming mode) but downshift to a considerably slower speed if they are not being fed data quickly enough to keep up with the tape write speed. If the drive has no data to write, the drive must stop, reverse position, and wait until it has enough data to start writing again. Drive manufactures call this the **shoe-shining effect** as the read/write mechanism moves back and forth over the same spot on the tape. In addition to slowing tape performance, it puts undue stress on the tape medium.

Therefore, if the server cannot provide data quickly enough, backup speed is dramatically reduced. For example, if network congestion is slowing the data from getting to the tape host, backups may be significantly slower than if congestion is not an issue. Many times, we've been asked to diagnose problems with slow backups only to find that the network in place is slower than the maximum write speed of the tape unit.

Restores will also be as slow as the slowest link, but there are additional factors. Finding a single file on a tape can take as long as a full disk restore itself. First, the system must skip other volumes stored on that tape. Then the system must read the particular volume to find the particular file to be restored. If the tape mechanism has no ability to fast-forward or skip to a particular data segment, this can be painfully slow.

Restoring an entire disk is extremely slow, too. The main issue on restore speed is not drive read speed but file system write speed. Writes are much less efficient than reads on almost every file system, and reconstructing a file system is often worst-case performance, particularly with journaled file systems. We've seen it take 5 to 15 times longer to restore the disk drive as it was to back it up. This is a very nasty surprise for most people.

If the server is able to receive data quickly enough such that the tape drive can stay in streaming mode, the restore can happen at maximum speed. However, if the tape drive's data buffer fills up, the drive will slow down the tape speed or, possibly, stop the tape mechanism completely. Rewinding to the proper position and getting back up to speed is a huge delay.

When building a backup and restore system, you must take into account the speed of the various interconnections and plan to make sure that the slowest link does not prevent you from meeting your time goals. It is common to use a dedicated network used exclusively by file servers to talk to their backup host. One of the first benefits that popularized SANs was the ability to move backup traffic off the primary network.

To alleviate such performance problems during backups, it is common to use a disk drive as a buffer. Previously, systems backed up data by copying it from one server to a tape unit on a centralized backup host. Now it is common to install a lot of disk on the backup host. Servers back up their data to the disks on the backup host, often one file per disk volume per server. The backup host now can write the completed backup files at full tape speed. It is common to see configurations in which all servers write their backup data at night, and the backup host spends the day writing out the data to tape. This is known as disk-to-disk-to-tape (D2D2T). It works better because local disk access is more deterministic than access across the network. Rather than having to engineer things so that the data can flow the entire path at the speed required for the tape drives, one must ensure only that such speed can be achieved from the local disk to the tape unit.

The only way to know for sure whether your time goals have been met is to try it. Timing both a test backup and a test restore can validate your design. Over time, experience will help you determine what will work and what won't. However, it can be difficult to gain usable experience when backup and restore systems tend to be reengineered every couple years. You can instead rely on the experience of others, either a friendly sales engineer or a consultant who specializes in backup and restore systems.

26.1.7 Consumables Planning

Your policy and schedule affect how quickly you will use consumables: tapes, tape cleaners, and so on. This too requires doing math. Using our example policy again, incrementals can be recycled after being stored 6 months, and full backups, except what is set aside as archives, can be recycled after 3 years.

Initially, there are no tapes to recycle. For the first 6 months, new tapes must be purchased for everything you do. Mathematically, you can project how many tapes will be needed by examining the schedule. Suppose that 6 days a week, 8 tapes will be used per day. That is 48 tapes a week, or

1,248 tapes for the first 6 months. Digital linear tapes (DLTs) cost about $80 each, or about $99,840 for the first 6 months.[6]

Because the cost of tapes is continually shrinking, we recommend purchasing them in monthly or quarterly batches. A rule of thumb is to make the first batch a double batch to establish a cache of blank tapes in case future orders are delayed. Otherwise, the cost of tapes often decreases more quickly than the volume discounts you might receive by purchasing large batches up front.

In the second 6 months, you can recycle all the incrementals, needing to purchase new tapes only for full backups. Let's assume that 9 tapes per week are full backups and that your incrementals are growing at a rate that requires you to purchase an additional 1 tape per week. Thus, you will need only 260 tapes in the second half of the year, costing $18,200 if you assume that the cost per tape has dropped to $70 by then. If these estimates are correct, recycling tapes will make your budget for tapes in the second 6 months: only about 18 percent as much as what you paid in the first 6 months:

Tape cost (first year): $118,040

The second and third years should also require about 260 new tapes per 6 months, or $36,400 per year:

Tape cost (second and third years): $36,400/year

Tape cost (first 3 years): $190,840 total, or $5,301/month average

After 3 years, you can recycle all tapes from the first year (1,508 tapes), except those marked as archival. If you do full backups every 14 days, the archival tapes should be all the full-backup tapes created in the first 2 weeks of any quarter, or 72 tapes per year ($9 \times 2 \times 4$). The remaining tapes total 1,436. Thus, you need to purchase only about 70 to 80 tapes per year. Assuming $70 per tape, your budget for new tapes is reduced to $5,000 to $6,000 per year:

Tape cost (fourth and future years): $6,000/year

Tape cost (first 4 years): $196,840 total, or $4,100/month average

Although the fourth year is the least expensive, it is likely the last year before you must upgrade to new technology with an incompatible medium.

---

6. And you thought that a jukebox was expensive!

If the old system is still around serving legacy systems, the tapes available for recycling should be sufficient for your diminished needs.

Let's look at how things would be different if the policy kept full backups, except for archival copies, for only 1 year. The 4-year tape cost will be significantly lower. During the second and future years, you'd be able to recycle all tapes except the 72 tagged as archives. The second, third, and fourth years would cost less than $6,000 each:

Modified policy 3-year cost: $129,240 total, or $3,590/month average

Modified policy 4-year cost: $134,840 total, or $2,809/month average

This single policy change didn't affect the first year cost at all but reduced both the 3-year and 4-year average cost by approximately 32 percent.

When setting the backup and restore policy, technical people commonly want backups that are retained forever, and financial people want a policy that saves as much money as possible. To strike a balance requires calculations based on your best predictions on the cost of consumables. It can be helpful to show people the cost models of what they have requested.

26.1.8 Restore-Process Issues

Important issues involving the restoration process require a lot of thought and planning. First, it is important to set expectations with customers. They should know what the backup policy is and how to request a file restore. Even a simple explanation such as this is sufficient:

> Backups are performed only on data stored on servers (your PC's Z: drive, or UNIX /home directory) every night between midnight and 8 AM. *We never do backups of your PC's local C: drive.* If you need a file recovered, go to [*insert URL*] for more information, or send email to "help" with the name of the server, the file's complete path, and which date you need the restore from. Barring problems, simple restores are done in 24 hours.

It is a good idea to include this information in any kind of new-user orientation documents or presentations and have it as a banner ad on your internal web portal. If your policy excludes certain machines from being backed up, it is particularly critical that people are aware of this.

You must think about the security implications of any restore request. Does this person have the right to receive these files? Will the file permissions and ownership change as a result of the restore? Will the data be restored to the same place with the same permissions or to a new place with possibly different security implications? Will it overwrite existing data?

There is a critical security issue here: Restore requests must be validated. Millions of dollars of security infrastructure can be defeated by a careless restore. Obviously, a restore of files to someone's directory on the server they originated from has few security implications. However, restoring a directory that is part of a project to someone's home directory may have security implications, especially if the person is not on the project.

Although this kind of security attack may sound rare, it is a bigger risk as larger domains of control are outsourced. In a small company, it may be normal for a manager to request a restore of files from the directory of a staff member, and the SA can verify that the staff/manager relationship is valid because everyone knows everyone. However, in a 50,000-person company, how do you verify who is in which organization? Therefore, as a company grows larger, it becomes more critical that a well-defined procedure exists for validating restore requests.

It is key that multiple people be able to perform restores, not only the person who designed the system. Commonly, the engineer who designed the system invests time in automating the daily ritual of changing tapes so the process is as simple as possible. This allows a lower-paid clerk to do the task. However, designers often forget that it isn't wise to be the only person who knows how to do a restore. The restoration process should be well documented. The documentation should be kept online, and a printed version should be stashed on or near the backup hardware. The amount of effort taken to document and train people on a type of restore should be proportional to how often the restore is requested. Many people should be trained on the most common request: simple file restoration. This procedure should be easy to follow. A couple of people should be trained on how to restore an entire disk volume. This may require additional technical knowledge because it may involve replacing failed disks or knowing who has hardware training. Finally, a few senior SAs should be trained on how to restore a failed boot disk. This may be difficult to document because every server is a little different, but the key issue to document is how to do a restore on a system that is in some half-up state or how to do a restore when the machine with the tape inventory is down. All these documents should list the customer-support contact information for all vendors involved, as well as the maintenance contract numbers and passwords required to receive service.

26.1.9 Backup Automation

Not automating backups is dangerous and stupid. It is dangerous because the more you automate, the more you eliminate the chance of human error. Backups are boring, and if they aren't automated, they will not be reliably done. If they aren't done properly, it will be very embarrassing to have to face your CEO's question: "But why weren't there backups?"

Three aspects of the backup procedure can be automated: the commands, the schedule, and tape management and inventory. In the early days, there was no automation. Individual commands were typed by hand every time backups were done. Often, backups were started by the last shift before leaving for the night. The schedule was simple. There was little or no inventory except the labels on the tapes. The first step in automation was scripts that simply replicated those commands that were previously typed manually. However, deciding what was to be backed up when was still a human task, and very little inventory management was done. Soon, software implemented the scheduling algorithms that humans had done manually. Eventually, the algorithms were improved, offering dynamic schedules that went beyond the scope of what humans could reasonably do. Finally, the task of physically manipulating tapes was automated through the use of jukeboxes. Automated systems alerted a clerk to remove a certain set of tapes from a jukebox and to replace them with new tapes. With a well-maintained inventory, a fully automated system can even automate the process of tracking which tapes are to be recycled and printing reports of tapes that are due for recycling.

Not all sites need such sophisticated automation, but all sites need to have at least the first two levels of automation in place. All this may seem obvious, but every site has one or two machines that have manual backups. Often, they are outside a firewall and unreachable from the central backup system. It is critical to introduce at least simple, rudimentary automation for these systems. If it is not automated, it will not happen.

We harshly call failing to automate backups stupid because manual backups are a waste of skills and time. With automation, the daily task of performing backups can be done by someone who has a lower skill level and therefore will be less expensive. Having a highly paid SA spend an hour a day changing tapes is a waste of money. Even if it takes a clerk twice as long to perform the function, it will be less expensive because during those hours, highly skilled SAs will be able to work on tasks that only they can accomplish.

This is why corporate executives do not send their own faxes.[7] It is better business practice to have executives do things that only they can do and to move all other tasks to lower-paid employees.

The only thing worse than no automation is bad automation. Bad automation automates many aspects of a task but does not alleviate the think work that must be done. Good automation doesn't simply do stuff for you; it reduces the brainwork you must do.

Backup System That Required Brainwork

Once upon a time, an SA had to reckon with a backup system that automated the major aspects of the task at hand and even printed pretty labels for the tape covers. However, the system failed to reduce the thinking aspect of the job. The software did a grand job of issuing the right backup commands at the right time, used a highly dynamic schedule to optimize tape use, and dealt with the security and political issues that were in place, which had the side effect of requiring about ten small tape drives in the main data center and an additional ten scattered in various labs around the building. (This was before tape jukeboxes were inexpensive.) However, every morning, the SA responsible for backups had to review 20 email messages, one for each tape unit, and decide whether that tape had enough space remaining to fit the next day's backups. To change a tape, a program was run, and much later, the tape was ejected. As a result, it took an hour or two to complete the daily tape changes. The SA, being lazy, did not want to think through 20 tapes per day and make a decision for each one. He knew that eliminating this daily task would be like gaining 5 to 10 hours of additional time for other projects.

His solution was based on his realization that he could buy more tapes but not more time. He noticed that the tape drives connected to large servers needed to be changed often, whereas the tape drives scattered in labs required infrequent changes. Rather than spending each morning with an hour of fretting over which tapes should be changed to optimize tape use, stop world hunger, and find a cure for cancer, he simply stopped changing tapes on Tuesdays and Thursdays. That gained him nearly 4 hours. If a new tape was started on Monday, Wednesday, and Friday, the risk of filling a tape by the next day was quite rare. He had not noticed this pattern previously because he hadn't spent the time to study the logs in that much detail. The time gained would be more valuable than the occasional full tape/missed backup situation. Next, he determined that the tape drives in the labs filled up very rarely, and he eliminated the grand tour of the facilities to change all the lab tape drives, except for once a week. That gained about 3 hours. By restructuring how the tape changes were performed, he gained an additional day[8] of time each week.

---

7. The person in the back row who is trying to point out that many executives can't figure out how to operate a fax machine should please sit down.

8. The sum of 4 + 3 is an eight-hour day for large values of three.

> The software being used was homegrown, and it would have been politically difficult to replace it before the author left the group, which he eventually did. Until then, this new process was a real time saver. In fact, the new procedure was so simple to explain to others that the SA was able to shift the daily process to a clerk, thus eliminating the task from his daily workload altogether. Victory!

Manual backups and homegrown backup software used to be very commonplace. Tracking new technologies, hardware, and OSs is costly. The more complicated backup requirements become, the more reason you have to purchase commercial software rather than trying to build your own system. With commercial products, the cost of development and support of the software is divided over their entire customer base.

> **Automated Backup Permits Delegation**
>
> A good friend of ours, Adam Moskowitz, was determined to build a backup system that was so automated that he could delegate the daily work to his company's secretary, at least most of the time. Each day, the system sent email to her and Adam with the status of the previous night's backup. The message included instructions about which tapes to change or stated that there was a problem for Adam to fix. Adam automated more and more of the error situations so that over time, there was less and less for him to do. Soon months would pass without requiring Adam's intervention.

26.1.10 Centralization

Another fundamental design goal of modern backup systems is centralization. Backups should be centralized because they are expensive and important. Making the right investments can spread the cost of the backup and restore system over many systems.

Two major costs can be reduced through centralization. Tape changes are costly because they are labor intensive. The equipment itself is costly because it involves precision mechanical parts spinning at high speeds. The tolerance for error is low.

Without centralization, a tape unit must be attached to every machine that needs to be backed up, and someone has to be paid to walk to every machine to change tapes. The result: paying for many expensive pieces of hardware and a large amount of physical labor.

Network-based backup systems let you attach large backup machinery to one or a few hosts that contact others to initiate backups. Network-based backups were adopted once networks were plentiful and reliable.

Jukeboxes are large devices that hold dozens, hundreds, or even thousands of tapes and contain robotic arms that shuttle tapes from their storage locations into one of multiple tape units. Jukeboxes are expensive, but their cost is amortized over all the systems for which they perform backups and vastly reduce labor costs. Tape drives, being mechanical, often break. The right software can detect a broken tape unit and simply use the remaining units in a jukebox to complete its tasks. Without network-based backup systems, you must either forgo backups on a system if its tape unit has died or install an extra tape unit on each system to ensure that there will always be one working tape unit. Certainly, a jukebox is less expensive than that! Jukeboxes also enable much of the sophisticated automation described elsewhere in this chapter.

26.1.11 Tape Inventory

A pile of backup tapes with no index or inventory is only slightly more useful than no backups at all. The inventory is critical to being able to do restores in a timely manner. Large, automated backup systems maintain that inventory online. Often, special precautions must be taken in backing up the inventory, because the system that does the backups will want to update the inventory as it is being copied. You might consider printing a minimal tape index at the end of your nightly backups and keeping those printouts in a notebook. The inventory is a good candidate for storage on a system protected with RAID or similar technology.

Being able to restore files is dependent on the quality of your inventory. The better the inventory is, the more quickly the restore can be done. If there was no inventory, you would have to read tapes in reverse chronological order until the needed data was found. If the inventory lists only which partitions are on which tape, you would have to read each tape with data from that partition until the requested file was found. If the customer can remember the last time the file was modified, this can help the search, but it would still take a long time. Full restores would not be so impaired.

If the system stores a file-by-file inventory of each tape, the entire search process can be performed quickly in database queries; the exact tapes required would then be loaded. For example, if a couple of files on various directories plus a couple of entire directories need restoration, the software can deduce exactly which full and incremental backup tapes have the data that needs to be restored. All the required tapes would be loaded into the jukebox, and the software would perform all the restores, using all the available tape drives in the jukebox.

Keeping a file-by-file inventory requires a lot of disk space. Some commercial products can strike a balance by maintaining the file-by-file listing for recent tapes and a simple partition listing for all others. The file-by-file listing can be reconstructed on demand if older files must be restored.

Software should be able to rebuild the inventory if it is lost or destroyed. In theory, you should be able to load the jukebox with the most recent tapes, click a button, and in hours or days, have rebuilt the inventory. A site could do backups by night and inventory reconstruction by day.

A good inventory should also track how often a particular tape is reused. Most tape technologies become unreliable after being reused a certain number of times. You should expect backup software to be able to tell you when to destroy a tape.

In extreme situations, you may need to do a restore without access to the inventory, without access to a license server, and without the complete backup system working. Although a good inventory is critical to normal operations, make sure that the system you use doesn't prevent you from reading the data off a tape when you have nothing but the tape and a manual. Look for all these features when selecting your backup and restore solution.

26.2   The Icing

Now that we've described the fundamentals of a solid, mature backup and restore system, certain things need to be established to maintain this system well into the future. First, you must perform fire drills to ensure that the system is working. Off-site storage of tapes protects the backup media that you've worked so hard to generate. We end with a technical yet somewhat philosophical explanation of why a backup system is always one step away from needing an upgrade.

26.2.1   Fire Drills

The only time you know the quality of your backup media is when you are doing a restore. This is generally the worst time to learn that you have problems. You can better assess your backup system if you do an occasional fire drill. Pick a random file and restore it from tape to verify that your process is working.

644   Chapter 26   Backup and Restore

Automated Fire Drill Requests

The first time Tom saw a backup fire drill was when he was working with Tommy Reingold at Bell Labs. Tommy wrote a small program that would randomly select a server, then randomly select a file on that server, then email the SAs to ask for a copy of that file as it was a week ago. He was able to sleep better at night knowing that these weekly requests were satisfied successfully.

It can be useful to do an occasional fire drill that involves restoring an entire disk volume. The speed at which an entire disk volume can be restored is often unknown because it is so rarely requested. Restoring a file, or even a directory of files, as regularly requested by customers will not help you determine how long a full disk restore will take, because of the huge difference in the quantity of data being restored. Bottlenecks go unnoticed until an emergency happens. It is better to restore an entire disk volume occasionally than to discover a bottleneck when you are under the gun to bring a system back into service. When doing these fire drills, it is important to time them and monitor such things as disk, tape, and network utilization. If you are not seeing the performance you expect, you can review the statistics you have collected to help determine what needs to be improved.

If you think that you don't have enough free disk space to do a full disk fire drill, you might want to do this whenever you have installed a new server but before it goes into production. You should have at least one spare partition available, and the drill will be a good burn-in for the new hardware.

If some tapes are stored off-site, the fire drills should include both off-site and on-site tapes to completely exercise the system.

The person who verifies that the data recovered in the fire drill is valid should not be the same person who is responsible for performing the backups. This creates a system of checks and balances.

26.2.2 Backup Media and Off-Site Storage

Backup tapes must be stored somewhere safe. It doesn't make sense to spend large amounts of money and time on security systems to protect your data yet store backup tapes in an unlocked room or cabinet. Your backups are the company's crown jewels. Finding secure and convenient storage space for them can be difficult in today's cramped office buildings. However, a set of well-locked cabinets or a large safe in an otherwise unsecure room may be sufficient.

If your backups are to hedge against the risk of a natural disaster that would destroy your entire machine room, they should not be stored in the machine room itself or in a room that would be flooded if your data center were also the victim of a broken pipe.

Off-site storage of backup media is an even better idea. A set of backup tapes or archival copies are kept at a safe distance from the computers that generated them. This need not be complicated or expensive.

The off-site storage facility can hold the backup tapes or copies of them. It is a trade-off in convenience versus risk. Storing copies hedges against the risk that the tapes may be damaged or lost in transit. However, making the additional copies may be laborious. Instead, the tapes usually are stored off-site. This affects your ability to do restores in a timely manner. You may choose to keep last month's full backups off-site, seeing that most restore requests are from the current month's backups, and customers should understand that restore requests from tapes that are more than 30 days old but newer than 60 days may incur a delay.

When selecting an off-site storage facility, consider all the same things that should be considered for the on-site storage facilities: Is the space secure? Who has access to the facilities? What policies, guarantees, or confidentiality contracts are in place? There are many ways to go about this, ranging from informal systems to using large commercial digital warehouse services.

Informal Off-Site Storage

In some situations, an informal policy is sufficient. A fledgling start-up had a policy that every Wednesday, the head of its data processing department took home the backup tapes that were 1 week old. On Wednesday morning of the following week, she brought in the tapes she had brought home the week before. One concern was that if she were in an auto accident, the tapes could be destroyed. The risk could be reduced by increasing the cycle to once a month. The risk could be completely eliminated by having her bring only copies of the tapes home. The other concern was the security of her house. The company provided a fireproof safe for her house to store the tapes in. The safe was secured so that it could not be stolen.

Many companies use an off-site records-storage service. This used to be a luxury service that only big financial companies used, but it has grown into a large market that serves all. These services provide pick-up and drop-off service, a 4- or 8-hour turnaround time on requests to have particular tapes returned, and so on. Although their cost may sound prohibitive initially, they save a lot of hassle in the long run. They can also provide suggestions about typical policies that companies use for off-site storage. They even provide cute little locked boxes for you to put your tapes in when they are ready to be picked up.

There are security issues with storing tapes off-site. A third-party company paid to store the tapes must be bonded and insured. Read the contract carefully to understand the limits of the company's liability. You'll find it disappointingly small compared with the value of the data on the tapes. The horror stories are true. We've gotten back other people's tapes from storage facilities. In one case, we were not able to retrieve a tape that was sent to them for storage and had to request the tape that contained the previous backup of that file. The author of the file was not happy.

It is important to keep good track of what tapes are sent out and to record every tape that is received back. Audit this tape movement and watch for mistakes; mistakes are an indicator of overall quality. This can be your best defense. Imagine not being able to retrieve a critical tape and later finding out from your operators that occasionally, the wrong tapes come back. Look for tapes that should have come back but didn't, tapes that shouldn't have come back but did, and tapes from the wrong company coming to you. If you are going to bring a complaint to the vendor, it is critical to have a written log of every mistake made in the past. Obviously, if these mistakes aren't one in a million, you need to change vendors.

Homegrown Off-Site Storage

Companies with multiple buildings can provide their own off-site storage systems. One division of a company had its people spread out across two buildings that were 40 miles apart. The people exchanged tapes on a regular basis. Because they were all one division, they could even perform quick restores across their corporate network if waiting an hour or two for delivery was unreasonable.

Networked Off-Site Backups

A research center in New York had a lot of bandwidth between its two facilities and discovered that it was nearly unused at night. For several years, the facilities performed backups for each other's site over this WAN link. This had the benefit of making all tapes off-site. The bandwidth between the two facilities was large enough that

> restores could still be done in a reasonable amount of time. The management figured that it was an acceptable risk to assume that both buildings would not be destroyed simultaneously.

As network bandwidth becomes cheaper, the economics of performing backups to other sites via a network becomes more reasonable. Commercial backup services have sprung up within Internet colocation facilities to service the needs of dot-coms. This is easy because extremely high-speed networks can be installed within a colocation facility. As bandwidth becomes cheaper and over-the-network backup technology becomes more reliable, secure, and accepted, we foresee this kind of service becoming even more common.

> ❖ **Internet-Based Backup Systems**   When Tom was 13 years old, he thought that an over-the-network backup service would be a fine idea but was discouraged when he realized that it would take hours to back up his 160KB floppy disks over his 300-baud modem. When cable modems and xDSL service brought high-speed Internet access to homes, companies sprang up offering over-the-net backup services. Even without high-speed access, these services are fine for backing up small things, such as a student's doctoral dissertation. Tom started backing up his personal computer to one of these services the moment he got cable modem access at his house to vindicate his age-13 inventiveness.

26.2.3 High-Availability Databases

Some applications, such as databases, have specific requirements for ensuring that a backup is successful. A database manages its own storage space and optimizes it for particular kinds of access to its complex set of data tables. Because the layout and data access methods are usually opaque to the backup software, the database usually is written to tape as a single unit, or file. If the data in that file changes as it is being written, information may be lost or corrupted because the records for locating the data may be missing or incorrect on the backup tape. Databases often need to be shut down so that no transactions can occur during the backup to ensure consistency.

If the database has high-availability requirements, it is not acceptable to shut it down each night for backups. However, the risks associated with not doing a backup or performing the back up while the database is live are also unacceptable. Some vendors of backup software offer modules for performing backups of particular databases. Some of these substantially reduce the risks associated with a live database backup. However, it is generally safest to back up the data when the database is not running. This is usually achieved by having the database mirrored, using RAID 1 + 0, for example. The database can be stopped long enough to disconnect a mirror. The disconnected mirror disks are in a consistent state and unaffected by database transactions and can be safely written to tape. When the backup is finished, the mirror disks can be reconnected to the live database, and the mirror will be brought back up to date automatically.

In many environments a high-availability database is triply mirrored: one set of disks actively mirroring the database and one set detached and being backed up.

26.2.4 Technology Changes

Free your mind of the notion that there is one good piece of software or hardware that you will use for backups during your career as an SA. Instead, start thinking in general terms and move with the changes in technology.

There is one constant in backup and restore systems: Disk technology and tape technology keep leapfrogging each other, never at the same pace. Embrace this rather than fight it. Some years, tape technology will zoom ahead, and you'll feel as though you can back up anything. Other years, you'll see disk technology be ahead and wonder whether you will ever be able to back up all that you have. To understand why this happens, let's look at the historical growth patterns of each technology.

Disk size grows in small increments. Every couple of months, slightly larger drives are available. Overall disk capacity doubles every 15 to 18 months, and, historically, applications have been quick to use what is available. This means that about every other year, you will be backing up disks that contain twice as much data.

Tape capacity over the years has grown in larger leaps but spread out over years rather than months. Consumers are less willing to upgrade tape-backup hardware, and therefore the industry tends to provide forklift upgrades every 2 to 3 years. Resist the urge to upgrade your tape technology very often, because it simplifies life to not have to deal with many, many different tape formats. Most sites tend to use primarily what was the latest technology when their system was installed and may also have a couple of legacy systems on the old platform. These legacy systems either haven't been upgraded yet or are to be decommissioned soon, and upgrading the tape technology would be a waste of money. They then retain one or two tape drives for all previous tape technologies that they still have in their archives.

Keep One Nine-Track Tape Drive

Here's a way to amass favors owed to you. An SA at a large company discovered that he was the only person in the main complex with the ability to read those old reel-to-reel nine-track tapes. Although it was rare that anyone needed to read such a tape, anyone who did need such a tape read was desperate to do so. Outside companies will do tape conversions at a very high price, and he knew that people within the company would not want to pay such fees. He made sure that the tape drive was in a place that he wouldn't mind visitors using and attached it to a machine on which he could create guest accounts. Every year, he gained a couple valuable favors, which he redeemed later. It also helped him gain a reputation as a nice guy, which can be more valuable in a large company than you would expect.

The unbalanced growth of disk and tape technologies affects how you can do backups. In the old days, it was extremely difficult to split a backup of a single partition across two tapes.[9] Most backup software was homegrown and tapes were small. Therefore, when QIC tapes could store 150MB, SAs would split disks into partitions of 150MB. Then 8-mm tapes with 2.5GB capacity became popular because disks were commonly holding half to a full gigabyte. SAs thought that their problems with mismatched tape and disk sizes were over; data disks could be one huge partition. The upgrade to 5GB-capacity 8-mm tapes came around the same time as disk capacity grew to 4GB. However, when disks grew to their next leap (9GB), the tape industry had not caught up. This stalled the sale of these larger disks and was a boon to the commercial backup software industry, which could invest in making software to drive jukeboxes and handle the complicated task of splitting backups over multiple tapes. Next came DLT technology, which could hold 70GB, again leapfrogging disk size. And history repeated itself when disks grew beyond 70GB.

What can we learn from this? Change is constant. Trust your vendors to provide leaps in both areas, but don't be surprised when they become out of sync.

26.3 Conclusion

This chapter is about restores, for which backups are a necessary evil. This is a policy-driven issue. We are continually surprised to find sites that do not predicate their backup system on a sound policy.

---

9.   It still can be a risky thing to do; most systems put the index only on the first tape.

There are three kinds of restore requests: accidental file deletion, recovery from disk failure, and archival. Each of these has different SLAs, expectations, and engineering requirements. More important, each serves distinctively different customer groups, which you may want to bill separately. The policy is set based on these parameters.

Once a policy is in place, all decisions flow easily. From the policy, you can develop a backup schedule that is a specific list of which systems are backed up and when. One of the most difficult parts of determining the schedule is deciding how many days of incremental backups should be done before the next full backup. Current software does these calculations and can create a highly dynamic schedule. The policy helps you plan time, capacity, consumables, and other issues. Communicating the policy to the customers helps them understand the safety of their data, which systems are not backed up, and the procedure they should use if they need data restored. Making customers aware of which systems are not backed up is important.

A modern backup system must be automated to minimize human labor, human thought, human decisions, and human mistakes. In the old days, backups were a significant part of an SA's job, and therefore it was reasonable that they consumed a significant amount of an SA's time. Now, however, an SA is burdened with many new responsibilities. Backups are a well-defined task that can, and should, be delegated to others. We delegate the creation of the software to commercial vendors. We delegate the daily operational aspects to clerks. We can even delegate simple restores to the customers who request them. We focus our time, instead, on designing the architecture, installing the system, and handling the periodic scaling issues that come up. All this delegation leaves us more time for other tasks.

Modern backup systems are centralized. Doing backups over the network to a central, large backup device saves labor. The cost of large jukeboxes is amortized over the number of machines it serves.

Well-architected backup systems have excellent inventory systems. The system must have an excellent file inventory so that restores are done quickly and an excellent tape inventory so that tapes are recycled according to schedule.

We've also learned that backups cost a lot of money, both in equipment cost and consumables. Section 10.1.2 discusses the economics you can use to justify systems that reduce risk.

Backup technology is changing all the time. As disk capacity grows, SAs must upgrade their ability to maintain backups. They must free their minds of the notion that any backup and restore system they install is their final solution. Instead, they must be prepared to scale it continually and to replace it every 3 to 5 years.

Once the basics are in place, a few icing issues can be addressed. First, the validity of backups must be tested with fire drills. To do that, select a random piece of information and verify that you are able to successfully restore it. Second, safe, off-site storage for the backup media must be established. Backups should not be kept in the same place as the computers they are backing up.

Restores are one of the most important services you provide to your customers. The inability to restore critical data can bankrupt your company. The flawless execution of a restore can make you a hero to all.

Exercises

1. What is your restore policy? Do you have to work within corporate guidelines? If so, what are they? Or is your policy created locally?

2. Tables 26.1 and 26.2 do not take into consideration the fact that tapes are usually changed every day, whether or not they are full. Why are the examples still statistically valid? Why might it be a bad idea to put multiple days' backups on the same tape?

3. Some vendors' incremental backups record only files changed since the last incremental. How does this affect how restores are done? What are the pros and cons of this technique?

4. Vendor terminology for "incrementals" varies. How would you construct a test to find out what variation a vendor implements? Perform this test on two different OSs.

5. What are the benefits and risks of using a backup system that can continue a dump onto a second tape if the first tape gets full?

6. The example in Section 26.1.7 assumed that tapes could be recycled with no limit. Assume that a tape can be used 15 times before it must be discarded. Calculate how many tapes would have to be discarded each year for the first 4 years of the example.

7. Section 26.1.7 didn't calculate how much would be spent on cleaning tapes. Assume that drives need to be cleaned every 30 days and that a cleaning tape can be used 15 times. Calculate how many cleaning tapes are required for the two examples in Section 26.1.7.

8. Section 26.1.7 assumed that the amount of data being backed up didn't change over the 4 years. This is not realistic. Reproduce the calculations

in that section, based on the assumption that the amount of data stored doubles every 18 months.

9. Section 26.1.7 specifies a particular tape-reuse regiment. What if new tapes were to be reused only ten times? What if tapes kept forever were to be new tapes only?

10. What aspects of your current backup and restore system should be automated better?

11. "A modern backup system must be automated to minimize human labor, human thought, human decisions, and human mistakes." What point is being made here?

Chapter 27

Remote Access Service

A remote access service gives authorized individuals a way to access the company network from home, customer sites, or other locations around the country, the continent, or the world. In the early days, it was something that weird technical people wanted so that they could do extra work from home out of normal working hours. More recently, it has become a core service that everyone in a company uses. Now telecommuters and road warriors work outside the office, connecting only for specific services.

Remote access is achieved in many ways, but there are two main categories. Some forms connect a computer directly into the network: dial-up modems, ISDN, and so on. Others connect to the Internet—WiFi, cable modems, DSL, Ethernet, and so on—and then from there somehow tunnel or VPN into your network.

Many problems get lumped together as remote access. One aspect of remote access is that people want to be able to check their email and to access data when they are on the road. Almost as common is people wanting to work from home in the evenings, weekends, a few days a week, or full time. Another aspect is that some people are semipermanently stationed at a customer's site but still need to be able to access the corporate network on a regular basis. This chapter shows how all these aspects have slightly different requirements but also much in common.

Remote access is one of the areas in which technology is continually changing. This chapter looks at how that affects the design and administration of a remote access service but does not examine what technologies to use, because that will have changed even between the time of writing and publication. The information in this chapter should give you a basis for evaluating current technologies and solutions and making architectural decisions.

27.1 The Basics

To provide a remote access service, you should start by understanding your customers' many and varied requirements. You should also decide with your customers what service levels the SAs will provide for the various aspects of the system and document those decisions for future reference.

Once you have defined the requirements and the service levels, you are ready to build the service or to not build it. One of the basics of building a remote access system is to outsource as much of it as possible. However, several components must be built or managed internally to the company. In particular, the security aspects of authentication, authorization, and maintaining perimeter security should be managed internally.

27.1.1 Requirements for Remote Access

The first requirement of a remote access service typically will be assumed and not explicitly stated by your customers: Everyone must have access to a low-cost, convenient remote access solution. If the SA team does not provide one, customers will build something for themselves that will not be as secure or well managed as the service that the SAs would provide. It is quite likely that the SAs will ultimately be expected to support the service that their customers have built when it develops problems. It typically also will be more difficult to support than an SA-built service.

The other requirements are based on how the customers intend to use the remote access system. The most common customers of remote access are people who are traveling and want to check or send email. Other common customers are people who want to log in for an hour or two in the evening to catch up on a few things. These different groups of people have something in common: They use the remote access service only for fairly short periods of time. They differ in that one group expects to be able to use the service from anywhere; the other, to use it from home. The requirement that they both introduce is that they need a reliable and economical way to connect to the office network for short-duration connections. Neither group needs very high bandwidth, but they both want as much as they can get. Where they differ is that the people who are traveling need to be able to connect from anywhere they may travel. Depending on the company, that area may be a small region or the entire world. To provide global remote access, the technology used must be ubiquitous. When setting up a remote access system for these customers, it is important to know what the coverage area needs to be for the service and what the cost model is for the different areas.

If people want to work from home on a regular basis, three primary things need to be taken into account. First, outages will have a significant impact on the day-to-day work of those people, so the service they use must be reliable. Second, they will need high-speed access because the speed of the connection will affect their day-to-day productivity, and they will typically be doing tasks that require higher bandwidth and/or faster response time. Finally, the economics are different from the occasional or short-time user. A person who is working from home is typically using the remote access service for 8 to 10 hours a day. Per minute charges add up rapidly under this usage profile, so always-on connections may be cheaper.

Often, people within the company may want to use a high-bandwidth Internet connection that they have access to at a conference or at home. This situation is particularly common in technical companies and often requires a very different technology from what is used to meet the requirements described earlier. It requires encryption between the person's computer and the corporate network because company-confidential information is being transmitted over the public Internet and can be intercepted. Transmission of information unencrypted over the Internet may also be considered publication of the information in legal terms, which causes the company to lose intellectual property rights. In addition, transmitting passwords unencrypted over the Internet is a sure way to get broken into. Typically, the server side of this encrypted connection is part of the corporate firewall. The encryption mechanism needs to provide access to everything that the person needs on the corporate network, be reliable, and have reasonably high throughput.

The service also needs to cater to people who need to access the network from another company's site, such as support engineers or consultants working at a customer site. This scenario introduces the added complexity of combining the policies, security, and practical issues of two, possibly unrelated, sites. These people usually are not in a position to be demanding of the customer, so they need to be able to work with whatever restrictions are in place rather than try to change the security policies or the firewall rules. Typically, bringing an always-on line of some description to the person's desk at the customer site is not an acceptable solution for either company's security team, because the person needs access to both networks and may inadvertently bridge them together. Sometimes, adding an analog line to the person's desk is acceptable but not usually. The usual method involves building an encrypted channel between the person's machine and the company firewall, crossing the customer's firewall and the Internet. This means that you need to provide a remote access mechanism that is likely to be permitted to pass through most firewalls, as they typically are configured, and that is not too difficult to add to firewalls that don't already permit it.[1] It also needs to be flexible enough that the person can access everything needed on the corporate network. That often is not as easy as it may sound, because some applications use protocols that are difficult to tunnel across some of the encryption mechanisms that meet the other requirements. Some compromises may have to be made between the various requirements to find products that will work. Ideally, this situation should be able to use the same software as was selected for the high-bandwidth, no-firewall situation described earlier, but that may not be the case. Supporting these people with remote access is often the most difficult challenge, especially because each customer site will have different security policies that must be followed or risk an embarassing situation.

Because of all the different requirements that remote access services may be expected to meet, they normally are composed of several components, each of which supports one or more of the groups of people described.

27.1.2 Policy for Remote Access

Before starting to provide a remote access service, the company must define a policy for remote access. The policy should define acceptable use of the service, the security policies surrounding the service, and the responsibilities attached to having access to the service. The policy should also state who gets what kind of remote access and who pays for it. Section 11.1.2 discusses the remote access policy and other security policies in more detail.

27.1.3 Definition of Service Levels

It is important to clearly define the service levels for the various remote access services in consultation with the customers of those services. Remote access can be a sensitive area because failures are discovered by people who want to do some work and are unable to do anything until service is restored. This is frustrating for them and can cause the problems to have a high visibility. If the service levels are clearly defined, communicated, and understood before problems arise, the customers should know what to expect for an estimated time to repair (ETR), which should reduce tension and frustration levels.

A lone SA at a small site should negotiate service levels that permit her to get some sleep in order to function properly during the day. Large

---

1. A new protocol is not too difficult to add if it uses only one TCP port and doesn't have security issues for the client side, such as permitting tunneling back to the client network across established connections.

organizations with a 24/7 helpdesk should have more customer-oriented service levels. The helpdesk staff should be trained on the remote access service and when to escalate problems. New services that are in a trial phase should have lower service levels because the helpdesk staff will not be fully trained, and only a few senior SAs will be familiar with the trial service. However, customers of the trial service should have a backup access method. Services that are being phased out and used by only a few people are also candidates for lower service levels, because new staff may not be trained on old technologies.

Choose Customers for Trial Services Carefully

Several years ago, a software company was introducing an ISDN-based higher-speed remote access service. The first stage of this project was to determine what equipment to use for the corporate side and the home side of the connection, testing reliability, compatibility, feature sets, and scalability. A couple of possibilities for each end of the connection had been identified and needed to be tested. The network team planned to use only a few SAs for the initial tests, so the SAs could help with the debugging. However, several people in engineering demanded the service, saying that they would build it themselves if the SA team did not deliver it quickly. The director of the SA team explained to engineering that the service would be available shortly, because initial trials were beginning. The engineering directors identified some engineers who were working from home and desperately needed higher-speed access and asked that they be included in the trial. The SA team had to agree to ensure that the engineers did not build their own service. The network team made it clear to the engineers who participated in the trial that this was not yet a service and that outages could potentially last for several days, so they were not to rely on it and must have a backup access method. However, it was not long before one of the engineers on the trial program had a problem with his ISDN connection and quickly escalated it through his management chain so that it became a top-priority trouble ticket, requiring SAs to pay attention to it rather than to many tickets relating to supported services. He was not an appropriate trial customer, because he became reliant on the higher-speed instantly and was not tolerant of outages or willing to revert to the old dial-in access method.

The root of the problem was that the ISDN investigation project was not funded until the engineers were already clamoring for it, which was more than a year after the budget request had been made by the network architect who had foreseen the need. At that stage, it was impossible to restrict the trial team to appropriate people, which led to lots of stress and frustration for both the SAs and the engineers.

Major bandwidth increases are addictive. Reverting to the old system is not an option after using a faster one, no matter how clear the SAs try to be about the service levels that can be expected of the prototype service.

A new service must have passed the initial prototyping phase, and at least the customer-side equipment must be determined, before early adopters are given access to the system; otherwise, it is a recipe for disaster. Try to squeeze important projects like this into the budget before they become political disaster areas, even if they are not officially funded.

27.1.4 Centralization

Remote access is an area that benefits from centralization. From a security standpoint, the authentication component of the remote access service must be centralized to ensure proper auditing and access control. From a cost standpoint, new technologies are emerging all the time, and the research costs for how best to implement and support a new technology are high and so should not be duplicated across the company. Also, significant economies of scale can be achieved in concentrating all the usage onto centralized equipment and lines. The ultimate form of centralization is to outsource the remote access service.

27.1.5 Outsourcing

The best way to deal with the continually changing technologies in the remote access area is to get someone else to do it. It is a losing battle to try to keep evaluating new technologies and figuring out how to scale and support them, only to replace everything within a year or two with newer technology.

Several remote access outsourcing companies, usually ISPs, can take on at least some aspects of a company's remote access service. One way they can do it is by installing VPN software on the customers' machines, with the customers dialing into the ISP's normal modem pools or other connection options, and using a VPN to connect to the corporate network. Another is through the use of virtual circuits that set up security filters and route customers' traffic based on the customers' authenticated identities. The customers usually use modem pools dedicated to this service offering from the ISP and dedicated connections from the ISP back to the company.

A more immediate benefit of outsourcing remote access is that the time spent supporting it is dramatically reduced. The cost becomes a visible, predictable number that can be in the budget rather than a hidden, unquantifiable, variable number. A predictable charge is good for cost management and budgeting. From the SA's point of view, outsourcing remote access means fewer support calls out of business hours and not having to track down the errant broken modem that is preventing customers from dialing in. Some outsourcing services may deal with all remote access issues; others may deal with everything except the VPN software, for example. Anyone who has had to support a modem pool will appreciate that getting someone else to do it is desirable.

The economies of scale mean that it is easier and more cost-effective for the outsourcing company to evaluate new technologies and how to support them. It is part of their core business, so evaluation projects will be funded.

Some aspects of remote access should not be outsourced. In particular, the authentication database should be maintained within the company so that it can be incorporated into the exit process for departing employees and contractors, can be audited, and can be used to handle sensitive terminations discreetly at short notice.

When a company decides to outsource any part of the computing environment, the SAs must choose the outsourcing vendor carefully. The vendors should be evaluated on the following criteria:

- *Coverage area.* The outsourcing company should cover at least the areas that the customer base needs, which includes both employees' homes and the areas to which people are likely to travel. It is best to find an outsourcing company with global coverage and an option to select and pay for smaller coverage areas. You can expand to larger coverage areas when necessary. An area can be considered to be fully covered if any connection to the remote access service within that area is charged at local rates or is free of charge to the caller, other than the remote access provider's charges. It may be less cost-effective to outsource if you require only a small coverage area.

- *Supported technologies.* Evaluating the outsourcing companies also involves looking at what technologies they support and their rate of technology adoption. If they don't keep up with new technologies, the problem of customers' building their own faster remote access system will raise its head.

- *First-level support.* Does the outsourcing company provide first-level support, or does it provide support only through escalation from the SA staff? Although problems that may be related to misconfiguration of the customers' machines could be solved by internal SA staff, they will not be as familiar with a service that was not built in-house and will not have access to all the relevant parts of the system for debugging problems. The extra level of indirection also costs time in resolving the customer's problem.

- *Service-level agreement.* It is important to get and evaluate a written SLA before selecting an outsourcing vendor. What do the response times look like? What nonperformance clauses are there? How can you track the vendor's performance? What speed and latency is typical, what is guaranteed?

- *Billing structure.* What is the cost model and the billing structure for the service? Ideally, all costs should be incorporated into the outsourcing company's charges so that the company and the employees do not have to deal with filing and processing expense reports for remote access. Understand what all the costs are and how they differ across service areas. Check whether it is possible to maintain for the outsourcing vendor a database that maps users to departments that the outsourcing company will then use to bill each department separately or at least provide a cost breakdown for the company.

- *Authentication interface.* Check what mechanisms the vendor supports for authentication. The vendor should support a few standard authentication and authorization protocols so that the SAs can choose an appropriate protocol for use with their authentication scheme. The vendor must have a facility for the authentication and authorization database to be managed by the customer company.

- *Security.* The security team at the company still has responsibility for the site's overall security, which includes the outsourced remote access system. The security staff must liaise with the outsourcing company to ensure that appropriate security is maintained within the remote access architecture, perhaps by implementing something at the corporate site that works in conjunction with authentication information passed along by the outsourcing vendor. Find out what its security architecture is and the options available before selecting the outsourcing company.

- *End-to-end bandwidth.* Be sure that you have enough bandwidth to the access point. Many times, we have seen network bottlenecks at the service provider or where they connect to the network. Estimate the peak number of users, how much bandwidth each might use, and multiply. If you outsource the dial-up component, make sure that your fixed line to the dial-up provider is big enough to handle expected user loads; if you provide access via the Internet using VPNs, ensure that you have enough bandwidth to handle this traffic on top of the rest of normal traffic. Also verify that any equipment that will terminate VPN connections has the CPU capacity to handle the peak number of connections. Encryption is CPU insensitive.

Take the time to do the vendor evaluation thoroughly and to make the decision carefully. It is difficult to change remote access vendors if it doesn't work out, because it involves changing configurations, and perhaps software, on everyone's machines, as well as ordering new lines to all the places that had permanent connections to this vendor and giving everyone the new information they need to carry with them when traveling.

27.1.6 Authentication

The authentication and authorization system is one component that always should be built and maintained in-house, even if everything else is outsourced. All remote access methods should use the same authentication database to reduce administrative overhead and the chances that one of the databases might be overlooked when disabling employees' access after they leave. There can be many interfaces into that database through different protocols, if necessary.

The authentication mechanism should use one of the many available one-time password, or token-based, systems. It should not be based on reusable passwords. Small companies may have to start with a simple password-based system for cost reasons, but they should budget for switching to a more secure system as soon as they can.

27.1.7 Perimeter Security

The remote access service is part of the company's perimeter, even if it is outsourced to another company. If the company bases some of its security around having a secure perimeter, that perimeter must be maintained. Remote access services can breach the perimeter security through misconfiguration of some of the components. In particular, hosts or networking equipment can be configured for dynamic routing with no restrictions on what traffic they route or what routes they propagate. This can result in the remote access service's providing a back door into the network.

Restrict Traffic and Routing Across Remote Access Links

A married couple worked in the computer industry, at one point, for direct competitors. Both companies used perimeter security models. Both companies installed a high-bandwidth remote access service to their employees' homes. The couple had a home network in the house with some shared resources, such as a printer. The networking equipment from each of the companies was not restricted in what traffic it would route or what routes it would propagate. Each company ended up with a full routing table for the other company. Company A used the same DNS table inside and outside the company, which resulted in company B's mail servers sending all mail for company A across the couple's home network directly to the internal mail server. The problem was spotted and traced only when one company noticed that the mail headers were not quite right.

The companies should have restricted what routes could get into their network tables and should have installed at least minimal security on these connections that restricted traffic to go to and from only the one authorized host on that connection. These measures would prevent the accidental connection of two networks but not deliberate break-in attempts. More complex security measures and policies are needed to fully secure these remote access connections.

27.2 The Icing

There are a few ways to improve on a remote access service once it is up and running. For people who work from home on a regular basis, consider their other business needs beyond simple network access. Look at ways to reduce costs and automate some of the cost-analysis components. For SAs who are providing remote access services, there are some ways to keep up with new technologies without making remote access support a complete nightmare.

27.2.1 Home Office

Remote access is only part of a complete teleworking solution. Working from home inevitably involves more than simply establishing network connectivity. Frequently, the SA team is called on for solutions to other problems.

One problem that directly affects the SA team is the issue of who provides the home office equipment, who supports it, and to what level. Support that requires a visit to someone's home to install new equipment or fix broken equipment is very expensive to provide. The SLA must be very specific on these issues, and if that level of support is provided, there must be a model for recovering those support costs from the home employee's department.

The other issues that inevitably arise are that the employees working from home need to make business calls, send and receive faxes, print, photocopy, and initiate and participate in conference calls. Depending on their jobs, they may want to be able to be connected to the network, on the telephone, and still able to receive a fax. They also don't want to have to go through their phone bills and expense back all the business calls every month. The company may want to consider remote access services that include telephony or to simply install additional phone lines that are billed back to the company. If the lines can't be billed directly to the company, the time employees spend on filing expense reports for their individual bills can be a large hidden cost; the cost is not simply employee time but also in the customer frustration the service may generate. The SA team should bear these requirements in mind when deciding on the home office remote access solution and be ready to provide a solution for the customers.

The other issue that arises for people who work from home is that they feel that they are losing touch with what is happening at the company because they are not involved in corridor conversations or group meetings or lunches. Look for ways to break down the distance barrier and make casual communication easier. Some common solutions include one-on-one video-conference systems and equipping all conference rooms with the ability to broadcast presentations over the network.

27.2.2 Cost Analysis and Reduction

Remote access costs can accumulate quickly, and they are typically hidden from those who incur them. Once the remote access system is operational, look at ways to reduce the costs without adversely affecting the service. Most remote access services provide toll-free numbers for people to call, which have high charges for the company. Providing local dial-up numbers in a high-volume area and converting people to that number can reduce costs.[2] Also, look at the people who use the service the most (from a fixed location) and see whether an always-on connection to that location is possible and would prove more cost-effective. Automate as much of this process as possible, including a notification mechanism for people who are using the toll-free number when they could use a local number instead.

---

2. This is particularly applicable in countries that have free local calling or even flat-rate local calls but is not so useful in countries that charge per minute for local calls. Avoid this approach if it will lead to people expensing their dial-up costs.

Case Study: Reducing Costs by Billing Analysis

Lucent was able to significantly reduce the cost of its dial-in service by using some interesting techniques. The system provided modem pools in areas that were highly populated by employees, so that the calls would be local and therefore toll-free. People who were not local to a modem pool expensed portions of their phone bills, which was time consuming for employees, expensive to process for Lucent, and wasteful because the individual's per minute charges were often higher than Lucent could negotiate with phone companies. The use of a toll-free (1-800) phone number greatly reduced the expense-report process and saved costs. The 800 number was sophisticated enough to direct the call to the nearest modem pool and to route around modem pools that were low on capacity. The toll-free number was so convenient that sometimes people used it even though there was a local number that was less costly to the company.

A system was created that detected the phone number of the incoming call and dynamically generated a sign-on banner that would alert the caller to the phone number the person should call instead. If the user had dialed in via the most cost-effective phone number, the normal banner would be displayed. Billing records were examined, and employees not dialing the most cost-effective dial-in numbers received email once a month, explaining how much money they would have saved the company if they had dialed the right number.

When VPNs were first being introduced, billing records were used to identify which users could be supported for less money if they used a VPN service over an always-on Internet technology, such as cable modems and xDSL. People whose conversions would save the company the most money (the top 10 percent) were actively sought out to be some of the first customers for this new service. From time to time, billing records were again examined to identify new candidates.

27.2.3 New Technologies

SAs who have to build and support remote access services are faced with the problem of trying to keep up with new technologies and deciding which ones to implement. The SAs then need to support all the new and old technologies simultaneously, which leads to ever-increasing support costs. Traditional modems have a benefit in this area, in that they are backward-compatible. It is possible to upgrade the company modem pool to the latest, fastest technology and still support all the people who have older modems. Other remote access technologies do not have this benefit.

Introducing a new technology increases the support costs significantly until that technology has been widely adopted and is well understood. Supporting old technologies also has a high cost: The equipment becomes less reliable, and SAs are less familiar with the system when only a few people use it.

The key to keeping support costs under control is to avoid the high support costs at the end of the curve, when an old technology is still in use by only a few people. Do this by supporting at most two technologies, in addition to traditional modem dial-in access. When a new technology is going to be deployed, aggressively phase out the older of the two existing technologies by converting those people to a newer technology and having a hard cutover date when the old service will be discontinued.

27.3 Conclusion

Supporting a remote access service can be a very time-consuming and thankless task. Technology moves rapidly, and your customers want to move with it, but you may not be funded for it at the right time. Understand the requirements before attempting to build a remote access service; they may be many and varied. Define a remote access policy that customers must agree to before they have access to the service. Agree on and communicate service levels for the various components of the service.

The remote access service benefits from centralization because of the rate of technological change. It is a good area to outsource to benefit from the economies of scale and large coverage areas that an outsourcing vendor can achieve. The major benefit of outsourcing is that it relieves the SA team from the burden of maintaining a modem pool and debugging remote access problems. Keep control of the authentication and authorization components of the remote access service, however, and pay attention to the security of the service, particularly if your site relies on perimeter security.

Improve the remote access service by solving some of the other home office issues before they even arise. Find ways to reduce costs, and automate as much of that as possible. When faced with the challenge of supporting a remote access service, control the support costs by limiting the number of technologies in use.

Exercises

1. What technologies does your remote access service support? Which of these is the most expensive to support, and why?

2. What is the next access technology you will adopt? Describe what will be involved in adopting it.

3. What is your site's remote access policy? How is it advertised to the customers?

4. What requirements does your remote access system have to meet?

5. Follow a new hire through the process of procuring remote access services from your organization. Watch, but don't help, the person find out what is available, sign up for the service, complete the installation, and become functional. What should be improved about the process to make it a more pleasant experience for the customer?

6. How would you provide remote access for employees who are at a customer's site? What compromises would you need to make?

7. What are your site's service levels for the various areas of your remote access system?

8. If you do not outsource any of your remote access, what would the cost of outsourcing it be? How does that compare with the cost of supporting it in-house? What would the benefits be? What would the disadvantages be?

9. If you are outsourcing some of your remote access, how did you decide what parts to outsource, and how did you determine the vendor?

10. What authentication mechanism do you use for your remote access service?

11. How many authentication databases are there in your system?

12. What security controls are on your remote access service?

13. How many people in your company work from home on a regular basis? What is the support model for the equipment in their homes? What services does the company provide beyond simple network connectivity?

14. If you were to design a remote access service to support people who work from home within a reasonable distance of the main office, what support model would you choose? What technology would you use, and why? How would you support your customers' additional needs, such as phones and faxes? How would your answer change if the people were 2,000 miles away from the nearest office?

15. How could you reduce the costs of your remote access service?

Chapter 28

Software Depot Service

A software depot is a way of making a large number of software packages available to many hosts. UNIX has a tradition of a globally accessible `/usr/local/bin` that is shared among all hosts in a cluster. Windows sites have a different tradition involving a repository of installable packages.

UNIX is known for providing a large number of tools to do various tasks. However, this number seems small compared with the number of tools that are available for free via the Internet. Selecting and installing these tools is a huge responsibility. Replicating these tools to dozens, hundreds, or thousands of machines is impossible without automation. If a software depot is not provided, nontechnical customers will simply lack these tools and will not reach their full productivity; technical customers will install these tools themselves, most likely duplicating the work of others doing the same. Either way, customers will lose productivity if the SAs do not provide this service.

A good software depot makes the most anemic operating system rich and useful. It can become easy for customers to take the benefits for granted.

We Forget How Bare Vendor Installations Can Be

On a mailing list, a Solaris user asked how she could download a web page to disk in a shell script. One reply stated that it was a shame that she wasn't using Linux, because she would then have access to a great program called `wget` (Niksic 1998). Tom was surprised because he had `wget` on every machine of every UNIX and UNIX-like OS to which he had access. He had forgotten that not everyone's UNIX environment included a rich software depot that tracked all the latest software. If your software depot is rich and widely distributed to all machines, customers will forget that it isn't part of the vendor's OS. This incident made Tom realize that much of the attractiveness of Linux distributions is that they include such a rich collection of tools without requiring a full-time software depot maintainer, unlike Solaris. It was a luxury he'd always had

---

> and therefore had taken for granted. (*Note:* Solaris has greatly improved in this area recently.)
>
> Conversely, although this reduces the barrier to entry, it makes future upgrades more difficult. Upgrading to a new release of any of those packages requires work on each and every machine, because they are not accessing a repository shared over a network. Sites that have adopted Linux have had to refine or rewrite their software depot systems in response, maintaining a depot of Linux packages and automating the controlled introduction of such packages to all machines.

Historically, Windows and Unix depots tend to be very different. Windows depots tend to be repositories of software to be installed, and Unix depots tend to be repositories of software used in real time from the depot.

Unix software often is delivered in source form with an installation process that is much more complicated than the average customer could follow. Even commercial Unix software can be equally difficult to install. The installation of Unix software often requires root access, something that Unix users don't tend to have. In Unix environments, therefore, it is wise to have one person or a team of people build packages and distribute them to all hosts, often keeping hundreds or thousands of hosts in sync. This centralization leverages expertise. Often, Unix software is not installed on the local machine but is simply made available on a file server, such that one may mount the depot at a particular directory—for example, /sw or /opt/net—and add the location to your $PATH—for example, /sw/bin or /opt/net/bin—and use the software right off the server. Such a system can be exported read-only so that clients cannot accidentally or maliciously modify the contents.

Windows software depots usually take one of three forms. One form is a **network disk** that includes certain software packages specifically written to run off a network disk. The first execution of such software installs the necessary local files and registry settings. Another form is some kind of **network-based software push system**, such as Microsoft's System Management Service (MS-SMS), which lets centralized administrators push packages to all machines. The last form that this takes is the **distribution-server model:** A repository of software packages—usually, .ZIP files—is made available to the local community for manual installation.

The technical difference is that Unix software generally can be installed on the network disk, and then all clients that mount that disk can use the software. Windows systems generally do not use this model, because registry settings must be set by an installer program before the application will work.

For the purposes of this chapter, *Windows software depot* means the distribution-server model, whether the installation files are accessed via the web or a network share. Running software off a network disk is similar to Unix software depots and such systems as MS-SMS (discussed in Chapter 3).

Software depots often are thought of as something found in corporate or university general-purpose computing platform environments rather than, for example, e-commerce sites that need to tightly control which software is on which hosts. Although the number of software packages may not be as large in e-commerce environments, important principles, such as consistency and leverage, still apply.

28.1   The Basics

We begin by understanding the business justifications and technical requirements of software depots. Then we discuss the policies and documentation you should create. With those foundations, we follow the process of selecting from the many preexisting software depot management packages and then design simple software depot systems for both Unix and Windows systems. The system we design fulfills our requirements and requires very little programming.

28.1.1   Understand the Justification

A software depot is a customer service that finds, installs, and maintains a library of software. Considerable cost savings can be achieved by reducing duplication of effort through using a software depot.

A depot saves people from searching for the software on the Internet, provides a simple cache that saves network bandwidth, and consolidates software purchases. (Section 21.2.1 describes the economic benefits and ramifications of volume software purchasing.)

Without a depot, customers and fellow SAs will waste a lot of time searching for software on the Internet, in catalogs, and other places. The depot provides a single place for customers to look for software. Without a depot, software will be installed in many places around the network. The people who maintain software depots are librarians. They cull through new software and select what they feel their customers will need. They also take requests.

If one person has requested a package, there is a good chance that other people will find such software useful, too. Self-supporting subcommunities may spring up around certain packages.

Depots leverage software installation expertise. Compiling and installing software can be difficult, something that experienced SAs may forget after doing it so often.

SAs who maintain packages should always be watching for and installing new versions of a package as they are released. Bug fixes, especially security-related bug fixes, are particularly important to look for. Maintaining a centralized depot ensures that all customers have access to the updated release if a push model is used.

The consistency that comes from having the same software on all hosts benefits SAs and customers alike. SAs benefit because their effort is leveraged to all hosts. Customers benefit because all machines that access the depot become somewhat interchangeable. Customers can select hosts based on their hardware differences, such as speed, memory, and so on, rather than which software packages are available.

Small sites often believe that they don't need a software depot. We assert that all machines need a consistent layout for storage of software; otherwise, the inconsistencies will create a rat's nest of confusion. Although they may not need a complicated depot system, a consistent layout and process is important as small sites grow into larger sites. Small sites should be on the lookout for signs that they are growing and would soon benefit from a more complicated software depot. Some warning signs are that you find yourself micromanaging your software library, duplicating the build process unnecessarily, and having an inconsistent set of software packages on your machines.

28.1.2 Understand the Technical Expectations

A software depot must be based on the requirements of the people who use it. Get an understanding of what customers want from a depot. Their needs could be narrow or broad, constrained by management or legal requirements, or not limited at all. Customers may also have need to have multiple versions of a key tool, such as a compiler, available simultaneously while they cut over to a newer version.

Consider the reliability requirements. If the files are stored locally, there is less concern, because local files tend to be available if the machine is available. If the files are on a remote file server, network and server reliability and scaling are factors. If the depot is more like an FTP server that is accessed occasionally, customers will be more tolerant of outages. If you need even higher levels of reliability, consider using replication or RAID techniques, as described in Section 25.1.1.2, to increase the chance that the depot will be available.

28.1.3 Set the Policy

There needs to be a policy that describes who can contribute software packages to the depot. It can be dangerous to permit anyone to provide software that everyone will run. Someone could install a Trojan horse, a malicious program with the same name as some other program. Or someone who is not aware of all the customer requirements might upgrade a tool and inadvertently create compatibility problems. The policy should address the following questions.

- Who may build and install packages? There might be one or more people who do this as their full-time job. Maybe all SAs can create packages, but one person does a quality-control check and installs the package. Maybe certain customers are able to update certain packages, but the initial installation must be gated by an SA.

- What happens if the maintainer leaves the organization? If particular packages are maintained by a particular person, the policy should specify what to do if that person leaves.

- Which OSs are supported? Is there a depot for each OS in use, or only a few? In UNIX, it is possible to have one depot for all OSs and to use **wrapper scripts** to work around system differences. A wrapper script is a batch file that discovers what platform it is running on and calls the appropriate binary. Usually, the binaries have been renamed so that the wrapper script can have the name that customers expect to type. Wrappers can set environment variables, verify that configuration files exist, and so on. Alternatively, if there is a depot for each OS, are packages expected to run on all releases of that OS, or are wrappers used when different binaries are required even for different versions within that OS?

- If you do use wrappers, is there a standard wrapper or template that everyone should adopt?

- How are upgrades handled? When there is a new release of a package, who is responsible for installing it?

- How are bugs handled? Is the maintainer expected to try to debug open source packages, or are customers simply told to report the bug to the maintainers and wait for the next release?

- How are packages deleted from the depot? Many sites have a strict deletion policy. Packages may be deleted as the official development environment progresses to newer tools, or packages may stay around forever, simply depending on the fact that only popular packages are carried forward to the new depot created for the next release of the OS.

- What is the scope of distribution? Is this depot for a cluster, a department, or an entire enterprise?

- How do customers request that packages be added to the depot? Is there a depot committee that decides these things?

The policy must be advertised and published, preferably where customers will see it.

❖ **Tracking Licenses**   Section 12.1.5 contains two low-effort techniques for tracking software licenses.

28.1.4 Select Depot Software

For UNIX systems, we recommend selecting an existing depot management system rather than writing one from scratch. Even if you feel that your environment is particularly special, customizing an existing package is easier than inventing a new one. Many free software depot packages are available. Depot (Colyer and Wong 1992) is one of the seminal software packages to administer software depots. Many other packages are available, such as LUDE (Dagenais et al. 1993), Modules (Furlani and Osel 1996), and SEPP (Oetiker 1998b). GNU Stow (Glickstein 1996) is a useful tool for managing UNIX symbolic links in a depot.

For our definition of a Windows software depot, there are also choices. You can make a network directory share an FTP server or a web site that provides the software. Section 28.1.6.2 describes how the questions of organization and documentation of the Windows depot can be addressed in the architecture of the depot system.

Your company may already have a legacy repository system. In that case, decide whether it would be better to augment the existing system or to deploy an entirely new one.

28.1.5 Create the Process Manual

No matter what software you choose, it is important to document the local procedure for injecting new software packages into the system. Although the documentation that comes with the package manager is useful, this document should include local specifics, such as the names of the hosts that control the system and so on.

After people have used this documentation to inject a couple of packages, it can be useful to create a shorter quick guide that summarizes the steps without much explanation as to why they are doing each step. This document simply helps the experienced SA not to forget any steps. The SA should be able to cut and paste command lines from this document into a shell so that the process goes quickly.

28.1.6 Examples

28.1.6.1 UNIX

We now describe a simple yet powerful software depot for UNIX. It can be used on a single system, as well as a medium-size distributed network. It can be extrapolated for large networks with a little automation.[1] In our example, the packages we are installing are various versions of the programming language `perl` and the mail reader `mutt`.

Packages are built on a particular server for each OS being supported. It is important to document which build machines are used so that the process can be repeated exactly. This makes it easier to track down problems, especially strange library issues that pop up now and then.

The source code for each package is stored in `/home/src`, with a subdirectory for each package. Inside the subdirectory are the `tar` files for all the versions of the package that are currently supported, along with the untarred source code where the builds are performed. For example, `/home/src/perl` might contain `perl-6.0.tar.gz` and `perl-6.1.tar.gz`, as well as appropriate subdirectories. In multi-OS environments, another subdirectory level may separate the copies of source code compiled for each OS, though some packages use the `VPATH` facility in `make` to permit one copy of the source to be used when building for multiple OSs.

Also in `/home/src` is a script named `SOURCEME`, which is sourced to set up the build environment properly. If a special environment is required for a particular package, a `SOURCEME` file specific to those requirements is stored

---

1. We would like to specifically recommend against installing third-party software directly in `/bin` or `/usr/bin`, as other books and articles have recommended. It is too difficult to track changes when you are modifying the vendor-provided namespace.

within the package subdirectory: for example, /home/src/perl/SOURCEME or /home/src/perl/SOURCEME-6.1. Creating such a file is a small time investment that promotes institutional learning, results in less reinventing of wheels, and leaves a paper trail for future SAs who must repeat the process. The large effort to build the first release of a package is leveraged when the newer releases arrive.

Packages are installed in directories that encode the name of the package and its release number. For example, /sw/perl-6.0 would contain a bin, man, and lib directory of Perl 6.0. Other packages might be stored in /sw/perl-6.1, /sw/mutt-1.2.6, and /sw/mutt-2.0.1. This enables the SAs to satisfy a requirement to maintain multiple versions simultaneously.

The name of the package without a version number is a link to the latest supported release of that package. For example, /sw/perl would be a symbolic link pointing to /sw/perl-6.1. This means that to specifically use the older, 6.0, release of perl, you would include /sw/perl-6.0/bin in your PATH.[2] However, to go with the flow and use the latest stable release of Perl, you would include /sw/perl/bin in your PATH.

New packages can be installed and tested before they are released to the general public by simply not updating the generic (/sw/perl) symbolic link until that release is ready for public use. For example, if Perl 6.1 is in common use and Perl 7.0 has just been released, this new release would be installed in /sw/perl-7.0. Testers could include /sw/perl-7.0/bin in the front of their PATH. After they certify the new release, the /sw/perl symbolic link is adjusted to point to the 7.0 directory. Because of the way symbolic links work, processes currently accessing the older version will usually continue to operate without trouble, because the old version isn't removed. Instead, only new invocations of the software will see the new package.

If you used the system as described so far, each user's PATH would be very long and difficult to manage if there were many packages. To solve this, create a directory called /sw/default/bin that includes symbolic links to all the most popular programs. Now, typical depot users need to add only this one directory to their PATH to access the typical software. For example, /sw/default/bin/perl would be a link to /sw/perl/bin/perl. Similar links

---

2. You should also include /sw/perl-6.0/man in your MANPATH. In the future, any time we suggest adding something to your PATH, we will assume that the appropriate man directory is added to your MANPATH.

would be included for other parts of the Perl package, such as a2p, s2p, and perldoc. Note that these links would be relative to /sw/perl rather than /sw/perl-6.1 because /sw/default/bin should refer to what most people commonly need, not specific versions. Also, if a new version of Perl were installed, it would be a bother to have to update all the links in /sw/default/bin. Someone who wants access to the entire package can add the package's bin directory to the PATH.

Guessing at the popular programs in a package can be hit or miss, but without automation, it is easier to guess than to create links for every item in a package. A little automation can help here by making it just as easy to link to all the files in the package rather than to what the SAs think the typical customer will want. A program such as GNU Stow (Glickstein 1996) can be used to manage the symbolic links. Stow is easy to use and always generates the minimal number of symbolic links such that it becomes just as easy to generate symbolic links for all the binaries in bin, as well as man pages, libraries, and other files.

So far, what we've described works for a single host. For a network of hosts, we want to give clients access to the same software. We can do this by copying the packages to the appropriate machines, or we can provide access over the network, possibly via NFS. We can use the automounter to make the /sw of other servers appear on the clients.

Assuming that bester is the file server that supports the Solaris 8.0 hosts, the automounter map of /sw for Solaris 8.0 might look like this:

```
default        bester:/sw/default
perl-6.0       bester:/sw/perl-6.0
perl-6.1       bester:/sw/perl-6.1
perl           bester:/sw/perl-6.1
mutt-1.2.5     bester:/sw/mutt-1.2.5
mutt-1.2.6     bester:/sw/mutt-1.2.6
mutt-2.0.1     bester:/sw/mutt-2.0.1
mutt           bester:/sw/mutt-2.0.1
```

When Solaris 9.0 is introduced into the environment, the automounter map for Solaris 9.0 systems is created by copying the map from 8.0. However, not all packages compiled for Solaris 8.0 are binary compatible for Solaris 9.0. Specific packages that require recompilation can point to those new binaries. In our example, mutt is binary compatible across Solaris 8.0 and 9.0, but Perl requires recompilation. Supposing that our Solaris 9.0 server is named `lyta`, our 9.0 map would look like this:

```
default       lyta:/sw/default
perl-6.1      lyta:/sw/perl-6.1
perl          lyta:/sw/perl-6.1
mutt-1.2.5    bester:/sw/mutt-1.2.5
mutt-1.2.6    bester:/sw/mutt-1.2.6
mutt-2.0.1    bester:/sw/mutt-2.0.1
mutt          bester:/sw/mutt-2.0.1
```

Note that `perl-6.0` is missing. This is to demonstrate that obsolete packages are not brought forward to new OS unless specifically requested.

You can adapt a couple of policies to support older OSs. Obviously, a new package should be built for the latest OS. However, if it requires special recompilation for older OSs, you can end up spending a lot of time and effort to support only a few legacy hosts. You might decide that the current and one previous release of an OS will have actively maintained depots. The depots for older OS releases are frozen in time, except possibly for security-related fixes. This means that host `bester` can't be decommissioned until it is the last Solaris 8.0 host. Alternatively, the data can be copied to any NFS server, and, after a simple adjustment to the automounter map, `bester` can be decommissioned.

Additional OSs can be handled the same way: one tree per OS and an additional automounter map configured on the clients. These new depots usually will start out nearly empty because it is rare that any package can be reused for a completely different OS.

The reliability requirements gathered for your depot often can be implemented using automounter features. Replication can be handled by using the more sophisticated automounter syntax options that let you specify multiple servers. In fact, some automounter implementations permit maps to make decisions based on which OS the client uses. In that case, one supermap can be created that does the right thing, depending on what OS is in use and which servers are up.

Managing symbolic links and the many automounter maps can be a hassle. Even if a new package is binary compatible across many OS releases, many automounter maps must be updated. Odd problems can appear if the maps get out of sync. Humans aren't very good at keeping such things in sync, but computers are. Therefore, it can be useful to automate this process to reduce mistakes and hassle. Create a master file that describes the various packages, versions, OSs, and servers. Use this master file to generate the automounter maps and the GNU Stow commands that need to be run. A program such as make can automate all the preceding so that you have to edit only the master file and type make. (Many system administrators don't think of using make to automate tasks. However, it can be extremely useful whenever one has a series of tasks that depend on one another.)

Following our example, we introduce talia, a server that is redundant for lyta in that it provides the same software on a different host. The master file might look like this:

```
default        sol80          bester         /sw/default
default        sol90          lyta,talia     /sw/default
perl-6.0       sol80          bester         /sw/perl-6.0
perl-6.1       sol80          bester         /sw/perl-6.1
perl           sol80          bester         /sw/perl-6.1
perl-6.1       sol90          lyta,talia     /sw/perl-6.1
perl           sol90          lyta,talia     /sw/perl-6.1
mutt-1.2.5     sol80,sol90    bester         /sw/mutt-1.2.5
mutt-1.2.6     sol80,sol90    bester         /sw/mutt-1.2.6
mutt-2.0.1     sol80,sol90    bester         /sw/mutt-2.0.1
mutt           sol80,sol90    bester         /sw/mutt-2.0.1
```

Using such a master file requires defining a standard way of specifying OSs. In our example, we defined sol80 and sol90 to mean Solaris 8.0 and Solaris 9.0, respectively. Some companies have created complicated codes to specify an exact vendor, processor, OS, and OS release 4-tuple, but we recommend that you keep it simple and use codes that you understand.

Deleting packages is as easy as removing the directory from the server and deleting the appropriate lines from the master file. A more conservative approach might be to rename the directory on the server so that it cannot be accessed. It is prudent to not delete the files for a week or so. If someone complains that the package is missing during that time, it can be added back easily. (Of course, the removal should be announced to your customers, using whatever method is appropriate for your site.)

The system as described has the potential to infinitely increase in disk utilization until it exhausts all available disk space. However, we find that the system manages disk space on its own. Now and then, new OSs are adopted that are incompatible enough that none of the previous packages can be carried over into the new automounter map. Rather than rebuilding every single package for the new OS, usually only the critical and popular packages get rebuilt. Eventually, the legacy OSs are eliminated from the environment, eliminating older, unused packages. As long as this happens, the system is relatively self-limiting in its disk consumption.

Control over who can add packages in this system is based on the UNIX permissions of the files and directories involved. Obviously, all these packages should be read-only for all nonprivileged users. In fact, you should NFS export the packages as read-only when possible.

If customers would like to be able to maintain software in this tree, it is best to have them hand the software to an SA who installs it. This ensures that the installation media has been archived in a central place. If the software is distributed in source code form, this prevents the situation in which the only person with the source code leaves the company.

It can be useful to provide an area where customers can install software on their own to share with others. This delegates work away from the SAs, which is always a good thing. The additional control given to the package owner means that he can provide rapid updates. Without this ability, sharing of such software often will involve customers including other customers' `bin` directories in their `PATH`s. That generally isn't safe practice. Given the system as described so far, we can extend it to permit this kind of customer-initiated software. You can create a `/sw/contrib` directory that is writeable by any user ID, possibly only from a particular host. Customers can create subdirectories in this area for packages they wish to install. A couple of rules should be put into place to ensure some reasonable security. Obviously, if anyone installs virulent software, it can be traced to the source, because that person owns the files that were installed in `/sw/contrib`. That is usually enough incentive to be careful selecting what is installed. The person who owns the files should be responsible for supporting the package.

It would be unreasonable to expect the SAs to support a homegrown package in `/sw/contrib`. Another precaution is to forbid people from including `/sw/contrib` directories in their `PATH`. Sadly, this can be enforced only through education and peer pressure. Rather than directly adding such packages to their `PATH`s, people should create symbolic links from `$HOME/bin` to the specific program in `/sw/contrib` that they need to access. Although this isn't perfect, it balances convenience with safety. You should document the policies related to the `/sw/contrib` directory in a file named `/sw/contrib/POLICY`, or at least use that file to direct people to a web page that explains the policy.

One advantage of the system we've described is that it doesn't require the use of wrappers. We've seen well-written wrappers and poorly written wrappers, and, in our experience, we'd prefer to see no wrappers at all. Wrappers sometimes have strange effects on programs that react badly to being renamed, take options in a strange format, and so on. In UNIX, a wrapper that starts with `#!/sw/bin/perl` will not work if `/sw/bin/perl` is itself a shell script—first line starts with `#!/bin/sh`. Of course, there surely will be an extreme case in which wrapper is still needed. You might put all wrappers in a special area, such as `/sw/wrappers/bin`, or they can be directly installed in `/sw/default/bin`. Some feel it is more pure to have only symbolic links in `/sw/default/bin`; others feel that symbolic links and wrappers can share that space.

These wrappers might set environment variables and then call the program in the package's `bin` directory, or they may do a lot more. If you have a highly technical customer base, a sufficient wrapper might simply print out instructions on how to set the environment so that the program they are trying to run is accessible.

Wrappers can be a slippery slope. If you use a wrapper to avoid creating an automounter map for a new OS release, suddenly there may be many more wrappers to maintain. It's better to invest a little time to make it easy to create new automounter maps than to start creating wrappers.

This system can grow quite large by adding packages, replicating the various packages onto additional servers, and creating new automounter maps for new OSs. As it grows, it makes sense to automate these processes, especially replication.

In this section, we have described a simple yet powerful software depot for UNIX. It leverages off preexisting elements, such as the UNIX permission system, automounter, and NFS. It is self-documenting—the master file and file system layout describe the system itself. It is simple enough to be sufficient for a single host or a small cluster, and it has a clear path to growing to larger, even global, systems.

28.1.6.2 Windows

Windows environments historically have more self-administered hosts than UNIX environments do. The traditional Windows software depot is more akin to an FTP server or a file server directory that contains installable packages—.ZIP files or self-installing .EXEs—of software that can be installed by the PCs' users.

Environments differ in their policies regarding self-installed software. Some completely forbid it, others permit only approved software to be installed, and others allow users to install whatever they want on their PCs. A software depot should reflect this policy.

Here is an example of a simple software depot that would be suitable for an environment in which certain products are approved for all systems, but others have special installation prohibitions and controls. In this depot, a "share" is created on a Windows (CIFS) file server named `software`. The users would access it as `\\server1\software`. Within it, they would find a document named `POLICY` explaining the general policy toward user-installed software on PCs and specific policies related to particular software packages. For example, it might explain how to acquire licensed software. There would also be a series of directories, as follows:

- *Standard.* This directory contains software that has been approved for all machines but not installed by default on newly delivered PCs. This is the first place people would check when they want to see whether a piece of software is available in the depot. Site-licensed software might be appropriate here.

- *Preinstalled.* This contains software that should already be installed when PCs are delivered and/or is updated automatically via MS-SMS. Although redundant, it is useful to have the preinstalled software available for reinstallation or for installation on machines that escaped the regular PC deployment process. Example software found here would include site-licensed software, such as WinZip, virus scanners, and office suites.

- *Disk images.* This directory contains images of CD-ROMs and DVDs that have been licensed or whose license permits free distribution. For example, images of BSD and Linux distributions belong here. The benefit of providing these images here is that it saves bandwidth at your Internet gateway.

- *Experimental.* This is for software packages that are not yet approved but are being considered for approval. This directory might be password protected or may have a restrictive access control list (ACL), so that only evaluators are able to access the contents.

- *Admin.* In here are tools that only SAs should access, or more important, software that is specially licensed. This should be a password- or

ACL-restricted directory that only the SAs can access. The directory structure inside this area may include standard, preinstalled, disk images, and experimental directories. One way of handling licensing issues is to require that software without site licenses be installed by an SA or someone trusted to follow all the license procedures. For example, the person might verify that the software license was acquired for this particular host before it is installed. If software is prepurchased in bulk, as described in Section 21.2.1, the SA might simply record this installation as consuming one of the prepurchased licenses.

Each directory may contain subdirectories for various flavors of Windows where version-specific packages are stored. There may be a directory named Obsolete where old packages that are no longer supported are moved. Although such old packages shouldn't be needed any more, emergencies do occasionally arise in which having the old packages around is beneficial. It's a balance of risk management versus disk space.

It is useful to create a directory for each package rather than having a single directory full of packages. Package names are not always understandable to the casual observer, whereas directory names can be very specific: `FooSoft Accounting Client 4.0` is more clear than `FSAC40.ZIP`. Most packages include a separate `README` file, which should be in that directory. If packages are all stored in one directory, there is a good chance that the names of the `README`s will conflict.

For every directory, it is useful to create a document by the same name—with the addition of `.txt`, of course—that includes notes about the software, what the license restrictions are, and whether there are any special installation tricks or tips. You should adopt a standard format for the first part of the file, with free-form text following.

If the software depot is extremely successful, you might choose to replicate it in various parts of the company. This can save network bandwidth, improve installation speed, and offer more reliability. The point at which such replication becomes useful is much different from that with the UNIX depot. Windows software depots are relatively light on networks compared with the network activity required for a UNIX depot that accesses the network for every execution of a program. A Windows software depot is also less real time than UNIX depots, because installation happens once, and the server is not accessed again. An occasional slow install is painful but not a showstopper. However, slow NFS access to a UNIX depot can destroy productivity.

For these reasons, you may choose not to replicate a Windows software depot but instead simply locate it somewhere with excellent network connectivity.

In this section, we have described a simple yet powerful software depot for a Windows environment. It takes into account the unique culture of Windows systems with respect to software installation. It requires no software, unless replication is required, at which time one of many fine directory replication systems can be used. It leverages the access controls of Windows' CIFS file access protocol to restrict access as needed. It is self-documenting, because the directory hierarchy describes what software is available, and local installation notes and policy documents can be colocated with the packages for easy access.

28.2 The Icing

Although the purpose of a software depot is to provide the same software to all hosts, the icing is to be able to provide customizations for various hosts. Here, we include suggestions for handling a few frequently requested customizations: slightly different configurations, locally replicated packages, commercially licensed software, and smaller depots for OSs that do not receive full support.

28.2.1 Different Configurations for Different Hosts

A commonly requested feature of UNIX software depots is the ability to have slightly different configurations for certain hosts or clusters of hosts. If a package's configuration must vary wildly from host to host, it may be useful to have the configuration file in the depot simply be a symbolic link to a local file. For example, `/sw/megasoft/lib/megasoft.conf` might be a symbolic link to `/etc/megasoft.conf`, which could contain specific contents for that particular host.

If you might want to choose from a couple of different standard configurations, they could be included in the packages. For example, `/etc/megasoft.conf` might itself be a symbolic link to one of many configuration files in `/sw/megasoft/lib`. You might have standard server and client configurations (`megasoft.conf-server` and `megasoft.conf-client`) or configurations for particular customer groups (`megasoft.conf-mktg`, `megasoft.conf-eng`, `megasoft.conf-dev`, and `megasoft.conf-default`). Because the series of symbolic links bounce from the depot to the local disk and back to the depot, they are often referred to as bounce links.

28.2.2 Local Replication

If your UNIX depot is accessed over the network, it can be good to have commonly used packages replicated on the local disk. For example, a developer's workstation that has disk capacity to spare could store the most recent edition of the development tools locally. Local replication reduces network utilization and improves performance. You should make sure that access to a local disk is faster than access to a network file server, which is not always the case. The problem becomes managing which machines have which packages stored locally, so that updates can be managed.

Depot management software should make all this easy. It should provide statistics to help select which packages should be cached or at least permit SAs and customers to indicate which packages should be replicated locally. In our UNIX example, if a sophisticated automounter is used, it can specify that for a particular machine, a package can be found on a local disk.

New releases of packages require special handling when local replication is being performed manually. In some systems, a new, uncached release overrides the local copy. If the intention was that customers always see the most recent release of a package, the right thing would happen, though performance would suffer if nobody remembered to copy the new release to this machine's local disk. It's better to have the right thing happen slowly than the wrong thing happen with excellent performance. On the other hand, if someone directly changed the master copy of a package without changing the release number, the SA must remember to also update any copies of the package that may be on other clients. This can become a management nightmare if tracking all these local copies is done manually.

Replicating software depot files locally may have impact on backup policies. Either the backup system will need to be tuned to avoid backing up the local repositories, which, after all, can be restored via the depot management software, or you have to plan on handling additional data storage requirements. The benefit of backing up the locally replicated software is that full restore reflects the true last state of the machine, software and all.

The general solution to this is to use an NFS cache, whereby files accessed via NFS are cached to the local disk. NFS caches, such as Solaris's `cachefs`, work best on read-only data, such as a software depot. Such a system has a huge potential for performance improvement. Most important, it is adaptive, automatically caching what is used rather than requiring SAs to manually try to determine what should be cached and when. It is a set-it-and-forget-it system.

28.2.3 Commercial Software in the Depot

Including commercial software in the depot is as difficult as the software's license is complex. If there is a site license, the software packages can be included in the depot like anything else. If the software automatically contacts a particular license server, which in turn makes a licensed/not licensed decision, the software can be made available to everyone because it will be useless to anyone not authorized.

If, however, software may be accessed only by particular customers, and the software doesn't include a mechanism for verifying that the customer is authorized, it is the SA's responsibility to make sure that the license is enforced.

In our Windows depot example, we discussed gating licensed software installation by requiring SAs to perform the installation. A UNIX environment has additional options. If the software is licensed for all users of a particular host, the software can be installed on that host only. You should install it in the usual depot nomenclature, if possible. (In other words, depot management software shouldn't panic when it detects locally installed software in its namespace.) Alternatively, a UNIX group can be created for people who are authorized to use the software, and key files in the package can be made executable only by members of that group.

UNIX environments often face a situation in which various small groups all use the same software package, but a different license server must be accessed for each group.[3] This is another problem that can be solved using the bounce-link technique to point different clients to different license files.

Having complex requirements for software distribution is a common problem (Hemmerich 2000). It is an area that people are continually trying to improve. Before trying to solve the problem yourself, look at the past work in conference proceedings and journals for inspiration. Someone may have solved your exact problem already.

28.2.4 Second-Class Citizens

Software depots also need to handle off-beat OSs that may exist on the network. These hosts, often referred to as second-class-citizens, are OSs that do

---

3. We recommend centralizing license servers, but we include this example because we often find that for political reasons, they are not centralized.

not receive the full support prescribed for first-class citizens (see Section 3.1) but exist on your network and require minimal support. The support that second-class citizens receive might simply be the allocation of an IP address and a few other simple configuration parameters to get the device up and running.

The software depot required for second-class-citizen OSs tends to be minimal: applications required for the special purpose of that machine, possibly compilers, and the tools required by the SAs. We explicitly recommend against trying to provide every package available in the full depots. It would be a huge effort for little gain.

It is important to have a written policy on second-class-citizen OSs. Indicate the level of support to be expected and areas in which customers are expected to provide their own support. The policy for a small software depot should specify a minimal set of packages customers should expect to find in the depot.

We recommend a few groups of tools that should be included in a small depot. Install the tools needed for the purpose of the machine. For example, if this machine is for porting software to that OS, install the appropriate compiler tool chain. If the host is for running a particular application or service, install the required software for that. The tools required for SA processes—automated and otherwise—should also be installed. These include inventory collectors, log rotators, backups, software depot updates, debugging tools, and so on. Finally, every company has a short list of convenience tools that can be provided for your own benefit, including the command line version of the corporate phone number lookup software, minimal email ("send only") configurations, and so on.

❖ **A Tool Chain**   A *developer's tool chain* is the specific software required to build software. In some environments, this might involve software from various vendors or sources. This usually includes build tools, such as `make` and `autoconf`, compilers, assemblers, linkers, interpreters, debuggers, source code control systems, such as SubVersion, CVS, Perforce, ClearCase, and SourceSafe, and various homegrown utilities that are involved in the development process. The term *chain* refers to the fact that one tool often leads to the next, such as the compile/ assemble/link sequence.

28.3 Conclusion

In this chapter, we have discussed software depots. Software depots are an organized way of providing software packages to many hosts, though having a good organization is useful even for a single host. A good software depot provides a ubiquitous set of tools that become as much a part of the culture of your customers as the network itself.

Windows systems usually handle software depots differently for historical, technical, and cultural reasons. Windows depots tend to be repositories of software to be installed; UNIX depots, repositories of software used in real time from the depot.

Sites should have a written policy regarding various depot issues: how and by whom packages get installed, what systems receive the services of the depot, how requests and support issues are handled, and so on.

We described simple depots for both UNIX and Windows environments, showing that policy and organization are key and that an extremely powerful depot can be created with very little software. There are many open source packages for maintaining depots, and thus we recommend against creating one from scratch. Find one that you like, and modify it to suit your needs.

Although the purpose of a software depot is to provide the same software to many hosts, you eventually will receive requests to have customizations for particular hosts or groups of hosts. We discussed the most common kinds of requests and some simple solutions.

Exercises

1. Describe the software depot used in your environment, its benefits, and its deficiencies. If you do not have a depot, describe where software is installed and the pros and cons of adopting one.

2. What are the policies for your software depot? If you do not have any policies or do not have a depot, develop a set of policies for a depot at your site. Justify the policy decisions made in your depot policy.

3. In the UNIX example (Section 28.1.6), what happens to `perl` modules and other add-on packages? How would you handle this situation?

4. Compare your software depot to one of the samples described in this chapter. How is it better or worse?

5. A good software depot management system might also track usage. How might usage statistics be used to better manage the depot?

6. If you are at a small site that does not require a complicated software depot, describe what kind of simple software depot you do have. At what point will you have grown to require a more complicated depot? What might that look like? How will you convert to this new system?

7. Develop a set of codes for each of the OSs and the various versions of each OS in use at your location akin to what was used in Section 28.1.6. Explain and justify your decisions.

Chapter 29

Web Services

Managing web systems has become such a large and important part of system administration that specific techniques and specialities have developed outside of simply loading Apache or IIS and providing content. In theory, we have already covered all the material required to run a web service or web-based application successfully. Simply buy server hardware, install the right services, put it on a fast network, with carefully considered namespaces in a data center, document everything, create a solid disaster-recovery plan, be mindful of the security issues, debug problems as they happen, adhere to strict change-management controls, upgrade it as required using a good maintenance window strategy, monitor it for problems and capacity planning, provide plenty of data storage, and make sure that you have a good data backup and restore system. It's all right there in Chapters 4–10, 11, 15, 17, 18, 20, 22, 25 and 26. However, some specific techniques and issues are still underserved by those chapters.

A web site is a way of presenting information and applications to users using a client/server model. Web content is usually accessed by a client program called a **browser** but can be accessed by any program that speaks HTTP. The web server delivers documents called **pages**, formatted in HTML, as well as any content specified in the HTML page, such as embedded graphics, audio files, and so on. Sometimes, the content includes programs written in languages, such as JavaScript, that will be run by the client browser.

The web is based on open standards, which means that they are developed by an international committee, not a single corporation. They can be used without paying royalty or licensing fees. Web standards are defined by the World Wide Web Consortium (W3C), and the underlying Internet protocols are defined by the IETF.

The benefit of web-based applications is that one browser can access many web applications. The web browser is a **universal client**.

Web applications and small web servers are also present in firmware in many devices, such as small routers and switches, smart drive arrays, and network components.

> ❖ **The Power of Open Standards**   Imagine if instead of using open standards, one company set the standards and charged royalties to use them on a web site or in a browser. The web would never have been as successful. In fact, one attempt at just such a thing was attempted shortly before the web was becoming popular: Network Notes was a collaboration of AT&T, Lotus, and Novell. One could use only the Novell/Lotus software and only the AT&T network and could communicate only with other people using Network Notes.
>
>   People weren't willing to pay money for the software, because there were no sites to visit; nobody was willing to build a site, because nobody had the software to access it. The vendors weren't willing to give the software away for free, because they had to recoup their development costs.
>
>   Even if the service had become popular, innovation would have been stifled in other ways. Without the ability for vendors to make their own client software, nobody would be able to experiment with building browsers for other devices. Cellphone-based browsing might never have happened.
>
>   This is relevant because even with the success of the Internet, companies continually bullheadedly repeat these mistakes. There are continual attempts to extend web browsers in ways that lock customers in; rather, they are locking potential customers out.

29.1 The Basics

In this section, we explain the building blocks that make up web service, the typical architectures used, and the measures needed to provide service that is secure, scalable, monitored, and easy to manage.

29.1.1 Web Service Building Blocks

A **uniform resource locator** (URL) is the address of information on the web. A URL consists of a host name, and the path to the resource, for example, http://www.EverythingSysadmin.com/.

A **web server** receives HTTP requests and replies with data. Some typical web server software packages are Apache HTTP, AOLServer, and Microsoft IIS.

The reply is usually a static file. However, the reply is sometimes generated on demand, using the Common Gateway Interface (CGI). The generated, or dynamic, content is often the result of a database query. There are two variations of CGI scripts: GET and POST. GET takes inputs—values assigned to variable names—and uses them to read a result. For example, http://google.com/finance?q=aapl is a GET request. POST takes inputs and uses them to do some mutation, such as update a shopping cart, post to a blog, or delete a file.

POST does not put the input in the URL but inside the HTTP request itself. Therefore, the input can be much longer, as it does not have to abide by the length limits of URLs.

The important point here is that GET is read-only and that POST is an update. When it crawls the web to build its search corpus, a search engine does not follow POSTs. There are famous cases in which programmers accidentally made an application in which a DELETE button was a GET instead of a POST; every time a web crawler found that site, all the data was deleted.

Other technologies for dynamically generated web pages include in-line interpreted code using such systems as PHP (www.php.net) and Microsoft's Active Server Pages. An otherwise normal HTML web page is stored on the server, but embedded in it are special instructions that the web server interprets prior to serving the page. An instruction might be to perform a database query and turn the results into a table. What the user sees is a web page with a dynamically generated table in the middle.

The **web client** receives the page, interprets it, and displays it for the user. The web browser is a **universal client**. Previously, every server application required the deployment of specific client software, which stalled progress. What makes the web revolutionary is that new services can be created without requiring new client software.

The browser interprets and displays the page that was served. HTML is interpreted and displayed. Sometimes, an embedded language is included and is interpreted on the client, such as ECMAScript, commonly known as JavaScript. Other file formats require interpretation, such a photo formats, video, audio, and so on.

AJAX is not a protocol but a technique for creating interactive web pages. They are often as interactive as traditional PC applications. The server is contacted only at appropriate times for updates and major state transitions, which reduces server load and improves responsiveness. The term refers to its two building blocks: asynchronous JavaScript and XML. The user interface is implemented mostly in JavaScript, which is able to asynchronously contact the server for additional information as required rather than wait for a user to click a SUBMIT button, as in HTTP GET and POST operations.

Web clients exist outside of computers and are now in mobile phones, televisions, and kiosks. Even home appliances configure themselves by using HTTP to draw a configuration file from a central server, or using HTTP POST requests to connect to the manufacturer to request service.

In 2007, nearly 1 billion people in the world access the Internet exclusively from mobile phones. Millions have never seen the Internet used from a computer.

Many data formats are used on the web. A web server generally outputs web pages, multimedia files, or errors.

Web pages are generally in HTML or an HTML derivative, such as XHTML, DHTML, XML, and so on. Some of these formats are old and discouraged; others are new and evolving. Multimedia files include pictures, audio, and video. New multimedia formats arise all the time. Usually, data cannot be used until the last byte is received, though web browsers do an excellent job of displaying partial results as data is received to make the viewing experience feel faster. However, some multimedia uses **streaming** formats, which are intended to be displayed in real time and provide pause, rewind, and fast-forward features. Streaming is particularly important for live audio and video. It wouldn't make sense to download a day's worth of live radio content and then listen to it after it has completely downloaded. With an audio streaming format, live radio can be listened to live.

Many special-purpose formats exist and are often built on top of other formats. XML is an excellent format for making other formats, or **microformats.** One popular microformat is an **RSS feed,** a format that lists a table of contents of a resource, such as a blog or news site. Wiki sites (see Chapter 9) often present a list of the most recently modified pages as an RSS feed. Special RSS-reading software scans many RSS feeds and displays new content to the user.

HTTP requests that fail have a standard set of error and status codes. Their meaning is usually not important to users but is very important to SAs. The codes are three-digit numbers. The first digit is 1, for informational; 2 indicates success, 3 indicates redirection, and 4 indicates an error. Following are the most common codes:

- *200* (OK); request completed
- *301* (Moved permanently); Implication: We wish you'd remember the new URL and go there directly next time
- *302* (Redirect to specified URL)
- *307* (Redirect to specified URL as a temporary measure)
- *401* (Please try again with authentication)
- *403* (Unauthorized, wrong password, or other issue)
- *404* (No such page found)

SAs often need to know these error codes to debug problems or to provide better service. For example, when debugging authentication problems, it is important to know that a page that requires authentication is generally first requested without authentication and the browser receives code 401. The page is then rerequested with authentication information attached: for example, username and password. Error 404, page not found, is important because although one still receives a page, it is an error message, not to be confused with a true web page. This error page can be customized.

29.1.2 The Webmaster Role

The webmaster is the person who manages the content of a web site, much as an editor manages the content of a newspaper. She is responsbile for setting web site policy. This role is often confused with the web system administrator, who sets up the server, software, and so on. A webmaster is involved in content; a web system administrator maintains the technical machinery—physical and virtual—that makes up the web site.

This confusion is understandable because at small sites, the same person may do both jobs, but even large sites confuse the two roles when management is not technical. Reenforce the difference by clearly explaining it to managers in terms that they understand, putting the two roles in different departments or two different budgets.

For SAs who find themselves forced into webmaster duties, we make the following recommendation. Focus on enabling people to do their own updates. Create the structure, but use software that makes the web site self-service.

If you are required to update web pages, get agreement on a policy so that such requests are not a surprise. There are plenty of stories about SAs being ready to leave for the weekend when surprised with a request to make a series of updates that will take hours. Set up an SLA specifying that changes must be requested a certain number of hours or days in advance or outlining a schedule, with major updates on Monday, minor updates done with 8 hours, and a process for handling emergency requests, for example. If at all possible, be involved in the processes that lead to changes to the web site so that there are fewer surprises. More examples are listed in Section 29.1.8.2.

29.1.3 Service-Level Agreements

Like any other service, a web service needs an SLA and monitoring to ensure compliance. Many customers are used to thinking of the web as a 24/7 critical service, but the SLA of an individual web service might be quite different. Most internal web services will have the same SLA as other office services, such as printing or storage.

If in doubt about the appropriate SLA for a web service, ask the customer group using it. Ideally, as with any SLA, the service level should be set by collaborating with the customer community. We suggest that you resist setting any SLA that does not allow for periodic maintenance, unless the service is built out on redundant infrastructure. If the service is provided by a single host or a shared web host and is required to be available around the clock, it is time to have a discussion about increasing the redundancy of the service.

Metrics that are part of a web SLA should include the latency for a certain level of queries per second (QPS). That is, how long should a typical query take when the system is under a particular load? Latency is usually measured as the time between receipt of the first byte of the request and sending of the last byte of the answer.

29.1.4 Web Service Architectures

Different types of content require different serving infrastructures. A single web server serving an unchanging document has different needs from a page serving dynamic pages. Web servers that will be accessible from the Internet rather than only within an organization require particular attention to security.

29.1.4.1 Static Web Server
A static web server is one that serves only documents that don't change or change rarely. The documents are static in that they are read directly

from disk and are not altered in the process of being delivered by the web server. The documents themselves are normal documents of any type, such as web pages, images, word-processing documents, images, spreadsheets, and so on.

The documents are served out of the **document root**. If it is a shared volume, subdirectories with appropriate permissions can be created for various customer groups. Each group is then able to publish information simply by creating and updating files. Web pages can be edited with normal office applications or with special-purpose web editing packages available for most desktop systems.

At high QPS rates, it is important that such a server have enough RAM to cache the most commonly requested files.

29.1.4.2 CGI Servers

CGI servers generate pages dynamically as described before. Because a large amount of work is done for each page, these servers often cannot serve as many pages per second as a static server can.

At high QPS rates, such a server must have enough CPU resources to keep up with demand. The software may also have other dependencies, such as RAM and network.

29.1.4.3 Database-Driven Web Sites

One of the most common types of web application is accessing and modifying information in a database. Examples of database-driven web applications are updating your preferences on a social-networking site, online shopping catalogs, or choosing which classes you want to take next semester. Web applications are replacing paper forms and allowing people to interact directly with a database.

Database-driven web sites create a template for a particular type of data rather than individual web pages. For example, a web-based bookstore does not need to create a web page for every book it sells. Instead, its catalog is stored in a database, and any particular item can be displayed by filling in the template with information from the database. The information may come from multiple sources, with pricing and availability coming from separate databases, for example. To make a global format change, one simply updates the template.

Imagine if a menu had to be changed and required every page on the site to be manually edited. The site would be unmanagable. Yet we are continually surprised to find web sites that started out manually updating every page and have not yet migrated to a database-driven system. As the SA, it is your job to encourage such sites to move to a database-driven model as early as possible.

At QPS-second rates, such a server must be scaled like any database, with the usual database performance-tuning tools that are available.

29.1.4.4 Multimedia Servers

A multimedia server is primarily a web server that has content that includes media files, such as video or audio. Media files are often very large and sometimes are accessed through some type of special client or browser to comply with digital rights management. When serving media files, the underlying data storage and network bandwidth capabilities become more important.

Media servers provide **streaming-media** support. Typically, streaming media is simply using a web application on the server to deliver the media file using a protocol other than HTTP, so that it can be viewed in real time. The server delivers a data stream to a special-purpose application. For example, you might listen to an Internet radio station with a custom player or a proprietary audio client. Often, one purpose of a media server application is to enforce copy protection or rights management. Another purpose is to control the delivery rate for the connection so that the data is displayed at the right speed, if the web site does not allow the end user to simply download the media file. The application will usually buffer a few seconds of data so that it can compensate for delays. Streaming-media servers also provide fast-forward and rewind functions.

When operating a media server that is transmitting many simultaneous streams, it is important to consider the playback speed of the type of media you are serving when choosing the storage and network capabilities. In Chapter 25, we mention some characteristics of storage arrays that are optimized for dealing with very large files that are seldom updated. Consider memory and network bandwidth in particular, since complete download of a file can take a great deal of memory and other system resources.

Streaming-media servers go through great lengths to not overwork the disk. If multiple people are viewing the same stream but started at different times, the system could read the same data repeatedly to provide the service, but you would rather avoid this. Some streaming applications will read an entire media file into memory and track individual connections to it, choosing which bits to send to which open connections. If only one user is streaming a file, keeping it in memory is not efficient, but for multiple users, it is.

With this method, performance is superior to reading it from disk but can require a lot of memory. Fortunately, there are alternatives.

Other implementations read in a fixed amount of the media file for each connection, sending the appropriate bits out. This can be very efficient, as most operating systems are good at caching data in memory. An hour-long video clip may be several gigabytes in size. But the entire file does not need to be in system memory at once, only the several megabytes that the application is sending next to each open connection. Customers who connected within a short time of one another will see good response, as their segments will still be cached and won't need to be read from disk. This approach gives quick response owing to cache hits but allows more efficient resource use.

For any kind of streaming-media server, CPU speed is also an issue. Sometimes, an audio or video file is stored at high quality and is reencoded at a lower resolution on demand, depending on the needs of the user requesting it. Doing this in real time is a very expensive operation, requiring large amounts of CPU time. In many cases, special-purpose hardware cards are used to perform the processing, leaving the CPU less loaded and better able to do the remaining work of moving the data off the disk, through the card, and onto the network.

> ❖ **LAMP and Other Industry Terms**   Certain technology combinations, or platforms, are common enough that they have been named. These platforms usually include an OS, a web server, a database, and the programming language used for dynamic content. The most common combination is **LAMP:** Linux, Apache, MySQL, and Perl. LAMP can also stand for Linux, Apache, MySQL, and PHP; and for Linux, Apache, MySQL, and Python.
>
> The benefit of naming a particular platform is that confusion is reduced when everyone can use one word to mean the same thing.

29.1.4.5 Multiple Servers on One Host

There are two primary options for offering a separate server without requiring a separate machine. In the first method, the web server can be located on the very same machine but installed in a separate directory and configured to answer on a port other than the usual port 80. If configured on port 8001, for instance, the address of the web server would be http://my.web.site:8001/. On some systems on which high-numbered ports are not restricted to privileged or administrator use, using an alternative port can allow a group to maintain the web server on its own without needing privileged access. This can be very useful for an administrator who wishes to minimize privileged access outside the systems staff. A problem with this approach is that many users will simply forget to include the port number and become confused when the web site they see is not what they expected.

Another option for locating multiple web sites on the same machine *without* using alternative ports is to have multiple network interfaces, each with its own IP address. Since network services on a machine can be bound to individual IP addresses, the sites can be maintained separately. Without adding extra hardware, most operating systems permit one physical network interface to pose as multiple *virtual interfaces* (VIFs), each with its own IP address. Any network services on the machine can be specifically bound to an individual VIF address and thus share the network interface without conflicts. If one defines VIFs such that each internal customer group or department has its own IP address on the shared host, a separate web installation in its own directory can be created for each group.

A side benefit of this approach is that, although it is slightly more work in the beginning, it scales very nicely. Since each group's server is configured separately and runs on its own IP address, individual groups can, be migrated to other machines with very little work if the original host machine becomes overloaded. The IP address is simply disabled on the original machine and enabled on the new host and the web services moved in its entirety, along with any start-up scripts residing in the operating system.

29.1.5 Monitoring

Monitoring your web services lets you find out how well you are scaling, areas for improvement, and whether you are meeting your SLA. Chapter 22 covers most of the material you will need for monitoring web services.

You may wish to add a few web-specific elements to your monitoring. Web server errors are most often related to problems with the site's content and are often valuable for the web development team. Certain errors or patterns of repeating error can be an indication of customer problems with the site's scripts. Other errors may indicate an intrusion attempt. Such scenarios are worth investigating further.

Typically, web servers allow logging of the browser client type and of the URL of the page containing the link followed to your site (the referring URL).

Some web servers may have server-specific information that would be useful as well, such as data on active threads and per thread memory usage. We encourage you to become familiar with any special support for extended monitoring available on your web server platform.

29.1.6 Scaling for Web Services

Mike O'Dell, founder of the first ISP (UUNET) once said, "Scaling is the only problem on the Internet. Everything else is a sub-problem."

If your web server is successful, it will get overloaded by requests. You may have heard the phrase "the slashdot effect" or "they've been slashdotted." The phrase refers to a popular Internet news site with so many readers that any site mentioned in its articles often gets overloaded and fails to keep up with the requests.

There are several methods of scaling. A small organization with basic needs could improve a web server's performance by simply upgrading the CPU, the disks, the memory, and the network connection—individually or in combination.

When multiple machines are involved, the two main types of scaling are *horizontal* and *vertical*. They get their names from web architecture diagrams. When drawing a representation of the web service cluster, the machines added for horizontal scaling tended to be in the same row, or level; for vertical scaling, in groups arranged vertically, as they follow a request flowing through different subsystems.

29.1.6.1 Horizontal Scaling

In **horizontal scaling,** a web server or web service resource is replicated and the load divided among the replicated resources. An example is two web servers with the same content, each getting approximately half the requests.

Incoming requests must be directed to different servers. One way to do this is to use *round-robin* DNS name server records. DNS is configured so that a request for the IP address of a single name (www.example.com) returns multiple IP addresses in a random order. The client typically uses only the first IP address received; thus, the load is balanced among the various replicas.

This method has drawbacks. Some operating systems, or the browsers running in them, cache IP addresses, which defeats the purpose of the round-robin name service. This approach can also be a problem when a server fails, as the name service can continue to provide the nonfunctioning server's address to incoming requests. For planned upgrades and maintenance, the server address is usually temporarily removed from the name service. The name record takes time to expire, and that time is controlled in DNS. For planned maintenance, the expire time can be reduced in advance, so that the deletion takes effect quickly. However, careful use of DNS expire times for planned downtime does not help with unexpected machine outages. It is better to have a way of choosing which server to provide for any given request.

Having a hardware device to be a *load balancer* is a better solution than using DNS. A load balancer sits between the web browser and the servers. The browser connects to the IP address of the load balancer, which forwards the request transparently to one of the replicated servers. The load balancer tracks which servers are down and stops directing traffic to a host until it returns to service. Other refinements, such as routing requests to the least-busy server, can be implemented as well.

Load balancers are often general-purpose protocol and traffic shapers, routing not only HTTP but also other protocol requests, as required. This allows much more flexibility in creating a web services architecture. Almost anything can be load balanced, and it can be an excellent way to improve both performance and reliability.

One of Strata's early web service projects seemed to be going well, but the messaging system component of it was prone to mysterious failures during long system tests. The problem seemed to be related to load balancing the LDAP directory lookups; when direct connects to the LDAP servers were allowed, the problem did not appear. Some careful debugging by the systems staff revealed that the load balancers would time out an idle connection without performing a certain kind of TCP closure operation on the pruned connection. The messaging server application did not reopen a new connection after the old one timed out, because the operating system was not releasing the connection.

Fortunately, one of the SAs on another part of the project was familiar with this behavior and knew of the only two vendors (at the time) whose load-balancing switches implemented a TCP `FIN` when closing down a connection that timed out. The TCP `FIN` packet directs the machine to close the connection rather than wait for it to time out. The SAs changed the hardware, and the architecture worked as designed. Since then, the operating system vendor has fixed its TCP stack to allow closing a connection when in `FIN_WAIT` for a certain time. Similar types of problems will arise in the future as protocols are extended and hardware changes.

29.1.6.2 Vertical Scaling

Another way to scale is to separate out the various kinds of subservices used in creating a web page rather than duplicating a whole machine. Such vertical scaling allows you to create an architecture with finer granularity, to put more resources at the most intensively used stages of page creation. It also keeps different types of requests from competing for resources on the same system.

A good example of this might be a site containing a number of large video clips and an application to fill out a brief survey about a video clip. Reading large video files from the same disk while trying to write many small database updates is not an efficient way to use a system. Most operating systems have caching algorithms that are automatically tuned for one or the other but perform badly when both happen. In this case, all the video clips might be put on a separate web server, perhaps one with a storage array customized for retrieving large files. The rest of the web site would remain on the original server. Now that the large video clips are on a separate server, the original server can handle many more requests.

As you might guess, horizontal and vertical scaling can be combined. The video survey web site might need to add another video clip server before it would need to scale the survey form application.

29.1.6.3 Choosing a Scaling Method

Your site may need horizontal or vertical scaling or some combination of both. To know which you need, classify the various components that are used with your web server according to the resources they use most heavily. Then look at which components compete with one another or whether one component interferes with the function of other components.

A site may include static files, CGI progams, and a database. Static files can range from comparatively small documents to large multimedia files. CGI programs can be memory-intensive or CPU-intensive and can produce large amounts of output. Databases usually require the lion's share of system resources.

Use system diagnostics and logs to see what kinds of resources are being used by these components. In some cases, such as the video survey site, you might choose to move part of the service to another server. Another example is an IS department web server that is also being used to create graphs of system logs. This can be a very CPU-intensive process, so the graphing scripts and the log data can be moved to another machine, leaving the other scripts and data in place.

A nice thing about scaling is that it can be done one piece at a time. You can improve overall performance with each iteration and don't necessarily have to figure out your exact resource profile the first time you attempt it.

It is tempting to optimize many parts at once. We recommend the opposite. Determine the most overloaded component, and separate it out or replicate it. Then, if there is still a problem, repeat the process for the next overloaded component. Doing this one component at a time has better results and makes testing much easier. It can also be easier to obtain budget for incremental improvements than for one large upgrade.

29.1.6.4 Scaling Challenges

Scaling subsystems that rely on a common resource can be a challenge. If the web site contains applications that maintain state, such as which pages of a registration form you have already filled out, that state must be either maintained by the client browser or somehow made available to any of the systems that might handle the next request.

This was a common issue for early load-balancing systems, and Strata remembers implementing a number of cumbersome network topology architectures to work around the problem. Modern load balancers can track virtual sessions between a client and a web server and can route additional traffic from that specific client to the correct web server. The methods for doing so are still being refined further, as many organizations are now hidden behind network address translation (NAT) gateways , or firewalls that make all requests look as though they originate from a single IP address.

CGI programs or scripts that manipulate information often use a local lock file to control access. If multiple servers will be hosting these programs, it is best to modify the CGI program to use a database to store information. Then the database-locking routines can substitute for the lock file.

Scaling database usage can be a challenge. A common scaling method is to buy a faster server, but that works only up to a point, and the price tags get very steep. The best way to scale database-driven sites tends to be to separate the data into read-only views and read-write views. The read-only views can be replicated into additional databases for use in building pages. When frequent write access to a database is required, it is best to structure the database so that the writes occur in different tables. Then one may scale by hosting specific tables on different servers for writing.

Another problem presented by scale is that pages may need to pull data from several sources and use it in unified views. Database-replication products, such as Relational Junction, allow the SA to replicate tables from different types of databases, such as MySQL, Postgres, or Oracle, and combine them into views. We predict increased use of these types of tools as the need for scaling database access increases.

❖ **The Importance of Scaling**   Everyone thinks that scaling isn't important to them, until it is too late. The Florida Election Board web site had very little information on it and therefore very little traffic. During the 2000 U.S. national elections, the site was overloaded by people who thought that they might find something useful there. Since the web site was on the same network as the entire department, the entire department was unable to access the Internet because the connection was overloaded by people trying to find updates.

In summary, here is the general progression of scaling a typical web site that serves static content and dynamic content and includes a database. Initially, these three components are on the same machine. As the workload grows, we typically move each of these functions to a separate machine. As each of these components becomes overloaded, it can be scaled individually. The static content is easy to replicate. Often, many static content servers receive their content from a large, scalable network storage device: NFS server or SAN. The dynamic content servers can be specialized and/or replicated. For example, the dynamic pages related to credit card processing are moved to a dedicated machine; the dynamic pages related to a particular application, such as displaying pages of a catalog, are moved to another dedicated machine. These machines can then each be upgraded or replicated to handle greater loads. The database can be scaled in similar ways: individual databases for specific, related data, each replicated as required to handle the workload.

29.1.7 Web Service Security

Implementing security measures is a vital part of providing web services. Security is a problem because people you don't know are accessing your server. Some people feel that security is not an issue for them, since they do not have confidential documents or access to financial information or similar sensitive data. However, the use of the web server itself and the bandwidth it can access are in fact a valuable commodity to some people.

Intruders often break into hosts to use them for entertainment or money-making purposes. Intruders might not even deface or alter a web site, since doing so would lead quickly to discovery. Instead, the intruders simply use the resources. Common uses of hijacked sites and bandwidth include distributing pirated software ("warez"), generating advertising email ("spam"), launching automated systems to try to compromise other systems, and even competing with other intruders to see who can run the largest farm of machines to launch all the preceding ("bot" farms). (Bot farms are used to perform fee-for-service attacks and are increasingly common.)

Even internal web services should be secured. Although you may trust employees of your organization, there are still several reasons to practice good web security internally.

- Many viruses transmit themselves from machine to machine via email and then compromise internal servers.

- Intranet sites may contain privileged information that requires authentication to view, such as human resources or finance information.

- Most organizations have visitors—temps, contractors, vendors, interviewees—who may be able to access your web site via conference room network ports or with a laptop while on site.

- If your network is compromised, whether by malicious intent or accidentally by a well-meaning person setting up a wireless access point reachable from outside the building, you need to minimize the potential damage that could occur.

- Some web security patches or configuration fixes also protect against accidental denial-of-service attacks that could occur and will make your web server more reliable.

In addition to problems that can be caused on your web server by intrusion attempts, a number of web-based intrusion techniques can reach your customers via their desktop browsers. We talk about these separately after discussing web server security.

New security exploits are frequently discovered and announced, so the most important part of security is staying up to date on new threats. We discuss sources for such information in Chapter 11.

29.1.7.1 Secure Connections and Certificates
Usually, web sites are accessed using unencrypted, plaintext communication. The privacy and authenticity of the transmission can be protected by encrypting the communication, using the HTTP over Secure Sockets Layer (SSL) to encrypt the web traffic.[1] We do this to prevent casual eavesdropping on our customers' web sessions even if they are connecting via a wireless network in

---

1. SSL 4.0 is also known as Transport Layer Security (TLS) 1.0; earlier versions SSL 2.0 and 3.0 predate TLS.

a public place, such as a coffeeshop. URLs using https:// instead of http:// are using SSL encryption.

Implementing HTTPS on a web server is relatively simple, depending on the web server software being deployed. Properly managing the cryptographic certificates is not so easy.

SSL depends on cryptographic certificates, which are strings of bits used in the encryption process. A certificate has two parts: the private half and the public half. The public half can be revealed to anyone. In fact, it is given out to anyone who tries to connect to the server. The private part, however, must be kept secret. If it is leaked to outsiders, they can use it to pretend to be your site. Therefore, one role of the web system administrator is to maintain a repository, or **key escrow**, of certificates for disaster-recovery purposes. Treat this data like other important secrets, such as root or administrator passwords. One technique is to maintain them on a USB key drive in a locked box or safe, with explicit procedures for storing new keys, recovering keys, and so on.

One dangerous place to store the private half is on the web server that is going to be using it. Web servers are generally at a higher exposure risk than others are. Storing an important bit of information on a machine that is most likely to be broken into is a bad idea. However, the web server needs to read the private key to use it. How can this conflict be resolved? Usually, the private key is stored on the machine that needs it in encrypted form. A password is required to read the key. This means that any time a web server that supports SSL is restarted, a human must be present to enter a password.

At high-security sites, one might find it reasonable to have a person available at all hours to enter a password. However, most sites set up various alternatives. The most popular is to store the password obfuscated—encoded so that someone reading over your shoulder couldn't memorize it, such as storing it in base64—in a hidden and unique directory, so an intruder can't find it by guessing the directory name. To retrieve the password, a helper program is run that reads the file and communicates the password to the web server. The program itself is protected so that it cannot be read—to find what directory it refers to and can be executed only by the exact ID that needs to be able to run it. This is riskier than having someone enter the password manually every time, but it is better than nothing.

A cryptographic certificate is created by the web system administrator using software that comes with the encryption package; OpenSSL is one popular system. The certificate is now "self-signed," which means that it is as trustable as your ability to store it securely. When someone connects to the web server using HTTPS, the communication will be encrypted, but the client that connects has no way to know that it has connected to the right machine. Anyone can generate a certificate for any domain. If can be a client tricked into connecting to an intruder instead of to the real server, the client won't know the difference. This is why most web browsers, when connecting to such a web site, display a warning stating that a self-signed certificate is in use.

What's to stop someone pretending to be a big e-commerce site from gathering people's login information by setting up a fake site? The solution is an externally signed cryptographic certificate from a registered certification authority (CA). The public half of the self-signed certificate is encrypted and send to a trusted CA that signs it and returns the signed certificate. The certificate now contains information that clients can use to verify that the certificate has been certified by a higher authority. When it connects to the web site, a client reads the signed certificate and knows that the site's certificate can be as trusted because the CA says that it can be trusted. Through cryptographic techniques beyond what can be explained here, the information required to verify such claims is stored in certificates that come built into the browser so that it does not need to contact the CA for every web site using encryption.

The hierarchy of trust builds from a CA to your signed certificate to the browser, each level vouching for the level below. The hierarchy is a tree and can be extended. It is possible to create your own CA trusted by a central CA. Now you have the ability to sign other people's certificates. This is often done in large companies that choose to manage their own certificates and CAs. However, these certificates are only as trustworthy as the weakest link: you and the higher CA.

Cryptogaphy is a compute-intensive function. A web server that can handle 500 unencrypted queries per second may be able to process only 100 SSL-encrypted queries per second. This is why only rarely do web sites permit HTTPS access to all pages. Hardware SSL accelerators are available to help such web servers scale. Faster CPUs can do faster SSL operations. How fast is fast enough? As long as a server becomes network-bound before it becomes CPU-bound, the encryption is not a limiting factor.

29.1.7.2 Protecting the Web Server Application
A variety of efforts are directed against the web server itself in order to get login access to the machine or administrative access to the service.

Any vulnerabilities present in the operating system can be addressed by standard security methods. Web-specific vulnerabilities can be present in multiple layers of the web server implementation: the HTTP server, modules or plugins that extend the server, and web development frameworks running as programs on the server. We consider this last category to be separate from generic applications on the server, as the web development framework is serving as a system software layer for the web server.

The best way to stay up to date on web server security at those layers is vendor-specific. The various HTTP servers, modules, and web development environments often have active mailing lists or discussion groups and almost always have an announcements-only list for broadcasting security exploits, as well as available upgrades.

Implementing service monitoring can make exploit attempts easier to detect, as unusual log entries are likely to be discovered with automated log reviews. (See Section 5.1.13 and Chapter 22.)

29.1.7.3 Protecting the Content

Some web-intrusion attempts are directed at gaining access to the content or service rather than to the server. There are too many types of web content security exploits to list them all here, and new ones are always being invented. We discuss a few common techniques as an overview.

We strongly recommend that an SA responsible for web content security get specifics on current exploits via Internet security resources, such as those mentioned in Chapter 11. To properly evaluate a server for complex threats is a significant undertaking. Fortunately, open source and commercial packages are available.

- **Directory traversal** is a technique generally used to obtain data that would otherwise be unavailable. The data may be of interest in itself or may be obtained to enable some method of direct intrusion on the machine. This technique generally takes the form of using the directory hierarchy to request files directly, such as `../../../some-file`. When used on a web server that automatically generates a directory index, directory traversal can be used with great efficiency. Most modern web servers protect against this technique by implementing special protections around the document root directory and refusing to serve any directories not explicitly listed by their full pathnames in a configuration file. Older web implementations may be prone to this problem, along with new, lightweight, or experimental web implementations, such as those in equipment firmware. A common variation of this is the CGI query that specifies information to be retrieved, which internally is a filename. A request for `q=maindoc` returns the contents of `/repository/maindoc.data`. If the system does not do proper checking, a user requesting `../paidcontent/prize` is able to gain free but improper access to a file.

- **Form-field corruption** is a technique that uses a site's own web forms, which contain field or variable names that correspond to input of a customer. These names are visible in the source HTML of the web form. The intruder copies a legitimate web form and alters the form fields to gain access to data or services. If the program being invoked by the form is validating input strictly, the intruder may be easily foiled. Unfortunately, intruders can be inventively clever and may think of ways around restrictions.

  For example, suppose that a shopping cart form has a hidden variable that stores the price of the item being purchased. When the customer submits the form, the quantities chosen by the customer are used, with the hidden prices in the form, to compute the checkout total and cause a credit card transaction to be run. An intruder modifying the form could set any prices arbitrarily. There are cases of intruders changing prices to a negative amount and receiving what amounts to a refund for items not purchased.

  This example brings up a good point about form data. Suppose that the intruder changed the price of a $50 item to be only $0.25. A validation program cannot know this in the general case. It is better for the form to store a product's ID and have the system refer to a price database to determine the actual to be charged.

- **SQL injection** is a variant of form-field corruption. In its simplest form, *SQL injection* consists of an intruder's constructing a piece of SQL that will always be interpreted as "true" by a database when appended to a legitimate input field. On data-driven web sites or those with applications powered by a database back end, this technique lets intruders do a wide range of mischief. Depending on the operating system involved, intruders can access privileged data without a password, and can create privileged database or system accounts or even run arbitrary system commands. The intruder can enter entire SQL queries, updates, and deletions! Some database systems include debugging options that permit running arbitrary commands on the operating system.

29.1.7.4 Application Security

The efforts of malicious people can be made less likely to happen. Following are some of the fundamental disciplines to follow when writing web code or extending server capabilities. We highly recommend the work of James Whittaker[2] for further reading in this area.

- **Limit the potential damage.** One of the best protections one can implement is to limit the amount of damage an intruder can do. Suppose that the content and programs are stored on an internal golden master environment and merely copied to the web server when changes are made and tested. An intruder defacing the web site would accomplish very little, as the machine could be easily reimaged with the required information from the untouched internal system.

  If the web server is isolated on a network of its own, with no ability to initiate connections to other machines and internal network resources, the intruder will not be able to use the system as a stepping-stone toward control of other local machines. Necessary connections, such as backups, collecting log information, and installing content upgrades, can be set up so that they are always initiated from within the organization's internal network. Connections from the web server to the inside would be refused.

- **Validate input.** It is crucial to validate the input provided to interactive web applications in order to maximize security. Input should be checked for length, to prevent buffer overflows where executable commands could be deposited into memory. User input, even of the correct length, may hide attempts to run commands or use quote or escape characters.

  Enclosing user input in so-called safe quotes or disallowing certain characters can work in some cases to prevent intrusion but can also cause problems with legitimate data. Filtering out or rejecting characters, such as a single quote mark or a dash, might prevent Patrick O'Brien or Edward Bulwer-Lytton from being registered as users.

  It is better to validate input by inclusion than by exclusion. That is, rather than trying to pick out characters that should be removed, remove all characters that are not in a particular set.

  Even better, adopt programming paradigms that do not reinterpret or re-parse data for you. For example, use binary APIs rather than ASCII, which will be parsed by lower-level systems.

---

2. See www.howtobreaksoftware.com.

- **Automate data access.** Programs that access the database should be as specific as possible. If a web application needs to read data only from the database, have it open the database in a read-only mode or run as a user with read-only access. If your database supports stored procedures— essentially, precompiled queries, develop ones to do what you require, and use them instead of executing SQL input.

  Many databases and/or scripting languages include a *preparation function* that can be used to convert potentially executable input into a form that will not be interpreted by the database and thus will not be able to be subverted into an intrusion attempt.

- **Use permissions and privileges.** Web servers generally interface well with the authentication methods available on the operating system and have options for permissions and privileges local to the web server itself. Use these features to avoid giving any unnecessary privileges to web programs. It is to your advantage to have minimal privileges associated with the running of web programs. The basic security principles of least privileges apply to the web and to web applications, so that any improperly achieved privileges cannot be used as a springboard for compromising the next application or server. Cross-Site Reverse Forgery (XSRF) is a good example of the misuse of permissions and authentication.

- **Use logging.** Logging is an important protection of last resort. After an intrusion attempt, detailed logs will permit more complete diagnostics and recovery. Therefore, smart intruders will attempt to remove log entries related to the intrusion or to truncate or delete the log files entirely. Logs should be stored on other machines or in nonstandard places to make them difficult to tamper with. For example, intruders know about the UNIX /var/log directory and will delete files in it. Many sites have been able to recover from intrusions more easily by simply storing logs outside that directory.

  Another way of storing logs in a nonstandard place is to use network logging. Few web servers support network logging directly, but most can be set to use the operating system's logging facilities. Most OS-level logging includes an option to route logs over the network onto a centralized log host.

29.1.8 Content Management

Earlier, we touched briefly on the fact that it is not a good idea for an SA to get directly involved with content updates. It not only adds to the usually lengthy to-do list of the SA but also creates a bottleneck between the creators of the content and the publishing process. There is a significant difference between saying that "the SA should not do it" and establishing a reliable content-management process. That difference is what we address here by discussing in detail some principles of content management and content delegation.

Many organizations try to merge the roles of system administrator and webmaster or web content manager. Usually, web servers are set up with protections or permissions such that one needs privilaged access to update or change various things. In such cases, it "naturally" becomes the role of the SA to do content updates, even if the first few were just on a "temporary" basis to "get us through this time." An organization that relies on its system staff to handle web updates, other than the IS department's own internal site, is using its resources poorly.

This problem tends to persist and to grow into more of a burden for the SA. Customers who do not learn to deal directly with updating the content on a web site may also resist learning web tools that would allow them to produce HTML output. The SA is then asked to format, as well as to update, the new content for the web site. Requests to create a position for a webmaster or content manager may be brushed aside, as the work is already being done by the SA or systems team. This ensures that the problem stays a problem and removes incentive to fix it.

29.1.8.1 The Web Team

For both internal and external sites, it is very much to an organization's advantage to have web content management firmly attached to the same people who create that content. In most organizations, this will be a sales, marketing, or public relations group. Having a designated *webmaster* does not really solve the problem, even in very small organizations, as the individual webmaster then becomes a scarce resource and a potential bottleneck.

The best approach is to have a *web team* that supplies services to both internal and external sites. Such a team can leverage standards and software to create a uniform approach to web content updates. Team members can train in some of the more specialized web development methods that are used for modern web sites. If your organization is not large enough to support a web team, a good alternative is to have a *web council*, consisting of a webmaster and a representative from each of the major stakeholder groups, including the systems staff. Augmenting the webmaster with a web council reinforces the idea that groups are responsible for their own content, even if the work is done by the webmaster. It also gets people together to share resources and to improve their learning curve. Best of all, this happens without the system staff spending resources on the process.

Will They Really Read It This Weekend?

Many sites have what can be charitably described as a naive urgency regarding getting content updates out on their web sites. One of Strata's friends was stuck for a long time in the uncomfortable position of being the only person with the ability to update the web server's content. At least once a month, sometimes more often, someone from the marketing department cornered this person on the way out of work at the end of the day with an "urgent" update that had to go up on the server ASAP. Since the systems department had not been able to push back on marketing, even to the extent to get it to "save as HTML" from their word processors, this meant a tedious formatting session as well as upload and testing responsibility. Even worse, this usually happened on a Friday and ruined many weekend plans.

If you have not yet been able to make the case to your organization that a webmaster is needed and if you are an SA who has been made responsible for web content updates, the first step to freedom is starting a web council. Although this may seem like adding yet another meeting or series of meetings to your schedule, what you are really doing is adding visibility. The amount of work that you are doing to maintain the web site will become obvious to the group stakeholders on the web council, and you will gain support for creating a dedicated webmaster position. Note that the council members will not necessarily be doing this out of a desire to help you. When you interact with them regularly in the role of webmaster, you are creating demand for more interaction. The best way for them to meet that demand is to hire another person for the webmaster role. Being clear about the depth of specialization required for a good webmaster will help make sure that they don't offer to make you the full-time webmaster instead and hire another SA to do your job.

29.1.8.2 Change Control
Instituting a web council makes attaching domains of responsibility for web site content much easier because the primary "voices" from each group are already working with the webmaster or the SA who is being a temporary webmaster. The web council is the natural owner of the change control process.

This process should have a specific policy on updates, and, ideally, the policy should distinguish three types of alterations that might have different processes associated with them:

1. *Update*, the addition of new material or replacing one version of a document with a newer one

2. *Change*, or altering the structure of the site, such as adding a new directory or redirecting links

3. *Fix*, or correcting document contents or site behavior that does not meet the standards

For instance, the process for making a fix might be that it has to have a trouble ticket or bug report open and that the fix must have passed QA. The process for making an update might be that it has an approval email on file from the web council member of the group requesting the update before it is passed to QA and that QA must approve the update before it is pushed to the site. A similar methodology is used in many engineering scenarios, where items are classified as bug fixes, feature requests, and code (or spec) items.

Policy + Automation = Less Politics

When Tom worked at a small start-up, the issue of pushing updates to the external web site became a big political issue. Marketing wanted to be able to control everything, quality assurance wanted to be able to test things before going live, engineering wanted to it to be secure, and management wanted everyone to stop bickering.

The web site was mostly static content and wouldn't be updated more than once a week. This is what Tom and a coworker set up. First, they set up three web servers:

1. www-draft.example.com: The work area for the web designer, not accessible to the outside world

2. www-qa.example.com: The web site as it would be viewed by quality assurance and anyone proofing a site update, not accessible to the outside world

3. www.example.com: The live web server, visible from the Internet

The web designer edited www-draft directly. When ready, the contents were pushed to www-qa, where people checked it. Once approved, the contents were pushed to the live site.

(*Note*: An earlier version of their system did not include an immutable copy for QA to test. Instead, the web designer simply stopped doing updates while they reviewed the proposed update. Although this system was easier to implement, it didn't prevent last-minute updates from sneaking into the system without testing. This turned out to be a very bad thing.)

Initially, the SAs were involved in pushing the contents, from one step to the next. This put them in the middle of the political bickering. Someone would tell the SAs to push the current QA contents to the live site, then a mistake would be found in the contents, and everyone would blame the SAs. They would be asked to push a single file to the live site to fix a problem, and the QA people would be upset that they hadn't been consulted. Management tried to implement a system whereby the SAs would get signoff on whether the QA contents could be copied to the live site, but everyone wanted signoff, and it was a disaster: the next time the site was to be pushed, not everyone was around to do the signoff, and marketing went ballistic, blaming the SA team for not doing the push fast enough. The SA team needed an escape.

The solution was to create a list of people allowed to move data from which systems and the automation to make the functions self-service to take the SAs out of the loop. Small programs were created to push data to each stage, and permissions were set using the UNIX sudo command so that only the appropriate people could execute the particular commands.

Soon, the SAs had extricated themselves from the entire process. Yes, the web site got messed up. Yes, the first time marketing used its emergency-only power to push from draft directly to live, it was, well, the last time it ever used that command. But over time everyone learned to be careful.

But most important, the process was automated in a way that removed the SAs from the updates and the politics.

29.1.9 Building the Manageable Generic Web Server

SAs are often asked to set up a web server from scratch without being given any specific information on how the server will be used. We have put together some sample questions that will help define the request. A similar list could be made available for all web server setup requests. It's useful to have some questions that a nontechnical customer can usually answer right away rather than deferring the whole list to someone else.

- Will the web server be used for internal customers only, or will it be accessible via the Internet?
- Is it a web server specifically for the purpose of hosting a particular application or software? If so, what application or software?
- Who will be using the server, and what typical uses are expected?
- What are the uptime requirements? Can this be down 1 hour a week for maintenance? Six hours?
- Will we be creating accounts or groups for this web server?
- How much storage will this web server need?
- What is the expected traffic that this server will receive, and how will it grow over time?

29.1.9.1 Any Site

There are some basic principles to remember when planning any web site, whether it is for internal or external use. One of the most important ones is to plan out your URL namespace. The general guidance we provide in Chapter 8 will be very useful. It can be difficult and annoying to change URL references embedded in HTML documents, so it is worth doing right the first time. People tend to see particular URLs and make assumptions about what other URLs will work, so consistency tends to make a better customer experience.

For example, suppose that one could find a coworker's web directory online at http://internal/user/strata. When the company is acquired by another company, what happens to that URL? Will it be migrated to the new shared intranet site? If so, will it stay the same or migrate to http://internal/old-company/user/strata? Maybe the new company uses /home instead of /user or even has /users instead.

Plan out your URL namespace carefully to avoid naming conflicts and inconsistent or messy URLs. Some typical choices: /cgi-bin, /images, /user/ $USER, and so on. Alternatives might include /student/$USER, /faculty/ $USER, and so on. Be careful about using ID numbers in place of usernames. It may seem easier and more maintainable, but if the user shares the URL with others, an ID embedded in the URL would be potentially confidential information.

One important property of a URL is that once you share it with anyone, the expectation is that the URL should be available forever. Since that is rarely the case, a workaround can be implemented for URLs that change. Most web servers support a feature called *redirect*, which allows a site to keep a list of URLs that should be redirected to an alternative URL. Although the redirect commands almost always include support for wildcards, such as `my-site/project*` becoming `my-new-site/project*`, often there is much tedious handwork to be done.

A good way to head off difficulties before they arise is to use a preprocessor script or the web server's own configuration file's `include` ability to allow separate configuration files for different sections of your web site. These configuration files can then be edited by the web team responsible for that section's content changes, including redirects as they modify their section of the web site. This is useful for keeping the SAs out of content updates. The primary utility, however, is to minimize the risk that a web team may accidentally modify or misconfigure sitewide parameters in the main web server configuration file.

On most sites, customers want to host content rather than applications. Customers may request that the SAs install applications but will not frequently request programmatic access to the server to run their own scripts and programs. Letting people run web programs, such as CGI scripts, has the potential to negatively impact the web server and affect other customers. Avoid letting people run their own CGIs by default. If you must allow such usage, use operating system facilities that set limits for resource usage by programs to keep a rogue program from causing poor service for other customers.

Unless you are the one-in-a-million SA who doesn't have very much to do at work, you probably don't want to be responsible for keeping the web site content up to date. We strongly suggest that you create a process whereby the requester, or persons designated by the requester, are able to update the new web server with content. Sometimes, this merely means making the volume containing the web content into a shared one; for external sites, it may mean creating secure access methods for customers to update the site. An even better solution, for sites already using databases to store the kind of information they wish to publish on the web, would be a database-driven web site. The existing database update processes would then govern the web content. If there isn't already a database in use, this might be the perfect time to introduce one as part of rolling out the web server and site.

29.1.9.2 Internal or Intranet Site

For an internal site, a simple publishing model is usually satisfactory. Create the document root on a volume that can be shared, and give internal groups read and write permission to their own subdirectory on the volume. They will be able to manage their own internal content this way.

If internal customers need to modify the web server itself by adding modules or configuration directives that may affect other customer groups, we recommend using a separate, possibly virtual, server. This approach need not be taken for every group supported, but some groups are more likely to need it. For example, an engineering group wanting to install third-party source code management tools often needs to modify the web site with material from the vendor's install scripts. A university department offering distance learning might have created its own course management software that requires close integration with the web site or an authentication tie-in with something other than the main campus directory.

29.1.9.3 External Site

Externally visible sites should be configured in accordance with good security practices, such as blocking unused ports or being located within a firewall. If your organization does not have an external web presence and this server that you are creating would be the first one, it is important to ask whether the requester is coordinating the creation of the site with the appropriate parties in the organization. It will be necessary to structure the site to support an overall layout, and everyone's time will be spent more efficiently by doing some preplanning.

Having a web site involves four separate pieces, and all are independent of one another: domain registration, Internet DNS hosting, web hosting, and web content.

The first piece is registering a domain with the global registry. There are providers, or registrars, that do this for you. The exact process is outside the scope of this book.

The second piece is DNS hosting. Registration allocates the name to you but does not provide the DNS service that accepts DNS requests and sends DNS replies. Some registration services bundle DNS hosting with DNS registration.

The third piece, web hosting, means having a web server at the address given by DNS for your web site. This is the server you have just installed.

The fourth and final piece is content. Web pages and scripts are simply files, which need to be created and uploaded to the web server.

29.1.9.4 A Web Production Process

If the planned web site is for high-visibility, mostly static, content, such as a new company's web presence, we recommend instituting some kind of deployment process for new releases of the web site. A standard process that works well for many sites is to set up three identical servers, one for each stage in the deployment process.

The first server is considered a "draft" server and is used for editing or for uploading samples from desktop web editing software. The second server is a QA server. When a web item is ready to publish, it is *pushed to* the QA server for checking, proofreading, and in the case of scripts or web applications, standard software testing. The final server is the "live," or production, server. If the item passes QA, it is pushed to the production server.

Sites that are heavily scripted or that have particularly strict content requirements or both often introduce yet another server into the process. Often known as a *golden master* server, this additional server is functionally identical to a production server but is either blocked from external use or hidden behind a special firewall or VPN. The purpose of a golden master site is generally for auditing or for integration and testing of separate applications or processes that must interact smoothly with the production web server. The QA site may be behaving oddly owing to the QA testing itself, so a golden master site allows integration testing with a site that should behave identically to the production site but will not impact external customers if something goes awry with the test. It also represents an additional audit stage that allows content to be released internally and then handed off to another group that may be responsible for putting the material on the external site. Typically, only internal customers or specific outside partners are allowed to access the golden master site.

29.2 The Icing

So far, we have discussed all do-it-yourself solutions. The icing deals with ways to leverage other services so that SAs don't have to be concerned with so many smaller details.

29.2.1 Third-Party Web Hosting

A web-hosting company provides web servers for use by others. The customers upload the content and serve it. There is competition to provide more features, higher uptime, lower cost. **Managed hosting** refers to hosting companies that provide additional services, such as monitoring.

Large companies often run their own internal managed hosting service so that individual projects do not have to start from scratch every time they wish to produce a new web-based service.

The bulk of this chapter is useful for those SAs running web sites or hosting services, this section is about using such services.

29.2.1.1 Advantages of Web Outsourcing

Integration is more powerful than invention. When using a hosting service, there is no local software to install, it is all at the provider's "web farm." Rather than having expertise on networking, server installation, data center design, power and cooling, engineering, and a host of other skills, one can simply focus on the web service being provided.

Hosting providers usually include a web "dashboard" that one can log in to to control and configure the hosted service. The data is all kept on the hosted servers, which may sound like a *dis*advantage. In fact, unless you are at a large organization or have unusual resources at your disposal, most of the hosted services have a better combination of reliability and security than an individual organization can provide. They are benefiting from economies of scale and can bring more redundancy, bandwidth, and SA resources to bear than an individual organization can.

Having certain web applications or services hosted externally can help a site leverage its systems staff more effectively and minimize spending on hardware and connectivity resources. This is especially true when the desired services would require extensive customization or a steep learning curve on the part of current staff and resources yet represent "industry-standard" add-on services used with the web. When used judiciously, managed web hosting services can also be part of a disaster-recovery plan and provide extra flexibility for scaling.

Small sites are most easily solved using a web-hosting serice. The economic advantage comes from the fact that the hosting service is likely to consolidate dozens of small sites onto each server. Fees may range anywhere from $5 per month for sites that receive very little traffic to thousands of dollars per month for sites that use a lot of bandwidth.

29.2.1.2 Disadvantages of Web Outsourcing

The disadvantages can be fairly well summarized as worrying about the data, finding it difficult to let go, and wondering whether outsourcing the hosting will lead to outsourcing the SA. As for that first point, in many cases, the data can be exported from the hosted site in a form that allows it to be saved locally. Many hosting services also offer hosted backups, and some offer backup services that include periodic data duplication so a copy can be sent directly to you.

As for the other two points, many SAs find it extremely difficult to get out of the habit of trying to do everything themselves, even when overloaded. Staying responsive to all the other job duties of an SA is one of the best forms of job security, so solutions that make you less overloaded tend to be good for your job.

29.2.1.3 Unified Login: Managing Profiles

In most cases, it is very desirable to have a unified or consistent login for all applications and systems within an organization. It is better to have all applications access a single password system than to require people to have a password for each application. When people have too many passwords, they start writing them down on notes under their keyboards or taped to their monitors, which defeats the purpose of passwords. When you purchase or build a web application, make sure that it can be configured to query your existing authentication system.

When dealing with web servers and applications, the combination of a login/password and additional access or customization information is generally called a *profile*. Managing profiles across web servers tends to present the largest challenge. Managing this kind of information across multiple servers is, fortunately, something that we already know how to do (see Chapter 8). Less fortunately, the method used for managing profiles for web applications is not at all standardized, and many modern web applications use internal profile management.

A typical web application either includes its own web server or is running under an existing one. Most web servers do not offer centralized profile management. Instead, each directory has a profile method set in the web server's control file. In theory, each application would run in a directory and be subject to the access control methods associated with that directory. In practice, this is usually bypassed by the application.

There are several customary ways that web servers and applications manage profile data, such as Apache .htaccess and .htpasswd files, use of LDAP or Active Directory lookups, system-level calls to a pluggable authentication module (PAM), or SQL lookups on an external database. Any particular application might support only a subset or have a completely custom internal method. Increasingly, applications are merely running as a script under the web server, with profile management under the direct control of the application, often via a back-end database specific to the application. This makes centralized profile management extremely irksome in some cases. Make it a priority to select products that do integrate well with your authentication system.

When using authentication methods built into the web server software, all the authentication details are handled prior to the CGI system's getting control. In Apache, for example, whether authentication is done using a local text file to store username and password information or whether something more complicated, such as an LDAP authentication module, is in use, the request for the user to enter username and password information is handled at the web server level. The CGI script is run only after login is successful, and the CGI script is told the username that properly authenticated via an environment variable. To be more flexible, most CGI-based applications have some kind of native authentication system that handles its own username and password system. However, well-designed systems can be configured to switch that off and simply use the preauthenticated username supplied from the Apache web server. The application can assume that login was complete and can use the username as a key to retrieve the application's profile for that user.

29.2.2 Mashup Applications

One side effect of standard formats for exchanging data between web applications is the phenomenon called *mashup* applications. These can pose considerable scaling challenges.

A mashup is a web site that leverages data and APIs from other web sites to provide a new application.[3] Mashup applications simply take the well-formed output from one web service, parse out the data according to the schema, and remix, or mash, it into their own new application. The combinations are often brilliant, versatile, and incredibly useful. Application designers are creating increasingly complex XML schema for their application data.

An excellent example of a mashup application that reuses data in this way is HousingMaps, http://www.housingmaps.com, which shows interactive maps using Google Maps data, based on housing listings from the popular Craigslist site.

A mashup application has two parts and therefore two parts to scale. The first part is the portion of the mashup that its author wrote to glue together the services used. The second part is the services that are used.

Usually, the glue is lightweight, and scaling is a matter of the techniques listed previously. However, one should note that if the mashup is truly novel and innovative, the application may become wildly popular for a brief time and pose an unexpected load on your web service infrastructure.

The biggest issue is the services that the mashup depends on. These usually do the heavy lifting. For the SAs who run such a service, a suddenly popular mashup may result in an unexpected flood. Therefore, a good API includes limits and controls. For example, most APIs require that any user register for an identification key that is transmitted in each request. Keys are usually easy to receive, and approval is automated and instant. However, each key permits a certain number of queries per second and a maximum number of

---

3.   At least one unemployed developer has written a mashup to demonstrate his skills in an attempt to get noticed, and hired, by the company providing the API he used.

queries in a given 24-hour time period. These rate limits must be specified in an SLA advertised at the time that the user requests a key, and the limits must be enforced in the software that provides the service.

When a user exceeds the limits, this is an indication of abuse or an unexpectedly successful application. Smarter companies do not assume abuse, and some even maintain goodwill in the community by providing temporary rate increases to help applications over their initial popularity.

Since all queries are tied to the key of the user, it is possible to notice trends and see what applications are the most popular. This information can be useful for marketing purposes or to spot good candidates for acquisition.

When a rate limit is exceeded, the first step is to decide whether a response is warranted. If examination of your servers' logs reveals a consistent but unsupported referring URL entry, you probably should check out the application to see what it is and bring it to the attention of your web team and appropriate management.

A mashup application represents a critical learning opportunity for your organization. The existence of such an application, especially one being used enough to impact your normal web services, indicates that you have valuable data to provide. Some other data source is adding value to it in some way, and the business-process folks in your organization can get a lot of vital information from this. For that reason, we always recommend that any attempt to immediately limit access by the mashup application go through your normal channels.

If the use of your data represents an opportunity rather than an inconvenience for your organization, you may be asked to scale your web services appropriately or to facilitate contact with the mashup authors so that your organization can be credited publicly with the data.

If the decision is made to block usage of your web services by the mashup application, standard blocking methods supported by your web server or your network infrastructure may be applied. The API key can be disabled. It is advisable to seek the advice of your legal and marketing departments before initiating any type of blocking; having a policy already in place will improve the ability to react quickly.

29.3 Conclusion

The web is increasingly becoming a universal service delivery system in the organization, with the web browser client providing a common interface to multiple applications. Web services should be designed with the primary applications in mind so that they can be appropriately scaled, either by adding instances (horizontally) or balancing the load among different service layers (vertically). Installing a simple web site as a base for various uses is relatively easy, but making sure that the systems staff doesn't end up tasked with content maintenance is more difficult. Forming a council of web stakeholders, ideally with a designated team of webmasters, can solve this problem and scale as the organization's web usage grows. Another form of scaling is to outsource services that are simple enough or resource-intensive enough that the system staff's time would be better spent doing other things.

Exercises

1. What items need to be considered differently when providing external web services versus internal services to your organization?

2. How many cryptographic certificates are in use by your organization? How are they managed? What improvements would you make to how they are managed?

3. What methods does your organization use to provide multiple web sites on the same machine?

4. Give an example of a type of web-specific logging that can be done and what that information is used for.

5. Pick a web service in your organization, and develop a plan for scaling it, assuming that it will receive five times as many queries. One hundred times as many queries.

6. Is your organization's external web site hosted at a third-party hosting provider? Why or why not? Evaluate the pros and cons of moving it to a third-party hosting provider or bringing it internal.

Part V

Management Practices

Chapter 30

Organizational Structures

How an SA team is structured, and how this structure fits into the larger organization, are major factors in the success or failure of the team. This chapter examines some of the issues that every site should consider in building the system administration team and covers what we have seen in a variety of companies. It concludes with some sample SA organizational structures for various sites.

Communication is an area that can be greatly influenced by the organizational structure of both the SA team and the company in general. The structure of the organization defines the primary communication paths among the SAs, as well as between the SAs and their customers.[1] Both sets of communication are key to the SA team's success. The SAs at a site need to cooperate in order to build a solid, coherent computing infrastructure for the rest of the company to use. However, they must do so in a way that meets the needs of the customers and provides them with solid support and good customer service.

Management and individuals should work hard to avoid an us-versus-them attitude, regardless of how the organization is structured. Some organizational structures can foster that attitude more than others, but poor communication channels are always at the heart of such problems.

30.1 The Basics

Creating an effective system administration organization free of conflicts both internally and with the customer base is challenging. Sizing and funding the SA function appropriately so that the team can provide good service

---

1. Communications between SAs and their managers are also critical and can make or break a team. This topic is covered in detail in Chapters 33 and 34.

levels without seeming to be a financial burden to the company is another tricky area. We also examine the effects the management chain can have on that issue.

The ideal SA team is one that can provide the right level of service at the smallest possible cost. Part of providing good service to your company is keeping your costs as low as possible without adversely affecting service levels. To do that, you need to have the right SAs with the right set of skills doing the right jobs. Throwing more people into the SA team doesn't help as much as getting the right people into the SA team. A good SA team has a comprehensive set of technical skills and is staffed with people who have good communication skills and work well with others.

Small SA groups need well-rounded SAs with broad skill sets. Larger SA groups need to be divided into functional areas. We identify which functions should be provided by a central group and those that are better served by small distributed teams of SAs. We explain the mechanisms of the centralized versus decentralized models for system administration and describe the advantages and disadvantages of each approach.

30.1.1 Sizing

Making your SA team the correct size is difficult; if it is too small, it will be ineffective, and the rest of the company will suffer through unreliable infrastructure and poor customer service. If the team is too large, the company will incur unnecessary costs, and communication among the SAs will be more difficult. In practice, SA teams are more often understaffed than overstaffed. It is unusual, though not unheard of, to see an overstaffed SA team. Overstaffing typically is related to not having the right set of skills in the organization. If the SA team is having trouble supporting the customers and providing the required level of service and reliability, simply adding more people may not be the answer. Consider adding the missing skills through training or consultants before hiring new people.

When deciding on the size of the SA team, the management of the organization should take into account several factors: the number and variety of people and machines in the company the complexity of the environment, the type of work that the company does, the service levels required by various groups, and how mission-critical the various computer services are. It is a good idea to survey the SAs to find out approximately how much time each of them is spending supporting the customers and machines in each group, as well as the central infrastructure machines.

Fill in the *approximate* percentage of time spent on each category.
Please make sure that they add up to 100 percent.

	Percentage		Quantity
• Customer/desktop support • Customer server support • Infrastructure support		• Number of customers • Number of customer servers • Number of infrastructure machines	

Figure 30.1 Short form for gathering approximate numbers for prediction of growth rate

Ideally, your trouble-ticket system should be able to give you this information for a given period quite quickly. If it cannot, you can have each SA fill out a short form, such as the one in Figure 30.1 with approximate numbers. This information will provide a basis for deriving the SA team's growth rate that should keep the service levels approximately constant. It should also give insight into areas that consume a lot of SA time and allow you to look for ways to reduce support overhead.

Case Study: High Support Costs

When Synopsys did a survey of where the SAs were spending their time, the managers discovered that SAs were spending a lot of time supporting old, ailing equipment that also had high maintenance contract costs. Replacing the equipment with new, faster hardware would yield continuing savings in machine room space and labor. The managers used this information to persuade the group that owned the equipment to retire it and replace it with new machines. This enabled the SAs to use their time more effectively and to provide better customer service.

There is no magic customer-to-SA ratio that works for every company, because different customers have different needs. For example, a university campus may have 500 or 1,000 customers for every SA, because most of these customers do not use the machines all day every day, are reasonably tolerant of small outages, and generally do not push the hardware to its limits. In contrast, high-tech businesses, such as hardware design or gene sequencing, require more from their IT services and may require ratios closer to 60:1 or even 20:1. In software development, the range is even wider: We've seen each SA supporting as many as 50 customers or as few as 5. A nontechnical corporate environment will require about as many SAs as a technical one but with more focus on helpdesk, user interface, and environment training. Regardless, all organizations should have at least two SAs or at a bare minimum should have some way of providing suitable cover for their one SA if that person is ill or on vacation.

Machines themselves also require support time, independent of explicit customer requests. Servers require regular backups, software and OS upgrades and patches, monitoring, and hardware upgrades and maintenance. Some of this can be optimized and automated through techniques discussed elsewhere in this book, but there is still significant server maintenance time. Even if desktops are easily replaceable clones of each other, they also require support time, though it is minimal because you can simply swap out a broken machine.

In any reasonably large organization, some people will spend their time primarily maintaining infrastructure services, such as email, printing, the network, authentication, and name service. Companies that provide e-commerce or other critical web-based services to their customers will also require a team to maintain the relevant systems.

All these areas must be taken into account when sizing the organization. Customer-to-SA ratios are tempting, but they tell only half the story. Gather real data from your organization to see where SAs are spending their time. Use the data to look for places where automation and processes can be improved and to find services or systems that you may not want to support any more. Define SLAs with your customers, and use those SLAs to help size the SA team appropriately.

30.1.2 Funding Models

Money is at the center of everything in every business. How and by whom system administration is funded is central to the success or failure of the SA team.

The primary reason that the SA function is generally understaffed is that it is viewed as a cost center rather than as a profit center. Simply put, the SA function does not bring in money; it is overhead. To maximize profits, a business must minimize overhead costs, which generally leads to restricting the size and growth of the SA team.

Case Study: Controlling Costs

A midsize software company growing by about 30 percent annually was trying to control costs, so it restricted the growth of the budget for the SA team. The management of the SA team knew that the team was suffering and that there would be more problems in the future, but it needed a way to quantify this and to express it to the upper management of the company.

The SA group performed a study to determine where the budget was being spent and highlighted factors that it could not control, such as per person and per server support costs. However, the group could not control the number of people other groups hired or the number of servers other groups bought, so the SA group could not control its budget for those costs. If the budget did not keep pace with those costs, service levels would drop.

The most significant factor was how maintenance contracts were handled. After the first year, maintenance contract fees for machines under contract were billed to the central SA group, not to the departments that bought and owned the machines. Based on past trends, the group calculated its budget growth rate and determined that in 5 years, the entire system administration budget would be consumed by maintenance contracts alone. There would be no money left even for salaries. Last one out, turn off the lights (and sign the maintenance contract)!

Once the SA management was able to quantify and explain the group's budget problems, the CFO and his team devised a new funding model to fix the problems by making each department responsible for the system administration costs that it incurred.

You must be able to explain and justify the money that is spent on system administration if you are to avoid being underfunded.

It is difficult to show how the SA team is saving the company money when everything is running smoothly. Unfortunately, it is easier to demonstrate where the company is losing money by understaffing system administration after the infrastructure and support have deteriorated to the point that people working in the profit centers are losing significant amounts of time through computer and network problems. If a company reaches this stage, however, it is almost impossible to recover completely. The SA team will have lost the trust and cooperation of the customer base and will have a very difficult time regaining it, no matter how well funded it becomes.

You want to avoid reaching this state, which means figuring out a funding model that works. You need to be able to answer the following questions: Who pays? How does it scale? And what do customers get for their money?

The design of the funding model also has an impact on the organizational structure, because the people who are paying typically want significant control. Generally, SAs are either paid for directly by business units and report into the business units or are centrally funded by the company and form their own business unit. These are the *decentralized* and *centralized* models, respectively. It is not uncommon to see companies switch from one model to the other and back again every few years, because both models have strengths and weaknesses.

When a company changes from one model to the other, it is always stressful for the SAs. It is important for the management of the company to have frank, open meetings with the SAs. They need to hear management acknowledge the strengths of the existing structure and the problems that the group will face in maintaining those strengths. The SAs also need to be told frankly what the weaknesses with the current structure are and how the new structure should address those weaknesses. The SAs should be given a chance to voice their concerns, ask questions, and suggest solutions. The SAs may have valuable insights for management on how their existing strengths can be preserved. If the SAs are genuinely involved in the process, it has a much higher chance of success. Representatives from the customer groups also should be involved in the process. It needs to be a team effort to succeed.

The primary motivation for the decentralized model is to give the individual departments better or more customized service through having a stronger relationship with their SAs and more control over the work that they do. The primary motivation for centralizing system administration is to control costs through tracking them centrally and then reducing them by eliminating redundancy and taking advantage of economies of scale.

When it moves to a central system administration organization, a company looks for standardization and reduced duplication of services. However, the individual departments will be sensitive about losing their control and highly customized services, alert to the smallest failure or drop in performance after centralization, and slow to trust the central group. Rather than work with the central group to try and fix the problems, the various departments may even hire their own rogue SAs to provide the support they used to have, defeating the purpose of the centralization process and hiding the true system administration costs the company is incurring.

Changing from one model to the other is difficult on both the SAs and their customers. It is much better to get it right the first time or to work on incremental improvements, instead of hoping that a radical shift will fix all the problems without introducing new ones.

Funding the SA team should be decentralized to a large degree, or it will become a black hole on the books into which vast sums of money seem to disappear. Decentralizing the funding can make the business units aware of the cost of maintaining old equipment and of other time sinks. It can also enable each business unit to still control its level of support and have a different level than other business units. A unit wanting better support should encourage its assigned SA to automate tasks or put forward the funding to hire more SAs. However, when a business unit has only one SA, doubling that may seem a prohibitively large jump.

Given a time analysis of the SAs' work and any predefined SLAs, it is possible to produce a funding model in which each business unit pays a per person and per server fee, based on its chosen service level. This fee incorporates the infrastructure cost needed to support those people and machines, as well as the direct costs. This approach decentralizes the cost and has an added benefit that the business unit does not have to increase its SA head count by whole units. It does require rigorous procedures to ensure that groups that are paying for higher service levels receive what they pay for.

Ideally, the beneficiaries of the services should pay directly for the services they receive. Systems based around a "tax" are open to abuse, with people trying to get as much as possible out of the services they are paying for, which can ultimately increase costs. However, cost tracking and billing can add so much overhead that it is cheaper to endure a little service abuse. A hybrid method, in which charges are rolled up to a higher level or groups exceeding certain limits incur additional charges, may be workable. For example, you might divide the cost of providing remote access proportionately across divisions rather than provide bills down to the level of single customers. Groups that exceed a predefined per person level are also charged for the excess.

Naturally, for budget planning and control reasons, the managers want to either know in advance what the costs will be or at least have a good estimate. That way, they can make sure that they don't run over budget by having unexpectedly high system administration costs. One way to do this is with monthly billing reports rather than an end-of-year surprise.

30.1.3 Management Chain's Influence

The management chain can have considerable influence on how the system administration organization is run. Particularly in fast-paced companies, IT may come under the chief technical officer (CTO), who is also in charge of the engineering and research and development organizations. Other times, system administration is grouped with the facilities function and reports through the chief operating officer (COO) or through the chief financial officer (CFO). These differences have implications. If your CIO reports to your CTO, the company may view IT as something to invest in to increase profits. If your CIO reports to the CFO, the company may view IT as a cost that must be reduced.

When the system administration function reports through the CTO or the engineering organization, there are several beneficial effects and some potential problems. The most demanding customers are typically in that organization, so they have a closer relationship with the SAs. The group generally is quite well funded because it is part of a profit center that can directly see the results of its investment in system administration. However, other parts of the company may suffer because the people setting the priorities for the SAs will be biased toward the projects for the engineering group. As the company grows, the engineering function will be split into several business units, each with its own vice president. By this time, the system administration function will either be split into many groups supporting different business units or will report to some other part of the company because it will not be a part of a single "engineering" hierarchy.

A sad counterexample is the time that Tom met a CTO who misunderstood IT to the point that he felt that IT was unnecessary in a high-tech company because "everyone here should be technical enough to look after their own machines."

In contrast, reporting through the COO or CFO means that the system administration function is a cost center and tends to receive less money. The people the SA team reports through usually have only the vaguest understanding of what the group does and what costs are involved. However, the COO or CFO typically has a broader view of the company as a whole and so will usually be more even-handed in allocating system administration resources. This reporting structure benefits from a strong management team that can communicate well with upper management to explain the budget, responsibilities, and priorities of the team. It can be advantageous to report through the CFO, because if the budget requirements of the SA team can be properly explained and justified, the CFO is in a position to determine the best way to have the company pay for the group.

Equally, if SA groups report directly into the business units that fund them, the business units will usually invest as much into IT as they need, though quality may be uneven across the company. Every reporting structure has strengths and weaknesses. There is no one right answer for every organization. The strengths and weaknesses also depend on the views and personalities of the people involved.

The SA managers need to be aware of how their reporting structure affects the SA team and should capitalize on the strengths while mitigating the weaknesses inherent in that reporting structure.

Friends in High Places

Although being close to the CTO is often better in highly innovative companies, Tom experienced the opposite once at a company that was not as technically oriented. When Tom joined, he was concerned that he would be reporting to the COO, not the CTO, where he was usually more comfortable.

At this company, the COO was responsible for the production system that made the company money: Imagine a high-tech assembly line, but instead of manufacturing autos or other hard goods, the assembly line did financial transactions for other companies on a tight monthly schedule. The CTO office was a newly created department chartered with introducing some new innovations into the company. However, the CTO office hadn't yet established credibility.

Being part of the COO's organization turned out to be the best place for Tom's IT department. The COO held the most sway in the company because her part of the company was making the money that fueled the entire organization. As part of her organization, the IT group was able to work as a team with the COO to not only get proper funding for all the upgrades that the production part of the company needed but also influence the CTO's organization by playing the role of customer of what the CTO was creating.

When the COO wanted something, she had the credibility to get the resources. When Tom wanted something, he had the COO's ear. When the CTO and Tom disagreed, he had the ear of the person who fundamentally controlled the funding.

30.1.4 Skill Selection

When building an SA team, the hiring managers need to assemble a well-rounded team with a variety of skill sets and roles. The various roles that SAs can take on are discussed in more detail in Appendix A.

The duties of the SAs can be divided into four primary categories. The first is to provide *maintenance* and *customer support,* which includes the helpdesk (Chapter 13), server maintenance, second-tier helpdesk support, and whatever particular groups of customers get their own specialized support on a day-to-day basis.

The second category is *deployment* of new services. These implementers should be dedicated to their current projects so that they are not affected by urgent customer requests that can push the project completion date back.

Third is the *design* of new service architectures. The design team is composed of systems *architects* who investigate new technologies and design and prototype new services for the customers and other SAs. The design team must keep in touch with customers' needs through the other SA teams and is responsible for making sure that new services are planned and built in advance of when the customers need them.

If you have separate teams of SAs responsible for networks, databases, security, and so on, each of these groups must have staff who cover the range of categories that SAs encompass. There must be people to design, deploy, and maintain each supported area.

Finally, an SA team also benefits greatly from *senior generalists* who understand, in depth, how all or most of the components work and interact. These SAs are able to solve complex, end-to-end problems that may elude SAs who specialize in only one or two areas. The senior generalists are often referred to as *integrators* because they can integrate various technologies effectively to produce the best possible systems and services.

Overlap often occurs between the categories, particularly in smaller companies, in which one or two SAs need to fulfill all roles to some degree. In larger companies, the roles are typically separated. Junior SAs are often hired to work at the helpdesk. As they gain experience, they can move into second-tier support positions and later into deployment roles, day-to-day business unit support roles, or infrastructure maintenance roles. The most senior SAs typically fill the design and senior generalist roles.

In larger companies, finding ways to give the SAs a chance to spend some time in other roles, working with other teams, gives them growth and mentoring opportunities and helps to educate the rest of the team on their experiences and insights.

Rotating all the SAs through the helpdesk can give them valuable insight into the most common problems, some of which they may be able to fix permanently. It can also provide training opportunities for the junior SAs and faster call resolution for some more complicated calls. Helpdesk personnel can be rotated out of the helpdesk to give them a break and to enable them to spend a week being mentored through more senior work with customers or implementers.

Similarly, having implementers become involved in direct customer support should give them feedback on customers' needs and how well their services are performing. Involving the implementers in design work should provide them with extra challenges and can help get their feedback to the designers.

SAs in roles that do not normally require much customer contact, such as server maintenance, design, and implementation roles, can lose touch with the customers' needs. Rotating them through roles that require a lot of customer contact can keep them in touch with the company's direction.

When Things Are Dire, Hire Higher

Being able to hire a mixture of skills and skill levels is a luxury for sites that are doing fairly well. When things are going well, it is possible to hire junior SAs who will be trained and groomed by the senior SAs. Being able to promote from within is less costly than recruiting outsiders, rewards the best workers, and retains institutional knowledge. Promoting from within lets you hire junior people to back-fill vacated positions.

However, if an SA team is not doing well—systems are crashing regularly, customers are unsatisfied, morale is low, and so on—a different tactic is required. When things aren't going well, one needs to hire reform-oriented people. Highly skilled people with experience at well-run sites are more likely to be reformers.

When reforming a failing organization, or even upgrading an organization that is performing OK but needs improvement, start by hiring a few senior-level people who work well together. As things start to stabilize, give them the freedom to reorganize the team to use the more junior members as their experience dictates, or call for new junior members to be hired as described in the anecdote in Section 2.1.5.3. Good people know good people; their professional contacts will help find the right people.

Tom likes to say, "When things are dire, hire higher."

30.1.5 Infrastructure Teams

When a company grows, it should have people dedicated to infrastructure support. An infrastructure team will look after centralized services, such as authentication, printing, email, name service, calendar service, networking, remote access, directory services, and security. This team also will be generally responsible for automated services for the SAs who are providing customer support, such as the automatic loading, configuration, and patching of new machines (Chapter 3).

The infrastructure team must be a cohesive unit, even if it is spread over multiple locations. The company's infrastructure should be consistent and interoperable among all the sites. If different groups are running different pieces of the infrastructure, they may fail to agree on the protocols and interfaces between the components with adverse results.

Case Study: Distributed Network Support

A large multinational computer manufacturing company implemented distributed management of networks and computers. Responsibilities were split among IT groups; the central IT department handled the WAN, remote sites had a local SA, and each department at headquarters had its own IT group to handle system and network administration. At the time, the remote administration tools we take for granted today were not available.

In the early days, with 20 sites, it seemed simple enough to merely give each site a subdomain, a class C network, and provide the SAs with tools to easily generate DNS zone files. However, when the company had 200 sites with different administrators wanting to manage their subdomains slightly differently, whenever an administrator left the company, the SA team had a training problem. In addition, many disputes went unresolved because, in some cases, the management chains of the two disputing sides intersected only at the CEO level. No one could reasonably be expected to arbitrate and decide what should be done.

Having so many subdomains also increased the amount of work the SAs had to do whenever someone moved to a different department. Mailboxes had to be moved; mail aliases, internal mailing lists, and NIS maps had to be changed; the various modem pool authentication servers needed to be updated; and so on. With a proper, centrally managed system, only the mailbox might have to be moved, with a single corresponding mail alias change. But with so many changes needed, things were inevitably missed and mistakes were made.

The lack of a central system administration management structure was also expensive for the company in other ways: The numerous system administration groups were unable to agree on a network architecture or even on what network hardware to use. Overlapping duplicated networks were built with a variety of hardware. Incompatibilities among the hardware resulted in some communications being dropped. The network that resulted from this unarbitrated, decentralized process was unreliable and unsupportable, but each department continued to fund its own administration team and adamantly defend its territory.

Many years later, when all the tools for centralizing network management, including namespace control, network addressing, and many other aspects of site maintenance became available, the company still used its outdated and ineffective distributed administration model.

Each piece of infrastructure has its own particular way in which it must be built and supported as a coherent unit. All infrastructure services fall into disarray when different parts of them are managed by different groups that do not cooperate with one another. Organizationally, this means that it is advisable to create a centralized infrastructure group and plan for its growth as needed. When other regions need their own infrastructure SAs, those SAs should report to the central infrastructure managers rather than to regional SA managers.

A very user-visible example of this is email, which is part of the company's interface to its customers and to the rest of the world. A consistent look and feel—one email format used consistantly throughout the entire company, hiding server names, and so on—gives the company a professional image. Having a unified email architecture benefits SAs by being easier to debug and administer. Dedicated choke points where email enters and exits the company results in better email security, as filtering can be more comprehensive. All this requires cooperation between infrastructure teams across the globe.

Modern computing infrastructures rely heavily on networks and network services. If the network or network services architecture is badly designed or managed, it increases SA workload, cost, and customer dissatisfaction. If each site is permitted to be *creative*, the result is a management nightmare. Network design and implementation must be a cooperative effort, and, where it cannot be, well-defined demarcation lines must exist between the zones of the company that have internally consistent designs.

The security of the company as a whole is only as secure as the weakest link. If different groups have different standards and policies, it will be impossible to know how good the company's security really is.

30.1.6 Customer Support

Customer support is a key part of the system administration function. Customer support means making sure that customers can work effectively. That, in turn, means being part of the solution for all their computing needs. Customer support generally works best in a more distributed model, in contrast to infrastructure support.

Having dedicated customer support personnel helps align your response time with your customers' expectations. As discussed in Section 31.1.3, having personnel dedicated to quickly responding to short requests and passing larger requests on to back-office personnel matches response time with customer expectations.

Customers like to know who their support people are. Customers build a relationship with a person and become familiar with that person's way of working and communication style. They feel more comfortable in asking that person for help. They can be more confident that their SA will know the context of what they are doing and what services the department uses and how, and that the SA will know what assumptions can be made about the customer and the environment.

We mentioned earlier that choosing between centralized and decentralized models for the system administration organization has an impact on customer support and the relationships between the SAs and between the customers and the SAs. In the decentralized model, whereby each department or group has its own small SA team, communication with the customers is typically strong, but communication between the SAs is generally weak. The customers will have a more familiar relationship with their SAs but will ultimately suffer because of the lack of communication between the SAs. For example, if the SAs' efforts are not well coordinated, many tasks may not be automated; there will not be consistent machines, OSs, patch levels, and applications across the company; and some services that should be centralized may be implemented multiple times. All these will result in inefficiency and lack of reliability that will ultimately be detrimental to the service the customers receive.

In the centralized model, communication between the SAs is generally strong and communication with the customer base is weak. The centralized model can lead to an us-versus-them attitude on both sides. On the other hand, that is balanced by a generally stronger infrastructure and a more consistent and robust site. However, customers will probably feel that they are not getting the attention they need, and projects for individual departments may be delayed unacceptably in favor of infrastructure projects or projects for other departments. Each department will suffer from not having its own SA paying attention to its specific needs.

A centralized support model can result in customers talking to a different person each time they place a support call. Because the SAs all support so many people, the SA who responds to a support call may not know the department well and probably won't know the customer. This is not a support model that satisfies customers. A team of at most five SAs should support a customer group. Customers want to know their SAs and have confidence that the SAs are familiar with the department's setup and requirements. If a customer-visible SA team is larger than about five, divide the team so that each half of the team supports one half of that customer group. Another approach is to look at ways to reduce the number of SAs who provide direct customer support to that group by having some SAs work behind the scenes.

Some companies use hybrid models, in which each department or business unit has some dedicated SAs who report to the centralized system administration organization. This model is not perfect either, because some business unit SAs may be more vocal than others, causing some departments' needs not to be addressed properly by the automation and standardization performed centrally on behalf of the business units. Hybrid models have a lot of potential, but they can also introduce the worst features of both centralized and decentralized models.

Whichever model you use, be aware of its weaknesses and do what you can to mitigate them.

30.1.7 Helpdesk

The first tier of a helpdesk function is one that works best when centralized. This is the organization that receives initial problem reports and resolves basic issues but otherwise dispatches the request to the appropriate area. Customers want one phone number, email address, and web page for support requests. Customers don't want to know which particular department owns a given problem, nor do they want to risk their request getting lost between departments because the one that received it doesn't know who should resolve it.

Large companies need well-coordinated regional helpdesks, with each reasonably large site having its own. With multiple helpdesks, escalation procedures and call hand-off procedures become critical because some calls will cross regional boundaries. Large companies need to find the right balance between a tightly controlled centralized helpdesk that can handle all calls and smaller distributed ones that cannot handle all the calls but can provide a friendlier, more personal face on the system administration organization. Chapter 13 discusses creation and management of helpdesks in detail.

30.1.8 Outsourcing

Outsourcing the system administration function can seem an appealing option to some companies because system administration is not usually considered a core competency of the company. If system administration is not a key part of the company's business, the company may prefer to outsource the entire area to an outsource contract company. That way, the company has to negotiate only a contract and not worry about SA recruiting, compensation packages, retention, and all the other issues that are part of having employees.

For some companies, outsourcing makes sense. If a company is fairly small and has basic computing needs, negotiating a contract is easier than trying to hire an SA when the company has nobody who can evaluate the SA's skill level or performance. If not satisfied with the outsourcing company, the company can renegotiate the contract or take the more difficult route of replacing that company with a new one. It is not as easy to change or terminate an employment contract.

Other sorts of companies should not outsource their IT functions or should do so very cautiously. For e-commerce sites, IT and system administration are part of the core business. Companies that rely on highly available computer systems will find that outsourcing contracts becomes prohibitively expensive when their reliability needs are factored in. Sites dependent on cutting-edge technology often need to run their own systems as well, because outsourcing companies have their own technology standards, which are difficult for individual customers to influence. In complex environments, getting rid of a poorly performing outsourcing provider is more difficult. It is not easy to switch out one SA team for another without suffering a significant amount of degraded service and outages while the new team becomes familiar with the site.

Security is another sensitive subject in the area of outsourcing. If security is important to a company, particularly in the areas of information protection and handling customer-confidential information, the legal department should require strict confidentiality agreements and assurances about what companies the security contractors work for before, during, and after their work at this company. If a security breach can result in loss of customer confidence or otherwise severely affect the company's revenue stream, the security function should be one of the company's core competencies. In-house security staff have a stake in the company's success and failure, whereas the outsourcing company's liability will be limited in their contracts.

In companies that have a revenue-generating Internet presence or an e-commerce site, the SA function of maintaining this site is one of the core functions of the company. As a result, most companies are unwilling to outsource this area of their business. They want the people responsible for maintaining high availability on their Internet sites to have a personal stake in their success or failure. For companies that receive only a small amount of revenue from their Internet presence and do not otherwise rely on high-availability computer systems, staffing the SA team for round-the-clock coverage can be prohibitively expensive, with outsourcing proving a more financially attractive option.

Many companies outsource their Internet presence to some degree by putting their Internet service machines into a colocation (colo) center. The main advantage of a colo is that the service provider has redundant high-bandwidth Internet connections and highly redundant power and cooling facilities that are prohibitively expensive for most companies to afford on their own. Colocation has better economies of scale. Some high-end outsourcing companies also support the machines and the applications running on them. Others might have someone available to power cycle a given machine on request. As with other forms of outsourcing, it is important to have service levels defined in the contract, with financial penalties if they are not met. The service levels should include guaranteed bandwidth, response times on service calls, power and cooling, uptime, physical security, and network-availability guarantees.

Outsourcing is a sensitive subject on which many people have strong views. We have tried to present some of the pros and cons of outsourcing in different situations. More discussion of the topic is in Section 21.2.2.

30.2 The Icing

The icing of system administration organization is the ability to use consultants and contractors to help your team grow and build new services and infrastructure well, while still maintaining service levels. Used in the right way, consultants and contractors can give in-house staff opportunities to grow and gain experience. Used in the wrong way, they can offend, dishearten, and alienate the SA team.

We distinguish between consultants and contractors by their skill level and the work they perform. A consultant brings significant new and in-depth skills to the table, usually for a specific project. A contractor brings skills that the company may already have and performs tasks that the SA group already performs.

30.2.1 Consultants and Contractors

Consultants who are experts in their fields can be useful temporary additions to a system administration team. A consultant should be engaged for a specific project, such as designing and building a new service that needs to scale rapidly to support the whole company, in which in-house SAs may not currently have experience.

A successful relationship with a consultant will involve the SAs, particularly architects and implementers, in the project on which the consultant is working. The consultant should be willing to share ideas, brainstorm, and generally work with the team and should not dictate to them. A good consultant can bring necessary expertise and experience to a new endeavor, resulting in a better design and increased knowledge for the in-house SAs.

On the other hand, it is not good for the morale and success of an SA team to bring in consultants for the new and interesting projects while the in-house SAs deal with the day-to-day support and maintenance. The new service will not be as well supported as it would be if the in-house SAs were involved and understood the design. It may also not take into account local quirks or be as well integrated with other systems as it would be if local knowledge were used in the design. The in-house SAs will not get the opportunity to grow and learn new skills and will become dissatisfied with their positions, resulting in high turnover and unsatisfactory levels of customer support.

If new projects need to be implemented but the in-house SAs do not have time to participate, contractors should be brought in to back-fill for the in-house SAs' day-to-day tasks, not necessarily to implement the new service. The project will usually be more successful in terms of budget, features, and ongoing support and maintenance if the in-house SAs are involved, rather than giving it entirely to an outside team. Helping the SAs to participate in new projects through relieving their day-to-day workload will also lead to a stronger, happier SA team.

Rotating the in-house SAs who participate in the interesting projects so that all the SAs have a chance to be involved in a project also strengthens the team.

Contract One-Shot Tasks

Installing commercial data backup/restore systems is usually quite difficult. It's a lot easier the third or fourth time through, but most SAs never get to that point. A new data backup system is installed every few years.

Instead, it can be much more cost-effective to hire someone to do the installation. Find someone who has installed that particular system three or four times already.

Most backup software companies have a professional services group that will do the installation for you. We find these groups to be invaluable. They set things up properly and train existing staff on daily operational details.

In one situation, Tom saw an SA take 6 months to install such a system. He was constantly interrupted with other project work, which extended and delayed the project.

> The company was happy that it didn't pay the $10,000 that the professional services contract would have cost. Tom felt that the money would have been well spent. Many similar one-shot tasks benefit from hiring someone with experience.

30.3 Sample Organizational Structures

How do the various roles and responsibilities fit into companies of different sizes? How does being an e-commerce site change the organization of the SA function? What's different in academic or nonprofit organizations? We describe what the system administration organization should look like in small, medium, and large companies; an e-commerce site; and a university/ nonprofit organization. For these examples, a small company is typically between 20 and 200 employees; a medium-size company, between 200 and 1,000 employees; and a large company, more than 1,000 employees. These are approximations; a small company with dozens of locations has many of the needs of a large company.

30.3.1 Small Company

A small company will have one or two SAs, who are expected to cover all the bases between them. There will be no formal helpdesk, though requests should be funneled through a help-request tracking system. The SAs will be involved in customer support and infrastructure maintenance. However, usually only one of the SAs will be involved in designing and implementing new services as they are required.

As a small company moves beyond 200 employees and starts growing into a midsize company, its system administration organization will be formed. This intermediate time is when the big decisions about how to organize and fund system administration need to be made by the company's senior management. The formal helpdesk will be formed during the transitional stages and initially will be staffed by a rotation of SAs in customer-support roles.

30.3.2 Medium-Size Company

In a midsize company, the SAs start to specialize a bit more. A helpdesk team with dedicated personnel should have been formed before the company reached the 1,000-employee mark. The helpdesk will be expected to solve reasonably complex problems. SAs in customer-support roles may still rotate through the helpdesk to augment the dedicated staff. Some SAs will specialize in a specific OS; others will take on networking or security special-ties, initially as part-time responsibilities and later, as the company grows, as full-time positions. The architects generally will also be implementers and, ideally, should be capable of solving end-to-end problems involving several technologies. Customer-support personnel also can be included in the design and implementation projects by designating days for project work and days for customer-support work.

30.3.3 Large Company

A large company will have a high degree of specialization among the SA team, a well-staffed helpdesk with a clearly defined second-tier support team for the more difficult problems, small customer-support teams dedicated to vari-ous departments or business units, and a central infrastructure support group and a central security team. A large company will have at least one architect for each technology area and teams of implementers for each area. The com-pany may have regional SA organizations or SA organizations dedicated to subsidiaries or large business divisions. These SA organizations will need for-mal communication paths to coordinate their work and clearly defined areas of responsibility. They should all be covered by the same company policies, if possible.

30.3.4 E-Commerce Site

An e-commerce site is different from other sites in that it has two sets of computers, networks, and services that require different levels of availability and are governed by different sets of priorities. A problem with a revenue-generating system will always take precedence over an internal customer-support call because the latter is directly linked to the revenue stream.

To avoid this conflict of interest, a company with a large e-commerce site needs two separate SA teams: one to support only the Internet presence, and the other to support only the corporate systems. (This is often also required for Sarbanes-Oxley compliance.) There should be a clean separation between the equipment used for each entity, because they have different availability requirements and different functions. Sites where parts of the Internet service rely on parts of the corporate infrastructure inevitably run into problems. A clean separation is also more readily maintained if different SA groups are in charge of each area.

The composition of the corporate SA team depends on the size of the com-pany. The composition of the Internet service is somewhat different. It may have a helpdesk that is part of the customer-support organization.[2] Although that helpdesk may have second-tier support to which calls are escalated, there will not be small internal customer-support teams that serve each department. There will only be SAs who are responsible for the support and maintenance of the Internet service and architects and implementers who design and deploy enhancements to the service and scale the service to meet customer demand.

Google's Two IT Teams

Google has two different IT teams. The systems operations team maintains the internal IT systems. The site reliability engineering team maintains the systems involved in the web properties. Initially one team, the division has enabled the SAs to better meet business demands and creates an environment in which there is less conflict over priorities.

30.3.5 Universities and Nonprofit Organizations

It is important for nonprofit organizations to control ongoing costs. Typically, they have very limited budgets, so it is vital that all the money available for computing be used properly, with organizations and departments working together with everyone's best interest in mind. It is easier to control costs when services are centralized. However, universities often have small fiefdoms built around the funding that individual research groups or professors receive. It is in the best interests of the university or nonprofit organization to centralize as much as possible and to work as a team. To do so requires strong leadership from the head of the organization and good service from the central SA team.

Case Study: Use Limited Resources Wisely

Here's an example of what can happen if there is no budget for centralized services. A university department had a limited amount of money to spend on equipment. Several research groups within the department received additional money for equipment from their research projects. Equipment that was retired from use in a research group was given to the department to help support the undergraduate and infrastructure needs. The department had some glaring needs that it had been unable to fund. The backup system was able to accommodate only the machines that were

---

2. A helpdesk that supports external customers of the company, as opposed to the internal customers of the corporate SA team.

used by the undergraduates. There was no backup service for research computers. The servers that provided email, printing, software depot, and home directory services for the department were two unreliable machines that had been designed to be desktop workstations and were 7 years old.

However, there was no coordination within the department on how best to spend the money from research contracts. One professor had enough money from a research project to buy four or five high-end PCs with plenty of disk space, monitors, and suitable graphics cards. Instead, he decided to buy two of the most expensive PCs possible with superfluous but flashy hardware and additional processors that could not be used by the computational code that ran on the machine. Both PCs were given to one PhD student, who already had a high-end computer. They were largely unused. No machines were handed down to the department, and no consideration was given to purchasing a backup server for the research community in the department.

Professors were entitled to spend their own money and none of them were willing to spend it on something that would benefit people outside their group in addition to their own group. Instead, money was blatantly wasted, and the whole department suffered. Ultimately, the head of department was responsible for failing to motivate the professors in the department to work as a team.

30.4 Conclusion

The size and cost of the SA team is an area that is often closely watched. Where the system administration organization reports into at the vice presidential level can also have considerable impact on those two areas. A company typically wants to optimize its spending on system administration so that it has the smallest budget possible without adversely affecting other people in the company. The SA team in general, and its managers in particular, have a responsibility to help the company to strike the right balance. Optimizing the SA team to have the right mix of skills and positions within the team is one of the ways in which the system administration organization can help. Providing data on how and why other groups' spending affects the SA group's spending helps, as does suggesting and participating in funding models that make other departments more directly responsible for the system administration costs incurred, thus making the cost/benefit analysis for the profit centers more accurate.

Another hot area for the system administration organization is the debate on centralized versus decentralized system administration. Infrastructure functions need to be centralized to provide a smoothly running, reliable service. Other than the helpdesk function, the more direct customer-support roles can benefit from being less centralized, but there are many pitfalls to avoid in doing so. Communication levels between the SAs need to be maintained at a high level, the teams need to cooperate, and dispute resolution between groups should happen at a lower level in the management chain than the CEO.

Consultants and contractors can be used effectively as short-term resources to advance particular projects that would otherwise have to wait. However, they should be used in such a way as to give the permanent SAs the opportunity to get involved in these interesting projects, learn, and advance their skills. Using only short-term resources to build systems for the permanent SAs to support is not a recipe for success.

As companies grow, the SAs tend to become more specialized, focusing on particular areas, rather than being expected to solve everything. SAs face problems of scale in areas that do not arise in smaller companies. There often is more pressure to keep up with new technologies. Larger companies need architects for the various technology areas to look at the big picture and steer the group in the right direction. A large company also benefits significantly from having some senior generalists to solve difficult end-to-end problems.

Companies that provide a significant service over the Internet generally need two separate SA teams to maintain the two separate pieces of infrastructure. The team supporting the Internet service also needs a different mix of skills than that of a typical internal system administration support team.

Exercises

1. Is your system administration team centralized or decentralized?

2. Are there parts of your system administration team that are decentralized that might work more effectively if they were centralized? What problems do you think centralizing those groups would solve? What problems might it create?

3. Are there parts of your system administration team that are centralized that might work more effectively if they were decentralized? What problems do you think decentralizing those groups would solve? What problems might it create?

4. In what ways have consultants or contractors been employed effectively by your organization?

5. In what ways have consultants or contractors been employed ineffectively by your organization? How would you change what was done to make the relationship succeed and meet its goals?

6. How is your system administration organization funded? What are the problems with your current funding model, and what are the benefits? Can you think of ways that it might be improved? What data would you need to present to upper management to get your ideas approved?

7. What are the relationships among the various components of your system administration organization? Can you think of ways to get SAs involved in other areas periodically? What advantages and disadvantages would the team experience from implementing that idea?

Chapter 31

Perception and Visibility

When done correctly, system administration is like good theater: The audience sees a wonderful show and never realizes how many months of planning were required to create the show or how much backstage work was happening during the performance. The majority of the work required for any performance is invisible to the audience. SAs tend to work behind the scenes. Even so, the audience appreciates and values the show *more* by understanding what went into creating the production. The audience is more invested in the success of the theater if it feels some kind of relationship to its people.

Perception is how people see you; it is a measure of quality. **Visibility** is how much people see of you; it is a measure of quantity. This chapter is about how customers see you and how to improve their perception of you. You are a great person,[1] and we hope that this chapter will help you shine.

Customers' perceptions of you are their reality of you. If you are working hard but aren't perceived that way, people will assume that you are not. If they do not know you exist, you don't exist. If they know that you exist but have a vacuum of information about what you are doing, they will assume the worst. That's reality.

Many SAs feel that if they do the technical part of their jobs well, they will be perceived well and will be visible. This is not true. Many SAs feel that real SAs are concerned only with technical problems and that perception and visibility aren't their job or that this is what managers are for or that they have no control over how people perceive them or that this is all just a hunk of baloney. We hope to change your mind. To that end, we have tried to keep our examples as real and down-to-earth as possible.

---

1. Our publisher assures us that this book will be read only by quality people like yourself.

31.1 The Basics

This section is about perception. We've already established that you are a quality individual. Do people perceive you accurately? The basics of this chapter deal with improving how you are perceived and establishing your positive visibility. Every interaction with others is an opportunity to improve how you are perceived. The first impression that you make with customers dominates all future interactions with them. You must have a positive attitude about the people you support, because they will perceive you by your attitude.

Customers perceive the efficiency of the work you do not by how hard you work but by how soon their requests are completed. Therefore, we discuss a technique that lets you match your priorities to customer expectations of completion time. We end this section with a discussion of what we call being a system advocate—being proactive in meeting the needs of customers.

You are responsible for whether you are perceived positively or negatively. Take responsibility for improving how you are perceived. Nobody else will do it for you.

These are the key elements every SA must master to achieve positive visibility. Some of these are more appropriate for management to initiate, but others must be done on the personal level. After this section, we discuss techniques SAs can use to increase the amount of visibility they receive.

31.1.1 A Good First Impression

It is important to make a good first impression with your customers. If you get off on the wrong foot, it is difficult to regain their trust. On the other hand, if you make a good first impression, the occasional mistake will be looked at as a fluke.

Try to remember back to grade school on the first day of the school year, in particular. The kid who got in trouble that day was assumed to be "the bad kid" for the rest of the year. He was watched closely, was rarely trusted, and never got the benefit of the doubt. If anything went wrong, he was accused. On the other hand, some students were on their best behavior the first week of school. They went out of their way to be especially nice to the teacher. For the rest of the year, they could get away with occasional infractions or ask for and receive permission to bend the rules.

Think of the impression you make as a goodwill bank account. Every good thing you do goes into an account. You can survive one bad thing for every five good things in the account, if you are lucky. Making a good first impression starts that bank account with a positive balance.

If your first interaction with a customer is at an appointment, you can do many things to make a good first impression: Be on time or early, polite, friendly, and willing to listen. Humans are visual beings, so appearance and facial expression are two things people notice first. Smile.

Chromatically Different Hair

Dressing in a way that gives a positive first impression means different things at different companies. An SA we know wears baggy overalls and dyes her hair bright pink, the current rave fashion. She's quite a sight! For a while, she was an SA at a major company in Silicon Valley. When she was assigned to directly support a web farm for a small group of people, they were extremely respectful of and enthusiastic about her. One day, a peer told her that the reason she had gained such quick acceptance by the customers was that they figured that anyone who dressed that way and got away with it must be technically excellent.

Pay attention to what you wear. Being well dressed has different definitions at different companies—a suit is respected at some, mocked at others. Just because we are not as concerned about how we dress does not mean that others are the same.

The First Time I Met You

Tom ran into someone he hadn't seen for several years. The person casually recalled, "I still remember the silly T-shirt you were wearing the first time I met you!" First impressions are lasting impressions. Every day is a day you can potentially make a first impression.

What you wear on your face is also important. A nonexasperated, unruffled exterior is the greatest asset an SA can have. Smile now and then, or people will remember you as "the grumpy one."

Don't yell. Don't yell during a disagreement or because you are frustrated with someone in an otherwise calm situation. Yelling at people is bad. Really bad. The kind of bad that gets people demoted, fired, blackballed, or worse. When overheated or frustrated, it is nearly impossible to find something polite to say and if you do say something polite, it won't come out sounding that way. It is simply best to remove yourself from the situation. If you are so frustrated that you feel you are about to yell at someone, announce that you have to go to the restroom. It always works. Excusing oneself to go to the restroom is socially acceptable, even if you are in an important meeting, phone call, or standing in front of a down server with the CEO breathing down your neck. It's a convenient reason to take a break and cool off. Everyone understands what it means and why taking immediate action is required.

You have an existing installed base of reputation with your current customers, but it is extremely important to make a good first impression with each new person who is hired. Eventually, these "new people" will be the majority of your customers. Making a good first impression on new hires begins before their first day at work. You need to make sure that when they arrive, they will find their computers in their offices, configured, accounts created, and everything working properly.

On a person's first day, he can be nervous and afraid of his new surroundings. Having everything set up gives him a warm and invited feeling that affects his impression of not only the SAs but also the entire company. The SAs have an opportunity to establish a reputation for being organized, competent, and having the customer's needs in mind.

Businesses are realizing that a new hire's first day sets the tone for the employee's entire time with the company. A person arriving for the first day of work usually is highly motivated. To maintain this motivation, the person must be productive right away. Every day that the person is delayed from being productive reduces motivation. If you want high performance, make sure that new hires can get started right away.

S-l-o-w PC Delivery

A programmer in New Jersey told us that when she started working at a large insurance company, she didn't receive a computer for her first month. This may be acceptable for nontechnical jobs, but she was a programmer! Members of her group were curious why this upset her, because this was the status quo for PC deployment in their division. She was paid to do nothing for the first month, and everyone considered this "normal." This was a waste of company resources. The fact that fellow employees had grown accustomed to such slow response indicates that the SAs of this company had been doing an unimpressive job for a long time.

It is much better to use new PC deployment as a time to create positive visibility.

PC Delivery

At New York Institute of Technology, new PCs are delivered to faculty and staff in a way that generates a lot of positive visibility. The PCs arrive on a cart decorated with jingle bells.

Everyone knows that the sound of bells means that someone is getting a new PC. As the cart rolls down the hallway, a crowd gathers to see who the recipient is. Finally, the cart reaches its destination. Everyone watches as the PC is lifted off the cart and placed on the person's desk. The "oooos" and "aaaahs" sound like gifts being opened during a baby shower. Sometimes, people even applaud. (Of course, the PC has been preloaded and tested and is ready to be plugged in and used. Rehearsal makes everything perfect.)

To ensure that people have what they need on their first day, you should establish a process with the cooperation of other administrative personnel, often outside of the system administration team. Secretaries usually have a checklist of arrangements to make for all new hires. It is key to make sure that computing needs are on that checklist: finding out what kind of computer the person needs, procuring the computer, arranging the network jacks, finding out what the person's preferred login name is, determining what internal mailing lists the person need to be on, finding out what software is needed, getting the accounts created, and so on. If there is a standard desktop computer configuration, preconfigured machines should be on hand and ready to be deployed. Otherwise, there has to be a process whereby the new hire is contacted weeks in advance to arrange for the proper equipment to be ordered, installed, and tested.

On the employee's first day, the friendliest member of your SA team should visit the person to do some kind of in-person orientation, answer questions, and personally deliver a printed "welcome to our network" guide. The orientation process puts a face to the SA team. This is comforting to the customer. Customers don't like faceless organizations. It is easier to get angry at a person whom you have never met. The orientation is an investment that pays off with an improved relationship in the future.

Case Study: Orientation Sessions

If the SAs don't visit new hires to give them an orientation, someone else will. One company felt that doing such an orientation was a waste of time for the SAs and assumed that it would be an annoyance to new employees. Instead, a peer employee would brief the person about how to log in and during the process take time to bad-mouth the SA team or recount the last unplanned system outage. It was a long time before the SA team realized that this was happening and even longer before the SAs could turn the situation around and repair their reputation.

31.1.2 Attitude, Perception, and Customers

How people perceive you is directly related to the attitude you project. It is important to have a positive attitude because people pick up on your attitude very quickly.

The number-one attitude problem among SAs is a blatant disrespect for the people whom they are hired to serve. It is surprising how often we remind SAs that their users are not "lusers" or "pests with requests." They are the reason SAs have jobs. SAs are there to serve but, more important, to advocate for these people. The SAs and the computer users are all on the same team.

We advocate that SAs stop using the term *users* and replace it with the term *customers* (Smallwood 1992). This becomes a reminder that SAs are in a service industry, supporting the needs of these people instead of "pests" who make requests all day. Doing this can change SAs' attitudes dramatically.

It is very enlightening to work as a consultant; the customers are directly paying you for your SA work and will replace you if you don't meet their needs. It helps you to realize how much better things work when you treat your "users" as customers and really listen to what they need.

Conversely, an SA can get into trouble if she adopts the attitude that "the customer is always right." That's going too far. Part of an SA's job is to (politely) say no when appropriate. An SA can end up doing the customer's job if she does *everything* the customer requests. Instead, the SA must remember to help the customer help himself. It is a balancing act. The SA management needs to establish a clear definition of where to draw the line (see Section 13.1.5). It also helps to adapt an attitude of "just because I *can* do it doesn't mean I *should*." Teach customers how to do things themselves, provide documentation, make sure that they become good customers, the kind that don't ask time and time again how to do something. It is also the responsibility of an SA to politely reject requests that are against policy.

As an SA moves from customer support to higher-level roles, such as system architect, the "customer" relationship often gives way to a more collaborative relationship whereby the SA and the customer work together as a team. As this happens, you are trying to develop a "business partners" relationship. You work together to do what is best for the company and define a "scope of work" that delineates what SAs should do and what customers should do, but the customer relationship still should remain.

We've tried to role-model this language throughout this book. We've always referred to the people whom we serve as "customers," using the term "user" only when we mean someone who uses a particular device or service.

Another attitude problem SAs can develop is becoming frustrated by the fact that customers do nothing but bring them problems. SAs can develop resentment toward customers and want to avoid them or moan every time customers come to their offices. This is a bad thing. We hear such comments as, "Oh, great! Here comes another problem." This is an ironic situation because your job as an SA is to fix problems. If you get frustrated by the constant flood of problems, maybe you need a vacation (see Section 32.2.2.8). A more positive attitude is to address every "problem" as a puzzle, one that is a fun challenge to solve.

Related to that situation is the frustration that "All my users are stupid," or "Why do these people always call the help line with dumb questions?" Our reply: They wouldn't be calling if they knew the answer, and you wouldn't have been hired if you didn't know more about this than they do. "My users are idiots! They barely know anything about computers!" Our reply: They know enough to work for a company that is smart enough to hire someone like you who can answer their questions, and they know a lot more about their own areas of expertise than you do.

Create opportunities to interact with your customers in which they won't be coming to you with problems. Take the initiative to visit them occasionally. We'll have more suggestions later in this chapter.

Venting About Customers

An SA lost the respect of his customers and was later removed after an incident in which he loudly complained about them in the company cafeteria. His complaint was that although they were brilliant in topics outside of computers, he felt that their approach to computers was idiotic. He complained about them to no end while eating lunch and explained that he felt that it was beneath him to have to help them. One mistake he made was using the word *idiots* (and worse) to describe them. Another mistake he made was to misunderstand the hand signals all his coworkers were giving him to try to explain that the people he was talking about and their director were sitting at the table behind him. As you can guess, this issue was resolved by management at a very high level.

If your customers frustrate you, complain in private to your manager, and work on constructive solutions. Don't gripe about customers in public, and remember that email can be forwarded, chat windows can be seen by passersby, and conversations can be heard over cubicle walls. Venting is a much-needed form of stress release: Find the right forum for it.

You should adopt an enlightened attitude toward trouble reports. Requests from customers can be exciting challenges and opportunities to do a fantastic job, one of which you can be proud. When you integrate this attitude into your life, your customers will notice the difference in the service you provide. When replying to a customer's trouble ticket, end with a sincere note of thanks for reporting the problem: "Thank you for reporting this. It helped us fix the problem and find ways to prevent it in the future." It can make all the difference. Your attitude shows through in everything you do.

31.1.3 Priorities Aligned with Customer Expectations

The way you prioritize your tasks influences how customers perceive your effectiveness. You can make customers a lot happier if your priorities match their expectations.[2]

Customers expect small things to happen quickly and big things to take a reasonable amount of time. The definition of *big* and *small* is their definition, which is based on their perception of your job. For example, resetting a password, which is perceived as taking a minute or two, should happen quickly. Installing a new computer is perceived as a bigger process, and it is reasonable to take a day or two. When a critical server is down, customers expect you to not be working on anything but handling the emergency.[3] Therefore, you can make customers much happier if you prioritize requests so that emergencies are handled first, then quick requests, followed by longer requests.

In a given day, you or your group may complete 100, 500, or 5,000,000 requests. If you do them in the order that they arrive, your customers will

---

2. Thanks to Ralph Loura for this technique.
3. Console servers let you perform tasks on a server's console from your desk. However, customers may get the impression that you don't care about the down machine because you aren't in the machine room. It can be useful to assure them that you are virtually working in the machine room, perhaps inviting them to look at your screen.

not be extremely happy with your work, even though their requests were completed. Instead, you can do the same amount of work in a day but in a different order, and customers will be delighted because their expectations were matched.

A customer will be upset if told that his small request has to wait until you have completed a larger request, such as installing a new computer. Imagine how upset you would get if you had to wait for a one-page print job because someone was printing a 400-page report that was ahead of you in the queue. It's very similar. It is important, however, to make sure that big jobs are not postponed endlessly by small ones.

Such tasks as resetting a password also have this expectation because of the domino effect. Not being able to log in delays other tasks. A person who can't log in can't get other work done. However, replacing an old PC with a newer one is less likely to have this same quality, since the person already has a PC.

Quick requests are often easy to automate, so they become self-serve. You can arrange for a web page that will do the task for the customer. There may be a way that people can identify themselves in other ways that would lead to an automated password-reset system. Rather than personally handing out IP addresses, an SA can set up a DHCP server so that IP addresses are provided in real time, matching customer expectations without incurring any work on the SA's part. However, some devices can't use DHCP; in those cases, we have to do something a little more creative. It might not be worth the effort to develop a web page that lets customers allocate their own IP addresses. Instead, you might keep a list of the next ten available IP addresses on a pad of paper on your door. People can tear off the IP address they are going to use if they print their names in the right spot so you can later update your inventory. Creative solutions such as that can be fun to invent. Sometimes, the solution is as simple as keeping the spare toner cartridges near the printer so that the time to install them is not dominated by the time to walk to a distant supply room.

In addition to using this reordering technique on the personal level, you can use it throughout an organization. You can divide the SA team so that front-line support people perform requests that customers expect to see done quickly. Requests that will take more time can be passed on to second-tier personnel. Senior SAs can be in charge of larger projects, such as the creation of services. This division of labor enables you to ensure that your priorities are aligned with customer expectations and shelters people who are working on long-term projects from continual interruptions (see Section 32.1.2.1).

This may sound like something only large SA teams can afford to do, but even a team of two SAs can benefit from this technique. One SA can shield the other from interruptions in the morning and vice versa in the afternoon. This is called the mutual-interruption shield technique (Limoncelli 2005).

31.1.4 The System Advocate

Customers perceive you as being somewhere between a clerk who reactively performs menial tasks and an advocate who proactively solves their problems and lobbies for their needs. This section is about becoming an advocate, which we feel is the better position to be in.

On one end of the spectrum is what we call a system clerk, who is reactive rather than proactive. The clerk is told what to do on a schedule and does not participate in planning his work. Sometimes, the budget for the clerk comes from nontechnical budgets. A system clerk might spend the day installing software, performing backups, creating accounts by manually entering the various commands required to do so, and so on.

On the other end of the spectrum is the system advocate, who is proactive about her customers' technical needs, advocates those needs to management, automates the clerical tasks that she is asked to do, and is involved in the planning process for projects that affect her. Earlier, we discussed having new customers' machines and accounts set up on the day they arrive. To achieve that goal, the SAs must be involved in the hiring process. Becoming involved is the kind of proactive step that a system advocate would take.

Between the clerk and the advocate are an infinite number of gradations. Try to be conscious of where you are and what you can do to move toward being an advocate.

Becoming an advocate is a slow evolution. It starts with one proactive project. Being proactive is an investment that can have a big payoff. It consumes time now but saves time later. It can be difficult to find time for proactive work if you are having trouble keeping your head above water. Select one thing that you feel is achievable and would have a significant impact, or get your manager's suggestions. If your manager believes in the potential impact, she should be willing to reallocate some of your time to the project.

It is better to be the advocate, for many reasons. It's better for your company because it means that you are aligning your priorities with those of your customers. It puts your focus on where you can best serve the people who rate and review you. It is better for you because it develops your own reputation as a can-do person. People with such reputations have better chances during promotion opportunities. When raises are being calculated, it certainly helps to have a reputation for being the most helpful person in the group.

A large team usually will have the entire spectrum from clerks to advocates. The clerks are an important part of the team. The clerk role is where SAs get started and learn from others; they provide the advocates with useful assistance. Even the newest SA should adopt a proactive can-do attitude, however, and should work toward becoming an advocate. There is a big difference between a clerk being managed by SAs versus by customers. Being managed by SAs means being told the right way to do things and the opportunity to learn and grow. A clerk being managed by customers doesn't have the chance to learn from experts in the field and can feel isolated.

The biggest benefit comes from adopting the can-do attitude across the entire SA team. The team becomes an active, positive force for change within the organization. The team becomes valued as a whole. Many companies live and die on whether they have the right IT infrastructure to achieve their business goals. Be part of that infrastructure.

Following are some examples to illustrate the difference between how a clerk and an advocate would handle various situations.

31.1.4.1 Installing Software

You would think that installing software is fairly straightforward, but many subprocesses are involved. A clerk, for example, might receive the software to be installed from a customer who has purchased it. The customer may have ordered it weeks ago and is anxiously awaiting its installation. Often, in this situation, something goes wrong. The customer didn't know that there is a network license server and has licensed it to his own workstation instead. This breaks the strategy of having a few well-maintained and monitored license servers. More often, the installation fails because of something simple that takes a long time to repair. For example, the customer was expecting the software to be installed on a machine that is overburdened and shouldn't have new applications added to it; the license is to a host that is being decommissioned soon; or the system runs out of disk space. It can take a long time to resolve such obstacles before a second installation attempt can succeed.

While the clerk is congratulating himself for accomplishing the installation after overcoming so many obstacles, the customer is complaining to the SA's boss that he had to wait weeks until the software was installed. The customer has no understanding that, for example, installing additional disk space is something that must be planned. Nor does he understand that the addition of a new license server requires more monitoring and reliability planning and that by not leveraging the planned infrastructure, future work will require more effort for the SA team. There is no accounting for the real cost of the software, which should have included the cost of disk storage, CPU capacity, and the fact that the installation had to be performed twice because the first attempt failed owing to lack of disk space. The multiweek installation effort did not match the customer's expectation of a quick install after he received the media. As discussed in Section 31.1.3, matching the customer's expectations is critical.

A system advocate would be in a position to make the process go more smoothly. The customers would have known to involve the SA in the process from the beginning. The advocate would have interviewed the customer to get a basic understanding of the purpose of the software and performed capacity planning to allocate the proper disk, CPU, and network needs. A timetable agreed to by all parties involved would have avoided misunderstandings. The purchase would have included the software—possibly ordered by the SA to ensure correct licensing—as well as any additional disk, CPU, or network capacity. The problems, such as lack of disk space, could have been resolved while waiting for the software to arrive.

Such planning matches the software with the appropriate disk, CPU, and network capacity and gives the customer a better understanding of the SA processes and the SA a better understanding of the customer's needs. People value what they understand and devalue what they don't understand. Through this process, both sides value the other person more.

31.1.4.2 Solving a Performance Problem
A customer complains about slow system performance. A clerk might be told to upgrade the customer's machine to a faster network card because all customers assume that systems are always slow because of slow networks.[4] Little is improved after the installation, and the customer is not happy. The problem has not been properly diagnosed. In fact, many times we've seen this situation and the performance got worse. The PC now had a faster network card than the server and was flooding it with traffic. Upgrading the server was what would fix the problem.

An advocate would take a more active role by observing the problem— ideally, before the customer notices it if there is a good monitoring system

---

4. As a historical note: Before network-centric computing, the usual assumption was to blame a lack of RAM.

in place—using various tools to diagnose the problem and proposing a so-lutions. The advocate takes the time to explain the problem and the various potential solutions with enough detail so that they can select the best solution together. The proposal is presented to management by the customer, who is now capable of explaining the issues. The SA is in the room to support the customer if he stumbles. After management approves the purchase and the problem is fixed, the customer is very happy.

The result of such a team effort is a customer base that is more invested in the evolution of the network.

31.1.4.3 Simple Automation

The advocate manages time (see Chapter 32) to make time for projects that will prevent problems. She also creates additional time in her day by automat-ing her most time-consuming tasks. Automation opens doors to better ways of doing things.

The clerk might choose to put off all account-creation requests until a certain day of the week, then do them all in a batch. Customers see extremely poor turnaround time. The advocate automates the task so that creating accounts is simple and she can do them on demand.

Automating a task does not have to be extremely complicated. Don't get bogged down in creating the perfect system. A simple script that assists with the common case may be more valuable than a large system that automates every possible aspect of a task. For example, automating account creation is easy, except special cases, such as administrative accounts. Automate the 80 percent that is possible, and save those special cases for the next version of the program. Document the cases that require manual handling. Documentation is particularly important in these cases because the process is being done far less often, so it is easier to forget the nuances. Automation also hides how the normal cases are handled; thus, coworkers performing the special cases have no baseline against which to compare.

Rather than writing a script to automate things, one can write a script that outputs the commands that would do the task. The SA can review the command for correctness, edit them for special cases, and then paste them to the command line. Writing such scripts is usually easier than automating the entire process and can be a stepping stone to futher automation of the process.

Manually loading a machine's OS also can be a long process, especially if a series of from-memory customizations must be made. OS vendors pro-vide tools for automating installations that also automate customizations, as discussed in Chapter 3. The advocate takes advantage of these tools; the clerk continues manually loading OSs.

Automation is often done to improve repeatability or prevent errors and does not otherwise speed up the task. An easy sequence of commands that involved filenames that are easy to mistype is a good process to automate even if little time will be saved. The time savings come from not having to fix mistakes.

31.1.4.4 Automating Anything

The most important thing to remember when automating a process is to first do the entire process manually, then automate those steps exactly. After that, you can improvise, add features, or make this small program part of a larger superstructure. But first, you must do it yourself and automate your steps.

We know this from experience. We have seen many novice SAs struggle for weeks trying to automate a process, only to discover that they were trying to automate something that *they* weren't sure how to do! It's easy to get into this trap. On a theoretical level, people think that they know how to do it. It sounds easy, why would automating it be difficult? Why not simply start by writing code to do it? Instead, a lot of time is wasted because you don't know whether you can do something until you've done it.

As you manually perform the process, record what you do. Do the process; don't simply think your way through it. You are not as good at simulating a computer as a computer is. For example, if you were automating the creation of user accounts, record all the various steps as you do the process manually. Now test the account to make sure it works. You might find that you forgot something, requiring you to revise the process.

Once the steps are recorded, consider how to automate each step. Is there a command that performs that function? What happens behind the scenes when you click that button? Does it modify a registry setting? Run a program? Update a file?

Now write code to automate that one step. Don't wait until all the code is written to start testing. Test each step separately before adding it to your main program. Test the main program after each step's automation is added. Finding mistakes early on is key to writing solid code. This avoids the situation in which you find that a mistake made in the first step made the rest of your code useless. Even worse is discovering that fixing a problem in the first step has ramifications for the rest of the steps. Imagine if a particular variable established in the first step now needs to be an array of variables. Now all future steps that use that variable have to be modified. What if you accidentally don't change it everywhere? What if this radically changes the algorithms used in later steps? If those steps are already coded, you will find yourself hacking the code to conform to the variable, rather than writing it cleanly the first time. For these reasons, automating and testing one step at a time will produce a better system.

The Practice of Programming by Kernighan and Pike (1999) has excellent advice on such incremental development and testing of software. Bentley's *Programming Pearls* (1999) is an excellent book to read next if you find yourself developing more complicated algorithms.

31.2 The Icing

So far, this chapter has dealt with improving how you are perceived. The next level is to increase your visibility. We were talking about quality; now we are talking about quantity.

The SA's *visibility paradox* is that SAs are noticed only if something breaks. Achieving consecutive months of 100 percent uptime takes a huge amount of behind-the-scenes work and dedication. Management may get the impression that the SAs aren't needed, because it does not see the work required. Then a server crashes every hour until a controller is replaced. Suddenly, the SA is valuable. He is the hero. He is important. This is not a good position to be in, because people get the impression that the SAs do nothing 95 percent of the time, because they don't see the important, back-office work the SAs do.

One alternative is to maintain an unstable system so that the SAs are always needed and noticed. That is a bad idea. A better idea is to find subtle ways to make sure that the customers understand the value of what the SAs do.

You are responsible for the amount of visibility you receive. Take responsibility for achieving it. Nobody else will promote you except yourself.

None of these techniques should be attempted if you aren't providing good service to your customers. The keystone of good visibility is to already be doing good work. There is no point in advertising a bad product.

31.2.1 The System Status Web Page

A good way to be visible to your customers is to provide a web page that lists the status of your network. SAs should be able to easily update the status message so that when there are outages, they can easily list them. When there are no outages, the system should state so. The status should be time/date stamped so that people understand how current the information is. The page should have information about how to report problems, links to your monitoring systems, a schedule of planned outages, and news about recent major changes.

Most people start a web browser at least once a day. If the default web page is your status page, there is an opportunity to be in their field of vision quite often. Because customers can change their browser's default page, it is important to include content that is useful to the customers on a daily basis so that they are not tempted to change the default. Links to local weather, news, and corporate services can discourage people from switching.

A status web page sends a message that you care. If there is an outage being reported, it tells the customers that you are working on the problem and reduces the number of redundant phone calls complaining about the interruption.

A status message should be simple and assure people that the problem is being looked into. "Server sinclair is down; we're working on it." In the absence of this information, people often assume you are out to lunch, ignoring the problem, or ignorant of the problem. Taking ten seconds to give the status creates the positive visibility you desire.

As customers become accustomed to checking this web page, there will be fewer interruptions while you try to fix the problem. There is nothing worse than being delayed from working on a problem because you are busy answering phone calls from customers who want to help by reporting the problem. People will not develop the habit of checking this page until you consistently update it.

This can be a simple web page or as complicated as a web portal that delivers other news and features. Commercial and free portal software has a range of features and complexity.

Low-tech solutions also work well. One site simply put a whiteboard at the entrance to the machine room, and SAs wrote status messages there. If a method gets the message across, it is a good solution. This approach works well only in smaller environments where the machine room is convenient to the customers. At some sites, a webcam is aimed at the whiteboard to make it even more convenient to see.

31.2.2 Management Meetings

Although being visible to all customers is useful, a more targeted approach is also valid. A regularly scheduled one-on-one meeting with the head of each customer group can be very valuable. Often, each SA is aligned with one or two customer groups. A 30-minute meeting every 2 weeks with the manager of each group can keep him aware as to the projects being done for his people. The manager can stay abreast of what kind of work is being requested by his staff and help prioritize those projects. You will occasionally find the manager eliminating certain requests. The secondary purpose of such meetings should be to educate the manager regarding infrastructure changes being made that, although invisible to them, are being done to improve the network. This process goes a long way toward shedding light on the invisible.

31.2.3   Physical Visibility

When considering your visibility, consider your physical visibility. Where you sit may cause you to be out of sight and out of mind. If your office is hidden behind a physical barrier, you are projecting an image of being inaccessible and unfriendly. If your office is in everyone's view, you are under the microscope. Every break you take will be seen as slacking off. People will not understand that an SA's job involves bursts of activity and inactivity.

It is good to find a balance between being physically visible and invisible. A strategic way of managing this is to have a good mix of visibility within your team. People responsible for directly interfacing with customers and doing customer care should be more visible, whereas back-office programmers and architects should be less visible.

Office Location and Visibility

When Tom was at Bell Labs, there was an opportunity to move to new offices, owing to some renovation work being completed. His boss arranged for the customer-facing SAs to be relocated to offices on high-traffic hallways. Senior, more project-oriented SAs received offices at the end of dead-end hallways that received less walking traffic. The physical location resulted in better visibility for the people who should be seen and hid the ones who should not usually be interrupted.

Desk Location and Visibility

When Tom joined Cibernet, he was told to fix a problem in the London office, where people were bothering the senior SA with trivial matters that could be handled by the junior SAs. When he arrived at the office, he saw the problem immediately.

The office was set up in an open plan much like a call center, with the SA team at the far end. Because of the seating arrangement, a customer walking toward the SAs would physically reach the senior SA first. People were addressing their problems to the first SA they reached.

Tom rearranged where people sat and it greatly improved the situation.

31.2.4 Town Hall Meetings

Another way of increasing your positive visibility is to host regularly scheduled meetings open to all customers. Such meetings can be an excellent forum for bidirectional feedback. They can also be a disaster if you are unprepared. Planning is essential.

Some organizations have yearly town hall meetings, which usually include a high-level manager's presenting a "state of the network" address that reviews the last year's accomplishments and the next year's challenges. This is usually a slide presentation. One way to communicate that your SA team has division of labor and structure is to have different area heads present briefly on their domains, rather than have one person do the entire presentation. Question-and-answer sessions should follow each presentation. Meetings like this can drag on forever if not planned properly. It is important to have all speakers meet to plan how long each will talk and what each will say. Have a script that is reviewed by all speakers. Make sure that there is little redundancy and that everyone adheres to the schedule. Have someone to introduce people and to signal people when their time is up.

Some organizations host monthly or quarterly meetings. These user group meetings often are half entertainment (to draw people in) and half bidirectional communication. The first half may be a demo or a speaker. You might have a vendor come in to talk about something exciting, such as a future product roadmap or to introduce a new product. Avoid sales presentations. SAs might present an interesting new tool to the customers and spark interest by presenting plans for major network upgrades, information on hot topics, such as how to avoid spam, and so on. This is an excellent forum to present a dress rehearsal for paper presentations that SAs may be doing at future conferences, such as LISA. Doing this also communicates to the customers that the SA staff is receiving external professional acknowledgment of their good work. The second half is a bidirectional feedback session, such as a question-and-answer forum or a facilitated discussion on a particular issue. These meetings are also an opportunity to announce scheduled changes and explain why they are needed. Following is the format one organization uses for its quarterly user group meeting.

1. *Welcome* (2 minutes): Welcome the group and thank them for attending. It is a good idea to have the agenda written on a whiteboard so people know what to expect.

2. *Introductions* (5 minutes): The attendees introduce themselves. (For large groups, call for a show of hands for each team or other segment of the community.)

3. *Feedback* (20 minutes): Getting feedback from the customers is part art and part science. You want people to focus on their needs rather than on how those needs should be met. Consider taking a class on meeting facilitation if you feel weak in this area. Ask open-ended questions: for example, "If one thing could be improved, it would be...." "The single best part of our computing environment is...." "The single worst part of our computing environment is...." "My job would be easier if...."

   Keep a log of what participants suggest. A huge pad of paper on an easel is best, so everyone can see what is being recorded. Don't write full sentences, only key phrases, such as, "faster install new C++ releases" or "add CPUs server5." Once a sheet is filled, tape it to the wall and go to the next one.

   Do not reject or explain away any requests. Simply record what people say. To get the best responses, people must feel they are safe. People do not feel safe—and will stop talking—if every suggestion is answered with your reason why that isn't possible or is too expensive. However, be clear that recording an idea does not guarantee that it will be implemented.

   Be careful of permitting one talkative person to dominate the meeting. If this happens, you might want to use such phrases as, "Let's hear from the people in the room who have not spoken yet," or in extreme cases, you can go around the room, having each person answer the question in sequence, without permitting others to interrupt.

   Don't get stuck in an infinite loop. If you hit your time limit, cut off discussion politely and move on. People have busy schedules and need to get back to work.

4. *Review* (10 minutes): Review what you've recorded by reading the items out loud. Consider reviewing these lists with your management afterward to prioritize (and reject) tasks.

5. *Show and tell* (30 minutes): This is the main attraction. People want to be entertained, which means different things to different people. The best way to entertain technical people is to have them learn something new. Nontechnical people might want to learn about some mysterious

part of the system. Ask a vendor to present information on a product, have an internal person present some information about something he does or has found useful, or focus on a new feature of your network. This may be a good time to explain a big change that is coming soon or describe your network topology or some aspect of the system that you find customers often don't understand.

6. *Meeting review* (5 minutes): Have each person in turn briefly assess the meeting (less than one sentence each). For large groups, it can be better to have people say a single word or to simply raise their hands if they want to comment.

7. *Closing* (2 minutes): First, ask for a show of hands to indicate whether people thought the meeting was useful. Remind them that you are available if they want to drop by and discuss the issues further. Then, and this is important, thank people for taking time out of their busy schedules.

31.2.5 Newsletters

Many large system administration organizations produce a monthly or quarterly newsletter. Sometimes, these are excellent and useful to the customers, but we find that they are mostly ignored or backfire by sending a message that your team is more concerned with PR than with solving problems.

We feel that if you must have a newsletter, it should be simple and useful: a simple layout, easy to read. The content should be useful to the intended audience, possibly including frequently asked questions or an "ask the SAs" column that selects one question per issue to explain in detail.

If you have hired a full-time person to do nothing but produce the newsletter, you don't have a simple newsletter.

31.2.6 Mail to All Customers

Before major changes, such as those that might be implemented in a maintenance window (Chapter 20), send a brief email to all customers, telling them about the outage and what improvements they will experience afterward. Sending useful mass email is an art. Make it very brief and to the point. The most important information should be in the first sentence. Most people will read only the subject line and possibly the first sentence. Extra information for those who are interested should be contained in a few additional, brief paragraphs.

Include the text "ACTION REQUIRED" in the subject line if action is required. Then make that action clearly indicated in the body, and explain what will happen if action is not taken.

For example, a good mass email about system maintenance might read as follows:

```
Subject: No printing in Bld 1 and 2 SATURDAY MORNING

Printing in Buildings 1 and 2 will not work on Saturday,
June 24 between 8AM and 11AM because of essential system
maintenance.
    If this is a problem, please let John Smith know at
extension 54321 as soon as possible.
    The printing servers in those buildings are approaching
the end of their useful lives, and we anticipate that they
will become less reliable in a few months. We are replac-
ing them with new hardware now, so that we don't suffer from
reliability problems in the future. If you have further ques-
tions, please contact us by email at print-team@company.com.
```

On the other hand, an email sent to all customers that is wordier, like a traditional letter, is less useful. The following, for example, does not get the important point across quickly:

```
Dear all,

To serve you better, the system administration team monitors
all components of the system. We endeavor to anticipate prob-
lems and to fix them before they arise. To do so, we need
to occasionally schedule outages of some component of the
system in order to perform maintenance. We do our best to
schedule the maintenance at a time that will not adversely
affect any urgent work in other parts of the company.
    We have identified a potential problem with the print
servers in Buildings 1 and 2. We anticipate that those print
servers will become less reliable in a few months' time and
will then cause problems printing in those buildings. Because
of this, we have scheduled some time on Saturday, June 24
between 8AM and 11AM to replace those servers with new,
```

```
reliable  machines.  Because  of  that,  you  will  be  unable  to
print  in  Buildings  1  and  2  during  those  hours.

    If  the  timing  of  this  maintenance  window  will  interfere
with  some  urgent  work,  please  let  us  know  as  soon  as  possible
and  we  will  reschedule  it  for  another  time.  John  Smith,  at
extension  54321,  is  the  person  to  contact  about  scheduling
issues.

    As  always,  we  are  happy  to  answer  any  questions  that  you
might  have  about  this  maintenance  work.  Questions  can  be  ad-
dressed  directly  to  the  people  working  on  this  project  by
sending  email  to  print-team@company.com.  All  other  questions
should  be  addressed  to  helpdesk@company.com  as  usual.

    Thank  you  for  your  cooperation  with  our  ongoing  mainte-
nance  program.

The  SA  Team
```

Such email should always include two ways of contacting the SAs if there are questions or if someone has an issue with what is being announced. It is critical that this contact information be accurate. We've seen many complaints from people who received such a notice but for various reasons weren't able to contact the author. It is important that the various contact methods are two different means (email and phone, fax and phone, and so on), not simply, for example, two email addresses. Be sure that you aren't telling people, "If you're email isn't working, please send email to our helpdesk to have your problem fixed."

Mass email should be used only occasionally and for important changes. Too much mass email or mass email that is too wordy wastes everyone's time and will be seen as a nuisance.

Who Needs to Read This?

As part of the Google culture, all mass email begins with a statement saying who doesn't need to read the following message. Some real examples:

- "If you don't use [URL to internal service], you can stop reading now."
- "If you don't write C++ code on Linux, you can stop reading now."
- "If you don't use GFS or have no idea what GFS is, you can stop reading now."
- "If you haven't had a birthday in the last 12 months, you can stop reading this now."

> **Promote Services in Unexpected Places**
>
> Les Lloyd at Rollins College uses his email signature to advertise new features, upcoming training classes, and major planned outages.

31.2.7 Lunch

Breaking bread with customers is an excellent way to stay visible. Eating lunch with different customers every day or even once a week is a great way to stay in touch in a way that is friendly and nonintrusive.

> **Free Lunch**
>
> Tommy Reingold at Bell Labs watched the serial numbers on the trouble tickets that were generated. The creator of every 10,000th ticket is taken out to lunch. He pays for the lunch out of pocket because of the value he gets out of the experience. It's a simple, inexpensive thing to do that helps build the reputation of the SA team as being fun and interesting. This "contest" isn't advertised, which makes it even more of a surprise to customers when they win. It can be fun to watch people send an extra ticket or two to try to increase their chances of winning.

31.3 Conclusion

Do not leave perception and visibility to fate. Take an active role in managing both. Unmanaged, they will be a disaster. As we become conscious of these concepts, we quickly find many ways to improve them.

Perception is about quality, how people perceive you. Creating a good first impression is a technical issue that requires much planning. Establishing the processes by which new customers have their computers and all accounts the day they arrive requires coordination between many different departments. It is important that new customers receive some kind of orientation to welcome them to the network, as well as some kind of getting-started documentation.

We find that referring to "users" as "customers" changes how we treat them. It focuses our attention on the fact that we serve them. It is important to treat your customers with respect. There is no such thing as a "stupid" question.

We discussed using queuing-theory, a technique for reordering the requests that you receive, so that their completion time is aligned with the expected completion time.

We discussed the system-advocate philosophy of system administration. A system advocate is a proactive SA who takes the initiative to solve problems before they happen. Transforming a clerical role to a proactive system advocacy role is a change in attitude and working style that can dramatically improve the service you provide to your customers. It isn't easy, it requires hard work and an investment in time now for a payoff later.

Visibility is about quantity—how much people see of you. We discussed many ways to increase your visibility. Creating a system status web page puts you in front of customers' eyes daily. Meetings with managers help them understand what you do and help you maintain focus on their highest priorities.

The office locations of every member in your team affects your team's visibility. Customer-facing people should be in the more visible locations. Town hall and user group meetings should be held. Newsletters are often produced by SA groups but rarely read by customers. They are a lot of work to produce and too easy to ignore. Having lunch and social functions with customers is a simple way to maintain interaction.

Taking control of your perception and visibility is required to manage your and your team's personal positive visibility. Managing these things effectively enhances your ability to work well with your customers, increases your opportunities to serve your customers better, and has great potential to enhance your career.

Exercises

1. What is the first impression you make on your new customers? Is it positive or negative? What can you do to improve this?

2. Ask three customers what they remember about the first time they interacted with your SA team. What did you learn from this?

3. At your site, who gives new hires their first-day orientation?

4. Do the members of your team use the term "user" or "customer"? What behavior do you role-model for others?

5. When you need to vent about a customer, whom do you talk to and where?

6. Select ten typical customer requests, and estimate your customer expectations for how long they should take to be completed. Poll three customers for their expectations. How did you do? What did you learn?

7. In what way does your organizational structure benefit or hurt attempts to match customer expectations of completion time? How could this be improved? What do you do on the personal level in this regard, and what can you do to improve?

8. On a scale of one (clerk) to seven (advocate), where are you? Why do you say so? How did you decide on your rating? What steps can you take to move toward advocate?

9. Do you experience the system administrator's visibility paradox mentioned in Section 31.2? Give some examples. What can you do to turn this situation around?

10. Which of these projects would have the biggest positive impact on your organization's visibility: a system status web page, regular meetings with key managers, reorganizing the location of your and your team's offices, town hall meetings, user meetings, a newsletter, or having lunch occasionally with your customers?

11. Does your group produce a newsletter for customers? Poll five customers on whether they read it and what they find useful if they do. What did you learn?

12. Who on your team is best qualified to host a town hall meeting?

13. Discuss with your manager this question: What needs the most improvement: your perception or your visibility? What about your team?

Chapter 32

Being Happy

This chapter is about being a happy system administrator. Happiness means different things to different people. A happy SA deals well with stress and an endless incoming workload, looks forward to going to work each day, and has a positive relationship with customers, coworkers, and managers. Happiness is feeling sufficiently in control of your work life and having a good social and family life. It means feeling like you're accomplishing something and deriving satisfaction from your job. It means getting along well with the people you work with, as well as with the management above you.

Just as happiness means different things to different people, various techniques in this chapter may appeal more to some readers than to others. Mostly, we've tried to list what has worked for us. For example, of the hundreds of books on time management, we try to list the 10 percent of such books that apply to issues SAs face. If you think that books on time management are 90 percent junk, we hope that we've covered the remaining 10 percent for you here.

The happy SAs we've met share certain habits: good personal skills, good communication skills, self-psychology, and techniques for managing their managers. We use the word *habits* because people do them unconsciously, as they might tap their fingers when they hear a song on the radio.

These behaviors come naturally to some people but need to be learned by others. Books, lectures, classes, conferences, and even training camps teach these techniques. It's pretty amazing that happiness comes from a set of skills that can be developed through practice! Making a habit of a technique isn't easy. Don't expect immediate success. If you try again and again, it will become easier and easier. A common rule of thumb is that a habit can be learned if you perform the behavior for a month. Start today.

The goal of this chapter is to give you a taste of these skills and techniques and then refer you to resources for a more complete explanation.

32.1 The Basics

The basics involve being organized and being able to communicate well. Good follow-through is an important goal; it comes from being organized and requires good time management. Professional development is important, too. These basic skills are a platform on which you can build a successful career.

32.1.1 Follow-Through

Follow-through means completing what you committed to do. Happy SAs stay organized by maintaining a written or electronic organizer, or PDA, that records their to-do lists and appointment calendars. Organizing goes a long way to ensuring follow-through. Nothing is more frustrating to customers than dropped requests and appointments. You will be happier if you develop the respect that comes from having a reputation for excellent follow-through. This is one of the reasons that, throughout this book, we put so much emphasis on using trouble-ticket tracking software. Such software assures us that promises are not forgotten.

Your brain has only so much storage space, so don't overload it with items that are better recorded in your organizer. Albert Einstein is rumored to have been so concerned about making sure that 100 percent of his brain was used for physics that he didn't "waste" it on such silly things as what to wear—he had seven outfits, all the same—one for each day of the week—or his home address and phone number—he kept them written on a card in his wallet. When people asked him for his phone number, he advised them to look it up in the phone book. He didn't memorize it.

Your memory is imperfect. Your organizer, on the other hand, will not accidentally drop an action item or reverse two appointments. You should have a single organizer, so that all this information is in one place. This is better than having a million pieces of paper taped to your monitor. Combine your work and social calendars so that conflicts don't arise. You wouldn't want to miss that important birthday or anniversary or a meeting with a customer. Maintaining separate calendars at home and at work is asking for trouble. They will become out of sync.

A combined organizer should include your social events, anniversaries, doctor's appointments, non-work-related to-do items, and reminders of regular events, such as the dates for your next annual physical and your car's next inspection. Use your organizer to remind yourself of regular, repeating events. Include reminders to take breaks, to do something nice for yourself, and to compliment your significant others. Use your organizer to record the names of movies that you want to see so the next time you are at a video rental store, you aren't frustrated trying to remember that great movie that coworkers recommended. None of these things should be lost in a mess of notes taped to your desk or in your messy and imperfect brain.

Case Study: Dynamic To-Do Lists

In an attempt to achieve perfect follow-through, Tom maintains 365 to-do lists per year. He ends each day by copying the incomplete items from today's list to tomorrow's list. Already on tomorrow's page are items that he previously committed to doing that day. If he's overloaded, he can copy the incomplete items to lists even farther into the future.

In the morning, he reads today's list and tags each item that absolutely has to be done today. First, he works on those items. After those are completed and crossed off, he works on the remainder of the list. Previously, he felt it was impossible for an SA to prioritize; now, he is able to set priorities each morning.

When a new item is added, he writes it on the first day that he'll be able to work on it. Usually, that's today's list; other times, it may be a few days or months away. Previously, he felt that it was impossible for an SA to plan very far ahead; now, he is able to schedule work rather than always feeling pressured to do it right away or before he forgets.

Near the end of the day, he can see what hasn't been completed. If it looks as though he'll be missing a deadline he committed to a customer, he can call the person see whether the item can wait until first thing the next morning or whether it is so critical that he needs to stay late to work on it. Previously, he always felt pressured to work late every night or guilty over every missed deadline. Now, he can call people and renegotiate deadlines.

At the end of the day, the need to copy the incomplete items forward gives him incentive to not let one slip, because he will have to copy it more often. At the end of the day, every item has been somehow managed. It is either completed and crossed off or moved to a future date and crossed off. He receives a feeling of accomplishment and closure because every item has been "managed." Previously there was no feeling of closure, and every day he'd leave work feeling that there was no end in sight to all the work he had since there were so many open issues. Now he can sleep better knowing that he'd gotten the important things done and the others are no concern of his until the morning.

When writing monthly or yearly reports, rather than struggling to remember what he's accomplished, he has completed to-do lists as reference.

There are software packages, PDAs, and even web-based portals that automate this process. However Tom prefers to do this with a paper-based system because it is easier to write notes in the margin, and has zero reboot time. Tom draws a lot of diagrams, and that's easier to do with paper. The physical binder he uses is large enough to carry pens and sheets of paper, which is always convenient to have.

Having any kind of system is better than having no system at all. We believe this so strongly that we encourage employers to pay for employees' PDAs or old-fashioned paper organizers, even if they are used for maintaining both social and work information. We're not concerned with which system you use, but we are concerned if you aren't using any system.

Once you have been maintaining your organizer for a while, you will find that you can focus and concentrate better. You can focus better on what you are doing when you aren't also trying to remember what you are doing next, what you have to do next week, and whether that customer meeting is next Wednesday or the Wednesday after that. It's as if you can purposely forget things after you have recorded them in your organizer. Each morning, you can review today's items to refresh your memory and set your focus for the day. Let your organizer work for you; don't duplicate its work.

32.1.2 Time Management

Time management is about using time wisely. Rather than increasing productivity by working more hours, you can do more in the same amount of time by using a number of techniques and doing a little planning.

Work smarter, not harder. Customers don't see how hard you work. They see what you accomplish. Align yourself with this bit of reality. Anybody can work hard, and we're sure that all the readers of this book do. Successful SAs focus on results achieved, not on effort expended.

32.1.2.1 Difficulty of Time Management

Time management is extremely difficult for SAs because an SA's job is typically driven by interruption. People or other external events interrupt you with requests. So rather than working on your high-priority goals, you spend time responding to other people's requests, which are based on their priorities. Imagine trying to drive a bus from New Jersey to San Francisco if you stopped the bus every time a passenger asked you to. You might never get to your destination! Although it is valuable and interesting to have stopped at those locations, your job was to get the bus and the passengers to San Francisco. A critical step toward good time management for SAs is to break the cycle.

As discussed in Section 31.1.3, you can split your day, perhaps working on projects in the morning and responding to requests in the afternoon. If customers know that this is your work cycle, they will respect that and bother you only in the mornings for emergencies. If they don't, you can politely record their requests and tell them that you will get to them in the afternoon.

Alternatively, you can trade with a coworker so someone is always taking care of interrupts. Or you can simply arrive extremely early in the morning, when others aren't around to interrupt you.

When you are interrupted, you can deflect the interruption by writing the request into your personal to-do list and tell the person that you will get to the request later. Sometimes, you may be unable to write down a request. For example, you are walking through the lobby when Cindy Lou interrupts you with a request. In this case, it can be useful to explicitly state, "I'm not going to remember your request, because I can't write it down right now. Could you please send me an email?" People will appreciate the honesty if you do not sound rude or indignant. It is easy to come off sounding rude in this situation, so we recommend being extra nice. If a trouble-ticket system, such as the ones mentioned in Section 13.1.10, is used to drive your to-do list, it can be effective to ask the person to submit a ticket. It trains customers to use the channels that were set up just for them. It can be effective to show customers that you are taking them seriously by listening to them and telling them specifically how to phrase the request in the ticket system. You might say, "Could you create a ticket that says, 'Fix the DNS problem on server 5; John[1] knows what I mean.'" The customer will appreciate not having to spend so much time composing the message. The key to a good deflection is to not be perceived as rude and to help the customer get help.

32.1.2.2 Goal Setting
A common problem is to feel as though you are spinning your wheels— working hard month after month but not getting anywhere. You are spending so much time mopping the floor that you don't have time to fix the leak. You can break this cycle only by changing your behavior. We suggest *goal setting*. Take some time to set goals for the next month. Write down everything that comes to mind, in any order. Then prioritize them, and eliminate the low-priority items. Plan what smaller steps are required to meet the remaining goals. Prioritize the tasks that will bring you closer to those goals, and stop doing the things that won't.

Planning a year in advance may seem like writing science fiction, especially if you are in an environment in which things change rapidly. You might think it unreasonable to plan more than 6 months in advance at a start-up, but don't pressure yourself to have only hard "business" goals. Even at a start-up where quarterly goals aren't precise, you can have long-term goals: Fix or replace the four least-reliable servers, be on time for meetings more

---

1. Only if your name is John.

often than not, meet monthly growth plans on time, force yourself to take time for yourself, get a promotion, accrue a down-payment on a house.

One useful technique is to spend an hour on the first day of the month reviewing your accomplishments from the last month to see how they got you closer to your bigger goals. Then plan what you want to accomplish in the next month, possibly revising your 1-year goals. You can begin each week by reviewing your status. This has the effect of keeping your goals in the front of your mind. How many times have you gotten close to a deadline and thought, "Gosh, I can't believe I forgot to work on that!" Trust the process. It works.

32.1.2.3 Daily Planning

Again, planning is the key to successful time management. You should begin each day by reviewing your to-do list, prioritizing items, and fitting them into your schedule for the day. This 5-minute investment has a huge payoff.

Case Study: Putting It All Together

Speaking of early mornings, Tom finds that he can get more work done in the first hour of the day than the rest of the day combined, because there are no interruptions. People don't interrupt him, because they are aren't in yet or are too busy checking their email, preparing for the day, and so on. He used to spend his first hour reading email and visiting the various web sites (Adams 2000). One day, however, he realized that it would be better to use this most productive hour for something more, well, productive. Now, he starts off by checking his monitoring system for any red alerts and then his email box for messages tagged "urgent" but then resists the temptation to read the other messages.[2] He invests 5 minutes planning his day: First, he reviews, edits, and prioritizes his to-do items, possibly moving some items to tomorrow's list if there won't be time for them. He then schedules his day with a granularity of 1 hour. He blocks out time for meetings that he must attend. He blocks out a couple of hours for interrupt-driven tasks. He blocks out the remaining hours for his top-priority projects. The remainder of this first hour is spent working on his single highest-priority item. He even ignores phone calls. This first hour ensures that this most important project gets at least some attention every day. His most productive hour is spent on his most important tasks. He doesn't do this every day, but he always wishes he had. When he skips this step, important tasks get forgotten, appointments are missed, and schedules slip.

Chopping your day into 1-hour increments may not be right for you. Half-hour increments might be better or might totally stress you out.

---

2. Actually his monitoring system and email system send urgent messages to his pager so that he can avoid that step entirely.

Half-day increments might be better for you. Experiment a little and discover what works best.

Although the first hour of the day may be extremely productive because of the lack of interruptions, you are likely to find another time of the day that is extremely productive because of your biological clock. Some people find that their most productive hour is in the midafternoon or 6 PM or even 2 AM. There is no rhyme or reason to it; it's just the way people are built. Whatever it may be, plan your schedule around this. Schedule the work that requires the most thought, attention to detail, or energy during that hour. Your most productive hour might not be when you expect it. It might also change as you grow older, sort of the same way that your sleep patterns change as you grow older. The only way to find your productivity peaks is to slow down, listen to your body, and pay attention.

After reading the previous case study, you probably think that Tom is a "morning person." Amazingly, he isn't. Starting the day by working out a schedule wakes him up to the reality of what he needs to do that day. He finds the first hour so productive because of the lack of interruptions, not because his biological clock makes mornings a good time for him to work. His peak hour is 7 PM, especially if he had dinner at 5 PM.

32.1.2.4 Handling Paper Once

Time management books also recommend a couple of other techniques that bear repeating here because they are useful to SAs. One technique is to "touch every piece of paper only once." Process each piece of mail completely rather than sorting it into piles to process later. As you touch each item, examine it and decide whether you are going to throw it away without read it, read it and throw it away, deal with it and then throw it away, respond to it and then throw it away, or file it. Sometimes, dealing with an item means recording it in your to-do list. Other times, you can write your response in the margin and send it back to the party who sent it. The worst thing you can do is read it, then put it in a pile to be dealt with later: This means that you will have read it twice, which is a waste of time. Remember that everything you file creates more work when you go to clean your files or makes the effort of maintaining the file a larger task. File as little as possible. When in doubt, throw it out.[3]

---

3. Non-SAs might place such items in a "throw out in 30 days" folder that is emptied once a month. However, we find that SAs don't receive important items on paper. SAs receive important information electronically. Paper notifications that SAs receive tend to be from the company's nontechnical people who only want to bother us with useless information, such as the fact that because repairs will be made to the second-floor restroom, people should use the third-floor restroom in the meantime. We believe that the SAs reading this book are smart enough to go to the third floor on their own when they see that the second-floor bathrooms are being repaired.

If it was really important and you later find that you need it, you can contact the source for a new copy.

Email can be treated the same way. If you read each item and then keep it to process later, you are effectively doubling the amount of email you process. Instead, read and delete it, file it, paste it into your to-do system and delete the original, or forward it to someone else and delete the original. If you never delete email because you fear that you might need the message some day, configure your system to archive every message you receive in a "archive folder." You can then delete email without fear, because you know that you can refer to the archive. This archive can be rotated like log files, retaining only the last few months of email to conserve disk space.

Even better than doing all this yourself is to have an automated system do it for you. UNIX systems are known for having some excellent mail-processing utilities, such as procmail (van den Berg 1990). Tom lives by the phrase, "If you aren't using procmail, you're working too hard." Systems such as procmail allow you to set up filters to presort your email based on various criteria. Tom has a folder for each mailing list he is on and uses procmail to filter messages from mailing lists to the appropriate folder. This keeps his mailbox relatively clean. If he doesn't find time to read a particular mailing list for an entire week, he simply deletes the folder's contents: If it was earth-shattering news, he would have heard about it elsewhere or would have seen the fireball personally as it fell out of the sky. Filters also have the ability to call other software: procmail sends a copy of email to Tom's pager if it comes from his boss, has the word "urgent" in the subject line, or mentions the word "lunch." This ensures that his three top priorities receive immediate attention, yet he does not need to continually check for new email.

Tom also uses filters to archive all incoming email to a folder named after the current year and month. On the first day of every month, a cron job runs that compresses the archives that are more than 3 months old. Every now and then, he burns these archives into a CD-ROM and deletes any that are older than 1 year. This balances his need for a permanent record with his desire not to waste disk space.

Systems that Archive All Email

Google's gmail service saves all email messages by default and provides excellent search capability. Rather than spending time deleting or filing messages, one simply searches for messages in the archive when they are needed.

32.1.2.5 Staying Focused

Time management books talk a lot about staying focused. A common tip is that messy desks are full of distractions that make it difficult for the brain to focus. Extending that to computer users means also keeping a clean email box and a clean computer GUI desktop. The more icons on the screen, the more visual distractions present to make your mind wander. Instead, virtual screens can greatly help maintain focus by showing only the information on which you want to be focused. It may sound radical, but you also might disable any systems that let you know when you have new email and instead set aside a couple of small blocks of time each day during which you read email. Email can become one of the interruptions that prevents you from getting your job done.

32.1.2.6 Daily Tasks

If something must be done today, do it first. That ensures that it gets done. If there is a task that you have to repeat *every* day, schedule it for early in the day.

Case Study: Schedule Daily Tasks Efficiently

Tom used to have to change backup tapes every day. It took about 15 minutes if everything went right and an hour if it didn't. His plan, which didn't work well, was to start changing the tapes at 5:30 PM so he could leave by 6:00 PM. If he started at 5:30 PM but the task only took 15 minutes, he would then waste another 15 minutes because he didn't want to start a new project right before leaving. That would waste more than an hour a week. If he had been deeply involved in a project and lost track of time, he would find himself starting to change tapes when he was already late for whatever he was doing after work. He'd be late, stressed because he was late, angry while changing tapes because now he was going to be even later, and arrive at his after-work function stressed and unhappy. He tried changing the tapes first thing in the morning, but that conflicted with his attempt to use that first hour for his most important tasks. Finally, he settled on changing tapes immediately after lunch. This worked well and became somewhat of a ritual that got him back into work mode. If something has to be done every day, don't schedule it for the end of the day.

32.1.2.7 Precompiling Decisions

It is more efficient to make a decision once rather than over and over again. This is why compiled languages tend to be faster than interpreted languages. Think about what a compiler's optimizer does: It spends a little extra time now to save time in the future. For example, if a variable is added to a constant, the optimizer will eliminate this calculation if it determines that the constant is zero. An interpreter, on the other hand, can't do such an optimization because it would take longer to check whether the constant is zero before every addition than it would to simply do the addition. You can precompile your decisions the same way. Decide to do something once and retain that decision. When you are breaking your old habit, your mind might start to try to make the decision from scratch. Instead, distract your brain by replacing those thoughts with a mantra that represents your precompiled decision. Here are some mantras that have worked for us.

- *It's always a good time to save your work.* In the time it takes to decide whether it's a good point to save your work, you could have pressed the keys to have it done already.

- *Always make backups.* Always back up a file before making a change. Often, someone thinks that the change is so small that it can be undone manually. Then the person ends up making a big change. It's better to decide to always make a backup rather than spend time deciding whether to do so.

- *Record requests.* Rather than try to remember a request, write it down: Add it to your PDA, create a helpdesk ticket, write it on the back of your hand. Anything is better than trying to remember something. And yet, we find ourselves saying, "This is so important, how could I possibly forget it?" Well, the truth is that if it is that important, it's worth opening a ticket.

- *Change tapes M-W-F.* In Section 26.1.6, we discussed a backup system that required a lot of daily thinking to decide whether tapes should be changed. Instead, it was decided that time was more valuable than blank tapes, and tapes were simply changed on certain days whether it was necessary or not.

- *Take the PDA.* Tom was always trying to decide whether he should take his PDA organizer with him. It was obvious that it should be taken to meetings, but would he need it while working in a customer's office? He found that every time he was leaving his office, he was delaying himself to consider whether he would need his PDA. If he didn't take it but later needed it, he would revert to writing notes on tiny slips of paper that would invariably get lost. He also found himself losing his PDA, always finding it later in some office that he had visited to help a customer.

When going home at night, he'd pause to decide whether he should bring it home. If he left it at the office, he'd invariably end up needing it at home. If he did bring it home, the next morning he'd often forget it at home because he would not remember whether he had brought it home the previous night. The solution to all these problems was to precompile this decision: "Tom will always bring his organizer with him wherever he goes." As a result, he always had it when he needed it, whether he was in the office or at home. He never reverted to notes on slips of paper. It never got left at home because when he left for work, he knew it should be with him. He no longer lost it, because he developed the habit of making sure that he had it with him whenever he left a room. He was more focused because his brain didn't need to sidetrack to make an unrelated decision about his organizer every time he sprang into action. He saved time because he wasn't wasting it deciding the same issue over and over.

- *Sooner is better than later.* Our final example helps prevent procrastination. For smaller tasks, we suggest that "sooner is better than later." For example, Tom would often procrastinate on small items because if it is small, he could do it "any time." However, "any time" would rarely arrive. For example, when driving home late at night, he would notice that his car was low on gas. He'd decide that he could do it on the way to work the next day, especially if he could remember to leave a little early. As luck would have it, he would be late the next day, and needing to get gas would make him even later. After adopting this mantra, he would get gas at night when he realized that his car was in need.

    There are many similar situations in the life of an SA: Place the order now, make the phone call now, start the process now, and so on. When you start to debate with yourself about whether it is the right time to do these tasks, remind yourself that "sooner is better than later."

These precompiled decisions work well for us. You should take time to consider which decisions you find yourself making over and over again, and select one or two to precompile. You will lose a little flexibility, but you will gain a lot of other benefits. The mantras you develop will be specific to your lifestyle, dress, or possibly even gender. One woman's style of dress made it difficult to always carry an organizer. Instead, she always keeps a single sheet of paper in her handbag on which to scribble notes. Her mantra was, "When I sit down at my computer, I will transfer the notes from my sheet." Whatever works for your situation is fine.

32.1.2.8 Finding Free Time

Free time is hiding all over the place, but you have to look hard to find it. You can also create free time by getting rid of time wasters. Here are some easy places to look for spare time.

- Find a "light" time of the year. Software shops with a new release every 4 months usually have a 3- to 4-week "slow period" after each release. You might have spare time then, or that may be the busy time for you as you get things ready for the customers' busy periods. You may find that during their busy periods, nobody bothers you.

- Eliminate rather than automate. As SAs, we tend to accumulate things and then spend a lot of time managing what we've accumulated. We think we're improving our situation when we find better ways to manage our accumulated time wasters and often forget that we would save even more time by having a smaller list of things to manage in the first place.

- Stop reading Usenet Newsgroups. Period.

- Remove yourself from the two busiest mailing lists you are on. Repeat this once a month.

- Take advantage of mail-filtering software, such as `procmail`.

- Take advantage of the early morning: Come in an hour earlier.

- Shorten your commute to work by avoiding rush-hour traffic. Work odd hours. Determine your body's "alertness hours," and change your schedule accordingly.

- Take a 1-day time management class, or see whether there are any books on time management specifically for system administrators.

- Invest in training workshops or books that will enable you to automate tasks (write code) in less time. If you don't know `perl` and `make`, learn them today.

- Hold weekly or monthly meetings with your chief customer—a manager or a department head—to set priorities and eliminate superfluous items.

- Hire an assistant. A part-time assistant to take care of some of the clerical (tactical) tasks can free you for more important (strategic) duties and can be a great way to train someone to be an SA. Possible candidates: a local high school student, a technically inclined secretary, the person who covers for you when you are away, a summer intern, or an interested programmer. Students are particularly useful because they are inexpensive and are looking for ways to gain experience.

32.1.2.9 Dealing with Human Time Wasters

Sometimes, you find yourself dealing with people who lack good time management skills, and their ineffectiveness affects your ability to get your job done. We recommend three steps. The last one is quite extreme.

1. Coach these individuals. Help them see what is wrong with their processes, and encourage them to get help. Do this tactfully. People hate to be told that they are wrong; lead them to realize it themselves. Ask whether there is any way that you could help them get this done more quickly.

2. Work with their management.

3. If those first two steps are not possible—for example, you are dealing with this person for only a short time or the person is in a different part of your company (or a different company!) and coaching the person would be inappropriate and presumptuous—find a way to manage the person's time. This is a last resort. For example, your project is delayed because you are waiting for something to be completed by someone else. This person never gets around to your request because he is being interrupt-driven. In this case, make sure you are the highest-priority interrupt. If you have to, stand in his office until your request is complete. Ironically, this is exactly what you should *not* let anyone do to you. However, it's obvious that the person you are dealing with in this situation hasn't read this chapter. Don't let someone drowning in bad time management drag you down. (If you notice that people are doing this technique to you, maybe you need to reread this entire chapter.)

32.1.2.10 Dealing with Slow Bureaucrats

There are many techniques for dealing with slow bureaucrats. We'd like to point out our two favorites. The first technique is to befriend them. These people typically deal with an endless stream of faceless people who are angry and impatient. Be one of the pleasant people they talk with today. Give them a pleasant change of pace by being the opposite of the last ten people with whom they've dealt. They will work harder for you. Talk with them about things that might interest them, which may be entirely boring to you. Talk as if you've been friends forever, but be sincere. Ask them how their day is going, and offer sympathy when they tell you how overloaded they are. If talking via phone, ask how the weather is in their area. To really get on their good side, say something like, "Can you believe that latest decision by our CEO/president?" Although this may sound like a waste of time that slows you down, it's an investment that pays off in better service.

Our other technique works when you have to deal with the same person over and over. When a bureaucrat tells us that a request takes multiple weeks to complete, we often back off and conserve the number of requests that we give them so as to not overload them. That simply delays our own projects! Instead, do the opposite: give the person hundreds of requests at once. Rather than taking longer to complete, large requests usually get escalated to managers who have the authority to streamline processes, cut corners, or make special exceptions. For example, if each request requires individual approval, the manager will find a way to classify some or all of the requests that are similar and push those through all at once. A bureaucrat's job is to maintain processes that they themselves do not set and therefore cannot optimize. If the problem is the process, doing something unusual makes your request break out of that process. Then it is something that the person, or the person's manager, does control and thus can create a more efficient process.

32.1.2.11 Training

Time management training can be a small investment with a big payoff. It is very inexpensive compared with the potential productivity gain. Many internal corporate education centers offer 1- and 2-day time management classes. Take advantage of these internal courses, especially if your department pays for these with "internal dollars" instead of real cash. Most classes teach dozens of techniques, and each student finds a different subset of them useful. Enter such training with an open mind.

This section is only a brief introduction to time management techniques. Self-help books (see Lakein 1996, Limoncelli 2005, MacKenzie 1997) can help you develop the techniques listed earlier and much more. When you manage your time well, you get satisfaction from your sense of being in control of your working hours, and you are more productive. This makes you a happier SA.

32.1.3 Communication Skills

Learning to communicate well is crucial to being happy and successful in your job and in your personal life. All problems can be viewed as communication problems. In an office, two people who don't like each other simply haven't taken responsibility for learning how to communicate despite their disagreements. You shouldn't have to like someone to work with that person. You simply need to be able to communicate.

Even technical issues are communication issues: A dead disk on a server is a *problem* only if no one communicated that an outage would be unacceptable or if the communication was not listened to and acted on: for example, RAID should have been used to make the system survive single-disk failures.

Problems in life generally fall into one of four categories: my problems, your problems, our problems, and other people's problems. Each can be helped by a different set of communication skills.

1. *My problems:* When I have a problem, I need to make sure that I'm being heard. We will discuss a technique called "I statements."

2. *Your problems:* When you bring a problem to me, I need to make sure that I'm hearing you properly so that I can take appropriate action or help you troubleshoot. We discuss a technique known as "active listening."

3. *Our problems:* When you and I have a common problem, we need to be able to communicate with each other so that we can agree on a problem definition and action plan. If we then present that information to others, we'll use all the communication skills in this section.

4. *Other people's problems:* When other people have problems, I have to use discipline and not get involved. People spend a lot of time worrying about other people's problems. Instead, they should be focused on their own concerns. The communication skill required here is the discipline of minding your own business.

32.1.3.1 I Statements

I statements are a tool to help you make your point and also communicate the feelings you have. The value of an I statement is that it lets you get the issue off your chest in such a way that others can do something constructive about what you have said. You have given them a fixable problem statement. What happens as a result is usually positive. When we make our needs known, the universe tends to take care of us.

The general form is: "I feel [*emotion*] when you [*action*]." It makes people aware of the effect of their actions. This is much more effective than simply telling someone that you don't like a particular behavior.

An I statement expresses soft emotions—sadness or fear—rather than hard emotions—anger. It is said that underlying every hard emotion is a soft emotion. So, before you express your "I statement," figure out what the soft emotion is and express *that.* Those hearing anger will become defensive and will not hear you as well. Hearing fear or sadness makes people want to care for you and help solve your problem. Here are some sample "I statements."

- I feel hurt when you criticize me instead of my work.
- I feel unvalued when you credit my boss with the work that I did.
- I feel very happy that you completed the project on time.
- I feel frustrated when you demand reliability but won't fund the changes I recommend.
- I feel disappointed when I receive complaints from customers saying that you don't meet your commitments.
- I feel untrusted because you installed web-censoring software on our gateway.

32.1.3.2 Active Listening

Listening is more important than talking. That's why humans have twice as many ears as mouths. Active listening is a technique that ensures complete communication. We discuss three tools: mirroring, summary, and reflection statements.

Mirroring   You wouldn't trust a file transfer protocol that sent packets but never checked that they had arrived. However, many people talk and listen without ever pausing to verify that they are understanding what they hear. In effect, they treat conversations as two unidirectional packet streams. We can do better using active listening, or **mirroring**.

Active listening means that when the listener hears something, he seeks to understand what was said before he replies to it. Instead of replying with his next statement, he takes the time to *mirror* back what he just heard with an accurate but shorter statement. It's like verifying a packet checksum before you use the data.

If someone says, "People are complaining that the file server is slow," the listener might be tempted to offer a solution right away. Instead, it is better to say, "So you are saying that several people are complaining about the file server speed?" The speaker then sends an acknowledgment or correction: "Actually, Mark got a single complaint and passed it along." Now the listener understands the situation much better.

Mark forwarded a complaint about slow file server performance. Although all such complaints should be verified before they are fixed (see Section 14.1.2.3), Mark's technical competence can indicate whether the complaint has been filtered for validity already. Also, we now know that this information has been relayed twice, which indicates that information loss is occurring. The reaction to this complete information is much different, and more focused, than a typical reaction to the original statement.

Your interpretation of what someone said is based on your upbringing and experiences, which are completely unique to each person. The more diverse your organization is, the more important mirroring becomes. The more you deal with people from other parts of the country or other parts of the world, the more likely it is that the person you are speaking to has a different basis for semantic interpretation.

Don't Trust Your Ears

Tom was in a start-up that was struggling with only 10 people but had a promise of hiring 40 more people at the next round of funding, for a total of 50 people. The funding arrived but was less than expected, and the CEO told the team, "We'll have to make some changes because we will have a smaller team in the next year." The CEO meant that the 50-person goal was reduced, but everyone in the room thought he meant the current team of 10 would be reduced. Both interpretations are semantically valid, but active listening helped clear the confusion. Someone mirrored his statement by saying, "So I hear you saying that we're reducing our group rather than hiring new people." The CEO immediately realized that he was misunderstood and was able to clarify what he meant.

To sound as though you aren't challenging the person, it is useful to begin a "mirror" statement with "I hear you saying that . . . ." Once you understand the speaker, you can react to what you've heard. If everyone on your team uses that same phrase, it can become a quiet signal that active listening is being attempted and that you are trying to understand the person in earnest. This can be really useful, or it can become a running joke. Either way, consider it "team building."

Case Study: "Say Again?"

Standardizing on certain phrases sounds silly but can be useful. A small team worked in a noisy environment and often couldn't hear one another very well. This problem was made worse by the fact that listeners asking, "What?" sometimes sounded as if they were challenging the speakers, who then became defensive and reexplained what they had just said instead of simply repeating it. The listener, who simply wanted the last statement repeated, would become frustrated. The team members established the protocol of saying, "Say again?" to mean "Please repeat that, I didn't hear you," so that it was no longer confused with, "Are you nuts? Prove it!" An outsider listening to them saying "Say again?" all the time might have found it humorous to watch, but this protocol worked well for them the team.

Summary Statements   Summary statements occur when you pause the conversation to list the points made so far. A **summary statement** is a form of mirroring but covers more material. It is often useful after a person has completed several long points and you want to make sure that you heard everything and heard everything correctly. Sometimes, summary statements are used when you feel that people would benefit from hearing what they just said. Sometimes, hearing someone else summarizing what you've just said can be enlightening, especially if the person reframes the statements a little differently. Summary statements are also vital toward the end of a meeting to make sure that everyone leaves with an understanding of what's happened and what will happen next.

A summary statement should list the points in short, pithy statements. If people correct your summary, take the time to process clarifications and then repeat the summary statement. Sometimes, boiling down a person's thoughts helps the person solve his problem.

A sample summary statement would be: "Let me summarize what I've heard so far. You are upset at the way John treats you. You feel that he berates you at meetings, disagrees with the decisions you make, and takes credit for the work you do. This is making you very upset." A statement such as that tells the person that he is being heard and lets him verify that you didn't miss any of the key points.

Grouping the issues reframes them and draws out underlying issues that might need to be solved before the surface ones can be dealt with effectively. For example, "Let me summarize what I've heard so far. Two of your points seem to be problems resulting from lack of funding: We're short on staff and are dealing with underpowered servers that we can't afford to upgrade. On the other hand, four of your points are related to a lack of training: Josh is hitting the wall in his AIX knowledge, Mary doesn't understand the debugging tools we have, Larry hasn't learned Python, and Sue hasn't transitioned to MagentaSoft yet."

At the end of a meeting, a summary statement might sound like this: "To summarize: The problem is slow server performance. Customers are complaining. We've eliminated the possibility of an overloaded LAN or hot spots on the volumes. Sarah will check with the programmers to see whether their algorithms work well over a high-latency WAN. Margaret will find two clients and verify that they themselves aren't overloaded. We will revisit this next week." This lets everyone verify that they all agreed to the same thing. It can be useful to email such summaries to all the participants as a permanent record of the action plan and agreements.

Reflection   Reflection is a technique to assure people that their emotions are being recognized. This is particularly important when the person you are dealing with is angry or upset. The secret to dealing with angry people is to immediately do something to acknowledge their emotions. You must deal with their emotions before you can deal with resolving their complaints. This calms them down. Then you can begin to deal with the problem in a more rational manner.

The technique that we use here is referred to as **reflection**; you blurt out the name of the emotion you see coming from the person. It sounds simple and bizarre but is very effective.[4]

Suppose that someone came to your office and yelled, "I'm sick of the way the network is so damn unreliable!" The best response is to reply, "Wow! You are really upset about this!" This is much better than becoming defensive.

First, the person realizes that he has been heard. This is half the battle. Most of his frustration comes from feeling as though he is not being heard. It takes a lot of courage for him to come to you with a complaint. Maybe there have been other times that he was upset about something but didn't come to you. When he is in front of you and you acknowledge months of frustration instead of denying it or becoming defensive, this will calm him considerably.

Next, he will realize how he must look. People often get so enraged that they don't realize how angry they look. Reflection subtly tells him what he looks like, which can embarrass him slightly but will also help him regain composure.

Now he will start to collect himself. He may reply, "Darn right I'm upset!" This tells you that reflection has worked, because he is inadvertently using the mirroring technique discussed earlier. You can show openness to resolving

---

4. And we promise that you will feel silly the first time you try it.

the problem by saying, "So sit down, and we'll talk about it." At this point, he should calm down, and you can productively discuss the problem.

If not, draw on your active-listening skills—mirroring and summary statements—to discuss the emotional side of the issue. We can't stress enough that technical issues can't be solved until you've effectively responded to the emotional side of the issue. Once he has calmed down, be ready with your mirroring and summary statements to address the technical issue.

32.1.4 Professional Development

Professional development means receiving the training required to maintain and improve your skills. It also means associating yourself with the professional organizations of your field.

There may be professions that don't change much and don't require keeping up with the latest technology and techniques. However, system administration isn't one of them.

Learning new skills helps in your career and is fun. It is our experience that SAs tend to rank "learning new things" high on their list of fun things. Never turn down the opportunity to learn.

Reading can keep you up to date with new technology. There is a constant flow of new books, magazines, and trade and academic journals. We also recommend that you subscribe to the major trade journal of the industry that your customers work in so that you are familiar with the industry trends that concern your customers.

One-day workshops and training programs serve a different purpose than week-long conferences. One-day seminars tend to be *tactical*: focused on a particular technology or skill. Week-long conferences are *strategic*: offering opportunities to discuss broader topics, to network, to build community, and to further the craft of system administration as a respected profession. Week-long conferences have a powerful effect, providing a much-needed opportunity to relax, and they provide a supportive environment where you can take a step back from your day-to-day work and consider the big picture. Attendees return to their jobs brimming with new ideas and vision: refreshed, motivated, and operating with a new outlook.

Although this book does not endorse particular products, we can't hold back our enthusiasm for the USENIX (the Advanced Computing Systems Association) and LOPSA (the League of Professional System Administrators) organizations. We get a lot of value from the USENIX Annual Technical

Conference, Security Symposium, and LISA (Large Installation System Administration) conferences. There are many ways to become involved in these international groups, in addition to the various local chapters. Volunteering with these groups, writing papers, submitting articles to their newsletters, helping plan conferences, and speaking at their meetings can go a long way toward developing your reputation and career.

32.1.5 Staying Technical

We often hear SAs complain, "They're trying to turn me into a manager, but I want to stay technical!" and ask for advice about how not to be promoted. If this is your situation, there are a couple of things to remember. First, if your manager is trying to promote you to management, he means it as a compliment. Don't be offended. Although some SAs have negative opinions of managers, managers tend to think that management is a good position. Maybe he is seeing great potential for you. Take the suggestion seriously and consider it for a while. Maybe it is right for you. Do, however, remember that becoming a manager does mean giving up technical responsibilities; don't feel that you'll be able to retain your technical duties and adopt new responsibilities.

Some SAs slowly slide into management, adopting slightly increasing management responsibilities over time. Suddenly, they realize that they are managers and don't want to be.

To prevent this, you must be aware of what kind of tasks you are adopting. If you want to stay technical, it is important to discuss this with your boss. Establish that there is a difference between being the "technical lead" of a group and being "manager" of a group. Come to agreement on where the line is drawn: a litmus test, so to speak. Then you can both be aware of the issue. For example, a *technical lead* is part of the technical process of architecting and deploying a new system. *Management* tasks usually involve budgets, salary and performance reviews, and other human resources issues. We'll discuss more about career management in Section 32.2.3.

32.2 The Icing

Now that you can manage yourself, your time, and your career, these skills can combine to create some higher-level skills, such as the basics of negotiation, a little philosophy about loving your job, and managing your manager.

32.2.1 Learn to Negotiate

SAs need good negotiation skills because they are often dealing with vendors, customers, and their own superiors. Negotiation is the art of getting what you want. It requires all the communication skills described in the previous section and then some.

32.2.1.1 Work Toward the Win-Win

It is important to work toward a win-win situation. That is, negotiate toward an agreement that makes both parties successful. It is useless to negotiate vendors to a price so low that they cannot afford to give you good service or to be negotiated down to the point that you are not getting what you want. A win-lose situation is where you win and the other person loses. This is the second-best situation. In both lose-lose and lose-win situations, you lose, so always avoid them.

32.2.1.2 Recognize the Situation

The first step in negotiation is to recognize that you are in a negotiating situation. It may sound strange, but countless times, we've heard someone sign a contract yet later say such things as, "I should have asked for more money." or "Maybe they were willing to negotiate." This means that the person didn't pause to consider whether he or she should be in negotiating mode. It's always polite to say the magical incantation, "Is that negotiable?" when talking with customers, vendors, tech support personnel, auto dealers, and even parents.

When your team is in a negotiating situation, communicate this fact to the entire team. Call a meeting and explain what's happening. Knowledge is power, so make sure that the team knows what information should not be leaked.

Case Study: Prepare the Team and Prevent Mistakes

An investment firm learned that the high-tech start-up it was talking to needed the funding by a certain date. The firm was able to exploit this information to its benefit and the start-up's detriment. How did the investment firm learn this information? Members of the start-up freely gave out the information because nobody had told them not to provide it. This could have been prevented if the start-up members had been assembled and told the strategy, in particular which information to protect. There are ways to communicate urgency without losing leverage. They could also have designated a point person to communicate on particular sensitive points; other team members could refer information seekers to that person.

You also have to be conscious of the power dynamic. Who is the requester? Who is the requestee? Who holds the power in the negotiation? If you are in the power seat, you can control the negotiation. If the other party is in the power seat, you must be much better prepared to defend your requests. The requester is not always the person lacking power, nor is the person receiving the request automatically in power. The power dynamic is not static. It can change unexpectedly.

Power Can Shift

Tom was negotiating with a vendor who was in the power seat because Tom's company had a large legacy investment in the vendor's product and couldn't change vendors easily. However, one of the vendor's salespeople let it slip that if the vendor didn't book the sale by the end of the week, it would be counted toward the next year's sales quota. Now Tom was in the power position. He knew that the vendor would rather receive its commission on this year's balance sheet. When the salespeople wouldn't reduce their price, he introduced issues that would delay the contract being signed but promised that roadblocks would be cleared and the contract would be signed before the end of the week if he got the product at the price he wanted. They caved.

32.2.1.3 Plan Your Negotiations

Planning is important. Sit down with the people who will be on your side and decide what you hope to gain. Which of these do you absolutely have to have? Which ones are you willing to sacrifice? Which ones are somewhere in between?

Decide what elements need to be kept secret and how such issues will be contained. Discuss the power dynamic and how that affects the strategy. Script how the meeting will be conducted, what you are going to say, and what your reaction will be if certain issues are brought up.

It is important to know what you are asking for in specific terms. Nebulous requests can delay negotiations needlessly.

Case Study: Know Who a Vendor's Competition Is

In the early 1990s, Sun Microsystems and HP were at war for the workstation market. An SA found himself working at a company that used workstations from both companies. He found it useful to put a Sun poster on his office wall and drink coffee from a Sun coffee mug when HP salespeople visited him and the reverse when Sun salespeople visited. It was a subtle reminder that he could go elsewhere.

Case Study: Do Your Homework

Doing your homework can lead to a big payoff, especially if the other side hasn't done any. When Tom meets with vendors to renew a yearly maintenance contract, he always brings a stack of printouts, each page being a trouble ticket that the vendor did not handle well. On each one are handwritten notes from the staff person involved describing what happened. Although the mishandled tickets are always a minority, it isn't Tom's fault that the vendor never arrives with data to show this. The vendor is instead humbled by the physical depiction of its mistakes and more willing to negotiate. At key points in the negotiations, Tom picks a page, reads the note out loud, frowns, and sits quietly until the vendor responds with another concession. None of this would be so effective if vendors would only do their homework and arrive with statistics that show they do an excellent job on the majority of the service requests.

Other Techniques Require Rehearsal

Before some difficult price negotiations, Tom made his team rehearse the situation in which Tom would be angry enough to walk out of the room for a couple minutes. His team was to act nervous, be silent for a minute, then tell the salespeople, "We've *never* seen him so unhappy with a vendor." They then fidgeted nervously in their chairs until Tom returned. Practice makes perfect.

These last two examples involved hardball tactics that rarely should be used. They hurt the relationship between you and the other party and will burn you in the future. As we said earlier, it is better to strive for a win-win situation. Each negotiation is an opportunity to develop a positive relationship. The future payoff is immeasurable. There is only one time when such tactics should be used, and that is when you will never have to negotiate with that person again (Koren and Goodman 1992).

The last two examples were exactly that situation: After the negotiations, that salesperson was "out of the loop" until the contracts were up for renewal. These multiyear maintenance contracts virtually guaranteed that years from now, when the renewals were being negotiated, a different salesperson would be involved. Quarterly updates to the contracts were done through a customer-service hotline whose staff had no visibility to the harshness of the prior negotiations. The salesperson Tom normally dealt with for hardware purchases was not involved in the maintenance contract negotiations, and therefore no bridges were burned there. Finally, Tom knew that he was leaving that position and therefore would not be involved in the next renewal negotiation. If bridges were burned, his successor could use another famous technique: Blame the predecessor to get on the good side of a vendor. "Oh, *he* was a jerk, but *I'm* the nice guy. So let's begin this relationship with a fresh start." This trick works only once. If you are a harsh negotiator too often, people will eventually stop dealing with you.

Variety is good, too, as we see in the next example.

Use a Variety of Techniques

Tom had a manager who successfully repeated one negotiating tactic: She was so impossible to deal with that people always gave her what she wanted. He soon realized, however, that this was her *only* tactic. Soon enough, people avoided dealing with her altogether; her career stalled as she became isolated. Be wary of burning too many bridges around you.

32.2.1.4 Set the Format of a Negotiation Meeting

The general format for an effective negotiation meeting is to define the terms, get agreement on the common ground, and then work on the more difficult parts. It sets a positive tone early on to resolve the easy issues. If something thought to be easy starts to take a long time, table it until later. Often, you will get to the end of the list of issues only to discover that there is very little disagreement or that the one item that you disagree on can be dropped. Commonly, you will discover that both people are on the same side, in which case the negotiation should be more along the lines of seeking agreement and making commitments.

32.2.1.5 Additional Negotiation Tips

These tips relate to making requests and offers. They are particularly useful during salary negotiations but apply to all negotiations.

- *Ask for what you honestly, honestly want.* Don't negotiate against yourself. Some people start off with a reduced request because they are embarrassed by asking for what they want, feel guilty that they want so much, or think that their opponent will think it is unreasonable and will refuse to continue. Don't be silly! Reducing the request is your opponent's job, not yours. Don't do the other person's job. You'll get more respect if you are honest about asking for what you want. You'll be surprised at how many times the request is accepted. Your job is to ask. The other person's job is to agree or disagree. Do *your* job.

- *After you make a request or an offer, close your mouth.* You also shouldn't negotiate against yourself when making a request or an offer. People make the mistake of stating a proposal, getting nervous at the silence they hear, and immediately making a concession to sweeten the deal. Your job is to make the offer or request; their job is to accept or reject it. Sometimes, people are silent because they need time to think or because they are hoping to make you nervous so that you will upgrade your offer without even being asked. If silence makes you nervous, fill your mind by repeating the phrase, "The next person to talk is the loser." Give things time and wait for their response.

- *Don't reveal your strategy to your opponent.* Although you shouldn't be paranoid, you also shouldn't reveal your strategy to your opponent. Don't reveal how low or high you are willing to go, just the offer you are making at that point. If a real estate agent, recruiter, head hunter, or other such agent is negotiating on your behalf, the person really represents whoever is paying him. It is always acceptable to directly ask an agent, "Who pays your commission in this situation?" You don't want to be surprised to find out that it is you! If he won't tell you who pays him, he is not being ethical. Being told, "Oh don't worry, you don't have to pay a thing" means that he is being paid by your opponent. If he is paid by your opponent, he is an extension of your opponent and you should reveal only what you would reveal to your opponent. He may say that he represents you, but if he receives a commission from the employer, landlord, or whomever, he "represents your position" to the other side, but he is acting in your opponent's best interest. Therefore, if he asks how high (or low) you are willing to go, address him like you would your opponent: Reveal only your current offer. If he demands to know your low and high range so he "can negotiate on your behalf," give him an artificial range.[5]

- *Always refuse a first offer.* Every *first offer* has built into it some room for movement in case it is rejected. Therefore, always reject the first offer.

---

5. Speaking of not revealing your strategy: We would like you to know that we haven't revealed all our secrets, so don't try to use any of these techniques against us. We have countertechniques. Really!

(This recommendation is brilliantly demonstrated in the 1995 film *Clueless*). This trick works only once. Don't automatically think that if the offer was sweetened once, it can be sweetened again. If your opponent isn't willing to budge, put your tail between your legs and accept the first offer. This is a risky technique; use with caution. (This isn't a binary search; employers usually don't make a second iteration.)

32.2.1.6 Use Silence as a Negotiating Tool

As mentioned previously, being quiet is a critical negotiating skill. Silence from your opponent may simply mean that she is thinking, has nothing to say, or is trying to make you nervous. Most people get nervous when they hear silence during a negotiation and respond by offering concessions that haven't even been requested. Another important time to be silent is when you get to an agreement. We've seen two sides finally get to an agreement, only to have them ruined by someone bringing up new issues. You've got what you were asking for, so shut up!

Be Careful What You Say

A woman was moving to a different division for an opportunity that gave her a raise and a promotion. Her new boss told her what the new salary would be and then asked, "Would you like it to be more?" She replied, "Yes." She was dumbfounded that anyone would ask such a silly question. Is there any other answer she could logically give? He should have simply waited for her to sign the paper and offer more money only if she rejected the offer. Now that he had offered to increase her salary and she had agreed, he had no recourse but to increase the offer on the spot. She later commented that she wouldn't hire someone who answered no to such a question. To her, it would be like failing an IQ test. She also mentioned that she wouldn't let anyone who asked such a question work for her. The person might trade the family's last cow for magic beans.

Although all these negotiating techniques have worked for us, we're not high-powered negotiation experts. Luckily, some real experts have written books on the topic. Often, books are specialized for a particular profession or situation. There is no negotiating book specifically for SAs, but *The Haggler's Handbook* (Koren and Goodman 1992) is a very good general-purpose book and has the benefit of being one tip per page. You can read one page per day when getting dressed in the morning; in a matter of weeks, you will be a much better negotiator.

32.2.2 Love Your Job

The happy SAs we've met love their jobs. This isn't an accident. They didn't fall into jobs that they love; they worked in many jobs in many types of companies and started to realize what they liked and didn't like. They then could become more focused when job hunting. It can take years, even decades, to figure out what motivates you to love your job and find a job that provides those qualities, but it is something to think about as your career evolves.

32.2.2.1 Enjoying What You Do

The 1999 film *Office Space* makes an interesting point. Imagine that you've won the lottery and don't have to work anymore. What would you do to fill your time? Your answer is what you should be doing as a career. If you would spend your days rebuilding old cars, become an auto mechanic. Maybe you are an SA because you would spend your time playing with computers. What are the aspects of computing that you enjoy so much? Consider integrating those things into your career.

Following Our Own Advice

Christine has been a fan of Formula 1 racing since she can remember and has always wanted to work in that industry. She decided that it was time to pursue that ideal; after the first edition of this book came out, she started working in the Formula 1 racing industry. She loves her job and is glad that she took the risk of making a career change.

Tom has always wanted to be more involved in politics. In 2003, he quit his job and worked on a political campaign. He found it a very interesting and fulfilling experience and will look for other opportunities to get involved in political campaigns that he believes in. Campaigns are increasingly relying on technology to succeed, and he wants to be a part of that.

32.2.2.2 Being Motivated

Being motivated about your job is no accident. Satisfying, long-term motivators are different for different people. Money motivates people but only in the short term. We find that it doesn't sustain motivation very well. Some people are motivated by the good feeling they receive after helping someone. It sounds simple, but helping people is habit forming. The good feeling you get from knowing that you've helped someone is so powerful that once you've had a taste of it, you crave it even more. You want to return to that good feeling, so helping people becomes even more important, and you strive to help even more people. This is highlighted in the film *Scrooged*.

The compliments people receive are habit forming in the same way. A compliment propels one forward. Imagine every compliment you get from your boss propelling you, motivating you to continue to achieve great things.

The problem is that those compliments take a long path between your ear and the part of the brain that *accepts the compliment*. Somewhere in that path is a minefield known as your *critical inner voice*. Sometimes, that voice reaches up, grabs that compliment midair, and pours toxic waste on it. Then that compliment is tainted. By the time it reaches its destination, the toxic waste has corrupted the compliment into something that hurts you. Thus, instead of a stream of incoming compliments that propel you, you have a stream of negatives that sap your energy.

For some people, this critical inner voice is a small, manageable little beast. For some, it is a loud, bellowing giant. Therapy can help manage that giant by helping you deal with the source of the problem, be it an overly critical parent, an overbearing significant other, or shame.

Shame comes from feeling bad about something and holding those feelings inside rather than letting them out. People often feel that personal problems should stay at home and not be discussed at work, but bottling up these problems can be unhealthy and wreck your productivity. Suppose that one of your parents is ill and that you haven't shared this or how it makes you feel with your coworkers. The positive feedback you receive should make you feel good and motivate you, but instead the toxic shame of, for example, feeling that you aren't visiting your ill parent enough negates the compliment: "Oh, they wouldn't have given me that compliment if they knew what a terrible daughter I am."

Therefore, it is important to accept compliments. When people deflect compliments, they do a disservice to themselves. People tend to reply to a compliment with, "Oh, it wasn't a big deal" or "I did a small part; Margaret really did all the work." If someone is being polite enough to compliment you, be polite enough to accept the darn compliment! If you aren't sure what to say, a simple, "Thank you!" will suffice.

Shame can take other forms. Fears of racism, sexism, or homophobia can hold people back from reaching their full potential. You might invalidate compliments you receive if you feel that your manager is biased against your sex, race, religion, sexual orientation, or gender identity. You can turn these issues around by discussing these fears with your coworkers and working to gain a better understanding and appreciation for your differences. If your corporate culture discourages openness about personal issues, you may find it useful to at least open up privately to someone, such as your boss or a close coworker.

An Unsafe Workplace Is an Unproductive Workplace

A bisexual SA lost a week's worth of productivity because he overheard a coworker in the next cubicle saying that "queers should all be killed." Would it be safe for him to walk to his car after work if this coworker found out he was bisexual? Would the coworker sabotage his work? Every time he tried to work, the memory of his coworker's words distracted him. The next day, he brought up this issue to his boss, who refused to talk with the coworker or move the SA's cubicle. Eventually, the SA left the company. The manager could have saved the cost of recruiting and training a new staff person if he had taken the time to make it clear to the coworker that such comments are inappropriate in the workplace and that their company valued people by the quality of their work, not by their race, sexual orientation, gender, or other nonwork issues. The manager could have also explained that the diversity of the group was what made it strong.

32.2.2.3 Happiness

Cognitive theorists believe that being happy or sad is not driven by whether good or bad things are happening to people, but by how they react to what is happening around them. How can this be? Again, we return to the concept of the critical inner voice. Some people can shut down that voice when they need to; others pay too much attention to it.

For example, suppose that a tree falls on someone's house. One person might think, "Of course it fell on my house; I don't deserve a safe home." Someone else might think, "I'm glad nobody got hurt!" and look forward to the opportunity to redecorate once the repairs are complete.

The opposite situation can also be true. You typically would think that getting a raise would be a good thing. However, it might introduce a big barrel of worries for some people: "I'm already working as hard as I can; now they'll expect even more. I'm doomed to fail!" The first part of *The Feeling Good Handbook* (Burns 1999a) gives further examples, as well as some excellent solutions.

A little insecurity is normal and healthy. It keeps people out of harm's way and encourages people to "measure twice, cut once." However, too much can cause problems.

Luckily, you can retrain yourself. The first step is to recognize that this critical inner voice exists. People can be so accustomed to it that they believe it without pausing to evaluate what it is saying. Once you have recognized that it is speaking, pause to think about what it is saying. Consider the source. Is it simply doubting everything? Is it viewing the world as black and white? Is it repeating negative things you were told by outsiders?

Case Study: Consider the Source

One SA had a major breakthrough when he realized that his critical inner voice was always saying negative things that his hypercritical mother had said to him when he was young. In fact, the voice sounded like his mother's voice! He realized that these thoughts were simply echoes of the extreme negativity he had received as a child and were not useful bits of advice. He set out to develop the habit of ignoring those thoughts until they disappeared. It worked!

Retraining yourself is not easy, but it can be done successfully. Many people choose to do it with the help and guidance of a therapist. Others do it on their own. Burns (1999a) includes a large number of techniques and a useful guide to selecting the ones that are right for you. Take advantage of the confidential employee assistance program (EAP) if your employer provides one as part of its mental health benefits package.

32.2.2.4 Good Boss/Bad Boss
Your manager affects your ability to love your job more than the kind of work you do. *A bad job with a great boss is better than a great job with a bad boss.* Suppose that your job was the best, most fantastic job in the world. For example, suppose that you were being paid to eat chocolate all day. If your boss was a jerk, you would still hate your job. On the other hand, if you had a terrible job, a great boss would find a way to make it enjoyable. Our personal experience is that most people leave their jobs not because they don't enjoy their work but because they didn't like their bosses.

32.2.2.5 Accepting Criticism
In addition to accepting compliments well, it is important to take criticism well. Everyone receives criticism now and then. Some people interpret all comments as criticism; others let the smallest criticism wreck their self-esteem. That's not good. However, if you take criticism positively, it can help you change your behavior so that you improve yourself. Criticism is a good thing: It prevents people from repeating mistakes. Imagine how terrible it would be

if everyone made the same mistake over and over again! Rather than accepting criticism with disdain for the critic, it is healthier to thank the person for his honesty and think about what you can do better in the future.

It is important to distinguish between constructive and nonconstructive criticism. Nonconstructive criticism hurts feelings without helping the situation. Be careful of the nonconstructive criticism you give yourself: Don't "should" yourself to death. "Should" is a scolding word. When you think to yourself "Oh, I *should* have done such and such," you are scolding yourself about something you can't control: the past. It is much better to replace "I should have" with "next time, I will."

32.2.2.6 Your Support Structure
Everyone needs a support structure. Everyone needs someone to talk with now and then. Your support structure is the network of people you can go to when you need to talk about a problem. Having different people you can go to for advice on office politics, technical advice, and general life advice is very important when you feel that you are over your head. It takes time to develop these relationships. Sometimes, the right person is your spouse or significant other, a friend, a coworker or manager, or even an email list of people who share a common interest.

32.2.2.7 Ask for Help
It is important to ask for help. We find that SAs tend not to be very good at seeking help for personal problems and instead are likely to let a problem build up until they feel like exploding.

Maybe it is related to some "macho" culture of being self-sufficient. Maybe because they solve problems before their customers notice them, SAs expect other people to read their minds when they themselves have problems. Maybe it's because SAs are expected to solve technical problems on their own and try to carry that into their personal lives. Even when SAs do reach out for technical help, it is often to nonhuman resources: web pages, FAQs, and manuals. Even asking for help on electronic mailing lists has an air of not talking about your problems face to face.

Successful people know that it is not a weakness to ask for help. In fact, people respect someone who takes responsibility for getting help. It creates less of a burden on others to deal with a problem when it is small rather than when it has escalated into a large emergency. Most important, problems are solved more quickly when many people work on them. Share the wealth! Friends help other friends. It's like a bank account: You make a deposit when you help your friends, and you shouldn't feel bad about making a withdrawal every now and then.

Should Have Asked for Help

Everything would have been better if one SA had asked for help. He was going to present a paper at a very large SA conference. When he didn't show up at the designated time, 15 minutes before his presentation, the coordinators went through a lot of pain to reorder the other speakers. He did show up just moments before he was to speak, when the session chair was on stage introducing the replacement speaker.

He was late because he had brought only overhead transparencies rather than his laptop with the presentation on it. Seeing that all the other speakers were projecting directly from laptops, he asked a technician at the conference whether it was possible to use transparencies. The technician was unaware that such equipment was available and erroneously told him that it was not possible to use overhead transparencies. Instead of asking one of the conference coordinators for help, he got permission from his boss to rent a laptop for a large sum of money. The rented laptop ran only Windows, and his presentation had been written under Linux, so he then spent several hours retyping the presentation into Windows while his boss made the presentation available over the Internet in case he could find someone with a Linux laptop that he could borrow.

Had he asked for help, the coordinators would have been able to find transparency equipment or would have been easily able to find a Linux laptop for him to use. Instead, he created a lot of stress for himself and others and spent a large amount of money to procure a temporary laptop. He should have asked for help.

We have other similar anecdotes that involve other personal issues, such as finance, health, relationship and family problems, and even drug and alcohol abuse. In every case, the person's friends wished they had been called on sooner. That's what friends are for.

32.2.2.8 Balance Work and Personal Life

Finding balance between work and personal time is important to mental health. Although it can be gratifying to be a hardcore techie who works day and night, burnout will eventually become a problem. Taking time for yourself is key. Taking breaks during the day, getting regular sleep, having a social life outside of work, and not working yourself to death are all critical habits to develop.

Treat your significant other with the respect he or she deserves. Many SAs work so many hours that their significant others become "technology widows." That shows little respect for them. Family time[6] is important time; take time for them. Schedule it in your datebook. Give them the thanks and admiration they deserve. Put pictures of them on your desk, so you are always reminded that you do it for them (Crittenden 1995). The most valuable thing you can give your family is time. Nobody's last words have ever been, "I wish I had spent more time at the office."

Respecting your body is also important. Listen to your body. If you are tired, go to sleep. If you are hungry, eat. If you aren't feeling well, help your body repair itself. It's ironic that we often meet people who take care of immense networks but don't know how to take care of their own bodies.

Your employer gives you vacation time. Take it; the company gives it to you so you won't burn out and then be completely useless to the firm. Long ago, employers discovered that vacations benefit both the employer and the employee.

You don't do yourself or your company a favor by skipping vacations. Many times, we've heard from people who prided themselves for not having taken a vacation in years: "The company can't live without me" or claims that skipping vacations shows your dedication. Actually, the opposite is true. If you don't disappear for a week or two once a year, there is no way to discover whether your job is documented properly or that your fallback coverage is properly trained. It is better to learn what coverage is missing during a vacation that you return from rather than when you quit or, heaven forbid, get hit by a truck.

32.2.2.9 Awards Wall

Finally, we have one more recommendation for maintaining positive self-esteem and loving your job. Maintain an "accomplishment wall," a place where you post all the positive feedback you receive: a note from a customer that says thanks, awards you have received, and so on. Make sure that these are in a place that you see every day, so that you have a constant reminder of the positive things you've done. If you are the team leader, you might consider having such a wall for all the team's accomplishments located in a place that the entire team will see. When morale is low, you can look at the wall to remind yourself of times when people have said good things about you.

---

6. By "family," we mean a very wide definition. Single people have families, too. Some people have chosen families, rather than biological ones (Small 1993).

❖ **Electronic Accomplishment Wall**   Much positive feedback is received via email. We recommend that you save every thank-you you receive in an email folder named "feathers,"[7] because they are the feathers in your cap. When you write your yearly accomplishments list, you can review this folder to make sure that you didn't forget anything. On days when you are depressed or things aren't going well, pop open this folder and remind yourself that people have said good things about you.

32.2.3 Managing Your Manager

Let's discuss a little "boss philosophy" first. Your boss has a job to do. Her performance is measured by whether certain goals are achieved. These goals are too big for any one person to complete alone. That's why you exist. Your assignment is to do a bunch of tasks that equal a small fraction of your boss's goal. Your fraction, plus the fractions of all your coworkers, should complete those goals. Some people think of their jobs as the tasks they are assigned. That's not true. Your job is to make your boss a success. Amazingly, your boss is in the same situation. She has been assigned a small fraction of what her boss needs to accomplish. Her boss's boss and up the chain all the way to the head of your organization are in this situation. The total of all these little fractions is one big success.

Why should you care about your boss's success? First, a successful boss gets promoted. An ethical boss will take you along with her. Second, a manager has a limited amount of time and energy, which she will expend on the people who are most likely to help her succeed. To manage your boss, you are going to need her time and energy. Obviously, a manager is going to respect the wishes of a star performer more than those of a slacker.

Raise-Time Humor

A group of SAs were talking about the recent round of raises. A person who didn't get a great raise complained about someone rumored to have gotten a very good raise.

He griped, "That guy always gets big raises because he just does whatever our manager tells him to."

Someone responded, "How's that do-the-opposite-of-what-our-boss-wants strategy working for you?"

---

7. Thanks to Tommy Reingold for this name.

Managing is about steering the boat that other people are rowing. Turning the rudder points the boat in the right direction, but someone else has to do the work to get you to your destination. You may think that it is your boss's job to manage you, but the reverse is also true. You must manage your boss; steer her toward what will make you happy.

Case Study: Pleasing the Visionary

An SA joined a university to fix a crumbling, unstable heterogeneous network that needed the very basics of upgrades: quality wiring, modern switches and routers, uniform OS configuration, and so on. However, the dean thought himself to be quite a visionary and wasn't interested in projects with such little flair. He wanted futuristic projects that would bring status, such as desktop video and virtual reality systems. None of those projects could possibly happen until the basic upgrades were done. The SA couldn't get any of the fundamental problems fixed until he started explaining them to the dean as the steps required to achieve his futuristic goals. He explained to the dean that he was going to make him a success and that these were the steps along the way to that goal.

Now we can talk about managing your boss. The first part of doing so is to make your needs known. Managers can't read your mind, so don't get upset when they don't guess what you want. On the other hand, you also are not the only thing on your manager's mind. Respect that by not going overboard and pestering her. Strike a balance.

One need you should communicate, perhaps once or twice a year, is your career goal. This doesn't have to be a 20-page document supporting the reasons for your request, but it should not be simply mentioned in passing, either.

Steer Promotions to You

Tom claims that he never received a promotion for which he didn't directly ask. In college, he was a student operator at the university computer center. One day, he walked to the director's office and stated, "I want you to know that I want to be one of the student managers here, and I'll do what it takes to get there." At the end of the school year, he was told that if he worked hard and was on his best behavior for the entire summer, he would receive the promotion before the new school year. He worked hard and was on his best behavior and received the promotion.[8] History repeated itself in his future jobs.

---

8. It helped that he had a great boss.

Putting an idea in a manager's ear means that the next time the manager comes to the right situation, you will be a potential candidate. A good manager will immediately start coaching you to groom you into that position, testing the waters, and watching whether you show promise to successfully fulfill the role you have requested. The manager can structure your tasks and training in the right direction.

If you are unsure of your career goals, you might communicate a technical skill you want to develop. If you want to stay where you are, be sure to let your boss know that too!

Another steering technique is to let your boss help you with time management. When you have a completely overloaded schedule with no end in sight, let your boss set your priorities. Don't bring a complaint about being overloaded. Managers receive complaints all day long and don't want another one. Instead, bring your to-do list annotated with how long each item should take to complete. Explain that the total time for these projects is more than your 8-hour day (or 40-hour week), and ask for help prioritizing the list.

A typical manager will have several positive reactions. First, it's quite a compliment that you are seeking the manager's wisdom. Second, it makes the manager happy, because after a day of receiving selfish request after selfish request, you have come to her with a message that says, "I want to meet your top goals, boss; tell me what they are." This can be very refreshing! Finally, this gives your manager a clear view into what kind of work you do. Your manager may notice tasks that should be completely eliminated or may reduce your load by delegating tasks to other people in your team. Maybe that other team member made the manager aware that he wanted more of a particular kind of assignment, and this is your boss's opportunity to give it to him.

Finally, we'd like to discuss the concept of **upward delegation,** or delegating action items to your boss. Certain tasks are appropriate for upward delegation, and others are not. Your manager should be concerned with steering the boat, not rowing it. Don't delegate busywork upward. However, upward delegation is appropriate for anything that you feel you don't have the authority to do. Creating an action item for your boss is most appropriate when it will leverage the manager's authority to make other action items go away. For example, one might be having a difficult time making ad hoc solutions for individuals who need backups done on unsupported hardware. You boss, however, might have the authority to create a policy that only officially supported servers are backed up, with all other requests considered new-feature development projects to be prioritized and either budgeted or rejected like all new-feature requests. By using her authority to make or reiterate policy, she is able to remove an entire class of requests from your plate or possibly get funding to do the request properly.

> ### Use Your Boss's Power When Needed
>
> A group of SAs responsible for deploying PCs was missing deadlines because of an increase in custom configuration requests. These special requests required extremely large amounts of time. It turned out that many of these requests were not work-related. One request was for the SA group to configure a MIDI (synthesizer controller) card, something that was not required for the person's job. Another request was to create a dual-boot PC on which one of the partitions would be an OS that was not officially supported but had better games available for it. The SAs delegated to their boss the assignment to talk with the customers' director and deal with the situation. He explained that the SAs were not being paid to help with the staff's hobbies or children's entertainment. The manager was able to use his authority to save time for an entire team of SAs.

Sometimes, it is obvious when upward delegation is appropriate; other times, it is not. For example, when your manager asks you to do something, replying, "No, I think you should do it" always looks insubordinate. For example, if your manager asks you to give a presentation to people on a certain topic, a lousy reply is, "I'd rather you do it." A better reply is that you think it will be better received if it comes from the horse's mouth. That is leveraging the boss's authority. (You might then be asked to write the presentation, but the boss will present it.)

Upward delegations create more work for your boss, who is usually in a position to delegate work downward. Therefore, be careful with the quantity and timing of upward-delegation attempts. Don't do them continually; don't make them when at inappropriate times or during a heated discussion.

> ### Waiting List for Upward Delegations
>
> When should you make a request of your boss? Timing is everything. You might keep a mental list of items you want to ask for and pull out the most important one when you receive a compliment. It's difficult for a manager to turn down a *reasonable* request made immediately after having complimented you on a job well done or thanking you for saving the company money.

32.3 Further Reading

The habits listed in this chapter are difficult to develop. Books can help, as can workshops. Expect to be a little frustrated when you begin, but assure yourself that things will get easier as time goes on. One day, you'll notice that you've mastered the habit without realizing it.

Communication skills, negotiating, and follow-through are often the topics of books for salespeople. It can be useful to read such books and apply what you learn to your career. The classic books *The One Minute Sales Person* (Johnson 1991) and *The One Minute Manager* (Blanchard 1993) are full of advice that can be applied to SAs.

There are many excellent books on getting organized and setting goals. One is *Organizing from the Inside Out* (Morgenstern 1998).

There are many time-management books on the market. Allen's *Getting Things Done* (2002), is very popular, not to mention Tom's *Time Management for System Administrators* (Limoncelli 2005).

If you've never read a self-help book, it's difficult to imagine that a stack of paper with writing on it can solve your problems. Let us lessen that skepticism right here. Self-help books are great! However, let's be realistic: Only you can change you. Books only offer suggestions, advice, and new ways of looking at what you've been seeing all along. Not every book is going to be the right one for you. Maybe the way the author addresses the subject, the particular problems the book addresses, or the writing style isn't the right match for you. That is why you can find a dozen self-help books on any given topic, each with a different style to appeal to different people. We also recommend that you think critically about advice being offered before you try it. Be suspicious of any book that professes to fix all your problems. If it seems to good to be true, it probably is. All behavior modification requires some work, so disbelieve a book that claims otherwise. If it requires you to promote the techniques to others, we'd be concerned since a technique that works well doesn't require a pyramid scheme to sell it. We have tried to recommend timeless classics that have been on the market for a long time: books that have developed solid reputations for being effective. If you still doubt the usefulness of self-help books, put down the one you're reading right now.

32.4 Conclusion

It is important to be happy. It is important to be successful. These concepts are interrelated.

Successful people have excellent follow-through and focus, achieved by maintaining written or electronic to-do lists and calendars. This prevents them from dropping action items or missing appointments and deadlines.

Time management is a discipline that helps you accomplish your highest-priority goals. It is difficult for SAs to manage their time, because there is so much temptation to be interrupt-driven. SAs must set goals if they are to achieve them. Planning your day is a good way to stay on track. Reading email efficiently can cut your mail-processing time in half. Staying focused requires discipline also. If something is the highest priority, stay focused on it until it is done. Fill the wait time with your other priorities. Finding free time is a matter of eliminating the time wasters, not managing them better or doing them more efficiently.

We discussed communication skills such as "I statements" to make yourself heard, mirroring to confirm that you understand people, reflecting to deal with emotional people, and summary statements to verify that members of a group are in sync. These skills help someone deal with the four kinds of problems in the world: mine, yours, ours, and other people's. These communication skills are useful in your work, but they also are key to your personal life. In fact, they are the skills that are taught in marriage counseling. We hope that reading that section improves your relationships inside and outside of work.

Negotiation is about asking for what you want and striving for win-win situations. You should be aware of the power dynamic and how to shift it if you are not in a position of power.

Professional development is especially important in this continually changing high-tech field. One-day tutorials tend to be tactical (skills); week-long conferences tend to be strategic (vision). Both are useful and important.

We want you to love your job and be happy with it. That means maintaining good mental health, balancing stress, handling criticism, and taking care of yourself. You don't do anyone a favor by skipping vacations.

Managing your boss is a component of ensuring your happiness. This involves paying attention to her priorities so that she will pay attention to yours. Make your needs known. Attend to your manager's success. It is appropriate to delegate to your boss action items that leverage her authority to solve problems for many people who work for her.

The average person spends the majority of his waking hours at work. You deserve to be happy when you are there.

Exercises

1. Imagine that you've won the lottery and no longer have to work. What would you do? Why aren't you doing it now? How could you be doing it now?

2. What do you do to ensure good follow-through?

3. What percent of your day is interrupt-driven? What can you do to reduce the interrupt-driven nature of your job?

4. What are your goals for the next month, year, and five years?

5. How do you spend the first hour of your day? What can you do to make that hour more productive?

6. How do you manage your email? What strategy do you implement in your email filtering?

7. What time management training is available to you?

8. What tasks do you have to do every day or every week? When do you do them?

9. Name three low-priority items you can eliminate from your to-do list.

10. Name three time wasters you can eliminate.

11. What types of communication or interpersonal skills training is available to you?

12. How confident are you in your negotiation skills? How much negotiating do you have to do? How could you improve your skills?

13. Describe your last negotiation and what you could have done to improve it.

14. What are your primary outlets for professional development? What support do you receive from your employer for this?

15. Are you an optimist or a pessimist? Give two examples.

16. How accepting is your workplace to being open about your personal life? If your workplace does not condone this, who can you go to for support when you need it? Is your workplace safe?

17. Describe your support network.

18. When was your last vacation? Did you read your work email account during it? If you did, was it really a vacation? Do you promise not to read email on your next vacation?

19. Spend 15 minutes creating your awards wall.

20. Are your priorities in alignment with those of your boss? How do you know? How do you ensure that they are?

21. What is the next promotion you want? Who knows that this is your goal?

22. When someone who asked you to do something is standing in your office until you complete it, is the requester doing what is recommended in Section 32.1.2.9?

23. Describe the last time you needed to use upward delegation. How did your manager react? What will you do in the future to improve this?

24. What's your favorite self-help book?

Chapter 33

A Guide for Technical Managers

A technical manager is someone who understands system administration work in depth. She knows what is involved in running a site and working with customers. She probably used to be a senior SA but has now taken on a supervisory role. She probably is still involved at some level in the technical aspects of running the site. Her role includes mentoring more junior SAs and helping them to develop both their technical and interpersonal skills. The members of her technical staff look to her to deal with red tape or roadblocks they may come across in the course of their work, so that they can focus on the technical issues.

The technical manager also interacts with nontechnical managers in her management chain and throughout the rest of the company. She is expected to be able to communicate well with both nontechnical managers and her technical staff. She acts as a buffer and an interpreter between the two groups.

33.1 The Basics

To be a successful technical manager, you need to understand how to work with both nontechnical managers and your technical staff. Your technical staff people will consider that the way you deal with them is of utmost importance. If you fail to make them feel appreciated or to help them when they need you, the group will fall apart. If you fail to work well with the nontechnical managers in the company, you will not be able to set realistic goals, deadlines, and budgets for your group, and you will not be able to project a good image of your group to the company. These problems also will adversely affect your group.

In this section, we look at how to work with both your technical staff and the nontechnical managers in the company. We look at some of your responsibilities as a technical manager and prepare you for some of the decisions you will have to make in that position.

33.1.1 Responsibilities

The primary responsibility of a technical manager is to communicate priorities and provide the resources required to achieve the goals that have been prioritized. A technical manager has responsibilities to her staff, the company, and herself. She must keep her team's morale high and support the team members in what they do. She should take care of developing their careers and helping them improve their technical skills. She needs to provide vision to the group, keeping people focused on the direction they are going. She has a responsibility toward the company to keep her group performing well and within budget. She must manage all this while keeping herself sane and without falling completely behind on technology. She also must keep track of what her employees are doing without getting in their way.

33.1.1.1 Priorities and Resources

In theory, if a manager gives staff a prioritized list of things to do and enough resources to do them, everything will be fine. If only it were so simple.

The priorities usually come from the nontechnical management above the technical manager. The technical manager then determines the resources required and works with her management to acquire those resources.

One way to communicate those priorities is to establish SLAs for all the services being provided. This sets expectations. For example, an SLA for a helpdesk might include that requests sent via email must be acknowledged and categorized within 15 minutes during business hours and set expected time to completion for various categories of requests. For building an email system, the SLA might include uptime requirements, how many email messages the system should be able to transmit and receive each day, and how fast interactive response time should be for operations, such as reading a new message.

Another way to communicate priorities is to have written policies to guide the SA team. We feel that these three policies are the most important.

1. *How to get help* directs the customers on how to get the best service and when they can get service. It also helps your team by giving team members the ability to point people to the helpdesk when contacted inappropriately, such as at home, out of hours, or when the customer should have used the helpdesk. (See Section 13.1.6.)

2. *Scope of work* defines what, who, how, and where people work. What kind of machines/services are supported? Do SAs make house calls? Do they provide desk-side support, or must people bring their PC to the SAs? What do SAs do when asked to support nonsupported systems? This document is important because it tells SAs what they should be working on and empowers them to say no for all other requests. (See Section 13.1.5.)

3. *Definition of emergency* helps SAs disambiguate fact from fiction. Having a written policy helps SAs determine what a real emergency is. Everything else is not an emergency. (See Section 13.1.9.)

33.1.1.2 Structure

As the manager, your job is also to provide the structures that let people achieve their goals. This is often more important with more junior or less technical personnel who are not expected to be self-directed.

Using checklists to make sure that new computers are properly deployed is an example of a structure that lets people achieve their goals (see Chapter 3). With junior SAs, you might create the checklist for them, define the processes to complete each item in the checklist, and review the completed checklists. Senior SAs should be expected to create their own checklists and procedures, but you might have additions once the checklist is first drafted.

33.1.1.3 Team Morale

A technical manager must strive to keep her team's morale high. If morale is high, team members will be motivated to take on even the most arduous tasks, will enjoy their work, will work as a team, and will have low staff turnover. Hiring new staff will be easy. However, when morale is low, the team's productivity will go down, and turnover will increase. It will also be more difficult to hire new staff, because the interview candidates will sense the low morale in the group and not want to be a part of it. Most groups are somewhere in between, and the behavior of the team members also is somewhere in between. They are not willing to try to perform miracles on a daily basis; nor are they leaving in droves. If the technical manager performs her job well, the team's morale should be high. Section 34.1.2 discusses morale issues in more detail.

33.1.1.4 Removing Roadblocks

Another way to provide resources to your group is to restart stalled processes that have broken down and to remove roadblocks that are preventing work from getting done. In other words, grease the wheels.

There are a couple of ways to revive a stalled process. Sometimes, people aren't communicating, and you can connect the right two people. Sometimes, decisions aren't being made, often because people aren't sure of the proper direction, don't feel empowered, or are stuck in endless debates. You can intervene and recommunicate your vision, empower people to make the best decision, or communicate priorities to end the debate. These are all communication issues. It's your job to resolve them.

Being a good listener is important because problems often solve themselves when you simply listen to the people involved. For example, projects may be stalled because people aren't sure what to do and, in fact, neither are you. However, you can intervene and listen to people describe the situation. Making people explain a problem to a third party (you) forces them to think through the problem carefully. The solution usually becomes obvious, even if you didn't understand what they said. It is best to have them discuss the issue until the solution becomes apparent either to them or to you.

Removing roadblocks usually involves taking on the nontechnical, bureaucratic tasks so staff members have more time to focus on what they were hired to do: detailed technical tasks. For example, you might clarify a policy, negotiate with management to fund a project, purchase a time-saving tool, or empower people to say or do something they weren't sure whether they should do.

New technical managers often complain that they feel as though they aren't getting anything done, because they are used to having tangible results—machines installed, lines of code written—but their new role is more "soft issues." You might find yourself busy all day connecting people, removing roadblocks left and right, and enabling people to get things done but not have anything tangible to show for it. However, that is the nature of your job.

Often, one ends up in a meeting discussing how to solve a problem, with friction between those who favor a quick fix and those who want the long-term or permanent solution. A good way to manage this situation is to pause the meeting and reframe the discussion: Have the group brainstorm the best-possible permanent solution. Once that is settled, brainstorm to find a solution that is "good enough" to last until the permanent solution is ready. Breaking the process into two parts focuses the teams. Discussing the permanent solution first removes the distraction of trying to keep in mind the immediate problems. This is another way that a manager can provide the structure so that the team can achieve its goals.

One must decide whether it is best to skip either of the solutions or do both. There is a great likelihood that both solutions will be completed if the team is large and different people can work on each solution.

Implement the short-term solution and skip the long-term solution if a team is digging out of the hole (see Chapter 2) or has limited resources. Once things are stable, you can reconsider the long-term solutions. Maybe by then, there will have been staff turnover, with the new people bringing in new ideas.

On the other hand, the short-term solution sometimes relieves enough pressure on an understaffed team that the important long-term solution never gets started. That can be bad. An old saying goes, "There is nothing more permanent than a temporary solution."

It may be better to skip the short-term solution so that the team can focus on the long-term solution if the team is overloaded, understaffed, dealing with too many other crises, or has a problem completing projects. Ask the team, "What if we did nothing until the permanent solution is ready?" Sometimes, the team is shocked to realize that it wouldn't be so bad. The customers might suffer though a month of bad service, but maybe they are used to bad service already. Sometimes, customers have established their workarounds and would rather muddle through until the permanent solution is ready; it can be better than suffering through two upgrades.

A cost/benefit analysis can help determine whether the long-term solution is worthwhile. Sometimes, the technologies involved will be replaced in a year, making the short-term solution quite reasonable. Sometimes, as the manager, you know that a project will be canceled and that any effort on the long-term solution will be for naught.

The technical manager is often responsible for finding a political, policy, or financial solution. Consider fixing the problem upstream rather than downstream. Move up the management chain and have a problem fixed by changing a policy, removing restrictions, funding a replacement, or updating an SLA to reflect the true urgency of the situation.

As technical people, we love to solve problems with technical solutions: installing new software or using technology to try to control a situation. You can't solve social problems with technology. You can't solve the problem of people being rude in email by writing software to block angry phrases; people will simply get more creative. You can't reduce paper consumption by restricting how many pages a person can print each day; you'll find employees who are over their limit bothering people who are under their limit to print on their behalf. (Section 24.1.6 has better ideas.)

33.1.1.5 Rewards

As a manager, you must reward your staff. Rewards are very powerful. However, they also can be misapplied, with disastrous results. A book on managing people can give you a complete guide, and there are books specifically on this topic (Nelson 2005). We would like to highlight a couple of points.

Take the time to find out what motivates each person in your group. What is a reward to one person is punishment for others. Everyone is different. Pay attention to what each person in your group considers to be a reward. Keep notes in your PDA if it will help you remember. Publicly congratulating individuals for a job well done in front of their peers can be a hugely satisfying reward to some. An introvert might find that to be a painful experience. Patting someone on the shoulder and saying "good job" can be a powerful reward to some. Others may find that highly intimidating, and others may find it insufficient. One powerful reward for SAs is being given new assignments that are interesting to them. Each person finds different things to be interesting. Take notice of the types of assignments each staff person seems to enjoy doing. Usually, these will be the assignments that they do first when they are left to set their own priorities. You can also ask people what projects they like to do.

Reward the behavior you want to encourage. Never reward negative behavior. For example, if a staff member seeks your attention but goes about getting it by sending irate, argumentative email to you and your entire staff, don't use "reply all" to the email. That would be encouraging negative behavior. Instead, respond only when the person uses a proper communication channel. Although this will take a long time to produce the desired outcome, it will have a much more lasting result. Again, you must remember that different people find different actions to be a reward or a punishment.

Punishing negative behavior is a last resort. Punishing negative behavior is less effective than rewarding positive behavior. Think about when you were young and your parents punished you for doing something. Didn't it make you want to do that even more? The punishment also got you the attention you were craving, which means it was rewarding you.

If you must respond to negative behavior, do so in a way that doesn't reward the behavior. Returning to our email example, politely reply that such comments should be brought directly to your attention. If your reply addresses the person's points, you are training him to repeat the behavior in the future. If he was simply starved for attention, you have rewarded his technique by giving him the attention he craved.

People should be expected to do what is in their job description. They receive a paycheck for doing that work. Going beyond the call of duty, however, deserves to be rewarded with perks and bonuses. Confusing these two concepts can be a disaster. If you give a bonus or perk to people for doing their jobs, they will expect bonuses just for doing what they are paid to do. Soon there will be a sense of entitlement in the group.

Case Study: Bonuses Are for Special Deeds

A company distributed fake money (Lucky Bucks) to staff members who were doing particularly good work. Lucky Bucks could be redeemed for prizes. However, managers started handing out Lucky Bucks when nearly any task was completed. This was rewarding people for doing the things their job description entailed. As a result, the staff members became annoyed when they had to do anything without receiving a specific reward. The management had accidentally trained people to think that they should receive special celebrations for just plain doing their jobs. The staff became unmanageable. When the Lucky Bucks program was ended, the management had to spend years bringing back an appropriate work ethic. The management should have used discipline in handing out Lucky Bucks and rewarded only behavior that was extra special. In hindsight, management learned that if a program's goal was to encourage one thing, it should reward that one thing and nothing else.

Case Study: Special Achievements Deserve Bonuses

When Bell Labs was split between AT&T and Lucent, the SAs went through a lot of extra work to split the network on time. They received token bonuses when the project was complete (Limoncelli, Reingold, Narayan and Loura 1997). This is an example of a properly administered bonus. Such a large project was atypical and out of the scope of their job descriptions. The bonus was well received.

If the SAs had been hired specifically to split the network, a reward would have been appropriate only if it was rewarding an unexpected success, such as early completion.

33.1.1.6 Keeping Track of the Group

The technical manager is responsible to the company for keeping the group on track and knowing what her staff is doing. Some technical managers use weekly or monthly reports as a way to keep track of what everyone is doing. Others have regular one-on-one, face-to-face meetings with each staff member. If you arrange regular meetings, make sure that you don't schedule them more often than you can manage. Arranging meetings and then canceling them or showing up late is very annoying and demoralizing for your staff. It is better to arrange one meeting once a month that you always attend than to arrange one every week and show up to only one or two of them a month.

Meetings provide a good opportunity for dialogue that wouldn't otherwise occur. The manager can immediately address some concerns or answer some questions that an employee might not put in a report. If a manager does ask for reports, she must make sure that she sets aside time to both read them and respond to any issues raised in them. It is irritating and demoralizing for employees to have to interrupt their work to write a report that no one reads. It is also a waste of the company's resources.

Brief periodic reports can be useful for the technical manager to refer to when she needs to see whether her team can take on a new project or explain why the team doesn't have time to do something. However, there may be other ways to get that information, such as through the call-tracking system.

Case Study: Automated Reports

A technical manager at a midsize software company got automatic daily reports on what his staff people were doing by programming the call-tracking software to let him know which calls his team members updated each day and how much time they had spent on each of those calls. He was always able to discuss what people were doing at a moment's notice.

Another technical manager at a consulting company programmed the billing system to send him a list first thing in the morning of the hours that each of the consultants he was responsible for had billed the previous day. He always knew who was going to be low on hours for the week and when someone had stayed up all night working, even if the person was at a remote customer site.

Another technical manager wrote scripts to page him with calls in the call-tracking system that had not been updated in 24 hours, in addition to the daily reports. He worked in an Internet service company, where the calls were all customer problems rather than long-term maintenance projects.

Finding out what your staff is up to without interrupting members' work for status reports is often preferable to periodic reports. However, it does rely on discipline on the part of the staff to regularly update calls or enter billable hours, for example. If people do not update their calls, that also is necessary information for you; you should then find out why they haven't. There is a good chance that there is a problem with those employees. They may be overloaded, may have low morale, or may have bad work habits. In any case, you should talk with them.

Group meetings are also a useful way to keep track of what's happening and provide a forum to let everyone know what everyone else is doing. It is important for the group members to stay in touch with one another's work so that they can give input on other projects and know when another project may influence theirs.

It is also important for the manager to track her group's metrics. Somewhere in her management chain, the technical manager reports to a nontechnical manager. It is important for her to be able to demonstrate familiarity with and proper understanding and analysis of her department's metrics to build consensus with executive staff. No matter how important the technical manager thinks metrics are to her, the reality is that part of her job is to know her team's data better than anyone else so that she can communicate effectively with executive staff.

33.1.1.7 Support

The technical manager plays a supporting role for her team by handling bureaucratic tasks and supporting people in their interactions with the rest of the company. She should support them in the work they do. She should accept blame for failures that the group is responsible for, deflect the blame away from the team members, and not seek to assign fault to individuals while nonetheless expecting the team to do better the next time. The responsible individual should privately receive a warning rather than learn of the manager's dissatisfaction months later during performance reviews. On the other hand, she should make sure that the individuals in the team are recognized and rewarded for their successes rather than taking the praise herself. The technical manager should be able to derive satisfaction from seeing that her staff members are content and successful rather than from receiving praise for their accomplishments.

The technical manager also supports her staff by taking responsibility for contract negotiations and bureaucratic tasks: getting maintenance contracts approved and renewed, dealing with nondisclosure agreements (NDAs), and negotiating with vendors and the purchasing department, when necessary. The manager usually has the authority to sign contracts on behalf of the company or knows the proper channels to have such contracts approved, whereas the technical staff usually do not. She is also expected to be a better negotiator than her staff. By doing these tasks, she allows her team to concentrate on the technical tasks that they specialize in and enjoy, and she relieves them of the tedium of bureaucratic overhead. If some employees are interested in learning these skills, she should mentor them and give them the opportunity to relieve her of some of this work.

She should also support her team when members need to enforce company policy. At times, a policy may seem inconvenient to an SA's customer. The policy was implemented for a reason, and not enforcing it will ultimately be to the company's disadvantage. If the SAs are put into the position of saying no to their customers, they can seem unhelpful. If the no comes from someone of higher authority, it will be accepted more readily. Either way, it takes the onus off the SA. If it seems to be appropriate to have the policy modified, the manager should facilitate the effort herself or help her staff facilitate it.

Case Study: Enforcing the Policy

One technical manager was known for telling staff, "Your job is to say no. My job is to make it stick." If a customer pushed back about enforcing a policy, the SAs would explain to the customer why the policy existed and would help the customer achieve the end goal, which usually could be done via a different path that wouldn't violate any policies. However, if the customer still pushed back, the SAs could count on their manager to explain why the policy was in place and why it was going to be enforced. This let the SAs stay focused on their technical tasks rather than dealing with what was essentially a business issue.

Case Study: Let Me Be the Bad Guy

Another manager helped his SAs get through bureaucratic messes by letting himself be portrayed as the bad guy. This manager often told his staff, "Explain it to the customer; if the customer doesn't like it, blame me! Make me the bad guy!" This gave the SAs a tool they could use to deflect anger and save face. SAs would say to someone, "I understand your plight, but my boss won't let me, and you know how strict he is." Enough SAs used this excuse that eventually word spread. Corporate bureaucrats didn't want to have to face this mystery manager and reacted quickly to any requests from the group. Yet they never dealt with him directly.

The technique can be successful as long as it isn't overused. However, it works better when the customer in question is another staff member at the same level as or below the SA. If the staff member is at the same level as the SA manager or higher, we recommend that the SA escalate to his manager and let her deal with the problem directly and then escalate to her manager, if necessary. If the manager gets a reputation as someone who is impossible to work with, it can be bad for her career.

Standing by a Policy Need Not Be Humorless

Standing up for your SA team can also be done with a sense of humor. The following email was sent to users of a particular network after a series of outages.

```
From: Head of the SA Team
To: Users of this network
Subject: Network theft problem

    This is a quick note to enlist your support on a serious issue that involves
all of us.
    We are seeing an increasing rate of theft on our network. At least once
a week, the computer support team is diverted for an hour or two to track a
case of network theft.
    In all cases, we have identified the person who perpetrated the theft, and,
shockingly enough, in each case it has been one of our colleagues within the
department! What is even more shocking is that once confronted, the person
often shows no remorse and has little concern for the impact the actions have
had on peers.
    What am I talking about?
    It has become a common practice for people to steal an IP address without
registering it. They install a PC, workstation, or printer and simply use
an address they ''think'' is not used. Later on, when SAs are allocating
addresses for a new device, we discover a conflicting IP address already in
use on the network.
    This creates hours of wasted time each week for computing support and
affects users as a result of systems being down. We have had cases recently
in which people have used addresses already in use by critical servers,
printers, other people's PCs, and the like.
    This has the same effect as if someone walked up to another person's PC
when no one was around and pulled the network connection out of the back of
it. That person is affected, and the computing staff loses hours tracking
the culprit, diverting them from REAL work.
    Please obtain an IP address from the computing team BEFORE instal-
ling any new device on the network. Your coworkers will thank you.
    Thanks.
```

```
     P.S. If you are working in a lab where you have a need to dynamically in-
     stall and remove systems, we can arrange to assign you a block of IP addresses
     that you can cycle through or even arrange a custom DHCP configuration just
     for you.
```

Feel free to craft your own similar message, using this one as a base. In fact, this message was originally written by Ralph Loura and has been reused by many groups since.

33.1.1.8 Vision Leader

The technical manager is also responsible for having a vision for the group. She needs to know where the group is going and what its goal is. Setting an appropriate direction for the group requires being in touch with the direction of the company as a whole and figuring out how the group can help the company reach its goals. She should remind the group of its goals, to help keep people focused. These goals should include both long-term targets and shorter-term milestones so that the SAs can see the progress they are making toward the group's goal in the company's direction. The milestones might be annual or quarterly goals for the group. She needs to keep the vision consistent, because employees need to feel that their role is stable. SAs hate to feel that they are heading for point A one day and point B the next, especially when points A and B are in completely different directions. Because of day-to-day issues that arise, there are times when a short-term decision may seem contrary to what she previously told the staff. She should know how to explain how something that appears to be a shift in direction is in fact fulfilling a long-term goal.

Case Study: Explain Decisions That Appear Contrary to Direction

A technical manager of a customer-support organization had a staff of eight customer-support engineers (CSEs) supporting more than 180 customers and more than 200 technology and channel partners. The software product being supported was so complex that it took at least 4 months to get a CSE up to speed. The manager enforced the rule that partners calling for support on their own installations got lower priority than customers or partners calling on behalf of a customer. A week after he had started enforcing this direction, he found out that the company was negotiating a huge partnership deal and that calls from this potential partner should be made higher priority.

> He needed to communicate this message to his group without making them feel that the group's direction had changed.
>
> First, he told the group that this potential partner did not take priority over customers in production who were down, because that was a decision the executive staff would accept and understand. Then he explained that although customers are more important than partners, this particular partner was prepared to sign a deal that would allow them to be on site with dozens of customers. The more that the partner learned up front, the more calls it would be able to handle at customer sites and the less it would rely on the CSEs in the future. This would ultimately give all customers better support. The CSEs understood the decision in context. It made a short-term exception to the group's vision that the CSEs did not feel was contradictory.

Unless the company is floundering and changing its direction all the time, tying your group's direction to the company's direction should make sure that your vision can stay stable and consistent over time. In floundering companies, maintaining what is perceived as a locally stable vision can shelter the SA team from the morale-killing corporate instability. However, the manager should balance the need for sheltering the team with the need to keep her employees informed if it looks as though the company is going to sink. Part of managing people's careers is helping them to move on at the right time.

33.1.1.9   Coaching

The technical manager is also responsible for coaching her team. She needs to help people develop professionally and technically. A good coach needs infinite patience. People learn in different ways and at different speeds, but most people will not learn well or quickly if the person coaching them lets her frustration show. Coaching means taking the time to explain what to do and why and being there when people need help. It means watching them make their own mistakes and helping them to learn from them, without making them feel like bad people. It means making time for them. Typically, the junior SAs are the ones who need the most coaching. With practice, you can learn to give increasingly difficult tasks to people to develop their skills, letting them fail but encouraging them to continue. If they don't fail occasionally, you aren't increasing the difficulty quickly enough.

A big part of coaching is delegation. System administration is about controlling machines and networks, but delegation is about letting go of control and letting others be in control. They are opposing skills, and therefore many SAs need extra help learning to delegate.

When giving protégés increasingly difficult tasks, you have to let them fail and be supportive without getting angry. Remember that if they knew what they were doing, they would be doing it without your coaching. You are there to help them with the problems. Otherwise, you are like an auto mechanic who complains that people bring only broken cars to his shop.

Let People Learn from Mistakes

Once, Tom was coaching two engineers who were going to upgrade a link between two routers from 10Mb Ethernet (copper) to 100Mb Fast Ethernet (fiber). The two routers were in different parts of the building. He asked the two engineers to go to the server rooms and pantomime the change (see Section 18.2.5) to make sure that all the right connectors were delivered and that the fiber was the right length. He had done this in front of them during previous projects. They laughed at Tom for making this suggestion, and Tom had a feeling that they weren't going to do it. When the maintenance window arrived, they discovered that their fiber patch cord had the wrong type of connector. The maintenance window had to be rescheduled.

Tom could have gone behind their backs and done the checking himself. He also could have marched them down to the room to do the tests. Either would have been insulting and bad for morale. Instead, he checked to make sure that the project wasn't critical and could be delayed by a week or so without affecting other projects if something went wrong. The two technicians were adults and knew how to learn from mistakes. He noticed that on future projects, they pantomimed such changes without being asked.

When people get angry at someone who is learning, it is often because they feel that they are perfect, and dealing with people who aren't can be very frustrating. Experienced SAs know they're perfect: they know the process, are good at it, and have even developed some interesting little refinements that make the process go well. These SAs know all the keyboard shortcuts. It is difficult and frustrating to watch someone less experienced stumble through the process. But it took a long time for those SAs to become perfect and they need to let junior SAs take their time becoming perfect, too. It may take them longer to become perfect than it did for us, because we're so perfect, but they *will* get there some day. Remember this any time you forget to be humble.

Sometimes, no matter how hard you try, you will find yourself coaching someone who simply doesn't seem to get it. Try to understand where his confusion lies and how he is thinking, and then approach your teaching from that point of view. Always try your best and assume that you have a communication problem that you need to resolve, rather than giving up or getting frustrated. Occasionally, you will come across someone who learns a lot more slowly than you would like. Adjust your expectations accordingly, but don't stop trying. He will pick up more as time goes on. Some people learn best when left alone.

Coach people to document as they learn. It helps reinforce the learning process and builds a knowledge base. Even a cut-and-paste of what commands were used to achieve a goal is better than no documentation at all. (See Chapter 9, especially Section 9.1.3.)

33.1.1.10 Technical Development

The technical manager is responsible for ensuring that her senior SAs get to develop their technical skills and keep up with technological advances. She achieves this in several ways. She delegates to them large and complex tasks that she would otherwise have been more directly involved with herself. She makes sure that they attend relevant conferences and encourages them to write papers and otherwise participate in those conferences and other outside technical groups. Some companies allocate a certain amount of money and time per person for professional development. It is reasonable for an SA to expect about 40 hours of professional development a year. The technical manager is responsible for ensuring that her management understands the value of professional development and funds it appropriately.

The technical manager should also work with her employees to make sure that they get the most out of that money and that they share what they learn with the rest of the group. She should make sure that the group or department has a comprehensive library of technical books for her team to reference. She should also find opportunities to get her senior SAs involved in projects in other areas that they are interested in, to help them broaden their areas of expertise.

33.1.1.11 Career Paths

Career planning is often talked about but rarely done. A career path meeting is a time for the manager to listen to the employee talk about where he or she wants to be in 5 years. The manager must then consider how these desires can fit into the skills and roles that she requires in the group. Only then can she and the employee discuss what short-term and long-term objectives will meet those goals. The manager may learn that nobody in her current team wants to be in certain roles and therefore identifies roles that must be developed within the group or sought when hiring.

To do career planning right, technical managers should allocate an entire hour once a year with every staff member to focus solely on this topic.

It should not be the same meeting that includes the yearly performance review, as that praise (or reprimand) should not be diluted. The performance review meeting is for the manager to communicate to the employee. The career path meeting should focus on the manager listening to the employee.

This meeting is a learning experience for the manager, who might get some surprises: The introvert of the group wants to become the team leader, or the team leader wants to be coached to be the manager's successor. The manager might learn that someone is utterly bored and wants to change roles completely. It is easier to retrain someone than to hire an outsider, so these change requests should be encouraged. They also result in a cross-trained team.

Most people, especially younger people, don't know what their career path should be. The technical manager should make suggestions only after employees have exhausted their ideas of where they could go. Typical suggestions are along obvious paths: junior SAs to become intermediate and then senior SAs. She should help them to become proficient at what they do and then gradually increase the scope of their jobs so that they gain experience and proficiency in more areas. For intermediate SAs, she should watch as they develop, see what gaps they have in their expertise, and encourage them to fill those gaps. As they become more senior, she may want to encourage them to specialize in particular areas of interest.

Senior SAs are the most likely to suffer a career crisis. They have worked hard to reach this position, but now what should their goals be? For some, the answer is to encourage them to become more recognized and involved in the field. They should work toward advancing the profession of system administration by getting involved in organizing conferences, as well as presenting at them; or by working with the IETF or various open source communities to play a part in the specification and design of future technologies. Others may want to explore management as a goal. Give them the opportunity to manage some projects, supervise and mentor some more junior SAs, choose and manage contractors to help with particular projects, get involved in the budget process, and participate in cross-functional committee meetings on behalf of the group.

33.1.1.12 Budget

A technical manager is also responsible for her group's budget. She prepares a realistic annual budget request, including salary increases and bonuses, new staff, the costs of supporting the existing systems, scaling existing systems to meet the growth of the company, improving areas that are performing below the required service level, upgrading systems that will need upgrading, and funding the new projects required to keep the company moving with the times at an appropriate pace.

Once she has been given a budget, which may be less than what she requested for her group, she is responsible for making sure that her group remains within budget while achieving what it needs to achieve. If the budget is significantly below what was requested, she needs to identify the tasks that cannot be done while working to obtain additional funds.

33.1.1.13 In Touch with Technology

A technical manager has a responsibility to herself and to her staff to stay knowledgeable about new technology. She is the technical guide, mentor, and vision leader for the group. If she loses touch with new technologies, she will not be effective in setting an appropriate vision for her staff and leading the group toward it. Nor will she be as effective in coaching her staff and helping people to develop technically. She may even resist the introduction of new technologies because she is unfamiliar with them and does not feel comfortable moving the company in that direction.

33.1.2 Working with Nontechnical Managers

A technical manager should be able to work well with the nontechnical managers in her management chain and in her customer base. The key components of a successful relationship with nontechnical management are communication and setting and meeting expectations. Use graphs and quantitative data to address issues relating to the business goals of the company and of the group. The relationships with the nontechnical managers are key to the technical manager's success and job satisfaction.

Use Analogies They Understand

A technical manager had to explain what an Ethernet switch was to a financial director of his division. This was when Ethernet switches were new, and the proposal to upgrade the entire network from hubs to switches was going to be very expensive. He began by getting an understanding of technology the director *did* understand, which was mostly limited to telephone equipment. Therefore, he explained that the network was like a phone system. Right now, any two computers can talk to each other only at any given moment. All the others had to wait. The Ethernet switches, he explained, would let any two computers talk at any given moment rather than waiting. This the director could understand. The purchase was approved quickly because the technical manager found a way to communicate the value in terms the director could understand.

In general, other managers you work with will want to know that you and your team can accomplish what they need when they need it. They don't want to know the technical details of what you will need to do, and they expect you to figure out the requirements they want met. Make sure that any deadlines you set for yourself or your team are on the pessimistic side of realistic. It is better to give pessimistic estimates and surprise people when you are early than to disappoint customers by being late. Don't overdo it, though: If you are too pessimistic, people will find you obstructive and may go around you to make things happen.

Your direct management chain wants you to meet the deadlines it sets for you and to keep your customers happy. Management does not want to have to deal with complaints relating to you or your team but instead wants to know it can delegate things to you and be sure that they will be accomplished on schedule. If you can't meet a deadline or accomplish a task for your customers or your managers, they want to know as early as possible so that they can manage the impact of a slipped schedule.

The nontechnical managers with whom you work will also expect you to set direction for your group based on customer requirements. When they look for status, they want to know how you are performing in terms of the requirements and the goals and deadlines that were set. They generally do not want to be bombarded with technical details. However, if they do ask you to go into depth on technical points, do not be afraid to go right down into the details. If you are going too deep, they will stop you. Avoid vague generalities: Be definite and precise.

When working with your management chain, particularly on budget issues, justify what you need in terms of helping the company meet its goals or making your group meet the goals that have been set for it by the company. Management will need to be kept abreast of the large-scale tasks your group is working on, in order to answer accurately when asked by their peers and superiors. Keeping your management chain informed of what your group is doing is also important if you want to protect your group from being overburdened with extra work. If management doesn't know what your resources are allocated to, it may assume that it is nothing important and volunteer your group for extra projects, to the detriment of your existing commitments.

A basic expectation that nontechnical managers have of the technical staff is that they know, or learn, the requirements behind the tasks they are performing. For customer-support calls, knowing the requirements means understanding the root of the problem and the time constraints, as discussed in Chapter 14. For building a new service, it means understanding the customers' needs, how the service will be used, how it needs to scale, performance requirements, the support model, financial constraints, interoperability requirements, and all the other aspects that were discussed in Chapter 5.

Knowing the requirements and bearing them in mind as you work tends to keep you and your team more focused on the specific problem at hand. It is easy for an SA to lose focus when investigating one problem causes him to find others or when looking at ways to build a new service opens up all sorts of possibilities in other areas. This is known as **feature creep**. Your customers and your management chain expect you to use the requirements to direct your team's work, avoiding other interesting diversions to meet all your goals on time. Equally, they expect you to explore other possibilities that arise, if they are in line with the requirements. Deciding what to do is a matter of keeping the big picture in mind, not only the fine details of a particular part. The technical manager is the one who is expected to keep the big picture in focus and provide direction.

Communication with your management and customers should also be based on requirements. For example, if you are building a new service, your manager or a customer might want to know why your team is doing it one way rather than another. If you believe that your team's approach is better than what the other person proposes, use the requirements to express why. In other words, explain which requirements led you to choose this design rather than the other one. For example, it may be that your design is easier to support, it interoperates with other services, scales to the required size more cheaply or with better performance, can be implemented in the required time scale, uses more reliable systems, or has more of the required features.

Customer requirements are a significant part of any work that an SA performs. Finding out what those requirements are involves asking the right questions of your customers and listening to their answers, getting clarification where necessary. The process of building the list of customer requirements is an opportunity to build a cooperative relationship with the customers. It should also be used as a platform for giving the customers feedback and setting realistic expectations.

Clearly identifying the requirements and using them to direct your team's work results in faster problem resolution and better services, both of which lead to happier customers and happier managers.

33.1.3 Working with Your Employees

A technical manager's employees are a significant part of her job. She needs to keep their morale high and keep them happy to be working for her. She also needs to encourage them to perform well in their jobs and make sure that they know what is expected of them.

33.1.3.1 Be a Good Role Model

A manager influences the behavior of her group by the way she acts toward others, including her employees. If she is short-tempered and irritable, her employees will behave in a similar manner toward their customers. If she doesn't seem to care about her job, her group will mirror that in a lack of concern for its customers. However, if she treats her employees well, they will be attentive to their customers' needs. If she goes out of her way to help others, her employees will do the same.

The technical manager should take care to exhibit the behavior she would like her group to emulate. She leads by example, and the group will follow. She should see her employees as her primary customers and try to keep them happy. If they are happy, there is a much higher chance that they will keep their customers happy. If the group's customers are happy, her managers will be happy—with her, at least.

33.1.3.2 Treat Your Employees with Respect

Treating employees well is a key part of maintaining morale and loyalty. One way for a manager to show appreciation for her employees is to be aware of each group member's hire date and do something on their anniversaries. Something small that celebrates each person spending another year at the company makes the employee feel appreciated.

Another way for a technical manager to let her employees know that they are appreciated is to publicly acknowledge them when they do good work. Her compliments should be specific, sincere, and timely. Vague, belated, or insincere compliments can be demotivators. Excellent work that involved effort beyond the normal call of duty should be rewarded with at least a small bonus. Recognition and being made to feel important and valued are bigger motivators than money. However, lack of promised—or unrealistically expected—money is always a demotivator. Using money as an incentive can create an expectation that you can't maintain.

Recognition Is Important

A friend of Christine's worked at Xerox PARC during a turbulent period. Morale in the SA group was very low. Both managers of the group quit, and he was left as the acting manager. He had no budget for providing incentives. He spoke to the company cafeteria manager and asked whether he could give away a free lunch once a week to someone in his group, with the cafeteria charging the cost back to his department. The way that things worked in Xerox, internal money that didn't result in anyone receiving cash didn't count against the budget and so was essentially free. He then explained to his staff that each week at their staff meeting, they would recognize someone who had gone above and beyond the call of duty. He couldn't afford anything fancy, but he printed up little certificates with gold stars on them and gave away the free lunches. It was a huge hit. Morale improved, despite the fact that the cafeteria food wasn't even all that good. The recognition and the token reward were enough.

Recognition can be a double-edged sword. People who think that they've worked hard might feel underappreciated if someone else gets the recognition award. The comic strip *Dilbert* is full of stories of how recognition awards go awry.

Feedback should be timely and specific. If an employee fails in a particular task, he will usually know that he has done so. If it is not too serious a failure, take him aside and tell him not to worry about it and that everyone makes mistakes. Permit him to consider his failure in peace and to think about what he could have done differently. If it was serious, reprimand him, but be sure to do so in private. It is important to have a short conversation not long after the incident so that the employee does not brood over the mistake for too long and blow it out of proportion. Take the heat from the customers or your management on his behalf. He will know that you are aware of his error and will appreciate what you are doing. He will be determined not to put you in that position again.

However, people sometimes make mistakes and don't realize it. Some people don't have the same standards as you, and you need to explain to them that they've failed. Some people are convinced that nothing is ever their fault. You need to explain clearly to them that they are at fault. Only by understanding and appreciating their mistakes will they be able to improve.

When you reprimand someone, do so face to face, and be timely and specific about the behavior that needs to be changed. Reprimands should never be done in public. If you reprimand an employee in public in order to make a public example of him, you are showing a lack of respect toward those who work for you, and it will demotivate the entire team. That lack of respect will be mirrored back at you and may be reflected in the lack of respect shown to customers.

A manager should respect her staff by keeping people informed about important events that are happening within the group and the company. Strike a balance in doing so, however. It can be destructive and distracting to know every potential change when most of them don't happen. Significant news may need to be presented in the right way, so that it does not cause undue concern. However, it should be presented in a timely manner once it is certain. When a manager doesn't trust her employees to react in a calm, responsible manner to events in the company, she is showing them disrespect.

Lack of Information

At a small consulting company, senior managers were so paranoid about releasing to the employees any information that could be construed as bad news that it insisted on doing it themselves and refused to let the technical managers inform their staff people. This led to a lot of dissatisfaction among the technical managers and the staff alike. In one incident, one of the first five employees of the company found out that a key member of the company was leaving only through a companywide email news bulletin sent out by one of the founders. The newsletter mentioned the departure in an off-hand manner in the last paragraph. The employee was (understandably) so upset by the incident that from then on, his manager and a couple of others went against the management's instructions to the contrary and kept certain employees properly informed.

A manager should listen to her employees. They need to be able to discuss things that are on their minds. If they have a problem with a customer, a co-worker, or a vendor, or even have a personal problem, they should be able to talk to her about it. She needs to be available to her employees. She should always make them feel that their needs are important to her, even if she has other pressing work. Keeping the group working effectively will accomplish more than she can accomplish on her own. However, she also needs to find time to do her own work, without making her group feel neglected. Scheduled weekly meetings with each employee can go a long way toward reducing the number of times that she is interrupted during the rest of the week. These meetings don't need to be elaborate or long. They simply give the manager a chance to ask how things are going and whether she can help with anything. It gives the employee a chance to mention anything he thinks she might want to know about, without feeling as though he's making a big issue over it by making an appointment or interrupting her work to tell her. It should also make the employee more comfortable with the manager and generally improve the relationship. When she has a particularly tight deadline, a good way of ensuring that she is still in touch with important issues but is not involved in the lesser ones is to let her staff know that she has a deadline and to say that she will be closeting herself away but wants them to interrupt her if they need her help.

A technical manager generally likes to be quite involved with her staff and their projects. She is interested in how they are solving the problems they face and in the new technologies they are bringing into the company. However, she needs to be careful that her interest and her knowledge of how to solve many of the problems they might be facing for the first time do not lead to micromanaging her staff. Micromanagement is irritating to the SAs and demonstrates a lack of faith in their ability to solve the problems. You need to have faith in your staff. Encourage them to communicate with you on their progress and let you know when they would like to talk about the problems that they encounter, but do not look for progress reports several times a day or continually ask, for example, whether they have completed this task or spoken to that person yet. Respect their ability to do their jobs well, and give them the space to do so.

One way to do this is to ask them to write design documents for larger projects. It enables them to be creative yet gives you an opportunity, when proofreading it, to make constructive criticism. If you tend to micromanage people, send them off to write the drafts far away from you.

It is important for a technical manager to not only believe in her staff but also demonstrate to them that she believes in their ability to do whatever jobs she gives them. She should believe in them until they consistently give her reason not to. They should not have to prove themselves worthy of her trust; they should have it automatically until they show themselves to be unworthy of it.

33.1.3.3 Be Positive

One component of maintaining high morale in a group is to be positive about the group's abilities and direction. A technical manager should let her staff know that she believes in the individuals and will do what she has to do to get them what they need to be successful. She should never harp on how great things were in the past either with this group or elsewhere; instead, she should look forward to a bright future.

If she is a new manager brought in to manage a group that she has been told by her management is failing in one way or another, she should not show that she believes that the group is failing. She should be positive and should talk to the people in the group to understand their impressions of the group. She should not start changing things until she understands why things are the way they are and can determine what is good and bad. Gratuitous change indicates that she thinks they are doing everything wrong. However, she does need to address the problem reasonably quickly, whether it be real or simply how the group is perceived. If she fails to do so, she will lose the support of her management, without which she will be an ineffectual advocate for her group.

New Director

A system administration organization of 75 people got a new director, who was told by his management that the group he was taking on was dysfunctional and did not work as a team. Although the group did have problems, it also had a very strong team spirit. The director gave a speech on his first day about how he was going to build a team and how all the people at his previous company had loved working for him and cried when he left. The SAs left the meeting feeling that they were all going to lose their jobs to people from his old company and doubting their working relationships with other parts of the group. He also left them doubting his ability to run the group, because he apparently was out of touch with the group's biggest asset: its team spirit.

33.1.3.4 Give Clear Direction

A technical manager needs to make sure that everyone in the group understands the division of responsibilities within the group and that each person takes care of his or her own areas. She should make sure that each person is working only on the things that he is assigned to do and not working on other projects unless or until she agrees to it. She should let her people know that they if they take responsibility for meeting their deadlines and keeping their customers happy, she will take care of the things she is responsible for and will not feel obliged to micromanage them.

She needs to be clear about what she expects of them. If they frequently do not give her what she is looking for, she is probably not explaining herself clearly. If she believes that she is explaining herself clearly but is still not getting the results that she wants, she should ask the employee to explain back to her in detail what it is that the employee thinks she wants. This can lead to a useful dialogue if there is a misunderstanding. If there is no misunderstanding, at least she knows that there is a problem and can deal with it directly.

Don't assume that you are communicating well just because you know exactly what you want. It is not always obvious to others. Some managers don't realize that they are not explaining what they want clearly enough. They use what is sometimes called the "bring me a rock" management technique. The manager says to the employee, "Bring me a rock." The employee dutifully brings her a "rock." She says "No, no! Not rock! I wanted a *rock*!" The employee searches for a different rock, and so on, until he finally stumbles on the particular kind of rock that his manager wants. Over time, the employee usually learns what the manager is looking for when she asks for a rock, but only if the manager is consistent about the types of "rocks" that she likes. The rock may be a style of writing, a way of laying out project proposals, a budget request, a project design specification, a service implementation, or a solution to a customer's problem. It is anything that the manager asks for but does not describe or explain adequately. Working for a manager who uses the bring-me-a-rock technique can be very frustrating and usually leads to high employee turnover.

33.1.4 Decisions

Certain decisions usually fall to the technical manager to make. These include group staffing decisions and prioritizing and allocating tasks to the group members. The technical manager also often has to decide whether to buy a product to solve a particular problem or to build the solution in-house.

33.1.4.1 Roles and Responsibilities

The technical manager should consider the responsibilities of her group and the talents of the people in it when she is hiring new staff, as well as when she is allocating projects or areas of responsibility to the various team members. When hiring, she should look for gaps that need to be filled in terms of skill sets and personality types. Appendix A looks at the various roles that SAs can play. A technical manager should try to make sure that she has a good balance in the roles relevant to her area of responsibility. Chapter 35 discusses how to hire people who will work well in your environment.

Given the mix of people in her group, the technical manager should distribute the work load appropriately. When doing so, she must consider her people's talents, experience, and career growth. She needs to give them tasks that they are capable of handling, tasks that will stretch their skills and help them grow, and enough variety to keep the work interesting.

33.1.4.2 Priorities

The technical manager also must decide the group's priorities and negotiate them with her management and her customers. In making those decisions,

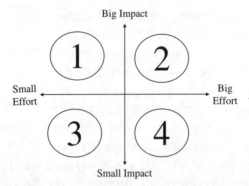

Figure 33.1 Setting priorities based on impact. (The numbers indicate the order in which tasks should be done.)

she should consider the importance or impact of a project and the amount of time and effort required to accomplish it. She should prioritize the items that will make the biggest impact over all others, as depicted in Figure 33.1.

It is easy to understand why you should put a high priority on doing projects that require little effort but would result in a big impact. It is easy to understand why the lowest priority is given to the other extreme: projects that require a large effort yet will have only a small impact.

The question becomes whether priorities 2 and 3 should be swapped. We claim that your priority should be on the biggest impact rather than the least effort. Otherwise, you will be distracted by easy projects that have very little benefit. It requires discipline to avoid these. They are inviting because of the potential for instant gratification; they will be accomplishments. You can spend months avoiding the high-impact projects by filling your day with "one more little task" that you want to do because it would be "so easy." This is one way that big projects get delayed. The technical manager must steer her team away from this trap.

Typically, if you have accurately understood the impact of and effort involved in each task, your management will support you in your decision. Your customers may or may not agree with where you rated their projects, because they may be biased against projects that aren't directly helping them. However, the projects of theirs that you rated as having the biggest impact should be the highest-priority tasks you do for their group, even if they are not the first priority overall.

Case Study: Bigger Impact, Better Results

A company had two systems that weren't under change management. One was surviving; the other was a disaster. Management decided to convert both systems to use the company's standard change-management procedures. Which should be converted first?

Consider the effort required: Project A would be the easier system to convert, because the team that put it together already used a fairly clean process that simply needed to be improved to meet corporate standards. Project B would be difficult to convert, because it had a more chaotic process. Based on the effort required, some people would do project A first. In fact, it might be a good "trial run" before the bigger project.

Now let's consider the impact of the two conversions. Project A's unofficial, but somewhat formal, processes kept it running fairly well. Moving it to the corporate standard for change management wouldn't have a very large impact. In fact, it could break an otherwise working system. On the other hand, project B's lack of formal processes resulted in a continual stream of problems and failures. Change management would help it greatly. The new, streamlined, process would free up four engineers to work on other projects rather than having them spend day after day chasing problems. That would have a large, positive impact on the small company.

Initially, management had planned on converting project A first: the path of least resistance. However, following the bigger-impact method helped management decide to start with project B. After both conversions were complete, the team was glad it had made this decision.

33.1.4.3 Buy versus Build

A technical manager is often faced with the buy-versus-build decision. Should she buy a product or assign team members to write the software themselves? This decision encompasses a continuum that includes buy, integrate, glue, or build, as follows.

- *Buy a complete canned solution.* Complete solutions exist in many industries, usually mature product spaces, such as word-processing applications.

- *Integrate or customize a product into the environment.* Larger applications require customization and configuration. An accounting system needs large amounts of customization to match your business needs. Helpdesk software needs to be configured to understand what products are being supported, who is being supported, and other workflow issues. If a system is completely configurable, small sites may find such customization to be as difficult as writing a system from scratch. Often, only large environments can benefit from highly configurable systems. Buying a system that is more configurable than the site needs often wastes time.

- *Glue together several products.* Often, the solution a site needs doesn't exist, but smaller systems can be combined to build a complete solution. The key is that some coding will be required to connect the components. The team's job becomes gluing them together. For example, rarely do different OSs handle user accounts the same way, but they can reference some kind of database. A site might deploy an SQL database and create the glue that lets each OS authenticate from it. Windows systems might create and delete accounts as they are added and deleted from the database. UNIX systems might generate their /etc/passwd files from dumps of the SQL tables or via stored SQL procedures (Finke 2000). Certain combinations of glued products become so commonplace that vendors spring up to provide preconfigured packages to fill the gap. These vendors can usually provide additional value or higher performance through expert customization. NetApp did this after seeing so many sites creating dedicated file servers out of UNIX boxes. The company provided network/NFS hardware accelerators with NFS and CIFS (common Internet file system) software and NIS for authentication. Mirapoint provided an integrated mail system after seeing so many people glue together mail servers out of a UNIX box, POP3 (Myers and Rose 1996) and IMAP4 (Crispin 1996) software, and an MTA, such as Sendmail or Postfix.

- *Build the solution from scratch.* The highest level of customization comes from this method. The technical manager and her team must go the entire route of gathering requirements, designing the architecture, implementation, testing, and deployment.

Each choice has positive and negative aspects. One end of the scale—buy—generally is believed to involve less work, have a faster "time to availability," and offer a lower cost in terms of human resources. On the other hand, these solutions are less customized and may have a steep learning curve. Support can be a positive and a negative thing: A commercial product—or commercial support for an open source product—will have a phone number that can be called when one has a question. On the other hand, it may be several long product cycles before bugs not considered urgent enough for a patch are fixed.

Building a solution from scratch has pros and cons, too. The solution is built to solve the exact problems that the group faces. It will fit with the existing environment, platforms, and methods. The cost is in time rather than in capital expense, which can be important in environments with little money to spend but a lot of people. Universities in particular often lean toward building systems from scratch because of their tight budgets and nearly endless supply of cheap labor. Another benefit of custom solutions is that they sometimes turn into products, or reseller/OEM (original equipment manufacturer) deals are made, or the authors gain fame through publishing their work either on the Internet or at conferences, such as LISA. The pride of creating original software can motivate the team.

Support after the initial team has gone away is a separate issue. Custom solutions can become a support nightmare after the programmers have left the group or graduated. Although commercial software vendors offer more reliable support, they too can discontinue support for older products or simply go out of business.

Given the positive and negative points on both sides, how does the technical manager make this decision? She must look at how she values what each method brings.

The prime reason for buying a solution is the faster time to availability. The prime reason for building a solution in-house is the ability to get features that aren't available externally. She must take an introspective look at why those features are required. Forgoing commercial software for a minor reason, personal biases, or antivendor feelings is simply wrong. On the other hand, a required feature sometimes is not available elsewhere because nobody has thought of it before. Developing a system in-house is worthwhile if you will receive value that commercial systems could not provide. This may lead to a competitive advantage.

Case Study: Building a Competitive Advantage

A manufacturer of Pentium-compatible CPUs was able to beat Intel's own ship date for a particular speed of processor because it had developed a batch-scheduling system in-house for easily doing large volumes of compute-intensive work. When the chip was announced, the manufacturer attributed its success to this custom solution; it couldn't have achieved this with commercial batch schedulers available at the time.

The chip design company even submitted a paper on its batch system at a USENIX LISA conference. The company didn't worry about releasing its secrets, because it knew that the competition would catch up by the time the conference rolled around.

A competitive advantage typically does not last long in our fast-paced computer industry. That should be taken into account as part of the decision process. A few months of being ahead of the game is often enough to gain a significant commercial advantage, though.

Custom solutions are common when an idea is new enough that commercial solutions are not yet available. However, the technical manager must pay attention to emerging commercial products and learn to acknowledge when a custom solution has been surpassed by one. For example, when UNIX was new, it was considered interesting and innovative to write yet another system for managing backups. Now, however, this is considered a "solved problem" for small sites and too complicated to build in-house for large sites.

Although the ability to gain original features is appealing, it is generally a good idea for the technical manager not to assume that the site's needs are very specialized and instead to seek out commercial packages to see what's available. She will at least learn of features she may not otherwise have thought of but may want to integrate or avoid. Along with reviewing the current popular products, she should review the proceedings of SA conferences, particularly the USENIX and LISA conferences.[1]

When commercial packages are used, it can be valuable for the technical manager or a senior member of the team to partner with the vendor to influence development decisions toward the new features that her site most needs. In cutting-edge environments, it can be useful to tell vendors that if you need this feature now, everyone else will need it next year. Large companies can use their financial muscle to influence such decisions. However, when a partnership is created, it is important to clearly define who owns the ideas; there may be intellectual property issues to consider.

A hybrid model is to use open source or commercial solutions that make good building blocks and perform the integration work yourself. Certain systems are designed to work this way. The difficult design and implementation work is done by the original author, but the customization you do makes it a perfect fit for your environment.

The buy-versus-build decision is one that comes up often, and yet there is no universal right answer. It comes down to issues of time, level of customization, and availability of features. As an industry matures, there are more commercial options. But the satisfaction of implementing your own brilliant idea cannot be overstated.

---

1. Available at www.usenix.org/.

33.2 The Icing

So, your group is now running smoothly, you have made the decisions you need to make, and you have all your responsibilities under control. What's next? We suggest some ways to make your team stronger. But more important, now that you have figured out how to keep your staff, management, and customers all happy, it's time to spare some thought for yourself. Work on your own career growth. Think about whether you can do something to give yourself a bit of extra job satisfaction.

33.2.1 Make Your Team Even Stronger

Consider ways to make the team stronger. Encourage teamwork and give employees an opportunity to learn by getting them to collaborate on larger projects. Get them to write conference papers together. Organize fun social events and include their families, such as a pot-luck dinner in a park, to which everyone brings something for the group to eat. Events can improve people's job satisfaction and relationships with others in the group. However, make sure that some people aren't left out of these events because of on-call support obligations or other work-related reasons. Someone who is left out starts to feel isolated, unimportant, and not part of the team.

The longer people stay with the group and the less turnover there is, the more they will feel part of the team and the more likely they are to stick with it through hard times. Figure out ways to retain your employees. Just as important as employee retention is hiring the right people. Make sure that the people you hire are good team fits. One bad fit can have a very bad effect on a group.

33.2.2 Sell Your Department to Senior Management

Make sure that senior management knows what your group does and how it benefits the company. The more visible your group is, and particularly the more visibly successful your group is, the more chance you have of getting the resources to help your people do their jobs and reward them for their work. Make sure that senior managers know about your group's contributions to major projects around the company. If someone works crazy hours to ensure that a demonstration at a conference or to a customer works flawlessly, make sure that the person gets credit and recognition for it. When your group introduces new services or upgrades an existing service, make sure that senior managers understand how it improves others' efficiency and saves the company money. Chapter 31 details ways to make the group's successes visible. It is vital to the ongoing success of the group that senior management recognizes the group as an asset to the company.

33.2.3 Work on Your Own Career Growth

Having helped everyone who works for you, spare a thought for yourself. Make sure that you get the recognition you deserve for your own accomplishments, as well as the reflected glory of your group's successes. Learn about the company's business so that you can relate better to your group's customers and make better decisions about which requests should take priority. Learn about business management so that you can relate better to the nontechnical managers in your management chain. Understand what they are looking for and why, so that you can meet their needs, and they will gain confidence in you and your team.

33.2.4 Do Something You Enjoy

Last but not least, consider how to keep yourself satisfied in the role of technical manager. Find a way to give yourself a task that you will enjoy as a break from your normal routine. For most technical managers, this means taking on some low-profile, low-urgency technical projects. A bit of technical work will provide a nice break from your other tasks and will help to keep you in touch with technology and the sorts of tasks that your staff people perform day to day.

33.3 Conclusion

A technical manager is someone who is expected to be both a senior SA and a manager. As a senior SA, she mentors more junior members of her group and acts as a technical resource for the group. As a manager, she needs to manage the budget, deal with contracts, and work with her managers and customers to try to keep everyone happy and her group going in the same direction as the rest of the company.

She is a role model and vision leader for her employees. She is the person to whom her management looks for information on what the SAs are doing. She is the person the customers' managers talk to for negotiating schedules and resource allocations for their projects.

Her primary responsibility is to keep her staff's morale high. To do that, she needs to treat employees with respect and reward them for good work.

She needs to keep them informed but not overwhelm them with the ever-changing whims of other groups. She needs to support her team and protect its members from the wrath of disappointed customers, as well as help them to improve in the future. She needs to promote their technical development and steer them along their career paths.

A manager is also required to make some decisions on behalf of the group. She needs to decide on the division of responsibilities within the group. She needs to recognize when she needs more staff and decide what roles the new staff members need to fill for the group. She also has to decide whether they should buy commercial solutions to solve particular problems or whether her staff should build the solution.

She also needs to take care of herself. She should make time for herself and do something that she enjoys, such as taking on a low-priority technical project that she can work on as a break from everything else.

People new to management might be interested in *The One Minute Manager* (Blanchard 1993) and a related book, *The One Minute Manager Meets the Monkey* (Blanchard Oncken and Burrows 1989). Both are short but extremely useful books.

Exercises

1. What attitude do you role model for the rest of your team to emulate?

2. Who was the best technical manager you ever had, and why? What faults did that person have?

3. Who was the worst technical manager you ever had, and why? What assets did that person have as your manager?

4. If you are a technical manager, what do you think you are doing well? What areas do you think you could improve?

5. Describe a group you worked in that had high morale. What factors do you think contributed to the high morale?

6. Describe a group you worked in that had low morale. What factors do you think contributed to the low morale?

7. Describe a situation in which the morale in the group you were working in dropped significantly. What factors do you think precipitated the fall in morale?

8. What do you do to let your staff people know that you appreciate their work?

9. What are you doing to help your staff's technical development? Is technical development adequately funded for your group?

10. Describe your relationship with your nontechnical manager. What were or are the primary difficulties you needed to overcome to make it a successful working relationship?

11. What kinds of rewards are given in your group? Based on the discussion in Section 33.1.1.5, are they being properly administered? What are the positive or negative results of these bonuses or perks?

12. What do you consider your primary responsibilities?

13. Describe a situation in which you had to make the buy-versus-build decision and you chose to buy. Why did you make that choice? With hindsight, was it the right choice?

14. Describe a situation in which you had to make the buy-versus-build decision and you chose to build. Why did you make that choice? With hindsight, was it the right choice?

15. Describe the division of responsibilities in your group. Is there anything that you think should be changed?

16. What do you do to treat yourself and keep enjoying your work?

Chapter 34

A Guide for Nontechnical
Managers

This chapter looks at the relationship between nontechnical managers and the senior technical staff in the system administration organization. The chapter examines the relationship between the SA staff and its management chain, as well as the relationships between the managers of the customer base and the senior technical SA staff. In particular, this chapter is geared for the nontechnical manager to which the system administration organization reports. Nontechnical managers may also wish to to consult Chapters 21 and 30, which cover system administration organizational structures, the strengths and weaknesses of the centralized and decentralized models, and how they affect the team.

Both the SAs and the managers have certain expectations of and responsibilities to each other. To form a good relationship, both parties must understand what those expectations and responsibilities are and how to meet them. Good relationships are based on mutual respect and good communication. This chapter includes techniques that encourage both.

34.1 The Basics

The primary responsibilities of the nontechnical manager responsible for a system administration organization are to set priorities and to provide resources while maintaining high morale.

All relationships are founded on communication, and the relationships that nontechnical managers have with the senior technical staff are no exception. We look at the ways in which both interpersonal communication and staff meetings can aid the nontechnical manager in improving communication with the technical staff.

To work well together, the SA team and manager need to have a shared vision. To help create this, the senior technical staff members should be asked to produce a one-year plan for each area of expertise, based on the information and direction that the manager gives them. The manager will use these statements in his budgeting and planning process, involving senior SAs through this entire decision-making cycle. Doing so can be a beneficial experience for everyone. It helps the SAs understand the direction of the company and makes them feel involved and invested in the outcome.

Providing SAs with opportunities to participate in professional development activities, such as conferences and training courses, is a necessary part of improving their performance and increasing their job satisfaction. SAs need to keep in touch with ever-changing technologies, and they typically enjoy doing so.

34.1.1 Priorities and Resources

The primary responsibility of the nontechnical manager in a technical system administration organization is to set priorities and provide resources. This is no different from any other management situation. However, a nontechnical manager may not always understand the details of the technical team's work and therefore needs more mutual respect and trust to be effective.

Communicating priorities is not only a matter of communicating direction but also facilitating the translation into language that everyone understands. The business-speak that makes sense to a nontechnical manager may be simply incomprehensible to technical people. This comes to a surprise to many nontechnical managers. Technical people are smart, but how could they be so ignorant at the same time? It isn't that technical people willfully ignore business-speak; it simply sounds funny to them, as though managers are inventing words all the time.

Providing resources usually means setting appropriate staff size and budget.

Steve's Best Two Bosses

An SA from New York described the two best bosses he ever had as follows. In both cases, they were senior VPs but were opposites in other ways.

The first had been in technical roles earlier in his career. When the SA brought up technical issues, the boss understood him. They could see eye to eye. They could work well together because they understood each other both technically and otherwise. The SA liked this boss.

The other boss, by contrast, had very little technical background. However, he and the SA had an excellent relationship because they respected each other's strengths and could work well together because they knew how to communicate on the things they needed to and accepted those boundaries. Their organization had specific goals related to new security initiatives that the company was adopting in response to new SEC regulations. The SA handled the technical side, and his boss worked to acquire funding to make the SA's plans happen. The SA's goal was to make his boss a success: The SA provided talking points that his boss could use when seeking the funding, as well as high-level milestones as well as progress information to instill confidence. Outside of budget and status, the boss usually didn't know what the SA was talking about. However, they could cooperate well and get the funding required to meet the business goals they had been assigned.

These two managers were complete opposites but were the best bosses the SA ever had. In both cases, they found ways to make their similarities or differences into assets.

34.1.2   Morale

For a team of SAs to work at peak performance, they must have high morale. When morale is high, they will do whatever is needed of them, even if it involves heroics and late nights. When morale drops, the staff will be no longer willing to put everything into a job that has become depressing and unrewarding.

Creating or maintaining high morale is easier said than done. System administration is very stressful. There can be an ever-increasing stack of work, clashing deadlines, some irate customers, lots of little crises, and occasional big emergencies. SAs need to spend time communicating with others, yet the stack of work is telling them to work continuously. This high-stress work life makes SAs very sensitive to the atmosphere at work and to feeling under-appreciated. A good nontechnical manager should figure out how to guide the group with a light hand and prevent outside influences from disturbing their workflow or upsetting morale.

Micromanagement reduces morale. A nontechnical manager should hand his staff goals, not solutions. The senior technical staff expect to be given high-level direction by their nontechnical managers, to be trusted to achieve those goals, and to give periodic progress reports. Micromanagement of projects distracts, slows down, and demoralizes SAs, as it does other technical staff. The SAs also expect their managers to assist in clearing any roadblocks they may encounter in trying to meet their goals and to fight for adequate funding so that the SAs can complete their projects and achieve the service levels expected of them. The nontechnical manager should also aim to act as a filter and a buffer from the stress of knowing all the things that might happen but don't, while giving the SAs enough advance warning of the projects that do happen.

The manager is the enabler. He enables his employees to do their jobs, while keeping the worst of the politics out of their way. A nontechnical manager should never try to make or direct technical decisions. When he has to override a technical decision for political reasons, he should explain to his people what the reasons were and why he did it; otherwise, they will resent him, and morale will plummet.

An uncertain future can completely destroy morale. Why work when you may lose your job? Why do a complete solution, with good documentation, reliability engineering, and so on, when you think that the group will not be around in a couple of months? Why do any long-term planning when the long-term plan for the group keeps changing? A large company is rife with rumors of reorganizations, layoffs, changes, and shuffles. It is the nontechnical manager's job to manage the effects of the rumors that get to the SA team. He should keep those potential changes in mind and inform senior staff members when a change looks probable. But he should make it general knowledge only after the decision has been made. Even if he is the person who must consider these potential corporate improvements, he must project an image of a solid future, or employees will leave left and right. It is important, however, not to give false or misleading assurances, or the staff will not trust him.

Case Study: Uncertainty Is Bad for Morale

A new manager didn't realize the importance of projecting a solid future and discussed every rumored change with his senior SAs. Every thought and notion about budget cuts, increases, shuffles, and reorganizations was discussed with the senior SAs. Soon, everyone in the group was convinced that management was out to kill the group, planned to downsize the company, was unhappy with the group, and so on. Why would management be proposing these changes if it wasn't unhappy with the team? In reality, it is management's job to always be thinking in terms of making changes that benefit the company. The previous managers had dealt with the same issues but hadn't exposed the SA team to any but the most likely situations. Thus, what the SA team saw was years of feeling as though it had a solid and predictable future, but now a year of continual threats of change. In fact, the changes happened at the same rate, but the perception was that now, there was less certainty about the future. SAs started leaving the team one by one. When certain senior SAs left, upper management panicked and had to educate the manager about the effect he was having.

This is not to say that management should make major decisions in a vacuum, without the consultation of the senior SAs. Rather, a balance must be achieved.

The SA team needs to know it can count on the manager for support. If he does not establish this reputation, the team members will leave for a company where they can get that support.

Support the Team

Here's how one manager sent a clear message to his team that the SAs were always supported if they acted honorably. An SA repairing one hard drive on a workstation accidentally reformatted a different drive on the machine. The deleted data had been collected in the field over the past 2 years and was not being backed up and could not be regenerated. Realizing that the situation could spin out of control, the manager took the SA, who was nearly suicidal with fear, out of the loop immediately. He met with the customers, explained what had happened, and took responsibility for the team's mistake. The customers were appropriately angry at the situation, but the manager stood up for his team. Having data on a workstation was against policy: All data was to be kept on the servers where backups were done. The disks had been attached to the workstation years ago and only with the agreement that the customers acknowledged that the data wouldn't be backed up and thus should be used only for temporary files and as a workspace. The SA's manager agreed to pay the full cost of a disk repair service, despite the high fee and no guarantee of success. The customers were not happy, but they respected the manager for sticking up for his team. (The fact that he was built like a football player may have helped here.) The SA was not publicly punished for what he had done. The week of living in fear for his job was certainly punishment enough, and we can assume that his yearly performance review was to be affected by this. The manager knew that the SA had learned his lesson and never talked about the incident except to say, "I'm sure you've learned a lot from this and will be more careful in the future."

The manager's actions spoke louder than words: Honest mistakes are part of the job, and his staff will receive his support if they work hard, are careful, and own up to their mistakes.

34.1.3 Communication

Members of the technical staff often can experience a language problem when talking to people who are not familiar with their areas of expertise. This problem can lead to a breakdown in communication. Typically, the technical staff will develop the habit of using vague generalities rather than giving details that may mean little to the listener. The senior technical staff members should be coached to learn the language of their nontechnical managers and customers and to use that language in their conversations with their managers and customers. That language is based on the requirements behind the work that the technical staff people are doing. The SAs should know the requirements that govern their work, base their decisions around those requirements, and discuss the project's progress in relation to those requirements.

Manager-Speak

To this day, Tom still isn't sure what managers meant by "synergy" in the early 1990s.

34.1.4 Staff Meetings

Formal staff meetings between SAs and their nontechnical manager help to keep the SAs in touch with what is happening in their group and within the company as a whole. Such quarterly meetings can be an opportunity for the manager to communicate the direction in which he wants the group to move yet empower individuals to decide how to meet those goals. These meetings require planning. He should meet with the senior SAs and script how the meeting should go. Just as he may not understand the SAs' technical jargon, they have an equally difficult time understanding management-speak and management's perspective. It is critical to review with a senior SA how various ideas will be presented so that they are understood and, more important, so that negative triggers are avoided. A bold statement that is meant to be empowering can be a disastrous demoralizing announcement when interpreted by SA ears. Discussing the outline, or script, for the meeting with an SA will avoid that problem.

Rehearse Executive Visits to Avoid Disasters

A company vice president once met with the SA team to show his support for the group. The meeting went very well until his last comment, when he unwittingly stepped into an area of hot debate. He didn't know that a particular issue had become dangerous to mention without upsetting people. Whereas the previous 45 minutes had gone swimmingly, the last 15 minutes were spent deflecting anger about the topic. The VP didn't think that the topic was significant and didn't realize how emotional it was for the team. He ended up looking as though he didn't care about the SAs. The meeting was such a disaster that the senior SAs called a team meeting later that day to try to recover from the damage done. They were not successful, and it took weeks to recover from the meeting. In that time, both a senior and a junior SA left the group. All this could have been avoided if the VP had met with the senior SAs beforehand.

Tom's high school drama teacher always used to say, "Never do anything in performance you haven't done in rehearsal." The VP would have benefited greatly from that advice.

The nontechnical manager also should encourage the team to have regular weekly meetings to maintain cohesion on technical issues. These meetings should function as opportunities for SAs to seek help from others or to become involved in projects or standards on which others in the group are working. These meetings can be a valuable way to keep the group united, involved, and happy.

SAs, like most people, want to know what is going on around them at work and to participate at least a little in projects that affect, or simply interest, them. Because many SAs, particularly those in direct customer-support roles, spend most of their time working with customers rather than with other SAs, they can feel isolated from the SA team. It is important to make them a part of the team and to involve them in the direction that the SA group takes in new technologies and standards. Regular staff meetings are a good way for SA managers to keep their teams unified and informed. These meetings enable team members to find out what others are working on, what issues or projects others anticipate, and where they can look for feedback on certain ideas or help with problems. The staff meeting should keep the SAs up to date with anything important that is happening elsewhere in the company. It can be used as a forum for regularly reminding SAs of important policies, procedures that should be followed, or internal standards.

These meetings are also useful because they may be one of the few times that front-line support people interact with back-line support or engineering. It is common at these meetings for back-line support to learn of systemic problems that they need to solve for the front-line personnel. It is also an opportunity for senior technical leads to educate the rest of the group on technical issues.

Case Study: Use Staff Meetings for Knowledge Transfer

One SA team's weekly meeting includes a 20-minute segment during which a senior SA explains some technical aspect of how the group's enterprise works. This gives senior SAs experience with presenting information and cross-trains the entire group on technical issues.

34.1.5 One-Year Plans

An SA's work is by nature composed of lots of small tasks and a few large ones. As a result, it is easy for an SA to lose sight of the big picture of what is happening in the company and the corresponding direction that her own work should take. Drawing up 1-year plans periodically can help to bring the big picture back into focus. It also helps the SA's manager and customers to plan better for the coming year.

Nontechnical managers should expect their senior technical staff to have a vision of the direction in which the company's computing environment is heading. The senior technical staff should anticipate new service requirements and necessary upgrades and should be thinking of ways to optimize SA tasks or otherwise improve service. A senior SA should always be looking at least a year ahead and planning the projects for the coming year so that they are evenly spaced out rather than all needed at once.

Of course, unexpected projects, such as a merger or acquisition, will always crop up, but the wise senior SA will be expecting the unexpected and will have leeway in her project schedule to accommodate those situations.

The nontechnical manager should require the senior technical staff to have a 1-year plan and to keep him apprised of it. It gives him the opportunity to figure out what, if any, money is available for those SA projects. It also gives him a chance to find the funding for the projects from groups that have an interest in seeing them succeed.

34.1.6 Technical Staff and the Budget Process

In addition to having the senior SAs creating a 1-year plan, it is important to involve the senior SAs in the budget process. Senior SAs should be able to build a detailed expenditure plan for the coming year, using their 1-year plan, their knowledge of day-to-day maintenance and growth issues, time scales for implementing projects, and staff availability.

Involving the senior SAs in the budget process gives them a forum for expressing their vision for their areas. It helps the manager to build a better budget by making him aware of all the projects, growth, and maintenance expenditures that the senior SAs foresee, rather than being surprised by them when an SA suddenly needs to spend money on something critical.

It gives the SAs an opportunity to explain what they need and why and to have some control over the funding in their areas. It also gives them some insight into one aspect of management, which may be helpful for those SAs who are interested in becoming managers.

> ### Include Technical Staff in the Budget Process
>
> A manager of the infrastructure team at Synopsys included the architect for each technology area in his budget process. When budget time was approaching, he asked his architects to build a list of projects and ongoing growth and maintenance work that they would like their groups to accomplish in the coming financial year. They had to prioritize that list. For each item, they had to estimate capital and noncapital expenditure and the head count required to meet that goal. They had to divide that expenditure into the quarters of the fiscal year in which they anticipated it would be spent. He also told them to draw a line through the list. Items above the line had to happen; items below the line would be good things to accomplish but were not critical.
>
> He took these lists and used them to compile his own prioritized list, grouping some items into a single line item and then drawing the line where he believed it should be. He also added salary and other information that only he had access to or responsibility for. That list was given to the director of the group, who compiled his list from all his sources, and so on.
>
> The manager discussed his compiled list with all the architects, using it as a vehicle to keep them informed of what other infrastructure areas were doing. As the budget process progressed, he kept the architects informed of the progress of the list and their line items. This level of involvement helped the architects to see a bigger picture of what was happening in the company and to understand why some budget items received funding and others did not. It also gave the architects a plan to follow for the coming year and let them decide, before problems could arise, how to cope without things that they felt were critical but that did not get funded.

The quarter-by-quarter budget should be used to check the group's progress against its goals. Putting this information onto a budget spreadsheet and making it available to everyone helps people to see what is going on in other areas. If something unexpected arises during the year, the managers can use the spreadsheet to figure out how to find the funding for it.

At some companies, it is important to spend the allocated money in the early part of the year because the budget can get cut during the year, taking away most or all of the unspent money. In such companies, the SAs should plan to spend the latter part of the year working on projects that do not require new equipment or that use equipment that was bought earlier in the year.

Some companies also automatically deduct a certain amount from every budget request. For example, the senior managers might look at the list of SA projects that they believe are reasonable and then deduct 25 percent from the requested amount. This approach to budgets is cultural within the company, and so everyone who knows about it then pads the budget by that amount to make sure that they get the amount they need. In such a company, it is important to recognize that budget cutting and padding go on. The nontechnical manager should make sure that he understands what the group's real needs are and should make sure that he does the right thing to meet those needs. If necessary, he should add in some projects that he can justify but that the group can manage without.

Once the budget has been decided on and allocated to the group, it is important that the nontechnical manager delegate the responsibility for completing the funded tasks and the authority for spending the budget to the technical manager. If the technical manager is given the responsibility, but not the authority, to spend the budget, she will become frustrated and eventually leave. Nothing is more demeaning than to be given the responsibility for something without the authority required to achieve the goal.

34.1.7 Professional Development

Providing SAs with opportunities for professional development is one of the key ways of increasing their job satisfaction. It benefits the company to keep them up to date on the latest technologies and methods for solving problems that they face in their day-to-day work. It also benefits the company to improve the SAs' skills and to keep them up to date on developments in, and the direction of, the industry. Professional development includes attending relevant conferences, taking appropriate courses, and having well-stocked bookshelves. The nontechnical manager of the SA team should make sure that each employee has some funding available to use for professional development.

Technology changes rapidly. Some estimate that 30 percent of the technical knowledge they need to know becomes obsolete every year. When SAs go long enough without training, it becomes difficult for them to do their jobs. It can be extremely frustrating to install this year's systems using guesses based on last year's knowledge. Eventually, this frustration becomes a morale problem and a risk to the quality of IT at your company. Professional development doesn't cost money, it pays dividends.

Managers should encourage the technical staff to attend conferences and courses to improve their skills and should be conscious of the different value proposition of one-day workshops versus week-long conferences. One-day workshops and training programs tend to be tactical, focusing on a particular technology or skill. Week-long conferences are strategic, offering opportunities to discuss broader topics.

Attending conferences enables SAs to keep in touch with the industry through formal presentations, vendor exhibitions, and simply talking to peers from many different backgrounds to learn from their experiences. The benefits of the so-called hallway track at conferences—chatting in the halls between sessions—where attendees share problems and ideas, cannot be overemphasized. A conference or training course is very intensive, but it also gives SAs some distance and perspective on their work, which can also help with sticky problems. Training should be off-site so that it is not interrupted. Ideally, both conferences and training should be out of town to give the SAs a chance to concentrate on professional development undisturbed. They should even be able to turn off their cellphones and pagers during sessions.

Junior SAs often benefit more from attending courses than conferences. Some specialized courses can also be useful to senior SAs. In addition to the content of the course, it enables the senior SAs to dedicate uninterrupted time—that they would otherwise be unable to find—to thinking about a particular technology in depth.

Many system administration tasks require an in-depth understanding of a protocol or how a particular technology works. It is impossible for an SA to keep all the details of every protocol and technology in his head, so he needs to have access to a good reference library at all times. Each SA should own the books that he uses most often, and, ideally, the company should have a large collection of system administration books available for reference.

We like to see companies allocate an allowance for each employee to spend on professional development each year. It covers some conferences, courses, and book purchasing for each SA. This approach ensures that all SAs can benefit from a development opportunity. Get the SAs involved in choosing how they want to use their allocation, and encourage them to make use of it. Professional development is in everybody's best interests, and positive encouragement makes the SAs feel appreciated and a valuable part of the company.

Professional development is also discussed in Section 32.1.4.

34.2 The Icing

When the basics of good relationships with the technical staff are covered, the nontechnical manager can consider a couple of things to get those relationships moving along even more smoothly. Rather than simply developing a detailed 1-year plan, the nontechnical manager should encourage the technical staff to sketch out a 5-year plan, too. He should consider how to incorporate those plans into the annual budget process to ensure that the funds they need for their projects arrive when they need them.

The nontechnical manager should also set up relationships between each customer-oriented technical staff member and a customer who can act as a single point of contact for the whole group. He should have the SA schedule regular meetings with that person to track hot topics and have the customer representative assist the SA in prioritizing tasks for the customer group and resolving priority clashes between people in the group.

The nontechnical manager also should try to learn about what the technical staff people in his group do. He does not need to become an expert in those technical fields, but understanding their work will help him communication with staff and customers.

34.2.1 A Five-Year Vision

In Chapter 5, we mentioned that when an SA builds a service, she should try to build it so that it will last for 3 to 5 years both because equipment tends to wear out—even systems with no moving parts—and because organic growth tends to require some kind of technology refresh approximately that often. The corollary is that she will need to upgrade services about once every 3 to 5 years. Somehow, rebuilding and upgrading services need to fit in between all the other projects that she has to do, and she still needs to have time for day-to-day maintenance and customer support.

Planning SA projects 5 years out is a good way to make sure that they all happen at reasonable times. Five years out? "But we don't know what's going to happen next week!" In fact, there are many long-term issues to be concerned with. Network technology tends to change enough to require new wiring every 5 to 10 years. The fast server installed this year will be the slowest server in 5 years, if the machine still exists. Network speed increases about an order of magnitude every few years, keeping pace with CPU speed. Completely new data storage paradigms have changed approximately every 5 years.[1] Long-term strategies that plan on machines being replaced or

---

1. It is interesting to note that every time data storage requirements have grown three orders of magnitude, the way we do data storage and backups has had to change almost entirely to be able to manage the additional space. Direct attached storage was fine for megabytes of storage, but network-attached storage lets us manage gigabytes; SANs made terabytes manageable, and parallel file systems are a necessity at the petabyte level.

upgraded at certain intervals should be reconsidered based on how the technology is evolving. Upgrades should be performed before the service starts falling apart. In many workplaces, it can sometimes take a few years of looking for budget allocation for a particular new service or upgrade before it is approved. Starting to ask for the money before the team really needs it can be a good way to make sure that the projects happen at a reasonable time. Obviously, the group needs the 5-year plan if the nontechnical manager is to look for money ahead of time. Be careful not to allocate the money before it can reasonably be used, however, or you risk losing it and not getting the budget for other projects in the future.

Case Study: Time Budget Requests Well

The senior network administrator at Synopsys had project scheduling and budget requests down to a fine art. He became good at predicting how many years he would need to request a budget for a particular item before it was allocated. He could nearly predict how many times his management team would put a given project "below the line" before they would get worried by how long they had been refusing this new service or upgrade and put it above the line. He planned projects and started looking for money for them far enough in advance so that he was always able to do the projects at the right time.

Each group needs a 5-year plan that takes into account the budget process and prepares senior management for upcoming projects. It is better for the nontechnical manager to do this rather than have each senior technical person try to do so.

For the 5-year plan, the nontechnical manager needs to have technical staff who are able to predict what new, up-and-coming technologies the company will want to use in the future, when the technologies will be mature enough to use, and when the customer demand for them will warrant the investment. Senior managers and customers will learn of a new technology and want to know when the company is going to provide that service. It is essential for the architects to stay on top of the new technologies and their maturities in order to help answer those questions sensibly and completely when asked. If an architect is unsure or can't give a good answer to the question, the group may be pressured to deploy the technology before it is sufficiently reliable and supportable. On the other hand, the SAs gain a lot of credibility and can ease the pressure for the new technology if their manager is able to answer such questions with: "We expect the technology to have developed to the point where it will be useful and stable enough for our purposes in 18 months, and we have tentatively scheduled an evaluation project for that time. We will be looking for the resources for that evaluation project in our next year's budget." If he does give an answer like that, he will need to be able to substantiate the time claim and explain why the team believes it is not ready for the company's use just yet. The architect should be involved in the conversation so that she can provide the details that the manager needs.

Start-up and e-commerce companies may find it impossible to plan 5 years down the road because growth is so explosive and failure rates are high. However, in this situation, the SAs are most likely much closer to the CEO and the vision of how the company will evolve. This can make it even easier to have a vision for the future than, say, at a large company where the SAs are buried five levels of management away from any kind of corporate strategic planning. If the company strategy is to be purchased by a bigger company, your 5-year plan is not to invest too heavily in long-term infrastructure. If the strategy is to expand by opening sales offices around the world, the group's plans can center on the different needs that such an environment would create, such as building a WAN and a network operations center. Even an amorphous vision of the future can give the team better direction than no plan at all.

34.2.2 Meetings with Single Point of Contact

In many places in this book, we emphasize communication between the SAs and their customers. Having regularly scheduled meetings with a single point of contact on the customers' team to track hot issues is a good way to formalize some of the communication. It does not replace the project-related, support-call-related, or other ad hoc conversations that the SA has with her customers; instead, it adds to them. The manager of the system administration organization should push the customer organizations into designating a single point of contact and making these meetings happen.

These scheduled meetings act as a focal point for both the SA and her customers. Before each meeting, both people should take some time on their own and with colleagues on their respective teams to consider what projects, maintenance, or problems the other party should know about. In the meetings, the status of previous issues should be tracked, and new topics should be discussed and added to the list. The SA can also use the list to prioritize tasks with the customer and to set realistic goals for new projects.

These meetings provide the customers with a valuable insight into what their SAs are working on. They give the customers status information on large projects and help them to understand why some of their jobs might be completed later than they would like. It allows someone in the customer's department to use his knowledge of his group's work to set priorities. The people in the group who have conflicting deadlines have to decide among themselves what their priorities are and communicate that to the SAs through their point of contact. This prioritization technique gives the responsibility for making those decisions to the right people, sets the expectations for the customers from the outset, and should result in the right decisions being made for the company. When SAs are forced to prioritize tasks without feedback from someone who is ultimately in charge of all the projects that rely on those tasks, they can make the wrong decisions or end up trying to accomplish everything in an impossible time frame.

The meetings actually save SAs' and the customers' time by avoiding frequent "status check" emails and conversations for the myriad tasks that the SAs are working on. The customers know what to expect and when to expect it, and they can quickly get a status update from their single point of contact or possibly through a web page, if the SAs track status there. The meetings are also a trust- and confidence-building exercise. No one likes throwing tasks into a black hole and hoping that they will be completed—or worse, expecting that they won't be.

Case Study: Weekly Meetings with Customers Save Time

One senior SA reluctantly began having weekly meetings with each department head in the cluster of groups that he supported. Initially, the meetings took an hour but eventually turned into short, 15-minute status updates as things settled down. When a large change was coming or if there was a problem, the meetings would increase in length until the issue was resolved. The meetings helped keep the SA focused on what was important to the customers yet also helped educate the customers about things that were important to the SA, such as taking a little longer on certain projects to make sure that they would scale or could be better supported, and so on. The result was that customer satisfaction increased dramatically because they felt that the SAs were listening to them. The SA was happier in his job because he was receiving positive feedback. One day, the SA told the person who had encouraged him to have these meetings that he was sorry he had resisted them. "I have the same work load and I'm doing the same amount of work, yet the customers are much happier and I'm much happier. Mathematically that doesn't make sense! It's magic!" Yes, it is.

Sometimes, customers will resist these meetings, and some will totally reject the idea. Ideally, they will hear from their peers how useful the meetings are for them and change their mind. Alternatively, you may choose other ways to increase communication with them. A department head once rejected the suggestion and said, "I'm happy with what you do. If something is wrong, don't I complain?" In fact, that person had a very good sense of what his own time management needs were and was very good about bringing issues to the SA rather than letting them fester. The greater need, however, was for communication in the other direction.

Not everyone can realistically have a single point of contact, however. SAs who are responsible for companywide infrastructure, for example, can't expect one person in the company to be able to identify everyone's needs or mediate in their priority negotiations. These SAs should gather all the infrastructure-related issues from the SAs who serve the customer base more directly and will need to do their own prioritization with the help of their management. In sensitive cases, they can bring together the single points of contact from the groups with conflicting requirements and look for them to come to some resolution. The manager of the system administration organization should also be available to help with such issues.

34.2.3 Understanding the Technical Staff's Work

A nontechnical manager should make his best effort to understand what his technical staff does. He does not need to become an expert in the field; rather, he should understand and appreciate what tasks they undertake and what is involved in the things that he and their customers request of them.[2] He will be better able to communicate with the technical staff and the group's customers if he understands what his staff does. Customers expect a certain level of knowledge from the nontechnical manager in charge of the group. He should try not to disappoint them, because it will reflect on his group. He will also be better able to represent the group's budget needs to senior management and be better able to negotiate with senior managers and customers on behalf of the group if he understands his employees' jobs. He will make better decisions with this knowledge. The team will be happier with the way he represents them and will also appreciate any effort he makes to understand what they do.

---

2. This book might be a good place to start for a nontechnical manager who wants to understand what SAs do!

> ### Learning Helps
>
> A manager found himself managing a group of technical people whose jobs entailed things that he had never been involved with before. He had a good relationship with them, but it noticeably improved when he did some reading about their jobs and demonstrated this new understanding to them.

34.3 Conclusion

A successful working relationship between nontechnical managers and the senior technical SA staff is built around communication and mutual respect. The nontechnical manager's job is to maintain morale by shielding the SA team from political issues and supporting the team members by going to bat for them in both good times and bad. Managers should keep SAs in the loop about what is happening in the company, particularly the areas that relate to the SAs' work but without speculating on every rumor. Formal meetings between the technical staff and their manager and between each SA and her customers' single point of contact are good ways to stay in touch.

Advance planning through 1-year and 5-year plans gives managers and customers confidence in the SAs and valuable insight into the work that they do. It also gives the managers the opportunity to look for budget allocations for the projects that the SAs foresee, rather than having to veto the projects regularly because of lack of funding. Involving the senior SAs in the budget process gives them insight into the way it works, which can aid their planning and give them good experience.

Exercises

1. How do you ensure that your priorities are communicated to the SAs?

2. How do you hold SAs to their commitments?

3. What is your group's 1-year plan? How well does the budget match it? How can you improve on that?

4. How has your company invested in the professional development of the SA staff in the last 3 years? How do you think it should progress in the coming years?

5. What conferences would your technical staff people like to attend? What do you feel the benefits are? How can you distribute conference

attendance fairly without jeopardizing your SA coverage during those conferences?

6. If you have regular staff meetings, do you keep your staff informed and cover the topics your team is interested in? How would you improve the meetings? If you don't have regular meetings, what would you use as an agenda for setting them up, and how often would you hold them?

7. Get your senior staff to sketch out a 5-year plan. How much do you think each of the projects on that list will cost?

8. Based on the 5-year plan and what you know of your budget process, when will you start looking for funding for each project?

9. Look at each of the customer organizations. Who would be the ideal single point of contact for your SAs in each organization? If you do not already have such a scheme set up, try setting up a test relationship and arranging regular status meetings between the appropriate SA and the single point of contact.

10. An anecdote in Section 34.1.2 involved defending the SA team even though a disastrous mistake had been made. Relate a similar situation that you have been in, or describe what you would have done if you were the manager in the anecdote.

Chapter 35

Hiring System Administrators

This chapter looks at hiring system administrators, focusing on areas that are different in some way from hiring other staff people. These items are the things that the SA staff and managers need to know. Everything else should be taken care of by the human resources department.

This chapter does not cover areas of hiring that are generic and apply across the board: compensation packages, on-call compensation, overtime pay, comp time, or traditional incentive schemes, such as stock options, hiring bonuses, and performance bonuses. Nor does this chapter look at how location, lifestyle, working from home, facilities for remote work, or training and conferences can factor into the hiring process.

Rather, this chapter covers the basics of how to recruit, interview, and retain SAs. It also looks at some things a company can do to stand out as a good company for which to work.

35.1 The Basics

The hiring process can be simplified into two stages. The first stage is to identify the people whom you want to hire. The second stage is to persuade them that they want to work for you.

Identifying whom you want to hire is in many ways the more complicated stage. To determine whether you want to hire someone, you must first know what you want the new hire to do and how skilled the person needs to be. Then you need to recruit the right candidates to get resumes from interested, qualified SAs. Then you need to pick the interview team and make sure that they are briefed appropriately on the interview process and determine who is tasked with finding out what information. The interviewers need to know how to interview the candidates in the particular areas of interest and how to treat the candidate during the interview process.

The second stage, persuading the candidate to work for you, overlaps a little with the first stage. The most important part of recruiting the candidate is doing the interview process well. The interviewers should show the best of the company and the position to the candidate, and the experience should make him want to work there. The timing also needs to be right; move quickly for the right candidates. We end the discussion with tips on how to avoid hiring by retaining staff.

35.1.1 Job Description

The first step in the hiring process is to determine why you need a new person and what the person will be doing. Figure out what gaps you have in your organization. Chapter 30 describes organizational structures and how to build a well-rounded team. That discussion should help you decide whom the new hire should be working with and what skill sets the person should have to complement the existing team's skills. Then think about what roles you want the new employee to take on, as described in Appendix A. This should give you an idea of the personality type and the soft skills for which you are searching. From this list of requirements, figure out which are essential and which are desired. You now have a basis for the job description.

Although time consuming, write a job description specific to every position. A written job description is a communication tool. Writing it is a catalyst that encourages team members to express their visions for the position, resolve differences, and settle on a clear definition. Once written, it communicates to potential candidates what the job is about. During the interview, it communicates a focus to the interviewers. When having to decide between two similarly qualified candidates, the job description serves to focus the decision makers on what is being sought.

A **job description** should include two parts: a list of responsibilities the person will have and a list of skills the candidate should have. To make it easy to write, and easy to read, make each job description a bulleted list, with the more important items at the top of the list. However, do not confuse a job description with a **job advertisement**, which is the job description revised for external consumption plus contact information, and any other legally required statements.

In Section 9.1.1, we discussed that documenting the tasks that you dislike doing makes it easier to delegate them. The next time you get the opportunity to hire, you can use the list of documents to help create the job description. The list of tasks you documented—and want to delegate—can be added to the list of responsibilities. The skills required to perform those tasks can be added to the list of required skills. The job description practically writes itself.

Two competing philosophies are related to filling an open position. *Hire the skill* means look for someone with the exact skills specified in the job description. Years later, you intend to find this person doing the exact same job he was hired to do, without variation. By contrast, *hire the person* means look for quality people and hire them, even if their specific skills only overlap what's listed in the job description. If you "hire the person," you are hiring the individual for his or her intelligence, creativity, and imagination, even if some of the specific credentials associated with the job you're trying to fill are lacking. These people may surprise you by changing a job so dramatically that the effort required is much less and the results are much better, perhaps through the elimination of unnecessary tasks, automating mundane tasks, and finding publicly available resources that accomplish the task.

It is easier to "hire the person" when you have many open positions, each requiring a different set of skills. If the first quality person you find has a few skills from each job description, you can redefine the position around that person. The next person you look for should have the remaining skills.

We tend to find ourselves hiring mostly senior-level SAs in such large quantities that we almost exclusively "hire the person." We recommend "hiring the skill" only for specific tactical instances.

Case Study: When to "Hire the Skill"

At Bell Labs, Tom's SA team "hired the person" for certain roles and "hired the skill" for others. For example, the senior SAs were expected to find creative solutions for the problems at hand. Those positions called for "hiring the person." On the other hand, a league of technicians who deployed new PCs needed only to start automated procedures to load the OS and then deliver the fully configured computers to the right office. For that role, "hiring the skill" worked best.

The hire-the-person strategy works only within limits. Make sure that you have something for the person to do. One Silicon Valley computer company had a strategy of hiring people because they were great, on the assumption that they would find projects on their own and do wonderful things. Instead, however, many of these people became lost, felt unwanted, and became extremely unhappy. Such a strategy works well for hiring researchers doing transformational work but not when hiring SAs.

Some candidates want to be very clear about what the job will be in order to decide whether it is something they want to do and if it will enable them to advance their career goals. These candidates will reject an offer of a job when the job duties are vague, or are unclear to them. Other candidates want to know whether there is flexibility in the job, so that they can gain experience in a variety of areas. In both cases, the interviewers need to know what the job entails and where it can be flexible, so that both sides know whether the candidate will be suited to the job. Be flexible if multiple positions are available. Some candidates may be perfect for part of one job and part of another. To maximize everyone's options, the interviewers should be aware of all the requirements in all the open job descriptions, so that they can talk to the candidate about other possibilities, if appropriate.

35.1.2 Skill Level

After building the basic job description, you should have a reasonable idea of the skill level required for the position. Ideally, map the job requirements to the SAGE skill levels described in their booklet *Job Descriptions for System Administrators* (Darmohray 2001). This has become the standard way of communicating such things in job descriptions, advertisements, and resumes.

The skill level of the person you hire has economic implications. To save money, some organizations believe in hiring the lowest-possible skill for first- and second-tier support. The theory is that the most common position to be filled should cost the least, using minimally trained people.

Other organizations prefer to hire people who are smart and highly motivated and are on the verge of being overqualified for the position. These people will be bored with the repetitive tasks and will eliminate them by instituting automation or recommending process changes that will continually improve the organization. In essence, these people will gladly put themselves out of a job because they know that their motivation will lead to other positions in the organization.

A talented, motivated SA who verges on being overqualified is worth more than two unmotivated, unskilled SAs who are hired to make up the numbers. The ideal candidate for the more junior position is bright and interested and has recently entered the field. If you invest in such people and give them opportunities to learn and do more, they will rapidly rise in skill levels, giving you ideal candidates for promotion into more senior positions that can be more difficult to fill. If you are lucky enough to hire people like this, make sure that their salaries and bonuses keep pace with their rising skill levels, even if it means pushing through special raises outside review periods. These people are valuable and difficult to replace, and they will be hired away by another company if you do not keep pace. Giving them extra raises outside of review periods also builds loyalty for the long term.

When rebuilding a struggling team, it is important to hire reform-oriented, senior-level staff people who have experience doing things "the right way" so that they are more likely to work to a higher standard. When a team is doing well, you have the luxury of hiring a mixture of senior and junior people to fill various specializations. The anecdote When Things Are Dire, Hire Higher in Section 30.1.4 has advice and examples related to this.

35.1.3 Recruiting

Once you have decided what position you are trying to fill and what skill level you are looking for, you need to find appropriate candidates for the job. The best candidates are usually found through personal recommendations from members of the SA team or customers. A recommendation from a customer will usually lead to a candidate who is good at all aspects of the job, including customer interaction and follow-through.

System administration conferences are also good places to recruit candidates. It may be possible to do some interviewing at the conference, and it is also possible for the candidates to talk to members of the SA team to find out what they are like and what it is like to work at the company. SAs who attend these conferences are often good candidates because they are keeping up with what is happening in the field and are interested in learning.

Use technology if you want to attract people who appreciate technology. Advertisements in newspapers are not going to attract the highly skilled, high-tech workers you are looking for. In our experience, advertisements on the web have a more effective reach than newspaper advertisements, even if the newspaper reaches more people.

The Internet is full of communities specific to particular skills; many of these communities have job-listing areas. By seeking out people in their community, one finds better candidates. For example, the FreeBSD community has a mailing list just for community members looking for jobs and those who want to hire them.

Many head-hunters specialize in SA recruiting and may have a useful database of SAs and the types of jobs that interest them. Your company's own web site should advertise available positions. If you do not list any openings on your own web site, people will assume that you aren't hiring.

There may be political barriers preventing job listings on your web site, but it is worthwhile to overcome those obstacles.

One problem that often arises in hiring SAs is that the human resources department does not fully understand SA resumes or SA job descriptions the way SAs do. The best recruiting campaign in the world will fail if the resumes do not get past the HR department. Excellent resumes often get rejected before they are even seen by the SA team because the HR person does not recognize that the resume is good, particularly if the company uses a computerized resume scanning and processing system. Such systems typically code for keywords and are fine if you want to "hire the skill" but not if you want to "hire the person" (Darmohray 2001). The best way to make sure that good resumes do not get discarded is to have one HR person assigned to hiring SAs and to have SAs and SA managers team up with her to gain an understanding of how to identify good and bad resumes, what is relevant for one position or another, and so on. Eventually, the HR person should be able to go through the resumes and pick out all the good ones. The HR person will tend to focus on keywords to look for, such as certifications, particular technologies, products, and brand names. We've had to explain terminology, such as the fact that Linux, IRIX, Solaris, and AIX all mean UNIX. Providing HR with a chart is an easy way to be helpful. We've also found it useful to give copies of the SAGE booklet (Darmohray 2001) to HR personnel.

Once trained, the SA managers can let the HR person do her job in peace and have confidence that she is not missing out on good candidates. Reward the HR person whom you have trained when she succeeds. Make sure she is the first person in HR to receive computer upgrades. Make all the other HR staff want to be the next to be trained.

Some companies do not trust their HR department to evaluate resumes at all. Instead, engineers or managers volunteer to take rotations evaluating resumes into "call," "don't call," and "maybe" piles. This can be especially useful when HR is still getting up to speed or when hiring is only an occasional task and training HR personnel would have little return on investment. Be sure that you have a mechanism to inform HR when you are expecting a resume from someone who deserves special attention: someone well known in the field, someone you've particularly recruited, or someone you otherwise know to be a good candidate.

Sometimes, a recruiter or someone from HR is the first person to talk to the candidate and does a phone screen. It is important to make sure that this first contact goes well. A recruiter who knows what to look for in the resume should also know how to perform a phone screen.

Bad Phone-Screening Alienates a Candidate

A large software company phone-screened a candidate for a software development vacancy. The candidate had a research degree in computer science and some software development experience. The HR person who performed the phone-screen asked the candidate to rate her programming skills against the other people she had worked with in the research group. The candidate tried to explain that everyone in the group was good at programming but that the ability to understand and solve the problems was the more important and relevant skill. Her interviewer didn't seem to understand what she was saying. At the end of the interview, the interviewer told her that it was interesting talking to her and that he had never spoken to a computer scientist, as opposed to a programmer, before. The candidate decided right then that there was no way she wanted to work for that company. Various recruiters and managers called her, trying to persuade her that she was interested in the job several times after she told them that she was not interested in pursuing the job. They also displayed some corporate arrogance: Even after she told them she had accepted another job, they couldn't understand why she was not interested because *they* were interested in continuing to interview her. This attitude confirmed her decision not to work for that company.

If your company has an in-house recruiter, an education process should be instituted. The best recruiting campaign in the world will fail if potential candidates think that your recruiter is an idiot.

35.1.4 Timing

In hiring, timing is everything. There is a brief window when someone is available and a brief window when you have open positions. The fact that those windows overlap at all and enable you to hire people is practically a miracle. Sometimes, positions open up just after an excellent candidate has taken a position elsewhere, or the perfect candidate becomes available right after the job has been offered to someone else. Sometimes, the timing mismatch is unavoidable, but other times, a company's inability to move quickly costs it the chance of hiring the best candidates.

When trying to attract SAs into a company that is meant to be a high-tech, fun company, the company needs to be able to move quickly in making hiring decisions. If a company delays too long in making its decision or has a long, drawn-out interviewing process, the best candidates already will have accepted offers somewhere else. Some companies even write the offer letter before the candidate arrives, particularly if the candidate is being flown in from far away. The offer can be made on the spot, and the candidate can stay for an extra day or two to look at housing and schools, if necessary.

A balance must be found between interviewing lots of candidates to find the best ones and moving quickly when a potentially suitable candidate is identified. Moving too slowly can result in losing the candidate to another company, but moving too quickly can result in hiring the wrong person.

Don't Rush a Hiring Decision

A midsize software company needed to hire a network administrator to develop network tools. The team interviewed a candidate who was reasonably well qualified, but his experience was on different hardware. He already had an offer from another company. The team knew that it had to make a decision quickly but was not sure about his skills or his team fit. The team wanted to do another round of interviewing, but there was not enough time. The team decided to offer him the job; he accepted the offer. Unfortunately, he did not work out well in that position or with the team. The team was stuck with the bad decision that was made under time pressure. Given more time and another round of interviews, the team might have decided against hiring him.

Hiring a new employee is a long-term commitment; it pays to take the time to get the right person. If the person is genuinely interested, he will ask the other company for more time to make a decision and should be given it, for fear of losing him by forcing his hand. All parties should take the time they need and give the others that benefit.

Strike While the Iron's Hot

A Silicon Valley start-up went bankrupt and had to let all its employees go on a Friday morning. One of those people was a well-known SA. Several companies rushed to employ him. During the following week, he had first- and second-round interviews with a few companies and at the end of the week had several offers and made his decision. One of the companies that he decided against did not have the right people interview him and had not trained the employees well in the art of interviewing, because it unintentionally told him why he should not work there. Another company that was very interested in hiring him was unable to move as quickly as the others and failed to have him even interview with the necessary people before the end of the week.

35.1.5 Team Considerations

It is important to make sure that the person you are hiring will fit into the team. One aspect of this is making sure that there aren't any serious personality clashes. A personality clash can lead to people not enjoying their work and using their energy in a negative way that lowers morale in the team.

Chapter 34 explains more about why low morale is bad for the team. The SAGE booklet *Hiring System Administrators* (Phillips and LeFebvre 1998) contains an excellent discussion on the psychology of hiring and how every new person who joins the group changes the team dynamic.

Sometimes, the decision is difficult because there may not be any obvious personality clashes, but the candidate has a different style from the rest of the team. This is where careful consideration of the job description before trying to interview candidates should help. The candidate's style of working may be something that the team is lacking and, as a result, all the interviewers will be aware that it is a desirable quality.

The Dilbert Check

One group always asked candidates to "relate the story line of your favorite Dilbert strip" as a way to see whether the person would fit into its fun-loving culture. There was no "right answer," but a lot was learned from which strip the candidate selected. Sometimes, it allowed the candidate to reveal the kind of coworker they didn't like to be with, which character they related to the most, or what their current job's work environment was like. Most important, it revealed whether the person could tell a joke. Nobody would be rejected solely on the basis of not being a Dilbert fan; however, it is interesting to note that one time, a candidate who had never heard of Dilbert had been hired and by some amazing coincidence, the person didn't work out and was encouraged to find work elsewhere. We are not recommending that someone shouldn't be hired just for not having heard of Dilbert, but that person will need special mentoring and a small budget to purchase the latest Scott Adams book.

The Other Dilbert Check

One candidate always made a point of looking at the cartoons pinned outside the offices and cubicles of the company at which he was interviewing. People tend to find cartoons funnier when they resonate with what happens at their own company. Looking at the cartoons people liked gave him a good insight into what it was really like to work at the company.

Know What You Are Looking For

A midsize company was trying to hire a second person for the security team. The SA organization was a young, dynamic, fast-paced, fast-growing team. The security SA's manager gave her the responsibility for choosing the right partner for the security team. However, the manager did not provide direction or advice on what was lacking in the organization. She interviewed one candidate who was well qualified but decided against hiring him because she was unsure of the team fit. He was a steady, reliable worker who always carefully researched and considered all the options, whereas the rest of the SA team was made up of people who made quick decisions that were almost always good but occasionally had negative repercussions. She was not sure how well he would get on in that environment. In retrospect, she realized that he was the ideal candidate, precisely because of his difference in style.

Another aspect of team diversity relates to cultural and ethnic diversity. Diversity in a team can be managed to garner excellent results. Everyone on a team brings a unique history and background, and these differences enrich a team. It's one of the ways that a group can make better decisions than a lone person. We all grow up with different experiences, based on our level of wealth, ethnic culture, stability, and myriad other issues. These experiences affect our thought processes; that is, we all think differently because of them. If we all had the same life experiences and thought the same way, we'd be redundant; instead, it is possible to manage diversity as your strong suit.

Three Different Backgrounds

Three SAs who worked together had very different upbringings. One had strict, religious parents who gave her a structured upbringing. Therefore, structure gave her comfort and security; everything had to be documented in detail before she could move forward. Another was kicked out of his house as a teenager when his parents found out that he was gay. He had to learn to survive on his own; he resisted structure and valued self-reliance. The third SA had been brought up in a very unstructured household that moved around the country a lot. He craved structure but expected unanticipated change. As a result, all three had relatively predictable work habits and design styles. Because they saw these differences as having many tools in their toolbox, it made for powerful results. Any design had to have enough structure to satisfy the first person, each component had to be self-reliant enough to satisfy the second person, and the system had to be able to deal with change well enough to satisfy the third. When documentation needed to be written, they knew who would see to its completion. This situation could have been a disaster if it had led to disagreements, but instead it managed to be their strength.

A manager must create an environment that supports and celebrates diversity rather than trying to fit everyone into the same "box." Model a willingness to listen and understand. Challenge the group members to under-stand one another and find best-of-both-worlds solutions.

Four World Views

Tom once interviewed the highest-performing engineering team in his division to find the secret of its success. One of the engineers pointed out that the four of them each came from very different religious backgrounds, each of which represented a different world view. He felt that this was the group's biggest strength. One's deity was inside us all, one's looked down on everyone with a mindful eye, another was at the center of everything, and another was out of reach to all but a very few. The world views were reflected in how they addressed engineering problems. Although they all had different world views, they all agreed that none was the right analogy for every engineering problem. Instead, each could perform his own analysis of a problem using very different philosophies. When they came together to share their results, they had a very thorough analysis. The discussions that resulted helped each member gain a deeper understanding of the problem, because each person tended to find different issues and solutions. Once they all saw eye to eye, they could design a solution that took the best aspects from each of their analyses.

Another aspect of the team picture is no less important: mentoring and providing opportunities for growth for the junior members of the team. Junior SAs need to be trained, and they also need to be given the opportunity to grow and demonstrate their talent, especially in their first SA job. It can be very worthwhile to take a risk on hiring a junior SA who seems to have potential if an appropriate mentor is available and can be assigned that role before the new hire's first day. Never hire junior SAs into positions where they will not get properly supervised and trained on a day-to-day basis. People hired into positions like this will not enjoy their work and often will make mistakes that other people have to correct. Hiring juniors into an SA role and giving them superuser access and insufficient mentoring is a recipe for disaster, and they are likely to create more work for others rather than relieve the work load.

Why Junior SAs Need Mentors

An ISP start-up split its SA organization into two parts to avoid a conflict in priorities. One team looked after the Internet service, and the other looked after the corporate sys-tems and networks. Senior SAs kept transferring from the corporate team to the service team; at one point, only a couple of junior SAs were left on the corporate team. The senior SAs on the service team answered questions and helped out when they could, but their priority was maintaining the service. One day, the root partition on the corporate mail server filled up. The junior SA who found the problem went looking for help from the senior SAs, but they were all heavily involved in some important work on the service and couldn't spare much time. She decided that the best thing to do was to find some large files that probably weren't used very much, move them to another disk partition, and create links to them from the original location. Unfortunately, she chose the shared libraries (the UNIX equivalent to Windows DLL files), not knowing what they were or the effect that moving them would have.

When she moved the libraries, she discovered that she could not make links to them, because that command no longer worked. As she tried to figure out what was wrong, she discovered that none of the commands she tried worked. She decided to try rebooting the system to see whether that fixed the problem. Of course, the system was unable to boot without the shared libraries, which made things worse. She ended up taking the mail server and another system apart in the computer room to try to boot the machine and recover it to a working state. As luck would have it, when she was in the middle of this operation, with computer parts strewn all over the floor, a TV crew that was doing a feature on the company came through the computer room and decided that she made for interesting footage. This added even more stress and embarrassment to an already awful situation.

Eventually, when the corporate mail server had been down for several hours and senior management was expressing displeasure, one of the senior SAs on the service team was able to break away and help her fix the problem. He also took the time to explain what the shared libraries were and why they were so critical. If she had had a mentor who was able to spend time with her and help her through problems such as this, the situation would have been resolved quickly without a huge outage and embarrassing TV footage.

35.1.6 The Interview Team

To evaluate candidates properly, the interviewers need to work as a team to find out whether the person has the necessary technical and soft skills and is a team fit. This is another situation in which the job description plays an important part. What exactly are the skills that the candidate is supposed to have? Divide the desired skills up into small, related sets, and assign one set of desired skills to each interviewer. Select the interviewers based on their ability to interview for, and rate the candidates on, a particular set of skills. Some people are better at interviewing than others. If you are doing a lot of hiring, make sure that they don't get totally swamped with first-round interviews. Consider saving them for the second round. Make sure that all the interviewers are aware of what skills they are interviewing for and what skills other people are interviewing for, so that there is minimal duplication and everything is covered. Only really critical skills should be assigned to more than one person. If two people are assigned to interview for the same skill, make sure that they ask different questions. Make sure that all the interviewers understand that all areas will be covered properly by someone, so that they are all comfortable in their team role.

If there are many openings, have the interview team cover the skills required across all the jobs. It will probably take a while to fill all the positions. As more positions are filled, the search can be narrowed and the skills needed restricted to cover the gaps that remain in the SA team's skill set. If there are many positions, describe them all to the candidate and, if appropriate, express willingness to have some crossover between the positions. Find out what positions the candidate finds the most interesting and appropriate for her skills.

Both the candidates and the team members will want to know with whom they will be working. It is vital that the candidates spend time during the interview process with the person who will be their manager and the people with whom they will work most closely. Give the candidate the opportunity to meet as many people in the team as possible, without making the interview process overwhelming and exhausting. Consider adding an internal customer to the interview team, which benefits the candidate and your relationship with your customers. Bring the candidate to lunch with two or three SAs. This gives her an opportunity to get to know some of her potential coworkers in a more relaxed environment, which should help her to decide whether she wants to work with your team. One common mistake is to ignore the person at lunch. Make sure that you try to keep the candidate involved in the conversation. Ask open-ended questions to encourage her to converse with the group.

Involve the Candidate

Tom once worked at a site that always took candidates out to lunch with the entire team to see whether the candidate fit in well with the group. Tom was appalled to watch as nobody spoke to the person. Tom tried to bring the candidate into the conversation, but the candidate would immediately be interrupted by someone, and the conversation would be diverted away from the candidate. As a result, Tom instituted "how to have lunch" training whereby everyone was forced to practice such useful phrases as, "Hey, that's interesting. Tell us more about that."

35.1.7 Interview Process

The most important point that all interviewers need to remember is to re-spect the candidate. The candidate should always leave feeling that the in-terview was worthwhile and that the people that he spoke to were the sort of people with whom he would like to work. He should have the impres-sion that interviewing him was the most important thing on the interview-ers' minds. Remember, you want the candidates to want to work with you. You want them to tell their friends that your company looks like a great place to work. They need to leave the building with their self-respect in-tact and liking the company. Other ways to show respect include the following:

- *Read the resume before you arrive.* Nothing insults a local candidate like being asked how the flight was or being asked to list information that is clearly available on the resume.

- *Be prompt for your interview; don't leave the candidate waiting.* The candidate has given up a lot of his time to come to the interview; don't make him feel that it was a waste of time.

- *Before meeting the candidate, turn off all radios, pagers, and cellphones.* Your company will survive for an hour without you, even if it doesn't feel that way. You don't want the candidate to feel as though the site is in such a bad way that he will never have a moment's peace. Nor do you want to waste precious interviewing time worrying about, or dealing with, problems at the site.

- *Show interest in the candidate.* Did he have a difficult time finding the place? Was the traffic bad? How is he finding the interviews so far? Would he like a drink or a quick break?

- *Make sure that everyone is asking different questions.* It shows the can-didate that the group communicates and works well as a team. It shows that thought and preparation went into the interview process. Answer-ing the same questions over and over is a waste of time for the candidate. Asking different questions also gives the interviewers a broader view of the candidate when they compare notes later.

- *Don't set out to prove you know more.* The point of the interview is to find out how much the candidate knows, not to demonstrate your own brilliance or to try to catch him on some insignificant little detail that most SAs will never come across in their careers.

- *Ease the candidate into it.* Start with relatively easy questions to give him a chance to build confidence, and gradually make them more difficult. This process will give you a good idea of the candidate's skill level and gives the candidate a chance to demonstrate his true skills, rather than succumbing to nerves and forgetting everything. It is in both parties' interests for the candidate to show his true skill level.

- *Don't prolong the agony.* When you find the candidate's limits in one area, back off and try to find his limits in another area. Give him a chance to build up confidence before probing his limits.

- *Try to identify your concerns as you go.* If you are unsure how he would respond in a certain situation, it is best to realize that during the interview when you have a chance to direct your questions to validate or disprove your concerns.

Take Care of the Candidate

An Internet start-up interviewed a senior SA who had been personally recommended and recruited by the two most senior SAs on staff. The interview time was 6 PM to 10 PM. The employees of the start-up were working late nights all the time and always ordered take-out dinners from nearby restaurants. During one of the interviews, someone asked the interviewer what he wanted for dinner but did not ask the candidate, who also had not eaten. The next interviewer brought in his dinner and proceeded to eat it in front of the candidate, without thinking to ask whether she wanted anything. The same thing happened during the second round of interviews. She was offered the job, and they were surprised when she turned it down. In the ensuing months, she talked to many people about the awful interview process and came across others who had undergone similar experiences and also turned the company down.

Successful interviewing requires preparation, practice, and coordination. Record your thoughts on the interview and the candidate as soon as you come out of the interview. Doing so gives you the freshest, most accurate picture of the candidate when the team gets together to decide whom to hire. It also gives you the opportunity to think about concerns that you may not have probed in the interview and to ask a later interviewer to direct some questioning toward those concerns.

One of the biggest mistakes that companies make is to "sell the company" only after they've asked enough questions to determine that the candidate is qualified for the job. They feel that anything else is wasting time with people who aren't going to be hired. As a result, qualified candidates walk away from an interview thinking, "What a boring company!" or possibly "What a bunch of jerks!" Instead, start each interview by explaining what a great company you have and why you personally like the company. This starts the candidate off feeling eager to join; it relaxes the person and makes the interview go more smoothly. It also puts you in better light. If the candidate isn't qualified for the position, he or she might have friends who are. Also, an unqualified person may be qualified later in her career, and it would be a shame if you've turned her off to your company by one bad interview.

35.1.8 Technical Interviewing

Technical interviewing finds out whether the candidate has the skills and knowledge required for the job. (Nontechnical interviewing is discussed later.)

Some interviewers should be assigned to interview the candidates for their technical skills. This task can prove to be a challenge in a field as broad as system administration. However, the job description should provide a basis for an approach to the technical interviewing. It should identify whether the person needs specific technical skills and experience or more general problem-solving skills, for example. Technical interviewing for an architect position should identify design skills rather than intimate knowledge of the latest hardware from a particular vendor.

The interviewers must pitch the interview questions at the right level. Architects should be presented with an architectural problem and asked to discuss the problems they see and how they would go about solving them. For senior SAs, the interviewer should pick an area of technical expertise that they both have in common and dig deep. Check for problem-solving skills and the ability to explain what the candidate is doing, in addition to being able to do the tasks. Intermediate SAs should have a reasonable breadth of experience, problem-solving skills, and the ability to explain what they are doing. Junior SAs should demonstrate that they have tried to understand what they were doing and how things worked beyond what their specific job required. Look for junior SAs who pay attention to detail and are methodical. When interviewing SAs with no previous experience, look for someone who has an interest in computers and in how things in general work. Have they written computer games or taken their home PCs apart?

When looking for problem-solving skills, it can be informative to see whether the candidate understands how things other than computers work.

Ask the person to explain how a couple of everyday items work, such as an internal combustion engine or a flush toilet. Find out what else the candidate fixes. Does she fix broken electrical appliances or blocked sinks or furniture? Does she know how to change the oil in her car or do any small jobs on it? Some people feel that the ability to read sheet music demonstrates logical, methodical thinking and good problem-solving skills. Come up with imaginative ways to figure out how the candidate thinks. Ask the person why manhole covers are round, and watch the person's deduction and logic as they figure it out. Ask the candidate to estimate the number of fax machines in Manhattan and see the logic they use to produce engineering estimates.

It is always good to look at candidates' past experiences and get their thoughts on them. For example, asking what accomplishment they are most proud of and why can give you a good idea of what they are capable of and what they see as difficult challenges to overcome. Ask them about situations they have been in that they wish they had handled differently and what they would have done differently in hindsight and why. You want to know that they can learn from their mistakes. Ask the candidates to describe a big mess that they have had to clean up, how it came into existence, how they fixed it, and what constraints they had to work under to fix it. The candidates will enjoy telling their stories, and this should provide insight into how they think and work. Ask them to tell you about a big project they have had to work on alone or in a team. If you are interested in a particular skill, ask the candidates about a problem that needed solving in that area. Ask them about a tricky problem you have encountered in that area, and see how they would have approached it. Most of all, get them talking about real-life experiences. It's easier and more interesting for them and gives you a better idea of what they are capable of than dry, "how does this work" questions.

Don't ask "trivia" questions—questions with a single, highly specific, correct answer. People can forget that kind of thing when under stress. If their job requires them to know which pin on a V.35 interface is used to transmit data, they can look it up when they have the job. General questions help you understand more about candidates than trivia. Trivia questions are also called "gotcha" questions because there is a temptation to say "Gotcha!" when the candidate doesn't know the answer.

We also dislike brain-teaser questions. We cringe when we see companies ask candidates to connect nine dots laid out 3 × 3 using four straight lines, without lifting your pencil from the paper. (www.everythingsysadmin. com/p/e). These questions have nothing to do with whether a person can do a particular job. In fact, we assert that they test only whether the candidate has heard the question before.

The secret to good interviewing is the follow-up question. The questions that you ask are minimally important compared to the follow-up question you ask in response to the candidate's answer. Here's an example:

INTERVIEWER: Do you know C++?
CANDIDATE: Yes.
I: Do you know how to set up MS-Exchange?
C: Yes.
I: Do you know Apache?
C: Yes.
I: Do you know PHP?
C: Yes.
I: Do you know SonicWall firewalls?
C: Yes.

Wow! What a great candidate. She knows everything from programming in C++ to setting up web servers, email servers, and even firewalls! However, we haven't asked any follow-up questions. Let's see how follow-up questions make the interview process gather more accurate information.

INTERVIEWER: Do you know C++?
CANDIDATE: Yes.
I: What was the longest C++ program you've written?
C: A 200-line program that reformatted CSV files into a template.
I: What made C++ the best language to use? Why didn't you use a language like Perl?
C: It was a homework assignment in a C++ class. I didn't have a choice.
I: What about C++ program you've written outside of school?
C: I really haven't written much C++.
I: Why might you choose C++ over other languages?
C: I don't know. C++ is difficult; I'd rather use something easier.
I: Do you have experience with Apache?
C: Yes.
I: Have you maintained an Apache system or set one up from scratch?

C: From scratch. I downloaded the package and installed it on a Linux system. I then maintained the site for the company. The design was done by a consulting firm, but I had to fix problems with its HTML and change the configuration to work with its CGI scripts.

I: When I run Apache, I see a lot of subprocesses. What do they do?

C: I've never really looked into that.

I: Can you take a guess?

C: Maybe they each take care of a different request?

I: Why would that be a good thing?

C: To split the load.

I: Well, the machine has only one CPU. Why would multiple processes help?

C: I don't know.

I: Let's move to another topic. Do you have experience with SonicWall Firewalls?

C: Yes.

I: In general, how does a firewall work?

C: (The candidate gives a very technical explanation of how firewalls work.)

I: In what situations might the state table fill?

C: (The candidate discusses long-lived sessions, timeouts, and ways to tune the timeouts for sessions. She also explains FIN packet process and other details.)

Because we used follow-up questions, we have a much clearer sense of the person's real skills. We see that the person has rudimentary C++ skills that haven't been exercised since college. At least the person understands some programming concepts. The candidates knowledge of Apache web servers is somewhat superficial but sufficient to run a basic web server. She doesn't know the internal workings of Apache, which would be important for massive scaling projects or debugging oddball problems, but the experience with changing the configuration to permit CGI scripts—if not done through a menu—shows real understanding. Finally, the firewall questions show that she has a deep knowledge of the subject, not only understanding how they work but also demonstrating experience with a common scaling issue.

In reality, nobody conducts a interview as bad as the first example. We exaggerated the lack of follow-up questions but not too much, compared to some interview processes we've seen. On the other hand, the second example reveals another deficiency in the interviewer's technique: Obviously, the interviewer was not well prepared. Studying the candidate's resume beforehand would have indicated that she is a network or security engineer, and the questions should have been directed to those areas. Questions about C++ and Apache might have been fine questions for later in the interview to see the breadth of her knowledge. However, asking the questions in that order must have made the candidate concerned that she was being interviewed for the wrong job.

Determine the limits of a candidate's knowledge by asking deeper and deeper questions until the person finally says, "I don't know." The downside of this technique is that candidates may feel that for every topic you touched on, they were unable to answer the last question asked; meanwhile you were pleasantly surprised that their "limit" was just fine.

Seeking out the limit of the candidates' knowledge in the areas they feel they are strongest is an excellent way to understand their primary knowledge. Then ask questions in related topic, areas to see how broad their knowledge is. To identify the starting topic, ask them where they feel they are strongest in a list of choices, such as network protocols (how they work), network equipment, operating system internals, and scripting. The topics should be based on the experience listed in their resume. Ask them to pick their single strongest area.

Do not ask them to rate their skills on a scale of 1 to 10 for each topic. A study by Kruger and Dunning (1999) suggests that unskilled people are unaware of their lack of skills and will overestimate them, whereas more skilled people are more aware of their limits.

> ❖ **Asking Candidates to Rate Their Own Skills**   Asking candidates to rate their own skills can help indicate their level of self-confidence, but little else. You don't know their basis for comparison. Some people are brought up being taught to always downplay their skills. A hiring manager once nearly lost a candidate who said that she didn't know much about Macintoshes. It turned out that she used one 8 hours a day and was supporting four applications for her department, but she didn't know how to program one. Ask people to describe their experience instead.

35.1.9 Nontechnical Interviewing

For nontechnical interviewing, it can be particularly useful to take a course on interview techniques. There are several approaches to interviewing. One that works well in our experience is behavioral interviewing, which looks at past behavior to predict future actions. This technique can also be used for technical interviewing. Questions are phrased something like: "Think of a time when . . . . Describe the situation to me, and tell me what you did." Do it in such a way that it is clear that you won't fault the candidate for this situation having arisen and that you simply want to know how he handled it. For example, you might say to an SA candidate "We have all experienced times when things have become really busy and something has fallen through the cracks or has been delayed. Think of a time when this happened to you. Describe the situation to me, and tell me how you handled it. What did you learn from the experience?" Ask about both good and bad things. For example, ask about the best project that the candidate worked on, and why he felt it was the best, and then ask about the worst one. Ask about the person's best and worst manager to find out what he likes and dislikes in a manager and what his working style is. This technique works better than an approach that asks the candidate how she *would* deal with a particular situation, because it is often easier for people to see how they should behave when asked in such an academic fashion. However, when these situations arise, there are other pressures and other factors that result in different behavior. Behavioral interviewing looks at how the candidate behaved in real-life situations.

The nontechnical interviews are used to evaluate the candidate's soft skills: how the person works in a team environment, relates to customers, organizes his time, whether he needs lots of direction or just a little, whether he likes a narrow job description or the opportunity to work in lots of areas, and so on. Typically, these questions have no right or wrong answers. The interviewing team needs to hear the answers to decide whether the person fits into the team, fits the particular position, or perhaps is more suited to another position.

For example, a company might interview a candidate who is very bright but is someone who completes 80 percent of the task and then loses interest because all the difficult problems have been solved. If this person can be teamed up with someone else who enjoys taking tasks to completion and will enjoy learning from the other person, he would be a good hire. However, if there is no one to pair with this person, he probably is not a good choice.

Try to find out what the candidate's work habits are. If he stays in touch with technology by reading mailing lists and newsgroups and by surfing the web, does he do so to the detriment of his other work, or does he find the right balance? The interviewer should get a good idea of the candidate's approach by chatting about how he keeps up with technology and what mailing lists he reads. Some people waste phenomenal amounts of time keeping up with the latest technology and lots of mailing lists. Such candidates can be fun and interesting to talk to but frustrating to work with if they don't get much real work done.

Gauge the candidate's interest in computers. If computers are the focus of his life and are his only pastime, he will burn out at some point. He may work long hours because he enjoys the work so much, but that is not healthy or a recipe for long-term success. He may also spend a large part of his time in the office playing with fun technology that has nothing to do with his work. Because he works such long hours and spends all his time with computers, it will be difficult for him to figure out how much real work he is doing and how much he is simply playing around. On the other hand, some candidates may be surprisingly computer-averse. They may not want to touch or see a computer outside of working hours. These people generally lead a sustainable lifestyle and will not burn out—they may have already had that experience—but they are less likely to be happy working lots of long hours. However, they are also more likely to be productive all the hours that they do work. They are also less likely to be the first to hear about a new technology or to try it and suggest introducing it. Although the ideal candidate should have a balance between these two extremes, some jobs are suited to people at either end of the scale. Again, the interviewers need to know what they are looking for in the candidate.

35.1.10 Selling the Position

Beyond finding out which candidates the team wants to work with, the interview is also the time to persuade candidates that they want to work for the company. The first step on that path is to respect the candidates and make sure that the interview process does not waste their time or leave them feeling humiliated. The people whom the candidates meet during the interview process should represent the best of the team. They should be people with whom the candidates will want to work.

The position itself is also important. Find out what the candidate is looking for and figure out whether you can offer that in this position. Does the candidate want to work in a specific area of system administration or with many different aspects? Let the candidate know whether the position can be made into what she wants it to be. Each interviewer should think about all the positive things about the company and the group and share those with the candidates.

Internet commerce sites, ISPs, and SA consulting companies can make the most of the fact that the SA function is part of the core business of the company, and so it is, or should be, well funded and viewed as a profit center rather than a cost center. We have always found it more enjoyable to work for companies that look to SAs as valuable resources that must be invested in rather than as overhead that must be reduced.

35.1.11 Employee Retention

Once you have hired a good employee, you want the person to stick around for the long term. What motivates SAs to remain at a company is different for different people, but some areas cover most people.

Demand for SAs follows the ups and downs of high-tech, as do SA salaries. Although salary is important—because, after all, no one wants to feel exploited—offering the highest salaries does not necessarily retain employees. Salaries should be competitive, but it is more important for the SAs to be happy in their work.

One of the secrets to retaining SAs is to keep their jobs interesting. If there are tedious, repetitive tasks, get someone to automate those tasks. The person who is creating the automation will enjoy it, the SAs who no longer have to do the repetitive task will appreciate it, and efficiency will be improved.

As with most people, SAs like recognition for working hard and doing a good job. Performance bonuses are one way to recognize employees, but simply thanking them in group meetings for the work they are doing can work just as well.

Appreciation and Enjoyment Are Key

A consulting company that had many excellent SAs was going through a turbulent period and losing a lot of staff. One SA who left commented that the senior management of the company had no idea what motivated people. Most of those who left were well paid, and all were offered a pay increase to stay. But as this departing employee put it: "People work for money; people work hard for appreciation; but people work the hardest when they love what they do. People are recognized as "the best" when they love what they do, where they do it, and who they do it for."

Good SAs enjoy working with other good SAs. SAs like to see important infrastructure projects funded and like to be a part of building good infrastructure. They like to see long-term planning rewarded. SAs like to feel that they are a part of the company rather than an unimportant, often ignored appendage. They like to have a good relationship with the people with whom they work closely, who generally are their customers. Although most SAs thrive on being busy, most do not enjoy being overloaded to the point that they are unable to meet customer expectations. SAs are often not the most communicative employees, but they like to be kept informed and expect their managers to notice when they are overloaded or when they pull off great feats. SAs also want to have the opportunity to advance their careers; they will move on if they know that they will stagnate where they are.

SAs also like "fun stuff." Fast connections to home, high-end laptops, and the opportunity to work with new technologies help to keep the appeal of the work environment high. Finding opportunities for SAs to work from home can also help retain them.

The final element in keeping most SAs happy is their direct manager. Some people like a friendly relationship with their manager; others prefer clear lines of management and the knowledge that their manager has faith in them and will support them in what they do. Chapters 33 and 34 examine the roles of technical and nontechnical managers in detail. People take jobs because of money, but people leave jobs because of bad managers. As discussed in Section 32.2.2.4, it isn't what you do, but whom you do it for.

35.2 The Icing

Once a company has mastered the basics of hiring SAs, the final thing to consider is how to make the company stand out as one where SAs will want to work. This section looks at some ways to get noticed.

35.2.1 Get Noticed

Employing some nontraditional incentives can help to get the company noticed and enhance its reputation as a fun place to work. For example, one company gave all interview candidates a Palm Pilot PDA—the current hot new product—at the interview. Another company had informal group outings to a nearby roller-coaster park, and the company bought season tickets for those who were interested. Another company had the latest video games and game controllers in rooms in a few buildings around the campus. Senior

SAs and some managers in another company developed a tradition of playing multiplayer computer games one night a week. Others arranged sports or games leagues within the company or against other companies. Although most of these activities are not of universal interest, they are interesting to enough people that they distinguish the company as being a fun place to work, which can even help attract employees who are not interested in the activity that is offered.

Other, work-oriented schemes can help to distinguish the company in a positive way. Several local SA organizations, for example, have regular meetings that need to be hosted somewhere. Hosting the local SAGE group or regular talks on a topic of interest to SAs one evening a month makes the company more attractive to SAs. Encouraging SAs to write and present papers and tutorials at conferences also demonstrates that the company is a good place for SAs to work and gets the company's name known in the SA field.

Ultimately, the aim is to get the company noticed and considered to be a fun place to work and a place that values its SAs. Be creative!

35.3 Conclusion

The secret to hiring is good planning and follow-through. Hiring SAs starts with a good job description. The job description helps to define the skill level required and the soft skills needed, and it helps to direct the interviewers' questioning toward relevant topics. It is also used for recruiting appropriate candidates. The best way to recruit good candidates is through personal recommendations from customers and staff. Other ways that are oriented toward technologically minded people are also good.

The skill level of the person hired has financial implications, and companies should be aware of the hidden costs of hiring underqualified staff with lower salary requirements. The interview process should give the candidate the opportunity to meet the key people with whom she will be working, if hired. The interviewers should represent the company at its best. They should respect the candidate and make sure that the interview experience is pleasant. The technical and soft skills required for the job should be divided among the interviewers, and they should all know how to interview for their assigned skills.

The secret to good interview questions is the follow-up. Questions should give the candidate a chance to shine by easing her into the questioning and letting her build confidence. This chapter looked at ways to assess problem-solving skills and design skills. Soft skills are just as important as technical skills. Interviewing courses can be very helpful for suggesting ways to accurately assess these skills in the candidates.

Once identified, the right candidate must be persuaded to take the job. This process starts with the first contact the candidate has with the company. The candidate must have felt respected and treated well throughout the interview process. Trying to recruit someone who has been offended in the interview process is hopeless. The compensation package is a part of wooing the candidate, but so are the positive aspects of working for the group, such as a cool staff or being well funded. Having a reputation as a fun place to work or a place that values SAs can help enormously in hiring the right employees.

After people have been hired, they should be retained. Interviewing is a costly process.

Exercises

1. Write a detailed job description for an open position in your group or for a position for which you would like to be able to hire someone.

2. Does your company hire people above, below, or at the skill level required for a position? Illustrate your answer with some examples.

3. Who in your group is good at interviewing, and who is not good at it? Why?

4. What roles do you think are missing from your team?

5. How diverse is your team? What could you do to recruit members whose ethnic and cultural backgrounds differ from those of the people currently employed?

6. Who would be able to act as a mentor for a junior SA, if your group were to hire one?

7. Are there junior SAs in your group who are not mentored? If so, what good and bad experiences has the junior SA had as a result of the lack of mentoring?

8. How have you made the interview process pleasant for a candidate in the past?

9. How have you made the interview process unpleasant for a candidate in the past? Why did that happen? What can be done to prevent that from happening again?

10. Write a job description for someone who would have the skills you feel are lacking in your team.

11. What technical questions would you ask of a candidate for the position for which you wrote a job description?

12. What nontechnical questions would you ask of a candidate for that position?

13. What are the best things about working in your current company?

14. What are the worst things about working in your current company?

15. What motivates you to stay at your current company?

16. If you needed to start looking for a job tomorrow, where would you want to work, and why?

17. How well does your company do at retaining employees? What do you think the reason for this is?

18. What do you think your company does or could do to stand out as a good place to work?

Chapter 36

Firing System Administrators

This chapter is about how to remove fellow SAs from your site because they've been terminated. Our wish is that you never need to use the information in this chapter. But the reality is that everyone will need to use this information someday. You may not be a manager saddled with the responsibility of deciding to terminate someone, but you may be the SA who must deal with the consequences.

This chapter is not about why someone should be fired. We can't help you there. It is instead about the technical tasks that must be performed when it happens. In fact, you might say that this chapter begins after the management decision has been made to fire someone and you must remove the person's access from the network.

Removing SAs' access against their will is a unique situation. SAs have privileged access to the systems and are likely to have access to all systems. Some SAs may know the system better than you do because they built it. On the other hand, the techniques in this chapter can also be used when dealing with an SA who is leaving a company on good terms. Whether people are leaving on good or bad terms, the potential for the situation to turn ugly makes them a liability to the company's computer infrastructure.

Large companies usually have procedures for removing access when someone leaves. Small- and midsize companies may have ad hoc procedures. We hope that this chapter can serve as a starting point if you need to establish a termination procedure.

The process described is not theoretical. It is based on the best current practices of the companies we have interviewed.

36.1 The Basics

From an SA perspective, the basic process of firing someone boils down to three issues:[1]

1. Procedure
   a. Follow your corporate HR policy: the most important rule.
   b. Use a checklist so nothing is forgotten.
2. Access
   a. Remove physical access: "Can he get into the building?"
   b. Remove remote access: "Can he remotely access our network?"
   c. Remove service access: "Have access rights to applications been withdrawn?"
3. Continuous improvement
   a. Have fewer access databases: The fewer points of control, the easier it is to lock someone out.

In this section, we discuss each of the areas in detail and follow up with anecdotes that show how they have been addressed in some real-life situations.

36.1.1 Follow Your Corporate HR Policy

The single most important rule is that you must follow the policies of your company with regard to firing people. These policies are written by people who understand the complex legal rules governing employee termination. Those people are the experts, not you. They have guidelines about what to say, what not to say, how to do it, how not to do it. Usually, this is such a rare and delicate event that someone from HR holds your hand throughout it.

HR might recommend any number of techniques, from calling the employee at home and telling the person not to come in to work again to something as confrontational as two security guards and someone from HR meeting the employee at his cubicle and informing him that his personal effects will be shipped to him, as the security guards escort him out of the building.

36.1.2 Have a Termination Checklist

Maintain a checklist of tasks to be performed when an employee is terminated. The first part should be constructed with help from HR. The second part

---

1. This model is an extension of the one described in Ringel and Limoncelli (1999).

should be the technical details of how to disable access. This list should be easy to update; any time a new service is added, it should be easy to add the associated termination procedure to this list. This list should be analogous to the checklist used when creating accounts but is likely to contain many more items for services that are not enabled at time of hire.

The benefit of using a checklist is that it eliminates the thinking required when someone is terminated. If you have to think about what is to be done, you may forget something. A checklist assembles all the knowledge in one place. Terminating someone is often an emotional moment, so you might not be thinking very well at the time. A checklist also provides a level of accountability. If you print the checklist and mark each item as complete, it creates a permanent record. In some environments, the completed checklist is handed to the IT director, who signs off on the completed termination.

36.1.3 Remove Physical Access

Physical access means, quite simply, "Make sure the person can't get in the building." Usually, this is the function of HR or corporate security. For example, HR should already have a procedure for retrieving the employee's ID badge, which is checked by guards at the building entrance. If card-key access is used, the card-key system must be programmed to deny access to that card-key regardless of whether it has been returned. Keys to any rooms must be retrieved or locks changed. Combination locks, safe combinations, and so on must be changed. Is there a barn, maintenance shed, shack, outhouse, dog house, or annex that has network connectivity? Check them too. Because physical instruments, such as doors and keys, have been around longer than computers, most companies usually have good procedures related to them already. Follow them. Very small companies might not have any kind of identification badge or similar system in place. In that case, have the receptionist and other employees been told what to do if they see this person in or near the building?

You must also schedule time for the SA to return any equipment that he may have at home. Any computers that are returned are suspect. The disks should be erased to prevent virus transmission.

36.1.4 Remove Remote Access

Remote access refers to the many ways someone might get into the networks. These include, but are not limited to, modem pools, ISDN lines, xDSL, inbound connections through a firewall, and VPN service. Access to all these systems must be disabled. This can be difficult if each is run by a different team or has a different access control system.

36.1.5 Remove Service Access

Service access refers to the applications and services that are inside the network. Each of these services usually has a password. Examples include POP3/IMAP4 (Crispin 1996, Myers and Rose 1996), servers, database servers, UNIX servers (each with its own /etc/passwd file to be checked or a global NIS or Kerberos database to be checked), NT Domain logins, SMB servers (NT File Server), Active Directory, LDAP, and so on.

The issues introduced so far relate to actions that are taken when someone is actively being removed. Logistically speaking, each issue can be assigned to a separate subteam: Managers can take care of the HR processes, corporate security ensures that physical access is removed, the remote access administrators have their tasks, and the SAs can focus on removing service access.

The process described so far is tolerant to some mistakes. Access is divided into three tiers: physical, remote, and service. Mistakes can be made at any one tier and access is still prevented. If, for example, a login on a particular service hasn't been disabled but the person can't enter the building physically or get in via remote access, he can't get to the account to cause any damage. If remote access is accidentally left enabled, damage is limited by all services being disabled.

The following anecdotes are true. The names have been changed to protect people's identities.

Firing the Boss

A large manufacturing company had to suspend, pending investigation, the manager of a team of SAs. This person had administrative access to all the systems in his domain and had access to the network via every remote access method that the system administration group provided.

Without the accused manager knowing, a meeting was called by the accused manager's director with the lead SA and corporate security. The corporate security officer explained the situation and the action plan. The lead SA was to change all the privileged-account passwords that evening; in the morning, the director would meet with the system administration group, without their manager, to inform them of the situation. They would be told to suspend all access to the systems. If something could not be suspended, access would be deleted. The system administration group was split into subteams based on remote and service access.

The lead SA spent the evening changing the `root` password on every system. In the morning, all the SAs were brought into a closed meeting and the situation explained to them. Corporate security took care of the physical access aspects. The system administration team was assigned the remote and service access issues. They brainstormed on each issue separately, which helped them maintain focus. All changes were logged, and logs were turned over to the lead SA.

There was one problem where, to make a long story short, if he had a photographic memory, he could have leveraged a form of remote access to gain access to the network. It was going to take a couple days to rectify this problem, and nothing could make that happen any sooner. Even so, the risk of that happening was considered to be low, and the system administration team was confident that physical and service access had been completely removed and logs could be monitored for intrusions. In other words, they were confident that doing a complete job on two of the tiers would compensate for being incomplete on the third tier.

During the investigation, the accused manager resigned. The logs of what access had been removed were useful as a checklist of what access had been suspended and now needed to be deleted.

The process worked very effectively. There was increased efficiency from splitting into teams. The potential problem with remote access was compensated by effectively removing all other access.

Removal at an Academic Institution

Academic entities tend to be very astute about termination procedures, as they often have batches of terminated accounts at the end of every academic year. The university setting is a good example of how "practice makes perfect." However, this anecdote involves someone with privileged access to many machines.

At a large state university, a long-time operator with `root` access to all UNIX systems was to be terminated. She had been employed for so long that there was a concern that eliminating all access might be impossible. Such a situation had never been encountered previously.

Because all access could not be disabled instantly, there were concerns that the operator would be able to get back into the system. Not that retribution was expected, but the university couldn't take that risk. Because this was a public university, physical access to the building could not be eliminated, but card-key changes prevented the operator from gaining direct physical access to sensitive machines. Remote access could not be disabled, because the large university did not use a firewall.

After some discussion, it was decided to use the following procedure: A small team was assembled to list all the access she had and how to disable each, including card-key and host access. When the designated time arrived, she was told that her boss needed to speak with her in his office. The two offices were in opposite parts of the building, and the trip would take at least 10 minutes. During that time, all the senior SAs would work to disable her access. By the time she reached her boss's office, all her accounts would be disabled.

Because the operator had such pervasive access, the only way to ensure complete coverage was to take such extreme caution.

Amicably Leaving a Company

An SA at a small software development company announced he was leaving and offered one month's notice to help the company transition. The SA was actually involved in interviewing a replacement. All responsibilities had been transitioned by the termination date. On his last day, the SA walked into his boss's office and became `root` in a window on his workstation. While the boss watched, he disabled his own regular login. He then issued the commands to change the password of various routers and let his boss enter the new password. He then repeated this for a few other system accounts. Finally, he issued the command to activate the "change `root` password on all systems" procedure and let his boss enter the new password. The boss was shocked that the soon-to-be ex-employee was doing such a complete job of transitioning duties and deleting himself from the system. Finally, the SA put his card-key and physical keys on the boss's desk and left the building. About 2 weeks later, the ex-employee remembered that he had forgotten to change the password on a particular nonprivileged system account on a machine that had a modem directly attached to it. The ex-employee reports that he confirmed with former coworkers that the ex-employer didn't disable the account until he notified them of the error.

With one exception, the termination was complete. However, the exception crossed the remote and service tiers because the account (service access) was on a host that was directly connected to the outside world (remote access). Also, it was unsafe for the new passwords to be set in front of the exiting employee, who could have been watching the keyboard. The employee also could have recorded the new passwords as they were being set. The garden-variety `script` command on UNIX does not record nonechoed input, such as passwords, but there are plenty of keyboard-capturing utilities that do, on all OSs.

The company took a risk by not disabling access as soon as notice was given. However, it was a reasonable risk to take considering that it was not an adverse termination.

36.1.6 Have Fewer Access Databases

In terms of what SA tasks must be completed, disabling access is all about updating access databases that specify who may do what: password files, RADIUS lists, network ACL settings, and Active Directory are all access databases. There is less work to do if there are fewer of these databases. Therefore, system architects should always attempt to design systems with as few such databases as possible.

Part of the process involves brainstorming to try to remember all the ways in which access must be disabled. This process can be aided by having a good inventory and mechanisms to control the global environment based on updates to the database, as described in Section 8.2.2.

36.2 The Icing

Now that we have covered the basics, certain operational policies can make the process smoother and reduce risk.

36.2.1 Have a Single Authentication Database

Although having fewer access databases is a benefit, having all services authenticated off one database brings about a new paradigm. This is easy to do if all services are controlled by handheld authenticators (HHA) that access the same database.

In the first case study (Section 36.1.5), access to many services—VPNs, in-bound `telnet` through the firewall, `root` access, and so on—were controlled by a single HHA system. Disabling the manager's record in the HHA database resulted in immediately disabling many services at the same time.

This does not relieve SAs from deleting the person from the individual services' configuration files. An HHA system provides authentication information, not authority. That is, the HHA tells the service who is knocking at the door, not whether the person should be let in. That decision is left to the local service. For example, an HHA-based replacement for the UNIX `/bin/su` command would query the HHA server to find out who entered the command, but the software normally has a local configuration file that indicates who may become `root`. With the HHA disabled, nobody will ever authenticate to that user, but this does not make a username listed in that configuration file a moot point. Processes are not killed; `cron, at`, and other automated systems may continue to run. Eventually, all references to the person must be removed or deleted.

Having all those local configuration files and access databases centralized into a single database is the next advancement that we are looking forward to. LDAP, Kerberos, NDS, and other technologies bring us closer to that goal.

36.2.2 System File Changes

If someone suspects that he may be fired, he may create a **back door**—a secret way to get into the system—or plant a **logic bomb,** or software that causes damage once he has gone. Ideally, you can take a snapshot of all software before the person becomes suspicious and compare it to the running system on a regular basis. However, that is time consuming, requires a lot of storage, and would easily tip off the person that something is about to happen.

However, no suspicions can be raised if such a thing is always done. Programs that checksum system files and report changes are commonly found. The earliest to achieve popularity is named Tripwire. If this process is an automated system that is used regularly to notice external intruders, system failures, or other problems, it will be much easier to use it without raising suspicion. However, care must be taken to make sure that that person being fired doesn't update the database so that his changes aren't noticed.

Such a system is an excellent measure to detect any kind of intrusions. However, it is time consuming to process all the false-positives. The issue becomes scaling it to too many machines.

36.3 Conclusion

Firing SAs isn't fun or easy, but sometimes it has to happen. The basics are very simple. The most important rule is to follow the policies of your HR department. HR personnel are the experts, and you are supporting their process. Three tiers of access must be removed: physical access, remote access, and service access. The primary benefit of the three-tier model is that it provides a structured, rather than ad hoc, approach and is tolerant of mistakes made at any one level. Architectures that seek to minimize the number of access databases and a well-maintained inventory ease the process considerably.

In creating a checklist for all the manners of access to be disabled, one might begin with the new-hire procedure as a starting point: Whatever is done for a new hire must be undone for a termination. Although no checklist is complete, we have assembled several checklists of things to disable in the event of termination:

- *Physical access.* Change combination locks, all applicable safe combinations, and locks on doors with keys, even if they are returned. Remove access for all buildings: for example, remote locations, shacks, and utility buildings.

- *Property surrender.* Have the ex-employee turn in keys, card-keys, badges, HHAs, PDAs, and any company-owned equipment at home.

- *Remote access.* Modem pools, ISDN pool, VPN servers, in-bound network access—that is, `ssh`, `telnet`, `rlogin`—cable modem access, xDSL X.25 access.

- *Service access.* Remove access from database servers, NIS domains, NT domains, superuser access IDs, Netnews IDs, password files, and RADIUS servers.

The icing is a set of design and operational factors that better prepare a site for these unlikely but important tasks. The fewer the administrative databases, the easier the task will be, but if they are all tied to a single authentication database, the entire process becomes much simpler. Regularly maintained file checksum histories provide a way to detect and prevent back doors and logic bombs.

Dividing the process into HR policy and physical, remote, and service access brings clarity to the process. The process can be explained easily. The staff can be divided into a physical team, a remote team, and a service team. Each team can then work with complete focus because it has only one task.

This process works best when one can leverage the infrastructure that should be in any system. A solid security infrastructure keeps the wrong people out. Having a single (or few) administrative databases, such as a well-implemented HHA architecture, makes disabling all access from a central place a snap. Properly documented environments and well-maintained inventory improve one's ability to disable all access quickly. Routine Tripwire runs and system-monitoring processes are some of the automation that may already be in place at a site. The better the infrastructure is, the easier this process becomes.

The process described in this chapter handles the extreme case of terminating an SA but is also a useful model to consider when anyone leaves a company, simply leaves your domain of support, or changes jobs within a company and should no longer have privileged access to the systems she previously administered. We don't cover those topics directly. We felt that it would be more interesting to cover one extreme case and leave the others as an exercise to the reader.

Our discussion of this topic has been restricted to the technical side of the process. The nontechnical side, the human side, is equally important. You are changing this person's life in a very profound way. The person has bills to pay, a family to support, and a life to live. Corporate policies range from "get them out the door immediately" to "we're laying you off in six months." There are potential problems with both, but from our point of view, the latter not only works best but also shows trust and respect. This issue is not so much for the benefit of the person being laid off as for the benefit of those remaining.

Exercises

1. When someone is fired, does HR know whom to contact in the IT organization to have the person's access disabled?

2. In your current environment, what must be disabled if you were to be fired? Outside of checking individual hosts for local accounts, how many individual administrative systems did you have to touch?

3. What improvements to your system could make it easier to disable your access when you are fired?

4. A system like Tripwire causes periodic points of filesystem I/O. How does that affect the planning and deployment of such a system? How is this different for a file server, an e-commerce server, and a database server?

Epilogue

We began this book asking for a concise definition of system administration. Now we're no closer to an answer. If anything, we've broadened the definition. Rather than building a crisper definition of system administration, we've discussed customer support, repair, operations, architecture definition, deployment, disaster planning, and even management skills. System administration is an extremely broad field, and no simple definition can cover it all.

We hope that you've learned a lot from reading this book. We've certainly learned a lot by writing it. Having to put into words things that had become second nature has forced us to think hard about everything we do, every habit we've developed. The peer-review process stands us naked in front of our mentors and comrades to receive criticism of our fundamental beliefs. We're better for writing this book, and we hope you are better for reading it. We hope that some day, you write a book and enjoy the same exhilaration.

The most exciting part of this book has been to record, in such a permanent form, the rants and anecdotes that we have accumulated over our careers. We respond to certain technical and nontechnical issues by getting on our soapboxes to expound our opinions. These monologues are refined every time we repeat them, until we find ourselves repeating them word for word, over and over again. We can honestly say that this book includes every tub-thumping rant we authors blurt out with Pavlovian predictability. With a little bit of luck, these rants will stand the test of time. This book also captures every useful anecdote in our library of experience. Each anecdote teaches an important lesson or two. We can rest assured that these anecdotes will not be lost, and we can safely look forward to all the new anecdotes we will accrue in the future.

System administration is a culture. Every culture has its anecdotes, myths, and stories. It is how we pass our history to new generations and propagate the lessons and values that are important to us. We learn best from hearing our culture's stories and anecdotes. We enrich the culture every time we share a new one.

We'd like to share with you one final anecdote.

A Concise Definition

A facility had several researchers from a variety of universities visiting for the summer. That autumn, after they left, the SAs had to decommission their computers and clean the large room they had been sharing. The SAs found a scrap of paper that had been taped near the phone. It simply said, "Makes things work," followed by the phone number of the SAs.

It was absolutely the highest compliment they had ever received.

Appendixes

The Many Roles of a System Administrator

This appendix is heavy on philosophy. If that turns you off, you can skip it, but we think that it will help you think about your place in the universe or at least your role within your company, organization, or SA team. Examining your own role within an organization helps you focus, which helps you do a better job. It can give you a long-term perspective on your career, which can help you make the big career decisions necessary for having a happy and successful life.

This can also give your organization a framework for thinking about what roles they want you to play. Each of these roles in some way affects your organization. This is by no means a complete list; however, it is a very good starting point. You should use this list to consider what roles are missing in your organization and perhaps to start on a quest to fill them.

It is interesting to think about which and how many of these roles you are asked to play as your career moves forward. The list can help you plan your career. Some entry-level SAs are asked to play single roles and grow into more roles as they gain experience. Sometimes, SAs start out flooded with many roles and specialize as time goes on.

A small site may require its single SA to take on many roles. As the organization grows, certain roles can be transferred to newly hired SAs. Sometimes, you discover that you don't enjoy a particular role and look to avoid it when you change jobs. Thinking about these roles may also help guide your career with respect to what kinds of companies you decide to work for: Small companies tend to require people to fill multiple roles, larger companies tend to require people to specialize, and megacorporations have people so specialized that it can seem bizarre to outsiders. Technology companies respect and reward those who play the role of pushing for new technology, whereas other companies often discourage too much change.

A.1 Common Positive Roles

Some roles within a company are more critical than others; some are good and some are bad. Here we list many common roles, the value they provide to the company, how those people derive satisfaction from the job, and what customers tend to expect from them.

A.1.1 The Installer

Some people view an SA as the person who installs "stuff." This is the role that customers see most often, and so is most often associated with the career of system administration. The customer rarely sees the other, possibly more critical, positions, such as the people who design the infrastructure.

The value to the company of Installers is their ability to follow through and see that the job gets done. They are often the final and most critical link in the deployment chain.

When installation is being done on a large scale, the item that is being installed is usually preconfigured at some central location. Installers are trained on the specific situations they are expected to see and have a second-tier resource to call on if they come across an unexpected situation. In that case, the kind of person who makes a good Installer is one who enjoys meeting and helping the customers and gets satisfaction from doing the same task well many times over. On the other hand, in smaller deployments, the Installer is often expected to be a higher-skilled person because more unexpected situations will be encountered.

When you are the Installer, it is important to be friendly and polite. The Installer is the public face of the organization; people will assume that the entire organization acts the same way that you do.

A.1.2 The Repair Person

Things break. Some people view an SA as a Repair Person. Just as people call a dishwasher repair person when their dishwasher breaks, they call a computer Repair Person when their computer breaks. SAs also repair bigger and sometimes more nebulous things, such as "the Internet" and "the database." Whether the real problem is simply a broken cable or a much larger problem is of little interest to the customer.

The value to the company of Repair People is their ability to bring the company back to life when technological problems stall a business. Repair People receive satisfaction from knowing they've helped one person or the entire company. They enjoy the challenge of a good puzzle or mystery.

When you are the Repair Person, customers want to know that you are concerned about their problems. They want to feel as though their problems are the most important problems in the world.

A.1.3 The Maintainer

The Maintainer is the person who keeps previously built systems going. Maintainers are very good at following the instructions presented to them, either in a written manual or through training. They do not seek to improve the system; they are willing to maintain it as it is.

The value to the company of Maintainers is bringing stability to the environment. These people are not going to break things trying to improve them or replace them; nor do they spend all day reading magazines about new things to install. Once companies spend money to install something, they need it to be stable long enough to pay for itself before it is replaced with something newer.

Maintainers receive satisfaction from knowing that their work is part of the big picture that keeps the organization working. They tend to be glad that they aren't the people who have to figure out how to design and install the next generation of systems and may even have disdain for those who wish to replace their stable system with something new.

When you are the Maintainer, customers want two opposing things: They want to know that you are maintaining the stability of their world, and they want you to be flexible when they seek customizations.

A.1.4 The Problem Preventer

A role that is invisible to most customers is the Problem Preventer, who looks for problems and fixes them before they become visible. Problem preventers do the behind-the-scenes planning and preventive maintenance that keeps problems from occurring at all. A good Problem Preventer collects metrics to find trends but also has an ear to the ground to know what future problems may arise.

The value to the company of Problem Preventers averting problems, which is less costly than fixing problems when they happen.

Problem Preventers receive satisfaction from knowing that their work prevented problems that no one even knows could have happened. Their joy is private. They enjoy thinking in the longer term rather than getting immediate satisfaction from solving an emergency.

Typical customers do not know that this person exists, but their management does. The managers expect this person to have the same priorities that they do.

A.1.5 The Hero

The SA can be the Hero who saves the day. Like the firefighter who pulls people out of a burning building, the Hero receives adulation and praise. The network was down, but now it is up. The demo wasn't going to be ready, but the SA worked all weekend to bring the network to that part of the building. Heroes get satisfaction out of their jobs from the praise they receive after the fact.

The value to the company of Heroes is huge: Management always rewards a hero. Ironically, Problem Preventers often must struggle to get the same positive visibility, though their contribution may be as or more valuable.

Heroes receive satisfaction from knowing that they hold the key to some knowledge that the company could not live without. The Hero role is not one that promotes a healthy nonwork life. Heroes give up nights, weekends, and vacations, often with no notice. A personal life takes second priority. Eventually, Heroes burn out and become Martyrs, unless management finds some way to help them manage their stress.

Customers expect the Hero to be anywhere at any time. Customers would prefer to deal only with the Hero, because this dashing superstar has become someone on whom they can rely. However, customers need to learn that if they get what they want, the Hero will burn out. New Heroes take a while to find.

A.1.6 The "Go To" Person

This person has gained the reputation of being the one to solve any problem. Go-to people are a little like Heroes, but are more coordinated and more infrastructure-related. Instead of running around putting out fires or repairing a server starting at 3 PM Friday and finishing at 3AM Sunday morning, this is the person management will go to when large-scale deep-knowledge issues are involved. Management knows that the go to person will get to the bottom of the problem, work out the underlying problems, and fix them. It could be an infrastructure issue—tuning a parameter on a database—or a process issue: how to ensure that new users have a common configuration, the need to create a new automation system, or almost anything.

The value of having a go to person around is to get things done when others don't.

Like the Hero, this person can burn out if overused, but when he does the job, he gets the satisfaction of knowing that his solution will become part of the standard procedures going forward.

Customers expect a go to person to follow through when they agree to solve a problem and to be able to give accurate time estimates, or at least periodic status updates until a time estimate can be given.

A.1.7 The Infrastructure Builder

A corporate network depends on a lot of infrastructure: DNS, directories, databases, scripts, switches, and so on. None of this is seen by the typical customer, except when an outage is explained after the fact with mysterious phrases, such as "It was a problem with the DNS server."

The larger the company, the more valuable Infrastructure Builders become. A good infrastructure is like a solid foundation on which a house can be built. You can build a house on a shaky foundation and adjust for it with more complicated and costly house designs, but in the long run, it is cheaper to have started with a solid foundation. A tiny company has almost no infrastructure. Larger companies get benefits from amortizing the cost of a quality infrastructure over larger and larger customer bases. When small companies grow to become large companies, often what makes this go smoothly is having had the foresight to employ SAs who "think big" about infrastructure.

Infrastructure Builders get satisfaction from doing long-term planning, taking existing systems and improving them, scaling large systems into humongous systems, and overhauling legacy systems and replacing them with newer systems. Infrastructure Builders are proud of their ability to not only build extremely huge systems but also coordinate elegant ways to transition to them.

When you are the Infrastructure Builder, you have two groups of customers. The general customer population wants the computer infrastructure to be reliable and wants new infrastructure to be deployed yesterday. Your other customers are the SAs whose systems sit on top of the infrastructure you are building. The SAs want documentation and an infrastructure that is reliable and easy for them to understand, and they want it *now*, because when you miss a deadline, it makes their projects late too.

A.1.8 The Policy Writer

Policies are the backbone of IT. They communicate the wishes of the top corporate officials and dictate how things should be done, tell when they should be done, and explain why they are done. SAs are often asked to write policies on behalf of management. Social problems cannot be solved by technology. Some social problems can be only solved by written policy.

The value to the company of Policy Writers is that they solve some problems and prevent new ones. Policies are a communication tool. As a company grows, communication becomes more difficult and more important.

Policy Writers gain satisfaction from knowing that their knowledge, skills, and personal experiences contributed to a policy that improved an organization. They also enjoy being facilitators who can obtain buy-in from many different communities.

When you are the Policy Writer, customers expect you to seek their input. This should be done at the beginning of the process. It disempowers people to ask for their opinion after the major decisions have been made. Your willingness to listen will be appreciated.

A.1.9 The System Clerk

System Clerks have very little power or decision-making responsibilities. These SAs are given instructions to be followed, such as "Create an account for Fred" and "Allocate an IP address." If the System Clerk works as an assistant to a higher-level SA, this can be a fine arrangement. In fact, it is an excellent way to start a career. However, we have seen System Clerks who report to nontechnical managers, who get frustrated when the Clerk is not able to tackle things outside his normal duties.

The value to the company of System Clerks comes from performing the tasks that would otherwise distract senior SAs from more specialized tasks and providing coverage for SAs when they are away. A System Clerk is also an excellent candidate to fill a more senior SA position as it opens. The Clerk already knows the environment, and the hiring manager knows his personality. However, if the environment has no senior SAs, the value provided is often that of a scapegoat for a bad computing environment, when the real problem is management's lack of understanding about how to manage technology.

The Clerk receives satisfaction from a job well done, from learning new skills, and from looking forward to the excellent growth path ahead of him.

When you are the Clerk, customers want their requests to be performed immediately, whether that is reasonable or not. Chapter 31 has more information about dealing with this situation.

Case Study: Site with Only System Clerks

A site needs a balance of senior-level SAs and Clerks. There once was a site that had only System Clerks. Their training included rudimentary UNIX skills: perform backups, create accounts, allocate IP addresses and IP subnets, install new software, and add new hosts. The Clerks fell victim to the "we can always add one more" syndrome: new allocations were blindly made as requested, with no overall plan for increasing capacity. For example, a new host would be added to a subnet without any network-capacity planning. This worked for a while but eventually led to overloaded subnets.

Customers complained of slow networks, but the Clerks did not have the network engineering skills to fix the problem. Customers solved this problem themselves by requesting private subnets to gain their own private dedicated local bandwidth. The Clerks would happily allocate a new IP subnet, and users would connect it to the rest of the network via a routing-enabled workstation with two NICs. These interconnections were unreliable because hosts route packets slowly, especially when they become overloaded. The more overloaded the main networks became, the more dedicated subnets were created. Eventually, much of the slowness of the network was caused by the slow interconnections between these private pools of bandwidth. The company's compute servers also suffered from the same lack of capacity planning. The customers installed their own compute servers, even though the performance problems they were trying to work around were most likely related to the slow host-based routing. These new, fast servers overpowered the 10Mb network, particularly because they were often an order of magnitude faster than the hosts doing the routing.

By the time the organization hired a senior-level SA, the network was a swamp of unreliable subnets, badly configured compute servers, and antique file servers. The network had 50 subnets for about 500 users. It took nearly 2 years to clean up the mess and modernize the network.

A.1.10 The Lab Technician

The Lab Technician is an SA for highly specialized equipment. For example, in a chemical research firm, the Lab Technician may be responsible for a small network that connects all the scopes and monitoring devices. At a telecommunications manufacturer, the Lab Technician may maintain all the equipment in a protocol-interoperability room having one of every version of a product, the competition's products, and a suite of traffic generators. The Lab Technician is responsible for installing new equipment, integrating systems together for ad hoc projects,[1] and being able to understand enough of her customers' specialties to translate their needs into the tasks she must perform. The Lab Technician usually has a small network or group of networks that connect to the main corporate network and depend on the main corporate network for most services; if she is smart, she also makes friends in the corporate services area to pick their brains for technical knowledge.

The value to the company of Lab Technicians is letting the researchers focus on designing the experiments rather than executing them. Lab Technicians also add value by their vast knowledge base of technical information.

The Lab Technician derives satisfaction from getting an experiment or demo successfully completed on time. However, if she does not get direct congratulations from the researchers she serves, she may grow resentful. Lab Technicians need to remember that their researchers are grateful, whether they express it or not. Researchers will have Technicians who stay with them longer if the Technicians are included in recognition ceremonies, awards, dinners, and so on.

When you are the Lab Technician, customers want to know that something can be done, not how it will be done. They want their requirements met, though it is your responsibility to draw out of them what those requirements are. Active listening skills can greatly help in this area.

A.1.11 The Product Finder

The Product Finder reads every technology magazine and review so that when someone asks, "Is there a software package that compresses widgets?" he can recommend not only a list of widget compressors but also ways to determine which is the most appropriate for the particular application. He also knows where to find such a product or where to look for one.

The value to the company of the Product Finder is his ability to stay on top of what's new. Managers should not watch this kind of person closely, because they will be appalled to discover that he spends half his workday surfing the web and reading magazines. Managers must weigh that against the time this person saves for everyone else.

---

1. In most labs, they are all ad hoc.

Product Finders receive satisfaction from having all the right resources. These people can be annoying to others in the group, even those they help, because everyone would like to have the time to surf the web and keep in touch, but most people (necessarily) have other priorities.

When you are the Product Finder, customers want summaries rather than details. If you provide them with every detail that you've learned on the subject in a long rambling story that takes hours to read, they will shy away from you. Be concise.

A.1.12 The Solution Designer

Solution Designers play a key role in a company. On hearing of a problem, they soon have a solution that is better than anyone would have expected. This may solve a small issue, such as installing an e-fax server to make it easier to send faxes, or it may resolve a large issue, such as creating an electronic version of a paper process. Unlike Product Finders, Solution Designers are more likely to build something from scratch or to integrate some smaller packages.

The value to the company of Solution Designers is their ability to remove roadblocks and simplify bureaucratic processes.

The Solution Designer receives satisfaction from knowing that her solutions are used, because usage indicates that people like it.

When you are the Solution Designer, customers want to see their aspect of the problem solved, not what you may perceive as the problem or what would save the company money. For example, if expense reports are faxed to headquarters (HQ), you might create a way for the data to be entered electronically so that HQ doesn't have to retype all the data. However, your customers aren't helped by saving time at HQ; they simply want the preparation to be made easier. That would be solved with a better user interface or a system that could download their corporate credit card bill off the service provider's web site. Your customers wouldn't even care if the output was then e-faxed to HQ for manual reentry.

A.1.13 The Ad Hoc Solution Finder

The Ad Hoc Solution Finder can, on an emergency basis, create a solution to a seemingly impossible problem. This is the person who magically yet securely gets network connectivity to the moon for your big demo to the moon men. These people may know more about the tools than the average person who uses the tools, possibly from dissecting them. Unlike the

Hero, who usually puts out fires by fixing problems, this person builds solutions.

The value to the company of Ad Hoc Solution Finders is their ability to find solutions that work around the fact that technology is not as flexible as some special situations require or that your corporate network has weaknesses that you have not invested in fixing. The former is a situation that gets better over time. The latter indicates a lack of proper technology management.

The Ad Hoc Solution Finder receives satisfaction from saving the day. Like the Hero, the Ad Hoc Solution Finder can get burned out from being overloaded.

When you are the Ad Hoc Solution Finder, customers want miracles to happen and don't want to be reminded that the emergency could have been prevented through better planning by the company, which is rarely their fault.

A.1.14 The Unrequested Solution Person

Some SAs find themselves providing solutions that weren't requested. This can be a good thing and a bad thing. One SA was rewarded for installing for his users a paperless fax system that wasn't requested but soon became a major productivity enhancement. It was based on free software and used their existing modem pool, so the tangible cost was zero. This same SA was once reprimanded for spending too much time on "self-directed projects" and was encouraged to focus on his assigned tasks.

The value to the company of Unrequested Solution people is, they are usually close to the customers and positioned to see needs that upper management wouldn't see or understand. These SAs may also be more aware of new products than their less technical customers.

Individuals in this role receive satisfaction from discovering that their guesses of what might be useful turn out to be correct.

When you are in this role, customers want you to guess correctly what will or won't be useful to them; talking with them regularly at appropriate times is critical. They will be concerned that these new projects don't interfere with your assigned project's deadlines, especially when that would result in their missing their deadlines. Management will be concerned about the cost of your time and of any tangible costs, especially when an unrequested new service does not get used.

A.1.15   The On-Call Expert

The On-Call Expert is always available to give advice. This person has established herself as knowledgeable in all or most aspects of the system. Sometimes the On-Call Expert has a narrow focus; other times, she is an all-around expert.

The value to the company of On-Call Experts is that people have someone to call when they need advice, whether for an exact answer or simply a good starting point for research.

The On-Call Expert receives satisfaction from helping people and from the ego trip that is inherent to the role. Because technology changes quickly, she requires time to maintain her knowledge, whether that is time spent reading magazines, networking at conferences, or experimenting with new products.

When you are the On-Call Expert, you must remember to help people help themselves. If you don't, you will find yourself overcommitted.

A.1.16   The Educator

The Educator teaches customers to use the services available. The Educator may stop by to fix a problem with a printer but stays to teach the customer how to better use the spreadsheet software and finds himself writing most of the user documentation.

The Educator is valuable to the company because his work results in people working more efficiently with the tools they have. The Educator has close interactions with customers and therefore learns what problems people are having. He becomes a resource for finding out what the customers need.

The Educator receives satisfaction from knowing that his documentation is used and appreciated and from knowing that people work better because of his efforts.

When you are the Educator, customers want you to understand their jobs, how they work, and, most important, what it is in their tools that they find confusing. They want documentation that answers the questions they have, not what the developers think is important.

A.1.17   The Policy Enforcer

The Policy Enforcer is responsible for saying no when someone wants to do something that is against policy and also shuts down violators. The Policy Enforcer depends on two tools equally: written policies and management support. Policies must be written and published for all to see. If the policies are not written, enforcement will be inconsistent because he will have to make up the rules as he goes along, and his peers may enforce different ideas of what is right and wrong. The second tool is management support. The policy has no teeth if management bends the rules every time someone requests an exception. A manager shouldn't sign off on a policy and then continually sign off on requests for exceptions. Often, the Policy Enforcer has the authority to disconnect a network jack if the violation is creating a global problem and the violator cannot be contacted in a reasonable amount of time. If the management does not support the Enforcer's decision, he can't do his job. If management approves a policy but then permits an exception after the Enforcer says no, he loses authority and the will or reason to continue.

The value to the company of the Policy Enforcer is that company policies are carried out. Lack of follow-through on an important policy defeats the point of having a policy.

The Policy Enforcer receives satisfaction from knowing that he is actively trying to keep the company following the direction set by the management and from being chartered to steamroller through the site ensuring compliance.

When you are the Policy Enforcer, customers want to get their jobs done and don't understand why so many roadblocks (policies) are preventing them from doing that. Rather than saying no, it can be more useful to help them by understanding what they are trying to achieve and helping them reach that goal and stay within policy. If you do not like to be in this role but feel trapped in it, you might consider assertiveness training or such books as *When I Say No I Feel Guilty* (Smith 2000).

A Policy with Exceptions

A site had a security policy that created a lot of extra work for anyone who wanted to abide by it. For a web site to be accessible from outside the firewall, the site had to be replicated on the outside rather than by poking a hole in the firewall to let outsiders access the internal host. This replicated site could not make connections back into the company. If it needed access to an internal service, such as a database, that service also had to be replicated. Making a service completely self-sufficient was very difficult. Therefore, when the Policy Enforcer rejected a request, the employee would cry to management, and an exception would be granted. Eventually, enough holes were poked in the firewall that the policy didn't mean anything.

The Policy Enforcer proposed a revision to the policy that simply reflected management's behavior: Holes would be poked if the cost of replication would exceed a certain number of hours of work. Management was in a furor at the proposal because it was not how it wanted security to be done. The Policy Enforcer pointed out all the exceptions management had made. Although old exceptions were grandfathered, management became much better at supporting the Policy Enforcer after the revision. If management wasn't going to support the policy, the Policy Enforcer shouldn't have to, either.

A.1.18 The Disaster Worrier

Someone in the group should be worried about things going wrong. When a solution is being proposed, this person asks, "What is the failure mode?" Of course, the Disaster Worrier can't drive all decisions, or projects will never be completed or will be over budget. This person needs to be balanced by an optimist. However, without someone keeping an eye out for potential disasters, a team can create a house of cards.

The value to the company of the Disaster Worrier is felt only in times of emergency. Half the system is failing, but the other half keeps working because of controls put in place. General system robustness can be the result of this person.

This person receives satisfaction from ensuring safety and stability.

When you are in this role, others around you may get tired of your constant push for belts and suspenders. It is important to pick your battles rather than have an opinion at every turn. Nobody likes to hear such laments as, "That wouldn't have failed if people had listened to me" or "Next time, you won't be so quick to ignore me!" It may be better to share responsibility rather than place blame and refer to future improvement rather than gloat about your expertise: "In the future, we need to write scripts that handle disk-full situations." Gentle one-on-one coaching is more effective than public bemoaning.

A.1.19 The Careful Planner

The Careful Planner takes the time to plan each step of the project in which she is involved. She builds good test plans and is never flustered when things go wrong, because she has already figured out what to do.

The value to the company of the Careful Planner is that she completes important tasks reliably and flawlessly.

This person derives satisfaction from completing a task and knowing that it is really finished and watching the first customers use it without a hitch. She takes pride in her work.

When you are in this role, others come to rely on your work being flaw-less. You are often given the tasks that cannot afford to fail. Continue to work as you always did, and don't let the importance of the tasks weigh you down. Be aware that your meticulous work takes time and that others are always in a hurry and may get agitated watching you work. Make sure that you develop a talent for predicting how long you will need to complete a task. You don't want to be seen as someone who couldn't meet a deadline if it walked up and introduced itself.

A.1.20 The Capacity Planner

The Capacity Planner makes the system scale as it grows. This person notices when things are getting full, running out, or becoming overloaded. *Good* Capacity Planners pay attention to utilization patterns and are in tune with business changes that may affect them. *Great* Capacity Planners install sys-tems that do this monitoring automatically and produce graphs that predict when capacity will run out. Vendors can help Capacity Planners by docu-menting data that they would find useful, such as how much RAM and disk space are required as a function of the number of users.

The value to the company of Capacity Planners is that traffic jams are prevented. This is another role that goes unnoticed if the job is done properly. This person also helps the company fix the correct problem the right way. (Too many times, we've seen departments trying to speed up a server by adding more RAM when the real problem was an overloaded network connection, or vice versa.)

The Capacity Planner receives satisfaction from knowing that problems are prevented, that people heed warnings, and from finding the real source of problems.

When you are the Capacity Planner, customers want you to have accurate data and solutions that won't cost any money. It is your job to justify costs. As always, explaining things in the customer's language is critical.

A.1.21 The Budget Administrator

The Budget Administrator keeps tabs on how much money is left in the budget and helps write the budget for next year. This person knows what the money is meant to be spent on, when it is meant to be spent, and how to make the budget stretch farther.

The value to the company of the Budget Administrator is to keep SA expenses under control, ensuring that the tasks that need doing are funded—within reason—even if they are unexpected, and providing reliable figures so management can perform financial planning for the coming year.

The Budget Administrator receives satisfaction from staying within budget and still managing to fund extra, important projects that were not budgeted for.

When you are the Budget Administrator, customers want you to stay in budget, to prepare a good budget plan for the next year, to accurately evaluate what the most important projects are, to make sure that all the critical tasks have funding, and to show how the money they let you spend is benefiting them.

A.1.22 The Customer's Advocate

The Customer's Advocate can help a person speak up for her needs. He is the translator and lobbyist positioned between the customer and her management. The Advocate doesn't simply recommend a solution but also coaches the customer on how to sell the idea to her boss and stands by during the presentation in case she needs help.

The value to the company of the Customer's Advocate is to help the customers get what they need despite red tape and communication barriers.

The Advocate receives satisfaction from knowing that he has helped someone. He also knows that by interfacing with management, he is able to put his SA team in a good light and to perform the role of the helpful facilitator. Often, you help a customer get what she needs by working the system rather than going around it. This is especially valuable if you also created the system.

When you are the Advocate, customers want you to understand them before you start suggesting solutions. The customers want you to understand their technical needs as well as soft issues, such as schedules and budgets.

A.1.23 The Technocrat

The Technocrat is the advocate for new technology. When a system needs to be repaired or replaced, he puts more value in the new system because it is new, even if it still has bugs. He disdains those who seek comfort in old systems that may be "good enough." The Technocrat can provide good counterbalance to the Disaster Worrier.

The value to the company of the Technocrat is that he prevents the company from becoming technically stagnant.

The Technocrat receives satisfaction from being surrounded by the latest new technology—dare we say new-toy syndrome.

When you are the Technocrat, customers want you to focus on the real value of a solution rather than that newer is better.

A.1.24 The Salesperson

The Salesperson is not limited to tangible items. She may be selling a particular policy, new service, or proposal. She may be selling the SA team itself, either to upper management or to the customers. A Salesperson is concerned with finding the needs of customers and then convincing them that what she has to sell meets those needs. New services are easier to sell if the customers were involved in the specification and selection process.

The value to the company of the Salesperson is that she makes the SA team's job easier. A great system that is never accepted by the customers is not useful to the company. A great policy that saves the company money is not helpful if the customers work around it because they don't understand the benefits.

The Salesperson receives short-term satisfaction from "making the sale," but for real, lasting satisfaction, the Salesperson must develop a relationship with the customers and find herself feeling that she truly helps the customers in a meaningful way.

When you are the Salesperson, customers want to have their needs understood and appreciated. They want to be talked with, not to.

A.1.25 The Vendor Liaison

The Vendor Liaison maintains a relationship with one or more vendors. She may know a vendor's product line better than anyone else the in the group and be privy to upcoming products. She is a resource for the other SAs, thus saving calls to the vendor's salesperson.

The value to the company of the Vendor Liaison is having someone who understands and is dedicated to the company's needs dealing with a vendor. Having a single point of contact saves resources.

The Vendor Liaison receives satisfaction from being the expert that everyone respects, from being the first to know about vendor news, and from the free lunches and shirts she receives.

When you are the Vendor Liaison, customers want you to be all-knowing about the vendor, open-minded about competing vendors, and a harsh negotiator when getting prices.

A.1.26 The Visionary

The Visionary looks at the big picture and has a vision of where the group should go.

The value to the company of the Visionary is keeping the group focused on what's next.

The Visionary receives satisfaction when he looks back over the years and sees that in the long term, he made a difference. All those incremental improvements accumulated to meet major goals.

When you are the Visionary, customers want to know what's happening next and may not be too concerned with the long term. Your team's reputation for being able to execute a plan affects your ability to sell your vision to the customers.

A.1.27 The Mother

The Mother nurtures the customers. It's difficult to explain except through example. One SA spent her mornings walking through the halls, stopping by each person's office to see how things were. She would fix small problems and note the bigger problems for the afternoon. She would answer many user-interface questions that a customer might have felt were too small to ask the helpdesk. The customers were making a big paradigm change (from X Terminals to PCs running X Terminal emulators), and this mothering was exactly what they needed. In her morning walks, she would answer hundreds of questions and resolve dozens of problems that would otherwise have been tickets submitted to the helpdesk. The customers got very used to this level of service and soon came to rely on her morning visits as part of what kept them productive.

The value to the company of the Mother is her high degree of hand-holding, which can be critical at times of great change or with nontechnical customers. The personal contact also ensures a more precise understanding of the customers' needs.

The Mother receives satisfaction from the personal relationships she develops with her customers.

When you are the Mother, customers want to know that their immediate needs are being met and will put less emphasis on the long-term strategy. You must remember to keep an eye on the future and not get too absorbed in the present.

A.1.28 The Monitor

The Monitor notices how well things are running. Sometimes, the Monitor uses low-tech methods, using the same services that his customers use. Although the SAs may have a private file server, this person stores his files on the file server that the customers use, so he can "feel their pain." As this person becomes more sophisticated, he automates his monitoring but then watches the monitoring system's output and takes the time to fix things rather than simply clear the alarms.

The value to the company of the Monitor is that problems are noticed before customers start complaining. This can give the perception of a trouble-free network.

The Monitor receives satisfaction from being the first to notice a problem, from knowing that he's working on fixing a problem before customers report it, and from knowing that problems are prevented by monitoring capacity issues.

When you are the Monitor, customers most likely don't know that you exist. If they did, they would want your testing to simulate their real workloads: end-to-end testing. For example, it isn't good enough to know that a mail server is up. You must test that a message can be submitted, relayed, delivered, and read.

A.1.29 The Facilitator

The Facilitator has excellent communication skills. He tends to turn impromptu discussions into decision-making meetings. He is often asked to run meetings, especially large meetings in which keeping focus can be difficult.

The Facilitator adds value by making processes run more smoothly. He may not take on a lot of action items, but he gets groups of people to agree to what needs to be done and who is going to do it. He keeps meetings efficient and fun.

The Facilitator receives satisfaction from seeing people come to agreement on goals and taking initiative to see the goals completed.

When you are the Facilitator, the other members on your team want you to facilitate all their discussions. It is important to coach other people into being facilitators and to create an environment in which everyone has good communication skills.

A.1.30 The Customer/SA

Sometimes a customer is also an SA, perhaps because a customer has certain responsibilities that require privileged access or used to be an SA and retains some of those responsibilities.

The value to the company of the Customer/SA is filling in when other SAs are on vacation. In fact, in situations in which there is only a single SA, it is useful to coach one of the customers on daily operational issues, so he can provide vacation coverage. Having an additional person who can change backup tapes, create user accounts, and solve the top-ten most frequent problems can be very useful.

The Customer/SA receives satisfaction from the role if he holds SAs or superuser access in high esteem. Alternatively, he may receive some kind of "combat pay" for being cross-trained.

When you are the Customer/SA, the main SA team wants to know that you aren't interfering with their plans, are following the right procedures, and are upholding the same ethical practices as they are. The other customers want to know that you will be able to keep things running when called on to do so.

A.1.31 Customer Support

The Customer Support SA views his job as being centered on the human customer making the request rather than on the technical processes that he is involved with. He views his job as helping customers with the system, which is quite static. Major changes to the system come from external forces, such as a systems programming group.

The Customer Support SA adds value to the company by being the day-to-day human interface to the full SA team. Most customers never see any back-line support.

The Customer Support SA receives satisfaction from the personal relationships that he develops and the warm glow of knowing that he has helped a real live human.

When you are the Customer Support SA, customers want their issues dealt with on their schedules. If they perceive the situation to be an emergency, they expect you to stop everything and help them.

A.1.32 The Policy Navigator

The Policy Navigator understands the rules and regulations of the bureaucracy and can help others navigate through or around them. The Navigator can help someone get through a process or work around a policy without violating it.

The Policy Navigator adds value to the SA team by getting things done more quickly when having to deal with the system, and, when needed, working around the system without getting into hot water.

The Policy Navigator receives satisfaction from knowing that her connections and knowledge have contributed to a project.

When you are the Policy Navigator, your customers want things to get done, regardless of whether you stay within the system. This can put you in a difficult situation when it seems to the customer that it is easier to violate policy or work around the system.

A.2 Negative Roles

The following sections describe some negative roles that you want to avoid.

A.2.1 The Bleeding Edger

Sometimes, an SA can be so excited by new technology that he seeks to unleash it on the customers before it is ready. Rather than being on the leading edge, he keeps the company on the *bleeding edge*. In this case, the customers always seem to be enduring the pain of buggy new services.

A.2.2 Technology Staller

The counterbalance to the Bleeding Edger is the person who stalls on the use of any new technology. This risk-averse person sometimes has a favorite excuse, such as not being satisfied with the back-out plan. She is happy with the current OS release, the current OS distribution, the current brand of computers, amount of bandwidth, and type of network topology. The Staller doesn't see the lack of technology refresh and the problems that it has created. Ironically, this person used to be on the cutting edge but has now become stuck in a rut. She may have been the person who eschewed the mainframes and adopted UNIX or laughed at the workstation users who wouldn't adopt PCs. However cutting-edge she once was, she has found something she is comfortable with and now has become the person she used to mock years ago.

A.2.3 The SA Who Cried Wolf

This person is worried about things that aren't happening or are unlikely to happen. Much of system administration is about managing risks, but this person thinks that all risks are unacceptable. This person slows projects from getting off the ground. He predicts doom or failure without hard facts to back it up. Sometimes, he is simply uncomfortable with anything he isn't in control of or about which he isn't educated. Sometimes, this person will waste a lot of time working on problems that aren't even on your radar and ignore more pressing problems. The biggest danger with this person is that when he is correct, he will be ignored.

A.2.4 The Cowboy

The Cowboy rushes into fixing systems or implementing new services without proper planning, thinking through the consequences, or developing a back-out plan. He does not bother to ask his manager beforehand or to check with the customers. He does not test his work properly to verify that it is working, and he goes home without telling anyone what he has done. He sees himself as talented and fast-working and thinks that others try to put too much red tape in his way and that they are unappreciative of his talents. The Cowboy doesn't document anything and simply knows that he is invaluable to the company.

The Cowboy

A midsize computing hardware manufacturer had a Cowboy in a senior SA position. His management had brought in a consulting group to rearchitect the network and to build a transition plan from the old network to the new one. The plan was agreed on, the equipment was ordered, a schedule was laid out and agreed on with the customers, and test plans were being built with the customers. The day that the new equipment arrived, the Cowboy stayed late, ripped out the old network equipment, and installed the new gear. He did not use the new architecture; he ignored all the components of the transition plan that were intended to solve unrelated problems that could be solved by the process of the transition; and he did not do much, if any, testing. The next day, when people returned to work, many of them found that they had no network connection: the CEO, the entire customer-support department, the Cowboy's management chain, and many of the engineers. The helpdesk and the rest of the SA group had no idea what had happened, because he had not told anyone, and he didn't bother to arrive at work until much later in the day; after all, he had stayed late! He was still proud of what he had done and unrepentant because he viewed the transition plan and test plan as a big waste of time and money. He enjoyed showing that he could do it on his own in a few hours, when the consultants were taking so much time over it. He was oblivious to the cost of the major outage that he had caused and the damage he had inflicted on the SA group's reputation.

A.2.5 Slaves, Scapegoats, or Janitors

Sometimes, SAs are in the role of being Slaves, Scapegoats, or Janitors. Slaves are expected to do tasks without question, even if they might be able to suggest better processes if they were told the big picture. Sometimes, others use SAs as Scapegoats. All bad things that happen are blamed on the SAs. The SAs are blamed for a project being late, even if the customers weren't communicating their needs. Sometimes, SAs are thought of as Janitors: people who aren't valuable to the company's direct business but unskilled workers who are purely overhead. All three of these roles are problems with management's not understanding the purpose of SAs in their own organization. However, it is the SAs' responsibility to fix these problems by increasing communication and working on their team's visibility within the organization.

A.3 Team Roles

Within an SA team, some roles, with the exception of the Martyr, should be a part of every team.

A.3.1 The End-to-End Expert

The End-to-End Expert understands the technology being used from the lowest to the highest levels. She is critical for solving obscure problems, as well as major outages. Obscure problems usually are the result of multiple simultaneous failures or strange interactions between different areas, and they require expertise in all areas to be able to solve them. Major outages affect multiple subsystems and require a deep understanding of the overall architecture to pinpoint the real problem.

A.3.2 The Outsider

During a prolonged outage, the people working on the problem sometimes get the SA equivalent of writer's block. They're going in circles, unable to make a significant improvement in the situation. The role that is most useful here is the Outsider bringing a fresh viewpoint to the situation. By making everyone explain what has happened so far, people often realize the solution. Sometimes, the role of this person is to encourage the others to seek outside help or escalate the problem to higher authorities or to vendor support. Other times, this person's role is to simply recognize that it is time to give up: There is a back-out plan and it should be implemented.

A.3.3 The Level-Focused Person

Another role is the person who decides at what level to solve a particular problem. People always tend to think that problems can be solved at their own level. Technicians think they need to work harder. Programmers think that they need to introduce new software to fix the problem. However, an important role is the person who has an understanding of all the levels, including management, and can judge where best to solve a problem. After weeks of trying to solve a problem, this is the person who suggests that it would be less expensive and possibly more effective to simply get a higher level of management to announce that a certain practice is not allowed. It may be better to find the first manager up the organization chart who out-ranks the two bickering customers and give the problem to her to solve. This is also the person most likely to quote the old Internet adage: "Technology can't solve social problems," then seek a policy change.

A.3.4 The Martyr

The Martyr feels that nobody else has as much work as he does. Resentful of the fact that nobody else works the long hours that he does, and unhappy with his lack of social life or financial success, he's unable to understand how other people can "make it" when they do so little. This person spends a lot of time bemoaning the problems of the world—mainly his world. This can happen as a result of simple burnout or, more complexly, low self-esteem.

Burnout happens when a person does not balance work with recreation. Sadly, in today's fast-paced, modern culture, some people grow up not learning the importance of relaxation. They feel that they must always be "at work." This extreme work ethic may be the secret to their success, but without the mental equivalent of preventive maintenance, it leads to burnout. At that point, working harder only makes the situation worse. People who have reached this extreme may not be helped by a quantity of time off; and might be even more resentful if they have nothing to do.

Self-esteem is something we learn (or don't learn) when we are young. Cognitive theorists believe that our mental state—whether we are, by default, happy or sad—is not a sign of whether good or bad things are happening to us but of how we react to whatever is happening to us (Burns 1999b). We can even be unhappy in response to good events if our self-esteem has been damaged to the point that no matter what happens, we feel worthless. When this happens, we turn around good news and events and change them into things to worry about: "He liked my work on that project! What if I can't meet those expectations every time? What if my coworkers become jealous and resent me?" Various therapies are designed to help people in this situation (Burns 1999a).

A.3.5 Doers of Repetitive Tasks

Some personality types lend themselves to doing repetitive tasks. These people should be valued because they solve immediate problems. This book can't stress enough the importance of automation, but some tasks can't be automated, such as physically delivering new machines, or are not repeated enough to make it cost-effective to be automated. This role is an important one for the team. This person can take on the load of repetitive tasks from higher-skilled people. These smaller tasks are often excellent training for higher-level tasks.

A.3.6 The Social Director

The Social Director boosts team spirit by finding reasons for the group to celebrate together; people's birthdays, anniversaries, and hiring dates are just a few. Getting people to relate to one another in a nonwork context can build team cohesion. The key to success in this position is to make sure that people don't feel imposed on and to make sure that you don't overdo it and risk the boss considering you a time waster.

Monthly Birthday Lunch

One SA team had a policy of going out to lunch once a month. The people with birthdays that month didn't have to pay and were responsible for coordinating the next month's lunch. It was a valuable team-building tradition. Because of a couple of factors, the tradition stopped for a year. To restart the process, the team held a lunch for anyone who had a birthday in the last 12 months, and the boss paid the entire bill.

A.3.7 Mr. Break Time

During an emergency situation, it is key to have someone who notices when people are becoming exhausted and encourages them to take a break. People may feel that the task is too important to stop working on it, but this person realizes that nothing is getting done and that a break might refresh people. Tom is known to disappear and return with pizzas and drinks. Often, by walking away from a problem for a time, people will think about it differently and come up with better solutions.

There are other roles that exist in an SA team, but we feel that the preceding ones deserve highlighting.

A.4 Conclusion

We hope that as you read this appendix, you found one or more of these paragraphs to be like looking into a mirror and seeing yourself for the very first time. Now you can be conscious of what motivates you and how you fit into your team.

This may help you realize that you play many roles in your organization and may play a special role on your team. You wear many hats. As you wear each hat, you can be conscious of the value you should be providing to the company, what motivates you, and what customers expect from you.

Maybe you learned something good or bad about yourself. Maybe you learned something new about yourself or validated feelings that you already had. It may convince you to seek personal improvement in an area of your life. The next time you consider a career change, you might spend more time thinking about the roles you like to be in or the roles that match your skills and compare those to the roles you will be asked to play in the new position. Don't be worried if you feel that every role appeals to you. Maybe that is your destiny in life, or maybe as you gain more knowledge and experience, you will find new clarity in your feelings about these things.

Maybe this appendix made you realize that your organization is in dire need of one of the roles described here. Maybe you've noticed something missing from your SA team. Maybe you should try to take on that role more often, encourage others to take on that role, or look for those skills the next time you hire someone. You may realize that your organization has too many people in a particular role, which indicates that you need balance. Maybe this appendix helped you notice that a certain person is fulfilling a negative role and needs coaching to change.

938   Appendix A   The Many Roles of a System Administrator

Maybe this appendix made you realize that people on your team all play too many roles or don't play enough roles or the roles aren't balanced.

Most of all, we hope that this part of the book helped you understand the people on your team who are not like you. Now you can appreciate the value they bring to the team. A strong team includes people with different skills and from various backgrounds; each brings something unique to the table. Those differences do not divide a team but make it stronger. For that to happen, the team must be conscious of the differences and take time to value them rather than run from them.

Exercises

1. What roles do you see yourself in? (Don't be humble.) Do you want to remain in these roles? What unfamiliar roles appeal to you?

2. What roles did you see yourself in early in your career? How is that different from the roles you are in now?

3. What roles do you see yourself fulfilling in the future?

4. What personal changes would you like to make so that you can better serve in your role or move into new roles?

5. What roles do you not like? Why? How are they different from the roles you are currently fulfilling?

6. Determine which role each person on your team portrays. If you feel it wouldn't destroy your friendship, have the team members do the same thing, and share the lists. How much did the therapy bills cost?

7. Psychologists and managers know that other people cannot be changed; they need to see the need for change themselves and decide how to make the change on their own. Did this chapter make you realize that someone on your team is fulfilling a negative role and needs to make some personal changes? How might you help that person see the need for change? Is that person you?

8. What roles are missing from your team? How can you develop those roles in your team?

9. This appendix does not contain a complete list of roles. What roles do you feel should be added to this list? How are they valuable to the organization or team, or in what ways are they negative roles? What are the motivators for these roles? What do customers expect from them?

Appendix B

Acronyms

AC	Alternating Current
ACL	Access Control List
AICPA	American Institute of Certified Public Accountants
AoE	Ata over Ethernet
ASP	Application Service Provider or Active Server Page
ATA	Advanced Technology Attachment
ATM	Asynchronous Transfer Mode
ATS	Automatic Transfer Switch
AUP	Acceptable-Use Policy
AUSCERT	Australian Computer Emergency Response Team
BGP	Border Gateway Protocol
CA	Certification Authority
CAD	Computer-Aided Design
CAP	Columbia Appletalk Protocol
CDP	Continuous Data Protection
CD-ROM	Compact Disk Read-Only Memory
CEO	Chief Executive Officer
CERT	Computer Emergency Response Team
CFO	Chief Financial Officer
CGI	Common Gateway Interface
CIAC	Computer Incident Advisory Capability
CIFS	Common Internet File System
CIO	Chief Information Officer
CMS	Content Management System
Colo	Colocation Center
CNAME	Common NAME (DNS record)
COO	Chief Operating Officer
CPU	Central Processing Unit
CSE	Customer Support Engineer
CSU/DSU	Channel Service Unit/Data Service Unit
CTO	Chief Technology Officer
DAD	Disk Access Density

DAS	Directly Attached Storage
DC	Direct Current
DHCP	Dynamic Host Configuration Protocol
DLT	Digital Linear Tape
DNS	Domain Name Service
DoS	Denial of Service
DR	Disaster Recovery
DSL	Digital Subscriber Line
EAP	Employee Assistance Program
EDA	Electronic Design Automation
EIGRP	Enhanced Interior Gateway Routing Protocol
EPO	Emergency Power Off
ERP	Enterprise Resource Planning
ESD	Electrostatic Discharge
ETR	Estimated Time to Repair
ETSI	European Telecommunication Standards Institute
EU	European Union
FAA	Federal Aviation Administration
FAQ	Frequently Asked Question
FC	Fibre Channel
FC-AL	Fibre Channel-Arbitrated Loop
FCC	Federal Communications Commission
FDDI	Fiber-Distributed Data Interface
FTP	File Transfer Protocol
GUI	Graphical User Interface
HBA	Host Bus Adapter
HHA	Handheld Authenticator
HTML	HyperText Markup Language
HTTP	HyperText Transfer Protocol
HVAC	Heating, Ventilation, Air Conditioning
ICS	Incident Command System
I/O	Input/Output
ICMP	Internet Control Message Protocol
IDF	Intermediate Distribution Frame
IDS	Intrusion Detection System
IEEE	Institute of Electrical and Electronic Engineers
IETF	Internet Engineering Task Force
IMAP	Internet Message Access Protocol
IP	Intellectual Property
IP	Internet Protocol
IS	Information Systems
ISDN	Integrated Service Digital Network
ISO	International Organization for Standardization
ISP	Internet Service Provider
IT	Information Technology

ITIL	Information Technology Infrastructure Library
KVM	Keyboard, Video, Mouse
LAN	Local Area Network
LDAP	Lightweight Directory Access Protocol
LOPSA	League of Professional System Administrators
LPDP	Line Printer Daemon Protocol
LISA	Large Installation System Administration
MAC	Media Access Control
MAN	Metropolitan Area Network
MAPI	Mail API, a proprietary licensed API not to be confused with IMAP
MDA	Mail-Delivery Agent
MDF	Main Distribution Frame
MIB	Management Information Base
MIDI	Musical Instrument Digital Interface
MIL-SPEC	U.S. Military Specifications
MIS	Management Information Systems
MONET	Multiwavelength Optical Network
MPEG	Moving Picture Experts Group
MPLS	Multi Protocol Label Switching
MRTG	Multirouter Traffic Grapher
MS-SMS	Microsoft's System Management Service
MTA	Mail Transport Agent
MTU	Maximum Transmission Unit
MTTR	Mean Time to Repair
MUA	Mail User Agent
MX	Mail Exchanger
NAS	Network-Attached Storage
NAT	Network Address Translation
NCD	Network Computing Devices
NDA	Non-Disclosure Agreement
NEBS	Network Equipment Building System
NFS	Network File System
NIC	Network Interface Card (PC Ethernet network card)
NIS	Network Information Service
NNTP	Net News Transfer Protocol
NOC	Network Operations Center
OEM	Original Equipment Manufacturer
OLTP	Online Transaction Processing
OPS	Operations Per Second
OS	Operating System
OSHA	Occupational Safety and Health Administration
OSI	Open Systems Interconnection
OSPF	Open Shortest Path First
OTP	One-Time Password
PAM	Pluggable Authentication Module

PARIS	Programmable Automatic Remote Installation Service
PC	Personal Computer
PCMIA	People Can't Memorize Industry Acronyms
PDA	Personal Digital Assistant
PDU	Power-Distribution Unit
PIN	Personal Identification Number
POP	Post Office Protocol
POPI	Protection of Proprietary Information
POP3	Post Office Protocol, version 3 (Not to be confused with MAPI)
PPP	Point-to-Point Protocol
PR	Public Relations
QA	Quality Assurance
QPS	Queries Per Second
QoS	Quality of Service
RADIUS	Remote Authentication Dial-In User Service
RAID	Redundant Array of Inexpensive Disks
RAM	Random Access Memory
RAS	Remote Access Server
RCS	Revision Control System
RF	Radio Frequency
RFC	Request for Comments
RIP	Routing Information Protocol
RMA	Returned Merchandise Authorization
ROI	Return on Investment
RPC	Remote Procedure Call
RTT	Round-Trip Time
RSS	Really Simple Syndication
SA	System Administrator
SAGE	System Administrator's Guild
SAN	Storage-Area Network
SANS	System Administration, Network, and Security
SAS-70	Statement of Auditing Standards, No. 70
SATA	Serial ATA
SCCS	Source Code Control System
SCSI	Small Computer Systems Interface
SCM	Software Configuration Management
SEC	Securities and Exchange Commission
SID	Security ID
SLA	Service-Level Agreement
SMB	Server Message Block
SME	Subject Matter Expert
SMTP	Simple Mail Transfer Protocol
SNMP	Simple Network Management Protocol
SOA	Start of Authority
SONET	Synchronous Optical Network

SQL	Structured Query Language
SSH	Secure Shell
SSL	Secure Sockets Layer
STP	Spanning Tree Protocol
SUID	Set User ID
TCP	Transmission Control Protocol
TDD	Test-Driven Development
TFTP	Trivial File Transfer Protocol
TLS	Transport Layer Security
TTL	Time to Live
UCE	Unsolicited Commercial Email
UDP	User Data Protocol
UID	User Identification
UPS	Uninterruptible Power Supply
USB	Universal Serial Protocol
URL	Uniform Resource Locator
UUCP	Unix-to-Unix Copy Protocol
VIF	Virtual Interface
VLAN	Virtual LAN
VPN	Virtual Private Network
VRRP	Virtual Router Redundancy Protocol
WAN	Wide Area Network
WAFL	Write Anywhere File Layout

Bibliography

Adams, S. 2000. *The Dilbert Principle*. Boxtree. www.Dilbert.com.

Albitz, P., C., Liu, and M. Loukides, eds. 1998. *DNS and BIND*, O'Reilly.

Allen, D. 2002. *Getting Things Done: The Art of Stress-Free Productivity*. Penguin.

Allen, J. R. 1999. Driving by the rear-view mirror: Managing a network with cricket. *First Conference on Network Administration (NETA '99)*, USENIX, Santa Clara, Calif., pp. 1–10.

Anonymous. 1997. The backhoe, natural enemy of the network administrator. www.23.com/backhoe/.

Archer, B. 1993. Towards a POSIX standard for software administration. *Systems Administration (LISA VII) Conference*, USENIX, Monterey, Calif., pp. 67–79.

Beck, R. 1999. Dealing with public Ethernet jacks—switches, gateways and authentication. *Proceedings of the 13th Systems Administration Conference LISA, (SAGE/USENIX)*, p. 149.

Bent, Jr., W. H. 1993. System administration as a user interface: An extended metaphor. *Systems Administration (LISA VII) Conference*, USENIX, Monterey, Calif., pp. 209–212.

Bentley, J. and Kernigan, B. 1991. A system for algorithm animation, *Computing Systems*, Vol. 4, USENIX, pp. 5–30.

Berkowitz, H. C. 1998. *Designing Addressing Architectures for Routing and Switching*. Macmillan Technical Publishing. ISBN: 1578700590.

Berkowitz, H. C. 1999. *Designing Routing and Switching Architectures*, Macmillan Technical Publishing. ISBN: 1578700604.

Berliner, B. 1990. CVS II: Parallelizing software development. *USENIX Conference Proceedings*, USENIX, Washington, D.C., pp. 341–352.

Bernstein, D. J. 1997. VERP: Variable envelope return paths. http://cr.yp.to/proto/verp.txt.

Black, D. P. 1999. *Building Switched Networks: Multilayer Switching, QoS, IP Multicast, Network Policy, and Service-Level Agreements*. Addison-Wesley.

Black, U. D. 2000. *IP Routing Protocols: RIP, OSPF, BGP, PNNI and Cisco Routing Protocols*. Prentice Hall. ISBN: 0130142484.

Black, U. D. 2001. *MPLS and Label Switching Networks*. Prentice Hall.

Blanchard, K. H. 1993. *The One Minute Manager*. Berkley Pub Group.

Blanchard, K. H., W. Oncken, and H. Burrows. 1989. *The One Minute Manager Meets the Monkey*. Morrow.

Bolinger, D. 1995. *Applying RCS and SCCS*. O'Reilly.

Braden, R. T. 1989. RFC 1123: Requirements for Internet hosts—application and support. See also STD0003. Updates RFC 822 (Crocker 1982). Updated by RFC 2181 (Elz and Bush 1997). Status: STANDARD.

Brutlag, J. D. 2000. Aberrant behavior detection in time series for network monitoring. *Fourteenth Systems Administration Conference (LISA '00)*, USENIX, New Orleans.

Burgess, M. 2000. *Principles of Network and System Administration*. Wiley.

Burns, D. D. 1999a. *The Feeling Good Handbook*. Avon.

Burns, D. D. 1999b. *Feeling Good: The New Mood Therapy*. Avon.

Chalup, S. R., C. Hogan, G. Kulosa, B. McDonald, and B. Stansell. 1998. Drinking from the fire(walls) hose: Another approach to very large mailing lists. *Twelfth Systems Administration Conference (LISA '98)*, USENIX, Boston, p. 317.

Chapman, D. B. 1992. Majordomo: How I manage 17 mailing lists without answering "-request" mail. *Systems Administration (LISA VI) Conference*, USENIX, Long Beach, Calif., pp. 135–143.

Chapman, R. B. and Andrade, K. R. 1997. *Insourcing After the Outsourcing: MIS Survival Guide*. AMACOM. ISBN: 0814403867.

Cheswick, W. R., and S. M. Bellovin. 1994. *Firewalls and Internet Security: Repelling the Wily Hacker*. Addison-Wesley.

Colyer, W., and W. Wong. 1992. Depot: A tool for managing software environments. *Systems Administration (LISA VI) Conference*, USENIX, Long Beach, Calif., pp. 153–162.

Comer, D. 2005. *Internetworking with TCP/IP*, Vol. 1. Prentice Hall.

Cox P. and Sheldon, T. 2000. *Windows 2000 Security Handbook*. McGraw-Hill Professional Publishing. ISBN: 0072124334.

Crispin, M. 1996. RFC 2060: Internet message access protocol—Version 4rev1. Obsoletes RFC1730. Status: PROPOSED STANDARD.

Crittenden, J. 1995. The Simpsons: [episode 2F10] And Maggie Makes Three, TV episode. www.snpp.com/episodes/2F10.html.

Crocker, D. 1982. RFC 822: Standard for the format of ARPA Internet text messages. See also STD0011. Obsoletes RFC 733. Updated by RFC 1123 (Braden 1989), RFC 1138, RFC 1148, RFC 1327, RFC 2156. Status: STANDARD.

Curtin, M. 1999a. Electronic snake oil, *;login:*, Vol. 24, USENIX, pp. 31–38.

Curtin, M. 1999b. Snake Oil Warning Signs: Encryption Software to Avoid. http://www.interhack.net/people/cmcurtin/snake-oil-faq.html.

Dagenais, M., S. Boucher, R. Grin-Lajoie, P. Laplante, P. Mailhot, and C. de Recherche Informatique de Montreal. 1993. LUDE: A distributed software library. *Systems Administration (LISA VII) Conference*, USENIX, Monterey, Calif., pp. 25–32.

Darmohray, E. T., ed. 2001. *Job Descriptions for System Administrators*, rev. and expanded ed. USENIX for/SAGE. www.sage.org/pubs/8_jobs.

Davis, C., P. Vixie, T. Goodwin, and I. Dickinson. 1996. RFC 1876: A means for expressing location information in the domain name system. Updates RFC 1034, RFC 1035. Status: EXPERIMENTAL.

Denning, D. E. 1999. *Information Warfare and Security*. Addison-Wesley. ISBN: 0201433036.

Dijker, B. L. 2000. Sage computing policies website. http://www.usenix.org/sage/publications/policies.

Dodge, J. 1999. Maybe Ascend should have bought Lucent, *ZDNet eWeek*. www.zdnet.com/eweek/stories/general/0,11011,385015,00.html.

Elz, R., and R. Bush. 1996. RFC 1982: Serial number arithmetic. Updates RFC 1034, RFC 1035. Status: PROPOSED STANDARD.

Elz, R., and R. Bush. 1997. RFC 2181: Clarifications to the DNS specification. Updates RFC 1034, RFC 1035, RFC 1123. Status: PROPOSED STANDARD.

Epp, P. V., and B. Baines. 1992. Dropping the mainframe without crushing the users: Mainframe to distributed UNIX in nine months. *Systems Administration (LISA VI) Conference*, USENIX, Long Beach, Calif., pp. 39–53.

Epps, A., Bailey, D. G. and Glatz, D. 1999. NFS and SMB data sharing within a heterogeneous environment: A real world study, *2nd Large Installation System Administration of Windows NT Conference*, USENIX, Seattle, Washington, pp. 37–42.

Evard, R. 1997. An analysis of UNIX system configuration. *Eleventh Systems Administration Conference (LISA '97)*, USENIX, San Diego, p. 179.

Feit, S. 1999. *Wide Area High Speed Networks*. Pearson Education. ISBN: 1578701147.

Fine, T. A. and Romig, S. M. 1990. A console server, *LISA IV Conference Proceedings*, USENIX, Colorado Springs, CO, pp. 97–100.

Finke, J. 1994a. Automating printing configuration, *LISA VIII Conference Proceedings*, USENIX, San Diego, CA, pp. 175–183.

Finke, J. 1994b. Monitoring usage of workstations with a relational database, *LISA VIII Conference Proceedings*, USENIX, San Diego, CA, pp. 149–157.

Finke, J. 1995. Sql_2_html: Automatic generation of HTML database schemas, *Ninth Systems Administration Conference (LISA '95)*, USENIX, Monterey, CA, pp. 133–138.

Finke, J. 1996. Institute white pages as a system administration problem, *10th Systems Administration Conference (LISA'96)*, USENIX, Chicago, IL, pp. 233–240.

Finke, J. 1997. Automation of site configuration management, *Eleventh Systems Administration Conference (LISA '97)*, USENIX, San Diego, California, p. 155.

Finke, J. 2000. An improved approach for generating configuration files from a database. *Proceedings of the 14th Systems Administration Conference LISA (SAGE/USENIX)*, p. 29.

Fulmer, K. L. 2000. *Business Continuity Planning: A Step-by-Step Guide with Planning Forms*. Rothstein Associates.

Fulmer, R., and A. Levine. 1998. Autoinstall for NT: Complete NT installation over the network. *Large Installation System Administration of Windows NT Conference*, USENIX, Seattle, p. 27.

Furlani, J. L., and P. W. Osel. 1996. Abstract yourself with modules. *Tenth Systems Administration Conference (LISA' 96)*, USENIX, Chicago, pp. 193–203.

Garfinkel, S. 1994. *PGP: Pretty Good Privacy*. O'Reilly. ISBN: 1565920988.

Garfinkel, S. and Spafford, G. 1996. *Practical* UNIX *and Internet Security*. O'Reilly and Associates, Inc. ISBN: 1565921488.

Gay, C. L. and Essinger, J. 2000. *Inside Outsourcing*. Nicholas Brealey. ISBN: 1857882040.

Glickstein, B. 1996. GNU stow. www.gnu.org/software/stow/stow.html.

Group Staff Outsource 1996. *Outsourcing*. South-Western Publishing Company. ISBN: 0538847514.

Guichard, J., and I. Pepelnjak. 2000. *MPLS and VPM Architectures: A Practical Guide to Understanding, Designing and Deploying MPLS and MPLS-Enabled VPNs*. Cisco Press.

Guth, R., and L. Radosevich. 1998. IBM crosses the Olympic finish line. *InfoWorld*. http://archive.infoworld.com/cgi-bin/displayArchive.pl?/98/06/e01-06.79.htm.

Halabi, S. and McPherson, D. 2000. *Internet Routing Architectures*. Cisco Press. ISBN: 157870233X.

Harlander, D. M. 1994. Central system administration in a heterogeneous unix environment: Genuadmin, *LISA VIII Conference Proceedings*, USENIX, San Diego, CA, pp. 1–8.

Harris, D., and B. Stansell. 2000. Finding time to do it all. *USENIX;login:* 25(6). www.conserver.com/consoles/.

Heiss, J. 1999. Enterprise rollouts with jumpstart. *Thirteenth Systems Administration Conference (LISA '99)*, USENIX, Seattle.

Hemmerich, C. 2000. Automating request-based software distribution. *Fourteenth Systems Administration Conference (LISA '00)*, USENIX, New Orleans.

Hogan, C. Formula 1 Racing: "Science in the fast lane," *Nature* 481 (Oct. 14, 2000: http://EverythingSysadmin.com/p/a).

Horowitz, M., and S. Lunt. 1997. RFC 2228: FTP security extensions. Updates RFC 959 (Postel and Reynolds 1985). Status: PROPOSED STANDARD.

Houle, B. 1996. Majorcool: A web interface to majordomo. *Tenth Systems Administration Conference (LISA '96)*, USENIX, Chicago, pp. 145–153.

Hume, A. 1988. The file motel—an incremental backup system for unix, *USENIX Conference Proceedings*, USENIX, San Francisco, pp. 61–72.

Hunter, T., and S. Watanabe. 1993. Guerrilla system administration: Scaling small group systems administration to a larger installed base. *Systems Administration (LISA VII) Conference*, USENIX, Monterey, Calif., pp. 99–105.

Jennings, R. W. and Passaro, J. 1999. *Make It Big in the $100 Billion Outsource Contracting Industry*, Westfield Press, ISBN: 096543110X.

Johnson, S. 1991. *The One Minute Sales Person*, Avon Books, ISBN: 0380716038.

Kantor, B., and P. Lapsley. 1986. RFC 977: Network news transfer protocol: A proposed standard for the stream-based transmission of news. Status: PROPOSED STANDARD.

Katcher, J. 1999. NetApp Tech Report 3070: Scalable infrastructure for Internet business. www.netapp.com/tech_library/3070.html.

Keagy, S. 2000. *Integrating Voice and Data Networks*. Cisco Press.

Kercheval, B. 1999. *DHCP: A Guide to Dynamic TCP/IP Network Configuration*. Prentice Hall.

Kernighan, B. W. and Pike, R. 1999. *The Practice of Programming*. Addison-Wesley. ISBN: 020161586X.

Knight, S., D. Weaver, D. Whipple, R. Hinden, D. Mitzel, P. Hunt, P. Higginson, M. Shand, and A. Lindem. 1998. RFC 2338: Virtual router redundancy protocol. Status: PROPOSED STANDARD.

Koren, L., and P. Goodman. 1992. *The Haggler's Handbook: One Hour to Negotiating Power*. Norton.

Kovacich, G. 1998. *The Information Systems Security Officer's Guide: Establishing and Managing an Information Protection Program*. Butterworth-Heinenmann. ISBN: 0750698969.

Kubicki, C. 1992. Customer satisfaction metrics and measurement. *Systems Administration (LISA VI) Conference*, USENIX, Long Beach, Calif., pp. 63–68.

Kubicki, C. 1993. The system administration maturity model—SAMM. *Systems Administration (LISA VII) Conference*, USENIX, Monterey, Calif., pp. 213–225.

Kuong, J. F. 2000. *Application Service Provisioning*. Management Advisory Publications. ISBN: 0940706490.

Lakein, A. 1996. *How to Get Control of Your Time and Your Life*. New American Library.

Lear, E., Fair, E., Crocker, D. and Kessler, T. 1994. RFC 1627: Network 10 considered harmful (some practices shouldn't be codified). Obsoleted by BCP0005, RFC1918 Rekhter et al. 1996. Status: INFORMATIONAL.

Leber, J. 1998. *Windows NT Backup and Restore*. O'Reilly.

Lee, D. C. 1999. *Enhanced IP Services for Cisco Networks: A Practical Resource for Deploying Quality of Service, Security, IP Routing, and VPN Services*. Cisco Press.

Lemon, T., and R. E. Droms. 1999. *The DHCP Handbook: Understanding, Deploying, and Managing Automated Configuration Services*. MacMillan.

Levitt, A. M. 1997. *Disaster Planning and Recovery: A Guide for Facilities Professionals*. Wiley.

Levy, E. (n.d.). Bugtraq. www.securityfocus.com/frames/?content=/forums/bugtraq/intro.html.

Libes, D. 1990. RFC 1178: Choosing a name for your computer. See also FYI0005. Status: INFORMATIONAL.

Limoncelli, T. A. 1998. Please quit. *USENIX;login:* 23, p. 38.

Limoncelli, T. A. 1999. Deconstructing user requests and the nine step model. *Proceedings of the 13th Systems Administration Conference LISA (SAGE/USENIX)*, p. 35.

Limoncelli, T. A. 2005. *Time Management for System Administrators*. O'Reilly.

Limoncelli, T. A., and C. Hogan. 2001. *The Practice of System and Network Administration*. Addison-Wesley.

Limoncelli, T., T. Reingold, R. Narayan, and R. Loura. 1997. Creating a network for Lucent Bell Labs Research South. *Eleventh Systems Administration Conference (LISA '97)*, USENIX, San Diego, p. 123.

Limoncelli, T. A., R. Fulmer, T. Reingold, A. Levine, and R. Loura. 1998. Providing reliable NT desktop services by avoiding NT server. *Large Installation System Administration of Windows NT Conference*, USENIX, Seattle, p. 75.

Lions, J. 1996. *Lion's Commentary on UNIX 6th Edition, with Source Code*, Peer-to-Peer Communications, ISBN: 1-57398-013-7.

Liu, C. 2001. The ties that BIND: Using BIND name servers with Windows 2000, *Linux Magazine*. www.linux-mag.com/2001-03/toc.html.

Locke, C., R. Levine, D. Searls, and D. Weinberger. 2000. *The Cluetrain Manifesto : The End of Business as Usual*. Perseus Press.

MacKenzie, R. A. 1997. *The Time Trap*. AMACOM.

Maggiora, P. L. D., C. E. Elliott, J. M. Thompson Jr., R. L. P. and K. J. Phelps. 2000. *Performance and Fault Management*. Cisco Press.

Maniago, P. 1987. Consulting via mail at andrew. *Large Installation System Administrators Workshop Proceedings*, USENIX, Philadelphia, pp. 22–23.

Marcus, J. S. 1999. *Designing Wide Area Networks and Internetworks: A Practical Guide*. Addison-Wesley. ISBN: 0201695847.

Mathis, M. 2003. The case of raising the Internet MTU, *Cisco200307*. http://www.psc.edu/mathis/MTU/index.html.

Mauro, J. and McDougall, R. 2000. *Solaris Internals: Core Kernel Architecture*. Prentice Hall PTR/Sun Microsystems Press. ISBN: 0130224960.

McKusick, M. K., Bostic, K., et al. 1996. *The Design and Implementation of the 4.4BSD Operating System*. Addison-Wesley. ISBN: 0201549794.

McLaughlin III, L. 1990. RFC 1179: Line printer daemon protocol. Status: INFORMATIONAL.

McNutt, D. 1993. Role-based system administration or who, what, where, and how. *Systems Administration (LISA VII) Conference*, USENIX, Monterey, Calif., pp. 107–112.

Menter, E. S. 1993. Managing the mission critical environment. *Systems Administration (LISA VII) Conference*, USENIX, Monterey, Calif., pp. 81–86.

Miller, A. and Donnini, A. 2000. Relieving the burden of system administration support through support automation, *Fourteenth Systems Administration Conference (LISA '00)*, USENIX, New Orleans.

Miller, A. R. and Davis, M. H. 2000. *Intellectual Property, Patents, Trademarks and Copyright in a Nutshell*. West/Wadsworth. ISBN: 0314235191.

Miller, M. and Morris, J. 1996. Centralized administration of distributed firewalls, *Tenth Systems Administration Conference (LISA'96)*, USENIX, Chicago, IL, pp. 19–23.

Moran, J., and B. Lyon, 1993. The restore-o-mounter: The file motel revisited, *USENIX Conference Proceedings*, USENIX, Cincinnati, pp. 45–58.

Morgenstern, J. 1998. *Organizing from the Inside Out: The Foolproof System for Organizing Your Home, Your Office and Your Life*. Owl Books.

Moy, J. T. 2000. *OSPF: Anatomy of an Internet Routing Protocol*. Addison-Wesley.

Myers, J., and M. Rose, 1996. RFC 1939: Post Office Protocol—version 3. See also STD 0053. Obsoletes RFC 1725. Updated by RFC 1957, RFC 2449. Status: STANDARD.

Mylott, T. R., III. 1995. *Computer Outsourcing : Managing the Transfer of Information Systems*. Prentice Hall. ISBN: 013127614X.

Nelson, B. 2005. *1001 Ways to Reward Employees*, 2d ed. Workman.

Neumann, P. 1997. *Computer-Related Risks*. Addison-Wesley. ISBN: 020155805X.

Niksic, H. 1998. GNU wget. www.gnu.org/software/wget/wget.html.

Norberg, S. and Russell, D. 2000. *Securing Windows NT/2000 Servers for the Internet: a Checklist for System Administrators*. O'Reilly. ISBN: 1565927680.

Northcutt, S. 1999. *G4.1—Computer Security Incident Handling: Step-by-Step*. SANS Institute.

Oetiker, T. 1998a. MRTG—the multi router traffic grapher. *Twelfth Systems Administration Conference (LISA '98)*, USENIX, Boston, p. 141.

Oetiker, T. 1998b. SEPP—software installation and sharing system. *Twelfth Systems Administration Conference (LISA '98)*, USENIX, Boston, p. 253.

Ondishko, D. 1989. Administration of department machines by a central group, *USENIX Conference Proceedings*, USENIX, Baltimore, MD, pp. 73–82.

Osterman, M. 2000. The Impact of Effective Storage Technology on Exchange TCO. http://www.cnilive.com/docs_pub/html/stor00.html.

Oppliger, R. 2000. *Secure Messaging with PGP and S/MIME*. Artech House. ISBN: 158053161X.

Peacock, D., and M. Giuffrida. 1988. Big brother: A network services expert, *USENIX Conference Proceedings*, USENIX, San Francisco, pp. 393–398.

Pepelnjak, I. 2000. *EIGRP Network Design Solutions*. Cisco Press.

Perlman, R. 1999. *Interconnections, Second Edition: Bridges, Routers, Switches, and Internetworking Protocols*. Addison-Wesley. ISBN: 0201634481.

Phillips, G., and W. LeFebvre. 1998. *Hiring System Administrators*. USENIX for SAGE, the System Administrator's Guild, Short Topics in System Administration #5.

Pildush, G. D. 2000. *Cisco ATM Solution: Master ATM Implementation of Cisco Networks*. Cisco Press.

Postel, J., and J. K. Reynolds. 1985. RFC 959: File transfer protocol. Obsoletes RFC 0765. Updated by RFC 2228 (Horowitz and Lunt 1997). Status: STANDARD.

Powell, P., and J. Mason. 1995. Lprng—an enhanced printer spooler system. *Ninth Systems Administration Conference (LISA '95)*, USENIX, Monterey, Calif., pp. 13–24.

Powers, D. P., and D. Russell. 1993. *Love Your Job!* O'Reilly.

Preston, W. C. 1999. UNIX *Backup and Recovery*. O'Reilly.

Rekhter, Y., Moskowitz, B., Karrenberg, D. and de Groot, G. 1994. RFC 1597: Address allocation for private internets. Obsoleted by BCP0005, RFC1918 Rekhter et al. 1996. Status: INFORMATIONAL.

Ressman, D., and J. Valdés. 2000. Use of cfengine for automated multi-platform software and patch distribution. *Fourteenth Systems Administration Conference (LISA '00)*, USENIX, New Orleans.

Ringel, M. F., and T. A. Limoncelli. 1999. Adverse termination procedures or how to fire a system administrator. *Proceedings of the 13th Systems Administration Conference LISA (SAGE/USENIX)*, p. 45.

Rothery, B. and Robertson, I. 1995. *The Truth About Outsourcing*, Ashgate Publishing Company, ISBN: 0566075156.

Schafer, P. 1992a. bbn-public—contributions from the user community. *Systems Administration (LISA VI) Conference*, USENIX, Long Beach, Calif., pp. 211–213.

Schafer, P. 1992b. Is centralized system administration the answer? *Systems Administration (LISA VI) Conference*, USENIX, Long Beach, Calif., pp. 55–61.

Schreider, T. 1998. *Encyclopedia of Disaster Recovery, Security & Risk Management*. Crucible Publishing Works.

Schwartz, K. L., Cottrell, L. and Dart, M. 1994. Adventures in the evolution of a high-bandwidth network for central servers, *Eighth Systems Administration Conference (LISA VIII)*, USENIX, San Diego, California.

Shapiro, G. N., and E. Allman, 1999. Sendmail evolution: 8.10 and beyond. *FREENIX Track: 1999 USENIX Annual Technical Conference*, USENIX, Monterey, Calif., pp. 149–158.

Small, F. 1993. Everything possible. In particular, the title song.

Smallwood, K. 1992. SAGE views: Whither the customer? *USENIX; login:* 17, pp. 15–16.

Snyder, G., T. Miller et al. 1986. sudo. www.courtesan.com/sudo.

SPIE. 2002. Optical security and counterfeit deterrence techniques IV, *Proceeding of SPIE* Vol. 4677. http://everythingsysadmin.com/p/h.

Spurgeon, C. E. 2000. *Ethernet: The Definitive Guide*. O'Reilly. ISBN: 1565926609.

Stern, H. 1991. *Managing NFS and NIS*. O'Reilly.

Stevens, W. R. 1994. *TCP/IP Illustrated, Volume 1: The Protocols*. Addison-Wesley.

Stewart, J. W. 1999. *BGP4 Inter-Domain Routing in the Internet*. Addison-Wesley.

Stoll, C. 1989. *The Cuckoo's Egg*. Doubleday.

Thomas, T. M. 1998. *OSPF Network Design Solutions*. Cisco Press.

Valian, P., and T. K. Watson. 1999. NetReg: An automated DHCP registration system. *Thirteenth Systems Administration Conference (LISA '99)*, USENIX, Seattle.

van den Berg, S. R. 1990. procmail. www.procmail.org.

Vegesna, S. 2001. *IP Quality of Service*. Cisco Press.

Viega, J., B. Warsaw, and K. Manheimer. 1998. Mailman: The GNU mailing list manager. *Twelfth Systems Administration Conference (LISA '98)*, USENIX, Boston, p. 309.

Williams, O. D. 1998. *Outsourcing: A CIO's Perspective*. CRC Press St. Lucie Press. ISBN: 1574442163.

Williamson, B. 2000. *Developing IP Multicast Networks: The Definitive Guide to Designing and Deploying Cisco IP Multicast Networks*. Cisco Press. ISBN: 1578700779.

Wood, C. C. 1999. *Information Security Policies Made Easy*. Baseline Software. ISBN: 1881585069.

Yeong, W., T. Howes, and S. Kille. 1995. RFC 1777: Lightweight directory access protocol. Obsoletes RFC 1487. Status: DRAFT STANDARD.

Zwicky, E. D., S. Simmons, and R. Dalton. 1990. Policy as a system administration tool. *LISA IV Conference Proceedings*, USENIX, Colorado Springs, pp. 115–124.

Index